The Totalitarian Exp[...] Twentieth-Century Europe

MW00657665

Italian Fascism, Soviet Communism, and German Nazism emerged at roughly the same time, in the wake of the First World War, and together they present some of the most perplexing questions in modern history. Each regime was characterized by the rejection of liberal individualism and parliamentary democracy—and by the mobilization of the masses for grandiose public projects. Indeed, each seemed to galvanize genuine enthusiasm for acting collectively, beyond immediate individual self-interest. At the same time, each engaged in coercion, violence, and sometimes terror or even systematic killing. Whereas the regimes of Hitler and Mussolini came crashing down in overt imperialism and war, the Soviet Communist regime survived the extremes of Stalinism, only to unravel two generations later. However, despite their ultimate failure, these unprecedented regimes have fundamentally altered our sense of the political spectrum, even the range of human and historical possibilities.

In this compelling study, David D. Roberts provides a challenging new understanding of totalitarianism by focusing on its historically specific dimensions. Rather than dismissing it in terms of national weaknesses or psychological aberrations, he shows how the totalitarian mode of collective action was a response to enduring tensions in the modern mainstream. By providing a fresh understanding of the novel aspirations fueling the three departures, *The Totalitarian Experiment in Twentieth-Century Europe* illuminates the practices of each regime, showing how the new mode of action yielded a characteristic combination of radicalization, narrowing, myth making—and disastrous failure. By assessing totalitarianism in a more deeply historical way, this study suggests how we might learn further lessons from this troubling phase of modern political development.

David D. Roberts is Albert Berry Saye Professor of History at the University of Georgia. Among his numerous publications are *The Syndicalist Tradition and Italian Fascism* (1979), *Benedetto Croce and the Uses of Historicism* (1987), and *Nothing But History: Reconstruction and Extremity after Metaphysics* (1995).

The Totalitarian Experiment in Twentieth-Century Europe

Understanding the Poverty of Great Politics

David D. Roberts

Routledge
Taylor & Francis Group

NEW YORK AND LONDON

First published 2006 by Routledge Inc.
29 West 35th Street, New York, NY 10001

Simultaneously published in the UK by Routledge
2 Park Square, Milton Park, Abingdon, OX14 4RN

Routledge is an imprint of the Taylor & Francis Group

© 2006 David D. Roberts

Typeset in Baskerville by Taylor & Francis Books
Printed and bound in Great Britain by
TJ International Ltd, Padstow, Cornwall

British Library Cataloguing in Publication Data
A catalogue record for this book is available from the British Library

Library of Congress Cataloging in Publication Data
A catalog record for this book has been requested

ISBN10: 0-415-19278-1 (hbk)
ISBN10: 0-415-19279-X (pbk)

ISBN13: 978-0-415-19278-1 (hbk)
ISBN13: 978-0-415-19279-8 (pbk)

Taylor & Francis Group is the Academic Division of T&F Informa plc.

To the memory of Mario Corsi (1923–2004)

For when truth enters into a fight with the lies of millennia, we shall have upheavals, a convulsion of earthquakes, a moving of mountains and valleys, the like of which has never been dreamed of. The concept of politics will have merged entirely with a war of spirits; all power structures of the old society will have been exploded—all of them are based on lies: there will be wars the like of which have never yet been seen on earth. It is only beginning with me that the earth knows *great politics*.

Friedrich Nietzsche, *Ecce Homo*, edited by Walter Kaufmann (with *On the Genealogy of Morals*) (New York: Random House [Vintage Books], 1969), pp. 326–7.

Why should mankind not have the right to experiment on itself?

Ivanov, in Arthur Koestler, *Darkness at Noon* (New York, Bantam Books, 1966), p. 132.

And, even among those who survive, what barriers of constraint and unfamiliarity will have arisen in these years—not only of physical separation, but of experience unshared, of different feelings and opinions? What ties will survive that strain?

Iris Origo, diary entry for February 13, 1944, *War in Val d'Orcia: An Italian War Diary, 1943–1944* (Boston: David R. Godine, 1984), pp. 141–2.

Contents

Acknowledgements

I welcome the occasion to acknowledge my debts to the many colleagues with whom I have had the good fortune to exchange ideas during the ten-year gestation of this book—and, in some cases, for many years longer. I have particularly valued the support and advice of Stanley Payne, who has followed this project from its inception. I also thank Abbott Gleason for his interest as the project took shape, Marion Deshmukh for her comments on a paper that sketched the present introduction, and Alberto Moreiros, former director of the European Studies Center at Duke University, for the opportunity to present aspects of my work both in a public lecture and in a faculty seminar under the center's auspices early in 2003. Exchanges with Walter Adamson, Roger Eatwell, Roger Griffin, and Robert Mallett stimulated me as the book took shape. I am especially grateful to Aristotle Kallis for his generous response to the original manuscript and his most helpful suggestions for improvement.

I first outlined the contours of this book in a lecture at the University of Rostock, Germany, in 1996, and I again thank Wolf D. Gruner of the Rostock history faculty for that invitation, and for the publication that followed as volume 10 in the *Rostocker Beiträge zur Deutschen und Europäischen Geschichte*. I have greatly appreciated Professor Gruner's continuing interest and support. The opportunity to team-teach a graduate colloquium with him at the University of Georgia in 1999 enabled me to work out a number of the ideas that found their way into the present chapter on Nazism. I also learned much from my conversations with Werner Mueller of the Rostock history faculty.

Among Italian friends, Domenico Settembrini, Luca de Caprariis, and Alessandra Tarquini have been particularly generous in sharing ideas. A memorable conversation with Renata Viti Cavaliere and Daniela Coli in Messina in 2002 has continued to inspire me in ways that those two friends could not have anticipated. I am also grateful to Emilio Gentile for his helpful critical reading of an earlier version of Chapter 6. Angela Schinaia and Marcello Mustè were most generous in showing me how to navigate the materials of the Fondazione Gentile at Villa Mirafiori in Rome. I am also indebted to the always helpful archivists of the Archivio Centrale dello Stato in Rome (EUR).

At the University of Georgia, my colleagues Alexei Kojevnikov, Nan McMurry, John Morrow, Miranda Pollard, Steven Soper, and Kirk Willis generously responded to queries, and Ronald Bogue, Jim Cobb, Will Holmes, John Inscoe, Thomas Peterson, and Thom Whigham helped to sustain my progress with their interest, questions, and suggestions. Conversations with my former colleague Douglas Northrop were particularly helpful as I sought to get a handle on the Soviet experience. Although they have not been directly involved with the present project, the opportunity to interact over the years with Ruth Ben-Ghiat, Alexander De Grand, Richard Drake, Raymond Grew, Marion Miller, Borden Painter, Marla Stone, and Robert Wohl has helped to stimulate the thinking that led to this book.

I am under no illusions that the thesis offered here will compel universal agreement. Indeed, in light of the controversial nature of the subject, it is especially important to emphasize that none of those mentioned above will endorse all aspects of my argument, and I alone am responsible for the points that I have chosen to emphasize and for any errors of omission or commission. But if, as is my fondest hope, the inevitable disagreements prove fruitful, all these friends, colleagues, and occasional antagonists share the credit.

In the lengthy gestation of this project, I found myself working with three successive sponsoring editors at Routledge, and I am very much indebted to them all. Heather McCallum signed it on and has continued to follow its progress from her subsequent posts. I have particularly valued her ongoing interest and encouragement. At the helm as I was doing the writing, Vicky Peters knew exactly when to tighten and when to loosen my leash. Liz Gooster was just taking over when the manuscript arrived, and I have appreciated her efficiency and support in the transition from review to revision to production. In addition, I thank Philippa Grand for her many efforts, Lucie Ewin for shepherding the book through the production process, and Dennis Hodgson for his exemplary work as copy-editor.

I am most grateful to Bibb and Diane Saye for their support of the Albert Berry Saye Professorship in History at the University of Georgia, which has helped to make my research and writing possible. I also thank the University of Georgia Research Foundation for the Senior Faculty Research Grant that enabled me to do research in Europe in 1999. As always, Beth would prefer to be mentioned as unobtrusively as possible—if I insist (as I do) on mentioning her at all. So I thank her here, at the end of a paragraph, for her patience and occasional impatience as I tried out ideas, periodically ranting and raving. Above all, she has helped me to maintain at least some sense of proportion as I have brought this lengthy project to completion.

The book is dedicated to the memory of the distinguished Italian philosopher and historian of philosophy Mario Corsi, who died in December 2004, shortly after I had completed the manuscript for the present study. Almost immediately after our first contact in 1990, he and I became fast friends, and I greatly valued his support and advice, as well as our many wide-ranging conversations about history, philosophy, and politics. He had followed the present project with interest, and I am profoundly sorry that he did not live to see the book in print. I offer this meager dedication to his memory as an indication of the deep affection and respect I had for him. His wisdom and uncompromising intellectual integrity remain an inspiration.

1 Layers, proportions, and the question of historical specificity

Unforeseen political departures between the wars

The novel political regimes that we associate with Mussolini, Stalin, and Hitler fundamentally altered our sense of the political spectrum, even the range of human and historical possibilities. Defying expectations, each emerged in the wake of the First World War spearheaded by a new elite that claimed to offer a new vision in response to inadequacies in what had seemed the political mainstream so far. Each rejected liberal individualism and parliamentary democracy, and each featured unprecedented mobilization for grandiose projects. Indeed, each seemed to galvanize genuine enthusiasm for acting collectively, beyond immediate individual self-interest. At the same time, each engaged in coercion, violence, and sometimes terror or even systematic killing. Whereas the regimes of Hitler and Mussolini came crashing down in overt imperialism and war, the Soviet Communist regime survived the extremes of Stalinism only to unravel, with a whimper, two generations later.

Although each failed disastrously, these regimes proved unprecedented, and their memory and legacy live on in numerous essential ways. We think of gulags and gas chambers, ritual and spectacle, Big Brother and the banality of evil, *Darkness at Noon* and *The Captive Mind*. For the vast majority, the images are profoundly negative, and the confident self-understanding of liberal democracy by the end of the twentieth century derived partly from the outcomes of those departures. But despite generations of indispensable specialized scholarship, we still have difficulty making sense of this set of episodes within the contours of our continuing political experiment, articulating what went wrong and what is to be learned. We proclaim "never again," but the imperative can be flabby, as if the lesson is that we must guard against evil. Distancing ourselves from the agents through moralism and reductionism, we fail to address much about how that earlier set of episodes relates to us. Although their outcomes may seem to warrant liberal triumphalism, those departures have occasioned some loss of nerve, some restriction in our sense of possibilities, even in our range of questioning.

So tangled are the issues that we have difficulty sorting out layers, proportions, and intersections, even the synchronic and diachronic range of whatever is to be understood. We tend to vacillate as we ponder the places of, and intersections between, suprahistorical evil, ongoing human propensities, our historically specific Western culture, specifically modern possibilities, common national peculiarities, and unfortunate contingencies. Although all three regimes clearly departed from what seemed the liberal mainstream, we face questions not only about how each was related to the other but also about the basis and extent of the differentiation from that mainstream. We have come to recognize, for example, that novel aspects of Nazi population policy were not as different from the contemporaneous practice of the democracies as we had long assumed.[1] So pinpointing origins or sources and the bases of the differences within the experience of the period comes to seem trickier than we had recognized. At the same time, we ask to what extent and in what ways these regimes were historically specific, perhaps even confined to a particular period that they themselves helped to define—and that is thus by now over and done with. Alternatively, in what sense might they be better understood as revealing ongoing problems, tensions, or possibilities?

Because the Soviet regime far outlasted the Italian and German regimes, we encounter questions about symmetry and even about the subject of the inquiry on the Soviet Communist side. Do we focus on Stalinism, as a delimited chapter, even a phenomenon in its own right, or on the whole Soviet experiment, which, in outliving the fascist regimes, raises questions that they do not? Did the Stalinist phase, especially as it emerged during the pivotal interwar period, in some sense determine what the overall Soviet experiment became?

Obviously, political and moral concerns have been and remain heavily implicated—and complicate any inquiry immeasurably. What we say about these earlier regimes might lend legitimacy to this or that form of neo-fascism or neo-communism. Moreover, a concern that to understand is to forgive still lurks in some reaches of the discussion. When we come to the extreme outcomes, especially the Holocaust, those like Emil Fackenheim and Claude Lanzmann have insisted that we simply focus on the evil, eschewing the historical account, which might produce the *illusion* of understanding but would necessarily be too neat, redemptive, even exculpatory.[2] Better that the Holocaust be left, in Lawrence Langer's haunting phrase, a "ruin of memory."[3]

Germans who suggest that Nazism was either an incomprehensible eruption of evil or a merely freakish concatenation after the dislocations of the Great War are charged with apology or bad faith.[4] Yet non-Germans who suggest that Nazism can be delimited as idiosyncratically German draw comparable denunciations. Whereas some level of uniquely German responsibility for the Holocaust is obvious, we assume, or insist, that the most troubling outcomes of Nazism grew from supranational processes that, by definition, implicate others, even the whole of Western culture.

Even before Hitler came to power in 1933, some, recognizing that something new and unexpected was emerging, sought to devise a comparative framework that would encompass Fascist Italy and the developing Soviet regime.[5] And the almost contemporaneous advent of Nazism and Stalinism by the early 1930s made the quest for new categories of understanding seem all the more pressing. However, there were obvious differences in origins and priorities—between

Communism and generic fascism, and even between Italian Fascism and Nazism. So in what sense the three regimes overlapped or criss-crossed, participated in the same wider departure, or even invited comparison, remained uncertain.

The advent of those regimes brought "totalitarianism" into our vocabulary. Coined by anti-Fascists in Italy in 1923, the term was quickly adopted by the Fascists themselves, becoming central to their self-understanding. Yet the Nazis came to eschew the category, especially because they saw in the Italian usage a commitment to conservative statism as opposed to the dynamism of movement or party. So the term was contested virtually from the start.[6] It continues in lay usage, although it is generally conflated with authoritarianism or the sort of nasty dictatorship that has been all too prominent in parts of the world in recent decades. At least for a time, however, specialists had plausible criteria of differentiation, and it was through the totalitarianism category that fascism and communism were most often considered in tandem. But even as used in scholarly discussion, that category proved notoriously inadequate and misleading, for reasons we will consider below. Still, the three regimes seemed to entail some common novel and historically specific dimension requiring *some* new category.

Playing with overlap and contrast can be a fool's errand, and we have had good reason to be dubious about questioning the three regimes together, especially because certain parallels were long played up for questionable political or ideological reasons. However, although we must obviously be true to the singularity of each case, the present study seeks to show how we might most fruitfully encompass all three. Although doing so affords a frame for comparison, which is surely self-recommending, my purpose is not simply "comparative" in a static sense, as if the point were ahistorical classification, generalization, definition— some science of political extremism. The central question concerns whatever common place the three regimes had in the wider modern political experiment that continues in us. So treating the three cases together entails not simply comparing them as parallel instances but backing up to probe the soil from which they emerged, seeking to understand any common elements in the diagnoses and prescriptions that, partly for idiosyncratic contextual reasons also to be addressed, led counter-elites in three major European countries to spearhead departures from the liberal Western mainstream in the wake of the Great War. Deeper understanding of that common layer illuminates not only the wider era but also each of the three regimes.

However, reference to the wider soil suggests a question from the opposite angle—and points us back to the issue of synchronic and diachronic range. If the soil is to be understood in broader, supranational terms, is it too conventional to focus on Russia, Italy, and Germany to the neglect of other regimes, movements, even individual figures who seem comparable on some level, and who thus might also illuminate the overall departure? Clearly, that departure was not limited to these three countries, but just how wide it was, and whom or what else it encompasses on the synchronic level, is beyond the purview of the present study. Conventional though they are, these three cases must be among those considered, and I believe them to be sufficient to reveal the supranational, historically specific dimension, in both origins and ensuing dynamic. I hope that the present study will prove helpful to others examining other instances from the same epoch. Although I will limit the synchronic purview to these three cases, I will consider in the concluding chapter the diachronic question of what has ended and what continues, or may continue, from within the wider framework of modern politics.

This enterprise requires considering antecedent ideas that responded to tensions in the mainstream development in the West. That dimension of "intellectual origins," in turn, implicates the interface of "theory and practice," itself fraught with conceptual pitfalls, quite apart from the special difficulties that these now detested regimes present. Indeed, facile ways of positing the theory/practice dichotomy have long impeded the necessary encounter.[7]

So the essential reconceptualization and synthesis require a broad brush and a certain reflexive thickness in light of the conceptual obstacles and ethical sensitivities at work. Indeed, so pervasive are the difficulties, as exacerbated by the limitations of longstanding assumptions and approaches, that only by first systematically questioning and even "unthinking" certain of our ways of tackling the issue can we open to a more convincing, more deeply historical understanding. Thus we will need to address the obstacles and uncertainties as we consider how we have come to approach the overall problem as we have. We will need to distinguish suprahistorical and historically specific national and supranational factors, sorting out layers and proportions. Such thickness is daunting, but in fact all studies, even those apparently most down-to-earth and atheoretical, presuppose something of the whole business—not only the proportions of the various dimensions but also something about theory and practice and the significance of intellectual antecedents.

As I will emphasize again and again, the *outcome* of the three regimes is not at issue. The phase they constituted in our ongoing political experiment was tragic, catastrophic—an enduring nightmare. Nor is the point that it could have turned out well, or better, were it not for certain contingencies. Contingencies there were, and we will need to consider them, but questioning the experience afresh enables us better to understand what we can now recognize as the originating flaws and thereby to grasp the *strength* of the contingency of the actual dynamic in each of the three cases. The outcomes were no accident, but how they followed from the initial aspirations is not obvious. Nor is the supranational, historically specific dimension of those aspirations themselves. A deeper understanding of all that fed the three departures and then produced their negative outcomes enables us better to distinguish what has ended, consumed by their failures, and what continues.

We recognize the need and the scope for fresh questioning thanks in part to the wider cultural changes generally lumped, *faute de mieux*, under the ambiguous term "postmodernism." This term has come to cover a hodge-podge of sometimes incompatible notions, some of which have bred confusion, especially regarding the place of "history" and the scope for historical understanding. But the postmodern turn can be understood as warranting, and showing the way to,

a deeper, more significant engagement with our own past. It entails, most basically, a deeper sense of historicity. That sense, in turn, has begun to affect our
sense of how things come to be through history, our conception of what history
encompasses, and our sense of our own place in history—as we both peer into
the past and generate the future through our aggregate response to the world as
it has become so far.

The change in our sense of how history happens has made us suspicious of
essentialism, teleological assumptions, and master narratives. Conversely, we have
become more sensitive to the place of contingency in history. Thus we are
prepared for a greater raggedness as we find responses to novel situations yielding
partially unintended outcomes that then demand further response. Each step
becomes possible only because of the often unforeseeable results of the preceding.
Thus we better understand that we cannot infer intentions, purposes, or origins
from outcomes, and we learn to beware of the teleological backloading that, in
the case at hand, has led us to take the most extreme outcomes, like the
Holocaust, as the keys to the originating aims.[8] If we privilege such extremes as
revelatory, we may not be able to understand even those outcomes, let alone the
larger phenomenon from which they resulted, for we miss the genesis of the wider
realm of possibility from within which they emerged, contingently.

However, we can allow scope for such disconnection between origins and
outcomes without invoking the fashionable notion of "discontinuity" or reducing
the phenomenon—limiting understanding—to synchronic slices. Although the
processes at issue in the present case were ragged, with contingency at every step,
the outcomes resulted from a continuous process. Even as we take care to avoid
overdoing conscious control or intentional direction, we can probe for an overall
dynamic that resulted from the effort to act on the basis of the originating aspirations. Even if not intended, some such dynamic might be discernible *ex post
facto*, proving at once characteristic and comprehensible in historical terms.

In terms of substance, postmodernism entails a new angle on modernity itself
as we pull back especially from the master narrative of "modernization." There
is still a modern mainstream, found in "the West," but it is less obviously the
privileged standard, and we open to uncertainties, tensions, creases in what had
long seemed the relatively smooth fabric of modern deployment. On that basis,
we recognize that restrictively "modern" criteria may have guided our questioning, even our selection of the evidence, as we have dealt with the interwar
regimes. Some such selection remains inevitable, but we open to a wider range of
evidence—and possible meanings.

Coming more genuinely to terms with our own historicity makes us more alert
to our own place in the continuing history we study. Our inquiries become more
reflexive as we recognize that our assumptions and categories are themselves
historically specific—and historical products. We grasp more deeply the sense in
which understanding is itself a historical process and part of the larger continuing
history in which we too are enmeshed as participants, even as we question the
past. Our efforts may have unacknowledged historical antecedents that shape our
questioning, delimiting what we are prepared to ask, to find, to hear.[9]

However, although reflexivity has become almost a buzzword, it is not easily encompassed in historical inquiry—especially an inquiry into the subject at hand. It means, most basically, that in approaching the three regimes we keep in mind that we know some of what we know only because of what they tried to do, the catastrophic outcomes of what they did. Indeed, their experience has affected our way of framing the basic categories that structure our understanding of our past, our present political world, and even our sense of human possibilities. Such categories as power, ideology, myth, and action, or freedom, reason, commitment, and responsibility, were not given once and for all, in some essentialist way, but were themselves contested—and are still contested, or potentially contested. We learn to take particular care with binary dualisms, recalling, for example, Jane Caplan's call for a riskier but potentially more illuminating approach *even* to Nazism and fascism, putting at issue the binary oppositions at work—rational/irrational, for example—so that we might question their positive terms.[10] As themselves in play in our continuing history, such categories are not as stable as we have long assumed.

We come to recognize that insofar as we have not been reflexive enough in approaching the problematic side of our recent political history, our use of the key categories may have been facile, even flabby. At the same time, we understand that we cannot grasp whatever fed into the regimes in question insofar as we engage it, place it, only in terms of our present understanding of the key categories, reflecting our knowledge of the outcomes.

Insofar as reflexive historical inquiry means not simply confirming but also testing our own categories and assumptions, it obviously entails risk—*genuine* risk. Although we are privileged in knowing outcomes, we are not so sure, as we ponder the original departures, about the meaning of the evidence; the ideals and aspirations at work may entail substance that proves category-stretching. However, if we are to learn more deeply from the totalitarian dimension of our own historical experience, we must be willing to loosen our categories, to put them in play, to recognize that at the outset of the departures at issue some of them were contested by people who may have been caught up in the same historically specific processes as we are and who may have cared as deeply for the world as we do.[11] Only on that basis can we genuinely engage those "Others" and thereby better understand how they became as different they did—and made such a mess of things along the way.

Classic totalitarianism, the nominalist reaction, and beyond

In the aftermath of the Second World War, with the Cold War heating up, intellectuals like Karl Popper, Hannah Arendt, J.L. Talmon, and Albert Camus sought to think big in an effort to devise the sort of framework that seemed necessary to understand the regimes that had emerged from the Great War. And the central interpretive category that emerged was "totalitarianism." Its resonance having evolved since its coinage in early Fascist Italy, the term afforded an influential way of conceiving the three regimes and a criterion for comparison between them for two decades after the Second World War.

The category proved problematic, however—most basically because it was used ahistorically. And much of what it seemed to connote in these classic early works seemed to melt away with historical research, which made it clear that totalitarianism, as it had come to be conceived, was not remotely realized anywhere. But it is worth recalling certain aspects of the classic model because it still affects our thinking about ideology, the state—movement relationship, the place of Fascist Italy, and even originating purposes.

Especially as systematized in the classic work of Carl J. Friedrich and Zbigniew K. Brzezinski, published in 1956, totalitarianism became a kind of political science classification scheme. Connoting a static system, the category fostered reification. That "totalitarianism requires" x was taken as an explanation for x; the fact that they were totalitarians explains what they did.[12] It was essentially taken for granted that the aim was top-down "total domination."

Hannah Arendt took a more historical approach in her pioneering *The Origins of Totalitarianism* (1951; augmented 1958), which sought to address precisely the long-term developments that led to the political departures after the First World War, but although it was not static, her argument, too, rested on reification and unexamined assumptions about purposes. Total control tended to take on a life of its own, as when she suggested that "those who aspire to total domination must liquidate all spontaneity."[13] To create totalitarian rule, "Stalin had first to create artificially that atomized society which had been prepared for the Nazis in Germany by historical circumstances."[14]

Moreover, Arendt's argument was teleological, for the implicit key was to explain the origins of certain extreme outcomes, taken as the revelatory core of totalitarianism. The Nazi and Soviet camps were the central institutions of totalitarian power, indeed, the laboratories in which "the fundamental belief of totalitarianism that everything is possible" was to be verified.[15] Only in the otherworldly setting of the camps, where the free human personality could be readily manipulated, could the totalitarians actually achieve the total domination they sought.

The synecdoche of the "camp" has continued to dominate, often fostering quick conflations. Consider, for example, Leszek Kolakowski's treatment of Trotsky's point that the state, prior to disappearing, intensifies its activity and "embraces the life of the citizens authoritatively in every direction." As Kolakowski saw it, Trotsky had depicted the stage of proletarian dictatorship "as a huge permanent concentration camp."[16] However, this is to misconstrue both Trotsky's aspiration and the place of the camps. Unpalatable though we may find it, Trotsky's intensification of the state is distinguishable from the camp world, and to understand either we must eschew such conflation and grasp the dynamic connecting them, the process whereby the vision led to a particular mode of practice that included the camps as part of a wider syndrome.

Returning to Arendt, why did the totalitarians seek "total domination" in the first place? Despite her way of portraying the camps as archetypal, she was quite explicit that the point was not simply power for its own sake. Total domination was not an end in itself but was somehow to implement and confirm the prior Marxian or social Darwinian ideology.[17] As Arendt saw it, in fact, common embrace of a totalist ideology was central to the convergence of the Nazi and Stalinist regimes, but in each case the ideology was unrealistic, especially because its claim of total explanation was incompatible with human creativity, which makes the world unpredictable. So the agents had to facilitate, even to force, the historical process that the totalist ideological supersense had anticipated in each case.

Arendt invoked ideology late in the argument in *The Origins of Totalitarianism*, taking the totalism for granted and without having treated the ideologies in question—Marxism and Darwinism—as always evolving bodies of thought. Nor did she consider explicitly why anyone would embrace such a totalist ideology, unrealistically positing predictability and denying creativity, in the first place. We can only assume some characterological basis—perhaps an intolerance for ambiguity, a fear of freedom—but the argument still gives pause because insofar as the totalist ideologies were in fact unrealistic, practice had to have rested on something other than ideology. But what was it, and what can we say about it and its origins? It surely begs the question to attribute the extra dimension to a need to force an unrealistic ideology. At the same time, the ideologies in question lay in uncertain relationship with the broad socio-political changes that Arendt associated with bourgeois hegemony. Each positing change over time, Marxism and social Darwinism were, in her account, "ideologies of motion" that somehow reflected the dynamism unleashed by the relentless bourgeois expansion of capital.

So whereas Arendt sought to attend to historically specific purposes, her reliance on ideology occasioned ambiguity. She was moving beyond the instrumental conception of ideology prominent in this early discussion, but she ended up fastening upon a common unrealistic totalism that proved weaker as an explanatory principle than she seems to have believed. However, some who posited an overarching totalitarian impulse took more seriously apparent differences in ideological content, based on such dichotomies as rationalism and irrationalism or Left and Right. To feature content was to turn not only from any accent on the merely instrumental uses of ideology but also from Arendt's accent on a common totalist form. Popper, Talmon, and Camus all addressed totalitarianism as a unitary though bifurcated phenomenon on that basis. But sometimes the two notions—that prior totalism in the ideology was the source of the totalitarian impulse, and that ideology was a mere instrument, serving the aim of total control—got lumped together, although they mixed uneasily at best. So whereas "ideology" was central to these early efforts to understand the new anti-liberal politics as totalitarian, the place of "ideology" was often a muddle, and the muddle still shadows the discussion. Difficulties with the ideology category especially complicated any consideration of intellectual antecedents, a point to which we will return in concluding this chapter.

Although Arendt viewed totalitarianism as an ongoing modern possibility, she portrayed it as encompassing Stalinist Communism and German Nazism archetypally, whereas she judged Fascist Italy to have been merely authoritarian, at least until its last phase, and thus peripheral to the overall consideration of totalitarianism.[18] Most importantly, Fascist Italy lacked the terror apparatus and camp system of the other two, but she also cited its apparent statism. Whereas Mussolini merely seized the state, taken to be the highest authority, genuine totalitarianism resides in a movement that claims superiority to the state and even aims to destroy it.

Arendt's way of framing the issue helped to lead others, too, to marginalize the Italian case as less than totalitarian for reasons that are by now familiar. Not only did it fail to produce an intrusive secret police and "terror," but the Fascist regime was a "dyarchy," with King Victor Emmanuel III remaining in place throughout Mussolini's tenure. And although the monarchy ended up so discredited that Italy opted for a republic after the fall of Fascism, its presence surely affected the regime's dynamic, helping to make it different from that of Nazi Germany—hence, most notably, the major difference in modes of ending. But the dyarchy notion, writ large, has long seemed to suggest Mussolini's compromise not only with the monarchy but with pre-fascist elites and institutions more generally.

The early Renzo De Felice offered a somewhat different note in insisting on the totalitarian potential in the dynamic fascist movement that emerged from the First World War, then grew in reaction to the socialist threat and helped to propel Mussolini into power. De Felice even accented the movement's leftist origins and, on that basis, its contrast with the Nazi movement. But, endorsing Arendt explicitly, he went on to insist that the fascist movement was tamed, neutered, by Mussolini and the merely authoritarian state.[19]

However, it would seem that an inquiry like Arendt's, into *origins*, could usefully have encompassed that totalitarian *aspiration*, whatever its successes or outcomes. Moreover, both Arendt and De Felice were quick to posit a particular dichotomy of conservative, authoritarian state and dynamic totalitarian movement that may not have done justice to the possibilities at issue. Fueled by opposition to a particular political regime or form of state, a movement may aim to create a different state, which then might be radically transformed, to expand, making it all-encompassing. The state could even be the vehicle for ongoing "dynamism," understood as ongoing action through mass mobilization, direct and constant participation, which might entail politicizing the workplace, leisure time, even the whole of life. From this perspective, the total domination of outgroups in camps would hardly be the *sine qua non* of totalitarianism. In short, the criteria that Arendt used to marginalize Italian Fascism may well have been too limited.[20]

Insofar as it connoted a self-perpetuating static system, the totalitarianism model was vulnerable with the mellowing of the Soviet system after Stalin's death in 1953. The active de-Stalinization under Nikita Khrushchev, especially, made it clear that the "system" could evolve. Then, especially during the

Vietnam era, it was widely charged that the totalitarianism category had been misused for political purposes as an aspect of Cold War struggles.[21]

More generally, the earlier efforts to encompass so much of the troubling contemporary political experience through "totalitarianism" came to appear moralistic, speculative, and/or reductionist. Especially among specialists, the limits of those efforts tended to discredit any attempt to treat the three regimes together, asking about common sources. By the later 1960s, however, plausible reaction against the earlier effort to think big, which had primarily involved philosophers and social scientists, not historians, combined with national preoccupations to lead scholars to a more delimited focus on the national level, and thus to an increasing nominalism in conceptualization and research.[22] This seemed to be a more genuinely historical approach after those earlier sweeping and speculative efforts. Each of the three regimes was best understood as an episode in its respective national history, reflecting national "peculiarities." Insofar as there might still be a common frame, as with Barrington Moore's synthesis of 1967, it was simply the embrace of dictatorship as opposed to democracy, from commonalties in the peculiarities, bound up with modernization and backwardness.[23] However, the tendency by the 1970s was to play down *any* supranational dimension, other than the inescapable suprahistorical, from power to evil. Accenting the disparity of Italian Fascism and German Nazism, De Felice noted in 1975 that the most important recent contributions to the analysis of Fascism had come from systematic research with a delimited national focus.[24]

This focus on the national level had two distinguishable but partly overlapping consequences: first, as for De Felice, differences and singularity stood out; and, second, in each instance the results of such specialized research seemed to show how little the earlier totalitarianism model, as a system of top-down, total control, accorded with the reality. So even if somehow we *were* to want to conceive the three regimes in common, "totalitarianism" would not be the appropriate category.

Indeed, totalitarianism served as a foil for a generation of scholars who usefully showed that "total control" or "total domination" was not remotely realized in any of the putatively totalitarian regimes. Evidence of Hitler's abiding concern with public opinion suggested anything but the top-down domination of the earlier image. Studies of structure revealed limits to Hitler's power that are now taken for granted. The Nazi regime's organizational chaos, its cauldron of petty ambitions and rivalries, seemed utterly at odds with any notion of "totalitarianism." The debunking went so far that one major scholar, Hans Mommsen, ended up characterizing Hitler as "a weak dictator."[25] It was suggested that even the Holocaust stemmed from a bottom-up structural dynamic, in response to contingent circumstances, not from a carefully orchestrated initiative by the leadership. Although some continued to insist on Hitler's intention, the scope for the countervailing "functionalist" argument suggested the dissolution of the earlier totalitarianism model, with its accent on total control.

The turn to history "from below" further rendered untenable the earlier image of totalitarianism as top-down domination of a passive society—or a society rendered passive. The *Alltagsgeschichte* of the 1980s placed Nazism in more plausible proportion by showing the considerable continuity with the pre-Nazi period on the level of everyday life. There was plenty of scope for ordinary Germans to go about their business, even to resist the totalitarian pretensions of the regime.

At the same time, the several waves of revision that began gathering force in Soviet studies by the 1970s further undermined the traditional model in various ways, even as such major revisionists as Stephen F. Cohen, Moshe Lewin, Sheila Fitzpatrick, and J. Arch Getty often disagreed sharply among themselves. Showing the scope for participation and pressures from below, Fitzpatrick highlighted the support that the Stalinist regime gained from the many who experienced upward mobility thanks to the terror of the later 1930s.[26] Even that terror was not as anomalous as it had sometimes seemed; it was a step toward a differentiated society in which various groups could negotiate in pursuit of their interests. If anything, this was closer to mainstream liberalism than to the earlier image of totalitarianism.

Even insofar as the Stalinist terror was indeed an anomaly, it did not necessarily confirm the classic totalitarian model. Although they differed crucially among themselves, and although they did not convince earlier revisionists like Fitzpatrick and Lewin, those like Getty, Gabor Rittersporn, and Robert Thurston portrayed the Soviet terror as the result not of intention and control from the top but of an inability to control, a process out of control.[27] So much for Arendt's notion that the camps and the terror, as outcomes, manifested the success of the leaders, at least in this delimited sphere, in actually achieving the total domination they sought.

For all their contrasting accents, the several revisionisms in Soviet studies seemingly exploded altogether the utility of totalitarianism—even as a way of understanding the internal dynamic of the particular Soviet regime, let alone some wider supranational phenomenon or process. And, more generally, there is by now near-universal agreement that insofar as "totalitarianism" connoted a fully unified and integrated regime exercising total domination, it set up an impossible standard, not only unrealized but unrealizable. So deflating the category, showing that it was not met, was easy, and doing so by now is to beat a very dead horse.

At the same time, the immediate political resonance of historical understanding for the three countries involved significantly reinforced the national preoccupation in historiography. In Germany, the *Historikerstreit* of 1986–87 was only the most noisy episode as some charged that too many Germans were still sidestepping the essential accounting with their own past, while others worried that obsession with the recent past was keeping Germans from digesting it, placing it historically, so that the country could become normal, moving on to play its rightful and essential role in the world. Either way, the key questions concerned Germany, and any effort to place the Nazi experience in broader perspective could appear to be sidestepping the essential national accounting, if not indulging in outright apology.

In Italy during the mid-1970s, De Felice's insistence that Fascism had achieved "consensus" by the mid-1930s challenged the self-understanding of postwar Italian political culture, resting on common anti-Fascism. By the early 1990s, with the end of the Cold War framework and with bribery scandals discrediting much of the political elite, the very legitimacy of the postwar Italian state sometimes seemed at issue in any effort to reopen discussion of Fascism—or the resistance to it.[28]

Politics and historical understanding were comparably intertwined in the Soviet Union. Before the collapse, from Khrushchev to Roy Medvedev to Mikhail Gorbachev, hopes for reform were very much bound up with interpretations of earlier phases of the regime. Once Communism fell, the political stakes were different but just as passionate, in light of concerns about Communist revival and the need to legitimate the shaky post-Communist order. Central to that effort was a renewed critical preoccupation with original Leninism, as a number sought to show that the whole Soviet regime was fatally flawed, even congenitally illegitimate, thanks to its Leninist origins. Such political concerns made it hard to take full advantage of the opportunity for new historical questioning that opened with the collapse of the Soviet regime.

In each case, climbing to some supranational level or backing up to some wider, longer-term perspective was arguably what was needed even to address the national preoccupations at issue, but immediate political questions fed those preoccupations in a way that tended to preclude any such wider frame. The mechanism sometimes worked indirectly, as the case of Ernst Nolte and the *Historikerstreit* reminds us. To find such a wider perspective was precisely Nolte's aim at the outset of the *Historikerstreit*, but his effort seemed extreme, too obviously exculpatory.[29] So, rather than placing Nazism in a better perspective, Nolte's effort seemed to manifest the ongoing danger that any such effort will slide into apology, even thereby nurturing some deleterious revival. And although this syndrome was especially prominent in the three countries at issue, it was at work everywhere, affecting the range of questioning about the three interwar departures.

Nominalism is an abiding temptation for historians in any case, and there remain powerful arguments for a nominalist approach in the case at hand. Concluding their widely read study of Nazi population policy, published in 1991, Michael Burleigh and Wolfgang Wippermann stressed "the specific and singular character of the Third Reich. . . . Its objects were novel and *sui generis*." And they warned that "existing theories, whether based upon modernisation, totalitarianism, or global theories of Fascism, [are] poor heuristic devices for a greater understanding of what was a singular regime without precedent or parallel."[30]

This was to suggest not only that Nazism must be studied on its own terms, but also that a comparative approach, which might seem self-recommending, could actually throw us off. In light of the preoccupation with the Holocaust, especially, any effort to try to place Nazism in some wider perspective could seem morally dubious. The determined insistence on singularity by Burleigh and Wippermann prompted the British scholar Richard Bessel to a defensive justification even for the two-way comparison between German Nazism and Italian Fascism.[31]

Bessel's defense was convincing precisely because some of the ongoing questions about the earlier political departures—including their most haunting outcomes—seemed by this point to demand a wider focus. Even as pressures toward nominalism continued, some scholars began to complain that national self-preoccupation was delimiting the focus excessively, restricting the range of questions. Writing in 1988, Tim Mason asked, in an obviously prescriptive mode, "Whatever happened to 'fascism'?"—as a historical problem, a focus for research.[32] The big questions surrounding generic fascism had faded as scholars zeroed in on particular aspects of the problem, including the Holocaust. And generic fascism might seem to afford the best focus for an expanded inquiry. During the 1990s, such scholars as Roger Griffin, Stanley Payne, Walter Laqueur, George Mosse, and MacGregor Knox contributed important works of comparison and synthesis, but renewed questioning on that level raised new uncertainties about the framework, the axes at work, once we transcend a national focus.

Omer Bartov well articulated the question as he lamented the tendency toward fragmentation that remained in the discussion of Nazism, even as scholars worked beyond the intentionalist/functionalist dichotomy. There was still a reluctance to try to place Nazism within the wider contours of Western development—perhaps as manifesting some inherent or aberrant crisis of that development.[33] Seeking to show the way, Bartov suggested that novel features of the First World War had afforded conditions of possibility for some of what happened later—including especially the industrial killing central to the Holocaust.

However, to invoke some crisis of Western development and the novelty of the Great War suggested the need and the scope for a focus wider even than generic fascism. And as Bartov was pointing in this direction, the term "totalitarianism" became more respectable. Although it sometimes crept back into the discussion surreptitiously, some restored it explicitly. But what did it mean, in light of all the research discrediting the earlier model?

The unforeseen collapse of Soviet Communism especially forced a reappraisal of categories, including totalitarianism, which perhaps had been the key in some sense after all. Surveying the whole Soviet experience in light of its failed outcome, Martin Malia applied the category, even suggesting explicitly that it might be used more widely. But his few passing references to the German and Italian cases were relatively conventional, and his sense of the origins of totalitarianism recalled some of Talmon's categories of two generations earlier.[34] At the same time, Malia, Abbott Gleason, and Jeffrey Goldfarb noted that the idea of totalitarianism had been essential to the emergence of "post-totalitarianism" in the thinking of those like Leszek Kolakowski, Adam Michnik, and Václav Havel in East-Central Europe during the 1970s and '80s.[35] Now somehow in decay, or ossifying, or hollowing out, "totalitarianism" was still meaningful, but it had to be understood as encompassing a phase that the earlier model could not remotely have accounted for. If it could wither up from within, hollow out and die, totalitarianism must have entailed an altogether different sort of dynamic.

Perhaps most symptomatically, the noted historian of Nazism Michael Burleigh backed off from the dismissal of totalitarianism that had attended his earlier insistence (with Wolfgang Wippermann) that Nazism was *sui generis* and without parallel. In his massive synthesis *The Third Reich: A New History* (2000), Burleigh explicitly embraced the totalitarianism category, which he defended effectively against the always too facile notion that it had been merely a Cold War tool. As he saw it, the longstanding way of lumping the Nazi and Soviet regimes remained entirely legitimate. At the same time, Burleigh linked totalitarianism to "political religion," a category becoming newly fashionable, although, as he made clear, it had been central to a series of earlier accounts, from J.L. Talmon to Eric Voegelin to Norman Cohn.[36]

However, Burleigh's new contribution proved ambiguous, for although his book was invariably illuminating on specific episodes and dimensions, his use of totalitarianism and political religion proved too conventional to enable him to place Nazism in a fresh perspective. Rather than try—or even to contemplate the need—to rethink the origins and dynamic of totalitarianism, he simply linked it to propaganda, terror, and ideological fantasy, made feasible by the technical reach of the modern state. The overlay of political religion boiled down to the faith of desperate people in a mock Messiah.[37] Those who embraced Nazism "abandoned the burden of thinking for themselves, in favor of what George Orwell described as the tom-tom beat of a latterday tribalism."[38] Burleigh surrounded these familiar notions with an overtly moralistic gloss through the liberal use of such notions as "moral collapse" and "criminal degeneracy."[39] So, in embracing totalitarianism, he was almost explicitly returning to older notions rather than seeking the fresh perspective that was coming to seem possible.

Meanwhile, the tendency to marginalize Italian Fascism as merely authoritarian had provoked periodic doubts, and some suggested that restoring the Italian case might serve the broader discussion. In a seminal article published in 1982, Meir Michaelis usefully countered many of the standard reasons for denying the applicability of totalitarianism to Italian Fascism, as given archetypal formulation by Arendt and developed further by the early De Felice. Emphasizing that the image of complete totalitarianism, which had afforded criteria for judging the Italian case, was the stuff of fictions not realized anywhere, Michaelis accented the parallels between Fascism and Nazism and argued that the oft-cited differences were simply matters of degree. The Italian fascists had sought to form a "new man," even going after Christianity and the Catholic Church in the process. The role of the SS was a differentiating factor, but that simply made Nazism a more radical form of fascism.[40]

At about the time that Tim Mason was asking what had happened to "fascism," implicitly calling for questions that would encompass Italy, Charles Maier explicitly insisted that any effort to better understand generic fascism and totalitarianism required renewed attention to Italy. With a nod to Arendt, Maier acknowledged the usual reasons for denying that Fascist Italy was totalitarian in practice, but he went on to insist that "Mussolini and [Alfredo] Rocco did envisage a new type of political control, qualitatively different from ordinary dictatorship in its effort to sway hearts as well as minds, mold youth, and reinvigorate national existence. It is a mistake and a disservice to make too light of Italian fascism."[41] So Maier insisted on the novelty of Italian Fascist approaches, implicitly as "totalitarian," although his assumption that what was ultimately at issue was merely "political control" perhaps begged the essential questions.

Meanwhile, the Soviet specialist Abbott Gleason, in his penetrating survey of the uses of the concept of totalitarianism, brought home the significance of its Italian origins.[42] Gleason was much struck by the ideas of the philosopher Giovanni Gentile, whose conception of the totalitarian state he found "extraordinary" and "prophetic." He concluded that "Gentile deserves to be called the first philosopher of totalitarianism."[43] Similarly invoking Gentile, the contemporary Italian historian Emilio Gentile (no relation) insisted, on the basis of effective reconceptualization and much new research, that totalitarianism best characterizes the core aspirations and even the direction of practice in Fascist Italy, despite all the obvious compromises.[44] His work of the 1990s showed that ongoing pressures from party rank and file forced a kind of totalitarian direction, even in the face of Mussolini's periodic compromises with established elites. Indeed, at issue for Gentile was explicitly a specifically "Italian way to totalitarianism," a notion that suggested not a static model or a substantial identity between the three regimes but simply that they shared a common core, a new form of political dominion in mass society.[45]

In the English-speaking world during the 1990s, partly in the wake of Emilio Gentile, but primarily from other sources, a number of mostly younger scholars, concerned with newly fashionable topics like aesthetics, spectacle, consumption, ritual, masculinity, and the body, similarly took seriously the totalitarian thrust of Italian Fascism.[46] Even those who accented the regime's ultimately reactionary function fastened upon radically new cultural dimensions that seemed to have grown, in ways that had not been fully understood, from mass democracy in a totalitarian direction. Taken together, these studies brought home the significance of the Fascists' pioneering use of ritual, spectacle, and new media for any effort to reassess the novel politics of the period. However, the rationale for this culturalist emphasis, and the placing of these innovations in the overall trajectory of Italian Fascism, remained uncertain.

So there seemed to be some common aspects to the three regimes, with common sources that seemed not to have been fully understood, even as there was ever-deeper awareness of the limits of the totalitarian model, based on top-down domination. Perhaps it was necessary simply to distinguish theory, or aspiration, from practice, or realization. Robert Thurston was typical of some in suggesting that "totalitarianism is of some use in thinking about what the Nazi and Soviet regimes wanted, but it does not have much to do with what they got," for state intervention "often produced disorder and other negative consequences for the regime."[47] Thurston's characterization of what happened is unassailable, but his conclusion about the applicability of totalitarianism to practice rests on the old model, positing an all-powerful Stalin and a concerted plan for total domination from above.

Although we do not find the old "top-down" domination in any of the three cases, neither is what we *do* find to be understood simply as the limits or absence of such domination. We seem to have a novel, largely unforeseen kind of inter-play between elites, spearheading new forms of action, and those caught up in the process from below. Recent revisionist studies of the Stalinist terror do not simply undermine the earlier model but reveal a complex interaction of center and periphery, above and below, essential to the most troubling features of the Stalinist 1930s. Indeed, it has become clear that those dimensions of Soviet prac-tice required the active agency of ordinary people.[48]

Even as *Alltagsgeschichte* and other inquiries "from below" helped to deflate the straw man of "total domination," they, too, revealed the ways in which ordinary people in Nazi Germany were caught up in an unprecedented dynamic that required—and invited—their active agency. Omer Bartov and Mary Nolan, for example, each noted how *Alltagsgeschichte* proved to have cut both ways: even as it demonstrated continuity, normality, and the scope for passive resistance, *Alltagsgeschichte* brought home the extent of Nazification and the degree of genuine belief and willingness to participate actively that resulted from it.[49] More generally, we increasingly note that Nazism invited new forms of partici-pation by an array of Germans, from ambitious experts to "ordinary men," whose roles were essential even to the most troubling outcomes. So we must get deeper into how the dynamic worked to absorb them, what they thought they were doing, what they experienced themselves as doing.

In the same way, Emilio Gentile's work features the ongoing totalitarian pres-sures from the Fascist Party in Mussolini's Italy—itself an elite in one sense, but also in a sense operating from below *vis-à-vis* the government. Gentile shows that the party was never checked or neutralized, despite a series of what were long viewed as definitive defeats, producing the triumph of the conservative state apparatus or, at best, of Mussolini himself.

If, in looking at the three regimes together, we find not simply a failure of total domination but a complex interaction essential to characteristically novel forms of practice, then we also face new questions about the originating elites—their purposes, their claim to legitimacy, their place in the overall dynamic and the modes of interaction with the rest of society that thereby opened up. In each case, we sense the need to get beyond the longstanding notion of domination/submission to ponder the place of genuine commitment and shared belief in the interaction of leaders and led.

So, although "totalitarianism" again lurks in the discussion, it does not simply portend a return to the earlier, discredited model, not even for Malia, long hostile to Soviet Communism. Even as they treat what they themselves call the totalitarian dynamic in particular instances, Malia, Gentile, and others have suggested, if only implicitly, ways in which we might step back and recast the category to get at wider processes or some common layer beneath or beyond any particular case.[50]

Given the baggage it carries, we may be tempted to jettison "totalitarianism" altogether. Deflated to historical size, however, the category affords the framework we need to approach the three novel departures in a way that illuminates wider origins, common features, and enduring significance. The key is to probe totalitarianism not as a form of rule or set of extreme outcomes but as a historically specific dynamic, which grew from aspirations that became possible only at a particular moment from within the ongoing modern political experiment, and through which certain extreme and unforeseen outcomes came to be. Although the dictators grasped certain contours and intended certain directions, no one set out to create what actually resulted, no one knew what totalitarianism was— because it was just then coming to be for the first time.

Communism and fascism, Left and Right

Before proceeding, we must tackle explicitly the most obvious objections to any attempt to treat the three regimes together. We still have plausible reasons to think in terms of the longstanding Left/Right axis, and certain differences between Communism and fascism that have long seemed fundamental may seem to outweigh any common features. From this familiar perspective, whatever commonality resulted on the operational level, the origins and meaning of the Communist and fascist departures were profoundly different. However extreme or distorted it became, the Soviet experiment remained linked to Marxism and thus, it would seem, to the progressive Western mainstream bound up with the Enlightenment. With fascism, in contrast, we may seem to have mere counterrevolution, or perhaps something less comprehensible, and even more distasteful, as nihilistic, atavistic, and irrationalist. However naive the Bolsheviks may have been about their overall prospects, they were energized by the belief that they were pursuing some such universalist vision, whereas the Nazi vision, especially with its accent on human differentiation and racial hierarchy, was manifestly exclusionist. And although Italian Fascism posited a community based on culture and not race, it was based on an exclusivist nationalism, whether or not it posited a hierarchy of nationalities. At the very least, Communism and fascism have seemed asymmetrical insofar as the former claimed to derive from a well-articulated prior ideology, while fascism has seemed to lack a comparable pedigree.

The Communists made a full-scale socio-economic revolution, overturning class relations and virtually eliminating private property. However wayward or excessive, this was the direction that had come to be expected of a genuine revolution. The two fascist regimes made no such revolution, and thus, from this perspective, the revolutionary claim of each is bound to seem a sham. Indeed, radical opposition to Marxism was central from the start to the self-understanding and practice of both. Each won lots of support from those fearing Communism, and anti-Communism gave each a measure of legitimacy with established elites. Many found the primary *raison d'être* for fascism in its capacity to head off precisely the sort of revolution that was in progress in Russia.

Still, it is easy to show that although support on the basis of anti-Communism was crucial to give both Fascism and Nazism the chance for power, the content of their respective departures from the mainstream went well beyond such delimited counterrevolutionary purposes. But even when we probe that content—motivating purposes, priorities, long-term goals, and overall self-understanding—fascism seems to have differed crucially from Communism in ways that can be understood in Left/Right terms. Virtually from the start, even many of those featuring totalitarianism as a way of characterizing a common novelty also insisted on the ongoing significance of the Left/Right axis. In J.L. Talmon's classic distinction, even within totalitarianism, the Left stood for universalism, individualism, and rationalism, as opposed to racial and organic thinking. However, impulses distinguishable in recognizably Left and Right strands could each take totalitarian form.[51]

Fascist Italy and Nazi Germany ended up military allies, ultimately fighting the Soviet Union, among others. Meanwhile, the growing threat from fascism during the 1930s was partly responsible for some of the excesses that marked Stalinism as a particular direction from within the Marxist—Leninist experiment in the Soviet Union. The overall mutual antagonism might suggest the need to stick to the longstanding Left/Right axis.

Even insofar as we fasten upon the murderous extremes of Nazism and Stalinism, we have long found reasons for distinguishing them. For Saul Friedländer, comparison with Stalinist mass murder points up the singularity of the Nazi extermination of the Jews. The crimes of Stalinism were committed in the name of an ideal that served as an explanation—and as the basis for the Communists' own self-understanding. But, said Friedländer, the Nazi accent on secrecy suggests that even the Nazis themselves never found a commonly understandable explanation for the genocide.[52] In the same vein, Omer Bartov accents the differences between Nazi and Soviet practice in the war on the eastern front. Even under Stalin, Bartov insists, the Russians were not trying to do to the Germans what the Nazis tried to do to the Russians. Cruel, dictatorial, even totalitarian though it was, the Stalinist regime, said Bartov, was not seeking to exterminate or enslave the peoples of East-Central Europe.[53]

The two fascist regimes went down in flames, not outliving their founders. The Soviet regime, in contrast, lasted several generations and then merely fizzled out—almost half a century after the collapse of Fascism and Nazism. Many have found in these latter a kind of self-destructive dynamism, whereas Communism, having survived Stalin, got bogged down in bureaucratic ossification and eventually succumbed to a kind of loss of will. This difference, too, might seem to be evidence that these regimes were so different, not only in motivating aspiration but also in practical dynamic, that to place them within the same framework obscures more than it illuminates.

Concern with difference and asymmetry tended to keep even those featuring totalitarianism from any sustained attempt to define the historically specific origins of totalitarianism itself. Insofar as they sought origins, it was essentially the origins of the Left and Right impulses, with the common totalitarianism generally reducible to some combination of ahistorical psychological propensities and methods of rule, including the advent of novel means of mobilization and control. However, recent cultural changes, especially with the end of the Cold War, have dissolved or at least called into question some of the earlier basis for accenting both Left/Right differentiation and asymmetry.

It has become clear that Cold War concerns cut both ways in our approaches to the Soviet experience—and affected our approach to fascism as well. The counterattack against the "totalitarianism" of the late 1960s was a volley in the Cold War battle, just as was the embrace of the category by the early 1950s. We need not accept all of Malia's provocative argument, to be considered in Chapter 5, to grasp his point that the new accent on social history, or history from below, that shaped Soviet studies during the 1960s and 1970s stemmed partly from an ideologically charged desire to explain the Soviet regime as the product of popular action—and thus as democratically legitimate.[54] In some of its expressions, that approach seemed to be congruent with the notion, associated especially with E.H. Carr and Isaac Deutscher, and also reflecting Cold War concerns, that under the circumstances the Soviet Union faced, Stalinism afforded the only viable way of carrying on the Bolshevik Revolution. For those taking this tack, the Soviet experiment remained potentially positive as the bearer of a universal principle, pointing beyond liberal capitalism. In other formulations, the accent was on "convergence" with the West instead. Under the Soviet circumstances of relative backwardness, Communism was progressive—as an alternative path to the same modernity.

Neither tack was sustainable in light of the collapse of the whole Communist system, but the alternatives that most obviously emerged as a result—especially liberal triumphalism and/or a renewed reading of the whole Leninist departure as a usurpation—entailed a delimited range of questions about what the Soviet experiment had entailed and meant. Especially when considered in light of the wider crisis of the Marxist Left—manifested by the decline, for example, of Italian Communism, long viewed as the most innovative in the West—there was scope for fresh questioning about the wider place of twentieth-century Marxism and especially the actual course of the Soviet experiment in light of its Leninist origins. It seemed possible that through the actual history something new and even more deeply different had come to be, something that none of the categories on the table could encompass.

It was partly because of the other side of the Cold War framework that fascism had so long been explained away as mere reaction, "counterrevolution," stemming from establishment interests and the traumas of petty bourgeois losers, who were resentful of, among other things, the emerging industrial proletariat, assigned by Marxism a uniquely progressive historical role.[55] In the same way, a kind of double standard led us to take Communism seriously, to credit its idealism and thus the rationale for Soviet practice, but to approach fascism in reductionist terms. The end of the Cold War helped to open the way to a more open, flexible approach toward fascism, especially with respect to its place in "modernity" or comparably overarching processes. On the most basic, almost trivial, level, this meant that rather than debunking, we recognize that there were opportunists and idealists on both sides, and that whereas the bases of the opportunism, as ahistorical, are easy to grasp in either case, those of the idealism may not be.[56]

Counter to the longstanding tendency to dismiss fascism in terms of some combination of nihilism, opportunism, class reaction, counterrevolution, and failed adjustment to modernity, Stanley Payne noted with approval in his author-itative synthesis of 1995 that fascism was increasingly viewed as "a revolutionary new epochal phenomenon with an ideology and a distinctive set of ambitions in its own right."[57] This was at least implicitly to warn against any conflation of fascism and Communism around the old notion of totalitarianism, but Payne was calling our attention first to precisely those revolutionary aspirations. And although there are reasons to focus our renewed questioning on generic fascism, to portray fascism as "revolutionary . . . in its own right" is to invite new ques-tions probing the interface between that revolutionary aspiration and its outcome with the dominant Marxian idea of revolution and *its* outcome in the Soviet Union. This would require backing up to re-examine the relationship between the evolving Marxist tradition and the ideas and aspirations that ended up feeding fascism. And doing so might call into question the Left/Right axis or transcend it altogether, at least as it has been brought to bear in the case at hand. At the same time, new questions about origins, aspirations, and resulting modes of operation might reveal parallels between the Communist and fascist experiments that the old totalitarianism category could not possibly have encom-passed.[58]

Just as we have become less prone to say that fascism had no ideological pedi-gree, while Communism did, we are less sure of the significance of the Soviet link to the earlier Marxian tradition. Indeed, the place of Marxism is doubly problem-atic in terms of our discussion. Never fixed or stable, Marxism encountered ever more insistent questions about priorities and strategy, even about its intellectual center of gravity, by the later 1890s, the period of the multi-sided revisionist chal-lenge. Facing a crossroads, if not a crisis, Marxism spewed quite disparate offshoots from within, even as it also began to attract the attention of major intel-lectuals with independent perspectives, including Emile Durkheim, Vilfredo Pareto, Benedetto Croce, and Max Weber. And we must ask how the new ideas that emerged related to the advent of the ideas and aspirations that led to fascism.

Second, whatever "Marxism" meant by that point, the extent to which, and the sense in which, it actually guided, or *could* have guided, practice during the formative period of the Soviet Union is not clear. Obviously, the Soviet leader-ship followed Marxism in emphasizing class antagonism and in assaulting private property as the two fascist regimes did not, but once we place those directions within the wider framework of Soviet practice, it is not clear that they indicate a qualitative difference from fascism. It is arguable that first with Lenin, then with Stalin, Soviet Communism entailed a double departure from Marxism, so that Soviet practice necessarily led into uncertain new terrain. Because Marxism was itself uncertain and unstable in important respects, we might need a wider array of admixtures, beyond the familiar standbys of Russian backwardness and personal idiosyncrasy, to understand the Soviet dynamic, whatever the claim of the agents to embody the Marxist tradition. That array might encompass antecedent diagnoses and prescriptions that intersected, on some level, with those that fed the contemporaneous fascist departures. Thus we might find areas of overlap that we have missed not just in the modes of operation but also in the sense of possibilities and priorities within the wider effort to create an alternative to the liberal mainstream. The relationship between fascism and Soviet Communism would thus have been more complex that the antithesis between "the emancipatory project" and reaction that for so long shaped discussion.

Although the mutual antagonism between fascism and Communism was crucial, its basis thus becomes less clear. Insofar as fascism emerged not merely as reactionary but as revolutionary in its own right, it could only have been as a competitor to the established Marxist tradition. The two sides competed for the post-liberal terrain, and their way of playing off and learning from each other helped to generate the unforeseen dynamic of the era.[59] The Bolshevik Revolution and the first phases of Soviet practice radically changed the political situation in Italy and Germany, not least in affecting what could now be imagined, what seemed to have become possible. Lenin influenced Mussolini, Mussolini and Stalin both influenced Hitler, and the advent of Nazism changed the situation for the Stalin regime in the Soviet Union. Indeed, there is plenty of evidence of mutual admiration and influence, rivalry and fear, all constituting a kind of web connecting the three regimes.[60]

In a sense, each saw itself as spearheading, in competitive interaction with the others, a reaction of youth and new vitality against the old bourgeois Europe. From the fascist perspective, Marxist hegemony within the revolutionary tradition was by now a central part of the problem precisely because Marxist categories and approaches seemed to obstruct diagnosis of the limits of the modern liberal order—and thus to obstruct prescription and overcoming as well. For their part, the Communists tried to dismiss fascism as merely reactionary, but in their more lucid moments they understood that the challenge was more complex.[61]

So, although their mutual antagonism might seem to indicate that Communism and fascism cannot be treated in tandem, the interplay between them suggests that they played off each other as rivals, contesting the same post-liberal terrain. And the scope for such competition especially raises questions even about the Left/Right axis, which was itself historically specific—a product of the French Revolution. Although characterological underpinnings can plausibly be suggested, the criteria of Left and Right were never altogether clear. Talmon's classic distinction, based on perceptions of human nature, surely retains some force; thus, for example, both De Felice and Michaelis were quick to embrace it. Yet it was symptomatic that they differed over where Italian Fascism fitted.[62] Moreover, even Talmon's criteria could blur with further historical experience.

The Left/Right axis was implicated in the dynamic and could hardly have stood up in its original form as experience gathered and political priorities changed. Thus that axis was itself open to question as the implications of the mainstream liberal democratic direction became clearer and as questions about the requirements for a systematic alternative emerged at the same time. Thinkers like Pareto, Georges Sorel, and Giovanni Gentile, seeking fresh approaches around the turn of the century, are notoriously difficult to place on any Left/Right axis. Pareto, especially, explicitly called into question the criteria and utility of the Left/Right distinction.

Even insofar as that distinction remained meaningful in something like its original terms, totalitarianism could become more relevant, overwhelming it, at some historically specific point, with the advent of new political possibilities. In an earlier work on some of the intellectual antecedents of Italian Fascism, I distinguished Left and Right on the basis of criteria akin to Talmon's. Italian fascism grew from recognizably Left and Right components—and the difference persisted within the Fascist regime, producing tensions that proved central to its dynamic and outcome. But they had something important in common—a novel sense of possibility, of the scope for unprecedented forms of collective, history-making action—that is usefully characterized as totalitarian. It was on that basis that they could work together as fascists.

Even our ways of distinguishing between the murderous extremes of Nazism and Stalinism may not convince insofar as we better frame the question of common totalitarianism. To gauge the significance of the asymmetries that Friedländer and Bartov noted, we would have to probe the dynamics of the two regimes more deeply.

Whereas the differences in longevity and in mode of ending are also significant, they do not rule out the possibility that there were significant common elements in the three dynamics at work. We would simply have to make sense of the fact that, as it turned out, regimes of this novel sort could go down in flames or gradually lose conviction and fizzle out. Even this difference might suggest not so much a radical disparity as a kind of paired opposition inviting deeper questions about common features in the internal dynamics of the three regimes.

In short, precisely because the Left/Right axis was not static, given once and for all, but historical, its structure and place were—and remain—open to contest. And such contesting proves to have been central both to the process that yielded the conditions of possibility for the new interwar regimes *and* to the competitive interaction between them. So the relationship of the Left/Right axis to totalitarianism is more complex than it first appears; it is not as if totalitarianism warrants one kind of inquiry, Left/Right another. The basis of the fascist/communist difference was never a given, but we might now be better prepared to address the questions that the emergence of fascism raised about the whole political spectrum.

Still, even insofar as fresh inquiry reveals commonalities not yet fully grasped, certain asymmetries between generic fascism and Soviet Communism are undeniable, and they produce awkwardness in any quest to encompass both. So we must take care to avoid forcing the argument, and I will not hesitate to treat some subset of the three when it seems to illuminate this or that aspect of the overall problem.

Layers, proportions, and modes of questioning

Even a preliminary effort to sort out conceptually the impulses at work in these political departures leads to the problem of—what shall we call them?—layers and proportions. At issue are the disparate categories of understanding, the place and relative importance of each, and the interface among them. Most basic is the interplay of what we take to be ahistorical or suprahistorical with what we take to be historically specific. The ahistorical encompasses an array of categories from evil and power to careerism and fear that obviously enter the discussion from very different angles. The historically specific, in turn, may be idiosyncratically national or supranational.

The national obviously encompasses an array from longer-term factors—such as Germany's putative *Sonderweg* or Russia's particular revolutionary traditions—to some immediate crisis. However, although any account must encompass both national and suprahistorical components, we sense that no matter how we shuffle and combine the elements from those two layers, we need something more, something supranational yet historically specific. Turning to this layer, we might think first simply of common features in idiosyncratic national contexts that differentiated some set of countries from the mainstream. Such common idiosyncrasy can itself encompass a broad array—from a common experience of a wider event like the First World War to peculiarities in industrial development, possibly stemming from idiosyncrasies of geography, demography, or resource base. Even when we move beyond common idiosyncrasy to factors not limited to the countries in question, certain sets of categories are relatively familiar. We may think first of the advent of new techniques, new means of rule. Adding that dimension to ahistorical personal propensities and historically specific national contextual factors may seem sufficient to understand the eruption of totalitarianism.

Yet we often assume that the supranational historically specific entailed more—most basically, that the totalitarian experience revealed hitherto unforeseen possibilities of modern secular mass politics. Omer Bartov had something on the same level in mind in arguing that the novel experience of the First World War was essential to establish the possibility of the subsequent industrial killing of the twentieth century. The common wartime experience added conditions of possibility for subsequent departures, even aspects of their content, although obviously it took other factors to differentiate those countries that actually engaged in industrial murder from those that did not.

But we often invoke broader and less tangible factors as well, encompassing aspects of the Enlightenment deployment or "modernity." Thus, for example, Zygmunt Bauman pinpointed modern bureaucracy and instrumental rationality as historically specific conditions of possibility for the Holocaust.[63] Although it was obviously not sufficient, without this particular supranational, historically specific dimension, the Holocaust could not have happened. Bauman's way of relating the historically specific, as modern instrumental rationality, to something ahistorical—in this case, the human ethical capacity itself—operates on precisely the level of questioning we need. We need to get at whatever was supranational *and* historically specific, beyond the familiar ahistorical psychological propensities and national situational factors that were obviously also at work.

But whereas those like Bartov and Bauman have offered valuable indications of the supranational, historically specific elements to be probed, we are only just beginning to discern the contours of an overall framework. The question concerns the extent to which, the sense in which, totalitarianism became possible, obviously together with alternative directions, only from within the modern framework. At issue is not merely the *means* for a novel totalitarian direction but rather whatever modern, historically specific sources can be found for the content of the underlying aspiration and the sense that it was desirable to move in that direction in the first place. In other words, the supranational, historically specific dimension may have been crucial to the direction and content of the departure, although it would have been neither a psychological source nor an immediate triggering mechanism. At the same time, however, a better understanding of that dimension would clarify how the undoubted nationally specific and suprahistorical dimensions came into play.

The complex triangular interaction among ahistorical, idiosyncratically national, and supranational historically specific factors affords an array of possibilities, rendering interpretation complicated indeed. Although some under-standing of layers and proportions is necessarily at work even in the most delimited, specialized account, the issue is rarely confronted explicitly, but it has crucial implications for modes of approach, the range of questions we are prepared to ask. As it has happened, certain combinations, certain modes of interface between the layers, have became paradigmatic, thus limiting the discus-sion. At issue is the scope for an approach that, while keeping the ahistorical and the national in proportion, explores supranational historically specific factors that may have been more central than we have realized.

However, we cannot expect some definitive, universally compelling argu-ment for any particular way of apportioning the layers. Proportions are indeterminate. To some extent, the way in which any of us sorts it out is a matter of prior disposition, a prior sense of how the world happens, which often seems to be beyond historical evidence or argument. In confronting the case at hand, some are prone to fall back almost immediately to ahistorical moral categories or to reduce to ahistorical psychological categories. Moreover, a complex hierarchy of agency and involvement is to be understood, from originating elites to those who played certain roles out of seemingly banal motives like careerism or fear. We could not possibly assess all the possibilities at every layer and specify the place of each in the overall phenomenon. Still, a deeper sense of what was at issue on the supranational, historically specific level can significantly affect our sense of the proportions and modes of inter-face between the layers.

To pinpoint the most salient obstacles to understanding, we must consider, in a preliminary way, some of the categories and modes of interface between the ahistorical and the historically specific and between the idiosyncratically national and the supranational historically specific. This will enable us to question, and to propose ways of expanding, the dominant ways of conceiving the interface among them.

The ahistorical encompasses an array starting with evil and power, which, in the case at hand, have proved to be bound up with a tendency to inflate or deflate, thereby delimiting the measure of specifically historical engagement and understanding. When stated abstractly, the danger of moralism is obvious, but it is worth pinpointing certain tendencies specific to the study of the three interwar departures. Especially in light of the most sensitive provisional or final outcomes, such as the Holocaust, and the terror famine and the "great terror" in the Soviet Union, a certain moralism seems to be *de rigueur*; to eschew it is to invite charges of insensitivity or even apology.[64] Preoccupation with the Holocaust, especially, has made us quick to invoke evil, even "the universality of evil"—a particularly fatuous example of the tendency toward inflating moralism.[65] As evil, the phenomena become so grandiose as to defy historical understanding. Yet in another sense, the moralistic inflation seems to afford us all the explanation we need: the agents were criminals, gangsters; that is why these terrible things happened.[66] And the lesson, the moral imperative, is clear: let us guard against the criminals and gangsters among us.

"Evil," at one end of the ahistorical spectrum, surely has a place in the discussion, but how it plays against the historically specific—whence the evil?—is much of what is to be understood. And to the extent that moral outrage in light of outcomes leads us to fasten upon ahistorical evil up front, we compromise the scope for asking the sort of questions that might enable us to understand how the evil came into the world, historically.[67] Indeed, such moralism feeds a tendency toward backloading or teleological approaches that take the Holocaust, for example, as a revelation of Nazism's deepest meaning, as what most needs to be explained, as opposed to one contingent outcome of a larger process.[68] Monstrous crimes there surely were, and they were no accident, but we compromise our chance to understand their sources if, imputing evil or criminality *a priori*, we fail to treat them in their historical genesis, with sufficient openness to historical contingency. Our tendency toward moralistic put-down distances us from the agents, makes them Other, and thereby precludes the measure of engagement necessary for that historical understanding. Yet such understanding is essential to underpin our own deeper moral response, including whatever variation on "never again."

Conversely, some of our accents seem, to some at least, to suggest a troubling moral indifference or relativism. Virtually from the outset of his sensitive examination of the quest to understand Hitler, journalist Ron Rosenbaum was struck by the scholarly reluctance to call Hitler evil, in the strict sense of doing wrong knowingly. Hugh Trevor-Roper's contention that Hitler was convinced of his own rectitude, that he really believed in what he was doing, troubled Rosenbaum, who kept asking how professional historians assess evil.[69] His concerns reflected the wider cultural fear that unless we deny any such rectitude and insist on evil up front, we merely relativize and even absolve.

Emil Fackenheim avoided the problem of relativism by insisting that Hitler did *not* believe it—he was play-acting. He was thus all the more evil, radically evil—even representing a new category of evil.[70] Thus we encounter the historicity of evil, a category explored still more explicitly by another of Rosenbaum's sources, philosopher Berel Lang, on the basis of a parallel argument for intended evil that we will consider in more detail in Chapter 7. Lang found intended evil to be the only way to make sense of the Holocaust, not just what the agents did but how they did it—the secrecy surrounding the project, for example. Indeed, Lang concluded that the Nazi agents knew it was wrong and did it "at least in part *because* it was wrong: wrongdoing had assumed for them the status of a principle."[71]

But to posit the historicity of evil obviously raises difficult questions about the interplay of ahistorical and historically specific conditions of possibility. At first glance, to posit intended evil may suggest reduction to some ahistorical character type, with the historical question concerning how those intending evil managed to attain the power actually to act on their intention. We seem to have the familiar combination of ahistorical psychology and national trigger, but to posit the historicity of evil is to suggest a deeper historical dimension to be addressed through research. The question concerns the historically specific sources of the novel intention. To address it requires probing for changes in the sense of the human place in the world, of human opportunity and responsibility, and their implications for previously elaborated moral categories. And this dimension may carry beyond Lang's sense of the possibilities altogether. What he could only attribute to intended evil may be better understood in terms of a wider, historically specific change in the possibilities for moral response. In other words, although moral categories are surely at issue, we may find supranational historically specific sources, beyond intended evil, that make deeper sense of the modes of action that Lang was seeking to understand. Whether this would simply return us to the relativistic rectitude argument that so troubled Rosenbaum would remain to be seen.

Assessing the place of "power" need not entail the special problems of moralism, but it too requires questioning the interface of an essentially ahistorical category with wider, supranational historically specific factors. That power is centrally at issue in the case at hand is obvious; a newly extreme concentration of power was central to all three new regimes. But why and how? Insofar as we focus on the leaders, we often posit mere megalomania, a desire for self-aggrandizement, power for its own sake. Although the leaders took advantage of newly available means, they seem, from this perspective, to have been driven by an ahistorical psychological propensity, obviously differentiated across populations. But although this still commonplace view is surely reassuring, even "power" may have a historically specific dimension, transcending mere ahistorical megalomania. So we must probe the basis for the greater concentration of power, which, too, may reflect a changing sense of human opportunity and responsibility, the need and scope to act in new ways. From this perspective, the psychological propensity was surely operative, but in interface with something at once supranational and historically specific.

Power is but the first wedge in a set of ahistorical psychological propensities that have long been taken as central to the totalitarian experience. An array of overlapping categories, all entailing a deflating reductionism, has seemed to afford modes of differentiation from the norm that are more broadly encompassing than the megalomania of the leaders. And obviously the relevant suprahistorical dimension depends on the level of involvement. We think of the "authoritarian personality" or some propensity toward violence or even sadism. We think of the paranoid propensities at work in what Umberto Eco has called "ur-fascism."[72] Also at issue are fanaticism, utopianism, Messianism, or the embrace of totalist ideology, all reflecting an intolerance of ambiguity and standing opposed to freedom and "the open society," which are surely self-recommending to normal people under normal circumstances.[73]

From Erich Fromm to Karl Dietrich Bracher, "escape from freedom" was taken to explain why the masses subordinated themselves to a dictatorial leader whose own purposes seemed readily comprehensible in other terms, from megalomania to fanaticism. The implied argument is that although such propensities are always to be found in some subset of the population, they take political form only under specific, extreme conditions, most immediately on the national level, although intermediate layers are generally implicated as well. At one point, for example, "escape from freedom" was associated especially with the historically specific insecurities of the lower middle class at a supposedly pivotal moment in the development of industrial capitalism. However, the direction has often seemed to respond to the wider, although still historically specific, disruptions of modernity itself. From such perspectives, national contextual features exacerbate supranational, historically specific strains to trigger the response.

Although this mechanism entails historically specific intervening layers, the essential content of the response is the latent ahistorical propensity of certain psychological types. But the approach may be limiting and reductionist in its understanding of the response in light of the supranational, historically specific categories potentially at issue. Indeed, as we saw to be the case with evil and power, even categories like freedom and authority may interface with the supranational historically specific in more complex ways than is conventionally recognized. Deeper attention to the supranational historically specific, in interaction with both the nationally specific and ahistorical propensities, may be necessary before we can understand how such differentiation became germane and then account for the content of the departures at issue.

Concerned especially with totalitarianism from the Left in his pioneering *The Origins of Totalitarian Democracy* of 1950, J.L. Talmon implied that the underlying source was an enduring psychological propensity, presumably differentiated across populations, that came to the fore with the familiar disruptions of the modern period. Talmon offered a good example of reductionist deflating as, seeking to draw out the wider lessons in concluding, he recognized that:

> the power of the historian or political philosopher to influence events is no doubt limited, but he can influence the attitude of mind which is adopted towards those developments. Like a psychoanalyst who cures by making the patient aware of his subconscious, the social analyst may be able to attack the human urge which calls totalitarian democracy into existence, namely the longing for a final resolution to all contradictions and conflicts into a state of total harmony. It is a harsh but none the less necessary task to drive home the truth that human society and human life can never reach a state of repose. That imagined repose is another name for the security offered by a prison, and the longing for it may in a sense be an expression of cowardice and laziness, of the inability to face the fact that life is a perpetual and never resolved crisis. All that can be done is to proceed by the method of trial and error.[74]

Although psychoanalysis is now less fashionable, even as simile, the notion that the key to understanding these reactions against liberal democracy is to unearth a pathological psychological tendency remains deeply ingrained. The same mode of thinking underlies Isaiah Berlin's way of locating Joseph de Maistre at the origins of fascism.[75] From this angle, there is indeed a crucial historically specific layer, but the key to understanding is the incapacity of some, in light of ahistorical psychological propensities, to handle the healthy liberal pluralism and openness that became possible with the modern world.

In the wider culture, such deflation/reduction entails a tendency toward flattening and stereotype. Not only is fascism routinely invoked as a term of political abuse, but even in sophisticated humanistic discussion it is often equated with cruelty, sadism, and kinky sex.[76] Such stereotyping then reinforces the tendency to reduce to the ahistorical—and thereby to distance the fascists and sidestep a deeper encounter. "Fascism" itself becomes an ahistorical psychological category, and understanding becomes circular: they did it because they were fascists.

Whereas the scope for a response like out-group hostility may be universal, idiosyncratic historical experience obviously can make racial hatred, for example, especially likely in certain countries. So it is possible that what our three countries had in common was some level of idiosyncratic experience that brought some combination of differentiating ahistorical psychological propensities to the fore. Once again, this is to limit the supranational historically specific to common national idiosyncrasy and to reduce the content of the departure to something ahistorical—authoritarianism, paranoia, hate. However rich the interface, from this perspective the content or substance of the common departure lies on that ahistorical level; the historically specific is simply the national context that opens the way for such universals.

Also at issue has been an ahistorical capacity for cruelty that is seemingly more prevalent than has hitherto been recognized, even latent in the vast majority of human beings, although it too becomes operative only under extreme circumstances. In light of the case at hand, that propensity has been widely discussed in terms of two famous but controversial sets of experiments, by Stanley Milgram and Philip Zimbardo, respectively, during the 1970s.[77] Milgram demonstrated the capacity of apparently ordinary people to inflict pain when following seemingly legitimate authority, especially instructions from those taken to be experts. Zimbardo's Stanford prison experiment suggested a tendency to resort to overt cruelty when in positions of absolute domination over others.

The results of each experiment seemed to undercut the importance of abiding psychological differentiation; under certain circumstances, the vast majority will respond in the ways indicated. What differentiates is not some ahistorical psychological propensity but the context, the triggering circumstances. And although we think of the national level first, Bauman suggested in *Modernity and the Holocaust* that Milgram's mechanisms came into play especially with the advent of modern bureaucracy and instrumental rationality.[78]

Although the propensities at issue for Milgram and Zimbardo could not have initiated these regimes, those capacities may have played a significant second-order role, carrying forward, even radicalizing, a process that could not have produced the same outcomes without them. But although it is easy to take the responses in question as automatic, as in a laboratory experiment, we must take care to ask, again, how the ahistorical propensity at issue interfaces with the terms of the historically specific triggering situation. At issue is not merely a simple juxtaposition or complement. We need to specify how the specific content of Nazism, for example, drew on such suprahistorical psychological propensities, then shaped them, perhaps intensified them, in certain ways. Even categories like power, authority, fear, expertise, and duty may entail a greater dimension of historical specificity than we tend to recognize.

The whole package of ahistorical categories, from power and evil to abiding personality differentiation, from careerism, conformity, and fear to fanaticism, sadism, and hate, surely has a place in the overall economy of inquiry and understanding. But despite all our efforts to avoid moralism or reductionism, there remains a tendency to invoke some subset of these ahistorical universals prematurely, *a priori*, as a ready-made explanation, without fully considering their interface with the other layers. Whether by an inflating moralism or a deflating reductionism, such categories shrink the area that demands genuine historical engagement with the agents responsible and with the wider situation from which their diagnoses and prescriptions emerged.

The undoubted place of the idiosyncratically national may invite its own form of reductionism. Whether we posit parallel histories or some common wayward-ness or idiosyncrasy, we are tempted to invoke the putative German *Sonderweg*, or Russia's relative backwardness, or the inadequacy of national integration in Italy, as a ready explanation. The national layer may seem sufficiently rich to have trig-gered the ahistorical psychological propensities on its own, so we neglect the interface of idiosyncratic national features with contemporaneous supranational, historically specific factors. Thus, although we may fasten upon such general factors as the dislocations of modernity or the advent of bureaucracy, we attribute much of the content of the supranational to ahistorical propensities. This, again, is to delimit consideration of the supranational historically specific. The challenge is to specify the factors operating on the national layer, their relative weight, and their modes of interface with factors on the other two layers.

Just as we might rely too heavily on the national, we might delimit it unduly—even from a plausible desire to ward off contextualist reductionism. Thus, for example, Bartov questioned the mix that Christopher Browning invoked to account for the willingness of the now familiar "ordinary men" of Hamburg Reserve Police Battalion 101 to kill defenseless Jews face to face. Whereas Browning relied especially on ahistorical factors, including the Milgram mechanism, in interface with the immediate German wartime context, Bartov suggested that these men might have been especially receptive to Nazi policies, or simply especially prone to following orders, in light of longer-term cultural traditions specific to Germany.[79]

There was nothing in Bartov's way of framing the question that inflated the long-term national unduly or precluded other variables. The significance of ahistorical propensities was still at issue, as were the more immediate contextual triggering mechanisms that Browning featured. At issue was simply the range of variables and the proportions between them, and Bartov was suggesting that Browning may not have afforded enough space to such longer-term national idiosyncratic factors. Perhaps even ordinariness had to be understood as more idiosyncratically national and less purely ahistorical than Browning had allowed.

Insofar as we find something in common on the level of national contextual idiosyncrasy, its significance may not be as obvious as we assume. To assess the issue requires attention to the interface between the idiosyncratically national and the supranational historically specific. As we will discuss in the next section, the paradigmatic way of conceiving that interface, fastening upon some common waywardness or backwardness, producing divergence from the healthy modern mainstream, is subject to question.

Because we must encompass three distinct layers, we must beware of certain tempting dualistic modes of thinking that may delimit or preclude prejudicially. Encompassing only two sides of the triangle, we assume that if it was not this, it must have been that. Thus even efforts to avoid a delimiting monism may reinforce our tendency to frame the alternatives in dualistic terms and thereby to sidestep explicit attention to the supranational, historically specific dimension.

Noting that some see apology in anything less than a 100 percent emphasis on the personal factor in the Soviet case, J. Arch Getty and Roberta Manning insisted convincingly that we need the contextual as well as the personal.[80] But that contextual is then too easily left national, with implicit supranational, historically specific factors left unexamined. Still more explicitly, Robert Thurston held that in approaching the Stalinist 1930s, as in approaching Nazism, we must get beyond attributing all the extremes to intention at the top and encompass the active role of ordinary people. Doing so, he noted, makes the overall phenomenon more disturbing, not less, for what is to be understood is not just a handful of criminals but a dynamic involving millions in one role or another. Thus Stalinist terror is not so easily packaged as an idiosyncratic national problem; it becomes, Thurston appropriately reminds us, a more insistently human problem instead.[81] But here again an appropriate objection against a single factor tends to leave us with just two categories, as Thurston tended to conflate "human" with ahistorical, with abiding human propensities or conditions. In the same way, insofar as we insist, for example, that the Holocaust was not just German, we tend to resort to the ahistorically human, perhaps even "the universality of evil," as opposed to anything supranational historically specific. The key is to avoid either/or by keeping all three layers in mind.

The interface of the ahistorical and the historically specific is obviously central to the question of the diachronic range of whatever possibilities came to light in the three regimes. Although the regimes themselves are obviously finished, we ask, to put it simply, whether we are to understand totalitarianism as an ongoing *human* possibility, as an ongoing *modern* possibility, or as an *"epochal"* phenomenon, characteristic of and confined to an era now over. The ahistorical impulses that played into the phenomenon continue by definition, but we generally agree that to some extent "totalitarianism" stemmed from conditions of possibility that emerged historically, becoming part of the human horizon in historical time. Some or all of those conditions may continue, some or all may have ended—even have been consumed through the experience of totalitarianism itself. But we have trouble even formulating the question coherently unless we better grasp the supranational, historically specific dimension in its interface with the other layers at work.

Although concerned only with the German case, Bartov explicitly addressed the three-way interface in noting that what especially troubles us about Nazism is "that incredible mixture of detachment and brutality, distance and cruelty, pleasure and indifference," which stemmed, as he saw it, from an explosive combination of modernity with "ancient prejudices, hatreds, and violent instincts."[82] By implication, the essentially ahistorical elements—even cruelty and sadism—might have remained merely latent, but they were somehow actualized with the advent of a particular historically specific situation. And although he recognized that the idiosyncratically German was essential as well, Bartov insisted that an essential dimension of that situation was supranationally modern, entailing the ascendancy of experts, especially the physician and the lawyer. Moreover, as we noted briefly above, he insisted on *industrial* killing, as opposed simply to ethnic cleansing or even genocide. And various aspects of the experience of the Great War, especially, made the scope for such killing, as well as the scope for expertise, particularly germane.

Still, although he was suggesting the kind of thing that might be involved on the supranational, historically specific level, Bartov was especially concerned with the origins of, and the ongoing scope for, modern genocide, as opposed to totalitarianism, as a new historical-political orientation from within which genocide was perhaps especially likely. The question is how we might address the supranational, historically specific level in the broader way necessary.

From modernization to contested modernities

Insofar as we encompassed it at all, our sense of the supranational historically specific long reflected a master narrative of modernization, entailing a particular, putatively universal model or standard of development that we have recently called into question, especially with the postmodern turn. From that long-standing perspective, variation was anomalous waywardness, *Sonderweg*. Or perhaps the anomaly lay simply in relative backwardness, which suggested the need for novel means to catch up. But we now begin to grasp how seriously that narrative delimited our range of questioning.

In the Italian and German cases, the departure from the mainstream was long attributed to the combination of an industrial bourgeoisie too insecure to produce a genuinely democratic polity and a lower middle class particularly threatened by the rise of industrial capitalism and, more generally, the whole modernization process. It mattered that in both countries, modernization took place against a backdrop of late unification and late but concentrated industrial-ization, to some extent fostered from above, by the state. From this perspective, Fascism and Nazism reflected a crisis in class relations and, in the last analysis, a revolt against modernity itself.

Luigi Salvatorelli's pioneering analysis of Italian Fascism in 1923, accenting the strains affecting "the humanistic petty bourgeoisie" in light of industrializa-tion, afforded categories that endured for the better part of a century.[83] Although bourgeois class interests fueled the Fascist reaction against the Communist threat, what made Fascism distinctive, novel, and, for a while at least, all too effective, was the "availability" of the resentful petty bourgeoisie to serve reactionary purposes. Certain seemingly modernizing aspects of Nazism were hard to square with the model, but Henry Ashby Turner gave classic expression to the consensus view by the early 1970s: Nazism embraced modern means to achieve anti-modern ends.[84]

The fact that, on one level, the Soviet experiment entirely eluded these terms seemed to confirm the primacy of the Left/Right difference, for whatever its excesses the Soviet experiment was surely modernizing—anything but some revolt against modernity. But it was viewed in terms of the same master narra-tive, which made its anomalies explicable in terms of the Russian empire's relative backwardness. And so powerful was "modernization" that as the Soviet regime matured after Stalin, some began to anticipate convergence with the Western mainstream, despite the radically different means adopted to that point.

This framework for placing the three regimes gradually disintegrated, although for somewhat disparate reasons, so the process was ragged, with the implications uncertain. The notion that Italian Fascism had been a revolt against modernity came to seem ever more dubious during the 1970s. Although Renzo De Felice had embraced the conventional wisdom at first, his accents changed as, pursuing his pioneering researches, he encountered the manifest inadequacy of the standard framework. Fascism, he came to argue, stemmed from the aspira-tions not of declining but of ascending middle-class groups frustrated with the seemingly limiting structures and modes of practice of liberal Italy.[85] At about the same time, A. James Gregor went a step further to argue that Fascist Italy was the paradigmatic developmental dictatorship.[86] To accent developmental dictatorship was still to explain Fascism's characteristic totalitarian qualities in terms of Italy's relative backwardness, but it was to do so on a basis essentially the opposite of "revolt against modernity."

Significant recent studies have sought to show how Fascism could have been modernizing up to a point yet betray anti-modern impulses or contextual features of relative backwardness at the same time. For Ruth Ben-Ghiat, Italian Fascism was a Janus-faced response to the challenges of modernity immediately after the First World War. Although modernizing in some respects, Fascism won support because it seemed to address longstanding Italian and supranational *anxieties* about modernity, which were escalating in the postwar world.[87] For Mabel Berezin, in contrast, Fascism sought modernization, and Italy's relative backwardness accounts for the anomalous features that resulted from that effort. Because Italy was relatively backward, its middle classes, in her terms, "quasi-educated," Fascism placed great store in ritual, as opposed to cognitive verbal content. Indeed, Berezin seems to have taken for granted that what the Fascists actually wrote about the situation and its possibilities could only have reflected Italy's relative backwardness.[88]

A perspective based on backwardness and modernization might warrant treating Russia and Italy in tandem. Having earlier fallen behind according to the standard criteria of modernization, each departed from the mainstream simply in devising extraordinary means in an attempt to catch up rapidly. To be sure, they both may have framed the effort in more grandiose terms, but in light of the power of the modernization–developmentalist escalator, catching up was all that, objectively, they could have been doing. The rest was myth. Insofar as we place them in that way, their political departures do not seem so anomalous after all, but neither do they illuminate wider ongoing processes that also involve those seemingly more advanced, more fully modern. But if, from more recent perspectives, any such accent on backwardness, modernization, and developmental dictatorship seems one-sided, what do we have instead?

It is surely possible that Fascism stemmed from a mixture of sometimes incompatible impulses, just as Ben-Ghiat proposed. But insofar as we eschew the master narrative of modernization, it may not be easy to distinguish anxious defense from a quest for an alternative modernity. The criteria were themselves at issue, and thus we cannot be sure what counts as what.[89] Insofar as we eschew the master narrative, we recognize that although pre-Fascist Italy was surely idiosyncratic, the idiosyncrasy cannot all be reduced to backwardness or waywardness. Response in light of that idiosyncratic dimension might simply reflect a different take on aspects of the wider modern situation that Italy shared to at least some extent with others. Insofar as, with Berezin, we make backwardness paramount *a priori*, we may delimit what we can find as we probe the sources and content of Italian Fascism.

In the Soviet case, too, it has become clear that the modernization model delimited our range of questions. Writing shortly after the collapse of Soviet Communism, Martin Malia asked how so many of those seeking to understand the dynamics of the Soviet experiment could have been so wrong for so long. He had in mind especially those revisionists who, accenting the scope for agency from below, ended up speaking of negotiation, pluralism, and modern convergence. Especially because of what Malia characterized as social science reductionism, including privilege to a certain conception of modernization, scholars had assumed that the Soviet Union must be like other modernizing societies—its experience could not have been unique or *sui generis*.[90] But those scholars could not even formulate a question that would allow as an answer what Malia himself took to have been the case—the primacy of politics and ideology, irreducible to class. Not that ideology had been neglected, but by restricting the range of questions about the overall dynamic, the modernization syndrome had precluded seriously probing the content and implications of the ideology, including its relationship to agency from below. Because mainstream scholars could not get at the actual content and dynamic, they were utterly unprepared for the outcome, the disintegration of the regime.

But Malia himself was only retreating so far from the master narrative, and thus his formulation, too, raised questions—precisely about ideology and the primacy of politics. Hostile to the whole socialist experiment, he invoked Russian backwardness to explain why Russia, almost uniquely in Europe, could provide the soil for the socialist idea actually to be tried out. Marxist socialism could only have come to power via Leninism, could only have been implemented via Stalinism. But the lineage from Marxism to Leninism to Stalinism has long been much contested, and to back up further from the master narrative might expand the range of possible ways of understanding the connective tissue.

In studies of Nazism, assault on the various ways of invoking waywardness or revolt against modernity has come from several angles, but in this case, too, what we are left with remains contested. In his assault on the *Sonderweg* thesis, Geoff Eley showed how it had stemmed from a too-limited master narrative based on a single assumed standard. Although Germany did indeed entail distinctive features, different from Britain, for example, those could not be understood as wayward in the sense of inadequately measuring up to such a standard. Nor did they leave Germany still backward. Thus, Eley concluded, we must focus on the relatively immediate socio-economic conjuncture that followed the First World War if we are to get at the conditions of possibility for Nazism.[91] Although Eley denied some single modernization standard, he still afforded privilege to socio-economic concerns.

Carrying the departure from the model a step further, Detlev Peukert, analyzing the crisis of the Weimar Republic, insisted that, although the economy was obviously central up to a point, the German debate over modernity could not be understood in terms of class. In turning from class to feature the intersection of generational experience with demographic trends, he was opening to a wider range of questions about the meaning of responses to the modern German conjuncture to that point. Pivotally at issue was the impasse of the effort of the Weimar Republic, seeking to build consensus under Germany's difficult circumstances, to create the first thoroughgoing welfare state. This effort carried Weimar beyond the mainstream modernity of Britain and France, which did not face comparable challenges. But the effort failed, and Nazi totalitarianism emerged as seemingly the optimum response to certain underlying tensions in modernity that Weimar's pioneering effort had brought uniquely to the fore. At work, Peukert insisted, was the quest for a modern alternative to democracy, with a greater role for scientific experts, not a failure to accommodate to modernity reflecting some German *Sonderweg*.[92]

Much new research similarly suggests that central aspects of Nazism are not so readily understood merely as modern means to anti-modern ends, let alone as resisting modernity or clinging to tradition. We think of eugenics, the gradual delimitation of traditional religion, the breaking down of class barriers, as well as the Nazi concern with ecology, holistic medicine, public health, and cancer research.[93] But, as with the Italian case, it is not clear how to fit the pieces together to make sense of the combination. Were the seemingly modern dimensions actually intended, or were they mere by-products—or even effects *counter to* Nazi intentions? Whereas Peukert argued explicitly that Nazi totalitarianism was an alternative modernity, Burleigh and Wippermann disputed suggestions that Nazism was modernizing, or manifested tendencies in all modern societies, and found the race-hygienic core essentially atavistic.[94] De Felice had fastened especially on racism in portraying Nazism as anti-modern, in contrast to Italian Fascism.[95] However, it may be that even this dimension was not so obviously anti-modern—once "modern" is no longer unidirectional and honorific. It surely depends in part on the sources of the racism, its place in the wider Nazi enterprise.

In probing the question of Nazism and modernity, Mark Roseman noted how the defeat of Nazism had affected the way in which modernity itself had come to be understood in the West. Aspects of wider interwar innovation and experience that paralleled Nazism were quietly buried, but Nazism thus came to seem all the more incomprehensible in light of the sanitized modern tradition. For Roseman, however, industrialization, rationalization, and secularization remained the central processes even with the postmodern break; the difference was that we were no longer confident in their benign outcome. Modernity was not liberating but entailed a new, potentially insidious quest for dominance and control, especially through state intervention.[96] Far from a "revolt against modernity," Nazism manifested modern possibilities in extreme, frightening form.

Roseman's point about the incomprehensibility that has resulted from the sanitizing of modernity helps us to understand the ongoing tendency to resort to suprahistorical power and evil; through such sanitizing, we have precluded *a priori* what may be the essential alternative modes of understanding. Yet to desanitize modernity in this way is obviously disorienting. Insofar as we do so, we recognize that we may not yet have confronted all that the totalitarians confronted—or felt, or sensed—as they veered from the mainstream. On some level, we may still be caught up, unawares, in the same processes that elicited their responses. This insight affords not a new set of answers but simply the scope for turning from one particular, long-privileged understanding of "modernity" and "modernization" to a broader set of questions about what modernity can entail, and thus about the place of the totalitarian departure. But even

Roseman may not open them sufficiently. The point would not be simply that Nazism, as a mode of domination, was modern after all, but that Nazism emerged and developed within a historical framework that was more open, with more room for novelty, experiment, and contingency, than our earlier understanding allowed. What "modern" was to mean next was being contested. Speaking of the interwar fascists more generally, Philip Morgan got it exactly right in concluding that "what they offered was an alternative 'modernity', not an alternative to 'modernity'."[97]

Insofar as we pull back from the master narrative, we recognize that the long-standing accent on modernization and a particular range of socio-economic categories unduly limited what we were prepared to hear. Even the notion, long taken for granted, that "social roots" or "social foundations" afford the key to understanding may have been prejudicial. One of the questions about human possibility at issue concerned precisely the relevance of the sort of socio-economic categories—class interests, bourgeois hegemony—that had assumed privilege especially with the master narrative of modernization. That aspect of "modernity" was much contested by the agents at issue, although ways of addressing it obviously differed radically in the three cases. So, even as we acknowledge that the familiar socio-economic factors were surely at work, helping to shape perceptions and responses to some extent, we no longer take them as privileged *a priori*.[98]

Retreat from "modernization" invites attention, *in a non-reductionist mode*, to other strands of our experience—religion, politics, our changing sense of human possibilities, of the human place in the world and in history. We recognize that reactions against the modern mainstream may have been fueled by a sense of possibility and desirability that made the frame of mind of the agents more different—in a historically specific sense, beyond mere ahistorical psychological differentiation—than we were initially prepared to grasp.[99] More generally, we recognize that insofar as we, tough-minded and cynical, reduce their aspirations to psychological propensities or socio-economic interests, we may lapse into mere anachronism and thereby preclude the understanding we seek. Indeed, our cynical proclivities may have resulted partly from the disastrous outcomes of what they did.

Moreover, insofar as we pull back from the master narrative of modernization, the layer of national idiosyncrasy need not be understood in terms of backwardness. But how are we to conceive it instead, and how did it come into play? If there is no norm, there can be no waywardness, for every way is unique; every nation has its own traditions and contingent circumstances helping to shape its direction. Still, the terms of the national distinctiveness had more explosive possibilities in some countries than others. Although we have become less likely to take it as normative, a mainstream modern development surely seemed evident at the time, especially in such countries as Britain, France, and the United States. And on the basis of distinctive national circumstances, some in Russia, Italy, and Germany were especially prone not only to question the mainstream but to claim the wherewithal to leapfrog over it. The question is the basis of this claim and whatever counter-mainstream content it proved to entail.

Insofar as we eschew the master narrative, we must be open to the possibility that the national contextual idiosyncrasies at issue suggested not waywardness or backwardness but, rather, tensions and uncertainties in the Western mainstream, even in the now dominant radical tradition, that were simply closer to the surface in Russia, Italy, and Germany. Thus those idiosyncrasies might have revealed problems, but also possibilities, that remained more hidden elsewhere. Insofar as that was the case, Russians, Italians, and Germans would have been especially likely to probe the weak spots and, on that basis, to seek to create an alternative—as opposed to simply trying to catch up.

As far as fascism is concerned, this is to point beyond even Roger Griffin's nicely nuanced characterization of fascism's revolutionary content, accenting national renewal, palingenetic myth, and the effort to create a "new man," all in response to perceived decadence.[100] Although Griffin was careful to accent the scope for future projection, as opposed to literal return or restoration, any such characterization may lead us to take comparable national weakness or wayward-ness as the key to the departure and to the very content of the alternative devised. From this perspective, such ideas of renewal were obviously less likely in countries more advanced and successful. But to question the master narrative is to open to the possibility that the ideal of renewal and creating a "new man" responded not just to idiosyncratic national problems but also to tensions in the mainstream itself.

If, as Ben-Ghiat recognized, anxiety concerning degeneration and demog-raphy, for example, was to be found all over the Western world after the First World War, is the point that Italy, as relatively backward and especially vulner-able, was quicker to react—indeed, that Italy was quicker to react precisely *because* it was backward and vulnerable? That would be the modern reading. Or was the Fascist departure a specifically Italian yet irreducible, innovative mode of action to address the wider Western concern? We cannot answer unless we probe, first, the sense of the world that seemed to show the way to that new mode of action and, second, the reasons that Italians might claim to be espe-cially positioned to spearhead it. What galvanized the Fascist departure, as a response to the modern, may have been less fear and defense than a new, ener-gizing sense of opportunity and responsibility to show the way beyond the modern mainstream.

From this perspective, the Russian departure, although more immediately revolutionary, was perhaps initially *less* innovative insofar as the agents sought to cling to a prior Marxist ideology that claimed to show the way beyond the liberal mainstream. Up to a point, Leninism was simply a strategic supplement—successful on one level, but on the basis of assumptions about the imminence of wider revolution that proved to be misplaced. As a mere supplement, it was not addressing deeper questions that might have been raised about Marxism and modernity. But Leninism had its own, more specific content, which has long been traced in part to some variation on Russian backwardness. However, insofar as Lenin's mode of questioning, even his invocation of idiosyncratic Russian revolutionary traditions, reflected a grasp of genuine tensions in the wider Marxist mainstream and a sense of the scope for an innovative alternative, the Communist departure, and claim to lead, is not so readily reducible.

Thus whatever common element fueled the three departures may not have been some waywardness compromising the scope for political normality but a sense of new political possibilities, including the scope to act in ways that the liberal democracies and the mainstream socialists could not—and thereby to respond in innovative ways to wider modern challenges. Conversely, the fact that this sense of possibility reached the threshold level, galvanizing counter-elites, in these three countries may have reflected common idiosyncratic contextual features not reducible to backwardness or waywardness.

Insofar as we are to expand the range of possibilities in this way, we cannot start by asking why the agents were *not* democratic, as normal and expected, why they were unable to handle freedom, pluralism, or "the open society."[101] To limit the framework by assuming that what is to be explained is why the conditions for normal democracy were not present, why the creators of these novel regimes were not good liberal democrats, is to delimit the scope for "positive" reasons for seeking alternatives to the modern mainstream in response to genuinely problematic or uncertain dimensions.

The key, then, is to be able to recognize, account for, and encompass any supranational, historically specific content not reducible to common waywardness or backwardness. Characterizations of the novel practice of the three regimes sometimes suggest, if only inadvertently, aspects of what we have missed, even as they also reflect the difficulty of apprehending the missing dimension. Indeed, uncertainties about levels, proportions, and the range of the supranational historically specific make it difficult even to formulate the questions.

Writing of the Soviet turn to crash industrialization in 1929, Moshe Lewin noted that "the sense of urgency of the whole upheaval is baffling: the pace imposed suggests a race against time, as if those responsible for the country's destinies felt they were running out of history."[102] Here is one of our finest historians of the Soviet Union admitting to bafflement—over the interface of a seemingly anomalous historical sense with the extraordinary collective action being attempted.

Pondering the limits of the "banality of evil" in understanding the Holocaust, Saul Friedländer noted a crucial admixture to be understood—an "extraordinary exhilaration" among the perpetrators stemming from a sense of the exceptional, apocalyptic, world-historical quality of the genocidal enterprise.[103] This syndrome seems anything but bland or banal, but where did it come from, and how did it play into the element of banality that was undoubtedly at work as well? We find a sense of something comparable in a number of the most sensitive studies of Nazi population policy and the Holocaust, although characterizations differ markedly, from J.P. Stern on "catastrophe-mindedness" to Berel Lang on intended evil. As Burleigh and Wippermann also invoked something along these lines, they were particularly determined to counter universalizing psychological explanations and especially the increasing tendency to link Nazism to directions inherent in all modern societies: "the bleak truth of the matter is that the self-appointed elite were intoxicated by the idea of actions which were secret, racially therapeutic, and which took them beyond what they regarded as an obsolete morality, and knowledge of which would go with them to the grave."[104]

But quite apart from how such people came to power, how could such a state of mind have come to be in the first place? Burleigh and Wippermann did not raise the question, especially, it seems, because of their plausible concern to avoid what seemed the increasing tendency to overemphasize the generically modern. But by implicitly conflating the supranational historically specific with the generically modern, they precluded questioning on the level upon which irreducible common origins and illuminating parallels might be found. In short, we must be open to the possibility that a supranational, historically specific dimension more delimited than modernity itself is to be understood. And something of the sort is precisely what seems to have been at work in the several examples just mentioned.

Disparate though the projects chosen were—from corporativism to crash industrialization to racial purification—all three departures entailed a new mode of collective action stemming from a new sense of possibility, even responsibility, characteristically mixing hubris with a certain shrillness, and generating a characteristic dynamic. The key is to probe the supranational, historically specific level for the sources, purposes, and practical implications of that new mode of action. Its relationship to earlier bodies of thought like Marxism and social Darwinism is part of the question. Insofar as those were not in fact blueprints for action, the new practice could not have been simply a matter of implementing, or forcing, a prior ideology. This suggests the scope for a richer content on the supranational, historically specific level than has been recognized. At the same time, any such content might have been undesirable, flawed, or risky in ways that we have not recognized as well.

The question of intellectual antecedents

To encompass such supranational, historically specific content, we need to examine antecedent ideas, to get at something like "intellectual background." But we thus encounter yet another layer of problems for, no matter what the historical problem, it is notoriously difficult to pin down whatever connection there might be between "intellectual origins" and subsequent political practice.[105] Indeed, a certain schizophrenia over the issue has long characterized the discussion of interwar totalitarianism. On the one hand, we ask how mere ideas could affect hard-headed practice—especially the practice of cynical dictators, with their emphasis on power and success. Insofar as a layer of ideas or ideology must be admitted, it has seemed readily delimited—as mere theory as opposed to practice, as a separate, distinctly secondary chapter on "culture," or as merely instrumental, serving as window dressing to hide the real, down-to-earth purposes, which have to do with interests and power. In some moods, on the other hand, we sense that the familiar, tough-minded emphasis on practice and power is one-sided, that reference to earlier intellectual innovation affords access to the deeper meaning of the departures in question.

Virtually from the start, many viewed fascism as the outcome of relativism, which seemed to explain its alleged activism, irrationalism, and/or nihilism. In the United States, pragmatism fell from favor during and immediately after the Second World War partly because it was widely argued that the pragmatic understanding of truth fed totalitarianism.[106] Although the Italian thinker Benedetto Croce traced both Fascism and Communism to "anti-historicism" in a deeply critical lecture at Oxford in 1930, others found the opposite relationship, and after the Second World War some claimed that Croce's radical historicism had "helped lay the intellectual foundations of Italian fascism."[107] Whatever the limits of any one of these diagnoses, they remind us of the longstanding assumption that important intellectual "foundations," or "roots," or "origins" lie back there somewhere, that such innovations mattered.

In a probing analysis of the issue, Stephen Aschheim suggested that our sense of the importance of ideas in our effort to understand political departures like Nazism stems in part from our prior proclivities. Pondering the relationship of Nietzsche to Nazism, he noted that "the preparedness to grant a connection in the first place is often a function of a particular a priori attitude to Nietzsche or a particular methodological approach to Nazism. Those inclined to structuralist and social history, for instance, are suspicious of any ideational or ideological account (let alone the particular Nietzschean strand)." Aschheim went on to note that "even for those sympathetically disposed to such analysis, the problem of assessing the role and influence, the 'causal' force, of ideas in history remains highly controversial."[108]

Although some measure of such temperamental difference will no doubt remain, I suggest that the difference is not rigid and impermeable. Some of the skepticism has stemmed from inflated claims and plausible uncertainty about the connections between intellectual innovations and subsequent practice. There is scope for clarification about uses, limits, and proportions, and such clarification might yield greater agreement about the role of antecedent ideas in the case at hand.

Because early ways of invoking ideas were often inflated, the subsequent debunking fed a tendency to denigrate any inquiry on that level. Considering the origins of Nazism, Geoff Eley pinpointed the problems with a once popular approach that, by selectively constructing a proto-Nazi intellectual lineage, taken to have been dominant among educated Germans, made Nazism the direct resultant of idiosyncratically German intellectual antecedents. Referring to Rohan Butler's *Roots of National Socialism* (1941), Eley sneered that "his method is to ransack the German past for any idea with the remotest resemblance to those of the Nazis." With such approaches, Eley went on, the ideas are lifted from their sensible contexts, and "the connections are made predominantly, even exclusively, in the realms of ideology and consciousness; the roots of Nazism are seen to lie in a particular frame of mind."[109] For Eley, the key was to attend instead to societal changes, especially forms of petty bourgeois mobilization and involvement, not least to understand the *reception* of whatever ideas were in play.

Eley even tarred Fritz Stern's noted study of proto-Nazi "cultural despair" in Germany.[110] And it is true that even some of the finest historians who have addressed intellectual antecedents have left an apparent disjunction between intellectual innovation and nitty-gritty practice. Too often the connection is merely suggested, with the actual relationship sidestepped. We are left unsure if, why, and how the antecedent ideas matter. And although our choice of ideas for emphasis is bound to reflect our preliminary sense of the phenomenon to be understood, the approach, as Eley noted, can entail arbitrariness in the selection of ideas to be featured.

The fact that the most basic categories at issue have proved so ambiguous has further warranted skepticism. Fascism was long considered bad because it was irrational, even nihilistic, but more recently, as the cultural signs have changed, fascism has come to seem bad as the extreme, garish revelation of the implications of the universalizing rationalism of the Enlightenment. According to Berel Lang, we must look not to Nietzsche, whom he exempts, but to the intolerant potential of Enlightenment universalism if we are to understand the worst features of Nazism.[111] Yet Jeffrey Herf argued against this whole interpretive tendency, which he plausibly traced back to T.W. Adorno and the Frankfurt School, and insisted that the problem with Nazism was precisely a *dearth* of rationality. If the effort to apply even such fundamental categories as rationality and irrationality yields such disparities, no wonder most prefer to concentrate on hard-headed practice.

The assumption that "ideology" is what is at issue has made it especially hard to grasp the possible place of intellectual antecedents and articulated ideas. The term suggests the sort of intellectual content to be understood and the mode of interface with practice to be expected—and may throw us off as to both.[112] Whether as a blueprint or as mere window dressing, ideology tends, as for Zeev Sternhell, to be taken as a unified whole. We assume we are seeking the origins of a coherent orientation or blueprint. For Sternhell, fascist ideology was central to originating aspirations, but in its archetypal Italian form it was immediately compromised as Mussolini came to power.[113] So as but one, largely marginalized component in the Fascist regime, ideology seemingly tells us little about actual practice. Others accent the merely instrumental role of ideology as part of a wider system of rule.

For some, in contrast, ideology as inherently totalist and unrealistic manifests an *a priori* fanaticism that is itself the key to explaining the troubling practice at issue. But we noted above that Hannah Arendt's treatment of ideology in those terms left an array of questions. Precisely because the ideology was inherently unrealistic, the action in question could not be understood simply as ideological implementation. In both the Nazi and Stalinist regimes the ideology had to be forced, so the action required some admixture standing in uncertain relationship with the original ideology. Crucially, then, the mere embrace of a totalist ideology does not in itself afford an explanation for the particular modes of action chosen. Even as Arendt invoked it, ideology could be no more than part of a larger mix that might well have included *additional* antecedent ideas whose place could not have been specified by the ideology itself. What we must understand is that larger mix and the place of any more delimited ideology within it.

The assumption that we are looking for some coherent ideology may lead in the opposite direction. When we find not coherence but unrealistic or contradictory or contested elements, we may conclude that there was no ideational content at all. Thus we may either assume mere power and opportunism or play up non-ideational dimensions like aesthetics, ritual, spectacle, and rhetoric. This latter direction has been especially evident in the innovative culturalist scholarship on Italian Fascism mentioned briefly above. For example, Jeffrey Schnapp, stressing ideological instability and tension, privileged spectacle in a way that rendered unnecessary any engagement with the texts, the ideological elements in play. Because they are easily shown to have been *not* unified, they are a tissue of contradictions that cannot have been very important to the regime and perhaps not even serious to their proponents. What matters is the aesthetic overproduction through which the regime sought "to compensate for, fill in, and cover up its unstable ideological core."[114] Because there was no unified ideology, we need not confront those ideological elements, or whatever we are to call them, and consider how—whatever the tensions or contradictions—they might not only have helped to shape originating aspirations but have figured in the contested practice of the regime.

Our thinking about how to encompass antecedent ideas remains underdeveloped, but the wider "postmodern" change in our historical self-understanding invites the deeper understanding we need. Several recent scholars, while addressing the connection between earlier ideas and aspects of the ongoing problem of Nazism or totalitarianism, have contributed significantly to the necessary clarification.

In his study of the Nietzschean legacy in Germany, Steven Aschheim well articulated what we miss insofar as we minimize the role of prior intellectual innovation. Even as he agreed with Eley about the excesses in earlier efforts to posit a connection, he deftly challenged Eley's quick dismissal of "frame of mind." Referring to approaches to Nazism that encompass Nietzsche, Aschheim noted that

> these exercises at least attempt to confront what much of recent historiography has attempted to duck: the vexed question of Nazi motivation and intent. This view implies that in some meaningful way Nazism was, at least in part, a frame of mind and that ideas (in their most general sense) were both central to its disposition as a historical project and to its subsequent comprehension.

Aschheim recognized that such explanations, too, have shortcomings and that

> clearly, for events as complex and thick as these, there can be no question of a theoretical or methodological monopoly. Nevertheless, explanations that

entirely dismiss Nazism's frame of mind and render ideational motivations as mere background leave an essential dimension untapped. In this respect the more conventional modes of historical analysis soon reach their limits and leave one with a sense of frustrating incompleteness.[115]

So the necessary complement requires encompassing intellectual antecedents—although in a way that, taking care with proportions, avoids exaggerating their importance.

In the same vein, Bernard Yack sought to contribute to a more nuanced understanding of the connection with earlier ideas in the face of an ongoing tendency to overdo them or misconstrue the relationship. The collapse of communism might surely have opened the way for a clearer understanding, but Yack noted that it seemed "to have produced only a revival of simplistic and misleading theories about the nature of modern revolutionary sentiments, the most popular of which locates the origins of totalitarianism in the wild and wilful visions of modern philosophers such as Rousseau, Marx, and Nietzsche." As an alternative, Yack sought to specify

> a subtler and more accurate account of the connection between philosophic ideas and modern revolutionary sentiments. Although I reject theories about the philosophic origins of totalitarianism, I still believe that philosophers make an important contribution to the peculiar breadth and intensity of modern forms of social discontent. But I locate this contribution more in their new ways of thinking about what is wrong with our lives than in their new visions of a healthy social order.[116]

For Yack, then, intellectuals are central not because they offer some specific blueprint that revolutionaries then follow but because they explain, obviously in some particular way, "why the world contains these sources of dissatisfaction. Their efforts inspire new longings for social change by focussing our discontent on the deeper obstacles to human satisfaction that they uncover. Moreover, different understandings of these obstacles will inspire very different kinds of social discontent."[117] In short, ideas "crystallize" or give shape to our inchoate frustrations and aspirations, our sense of problems and possibilities.

We tend to miss the importance of ideas, said Yack, because we have come to privilege certain contexts of expression in our quest for explanation. Thus the use of shared philosophical concepts appears more abstract than common economic interests or the shared use of language. But although they *seem* more concrete, these latter are no less constructions—abstractions from the context of acts of expression—than a shared set of concepts. The question, Yack stressed, is which context yields the greatest insight into the material at issue. And the answer is not to be determined *a priori* but only on the basis of historical research.[118] This was simply to invite more flexibility in the face of long-standing prejudices about theory and practice, abstraction and concreteness, soft and hard.

Berel Lang similarly insisted that historical understanding requires attention to antecedent ideas, first because ideas help to constitute the meaning of intentional action:

> Historical events in which human agents figure would be unintelligible as deliberate or intentional unless certain conceptual forms could be identified in them. Obviously, such events do not occur only as ideas, but it is by way of ideas that they are almost invariably defined internally and even more obviously retrospectively; its conceptual form is to this extent a characteristic of the event or act.

Not that ideas constitute a privileged causal factor, Lang went on, but to exclude them seriously compromises our ability to imagine and understand historical events.[119] As for how, more specifically, ideas interface with subsequent practice, he suggested that "ideas persist by clearing a conceptual space which their implications or affiliations then occupy."[120] Though cryptic, this formulation, like Yack's, suggests that we must be prepared for a more open and unstable relationship than merely direct influence.

In their different ways, these scholars specified why we must attend to the layer of prior intellectual innovation if we are to grasp the historically specific substance of later departures. But they also imply that we need to be at once broader and more precise in our sense of the possible connections between intellectual response and subsequent practice. We do not necessarily find some fully elaborated ideology but simply a cluster of ideas that make some human sense of novel situations. So, in the case at hand, we may well miss the crucial relationship between ideas and actions if we conceive intellectual or discursive content as some finished ideology, or as theory that might be opposed to practice. The practice to be understood may have been neither an attempt to implement an ideological blueprint nor an attempt to hide behind an ideological façade for sheer opportunistic purposes. It may have entailed instead a contingent and open dynamic in which ideas, the meaning of categories of understanding, were centrally involved—and contested.

The supranational, historically specific content that will prove central for us was bound up with "modernity," or the Enlightenment tradition, which had afforded not some privileged rational blueprint but simply a set of new possibilities and seeming imperatives articulated by those whom we call intellectuals. As experience revealed tensions and uncertainties within that tradition, intellectuals further articulated problems and possibilities, offered diagnoses and prescriptions, thereby putting into play various bits and pieces that then intertwined contingently in practice in unforeseeable ways. So we must analyze the layer of antecedent ideas as a contested field, probing for the gaps and tensions that emerged—even in what purported to be coherent ideologies—as the modern deployment continued and experience grew.

Greater openness to the earlier phases of that contesting is essential to widen our frame of understanding so that we might hear what the creators of our three regimes were saying—as opposed to what we expect, based on our contemporary categories, reflecting our knowledge of the outcomes. Insofar as we take, for example, reason/myth, or egalitarianism/elitism, or even individualism/vtotalitarianism as stable dualisms, our grid is too coarse to enable us to catch and sift the novel ideas in the contesting of categories at issue. Attending to their historicity, we may find the key categories more elastic, less certain in implication, than we expected.

Whether or not we find direct influence, the evolving web of articulations, diagnoses, and prescriptions may have helped to shape the frame of mind, the self-understanding, the sense of possibilities and thereby to constitute the field for subsequent political action. Attention to the contingent interplay between this supranational, historically specific layer of antecedent ideas and the more familiar national level would then enable us better to understand why, when counter-elites in Russia, Italy, and Germany spearheaded a departure from the liberal mainstream, they found certain directions at once possible and appropriate as they sought to affect what modernity was next to become.

2 Seams, creases, and the emergence of new conditions of possibility in the nineteenth century

Locating nineteenth-century novelty

Whatever the importance of ahistorical personality factors, we sense that the totalitarian departures would not have been possible in 1750, or even 1830, or even 1870—yet somehow, at some point, they became so. It became possible to worry about, to desire, to find necessary and possible, certain things for the first time. On one level, the First World War was crucial, even a *sine qua non*, but it could not have had the impact it did without the new layer of possibility that had emerged before. We must grasp the emergence of conditions of possibility on this necessarily abstract level even before considering how intellectuals responded by articulating the new problems and possibilities that seemed to have emerged. Even when they ask about "origins," most inquiries into the three interwar regimes do not consider this background layer explicitly, but any account presupposes some understanding of the elements in play and the interface between them, even some sense of what was normal and desirable. And certain ways have come to structure—and limit—our inquiries.

The conventional starting point for any effort to pinpoint such supranational, historically specific conditions of possibility is the Enlightenment break, or the advent of modernity, bound up with secularization, industrialization, and democratization. Obviously, the Enlightenment did not create a *tabula rasa*, and older questions—ancient liberties versus natural rights, for example, or the relationship between the passions and the interests—remained on the table. But the deployment that followed from the Enlightenment is surely central.

Let us first consider two common ways of conceiving the relationship between the baseline Enlightenment break and twentieth-century totalitarianism. Each affords a useful foil. Two major examples of each will help us to grasp the terms of the essential alternative.

First, perhaps what we need to understand is the nature and relative importance of some underlying strand laid down at the outset, as part of the Enlightenment break, and relatively constant thereafter. Indeed, whatever we find at this point might exhaust the supranational historically specific; grasping its interface with idiosyncratic national and suprahistorical dimensions would be sufficient to account for the totalitarian departure.

For a longstanding tradition, archetypal in J.L. Talmon's work, the condition of possibility for totalitarianism emerged essentially full-blown as an aspiration or vision from a combination of an ahistorical psychological propensity and the historically specific secularization and democratization that followed from the Enlightenment.[1] And for Talmon that totalitarian democracy remained an ongoing possibility. As in the passage quoted in Chapter 1, it stemmed from a quest for security in light of the disruptions of modernity—and thus suggests ideological fanaticism, implicitly attractive to particular psychological types. So Talmon was assuming an abiding continuum of differentiation, but the modern break into freedom and openness crucially brought it to the fore, made it operative.

We find a different way of bringing together the ahistorical and the historically specific in Zygmunt Bauman's widely admired *Modernity and the Holocaust*, which seeks precisely to specify the modern conditions of possibility, especially for the Nazi genocide but also for the Soviet gulags.[2] It took visionaries to initiate the process that led to the Holocaust, and their vision had roots in one Enlightenment strand, which Bauman characterized as the "gardening" impulse, the new sense of the scope, and perhaps the responsibility, for human beings to shape what was coming to seem a purely secular world. Indeed, human beings began to envision fulfilling, through scientific expertise, "the dream of an all-embracing order and harmony."[3] The scope for implementing the vision entailed a distinctively modern bureaucratic rationality. At the same time, the notion of gardening implied that the very existence of some subset of human beings might be incongruent with the vision of harmony; they would need to be separated or even eliminated.

For Bauman, this syndrome afforded the conditions of possibility for Auschwitz: "Modern genocide is an element of social engineering, meant to bring about a social order conforming to the design of the perfect society . . . . One can and should remake the society, force it to conform to an overall, scientifically conceived plan."[4] However, the gardening impulse comes to the fore particularly in times of deep social dislocation, when society seems at once especially pliable and especially to require forming. By implication, the familiar national factors, both longer-term and immediate, afforded the essential trigger circumstances in the German case, and Bauman found no need to analyze them. But he was not remotely suggesting that all modernity is "a Holocaust," only that "the Holocaust is a by-product of the modern drive to a fully designed, fully controlled world, once the drive is getting out of control and running wild."[5] And bureaucratic rationality, entailing distancing and segmentation, determined how an ahistorical dimension, in this case the abiding human ethical capacity, came into play. Always socially directed, morality in this case came to be muted, silenced, or redirected to become merely doing one's segmented task well.

Up to a point, Bauman, like Talmon, was pinpointing a supranational, historically specific element established essentially with the Enlightenment break and enduring thereafter. Insofar as we seek supranational, historically specific conditions of possibility for the Holocaust, we can simply invoke this syndrome without much attention to any historically specific interplay between the

Enlightenment break and the advent of Nazism. To be sure, Bauman's account of the need to draw societal lines, to classify and exclude, in response to Enlightenment indeterminacy helps us to understand what happened during the intervening period.[6] Yet certain variations in Bauman's language suggest a measure of uncertainty or tension that seems to demand deeper attention to the nineteenth century. The syndrome that results from his way of bringing the abiding human ethical capacity together with the historically specific break into modern rationality may be too static, thereby missing key aspects of the dynamic as modern development affected how that ethical capacity came into play.

Although the gardening impulse comes to the fore particularly in times of social dislocation, Bauman portrayed it as a more general modern tendency, bound up with a sense of the scope for, and desirability of, mastery and control. But even in its generic form, does it reflect hubris or a kind of shrill desperation? Sometimes Bauman portrays humanity as cocky, on the verge of "devising the perfect world order," a scientific utopia, through hyper-rationalism, but sometimes we seem to be caught up in a grim, endless battle against chaos. Which accents when, and why? Might some combination of hubris and shrillness be possible under certain circumstances?

As Bauman's use of the gardening metaphor suggests, the implications of the new sense of human responsibility and possible mastery could not have been encountered all at once. Such "gardening" could take varying forms as conceptions of political possibilities and priorities changed with experience, so to understand how the new sense of possibility and responsibility fed Nazism and the Holocaust, we must probe the actual history, with a sense of the initial tensions and uncertainties in mind.

The examples of Talmon and Bauman indicate the first of the two questionable tendencies in our ways of placing Enlightenment modernity. Even when we pinpoint a supranational, historically specific layer, we may tend to take the initial break as sufficient, to conceive the layer as relatively constant, and to move quickly to outcomes without attending to any dynamic in between. Yet such a dynamic was surely important as new possibilities played out and experience was gathered.

The second of the two baseline approaches affords greater significance to that dynamic as it developed—uncertainly, contingently—during the intervening nineteenth century, but thus the inquiry becomes far more complex, and it is not obvious what we must be prepared to hear. Desirable though it surely is, even attention to the intervening dynamic has proved to invite approaches that may throw us off.

In attributing totalitarianism to the *decay* of democracy, Meir Michaelis was more deeply attentive than Talmon to historical specificity.[7] However, the pejorative term "decay" may beg the question. The key is surely that totalitarianism was an *outgrowth* of democracy; it presupposed an experience of modern democracy that had not been possible in the Enlightenment, or in the age of Rousseau and Robespierre. And to grasp whatever relationship exists between totalitarianism and the Enlightenment requires examination of the nineteenth-century democratic deployment and the novel experiences and ideas that resulted from it.

One major variant treats the process in simple Manichean terms by positing a benign, rational Enlightenment tradition that gradually came under assault by an irresponsible or even malevolent counter-tradition. A major exemplar is Zeev Sternhell, who has long been recognized as a major, if not the major, authority on fascist ideology.[8] In his Manichean struggle, the counter-tradition, centered in France, took cultural form by the end of the nineteenth century and, assaulting the rational universalistic Enlightenment tradition underpinning liberal democracy, eventually led to fascism. For Sternhell, the Enlightenment tradition entailed a cluster of themes that fit neatly together, and the elements of the counter-tradition, such as anti-materialism, myth, elitism, and a cult of violence, similarly coalesced seamlessly.

From this perspective, the Enlightenment tradition entails rationalism, humanism, universalism, and liberal democracy—all surely self-recommending at first glance. But even these are not unproblematic, especially as we stir in other elements that come up crucially in Sternhell's account. For example, he seems to deplore market capitalism, yet it was bound up with the demand for individual freedom in the Enlightenment tradition. Does humanism entail an assault on private property? Do the rationalism and universalism he values entail the "materialism" that proved the first target of the negative counter-tradition? Whatever its claim to have applied reason to the problems of the eighteenth century, the Enlightenment had not settled, for an age of mass politics, a cluster of issues concerning the bases of political motivation, the place of materialism and idealism, the interface of economics and politics, and the respective roles of leaders, elites, bureaucracies, and popular participation.

Sometimes Sternhell seemed to recognize the plausibility of questioning aspects of the liberal political mainstream as it had settled out by the end of the nineteenth century, but he was quick to portray the answers in terms of categories long familiar in the interpretation of fascism: authoritarian discipline; a certain take on elitism, violence, and myth; and an effort to preserve private property behind an illusory façade of change and participation, class collaboration and national solidarity.[9] Questioning positivism slides into an aesthetic of violence; questioning the liberal parliamentary system seems necessarily to reflect a "fear of the masses."[10] Such ready answers seem surprising in light of the apparent plausibility of the questioning and the complexity of the issues raised by the counter-tradition along the way.

Sternhell's limits suggest the scope for treating the emerging new categories in a more open-ended way, not as a Manichean reaction against a normative tradition given in unproblematic form at the start. Even his own account suggests a complex, uncertain process, as new layers were added with experience, as outcomes unforeseeable at the outset provoked fresh responses.

Hannah Arendt examined the intervening period in a more open-ended way, probing precisely for some unforeseen supranational, historically specific dynamic that emerged as elements from the Enlightenment break played out. In her account, that process resulted from the interplay of interests, rights, and virtues, from the changing role of the nation, the state, and the political sphere, and from a new understanding of history and the scope for collective action. And it had led by the early twentieth century to a crisis of the mainstream tradition and thus to a particular contingent synthesis, the elements of which, although not totalitarian in themselves, afforded precisely the sort of supranational, historically specific conditions of possibility for totalitarianism that we need to grasp.[11]

Any effort to reassess "the origins of totalitarianism" must encompass Arendt's classic account of what the nineteenth-century triumph of "bourgeois society" proved to mean, what was thereby lost, and what unanticipated side-effects it entailed. She showed that although the original categories and relationships—such as nation and state, interests, rights, freedoms, and political virtue—were still at issue later on, experience had gradually yielded concerns and possibilities that had not been on the table at first and that could not be characterized in terms of the original Enlightenment categories. We will have occasion to consider the specifics of her argument at several points in the present chapter, but although she pinpointed the essential elements, her way of bringing them together and characterizing the resulting dynamic raised questions that suggest the need for a still more open-ended inquiry into the connecting tissue, based on a still more differentiated sense of what might have been happening between the Enlightenment break and the advent of the totalitarian regimes.

Most basically at issue, then, is scope for novelty from *within* the Enlightenment deployment. Genuine novelty defies existing categories, and we miss, or misconstrue, any such novelty insofar as we too readily subsume it within prior categories. Indeed, to make sense of what proves the essential expansion in the case at hand, we must attend to our own categories as we proceed.

It is a given, even a cliché, that whether experienced as a loss, as a liberation, as an opportunity, or as some combination, secularization was central to the modern break, which carried beyond traditionally religious sources of meaning. And secularization has long been linked to an inflation of the political sphere and the advent of new forms of politics. But secularization is perhaps too easily invoked, and the link to politics is perhaps so familiar that it keeps us from thinking through the radical novelty, and the scope for further novelty, that opened with the Enlightenment deployment.

Bernard Yack insisted that the secularization category, as usually applied, merely affords new bottles for old wine: abiding religious aspirations simply took new form. Thus, he argued, the category does not do justice to the novelty of the concerns and possibilities that became possible with the modern break itself. We must more radically embrace the scope for novelty to make sense of the characteristic new expressions of discontent, the longing for a world without social sources of dissatisfaction, that he found in a tradition running from Rousseau and the Kantian Left to Marx and Nietzsche. What came into the world with this tradition was *not* merely a secular translation of earlier religious categories— especially a substitute for the religious vision of redemption—or even some new way of understanding or experiencing abiding aspects of the human condition. Modernity generates its own sources of discontent, and thus the laments of "dehumanization," for example, were genuinely, radically new in ways that the usual understanding of secularization keeps us from grasping. And thus the ways of questioning how the humanity of human beings could be realized were novel as well.[12]

Yack forces us to consider the possibility that we cannot grasp the perceptions, aspirations, and frame of mind at issue in terms of prior categories but must think more deeply about the novelty of the break—and the ongoing novelty that was bound to result. For, to extend Yack's point, modernity generated not only its own sources of discontent but also its own sense of possibility and responsibility, which could not be understood simply as the secular equivalent of some abiding religious imperative. And thus the deployment, the chain of responses, was more unstable, more open-ended, than the secularization category suggests. What opened was a whole new universe of questions about human being and history, about how the world gets made or comes to be in history, about human mastery and human limits, about the scope for and meaning of collective action, about the relationship between individual experience, even individual self-realization, and collective world making. These were questions that had never come up before—could never have come up before. And only experience could provide answers—provisional answers.

Still, if we keep the scope for radical, ongoing novelty in mind, we may find "secularization" the best term for the aspect of the Enlightenment break under-lying the new sense of the challenges and possibilities at issue. Interwoven with secularization was the modern political experiment, still in progress. And it has entailed precisely the novelty, the historical specificity, that Yack had in mind.

Tensions in the liberal tradition

Liberalism, drawing on earlier departures, was the mainstream political direction resulting from the Enlightenment, although a tradition of criticism emerged in symbiotic relationship with it. The liberal tradition still has its critics, and Stephen Holmes's recent spirited defense reminds us that it has often been cari-catured.[13] But whereas we might find a certain *ex post facto* coherence to the liberal project at each moment in its evolution over the last three centuries, liber-alism was never a stable, unequivocal notion. Uncertainty and contest about its essential terms surrounded its gradual triumph during the nineteenth century. Thus, for example, Claude Lefort noted how dizzying were the implications of universal suffrage, although the basis for the concern has by now become almost impossible for us to grasp.[14] New questions emerged, especially as the institutions of parliamentary government settled out and as the scope for political action expanded. To get at the nineteenth-century dynamic, we must pull apart bits and pieces that have by now coalesced in a certain familiar and reassuring way. We can thereby see into the earlier tensions, gaps, and creases.[15]

Liberalism was wound around a demand for individual rights and freedoms in opposition to absolutism, including the right or freedom to pursue individual economic interests—thus the premium on "negative liberty," specifying limits to the state in order to preserve the sphere of the private individual, whose satisfaction was an end in itself. But although they seem self-recommending, did the accent on rights and freedoms optimally elicit the political capacity, even political virtue, of which human beings were, or might be, capable? Could human beings be genuinely fulfilled if that capacity somehow atrophied? And the relationships between individual and society, and between long-term and short-term interests, were also at issue. Drawing on longstanding notions as well as immediate experience, critics like Edmund Burke and Samuel Taylor Coleridge countered the liberal solicitude for the rights and interests of individuals by accenting the importance of tradition and society, understood not as the mere mechanical aggregate of existing, self-sufficient individuals but as a living, organic whole, pre-existing and shaping individuals. The pendulum swung back and forth until, by the end of the nineteenth century, Emile Durkheim was asserting the societal basis of individuality or personality, even as he sought to deepen the basis for liberal democracy.

For Hannah Arendt, what happened in the nineteenth century was above all the triumph of a particular understanding of the Enlightenment dispensation. Whereas critics and defenders alike had often assumed a neat congruence between the political and the socio-economic legacies of the eighteenth century, Arendt insisted on the difference between the citizen and the bourgeois. In a sense, in fact, they were rivals, and in the parlance that has come down to us, liberalism stood in uncertain relationship with an ideal or possibility best characterized as "republican." Arendt particularly valued that loosely republican strand as the basis for autonomous political virtue, a sense of responsibility for the public sphere, even for the state, which, despite its monarchical origins, had created, and now constituted, a stable sphere of law. The state asserted and protected "the rights of man" and, at least in principle, afforded individuals the scope for participation, as citizens, in the public world.[16]

At this early point, republicanism tended to associate the sense of responsibility for public affairs with a restricted elite, no longer a hereditary caste but comprising those economically independent. However, Enlightenment notions of universal reason implied that the criteria of differentiation could be education or expertise, which would afford more open access for individuals apart from economic means. Or one might simply start by positing the capacity for political virtue as universal, in some sense congruent with human ethical capacity. By the 1830s, Giuseppe Mazzini was invoking duties as opposed to rights on that basis. Individuals had the capacity to see beyond their own immediate interests to the well-being of the nation, understood as the concrete, historically given community; they genuinely fulfilled themselves only insofar as they did so.[17] From this perspective, the collective interest was not merely the sum of immediate individual interests. But how individual duties and virtues were to coalesce, and how they were to play against the seemingly legitimate pursuit of individual interests, remained uncertain.

For Arendt, the premium on political virtue was gradually marginalized during the nineteenth century with the ascendancy of the capitalist bourgeoisie pursuing its economic interests. Bourgeois ascendancy meant the relentless expansion of capital, the endless dynamism of competition and acquisition. For much of the century, that pursuit seemed to require *laissez-faire*, but with the expansion of both political access and international economic competition by the later years of the century, it became clearer that political power could be useful, even essential, to the pursuit of economic interests. In Arendt's terms, civic virtue was further marginalized as the state disintegrated into the arena for the clash of particular societal interests—superficially masked as party politics.

As a result of this dynamic, the state by the early 1920s was no longer the instrument of stable law, standing above particular socio-economic interests, but the instrument of what Arendt called the nation, understood idiosyncratically as the mere aggregation of those particularist interests. Reflecting the restless expansionism of bourgeois capital, the nation was bound up with "dynamism," "perpetual motion"—a new relationship with history. The expansion of capital beyond national borders produced imperialism, which tended to undermine the nation-state even as it also demanded the endless power generation that Thomas Hobbes had anticipated.[18]

One casualty of the whole combination was "the rights of man." Arendt well understood that even as it had emerged from the Enlightenment, the nation-state idea had entailed a tension between the state as legal guarantor of rights and the nation as a homogeneous and thus exclusive community.[19] Then the nation-state evolved in a particular way because of the combination of particularism and imperialism. Just as the degeneration into societal particularism compromised the state as a stable sphere of law, expansion beyond the nation-state meant encompassing groups that were outside the sphere of citizenship, rights, and legal protections. The weakening or erosion of both stable law and human rights opened the way for the totalitarians to operate unchecked, to seek and even to begin to exercise total power as they twisted "dynamism" and "endless power generation" to their own purposes.

Arendt was pinpointing elements that any account of the origins of totalitarianism must encompass: the place of interests and rights, the scope for political virtue, the tendencies toward particularism and the changing place of the political sphere, the generation and expansion of power, and the new sense of history that she had in mind in accenting "motion" and dynamism.[20] However, the sources and implications of each, and especially the relationships among them, are tricky indeed. For reasons we can consider better below, Arendt's way of bringing them together proved problematic, even arbitrary. If we pull back and disaggregate those elements, we note the scope for other ways of understanding the relationships between them and the overall dynamic to which each seems to have been central. The possibility emerges especially as we encounter a wider inflation of the political during the nineteenth century that cannot be attributed entirely to— and even stood in problematic relation with—bourgeois particularism.

In the French revolutionary period, political virtue, the "rights of man," and the demand for liberty could appear to mesh seamlessly, but ensuing practice brought questions to the fore. If the right to liberty meant especially *laissez-faire* and the pursuit of economic interests, and if virtue was to transcend such particularism in the pursuit of some longer-term societal or national interest, then the quest for an antidote to particularism did not necessarily entail priority for the securing of individual rights. Indeed, the priority might be to seek to nurture political virtue as opposed to securing rights.

At the same time, the tension between negative and positive liberty, familiar in one sense, and long lurking in discussions of totalitarianism, afforded a different angle on the individual–state relationship, partly because it had implications for the extent and purpose of the political sphere—and thus for the place of political virtue itself. From within the Enlightenment tradition, the demand for liberty was first "negative," the freedom of individuals *from* this or that, especially the absolutist state. Affording individuals a sphere in which they could do as they pleased, without interference, such freedom was bound up with the exercise of rights, including the right to pursue interests, but virtually from the start, discussions of freedom reflected a sense of the limits of any such understanding and imperative. Surely freedom, as a human attribute, was not to be conflated with mere caprice; nor, it seemed, could doing evil, or what is irrational or stupid, be understood as genuinely free. Kantian imperatives, especially, suggested that freedom required not just negative "freedom from" but positive self-direction and thus a rational choice by the individual. Freedom was bound up with individual self-realization.[21]

But from there the question grew more complicated, reflecting concerns that have informed discussions of freedom ever since. The "positive freedom" required for individual self-realization seemed to entail freely accepting the law, or the general will, as rational and necessary, even internalizing the state as the incarnation of reason—a notion long familiar through some mixture of Rousseau and Hegel. But the accents of Rousseau, Kant, and Hegel differed, and the relationship between self-realization and coercion proved problematic.

For Isaiah Berlin in a famous essay, Rousseau envisioned all sharing in a public power that could interfere with all aspects of individual life. Carrying a variation of this vision into practice, Jacobinism entailed severe restrictions on the "negative" liberties of individuals even as it sought to ensure positive liberty.[22] Thus the longstanding sense that we find proto-totalitarianism, even the origins of totalitarianism, in some amalgam of Rousseau and Robespierre. Berlin found echoes of the Jacobin imperatives even in the assertions of British idealists like T.H. Green a century later, that no one is free in doing evil, that to prevent such action is to enhance freedom.[23] Still, the French revolutionary terror had demonstrated that the temptation to impose the conditions for positive liberty could lead to terrible excess, including violations of negative liberty and the private sphere. Thus the overriding issue for liberals like Benjamin Constant was not who wields the authority, but how much authority could safely be entrusted to *any* set of hands.[24]

If freedom required accepting the universal claim of reason, what did the expansion of scientific reason mean for freedom? Auguste Comte asked "if we do not allow free thinking in chemistry or biology, why should we allow it in morals or politics?"[25] With the expansion of scientific knowledge, freedom might seem to entail following the experts in ever-expanding spheres of human activity. To refuse to follow scientific experts, to claim to make one's own decisions even in the ethical or political realms, could yield only caprice, not genuine freedom. Conversely, expertise might entail the obligation to compel freedom through education.

Together with "tyranny of the majority," this Comtean or positivistic tendency in light of the increasing vogue of science was one of the apparent threats to freedom that prompted John Stuart Mill's *On Liberty* of 1859.[26] The question, obviously, was whether the ethical and political were inherently outside the realm of scientific expertise. Even those recognizing the distinction in principle might find it blurring in particular cases as the sphere of the political expanded.

Despite an occasional idealist moment, the tendency in the English-speaking world has long been to understand liberty in the negative sense and to denigrate any notion of positive liberty. One typical characterization refers to "the concept of 'positive liberty' outlined in Hegel's *Philosophy of Right*, which is the cornerstone of *Rechtsstaat* liberalism: the belief that man achieves liberty only through the state as the incarnation of his rational consciousness. Once the state is identified with man's rational nature, he can be seen to be free when he is most coerced, resistance on his part being interpreted as the expression of irrational urges."[27]

But "coercion" is surely dehumanizing and to be avoided, by definition. Kant, addressing uncertainties in Rousseau, had specified that whereas individual freedom entailed the *correct* use of the human moral faculty, individuals acted freely only insofar as they understood why they ought to actualize their moral faculties correctly. Such understanding could not be coerced even by those with some superior understanding. So individuals could *not* be coerced to be free. This Kantian element remained in the mix but perhaps could be overwhelmed by other considerations. Still, such characterizations as the quotation above surely misconstrue the alternatives and restrict the ways of conceiving the relationships between individual, freedom, rationality, and state that opened with the Enlightenment break. The distinction between coercion and self-realization was not so easily drawn. Moreover, the German *Rechtsstaat* tradition, in its later nineteenth-century guise, tended to emphasize the state's essential role precisely in preserving a sphere of private individual autonomy and freedom. That role did not require parliamentary sovereignty, which, indeed, might make the state not only corrupt but also more intrusive, thereby diminishing the sphere of individual freedom. It did require the primacy of law, even equality before the law, and thus, as corollaries, even-handed bureaucratic procedure and protection of the interests of the whole against infringement by particular groups.

In light of the complexities, certain positions and combinations became marginalized along the way, and thus our background categories as we ponder the origins of totalitarianism tend to remain on a delimited axis, concerned with coercion and individual self-realization. From Rousseau, Kant, and Hegel early on, the implications of internalizing the norms of the state depended at least in part on how the state itself was conceived, its composition and range. In establishing the sphere of law, the state, most basically, provides individuals with security but also, more interestingly, with the scope for the realization of their rational natures. Was it up to the state actively to foster such freedom, which might require not only rationality but also virtue? As we will see, questions about state responsibility became ever more germane with the increasing sense of the scope for public education, even compulsory education, but also as individual freedom seemed to require a wider range of societal conditions that the state might foster.

More generally, the question of freedom was bound to become still more complex, with new tensions and uncertainties, as the political sphere took on increasing weight during the nineteenth century. The familiar, variously phrased distinction between "by whom?" and "how much?" I am to be governed misses certain of the possibilities at issue, but differences in characterizing the second term suggest directions for further questioning. Whereas for Berlin the question was "how far does government interfere with me?" the sometimes disillusioned liberal José Ortega y Gasset, comparing Roman and modern liberal notions in 1940, asked "*How far* will I let myself be ruled."[28] To suggest that we may rationally choose to be *more* governed—that we may be freer insofar as we do so—at least puts the question of extent onto the table. At issue is not simply rational recognition and internalization of the law as rational but rather the reach of the law, the public realm. But even Ortega's phrasing did not adequately convey the stakes of the issue, which concerned not simply passively "being ruled." At issue, rather, was first the scope for collective action but then also the *capacity* to act collectively, through the state. Freedom might be understood as *requiring* that capacity. Put simply, the question was not what happens to us individually but what we are capable of doing collectively, what we have the freedom to do collectively, through the political realm.

The scope for thinking beyond freedom as self-realization depended considerably on whether society itself was conceived in terms of equilibrium or as open and dynamic. In *On Liberty*, Mill added an essential dimension almost in passing in framing his argument for liberty in the language of utility, explicitly eschewing any appeal to rights or natural law.[29] Freedom was useful not so much as an instrument for the happiness of individuals but as the instrument for societal progress. At issue was no longer simply the original utilitarian criterion of the greatest happiness of the greatest number but how to foster the continuing innovation essential for that progress. At issue, in other words, was the broader *societal* implications of individual freedom—and the argument was now that *societal* well-being requires such freedom. Such well-being was conceived not in terms of equilibrium—governmental legitimacy, consensus, order, and security—but precisely as "progress," a priority reflecting a more dynamic historical consciousness. Individual liberty was precious as a source of creativity, but it was now understood instrumentally, not as a right, bound up with individual self-realization. And even as Mill emerged as a liberal icon, he drew criticism from a remarkable range of angles. For Willmoore Kendall, he had reduced society to a debating club, with everything to be questioned all the time, whereas for

Maurice Cowling his concern for freedom applied not to all, not to individuality *per se*, but only to an elite clerisy.

Whatever their validity, such criticisms make it clear that emerging questions about the interface between individual rights, societal interests, and freedom were not all confronted at the time and continued to lurk as creases or uncertainties thereafter. Insofar as society was caught up in a future-oriented dynamic, it could not be understood as an agglomeration of free individuals. But if individual self-realization could not be an end in itself, it might still require freedom—freedom exercised in a way that serves such dynamism. Although comparably emphasizing the supra-individual dimension of society, any such notion pointed well beyond the various romantic notions of organic belonging.

In a formidable assault on conventional dismissals of positive liberty, Charles Taylor sought to show the incoherence of the purely negative view of freedom as the absence of *external* obstacles. Genuine liberty necessarily had a positive dimension because it entailed "freedom to," "the ability to fulfill my purposes," or the capacity *genuinely* to choose for oneself. But individuals might misconstrue their own real purposes, so the obstacles to freedom could be internal as well as external. Even insofar as they actually address such internal obstacles, individuals may remain mistaken about their purposes and thus not be genuinely free as they act. So individual subjects cannot be the arbiters of their own freedom. In concluding, Taylor insisted that a second line of issues thus opens, concerned with whether genuine, positive freedom is realizable only in a certain form of society. More specifically, the question is whether his notion requires, as he put it, "justifying the excesses of totalitarian oppression in the name of liberty." Only our simplistic definitions of freedom, he noted, had enabled us to evade this crucial line of questioning.[30]

Although still concerned with individual self-realization and the scope for coercion, Taylor was usefully stretching the usual framework. Insofar as we better grasp the place of purposes and internal obstacles, we better understand the scope for others, including the state, to constitute the conditions for individual freedom and self-realization. Moreover, although he did not break it out and develop it, Taylor added an altogether new dimension in suggesting that freedom is not just "the ability to fulfill my purposes"; rather, we must conceive freedom "as being greater the more significant the purposes." To add this qualitative dimension was to open a whole new universe of questions—and precisely the right ones if we are to understand the emergence of the conditions of possibility for totalitarianism.[31]

The political departure that grew from the Enlightenment had demanded individual freedoms, and rights as the warrant for those freedoms, as well as equality under the law. But hard upon those demands, and in problematic relationship with them, came the question of participation in political life. Although Benjamin Constant and other early liberals had warned of the illiberal potential of democracy, an equal right to participate—to vote, to hold office—seemed to follow from the freedom to organize, to petition, and to pursue interests in light of individual rights. Indeed, perhaps such public participation was an end in itself—an aspect of human self-realization—and thus itself a right. Moreover, insofar as society is the sum of individuals, all have a stake in collective political decision, the pursuit of national or societal well-being.

Despite major differences in timetable and other particulars across Europe, the dominant direction of political change was toward expanded suffrage and parliamentary sovereignty during the nineteenth century, but no one could be sure what form "mass politics" would, could, or should take. No one could be sure how best to allow, invite, or demand participation, whether the point was to nurture political virtue, to represent individual interests, or to pursue some particular societal interest. The tendency was toward *representative* democracy, which meant that the nature of the suffrage system was crucial to the quality of participation that formal democratic institutions made possible. But even the optimal form for the suffrage—the base or unit of representation—was open to contest, especially as experience grew and political parties emerged. At issue was how best to represent individuals, to nurture political capacity and involvement, and to pursue the wider societal interest at the same time. And, addressing the other side of the coin, how did parliamentary government, as the capstone of the democratic process, actually work?

There had been objections all along, but by century's end the actual experience with democratic procedures and institutions was beginning to yield a characteristic set of disillusionments. Most obvious was the tendency toward particularism—the reduction of the polity to society, reduced in turn to narrow, competing interests—that so concerned Arendt. But liberalism was multifaceted and uncertain in its combination of rights, freedoms, interests, and virtues. It was one thing to lapse into "faction," based on different conceptions of the collective good, when reason and virtue had been expected to dictate the same course for all; it was quite another to lapse into particularism, the increasingly naked pursuit of interests. But was the tendency toward particularism the betrayal or the revelation of liberalism? The answer was not obvious, in light of tensions in the liberal notion of freedom and even in the overall self-understanding of "bourgeois society."

For Arendt, as we saw, the liberal model itself bred such particularism, which followed from the newly unchained pursuit of capitalist economic interests. Although that tendency had been linked from the start to the advent of bourgeois society, by the turn of the century the working class and others could hope for a piece of the action as the suffrage expanded and trade unions won a place. Whatever the relevance of class, politics seemed ever more the naked clash of particular interests, with any pretense of virtue stripped away. But by the 1920s there were plenty of disillusioned liberals who denied that such particularism had simply been inherent in liberalism as it had been spearheaded by the middle class during the nineteenth century.

In *The History of European Liberalism*, published in 1925, Guido De Ruggiero found liberal particularism a *degeneration*, for which he blamed Marxist materialism, its denial of even the possibility of virtue from within the capitalist framework. Responding to the Marxist declaration of class war, the bourgeoisie had responded in kind, essentially accepting Marxist reductionist categories and the need to fight back on those terms. It had thereby abandoned what, as De Ruggiero saw it, had earlier been a genuinely universal vocation. Drawing on a reading of Hegel earlier prominent in Italy, he insisted that liberal freedom had meant precisely the capacity to transcend particular interests, precisely the capacity for political virtue. In principle, that capacity was a human attribute, although De Ruggiero found it still confined to the educated middle classes at present. And as an antidote to the actual particularistic degeneration, he could do no better than simply recall the middle classes to their universal mission.[32]

Writing at about the same time, Ortega y Gasset similarly lamented the abdication by directing elites, which, as he saw it, had taken place not simply in the face of Marxism but in response to the rise of mass culture and politics more generally.[33] American democracy, Italian Fascism, and Soviet Communism manifested the same deleterious modern tendency as the masses, through the state, intervened in ever more aspects of life, using violence as necessary. Experience had revealed the centrality of the distinction between "culture classes," those individuals capable of independent decision, of making great demands on themselves, and the "mass men," who lacked these capacities—who were, indeed, especially intolerant of those who had them. Although in principle the elite was open, not defined in hereditary or traditional class terms, there was no way to raise the masses—all individuals—to the level necessary for liberal independence and virtue. As for De Ruggiero, the only antidote, as Ortega saw it, was for the directing elites to get their act together, to regain confidence in their universal vocation.

But did the liberal democratic form of mass politics really turn over political direction to ordinary people, genuinely empowering them? Or, despite the rhetoric of popular sovereignty, did parliamentary democracy leave them indifferent, incompetent, easily exploited by political elites pursuing their own narrow interests? Insofar as the latter, what did this outcome reveal about the *potential* political capacities of ordinary people? Did it indicate simply that the modern political experiment had so far failed to realize the promise of democracy to nurture the political capacity of ordinary people, or, as for Ortega, did it manifest some inherent differentiation in political capacity that was better faced explicitly? That experiment had been wound around a particular set of procedures and institutions and a particular delimited, if evolving, conception of the political. So whatever it had revealed so far was not necessarily definitive.

In short, it was possible to welcome the advent of mass politics even while questioning the liberal parliamentary system and the whole culture of liberalism. But those who did so did not agree about what was required to realize the deeper potential of modern mass politics. Insofar as parliamentary democracy had proved to mean elitism and exploitation, was the point to teach ordinary people how better to pursue their interests—to make the pursuit of interests more honest and equitable? Or did the political capacity to be nurtured revolve around ethical duty and responsibility and thus transcend that model of politics altogether? Either way, what changes to the culture and institutions of liberalism were necessary? If, conversely, it was essential to face up to differentiation and the inevitability and/or necessity of some form of elitism, was the key simply to recall traditional elites to their universal mission, as for De Ruggiero, or was the capacity to transcend particularism more likely to be found in some new elite?

At the same time, concerns about the limits of liberal democracy surfaced from another angle, concerning the place of the political in the lives of individuals. Especially as bound up with the pursuit of interests, parliamentary government, representation, and the suffrage system did not seem to satisfy emotional needs for a sense of community and shared involvement. Insisting that representative democracy did not exhaust mass politics and that, conversely, mass politics did not have to entail representative democracy, George L. Mosse built a distinguished career exploring the counter-tradition that developed almost immediately in Germany with the reaction against Enlightenment universalism. Seeking emotional satisfaction and community through ritual, commemoration, and other forms of shared participation, that counter-tradition then grew in symbiotic opposition as parliamentary government based on universal suffrage developed, becoming the mainstream understanding of democratic participation.[34]

By the end of the nineteenth century, intellectuals from Hugo von Hofmannsthal to Emile Durkheim found it essential to specify the limits of the liberal mainstream now that what it seemed to mean in practice was coming into focus. Because liberal democratic practice had yielded a certain political indifference or even alienation on the part of many, as opposed to political integration and shared meanings, it seemed to be essential to foster more constant and direct participation in public life or to nurture an aesthetic dimension, thereby capturing the imagination, satisfying emotional needs, and deepening social bonds.[35]

However, although this overall syndrome is by now familiar, it was not clear what such departures might involve or how they would intersect with mainstream political forms. Taken as ends in themselves, enhanced emotional satisfaction and a deeper sense of belonging might seem limited and merely static. Could they underpin wider and more effective forms of mass participation, whether in the pursuit of interests or the exercise of virtue?

Questions about political capacities and modes of involvement came to the fore in tandem with new questions about the scope of the political sphere and the role of government that also gradually emerged with experience. The first layer of priorities for the new liberal politics had been reasonably clear—to secure the formal bases for liberalism itself, which included moving in the twin directions of expanded suffrage and parliamentary sovereignty, although how far and how fast was much disputed. However, questions about the kinds of issue to be addressed through the liberal political order increasingly arose at the same time. Such questions about the scope of political decision led to questions about modes of collective action that led, in turn, to questions about individual obligations to the collective and collective obligations to individuals. It increasingly seemed that governments had to be proactive in creating the conditions for both full citizenship and societal effectiveness; it was not enough simply to provide order, or to guarantee rights, or even to afford a vehicle through which individuals might pursue their immediate interests.

This seemed to mean that government was responsible, to some extent, for making the individual an effective member of society and, conversely, that individuals had a claim on society that it was up to government to fulfill. Most basic was the responsibility for and the right to education, as the central mode of individual and societal improvement. But how far did education extend? There were comparable questions about public health, social welfare, and even population policy, including first the birthrate. There seemed to be a public interest in what might appear to be the most private of spheres—sexuality, reproduction, and the family. Whatever the specific answers, as societal obligation expanded, it became ever more difficult to maintain any neat distinction between public and private or between negative and positive liberty. And possible answers to the new questions were not easily squared with a liberal model reflecting a special solicitude for the rights and freedoms of pre-existing individuals.

Although he called for compulsory education, John Stuart Mill assumed that the free creative agency essential for societal utility would result from the responses of private individuals. Such remained the liberal faith, but if even freedom and individuality were to be understood in instrumental terms, was there not some public role to foster and even demand the input of individuals, however it was to be characterized? With the sense of socio-political opportunity and responsibility expanding dramatically, the anarchy of free exchange would not obviously produce the optimum result.

This whole range of questions suggested the scope for government to shape citizens, foster virtue, or at least equalize the pursuit of interests. To characterize the uncertainties and choices at issue in terms of value-laden binaries like rational/irrational, freedom/coercion, progressive/conservative, even public/private, misses the uncertainty and openness, the scope for experiment and contest, trial and error.

A sense of the scope for progress was implicit in this expanding range of questions. Up to a point, progress had seemed to entail achieving rights and freedoms, expanding the suffrage, and securing parliamentary sovereignty; or progress could be taken as the aggregate economic improvement that seemed to result from the pursuit of interests. However, bound up with the expansion of the political sphere, deeper questions about the human relationship with history increasingly came to the fore. By the later part of the nineteenth century, the scope for progress was widely cast in scientific terms through the various forms of developmentalism. These included particular readings of Marxism and Darwinism, which Hannah Arendt characterized as ideologies of motion and found essential to subsequent totalitarianism. Although developmentalism never posited some automatic progress, it was ambiguous with respect to human agency and responsibility. Most basically, it afforded human agents the assurance that, insofar as they grasped the principles of development, they could contribute to the benign direction of history. Still, to posit developmentalism was to posit a world so configured that history does not depend simply on our actions. By 1890, however, the difficulties with all forms of developmentalism were coming explicitly to the fore. Thus, for example, Sheila Faith Weiss, pinpointing the origins of eugenic thinking, noted that by the late 1880s "the necessitarian optimism that had been the hallmark of early social Darwinism had begun to dissipate"; the improvement that had earlier seemed automatic was now only a possibility, depending on human agency.[36]

Developmentalism had emerged in complex interaction with positivism, heir to Enlightenment confidence in the methods of the natural sciences and especially in the scope for applying those methods to the human world. Although it was notoriously varied and slippery, partly because it evolved for half a century and more after Auguste Comte coined the term, positivism as a general cultural orientation, loosely bound up with both materialism and naturalism, reinforced a certain reading of liberalism, taking society as a mechanical aggregate of autonomous, self-contained, "contractualist" individuals pursuing their own interests. Although positivism was subject to internal criticism on philosophical grounds, the waning of developmentalism, especially, raised questions about the positivist conception of human capacities, human agency, and the scope for collective action. And such questions were necessarily bound up with wider questions about the human place in history, about how history happens—or could and should be made to happen.

The question of systematic alternatives

Doubt, discontent, and criticism had accompanied mainstream liberal development virtually from the start. Whereas some of the opposition was merely conservative, a tradition of imagining, or at least longing for, a systematic alternative also developed among those who welcomed the modern Enlightenment break but believed the liberal dispensation inadequate to realize its promise, for both individual self-realization and societal effectiveness.[37] Such discontent and longing took philosophical form, but a more down-to-earth quest for a systematic alternative emerged as well. Marginalizing competing counter-traditions like Mazzinianism, the socialist tradition became the receptacle for ideas about and images of such an alternative. The philosophical and down-to-earth strands converged in Marxism, which emerged from within generic socialism to become the mainstream framework for conceiving a systematic alternative by the last decade of the nineteenth century.

This evolution nurtured categories that crucially shaped diagnosis and prescription thereafter. Most were morally freighted, and many quickly came to seem givens even as they remained uncertain and contested on another level. To understand the issues, the stakes, and the ensuing steps, we must try to conceive the framework as neutrally as possible, in terms of "modern mainstream" and "alternative modernity." To characterize either in the ways that came to be the dominant—even as capitalist, bourgeois, or liberal, even as individualism or socialism—taking such categories as givens, already begs essential questions.

As it emerged from the French Revolution, the socialist idea was most immediately a demand for an expansion of the democratic impulse to the economic sphere, based on a sense that economic inequalities would compromise formal legal and political equality and even the value of individual rights. However, it is crucial that "socialism," as an effort at systematic diagnosis and prescription, stemmed first from the political and secularization sides of the modern deployment, not from industrialization. Questions about industrialization and its effects became central from within the wider socialist quest for a superior mode of modern life. Still, socialism came to seem *the* post-liberal alternative, *the* privileged way of understanding the unfulfilled possibility, because it focused on economic relationships and thus quickly interfaced with industrialization and the accompanying, increasingly intrusive, "social question."

However, socialism thus became a bulky package, and concern for the social question and sympathy for the industrial workers could lead to an embrace of socialism without thinking through the relationship between immediate social issues and the realization of whatever the mainstream liberal model was taken to be frustrating—the capacity for political virtue, for example, or some wider societal interest. In short, the contingent confluence led social thinking—even about overarching human possibilities, responsibilities, and modes of fulfillment—in certain contingent, delimited channels. So although it was certainly plausible to believe that to address the condition of the workers was to foster some wider human value, it was also plausible to question any such link, first in theory, but then especially on the basis of experience.

Forced to bear such weight, the socialist idea was inevitably much contested as the tradition came to encompass competing strands from Saint-Simon to Proudhon to Bakunin to Lassalle, each offering a different sense of problems and solutions, a different way of arranging the components. And although the genius of Marxism, both as a recasting of Hegel and as a critique of capitalist civilization, is undeniable, elements of the wider tradition were marginalized as Marxism became dominant within socialism by the early 1890s. Specifying a particular understanding of problems, a particular model of change, and a particular conception of the post-liberal future, Marxism became the privileged framework for those pursuing socialism as the alternative to the liberal model.

In its Marxist guise, socialism could claim to be grounded in objective economics and thus scientific. But Marxism was attractive for further reasons, thanks especially to its Hegelian underpinnings, although the relationships between its components were blurry at the time of its late nineteenth-century ascendancy—and have occasioned waves of controversy ever since, especially once those Hegelian underpinnings became newly evident during the 1920s. The Hegelian dimensions of Marxism indicated that socialism was not primarily an economic system to replace capitalism but a political-cultural form expected to realize the human capacity for freedom and virtue that the liberal mainstream could not fully realize.

To be sure, Marxist materialism seemed to posit capitalism, not liberalism, as the target, and to feature a certain mode of political–economic interface bound up with the primacy of class relationships. But that materialism was embedded in a wider aspiration and vision, and it was that wider sense of possibility that led Marx to posit his materialist conception of history in the first place. The ultimate target was precisely the wider liberal dispensation, with its particular understanding of human possibilities and the human world. The aim was human self-realization, which would entail a new human relationship with history, transcending materialistic determination. That new human situation would give rise to a different relationship between the economic and the political, but details of post-capitalist economic organization were distinctly secondary.

With its materialist conception, Marxism linked liberalism to the ascendancy of a particular class; transcending liberalism thus entailed class struggle and proletarian revolution. In principle, however, liberalism did not have to be understood as *bourgeois* to be seen as limiting and subject to overcoming. And Marx could not deny that the capacity to see beyond was not limited to the working class. Indeed, classical Marxism bristled with difficulties about consciousness and agency that even the term "praxis," connoting some almost mystical unification of theory and practice, objectivity and subjectivity, could mask only superficially.

With the great age of positivism by the 1870s, Marxism became more unequivocally materialist, developmentalist, and deterministic. Socialism would result from the unfolding of the dialectical logic of capitalism. The proletariat was destined to become the universal class as a result of its objective circumstances, so questions about consciousness and agency could be glossed over. But thus the coming of a post-liberal order was contingent upon particular economic projections. As it began to seem, with experience by the 1890s, that capitalism was defying those projections, questions about theory and practice, objectivity and subjectivity, inevitably came to the fore within the Marxist movement.

So precisely as Marxism was establishing its hegemony in the new Second International, founded in 1889, it faced new uncertainties about strategic priorities that occasioned the several intersecting revisionist debates of the 1890s. The new and deeper questions about Marxist modes of action made clear the instability of the Marxist synthesis, the uncertainty of its center of gravity. At the same time, as we noted in Chapter 1, Marxism began to draw the scrutiny of outside intellectuals like Durkheim, Pareto, Croce, and Weber as it became a significant political force during the 1890s. Just what was this doctrine that now seemed to be taking hold even among industrial workers? On what grounds did it claim to rest on science, as opposed to mere ethical assertion, and to be universal, as opposed to a particular political program like any other? Marxism was intriguing, possibly effective or even valuable, but it seemed to be a synthesis of disparate elements that fitted together uneasily—and that might be disassembled.

If capitalism was not to be transcended because of its inherent contradictions, new questions had to be raised about the scope for action, for willed intervention in the historical process, to bring about the post-liberal alternative. And although they pointed in disparate directions, the revisionist answers had a family resemblance as each entailed a form of voluntarism, accentuating precisely the scope for history-making action even as developmentalist assurance faded. But thus, whatever the specific direction, it was necessary to reconsider the place of subjective consciousness and agency *vis-à-vis* objective economic class and to ponder the roles of will, spirit, commitment, values, myth, leadership, and organization.

If the proletariat was not becoming worse off under capitalism, its claim to a universal role, tricky in any case, became still more problematic. Did the industrial workers, or some subset thereof, necessarily have a privileged role in the revolutionary transformation that would afford a systematic alternative to liberalism? Insofar as the transformation was a matter of consciousness, the objective class substratum might seem less decisive. Marxists held to class categories, which seemed central to their claim to a privileged grasp of the revolutionary process in course, but the need more explicitly to encompass willed agency and consciousness brought to the surface the underlying tensions concerning objectivity and subjectivity in Marxism.

More generally at issue was the place of economic relationships and class differences in diagnosis and prescription. Experience to a certain point had afforded Marx a particular set of reasons for viewing capitalism as at once productive, homogenizing, exploitative, dehumanizing, and self-destructive. If capitalism was not undermining itself through the contradictions Marx outlined, it might still be the central problem, but it was essential to ask more nuanced questions about the relative importance of its various aspects, from private property to the anarchy of the market, from distributive justice to the conditions of production. The answers might suggest new ways of understanding the relationship between the political and economic spheres, even the need to back up further to rethink the place of capitalism and the economy in the modern complex that had seemed to suggest the need for a systematic alternative in the first place.

That line of thinking was bound to raise questions about Marxist internationalism, for even if Marx's analysis of the relentless, supranational dynamic of capital remained unassailable, capitalism at present—and seemingly for the foreseeable future—was differentially developed as the result of differing national circumstances. It made sense to ask about the factors that seemed to be retarding capitalist development, and thus the coming of socialism, in particular countries. And whatever the importance of the Second International, those factors might have to be addressed on the national level.

When those who had tried to understand problems and solutions from within the Marxist framework began to question and even disaggregate some of the components, they could ponder reconnection with strands of socialist thinking that had been marginalized with the ascendancy of Marxism. Whereas the insurrectionist Louis Blanqui, for example, remained superseded, others like Jean-Charles de Sismondi, Henri de Saint-Simon, Pierre-Joseph Proudhon, and Francesco Saverio Merlino offered insights that might contribute to the more nuanced understanding of the problem, the process of overcoming, and the nature of the post-liberal alternative that now seemed necessary.

But such questioning might lead beyond Marxism altogether. Even the long-standing assumption that "socialism," especially as primarily "economic" in some sense, was the antidote to the inadequacies of liberalism was historically specific, not a given. It might be possible to specify a post-liberal mode that would not be socialist in any usual sense but that might still claim to address the frustrations that had fed socialism in the first place. So it was possible even to ponder reconnection with strands of anti-liberal thinking like Mazzinianism that had been marginalized with the ascendancy of socialism. Indeed, the sense of what it was about liberalism that seemed to frustrate human potential might itself evolve with experience, and in that light the relevance of the various components of the alternative tradition could be, had to be, reassessed on an ongoing basis.

At about the time of the revisionist debates, the advent of trade unionism drew attention from across the political spectrum. By now it is widely agreed that the emerging unions, by constituting a "countervailing force," played an essential role in pursuing legitimate workers' interests. Yet the wider implications of the trade union phenomenon, its place in mainstream liberal society and in the quest for a systematic alternative, were not clear at the time.

Such group experience and activity might be understood as expanding the moral and political horizons of individual workers, thereby contributing, poten-tially at least, to the production of a more effective polity in this developing mass age. But insofar as trade unionism entailed a deepening class consciousness, it might enhance the scope for revolution, for better or worse. Or perhaps it portended mere "economism," the embrace of immediate economic aims *as opposed to* wider political horizons, whether mainstream or post-liberal—and again for better or worse. This might mean settling for a piece of the action within the existing system, thereby undermining whatever revolutionary poten-tial the industrial workers might have had, and reinforcing the particularistic thrust of the mainstream. Some conservatives, in contrast, saw the unions as the vehicles of particularist interests and thus as a threat to the sovereignty of a liberal state already threatened by particularism.

As experience prompted a widening range of questions, the universe of possible post-liberal responses expanded, but thus also the scope for complex competition for the post-liberal terrain. Yet Marxism, especially, had bequeathed a certain way of understanding bourgeois society and "socialism" as the alternative, as well as categories like class that continued to shape thinking on all sides, as De Ruggiero's defensive critique makes clear. Contesting those categories would be central to any post-Marxist effort to spearhead an alternative to the modern mainstream. Such simple dualisms as progressive and reactionary, modern and anti-modern, and rational and irrational could not possibly make sense of any such contest.

Hannah Arendt plausibly fastened upon Marxism in its developmentalist mode to make her point about the centrality of developmentalist "ideologies of motion" by the later nineteenth century. In both the natural and the historical worlds, she said, everything was coming to be viewed as a stage of development. Whereas formerly the function of the political had been to establish stable law as the framework for human action, even the political sphere now became an expression of motion. This "tremendous intellectual change" was at least indirectly bound up with the relentless dynamism of the bourgeoisie in its pursuit of economic advantage.[38]

In Arendt's reading, Marxism and Darwinism proved central to Stalinism and Nazism, respectively, precisely as ideologies of motion.[39] Yet, as we saw in the last chapter, she also attributed totalitarianism to an attempt to force ideologies that were in fact unrealistic precisely in their determinism, their denial of human freedom and creativity, their denial of the openness of history.[40] So the totalitarians had somehow concluded, if only implicitly, that they could not simply sit back and let history or nature take its course—or simply apply the ideology as if it was a blueprint. In Arendt's terms, then, those ideologies were important but not remotely sufficient to specify the modes of action needed, so her account leads us to ask what happened *between* the emergence of such developmentalist ideologies and the advent of totalitarian politics several generations later.

Comparable questions emerge from Bernard Yack's innovative exploration of the novel philosophical tradition that expressed discontent with "modernity" and a longing for some systematic, even "total," overcoming of what seemed its dehumanizing spirit. Running from Rousseau through the Kantian Left to Hegel, this tradition found twin culmination in Marx and Nietzsche, but for Yack that culmination was essentially an impasse stemming from the incoherence of the form in which the discontent and longing were expressed. I suggest that Nietzsche is better understood as one strand of the broad cultural response to something like that impasse—as part of the next step, in other words—and we will treat him in that light in the next chapter. In any case, it is Marx who most tellingly makes Yack's point about the incoherence and thus the impasse of the tradition at issue. And Yack's critique affords an insight into the instability of the contingent assemblage we find in the more general quest for a systematic alternative to the modern liberal mainstream.

Although highly abstract, Yack's account opened new questions about the quest for a systematic alternative by placing in fresh perspective the changing understanding of the human relationship with history that was centrally at work. We noted that Yack was so insistent on novelty and historical specificity that he questioned even the secularization category; what emerged with the Enlightenment break was not simply new bottles for old wine. At issue, rather, were a new set of frustrations and thus a new vision of overcoming.

In Yack's terms, a precondition for the new thinking was "historicism" in Montesquieu's sense, suggesting that each epoch has a specific character, its institutions and cultural practices forming an interdependent whole informed by the same spirit. But what Yack's figures derived from this historicism was not the centrality of historical embeddedness or historicity but essentially the opposite. Once we recognize that there is a single spirit, a coherent totality, we can hope, in the face of frustration or unhappiness, to overcome the particular limitations of our own epoch. Indeed, it becomes possible to conceive, for the first time, transcending any such determination. Precisely because society came to be understood as a coherent, historically specific totality, there seemed scope for rupture, for "total revolution."[41]

For Yack's tradition, total revolution was desirable because "modernity," as a historically specific, integrated form of social interaction, seemed to constitute a systematic obstacle to human self-realization. As Yack put it, it became possible to envision overcoming "the dehumanizing spirit of modern society as the obstacle to a world without social sources of dissatisfaction."[42] At first glance, this characterization, wound around a quadruple negative, may seem willfully bizarre, hopelessly abstract, or merely question-begging, but it usefully avoids any implication that a utopian blueprint or a secular version of an abiding religious aspiration was at issue.

As the tradition grew from Rousseau to Marx, there seemed scope not simply for Kantian inner moral freedom but also for external realization—to change the world,[43] but Yack found the whole tradition incoherent on several intersecting levels, and that incoherence portended a kind of impasse and dissolution. The question then becomes what connection, if any, this "longing for total revolution" had with later totalitarian politics. Yack was circumspect, eschewing any suggestion of direct influence, let alone teleological inevitability. He claimed not to account for totalitarianism or any political departure but simply to unearth a new layer, a new, specifically modern mindset. He was critical of J.L. Talmon both for assuming abiding religious underpinnings in the concerns at issue and for connecting them with twentieth-century totalitarianism by mere analogy.[44] Still, although he left the relationship uncertain, Yack implied that this tradition opened the way to the totalitarian departure, even that the contradiction he identified bears at least an indirect relationship with what proved to be the excesses, the self-defeating quality, of totalitarianism.[45]

So Yack's account invited questions about the terms of the contradiction, about how the impasse played out, and about what might have happened in response to the impasse—yet prior to the advent of the new totalitarian politics. In concluding that this whole way of representing discontent and hope for change was inherently self-contradictory, Yack suggested that the problem was not, as for Talmon, some psychological maladjustment but rather an irreducible intellectual incoherence in response to a novel situation, summed up as "modernity." Yack's protagonists did not adequately grasp the terms of this new situation or the scope for systematic alternatives to it, yet it mattered that those seeking such alternatives had framed the issues as they had, thereby laying down a particular layer of articulation, hope, and expectation. It meant that when the impasse was reached, it was experienced and understood in a particular way that forced a particular set of questions onto the table.

After developmentalism

So far, we have the impasse of Yack's tradition in tandem with growing uncertainties about Marxism and developmentalism, all against the backdrop of the tensions within the liberal mainstream that we encountered earlier. The tensions and uncertainties gradually produced a kind of pivot into a new set of questions, a new range of possibilities, that had not been present with the Enlightenment break. They revolved around a new sense of the human relationship to history and a new sense of the scope and meaning of collective action.

To better understand Yack's claim that the whole tradition of "longing for total revolution" was self-contradictory, we must probe the historically specific frustrations at issue. And we will need to transpose Yack's categories slightly to take best advantage of his insights into the novelty, for Yack did not specify precisely what was so frustrating about "modernity." He tended to take for granted a certain conception of individuality that itself had to be considered in its historical specificity, but what he found most basically at issue was the new sense of "historicist" cultural totalities itself; by implication, "modernity" was troubling precisely on this level of historical consciousness. The sense of cultural wholes brought home the dependence of individuality on a wider socio-cultural matrix. Yet frustrating though it was, that sense also suggested ways of over-coming the sense of limitation. Any such overcoming would necessarily entail unprecedented modes of human self-realization.

In Yack's terms, the sense that any institution or cultural norm that conditions our behavior will be dehumanizing invited an understanding "of man's humanity in terms of the individual's ability to resist external conditioning" for the first time.[46] We cannot historicize the problem without contradiction, however, because in doing so we will be historically specific and thus ourselves conditioned. As we do so, in other words, we can only be part of the history, the historically specific configuration, so once we understand ourselves as embedded in some historically specific totality, we could be self-creating, autonomous, genuinely free only with some leap out of history, with its finitude and particu-larity.[47] That is what Yack's figures implicitly demanded. But we *cannot* leap out of history; we will always be some particular, finite way, stemming from the particular totality in which we find ourselves. In this sense, we are always condi-tioned and thus dehumanized. We can never achieve full self-determination.

However, this limitation was surely not specific to "modernity", as distinguish-able from any other cultural whole. What was changing was obviously not the human condition itself but Western cultural self-understanding. And what rankled about modernity was precisely the deeper sense of historicity that it entailed. Emerging from within the framework of secularization, the notion of historically specific wholes brought home finitude, what it means to be historical, to belong to history, as never before. But the duality of historical embeddedness and complete self-actualization did not exhaust the alternatives. Indeed, to expe-rience that duality pointed to further questions about historicity, beyond the mere fact of embeddedness itself, and to further questions about the particular modern totality. Even insofar as we may remain endlessly conditioned, we seem collectively, on some level, endlessly to reconstitute our historically specific world as well. So the issue was not simply the opposition of human freedom, autonomy, and self-realization to *nature*, to natural necessity, as for much of the tradition that Yack dissected.[48] At issue, rather, was the human relationship to *history*, what history can contain, how it happens—the scope for human beings to make it, and to remake themselves and their world in making it. The questions emerged especially with Marx's effort to bring Hegel's vision down to earth. Could human beings somehow *master* history and *make* it congruent with human self-realization?

In Marx's way of positing a transition from the realm of necessity to the realm of freedom, Yack found the most telling variation on the fundamental contradiction in the whole tradition of longing for total revolution. Whereas Hegel had focused on mind or spirit, Marx fastened on the realm of production, which seemed concrete and realistic by comparison. And for Yack it was this attempt to add historical materialism to idealism that led Marx into contradiction, for he was forced both to affirm and to deny the humanity/nature dichotomy. Humanity realizes itself in the world through history, the process by which aimless nature is subordinated to human purpose. Yet Marx as would-be materialist ridiculed the idealist dichotomy upon which that notion rested and thereby suppressed his idealist understanding of man's humanity.[49]

In the same way, Marx followed Hegel in assuming that societies are totalities, but for Hegel the notion rested explicitly on idealist premises that Marx rejected in his quest for concreteness. Translating Hegel into materialist terms, Marx took the realm of production itself to be a coherent, purposive totality.[50] At the same time, Marx simply assumed that the social forces created by social interaction with nature constitute a single controllable force that in principle could be made to serve the common interest, as opposed to operating aimlessly, sometimes colliding with each other.[51] Even as he sought to deepen his argument after 1844, Marx said only that such social forces are the products not of nature but of hitherto existing men. But, Yack stressed, it is not enough to insist on the historical character of these forces. To show that no particular constellation is natural is not to show that there is anything other than, as Yack put it, "the changing configurations of forces that follow from the unintended consequences of individual actions." Moreover, Yack objected that "the mere knowledge that the forces governing social life are mediated by our actions does not necessarily grant us control over them." Indeed, nature may be easier to understand and control than the human world.[52]

In Marx, it became clear that the central question all along had concerned the scope for aggregate human agency and the sense in which history was, or could be made to become, a human product, a realm of freedom as opposed to "natural" necessity. Because he conflated various ways of understanding the humanity–history interface, various ways of experiencing collective action as history-making, orthodox Marxism was ambiguous and inherently unstable. Thus, by implication, the impasse that it reached in practice by the turn of the century, when, as we have seen, new questions about freedom, consciousness, and agency became central.

The question for us concerns the possibilities that opened with that impasse—and what happened next. Although Yack did not explore this layer, the contradictions he pinpointed help us to see why, when the aspiration of "total revolution" reached an impasse, the response led in the direction it did. For the new thinking necessarily reflected some of the terms of the old even as it sought a deeper understanding of the human relationship to history.

Yack suggested that grasping the incoherence of the notion of total, systematic overcoming may breed a sense of hopelessness. But it need do so, he concluded, only to the extent that we continue to take "modernity" to be a coherent whole, so that improvement is all or nothing. Once we uncover the self-contradiction in the premises of the totalist tradition, we see the scope for partial reforms and even partial revolutions.[53]

But this understanding of the alternatives is too limited to grasp the possibilities that opened with the impasse of the tradition that Yack dissected. Insofar as we posit total/partial in this dualistic way, we cannot understand how the subsequent emergence of totalitarianism related to Yack's tradition of longing, and especially the problems leading to its impasse. The incoherence of that tradition meant that it could not be implemented in a positive, direct way, but neither did subsequent totalitarianism simply betray, even if only indirectly, that incoherence and the resulting impasse, as Yack sometimes implied. Obviously, discontent with the liberal mainstream continued even after Yack's tradition reached its impasse, and some continued to find a systematically post-liberal order desirable and possible. The impasse of the earlier tradition opened a new layer of questioning about humanity, history, and the sense in which history is, or can be made to be, a human product. But such questioning promptly unearthed further uncertainties. How, for example, did individual self-realization relate to whatever measure of collective freedom was manifest in world making?

Yack's way of characterizing the impasse of Marxism points us beyond the standard but too simple dichotomies—freedom (or voluntarism) and determinism, idealism and materialism, even history and nature—and on to deeper distinctions concerning modes of human interface with the world through history and ways of conceiving modes of action in light of that relationship. In what sense have we always been making history, and what is the scope for doing it differently? Insofar as we necessarily remain embedded in some historically specific totality, can we proceed only in a blindly "anarchical" way, or is there scope for some departure, even some *radical* departure, into a more lucid mode of history making? Insofar as the limit was not simply economic necessity but the human relationship to history itself, could a qualitative change on that level rest on materialist underpinnings? Was it necessary to experience the dehumanization of industrial capitalism to grasp the need and the scope for alternative modes of history making?

By the end of the nineteenth century, such questioning was yielding a new way of framing the issues and the possibilities. To turn from an incoherent "longing for total revolution" did not have to mean embracing liberalism, pluralism, and the open society. On the contrary, outgrowing that longing opened the way to the intellectual conditions of possibility for totalitarianism.

Although, as we noted above, Yack plausibly worried that reliance on the secularization category may keep us from grasping the historically specific novelty of the longing for total revolution, his characterization suggests the sense in which the aspiration was secular and novel at the same time. At issue was the scope for a world without *social* sources of discontent—social as opposed to ontological, existential, or natural. However we characterize it, the contrasting asocial, ahistorical realm surely encompasses the things we cannot change, and which feed the religious impulse, including, for example, mortality and finitude at the outer limits. But how far does the universe of specifically *social* sources extend? Recent historians have delighted in showing that our experience even of mortality and finitude is socially constructed, historically specific; modern individualism entails a particular experience of each. So even in these cases, the borderlines are not simply given.

It was a premise of Yack's charge of incoherence that we cannot overcome historicity or historical embeddedness, which proves one aspect of finitude; in that sense historical embeddedness is not social, or historically specific. But in this case as well, we must attend not simply to what, from our perspective, seems objectively the case but to how that embeddedness was and is experienced. And we noted that whereas historical embeddedness itself was not new with the advent of modernity, it was experienced as such for the first time. Although we cannot coherently conceive historical disembeddedness, the experience of embeddedness might yield varied responses, as efforts to shape or even to reconstruct that experience socially.

At one extreme, even recognizing the impossibility of "total revolution" to transcend history altogether, it might be possible to specify a mode of experience from within which historical finitude might not weigh so heavily—indeed, would not weigh at all. And that, I have argued elsewhere, was precisely the point of a major strand in Nietzsche's mature thinking, wound around *amor fati*, eternal recurrence, and the innocence of becoming.[54] We will consider Nietzsche's response more systematically in the next chapter, but the quest for an altered human relationship with history could also lead to a new mode of self-conscious history making.

The range of the social as opposed to the ontological cannot be established *a priori*. The question concerns the scope for human action and the range of human responsibility: What can we, should we, *do*? That is *the* secular question, and when thus phrased it is immediately clear that what is at issue is not simply a secular version of religious redemption. The point would not be to answer the question definitively but to begin to act in a new spirit, recognizing that, from all we can tell, the question could have no definitive answer. As the notion of total overcoming proved incoherent, we came to experience the world as ever-provisional and incomplete. Action is ongoing in response to each historically specific resultant, and history continues as the result of whatever we do. From this perspective, "positive" freedom would entail the capacity to act not merely individually but collectively.

If the aim was no longer some global overcoming of modernity itself, it was necessary to think more precisely about historically specific discontents, assessing the relative significance of each and the relationships among them. Up to a point, doing so was congruent with Yack's alternative, accenting the scope for partial reforms and even partial revolutions. But he assigned that alternative to us of the present, not to those who followed most immediately from the impasse he specified. It became possible at that point to disassemble what had come to seem like dimensions of modern bourgeois society—capitalism, private property, exploitation, particularism, alienation, egotism, atomization, and separation, understood as a certain way of distinguishing public and private.

But the changing sense of the human relationship with history could itself affect the sense of the obstacles to be overcome and thus the priorities for present action. If there was scope for a more effective mode of collective, history-making action, the key was to pinpoint the requirements for it, including those aspects of modern or bourgeois society that presented obstacles. The first practical step was to create the instrument for positive freedom, to organize for collective action.

We find, then, that in terms of both the range and the mode of action, a new space opened beyond the duality of impossible totalism and the modern liberal mainstream. That space made possible a different politics, and although what seemed to follow was, in one sense, precisely the scope for Yack's "partial revolu- tions," Yack's way of embracing the total/partial dichotomy proves to be inadequate to encompass the range of possibilities. To be sure, if not total then partial, but what kind of partial? Paradoxical though it sounds, the conditions of possibility for totalitarianism emerged only when the scope for total revolution had faded and the priority became precisely partial revolution, understood in a particular, even "total," way.

Whereas the impasse of Yack's tradition meant a deeper sense of belonging to history, the waning of developmentalism opened possibilities in what initially seemed to be the opposite direction—toward openness, indeterminacy, greater scope for willed human agency. In fact, however, the outcomes of both develop- mentalism and the Yack tradition led onto the same terrain—the terrain from upon which the totalitarian departures became possible.

We saw that Hannah Arendt posited a fundamental incongruity between these totalist, deterministic ideologies and human freedom and creativity, which make the world unpredictable and open to novelty. Because of that incongruity, the totalitarians had to force reality to fit their essentially fictitious ideologies; hence the need for a particular new mode of human intervention—not simply to achieve power for its own sake but rather to confirm the prior, deterministic Marxian or social Darwinian ideology. Totalitarian practice, with all its aggres- siveness, took place "only for ideological reasons: to make the world consistent, to prove that its respective supersense has been right."[55]

It was thus that Arendt found the Nazi and Soviet camps revelatory of the underlying dynamic of totalitarianism. In the otherworldly setting of the camps, the totalitarians actually managed to reduce creative human beings to predictable automatons, marionettes, merely conditioned reflexes, and thereby to create the predictable world envisioned in the ideology.[56] Outside the camps, the totalitarians could approximate that control and predictability by keeping people in motion. Such perpetual motion, or dynamism, required terror to atomize society and thereby enable the rulers to do the work of history or nature without interference from human spontaneity, freedom, or creativity. However, such dynamism was ultimately self-destructive.[57]

Arendt was on the right track in implying that totalitarianism rested on some complex new relationship to the earlier ideologies, with their particular take on "motion" or history. Because these ideologies did not afford some blueprint to be followed, the totalitarians felt the need to *act* as never before—and to act in certain ways. As we noted above, that determination to act had to have entailed a crucial admixture, beyond the ideology itself. So the key was not ideological thinking *per se* but the break beyond it, and the question is how we are to conceive the sources and implications of the "post-ideological" admixture.

For Margaret Canovan, one of Arendt's most authoritative interpreters, the admixture resulted in

> "a uniquely modern combination of determinism and hubris. Totalitarians simultaneously committed two errors that might on the face of it seem to be incompatible: on the one hand they were determinists, surrendering human freedom to the march of forces they believed to be irresistible; on the other hand they were, in their restless activism, convinced that 'everything is possible'. The point (as Arendt sees it) is that modern men are tempted to purchase unlimited power at the cost of siding with inhuman forces and giving necessity a helping hand."[58]

Canovan went on to note that for Arendt, totalitarianism—and the more general modern danger that it manifested—entails surrender to inhuman or natural forces while simultaneously pursuing grandiose aims, even omnipotence.[59]

In *The Origins of Totalitarianism*, Arendt was quick to jump to the extremes of totalitarian practice while initially invoking the ideologies as if they were still available, completed and ready to be implemented. The admixture seemingly came into play only as the totalitarian agents found the ideologies unrealistic in practice—thus the need to force things, to do the work of history or nature. In her subsequent work, however, Arendt suggested a more complex connection between the prior ideology and practice based on a reading of the tensions and ambiguities in classical Marxism. Although that reading was largely congruent with Yack's, she, more explicitly than Yack, sought to specify how those tensions and ambiguities invited totalitarian politics—and informed totalitarian practice.

Arendt found Marxism ambiguous on the sense in which history is a realm of human freedom in the face of natural necessity. Tackling that ambiguity suggested the need to distinguish modes of human activity that Marx conflated or treated too loosely, modes that she came to distinguish as labor, work, and action.[60] Labor refers to "materialist" biological necessity, to activities like eating and reproducing that, although essential to maintain the species, are merely repetition.[61] Work, in contrast, is the creative human activity of shaping nature, making things that last, even including institutions and civilization itself. But work is still a matter of shaping *things*, and it necessarily entails violence and destruction. "Action" in Arendt's special sense is essentially political, involving human interaction, and properly entails a recognition of the plurality, freedom, and creativity of other human beings. Marx's failure to distinguish between the three invited confusion about the interface of freedom and necessity, about the scope for agency, about what could be done and needed to be done—and how it should be done. Marx thereby left uncertain the sense in which humanity can be said to make itself in and through history.

As Arendt saw it, those conflations and confusions opened the way for totalitarian excesses among Marx's followers, above all because political action became conflated with work, with making *things*. By conceiving the single process to which Hegel had reduced history specifically as a labor process, Marx encouraged the aspiration that man could make history by controlling or even speeding up this process.[62] Thus arose the characteristic totalitarian combination of surrender to necessity and hubristic confidence that anything is possible. Indeed, Arendt held that "Marxism could be developed into a totalitarian ideology because of its perversion, or misunderstanding of political action as the making of history."[63] This proved to be such a problem, as Canovan summarized Arendt's thinking, "because the notion of *making* history, taking one's future in one's hands and shaping it, always entails violence. Fabrication is a violent business."[64] In fact, from this perspective, making history in this strong sense is impossible because human beings cannot control events; they can act, but their actions tend to unleash processes that they cannot control.[65]

We will see that some such unleashing of out-of-control processes was indeed central to the characteristic dynamic of totalitarianism, but the source of that tendency is not so clear. Although Arendt's way of addressing ambiguities in Marx and of tackling more general questions concerning collective action and history making was surely promising, to fasten as she did on a combination of hubris and surrender to necessity was to miss too much of what happened as confidence in developmentalist ideologies of motion waned toward the end of the nineteenth century. The challenge was to find a mode of political action to interface with a world experienced as newly in motion as history but lacking any developmentalist frame. That mode lay more radically beyond surrender to necessity or inhuman forces than Arendt's characterizations suggested. But nether was it a matter of hubristic assurance that anything is possible.

In Arendt's reading, totalitarianism embraced, as a principle, motion as opposed to stable law—motion understood as irrational and bound up with a quest for total domination that, in turn, required a premium on perpetual dynamism. The notion of stable law, bound up with the guarantee of rights that she associated with political virtue, had been a major strand of the Enlightenment tradition, but it was undermined by bourgeois dynamism and particularism, which thereby opened the way to totalitarianism. It gives pause, however, that Arendt's case against the bourgeois order recalled the charge of the totalitarians themselves that the liberal accent on individual interests was not congruent with societal interest and did not draw out the deepest political capacities of individuals. Although the difference over individual rights remains crucial, we surely need a more nuanced way of considering how the unstable combination of interests, virtues, and rights played into the changing sense of history and on into the totalitarian departure.

For Claude Lefort, in contrast to Arendt, totalitarianism was to be precisely the *antidote* to the problems, including the threat of particularism, that emerged as the democratic revolution played out during the nineteenth century. And he got at that dimension especially because he understood even better than Arendt that a newly problematic historical sense, requiring some deeper engagement with history, was centrally at issue. He was thus also clearer on the basis of the "endless power generation" that Arendt invoked, drawing on Hobbes. So whereas Lefort encompassed some of the elements—history (motion), interests, power—that Arendt found central, he brought them together in a more illuminating way.

Like Arendt, Lefort insisted that totalitarianism was not mere despotism but something new, something supranational and historically specific. It stemmed from the democratic revolution in tandem with secularization, which left the world without foundations. In pondering responses to this newly secular world, Lefort explicitly insisted on the irreducibility of politics and even of "ideology," understood simply as the new form of representation and self-understanding called forth.[66] The scope for socio-economic reduction fell away, for there were no suprahistorical criteria.

Lefort argued effectively that totalitarianism was a break from *within* democracy; it was not simply a psychological response, of the sort Talmon posited, but a response to some of the paradoxes that the first phase of the democratic experiment had entailed. These were genuine paradoxes, being confronted for the first time, although we now have trouble re-experiencing them. By implication, in fact, the totalitarians grasped them better than those who moved more complacently into liberal democracy. So Lefort afforded greater scope than either Talmon or Arendt for a "positive" understanding of the moment of origins. It was not simply that the totalitarians could not adjust or catch up.

What did it mean that the democratic revolution played out in the context of secularization—loss of foundations, loss of transcendence? With political activity no longer stemming from or working toward some other realm, society was newly experienced as on its own, as self-generating—and thus "historical." In fact, Lefort emphasized that modern democratic society "is *historical* society *par excellence*."[67] Thus we see the particular resonance of its founding step, the elimination of monarchy, which had entailed a particular relationship of head to body and of both to the divine. Sustained by the divine, the prince stood above earthly law yet was still subject to a higher law. Eliminating monarchy dissolved the corporeality of the social and made visible, even tangible, the loss of transcendence.[68]

Indeed, Lefort emphasized, the new democracy entailed an unsettling indeterminacy on both the synchronic and diachronic levels. As a substitute for the integrity of the body—for the unity long embodied in the monarch—there was the prospect of universal suffrage, which initially seemed monstrous even to many liberals.[69] It meant that society was foundationless, self-generating, historically indeterminate, and subject to debilitating uncertainty about its sources of identity and legitimacy. Secular, democratic society is self-creating in history primarily, if not exclusively, through the pursuit of particular interests. As merely transitory and historical, a polity based on universal suffrage faced an ever-present threat of dissolution into societal particularism. In light of these difficulties, Lefort insisted that even the early opposition to universal suffrage could not be reduced to mere socio-economic interest.

For Lefort, centrally at work in the dissolution of the prior order was the changing status of power, which "is not, as a certain contemporary discourse naively repeats, a mere organ of domination: it is the agency of legitimacy and identity."[70] When power was detached from the tangible body of the monarch, becoming the power of no one, it risked losing its symbolic function—at a time when the increasing scope for particularist social conflict threatened society with collapse. So for Lefort, much as for Arendt, political power became identified with "society," with mere particularity, under the democratic dispensation. Those who exercised or aspired to power appeared concerned solely to satisfy their own interests, and thus the danger that power would come to arouse mere contempt on the part of those without it. At the same time, it became ever more difficult to conceive of autonomous political virtue, genuine public-spiritedness.

So despite important differences of emphasis, both Arendt and Lefort stressed that the dissolution of the political threatened as a result of the overall liberal dynamic of the nineteenth century. But Lefort was more convincing in portraying totalitarianism not as the outcome of particularist degeneration but as its would-be antidote. More generally, Lefort saw totalitarianism as the antidote to the radical indeterminacy of modern democratic society. Although it was historical *par excellence*, democratic society made its history only haphazardly; history merely resulted, as the outcome, at each moment, of the aggregate of individual decisions stemming from short-term particular interests. The obvious question, then, was the scope for an alternative relationship with history, an alternative mode of collective action, an alternative way of *making* history.

Such an alternative relationship lay at the core of Lefort's account of totalitarianism. What distinguished the totalitarian departure was a new way of conceiving the interface of history and politics, including the place of power and collective action, in light of the democratic revolution and secularization, and in light of actual experience with liberal democracy, which had manifested the interpenetration of particularism and historical indeterminacy. Parliamentary democracy did not exhaust the possibilities of the democratic revolution, and the antidote to dissolution and indeterminacy was to be found from within the democratic tradition—in the image of the people as one and society as homogeneous and transparent to itself, with mass opinion sovereign and normative. That antidote drew from the tutelary function of the state, increasingly evident in the expanding governmental responsibility for society we discussed above. For Lefort, then, the totalitarian aim was to reunify power and society, effacing all signs of social division, banishing "the indeterminacy that haunts the democratic experience."[71] Totalitarianism could provide, as the liberal model and the parliamentary system could not, a neo-democratic substitute for the lost coherence.

Although his way of tracing the totalitarian departure to a new historical sense was more subtle and convincing than Arendt's, even Lefort's conception of the challenge and response proved too limited to make sense of the historical-political possibilities that opened. To grasp Lefort's limits, we must wait until Chapter 8, after we have considered the practice of the three regimes. It is enough for now to note that even as he granted the totalitarians novel purposes based on novel experience, he assumed that their priority was to re-establish control and coherence in the face of "historicist" dissolution, even "to restore the logic of a 'society without history'."[72]

As Lefort saw it, totalitarianism revolved around a strong leader, the tangible symbol of power, as linked to bureaucracy, which sought mastery through regular and controlling procedures above the flux. But to establish our essential foreground sense of possibility, we must loosen the elements in the complex, highly uncertain cluster we now have on the table and note the scope for an alternative reading. Most basically, we must grasp the possibility that the point was not simply to hold society together, to prevent dissolution, to restore equilibrium in the face of the indeterminacy of history, but to make history in a new, more effective way. This would mean a different understanding of the dynamic that developed from the effort actually to create a new, post-liberal politics. Lefort was more explicit than Arendt in accenting the unintended consequences of that effort; the key was that even totalitarianism, with its bureaucracy, could not contain the open-endedness of history. Yet Arendt was closer to the mark in recognizing that "dynamism" was somehow central to the originating aspiration, not an unintended and unwanted by-product. Somehow we must encompass the most convincing insights of both thinkers.

Although developmentalism, premised on some form of historical lock-step, and the Yack tradition, with its longing to transcend historical determination, had been opposites in one sense, the fact that there had been both, and that each had proved inadequate, produced a particular interweaving of themes, concerns, and insights as a new layer of possibility began to emerge. If there could be *neither* predictable developmentalism, whether experienced as confining or reassuring, *nor* some global leap transcending historical specificity, the sense of the human relationship with history assumed a particular, somewhat tension-ridden content as history came to seem more obtrusive in one sense, more open-ended and contingent in another. It was more obviously *made* by us, yet we finite human beings come to understand ourselves as more fundamentally *shaped* by its results than we had recognized. It was more radically up to us, yet there was more that we might do—if we could find the way to do it. There could be no guiding telos, and surely no redemption, for history was endless and every moment provisional. That the consequences of collective action now seemed less predictable was a warrant not for passivity but for deeper thinking about possible modes of collective action. The challenge was thus to adjust to the opportunity and responsibility of ongoing history making from within the historically specific whole that shapes us and to which we respond, thereby endlessly recreating the world.

The deepening sense of historicity found expression in the generational thinking that became prominent around the turn of the century.[73] As human horizons and prospects came to seem more obviously historically specific, each generation had its historically specific possibilities and tasks. Thus individual experience itself came to seem generationally specific as never before.

The pivot beyond developmentalism entailed a particular variation on the new secular sense of opportunity and responsibility that Zygmunt Bauman characterized as "gardening," although with the unremarked ambiguity in valences that we noted above. Some of his characterizations accent hubris, a sense of great opportunity, but others, shrillness, a sense of grim responsibility and risk. The element of shrillness suggested that "gardening" could not be simply a matter of systematically applying reason or implementing a scientific blueprint, as Bauman sometimes suggested. The point for us is that the potential for such shrillness emerged especially with the break from within the Enlightenment deployment near the end of the nineteenth century. After a century of experience, the sense of the scope for gardening, to stick with Bauman's metaphor, took on a particular, distinctive combination of hubris *and* shrillness.

Although there is opportunity before us, our task of making a garden from the wilderness is never finished. Even within the plot we have marked out and cultivated, we must both nurture new plants and fight the weeds, which keep coming back. Gardening is not about creating some utopia but a relentless, endless, Sisyphusian struggle of humanity against—what? At some point, the gardening metaphor was no longer appropriate—indeed, using it today radically misconstrues the sense of the challenge that emerged. At issue, again, was not humanity *vis-à-vis* nature but humanity *vis-à-vis* history—history as endless and open-ended. Not only did the scope for some teleological overcoming and end to history fall away; even the scope for a weaker claim to privilege based on whatever assumption that history is on our side began to fade. Yet insofar as we could better grasp the challenge and opportunity, we might develop the new forms of political organization and collective action necessary to begin making history in our own way.

Stalin reduced the challenge to its essentials in his oft-quoted speech to a workers' conference in 1931. Responding to suggestions that the pace of the Soviet industrialization drive might be relaxed, he proclaimed:

> No comrades, the tempo must not be reduced. On the contrary, we must increase it as much as is within our powers and capabilities. . . . To slow the tempo would mean falling behind. And those who fall behind get beaten. . . . Do you want our socialist fatherland to be beaten and lose its independence? . . . We are fifty or a hundred years behind the advanced countries. We must make good this distance in ten years. Either we do this or they will crush us.[74]

So much for the notion that history is on our side. As we will discuss in Chapter 5, the imperative, and sense of the action in progress, that Stalin conveyed had only a residual relationship with Marxism; it had everything to do with totalitarianism.

The instrument for history-making collective action

New conceptions of power and freedom, of agency, participation, and collective will, began to emerge haltingly from the effort to determine how the essential new forms of collective action could most effectively be orchestrated. That effort required a renewed critical look at the mainstream to determine the scope for departure from the dominant liberal procedures and institutions, but also from the whole culture of liberalism, with its characteristic understanding of individual and society, of equality and differentiation, of the place of virtues, interests, rights, and freedoms. Even as developmentalism had waned, aspects of the wider positivist orientation had remained, giving a particular cast to the mainstream understanding of the key categories. With its tendency to view humanity in tandem with nature and to conceive society as an aggregate of rationally calculating individuals, positivism might seem a particular obstacle to the new self-understanding needed. The essential rethinking might even warrant some adjustment to what had become the dominant understanding of the *inadequacy* of the mainstream dispensation and thus of the requirements for a systematic alternative.

Most basically, freedom had to be understood in a newly positive way as the capacity to act collectively. And that capacity required a wider concentration of power. How to concentrate power more effectively was the first question, which led to the bases of both societal cohesion and societal differentiation. If action was to be collective in a new way, how was the collective itself to be conceived, and what were the conditions of societal effectiveness? A deeper consensus, a greater measure of common consciousness or homogeneity seemed to be necessary, but on what basis, and how might it be fostered? Insofar as the collective had to be shaped in new ways, in what measure was the process to be "negative," excluding certain groups, and in what measure "positive," drawing individuals in, more deeply including them, nurturing their capacities?

The very notion of homogeneity points to what may seem the most negative features of totalitarianism, which by now we almost define by its exclusion of certain groups and assault on individual rights. But we must understand how the sense that such homogeneity was necessary emerged in the first place, as part of the overall historical-political break at work. In light of the tragic excesses we know are coming, a demand for homogeneity suggests negative restriction and exclusivism. Even an accent on national identity seems to jostle with the individual autonomy and self-realization that we take as primary. Moreover, we are now more likely to value multicultural diversity—even to believe that it *enhances* societal effectiveness, quite apart from the rights of individuals. Indeed, we are quick to reduce any accent on national, ethnic, or racial identity to the insecurities of certain socioeconomic groups or to such ahistorical propensities as intolerance, hate, or out-group hostility, so it is hard to understand the developing sense that a deeper measure of homogeneity was necessary in light of the "positive" collective role that might now be played. But we cannot assess proportions and understand the ensuing dynamic unless we are prepared to grasp that first. Having done so, we can then make the crucial distinction between more radically, deeply *including* individuals, albeit at the expense of the liberal-positivist conception of individual autonomy, and *excluding* certain groups on the basis of putative *a priori* characteristics precluding their assimilation into the more deeply homogeneous community.

We noted that even John Stuart Mill's mode of future projection stood in tension with any understanding of society as the sum of empirical individuals, of the societal good as the aggregate of the satisfaction of those individuals. But the later historical-political break forced a deeper reconsideration of the relationship between individual and society. Insofar as society was "in motion," projected into the future, insofar as society was itself an instrument for action, it was no longer enough to say that all individuals were equally subject to the sovereign or even to accent the more active "plebiscite of every day," the sum of all the individual decisions to belong, to participate, that endlessly recreate the society. So as the concern for collective action became more explicit, the notion that society was the aggregate of empirical individuals—encompassing whoever turned up—became still more dubious. The more we think of society as history-making, the less the satisfaction of individuals could be taken as the end—as self-justifying. But this was not necessarily to shift, in a merely dualistic way, from a premium on individual happiness to the subordination of individuals to social ends. The liberal-positivist conception of the individual *vis-à-vis* society may not have adequately read individual capacities or the criteria of meaning and satisfaction for individuals, a point to which we will return below.

To attain the deeper homogeneity might require innovative roles for new elites defined by their grasp of the historical-political challenge and by their willingness to act on that basis. They could claim to know how to marshal the capacities of individuals, to form and focus the collective will, to create and concentrate power, and thereby to forge the collective instrument necessary for ongoing history-making tasks. What this would require in practical terms was not obvious, and differences in priorities were possible. Still, certain new directions were clear, especially the scope and need for more intrusive and actively managed programs in education, welfare, and population policy. At the same time, however, any such elite role seemingly stood in tension with the accent on a deeper homogeneity. That tension was central to a family of new questions concerning the importance of differentiation and thus the place for leadership, elites, and expertise within a more deeply homogeneous collective.

From Emile Durkheim to Giovanni Gentile, there was much new thinking about education around the turn of the century, including explicit concern with the scope for more actively educating for political virtue. Education might foster the sense of duty and responsibility that had not been adequately nurtured under the liberal-positivist dispensation, with its premium on rights, freedoms, and interests. But the line between education and indoctrination was obviously at issue, and Durkheim's influence on French education drew charges of republican tyranny.[75] Still, the question was being formulated for the first time in this dawning age of mass education and mass politics, and the answers were not obvious. The advent of compulsory mass education certainly opened new possibilities, and formal schooling was only one layer of the new mass civic education that might be possible. Wider forms of mobilization could educate as they also produced more constant involvement.

Beyond the scope for molding individuals were questions about the constituents of society—who might belong and on what basis. Society was readily understood in national terms: the nation was society in its concrete historical—and thus individuated—incarnation. Insofar as virtue meant a willingness to subordinate immediate self-interest to, and a sense of responsibility for, the wider community, the nation could be its object. Within the nation were institutions that had already concentrated the power to act collectively to some extent, and they might afford the basis for the further concentration needed. Moreover, as the sphere of collective action expanded, it was becoming ever clearer that nationality, the fortunes of the particular nation, could make a real difference to individual prospects. So even insofar as individual satisfaction was taken as an end in itself, it made sense to grasp the significance of nationality, to be concerned with the nation, to act in and through the nation to improve the nation. As we noted above, a sense that national prospects mattered was emerging even from within the socialist tradition. For all these reasons, the complex place of nationalism and national identity in the mix, as new questions emerged about individual, society, and collective action, cannot be grasped in terms of such dichotomies as irrational/rational or imagined/real.

But who could be part of the nation? In what sense was it inclusive and in what sense exclusive? The quest for a deeper homogeneity might lead in either direction. The scope for producing such homogeneity through new forms of education and mobilization might mean that anyone could be assimilated, anyone's capacities could be marshaled and focused in the necessary direction. Or that quest could yield a deeper sense of the significance of difference. Indeed, either tack might draw from the universalist side of the Enlightenment tradition, which, as recent scholars have shown, entailed certain paradoxes and opened the way to unforeseen possibilities.

Referring explicitly to the place of the Jews, Berel Lang suggested that Enlightenment universalism could mean something quite different from—even diametrically opposed to—the solicitude for minorities that we might assume to have followed. With the new universalism, anyone could belong, but rights presupposed full assimilation or, in a sense, deeper homogeneity. So whereas Hannah Arendt saw the Enlightenment-derived nation-state as potentially the guardian of equal rights for everyone, Lang noted that in asserting equal rights, the Enlightenment was also asserting the scope for denying that the different have any rights at all.[76] How those outside the domain were to be treated was not specified, but there was now scope for more radically setting them apart, even excluding them altogether.

As Lang had it, inclusion was initially a matter of choice, and what may seem decisive about the Nazi departure is that it precluded any such choice for the Jews. But that preclusion was one outcome of a longer-term dynamic that Lang illuminates up to a point. Although it afforded a first step, and an opening for further steps, Jewish emancipation obviously did not in itself mean assimilation. Some Jews chose to assimilate more fully than others, but the criteria of assimilation and the measure of assimilation expected by the majority were not obvious.

Taken in the aggregate, those like Jews distinguishable as minorities tended to assume that they could assimilate sufficiently to be fully part of the community and retain some measure of their distinctiveness at the same time. That combination surely seems the desideratum today, but Lang implied that, even with emancipation and increasing assimilation during the nineteenth century, insofar as some subset of the Jews remained at least somewhat separate, identifiable *as* Jews, they could seem less worthy of rights precisely because they had chosen to remain less than fully assimilated—even with full assimilation now available. So despite the measure of universalism in principle and of assimilation in practice, the Jews were potentially more vulnerable than before. On this basis, Lang insisted that Enlightenment ideas helped to establish the grounds of possibility and the ideational framework for the Nazi genocide.[77]

Lang helps us to grasp the dynamic at work, but it is not enough to pinpoint the greater scope for exclusion in theory that resulted from Enlightenment universalism. We must also encompass the actual nineteenth-century experience that brought to currency the merely potential demand for greater homogeneity that he pinpointed. It happened especially with the historical-political pivot by the late nineteenth century, as it came to seem that the range of collective action could and should be expanded.

Whereas Lang was referring to culture as opposed to race, Bauman, considering the paradoxical results of the Enlightenment from a different angle, showed how Enlightenment universalism could indirectly feed racism. Liberating though they were in one sense, the openness and indeterminacy of the new universalism threatened to frustrate the modern aspiration for self-administration and control. The use of racial categories afforded a new, seemingly scientific way for those in charge to classify people and establish boundary lines in a world of ascription and assimilation. But such racialism, in principle merely neutral, could easily become racism, entailing not only racial hierarchy but, under certain circumstances, the potential for those in charge to declare certain categories of people inherently resistant to such control, even immune to all efforts at amelioration.[78] In other words some, defined by race, could seem incapable of assimilating, of becoming part of the community, no matter how superficially willing they might be, no matter what the education to which they were subjected.

In their different but complementary ways, Lang and Bauman were implicitly addressing the issue of layers and proportions central for us—and, up to a point, accenting the role of an elusive supranational, historically specific dimension. Although each could surely allow that ahistorical psychological propensities were also at work, the key for both was that some ahistorical racism was not the key to understanding the Holocaust and that the crucial historically specific element was to be found in the deeper scope for exclusion implicit in modern Enlightenment universalism itself. By implication, it was the historically specific scope for totalitarianism that brought the racist possibility, in its own particularly dangerous, potentially exclusionary historically specific form, to the fore.

However, the question is why a deeper degree of assimilation and homogeneity came to seem a prerequisite in the first place. Lang and Bauman each posited a layer between the generic, ubiquitous modern possibility and the national trigger mechanisms, but it was relatively thin in each case. The demand for deeper homogeneity could not have come about, as Lang implied, just because there was still a recognizable Jewish community, despite the undoubted—and in many ways remarkable—degree of emancipation *and* assimilation that had taken place. Nor is it sufficient to point, with Bauman, to a generic desire for control and mastery in the face of modern openness and indeterminacy. To account for that demand, which made generic Enlightenment possibilities operative, we must grasp the terms of the historical-political break and the resulting historically specific imperative to create the capacity to act collectively in new ways.

It is crucial, then, that the process leading from the generic Enlightenment possibility to the Holocaust entailed several steps, that even in combination with national crisis it was not the Enlightenment possibility itself, any more than it was simply some ahistorical "hate," that produced the Nazi dynamic that led, in turn, to the genocidal outcome. Neither Lang nor Bauman provided a sufficient sense of what happened in between on the level of the supranational historically specific as new conditions of possibility emerged.

By following Lang's implication a bit further, however, we can grasp, in a preliminary way, the need for certain distinctions and the scope for certain dimensions to become conflated as the generic Enlightenment possibility became operative under the conditions afforded by the late nineteenth-century historical-political break. At issue is a sort of matrix involving individual and group, positive assimilation and negative exclusion. In terms of this matrix, Lang's point remained somewhat ambiguous. On the basis of the initial universalism, the scope for full assimilation was assumed, although those who did not assimilate might find themselves with no rights at all. The argument to this point was focused on individuals as opposed to a group defined *a priori*. In principle, individual Jews could choose for themselves, and those who assimilated would be as much a part of the community as anyone else. Even in shifting the focus to the scope for the negative, for the exclusion of those who did not assimilate, Lang was still nominally talking about individuals. Crucially, then, on the first level the scope for the negative, for exclusion, did not rest on the step into racism. The scope for the deprivation of rights and for exclusion from the community rested on a failure of assimilation and a threat to homogeneity for which the individual could be held responsible.

But it was continuing Jewishness that seemed to set those individuals apart, whatever the variable individual reasons why some chose to maintain a greater degree of distinctiveness than others. Thus the challenge and threat seemed to stem not from a collection of individuals *qua* individuals but from a group— readily understood, it seemed, in terms of *a priori* group characteristics. Yet even to conceive the inadequacy of assimilation in group terms was not in itself to posit biological racism, rigidly precluding the scope for individual choice. And it mattered that before the racial lines hardened, there had been this ambiguity on what it meant to stand even somewhat apart at a time when deeper homogeneity was coming to seem both possible and necessary. The ambiguity affected both the image of the necessary homogeneity and the scope for exclusion. It opened the way to telescoping the extreme, even pathological racism of some of the Nazi leaders and the wider sense that difference entailed a moral fault.

The fact that Hitler and his henchmen were able to galvanize support for, or at least acquiescence in, anti-Semitic policies that the vast majority of Germans would not otherwise have supported has become central to the problem of Nazism. Because of that ambiguity and telescoping, those who had not been especially anti-Semitic, but who bought into the image of enhanced effectiveness based partly on deeper homogeneity, could more readily accept exclusion on racial grounds even as they continued to find something unnecessarily extreme in the racist anti-Semitism of the leaders. Put differently, the leaders could not simply tap into or whip up some ahistorical hate, but they *could* portray difference as deleterious and, in light of the telescoping at issue, even those whose threshold of hate was not unusual could understand the difference in racial terms.

But exclusion, on whatever basis, was not in itself sufficient to produce the essential homogeneity in light of the legacy of the liberal/positivist/socialist mainstream model and the overall frame of mind it had come to entail. Exclusion was but a first step, essential to create the framework for the positive program needed to overcome that mainstream legacy. It could be done, but perhaps *only* from within a society in which the negative had been excluded. Certain groups were negative not simply because they were unassimilable but because they actually embodied the principles of fragmentation and division that would preclude the essential deeper homogeneity. But whatever the need for exclusion, that deeper homogeneity required not merely passive belonging— through common blood, perhaps—but a fuller, deeper commitment of individual ethical capacities.

At issue is what the new education and mobilization, even the more activist welfare and population policies, would have meant to those on the receiving end, those who could be *included*. The familiar distinction between "by whom?" and "how much?" I am to be governed is too restricted, too confined to the liberal range of possibilities, to encompass the post-liberal modes of participation, experience, and self-understanding that opened. In seeking to conceive post-liberal participation, we may think first of the now familiar forms of ritualized, aestheticized, or even sacralized mass politics that perhaps afforded, depending on one's perspective, a deeper sense of community and belonging or a mere diversion, the illusion of participation, leaving the elites unchallenged to rule in their own interests. But in light of the expanding scope for collective action, the new forms of involvement at issue could be more resonant than *either* of these characterizations suggests. The meaning of the departure depended on assessment of the liberal/positivist/socialist model, the extent to which it genuinely fulfilled human capacities.

Liberal-positivist individualism entailed a particular understanding of freedom and creativity, of the public/private distinction, of the scope for ethical political action, of the human place in history. But as the new historical-political terrain emerged, it became less clear that that understanding did justice to human capacities. What fulfilled individuals was not the pursuit of their own interests or even the exercise of liberal rights, especially privacy—whether the privacy of certain decisions and activities or the privacy of property, as if these were divorced from any wider societal meaning. Rather, as Marx had come close to specifying, self-realization entailed making, building, creating in tandem with exercising the ethical capacity. In light of the changing historical sense, self-realization thus seemed to require, first, the scope for involvement in collective action but then also a wider scope for such action and an enhanced capacity to act collectively. That capacity required a fuller concentration of power. From this perspective, then, satisfying participation did not mean simply sharing in static "governance," maintaining equilibrium, or even some deeper mode of belonging; it required involvement in collective, history-making action.

Even as certain liberal rights waned in importance, such participation might be conceived as presupposing certain rights of its own, or at least certain corresponding societal obligations. First was the right to an education that nurtured the human ethical capacity in a way congruent with the requirements for history-making action under the particular historically specific circumstances that the society faced. Whereas state education, for example, could earlier have seemed only to reproduce—to recall the language of Yack's figures—the abhorred "spirit of modernity," an alternative informed by precisely the new sense of human capacity for collective action could now be envisioned. This would be education informed by a sense of *alternative* modernity that was not alienating but fulfilling—fulfilling not in the incoherent totalist sense but in a more realistic modern way. More generally, in the new situation of collective historical responsibility, there might be a right to be made an effective part of society, even to be afforded a societal role congruent with the new societal action.

From within the new framework, what had seemed private decisions—like having or not having children—now had public, history-making implications. Thus individuals might come to experience even reproductive decisions, for example, as more virtuous, more fulfilling, more meaningfully participatory than the public decisions possible from within the liberal framework, accentuating the public/private distinction.

In short, despite the shrill edge of the new historical-political sense, an originating elite might claim to afford the masses the scope for deeper individual self-realization by drawing out and focusing individual capacities and expanding the scope for collective, history-making action. So an accent on differentiation and elites did not have to mean sacrificing individual satisfactions and capacities in a way that liberal democracy did not. But at issue is only the new range of possibilities, which also entailed the scope for indoctrination, coercion, and the mere shell of participation.

The question of differentiation involved not only the difficult matter of elites and masses but also, intersecting at an uncertain angle, the role for experts, who might become more central as there seemed more to be done. The place of experts in Nazism, especially, has attracted much recent interest, but it has seemed merely to confirm the negative side of modernity, bound up with a historically specific will to domination and control. Insofar as we invoke such prejudicial notions up front, we may preclude understanding of more subtle possibilities emerging with the new historical-political sense. To assess the departure and the resulting dynamic, we must start with a more neutral way of framing the new aspiration and direction in light of that changing framework.

Although earlier marginalized figures like Saint-Simon had had ideas about expertise that might seem newly relevant, the place of scientific expertise became especially germane in light of the dramatic scientific achievement by the late nineteenth century. The imperatives in the areas of public health, welfare, and population policy, especially, suggested the scope for experts to assume more overtly political roles. And insofar as conventional democracy portended leveling, mediocrity, even tyranny of the majority, democratic imperatives obviously stood in tension with the undeniable significance of such expertise. As an aspect of differentiation within homogeneity, experts might simply be afforded new roles in explicit defiance of any egalitarian imperative. But more subtly in question was how any political role for experts might mesh with the role of a new elite, defined by its grasp of the new scope for action and by the will and capacity to act. More subtly still, how did expertise play against the more general significance of will, commitment, or consciousness that might unite elites and masses *vis-à-vis* those—like the experts in question—claiming an expanded role based on superior reason? At issue was a complex three-way interaction, likely to yield an uncertain, fluid dynamic, with the outcome depending at least partly on the direction of the new history-making action in specific cases. Moreover, expertise could develop a momentum of its own, based on its own logic, and it could end up serving domination and control even if the momentum grew initially from other impulses. So we must place the dimension of expertise in proportion, as part of a much wider dynamic.

At the same time, the place of leadership, will, commitment, and consciousness stood in uncertain relationship with bureaucracy, already long familiar as the instrument for acting collectively, for carrying out public tasks, in a regular, organized, routinized, efficient way. Bureaucracy was seemingly bound to expand with any expansion in the range of collective action. In the person of the technocrat, the bureaucrat might even conflate with the expert. We noted that Claude Lefort viewed leader and bureaucracy as complementary in light of his conception of the totalitarian aim—to hold society together, to prevent dissolution, to restore or maintain equilibrium. But if, instead, the aim was to act in new, more grandiose ways, the interface of these components was less certain; indeed, they could end up conflicting. In fact, many have found a tension-ridden relationship between leader and bureaucracy, as we will discuss especially in light of the Soviet experiment in Chapter 5.

But at the time of the emergence of the new terrain, the place that bureaucracy might play in expanded collective action was simply part of the cluster of new uncertainties that opened. At precisely the same time, the scope for extraordinary new forms of leadership, seemingly bypassing bureaucracy through charisma, found exploration in the literature of Gabriele D'Annunzio and in the theory and practice of *fin-de-siècle* Viennese politics, made famous by Carl

Schorske.[79] Especially in light of the disillusionment with parliamentary government and the growing awareness of the significance of non-rational appeals, the new thinking about charismatic leadership seemed to point well beyond earlier notions of the "man on horseback" or "the hero and the crowd."

The place of bureaucracy is central to Bauman's conception of the supranational, historically specific dimension in *Modernity and the Holocaust*. Bureaucratization proved to follow, as a practical corollary, from the modern confidence in the scope for shaping the world through instrumental rationality. As such, it became bound up with changes in human ethical response in the process through which the Enlightenment deployment helped to feed the totalitarian extremes. But although he offers a useful starting point, Bauman's account proved limited because his way of interweaving bureaucratic tendencies with the changing place of the ethical did not do justice to the challenges and possibilities at work, especially with the advent of the new historical-political sense by the end of the nineteenth century. Although it requires looking ahead a bit, we can usefully consider the basis of his overall argument at this point so that we can be alert to certain alternative valences and ways of assembling the components as we proceed from here.

Bauman took it for granted that the societal basis of morality, derived especially from Emile Durkheim, had become axiomatic—certainly in sociology, but also more generally in modern culture. From this mainstream perspective, human ethical capacity is a societal construct, and moral behavior rests on internalizing the norms of the society generating the moral sense in the first place. But unless we turn from any such conception, we could condemn Nazis like Adolf Eichmann only on the basis of "victors' justice," for they were operating within their particular socially constructed ethical framework, as binding on them as ours is on us.[80] In one sense, this point is now familiar, almost a cliché, but addressing it substantively is not so easy—thus the force of Bauman's argument. In the face of the ongoing Durkheimian tendency, the Holocaust forces us to show why human ethical capacity is not simply a function of the particular culture, why even as social creatures, we remain autonomous moral agents who can and must make our own judgments.

To counter Durkheim, Bauman followed the lead of Emmanuel Levinas, who had sought to show that morality is not socially produced but is bound up with the human existential condition of being-with-others. Indeed, morality is the primary structure of intersubjective relationship, for that condition entails a sense of unconditional responsibility for those with whom we share a world. In that sense, the moral impulse and moral behavior are *social* but not *societal*— stemming from a particular context and training. The process of socialization consists not in the production of the inborn human moral capacity but in its manipulation, shaping, and channeling. And although such channeling always goes on, a decisive measure of individual autonomy and capacity for choice remains in any society.[81] Thus Bauman's important point that, in response to the Holocaust, resistance or assisting the victims proved to have no social correlation or determinant; such a response did not have to be socially produced but stemmed instead from irreducible individual moral conscience.[82]

Yet in the case of the Holocaust, most individual Germans did not resist or help the victims but went along with the process, doing their part on various levels of involvement. So how did the moral sense get blunted or twisted in this particular case? For Bauman, the primal human sense of moral responsibility emerges in face-to-face encounter and dissipates with distance. In modern society, that sense could be numbed or even silenced because of modern instrumental rationality and bureaucracy, which entail segmentation and distancing. These, in turn, make it possible to miss the wider implications of one's actions. The moral sense might be diverted into simply doing one's job well. At the same time, bureaucracy has an amoral momentum of its own; things get done simply because the mechanisms have been set up to do them. Without this historically specific modern syndrome, Bauman insisted, the Holocaust would not have been possible.[83]

Partly because of his way of framing the issue of lessons, which we will consider in Chapter 9, Bauman was quick to link the moral to the personal, rather than consider the implication—the changing implication—of the ethical in the wider ongoing Enlightenment project. Plausibly seeking to oppose a kind of humanism to modern social science and instrumental reason, he posited a particular variation on the familiar dualism that opposes reason, objectivity, science, and domination to morality, subjectivity, and the scope for sharing or resistance. But especially with the historical-political break, the lines were not so neat. Certain impulses could be radically opposed to scientific hubris but still implicate the moral capacity in new, specifically modern ways *that also carried the possibility of excess*. We miss the scope for any such direction if we stick to Bauman's duality of gardener/bureaucracy and existential/ethical.

Even the "gardening" propensity that Bauman found characteristically modern seems, on his account, not to entail some divergence from the ethical but to bring the ethical more dramatically, publicly, and politically into play. Put generically, secularization might seem to invite a deeper sense of human responsibility, a sense that our actions help to make the world and, insofar as we respond ethically, stem from our human care for the world. Still, in the mode of hubris, the responsibility is merely to apply science and instrumental reason, to act through rational bureaucracies, so in this mode the ethical seems to be implicated primarily in the negative way Bauman emphasized. The sense of face-to-face responsibility weakens as bureaucratic segmentation and distancing accompany the new action. But insofar as the valence of gardening, to stick to Bauman's term, tilts from hubris to shrillness, we find less scope for instrumental reason, let alone some scientific utopia. Having no rational blueprint to follow but only indications from science in a mixture with much else—from which it is up to us to pick and choose—we feel ourselves more on our own. The sense of responsibility deepens and may point us in new directions.

In short, the ethical capacity was bound to be differently implicated as the historical-political sense changed during the nineteenth century. As a new kind of history-making action began to become conceivable by the end of the century, the ethical could in a sense inflate, so that its focus became less interpersonal relations—how I interact with those around me—and more history-making, the endless scope for reconstructing the world through response in action. From this perspective, I experience my action as part of a collective enterprise, carried out "for love of the *world*," even as opposed to the person next door. This would mean a change in the very structure of the human existential situation, as, to at least some extent, being-with-others gave way to being-in-the-world-as-historical.

Such care is not primal, ahistorical, in the Levinas existential sense, but a moment in a supranational, historically specific deployment. Yet neither can we account for the novelty as *societal* manipulation and channeling. Such manipulation and channeling became central to totalitarianism in practice, but for the initiating agents the originating sense of new possibility and potentially expanded responsibility had to have come first; their responses transcended present societal values. But from within the new framework those agents created, it seemed essential to nurture and focus ethical imperatives in a newly overt way. However, the resulting moral sense differed from Durkheimian morality, which entailed doing what was expected in a society in equilibrium. Although the new totalitarian morality was certainly socially produced, it could implicate the human ethical capacity in a new way, especially because society was now projected into the future, caught up in history-making collective action.

We can best understand the difference, and what Bauman's dualistic framework precluded, if we turn from initiating elites to followers, those whose ethical capacities had been subjected to the particular societal manipulation at issue and who now themselves became agents on this or that level. The question is what would be entailed in conforming to a society that had to some degree internalized the inflated moral imperatives accompanying an accent on the need for expanded collective action.

Bauman's dualistic framework made him quick to assume, in dealing with the Holocaust, that what was to be understood was the mechanism that made the bureaucratic agents deaf to their own ethical call, that led them, at best, to channel their ethical capacities in delimited, narrowing ways. This was to miss the possibility that although segmentation and distancing were surely at work, even the bureaucrats were caught up in the process as willing and responsible moral agents who *did* understand the macro-event in which they were caught up and who experienced what they were doing as ethically fulfilling in a newly grandiose way. The question is not how they could have turned from what they knew to be right but how a new, historically specific way of engaging the ethical capacity overrode any such earlier sense.

To grasp the possibility would require a wider understanding than Bauman offers of the supranational, historically specific dimension at work. Just as nurturing and channeling moral imperatives under the circumstances of newly grandiose action would depart from the Durkheimian model, so would internalizing such imperatives. Jumping the gun slightly, we can say that what Nazism produced in Germany was not simply a society like any other, with its own norms binding on its citizens, but a new, particular kind of society, having been shaped by a new kind of political regime, doing a particular kind of unprecedented collective action, newly involving the whole society up to a point, precisely in light of the new historical-political sense. So we must ask broad questions about the difference that the creation of this new framework could have made. Participation in this particular regime might have engaged the moral capacity in ways Durkheim could not have imagined.

Conclusion: novelty within the modern deployment

We have seen that whereas it makes sense to locate the supranational, historically specific conditions of possibility for totalitarianism from within the Enlightenment dispensation, we cannot simply invoke generic implications of that break but must attend to the deployment during the nineteenth century. The intertwined process of secularization and democratization brought to the surface an array of tensions and uncertainties, some implicit from the start, others evident with experience. At issue were the fortunes of both the liberal mainstream and the mainstream socialist alternative. Along the way, phases from developmentalism to "the longing for total revolution" ran their course and fell away. As a result, historical-political possibilities emerged at the end of the century that could not have been foreseen when the Enlightenment deployment began. Now the modern political experiment came to entail new or deeper questions about the scope of human responsibility and human agency through the political sphere, about the uses of power, the requirements for collective effectiveness, the meaning of freedom, and the forms of participation.

The universe that opened was one that neither Rousseau nor Hegel nor even Marx would have recognized. When, as discussed above, Rousseau suggested that everyone might share in a public power that can interfere with all aspects of individual life, he certainly pointed beyond what would become the liberal mainstream in certain respects, but the new historical-political frame at the end of the nineteenth century afforded the scope for an altogether different understanding of positive freedom, based on a new way of being caught up in history. Now at issue was not freedom as the realization of reason or virtue, bound up with internalizing the general will as rational, but freedom as participation in ongoing, collective, history-making forms of action that required a new concentration of power. In their different ways, Hegel and Marx historicized the world as never before, but they still posited an *a priori* and teleological framework. The terrain that emerged, as that framework fell away, opened the way to questions and possibilities that we cannot grasp if we remain caught up in the categories of Rousseau, Hegel, and Marx. But so powerful have been certain categories and dualisms, as well as the legacies of the Enlightenment and the French Revolution, that it has proved exceedingly difficult to grasp this later break and the novelty it entailed. Thus, especially, we see the limits in our interpretive arsenal when we seek the sources of the totalitarianism that followed.

Addressing the "tyranny of the majority" category, Karl Dietrich Bracher suggested that Alexis de Tocqueville had had totalitarianism in mind as he groped to characterize the new political forms that were beginning to grow from mass democracy.[84] But it was only with the later historical-political syndrome that totalitarianism, as opposed to a democratic "tyranny of the majority," became possible. Indeed, totalitarianism is better understood not as the realization of such tyranny but as, in part, an attempted antidote; totalitarianism emerged with the sense that such tyranny was a danger—not because it threatened the rights of individuals but precisely because it portended the static complacency of the least common denominator. From the proto-totalitarian perspective, the form of modern mass politics that could yield a tyranny of the majority could not constitute the instrument for the collective action necessary. Conversely, because of this added historical dynamism, this expanded sense of what was to be done politically, totalitarianism proved to be more dangerous even than "tyranny of the majority"—and carried beyond anything de Tocqueville or even Mill could have foreseen.

The more grandiose action envisioned could include both apocalyptic exhilaration and bureaucratic routine, both new forms of mass mobilization and new political roles for scientific expertise, both a cult of leadership and hierarchy and a quest for more constant, even more meaningful, forms of participation. Although sometimes in tension or even contradictory, these elements formed a characteristic cluster that we will find in each of the three regimes. But with so much in play, differences in accent and direction could easily emerge from within the new terrain. Indeed, the tensions among the new themes opened the way to conflict even within each regime.

Partly because the terrain itself was deeply uncertain and tension-ridden, we cannot expect to grasp the possibilities and responses in either/or terms, as rational or irrational, modern or anti-modern, humanistic or anti-humanistic. Rather, we have a field of interacting components, reinforcing in some ways, conflicting in others, and their uncertain mutual implication was centrally at issue as the scope for a new kind of politics emerged.

The uncertain possibilities of the new terrain would become concrete only in contingent interface with subsequent layers, most obviously certain national experiences of the First World War. By then, however, intellectuals had begun to articulate the new terrain, assessing the tangle of possibilities within it and establishing new categories for diagnosis and prescription. Thus, when the war was reached, the prior experience of that new terrain channeled responses in certain explosive directions.

3   Some diagnoses and prescriptions

Liberal renewal and beyond

Before the First World War, the field of possibilities resulting from all we considered in the previous chapter began to assume a certain shape and structure through the mediation of intellectuals, who translated those abstract possibilities into relatively concrete diagnoses and prescriptions. Those coming later thus tended to encounter the new space through the mapping that these intellectuals had thereby offered. Although such intellectual articulations were obviously not sufficient in themselves, they were essential to the content, or substance, of the subsequent totalitarian departures.

That mediation involved much of a remarkable generation of intellectuals, and surely innovative response at this point did not lead inexorably to totalitarianism. On the contrary, a number of those responses sought, with at least some measure of success, to revitalize the liberal democratic tradition. There was Sorel but also Durkheim, Lenin but also Bernstein, Pareto but also Mosca, Gentile but also Croce. At the same time, some contributed to the subsequent departure even if they themselves remained committed to democracy. Moreover, the point is not to claim some definitive set of figures—*the* intellectual precursors or originators of totalitarianism. But each of those to be considered in this chapter drew out some of the new possibilities and ended up exerting a particular influence on the new "state of mind" to be understood. For the most part, they are the usual suspects, but treating them together, and playing them against the background layer we identified in the last chapter, deepens our understanding of the link between the new situation at the turn of the century and the subsequent totalitarian departures.

Even as these particular thinkers suggested new directions, what emerged from their collective efforts was still only raw material that remained molten, fluid. It could not have been foreseen how the bits and pieces might intersect and where they might lead, so there is nothing static or finished about the cluster that we encounter at this stage, prior to the First World War. The ideas at issue would continue to evolve with experience, and they would remain contested as part of the wider dynamic, even as their practical implications became clearer in the practice of the three regimes.

On this level of intellectual mediation, we begin to find distinctive national preoccupations and accents. Lenin and Gentile explicitly embraced idiosyncratic national traditions; Pareto was much concerned with specifically Italian problems; Durkheim, as French, was less alienated; Nietzsche sought to be the most cosmopolitan of intellectuals yet remained, in some ways, German, all too German. A general concern with population policy produced a stronger interest in eugenics, and thus the potential for more radical departures in some countries than in others. All this is familiar—and may tempt us to focus on parallel national histories. But to grasp not only supranational, historically specific origins but also the defining features of the common totalitarian dynamic that ensued, we must avoid any national reduction at this point and consider these ideas as a supranational cluster. Conversely, we want to recall the possibility that idiosyncratic national features, preoccupations, and traditions might uniquely have enabled intellectuals in particular countries to reveal wider tensions and possibilities. However, we will find this syndrome coming fully into play only with the national experiences of the First World War, in ways we will consider in the next chapter.

In light of the limitations that the practice of both liberal democracy and Marxist socialism seemed to betray, some of the most innovative thinkers around the turn of the century found it necessary to question both traditions in tandem and to rethink the interface between them. It was almost as if the components that had gone into the two strands needed to be melted back down so that they might be assembled in new ways. From very different angles, Eduard Bernstein, Emile Durkheim, and Gaetano Mosca each confronted some subset of the issues, yet each ended up seeking to renew the broadly liberal democratic tradition. However, even as they addressed present inadequacies in innovative ways, each left symptomatic new uncertainties that illuminate the departures of those who moved in other directions, creating a new radicalism with totalitarian potential. So we will find it useful to have these three thinkers on the table as we seek to pinpoint the bases of that more radical outcome.

Bernstein's innovative diagnoses and prescriptions stemmed from an empirical premise that few disputed explicitly, yet that raised the deepest questions about what radical politics was to entail at that point, for the foreseeable future—and perhaps from then on.[1] Whatever the potential value of Marx's dissection of the logic of capitalism, and whatever the ongoing value of Marx's critique of capitalist civilization, Marx appeared to have been plain wrong about what was, on the strategic level, an undeniably decisive datum—what the development of capitalist economy would entail. Insofar as the pauperization, the concentration of capital, and the intensifying crises he had famously anticipated were not in evidence, the developmentalist assurance of Marxism weakened, perhaps dissolved altogether. Where was a Marxist, or anyone seeking a systematic alternative to liberal democracy, to go from there? What was to be done?

Bernstein found the scope for a kind of synthesis transcending the theory and practice of both socialism and liberal democracy to that point. Socialists, he suggested, had been properly skeptical of parliamentary institutions, which had indeed functioned as the vehicles for bourgeois interests. But the link had been merely contingent. Liberal democracy was potentially broader than its current bourgeois form, and the aspirations that had fueled the socialist tradition required not the repudiation of liberal democracy but its full realization. So in proposing that socialists drop their revolutionary rhetoric and pursue reforms from within democratic institutions, Bernstein was not simply capitulating to bourgeois liberalism, with its particular conception of individual and society, its accent on interests and negative liberty. On the contrary, the new socialist direction could qualitatively transform the meaning of parliamentary institutions, which would become vehicles for the pursuit of justice—the core of the socialist aspiration all along.

Rather than stick with Marxian orthodoxy, eschewing ethical categories and claiming universal importance for proletarian interests, Bernstein essentially posited two human principles—the self-interested and the ethical, which transcends interests and fuels the pursuit of justice. Both were at work even in present society. The distinction between them had gotten linked to class for good reason, in light of experience, but it was arbitrary to insist on the class link in a deterministic, ahistorical way. The ethical capacity could bind together the like-minded, essentially in a reformist party, whatever their putatively objective class.

At the same time, with the new sense of the open-endedness of history, the socialist end blurred, and thus, in Bernstein's quickly famous formulation, the movement was everything and the end, nothing. Although socialism remained a goal or ideal, its meaning was dependent on the free play of social forces and so could not be specified *a priori*. In that sense, it was simply the direction or criterion as human beings went on indefinitely seeking justice. What mattered, in other words, was not to specify, let alone actually to realize, some final socialist goal but to respond continuously to present injustices on the basis of the principles that had inspired the socialist quest from the beginning. And insofar as the movement itself was the key for now, the socialist aspiration was not merely congruent with but actively required the freedom and openness of liberal democracy and parliamentary institutions.

At the same time, however, the pursuit would carry beyond what had come to seem the bourgeois principle and create something new, fulfilling human capacities as the bourgeois order had not. In fact, the interface between the longstanding socialist aspiration and the new historical sense opened the way to a more plausible understanding of, on the one hand, the human capacities that had remained frustrated under liberalism and, on the other, the desired alternative, which could now actually be realized—in the only sense possible. As we come to understand the post-liberal alternative, we realize that in pursuing the ever-receding goal of "socialism," we fulfill our ethical capacities and exercise our human freedom in a positive, public way. And democratic institutions afforded the appropriate mechanism for the ongoing, open-ended collective action at issue.

In the preceding chapter, we considered Bernard Yack's way of pinpointing a key contradiction in Marx, but we also noted the scope for a step beyond Yack's contradiction-ridden layer to tackle the questions about how history gets made, and about the scope for human agency, that that contradiction itself had helped to force onto the table.[2] Bernstein's alternative was not subject to Yack's contradiction precisely because it was not claiming some total grasp. It was partly thus that Alain Besançon, writing on Lenin, found Bernstein not simply one of several alternative revisions of Marx—on the same level as Lenin—but a complete departure from the ideological thinking, the potential for totalism, inherent in Marxism. Bernstein was not abandoning one system for another; he was abandoning the spirit of system itself.[3] And thus Besançon found him especially sympathetic.

But the range of alternatives and the implications of those available were not so obvious when Bernstein and Lenin offered their ideas, prior to the effort to act in terms of them. The question was what scope there might be for an alternative to liberalism more radical and desirable than Bernstein's but that comparably reflected the new sense of historical openness, that also made the end nothing, the movement everything. In any case, Bernstein's democratic socialist direction, self-recommending though it may seem, itself entailed tensions, as well as possible limitations and risks. At issue was the interplay between interests and ethical values, individual and collective response, and the particularism that parliamentary government so far had seemed to breed.

Bernstein was optimistically suggesting that the human ethical capacity might coalesce for effective collective action from within the present framework, without some radical departure. But could this really "just happen" if socialists turned their efforts to the pursuit of justice from within parliamentary institutions? As more was to be done collectively, and as what was to be done was the pursuit of *justice*, was the ethical capacity of present individuals sufficient, or did it need to be nurtured and focused? Although the movement was now everything, perhaps some image of the socialist end could serve as a kind of myth, galvanizing that capacity, despite the indeterminacy of the end.

Even as he suggested that liberal democracy had always expressed a demand for justice for individuals, Bernstein thought the collective interest would gradually become clearer, more and more predominating. But in light of the particularistic tendencies that the liberal parliamentary system had manifested, this was perhaps a sanguine reading of the possibilities. Could the direction he proposed in fact yield a qualitative transformation over the longer term, or would existing modes of practice and understanding absorb this new socialist thrust within a merely expanded bourgeois mainstream, simply making the pursuit of interests more universal and equitable? A more radical departure might be essential if the point was to transcend the liberal preoccupation with individual rights and interests and to yield a greater premium on longer-term community values. As a start, a greater emphasis on the longer-term implications of what present individuals do together might be necessary.

Bernstein's way of reassembling the pieces adumbrated the course of the socialist idea in Western Europe by the later twentieth century. And the outcome by that point might be viewed as the definitive dissolution of the quest for a systematic alternative. This is surely not to fault Bernstein, who had been remarkably independent and critical in raising the issues he did, and who remained courageous and innovative as challenges arose. But his was not the only way to reassemble the pieces in light of new experience and the changing sense of the obstacles and pitfalls, possibilities and desiderata. Others sought to reassemble the pieces in a way that would head off the negative possibilities that his moderate direction seemed to portend; indeed, the force of his argument added urgency to that effort.

Although he was no socialist, Emile Durkheim focused on much the same cluster as Bernstein, including the place of Marxism and the overall socialist idea, as well as the role the human ethical capacity could play in overcoming the contemporary social problem, however construed. But Durkheim's aims, reflecting a very different sense of the challenge, were considerably more conservative. He was seeking to shore up the French Third Republic, with its liberal parliamentary system, its Dreyfusard commitment to individual justice, and its willingness to check the power of traditionally illiberal institutions like the Catholic Church. But as Durkheim saw the situation, France, even as it enjoyed these republican blessings, was encountering a systematic problem that, he came to believe, was endemic in modern bourgeois society, at least as it had evolved so far. That problem was only now coming to light, so it demanded innovative diagnosis—and novel solutions.

Concerned that traditional sources of societal cohesion were eroding with the development of modern industrial society, Durkheim examined the implications of the modernization process for societal cohesion in his first book, *The Division of Labor in Society*, published in 1893. At this point, he was satisfied that a rational understanding of increasing mutual interdependence, wound around the division of labor, would afford the specifically modern sources of cohesion that were necessary, but over the next few years he came to doubt that any such mechanism could suffice. Most famously in *Suicide* (1897), Durkheim found a correlation between modernization and increasing rates of suicide, crime, divorce, alcohol abuse, and other destructive forms of behavior. Cohesion in the modern world seemed to require something beyond the rational recognition of mutual interdependence.

Meanwhile, as a pioneer seeking to establish the foundations of sociology as a discipline, Durkheim posited the social fact, irreducible to individual psychology, as an autonomous object of study. Although he had one foot in the positivist tradition, he was thinking beyond the loosely positivist conception of individual and society. Society was not simply an aggregate of autonomous, rational, "contractualist" individuals. It is, first, the common culture, including especially language, which precedes the individual and which the individual internalizes. Uniform subservience to social facts affords the level of societal homogeneity.[4] On this level, there could be no conflict between individual and society, for individuality could not be conceived apart from some such societal framework. Supra-individual culture afforded the basis for authentic individuality, which presupposed the capacity to function effectively in the particular society. The process of socialization was the underlying source of the human ethical capacity that, Durkheim eventually concluded, has society itself as its point of reference.

How, then, could the increasing incidence of destructive or deviant behavior be understood? It could be studied, measured, explained precisely *as* a social fact, irreducible to individual psychology or character. At the same time, it suggested that the socialization process itself had somehow become inadequate to the novel challenges of the modern world. For Durkheim, such deviance was a symptom of *anomie*, his still indispensable term for the insufficient internalization of societal norms that his empirical studies suggested was becoming a systematic problem in contemporary secular, liberal, industrial society. Just as the rational recognition of mutual interdependence was proving insufficient, the practices of liberal democracy were not involving individuals adequately in collective life, affording the essential sense of belonging, of full participation.

Did socialism promise a solution? Durkheim was willing to admit that the growing popularity of Marxist socialism among the disaffected was a significant symptom; expressing a longing for something better, it even reflected a worthy moral passion. But the Marxist diagnosis confused the terms of the problem. As Durkheim put it in 1899: "it especially would be a considerable step forward, benefitting everyone, if socialism would finally quit confusing the social question with the question of the workers."[5] There was indeed a "social question," and it was indeed bound up with the spread of industrial capitalism, although not in the way that Marx had described. Moreover, the workers might indeed have legitimate grievances, but the appeal of Marxism, based on Marx's way of bringing together the two problems, made it more difficult to address either. In seeking to persuade the workers that they were preparing for a universal role, overcoming the core social problem, by pursuing their own interests, Marxism not only stirred up class antagonism but also fostered envy and resentment, a lack of sense of limits, among contemporary workers.[6] The popularity of Marxism was merely a symptom of the underlying social problem—the weakening of social bonds in modern industrial society. The workers had no privileged role in overcoming that problem.

But how, then, could the problem be addressed? Whereas Durkheim, like Bernstein, was denying Marx's conception of the place of the ethical, he was also implying that it could not be enough simply to appeal to the ethical and, on that basis, to bring the right-minded together to pursue reforms. The key was to *generate* the ethical capacity that Bernstein had tended to take for granted. And Durkheim's way of thinking beyond the loosely positivist conception of individual and society suggested the scope for engineering, necessarily starting with initiative from "above," the deeper integration necessary to nurture that capacity. On that basis, in fact, it would be possible to foster both a more genuine, fulfilling individuality and a more effective society.

Durkheim proposed two concrete avenues. First, those in charge had to make the educational system more effective as a means of instilling a patriotic sense of belonging, of citizenship, of sharing the values of the whole society. Durkheim was a tireless advocate of education, stressing the novelty of the challenge and opportunity now before it.[7] But it was also necessary to devise new institutions, addressing what had proved to be the inadequacies of the liberal parliamentary system. To foster the moralizing sense of belonging, a new network of intermediate groupings based on occupation, or the workplace, would afford individuals a more constant and direct kind of participation in an expanded public sphere. Thus the "corporativism" that Durkheim advocated first in *Suicide*, then developed more fully in the preface to the second edition of *The Division of Labor in Society* in 1902.[8]

Virtually by definition, any accent on *intermediate* groupings can be read in two ways, as promoting the moralizing socialization and integration of "anarchical," egotistical, atomized individuals, or as promoting freedom and autonomy *vis-à-vis* a centralizing, inherently authoritarian state. Durkheim was seeking to provide new *public* roles for individuals, whose experience of participation could be enhanced precisely as the state expanded *its* roles. Indeed, such expansion required that more direct and constant participation. But because the state would be in a sense decentralized, brought down to earth, even as it expanded, it would not be experienced as authoritarian and aloof.

In proposing public roles for new occupational groupings, Durkheim was responding in part to the trade union phenomenon, seeking better to integrate into present society the workers attracted to Marxism. The union experience was surely moralizing and socially integrative on one level, but the use of the strike as the chief mode of collective action could seem unnecessarily chaotic and arbitrary as a way of making societal decisions, allocating resources, even pursuing the workers' interests. At best, the advent of trade unions manifested and reinforced the tendency of the bourgeois liberal dispensation to settle into interest group particularism. So although the union movement was valuable as an innovative response to modern experience, the present form did not exhaust its wider societal possibilities. It had to be determined what was essential to this promising new phenomenon and what was merely contingent, the result of the imperfect liberal dispensation so far.

Durkheim's corporativist thinking also reflected his interaction with Léon Duguit, the most influential French figure in the international direction, known variously as solidarism or juridical socialism, that brought together a number of leading legal scholars, economists, and other social thinkers around the turn of the century. Now virtually forgotten, this highly symptomatic current needs to be better known if we are to assess what seemed to be the new issues and possibilities emerging at this pivotal moment.[9] The thinkers involved noted that trade unions were only the most visible of the many new autonomous social groupings—trade associations, for example—that were emerging spontaneously, apart from the state. Although membership was generally voluntary, such organizations were sufficiently powerful to make binding rules on individuals. It seemed that society was spontaneously overcoming the atomization of liberalism, even, in a sense, expanding the realm of public law, denying, for example, an absolute right of individuals over their own property. Yet it was becoming clear, at the same time, that the state held no monopoly on legislative capacity. In short, the liberal distinction between public and private was blurring, even breaking down. Those like Duguit welcomed this phenomenon, which seemed to address the concerns that fed the socialist movement and, more generally, to promise the basis of a more effective modern society. But the phenomenon demanded adjustments in thinking about individual, state, and society and perhaps even in the actual juridical or institutional relationships between the state and this emerging network of societal organizations. By somehow integrating the unions, for example, into the state, it would be possible better to guarantee the workers' gains and to enrich the state, making it more truly the vehicle of the whole society, at the same time.[10]

The young Italian syndicalist intellectual Sergio Panunzio, later a major Fascist ideologue, addressed juridical socialism in what proved to be an especially symptomatic study in 1906.[11] Even as, predictably at this point, he attacked the current as bourgeois and insisted that only class struggle could afford the antidote to the contemporary social problem, Panunzio was clearly intrigued by the image of a dense network of societal organizations overcoming the individualistic particularism of liberalism. As he began to find conventional Marxian categories inadequate, his encounter with this movement informed his effort to rethink the scope for a systematic alternative and affected the content of the overtly totalitarian alternative that he gradually came to formulate.

Durkheim, like Duguit, viewed the emergence of unions and other societal organizations as a welcome means of strengthening the state, carrying it beyond its liberal incarnation so far. Through corporativism, it would be possible to elevate from private to public the organizational impulse that had led the workers into the unions. Moreover, Durkheim envisioned minimizing the role of strikes through compulsory arbitration, which would make wage earners less dependent on bargaining, arbitrary decisions, and contingent circumstances.[12]

But whereas Durkheim found innovative response essential, his thinking remained relatively conventional on several levels. In contrast to Bernstein, who in shifting to the endless pursuit of justice was embracing the newly open-ended conception of history, Durkheim sought simply to restore the equilibrium that he took to be the societal norm. Ordinarily, collective sentiments are genuinely internalized to form both a cohesive society and the foundation for individuality; it is anomalous when they are not. The disruptions of the modernization process were producing such an anomaly, and although it was necessary to intensify the sense of belonging in a mass, industrial, secular age, to do so was simply to restore normal equilibrium. The point was to integrate individuals into the existing society/polity of the Third Republic, not, as for Bernstein, to project endlessly into the future—and certainly not to create the instrument for some new and different kind of societal projection.

Depending on one's perspective, Durkheim's way of promoting civic patriotism and public-spiritedness could seem to promise a healthy antidote to the "negative, desiccated, ungenerous" individualism preached by the contemporary French moralist Alain, even to the egotistical premium on self-discovery explored (but not celebrated) in André Gide's *The Immoralist* of 1902.[13] Or it could seem conservative in the most dubious, ideological sense. Although he recognized, in principle, the possibility of "negative division of labor"—an incongruence between careers and talents—Durkheim played down objective socio-economic issues such as the distribution of wealth or the scope for social mobility through access to higher education. Because the problem was essentially subjective and moral, the solution was not to change socio-economic relationships but to socialize individuals more effectively—to change the way they *felt* about their place in society. And this entailed internalizing the norms of the particular society, feeling part of it.

Whether we take Durkheim as a progressive democrat or an anti-Marxist conservative, it is crucial that he was a liberal and not a totalitarian. But whatever his commitment to the Third Republic, his response helped to articulate new uncertainties, new concerns, and a new sense of the possibilities. Especially from within the framework of a more dynamic, future-oriented historical conscious-ness, his sense both of the deepening inadequacy of the liberal dispensation and of the antidotes possible and necessary could readily carry beyond his own commitment to liberal democracy.[14] In light of his arguments, it was easy to conclude that there was scope for still deeper and more meaningful integration if more was to be undertaken collectively. Even the significance of corporativist participation would vary with the reach attempted, the political meaning of the decisions being made in this new collective way. Insofar as it was bound up with more grandiose aims, the new corporativism would mean fuller integration but not mere conservatism. More generally, Durkheim was showing the scope to foster and channel the human ethical capacity through more constant mobiliza-tion and intensive socialization. So his diagnoses and prescriptions not only fed the wider sense of openness and possibility but also suggested the direction for a more radical step not merely to adjust liberalism but to carry beyond it altogether.

Gaetano Mosca is often linked with his sometime rival Vilfredo Pareto and their German-Swiss-Italian contemporary Robert Michels as constituting an Italian "neo-Machiavellian" school of political analysis. With the democratic experiment now fully under way, each sought to tear aside democratic ideals and the rhetoric of popular sovereignty to probe, with unsentimental realism, the actual functioning of parliamentary institutions. Dispassionate analysis exposed the elitism, hypocrisy, cynicism, and egotism that belied populist ideals and the pretense of equality. If anything, democratic notions served simply as myths enabling a new elite to maintain itself in power. Moreover, modern parliamen-tary politics had proved especially prone to debilitating forms of corruption. All three thinkers sought radically to rethink modern political possibilities in light of the disillusioning outcome so far. But unlike Pareto and Michels, Mosca concluded that, despite everything, what he most valued could best be served from within a liberal democratic framework, the essential terms of which had to be, and could be, understood afresh.

Beginning in the 1880s, Mosca responded critically to the practice of Italian politics, especially *trasformismo*, the system of political manipulation and coalition building that Agostino Depretis pioneered after the fall of the *Destra Storica*, the party of Cavour's heirs, in 1876. Based on shifting coalitions of interests, that system reached its culmination under Giovanni Giolitti from 1901 to 1914. Mosca offered his most systematic analysis in *Elementi di scienza politica* (1896), which was published in a substantially augmented second edition (1923), later translated as *The Ruling Class*. Seeking to pinpoint the sources of what seemed to be the endemic corruption of parliamentary government, Mosca highlighted the power of the elected representatives, who pressured the ministers to arrange favors for constituents from the courts and "the vast and absorbing bureaucratic machine." Thus, for example, speculative industrial enterprises won the government favors that they needed to survive. The toll was high not only in public funds but also "in moral atmosphere," for the whole system tended to undermine "any respect for equity and law." The problem was not simple venality but a conflict of interest inherent in the system; for the most part, the deputies generally wanted to serve the collective interest, but they also needed to get re-elected.[15] And is not one elected to serve local constituents?

In the second edition, published in the wake of Italy's postwar crisis, Mosca worried that the contemporary representative system bred "a relaxation of those forces of moral cohesion which alone are capable of uniting in a consensus of sentiments and ideas all the atoms that make up a people, and which, therefore, constitute the cement without which any political edifice totters and collapses."[16] Parliamentary democracy was apparently a path to societal dissolution. Democratic ideas had proved to be merely the "ruling formulas" that enabled the particular contemporary elite to justify its power.

Nowadays, the tension in representative systems between particular and general interests and the problem of "money in politics" are too familiar to require comment, but around the turn of century, with parliamentary democracy being widely tried for the first time, Mosca's analysis was at once novel and potentially explosive in implication. Whereas a sense of public-spiritedness had been essential to the self-understanding of nineteenth-century liberal elites, parliamentary government seemed necessarily to foster a mode of particularism that either undermined that public-spiritedness or exposed it as mere pretense. Yet the mechanism undermining the ethical was quite different from the bureaucratic distancing that Zygmunt Bauman had found central to the modern problem.

The reader of Mosca in 1896 might conclude that the problem stemmed from democracy, not liberalism, and that liberalism would not have had to have led to this form of democracy, based on parliamentary sovereignty. Indeed, Mosca's diagnoses seemed to confirm the contemporary German argument that what mattered was a *Rechtsstaat*, a state guaranteeing the law and thus a sphere of individual freedom. Such a state did not require the parliamentary sovereignty that Germany lacked; if anything, the contemporary Italian and French experience suggested that parliamentary sovereignty tended to compromise the integrity of the state as the guarantor of freedom and equal treatment under the law. Much concerned with "juridical defense," Mosca, too, worried that the particularist tendencies of the contemporary parliamentary system compromised that essential function of the state. But as found in the German *Rechtsstaat* tradition or in Mosca's concern with juridical defense, the liberal accent on private autonomy and freedom meshed uneasily with the expanding reach of the state, the assumption of wider societal responsibility.

After the turn of the century, Mosca, like Durkheim and others across the political spectrum, focused his attention on the growing trade union phenomenon.[17] And his accents were decidedly negative. The specter of public service strikes, especially, threatened the authority of a liberal state already tending toward particularist dissolution. With the quasi-revolutionary labor unrest that Italy experienced just after the First World War, Mosca warned that intermediate bodies like unions were undermining not only the sovereignty of the state but also, in light of the growing mutual interdependence occasioned by the modern division of labor, the whole social fabric.[18]

Still, although his analyses suggested the inherent corruption of parliamentary government and the inherent weakness of the liberal state, Mosca pulled back from any blanket rejection of liberal democracy. In light of the new, deeper understanding of the actual workings of modern politics, the best course was to face up to certain trade-offs and limitations and to move on from within a broadly liberal frame. We come to recognize that despite universal suffrage, majority rule, popular sovereignty, and juridical equality, power is always concentrated in one or more elites. But the inevitable elitism could take varied forms. The key for Mosca was to foster a pluralistic balance of opposing forces and thereby to prevent the concentration of power in a single elite. Even more important than the structure of the state was a broader societal pluralism enabling political, economic, social, intellectual, and ecclesiastical elites to balance and check each other. Moreover, elites could be more or less open to the principle of meritocracy, and open elites were much healthier in terms of both justice to individuals and societal effectiveness. Indeed, in light of experience, we come to understand that meritocracy is central to all we mean by democracy.[19]

Underlying a renewed liberal democracy for Mosca was the principle of moderation. Even meritocracy could not be pushed too far; as an absolute principle, it would not only engender a counterproductive level of competition but also undermine private property and the nuclear family. So the key was to avoid absolutes, to recognize trade-offs. Mosca shared the deepening sense of the heterogeneity of ends that we associate with Max Weber and Isaiah Berlin, and he anticipated the accents of those like Robert Dahl who, after the Second World War, would portray such societal pluralism as the key to modern democracy. By now, in fact, Mosca's pluralistic imperatives seem familiar and almost self-recommending. But his way of articulating what experience had revealed was to make certain creases in liberal democracy visible in his own time. And although he offered some innovative prescriptions, he had trouble fitting the newly shaped pieces together. Thus his thinking betrayed tensions, and some of his prescriptions could seem too cautious in light of what seemed to be the problems and the scope for alternatives. Those following his diagnoses might find a more radical, post-liberal prescription necessary.

Like Durkheim, Mosca recognized that societal consensus required an emotional tie and, again like Durkheim, he thought it could be fostered from within a liberal democratic framework. But Mosca responded far more conventionally than Durkheim, relying on mere patriotic exhortation. Even in light of the widespread labor unrest during Italy's postwar crisis, he could only call for the trade unionists to put national loyalty first, to listen to government leaders before the leaders of their own unions.[20]

From Mosca's perspective, it was the "anti-national" socialist orientation of the unions that made their growing power a problem and not a welcome instance of societal pluralism. But even should they shed what might be viewed as their adolescent socialist trappings, the unions would be just another interest group within a modern liberal pluralism, precisely as for later theorists of liberalism. Could any such "interest-group liberalism" suffice, in light of Mosca's ongoing concerns about the state's sovereignty and authority and its role in promoting juridical defense? Some of Mosca's concerns might seem to suggest that pluralism and patriotism could not suffice, that a new, more organic relationship between the state and the unions was necessary.

Although Mosca concluded that liberalism remained the best guarantee of individual rights and freedoms, the advent of intermediate organizations like unions suggested that securing such a private space for individuals, conceived in isolation, was not necessarily the issue. Insofar as the workers, for example, had an equal right to state protection, juridical defense had to encompass the workers not as abstract individuals but precisely as an organized group. From this angle, too, a new, more organic relationship between state and unions might seem to be called for.

Although the Italian Fascists routinely invoked his pioneering dissections of parliamentary government and democratic myths, Mosca himself remained firmly liberal in the face of the totalitarian temptation. Indeed, he concluded the second edition of his *Elementi* in 1923 with a moving call to Italian youth not to be so quick to give up on the liberal parliamentary system.[21] Retaining his Senate seat after Mussolini came to power, he spoke out against the Fascist regime periodically, then lived in silent opposition until his death in 1941. Whatever the tensions in the contemporary world, societal pluralism and moderation on the one hand, and individual freedom and justice on the other, remained more important to him than the capacity to forge a deeper consensus and to expand the reach of collective action.

Although they started from very different concerns, Mosca, Durkheim, and Bernstein each found something deeply inadequate about liberal democracy as conceived and practiced so far. Yet each also thought it possible to recast the liberal tradition in response to the tensions experience had brought to light. But playing off these three was another layer of thinkers who, finding themselves on the same new terrain, also responded to liberalism and socialism in tandem, but who were temperamentally more radical. They addressed, directly or indirectly, the tensions in the thinking of their more moderate contemporaries and began to articulate more innovative ways of understanding problems and possibilities.

Discerning the scope for a new radicalism

Like Mosca, Vilfredo Pareto translated a deep disillusionment with parliamentary government into a new conception of modern politics and society, accenting the role of elites and reducing democratic ideas to ruling formulas or myths. But, more deeply discontented, he found revolution necessary, although his conception of revolution utterly eluded—and explicitly challenged—the dominant Marxian terms. So whereas Pareto is justifiably lumped with Mosca up to a point, he proved to have more in common with his French contemporary, the more radical and disaffected Georges Sorel, with whom he was also often lumped during the Fascist period.

Coming of age a humanitarian, a rationalist, and a liberal democrat, Pareto was a passionate Dreyfusard and opponent of anti-Semitism even as he passed into his fifties late in the nineteenth century. But his liberal democratic sympathies had begun to erode during the 1880s when he, like Mosca, began probing the actual workings of parliamentary government. Having begun his academic career as an economist, Pareto showed how the links between protectionist interests and government underpinned Italy's transformist politics, with its influence peddling and managed elections. Even more cynically than Mosca, Pareto portrayed democratic ideals as mere myths, slogans, that enabled the Italian governing class to conceal its true nature. The bourgeoisie might once have believed in its universal mission, but by now the selfish, short-sighted parliamentary politicians did not genuinely entertain the democratic platitudes they professed. Masking ever more superficially the actual bourgeois preoccupation with narrow, short-term interests, the threadbare myths of democracy could not long afford a viable basis for social cohesion.

Yet for Pareto, as for Mosca, our experience with parliamentary democracy had revealed that differentiation and elitism are simply built in, never to be overcome altogether. We must simply adjust to the fact. So elitism was not itself the problem, and, conversely, the antidote was not simply to criticize elitism and promote egalitarianism. But in contrast to Mosca, Pareto judged the present manipulation and corruption to be symptoms of a problem too deep to be overcome from within the present democratic framework. Something about the liberal elite made it incapable of the leadership that a healthy society required.

Whereas Mosca was troubled by the challenge of trade unions to the sovereignty of the state, Pareto found much to admire in the energy and commitment of the fledgling labor movement. Around the turn of the century, he, like Sorel, was struck by the impressive discipline and solidarity that the workers demonstrated in the face of adversity, most dramatically during strikes. Contrasting sharply with the short-sighted, self-serving ethos of the bourgeoisie, these qualities suggested that the organized industrial workers potentially constituted a new elite capable of spearheading societal renewal.[22] Although, as Pareto saw it, Marxism was not convincing or even coherent, the doctrine clearly inspired the workers, enhancing their effectiveness, by suggesting that they were developing the capacity to forge an alternative to the bourgeois order. As they made their revolution, based on this self-understanding, they would restore to society the commitment and solidarity, the willingness to sacrifice for the collective, that the bourgeoisie by this point was undermining.

So on the basis of experience first with parliamentary government, but then also with both Marxism and the labor movement, Pareto recast the terms of the opposition that had emerged between the liberal mainstream and the mainstream socialist alternative. Most obviously, he was bidding farewell to the by then conventional Left/Right axis, which had afforded a credible way of differentiating political positions during the nineteenth century, but which seemed ever less meaningful as new challenges and possibilities opened. The questions about differentiation and egalitarianism partly at issue in earlier Left/Right debates were no longer at issue; what mattered was differentiation *between* elites, in terms of their societal roles and effectiveness. And although thinking in terms of socio-economic classes had become conventional, Pareto found that elite effectiveness had no necessary relationship with class. Rather, elites varied according to subjectivity, consciousness, collective psychology, even irreducible values, all of which determined how they would organize society—and how effective they could be. The qualities that attracted Pareto to the workers were not reducible to the proletariat's objective place in the economy—although they did have some experiential basis and could be nurtured further.

Pareto's effort to understand and characterize the differences between elites occasioned his pioneering effort to distinguish underlying motives, pseudo-logical rationalizations, the objective validity of ideas, and the social effects of ideas. He had already noted that the effectiveness of ideas did not depend on their rationality or objective validity. In their different ways, protectionism and Marxism were notable cases in point. So it was crucial to attend to the effectiveness of non-rational sentiments. From there, Pareto began to note that the rationalizations that people give for what they believe are only pseudo-logical and must be distinguished from the hidden, underlying motives for those beliefs. Rather than try to pinpoint the ultimate source of these underlying differences, Pareto simply assumed them from the manifest differences in the ways people behave and explain what they do. The differences in the kinds of reasons that people gave to justify their behavior afforded a more illuminating way of characterizing social grouping and differentiation than socio-economic class.

Quite apart from criteria of differentiation, Pareto was suggesting that purpose, meaning, and effectiveness could not be cleanly separated but were caught up in a web that had eluded prior thinking, especially as crystallized in "positivism"—positivistic though Pareto's own thinking obviously remained on one level. The "reasons" at issue are not necessarily rational; indeed, they are more like myths, although they may serve a "rational' function. Moreover, rational understanding is one kind of thing, the necessary action another. So reason is at once murky and not necessarily desirable. As conventionally invoked, the whole axis of rational and non-rational was too simple to be helpful.

Once he had specified the basis of the differential effectiveness between elites, Pareto fastened on the distinction between lions and foxes, his shorthand for the two basic types of elite. The lions have a strong sense of purpose, accent group solidarity, and are quite willing to use force and even violence if necessary. Indeed, the capacity to exercise force and use violence was a key manifestation of the commitment and discipline needed to forge an effective society. The lions are able to use violence *with a good conscience*, not as some sadistic indulgence but as an expression of their belief in the rightness of their cause, whatever it is. But Pareto noted what seemed to be a natural tendency even for the lions gradually to lose their defining qualities. They change from lions to foxes—short-sighted, egotistical, cynical, relying on guile, mere corruption. Much like Mosca, Pareto suggested that effective elites might delay this process of degeneration insofar as they remain sufficiently open to replenishing themselves with energetic new elements from below. But even if there is genuine social mobility, an entrenched foxy elite is likely to take in those most like themselves, not those with the necessary lion attributes. Sooner or later, as the hypocrisy and ineffectiveness of the foxes becomes ever more apparent, a new elite begins to form from below, as some among the masses come to see through the present ruling myths and to believe themselves capable of forging a superior order based on their own new beliefs. This new elite begins to prepare a revolution of lions, appealing to solidarity and self-sacrifice.

Pareto concluded that despite what democratic ideology had led the modern world to hope and assume, the electoral mechanisms of parliamentary democracy tend to produce an elite of cynical, corrupt foxes incapable of effective leadership over the long term. For example, the bourgeois elite that had established its hegemony after the French Revolution had substantially reshaped society in its own image, but as the bourgeois principle had come to seem ever more equivalent to cynical self-interest, that elite was proving incapable of fostering the shared beliefs and solidarity necessary for an effective society. The antidote was not individual self-realization or even individual moral worthiness but post-bourgeois societal effectiveness resting on some set of shared values and beliefs that genuinely bound people together, that nurtured discipline and self-sacrifice, that underpinned collective action. Such was the antidote that the proletariat seemed for a while to be capable of offering.

Even in his most systematic sociological work, *Trattato di sociologia generale* (1916), Pareto minced no words as he specified the positive uses even of violence in "a country on its way to utter ruin" thanks to a decadent elite unable to defend not only its own power but even the country's independence. In the revolt from below that would ensue, those from the subject class would "apply force on a large scale, and not only overthrow the [elite] but kill large numbers of them—and, in so doing, to tell the truth, they are performing a useful public service, something like ridding the country of a baneful animal pest . . . . Owing to them the social fabric is acquiring stability and strength." In the same vein, Pareto noted that the use of force was "the main duty of a ruling class."[23]

Pareto developed his innovative categories most immediately in response to the contemporary Italian situation, which seemed especially to elude the Left/Right axis and the conventional self-understanding of both liberalism and Marxism. Still, the Italian case simply brought to the surface the underlying problems of the modern liberal dispensation. What weakened Italy was not capitalism but a kind of decadence, or flabbiness, the result of the ethos fostered by an elite of foxes clustered around the parliamentary state. The political class in Italy was parasitical, not an instrument of the energetic industrial development the country needed. The present Italian elite seemed to be incapable of binding society in solidarity and leading it effectively. Only a revolution of lions, not piecemeal reforms, could address the problem, first by inculcating a new integrative ethos.

Pareto was comparable to Mosca in his critique of parliamentary democracy, his accent on elites, and his new, more complex understanding of the socio-political role of ideas and beliefs. But rather than, with Mosca, placing his hopes in exhortation and an ambiguous pluralism, he called for a full-scale post-liberal revolution spearheaded by a new counter-elite of outsiders. At the same time, Pareto was comparable to Durkheim in seeking a fresh understanding of what now seemed the inherently non-rational bases of social cohesion. And he too found the present outcome of the modern dispensation inadequate. He agreed that the problem, and hence the scope for solution, was bound up with values, sentiments, or collective psychology, as opposed to apparently more objective socio-economic factors. But Pareto did not share Durkheim's assumption that a society is normally in equilibrium, that the priority at present was to find better ways of integrating individuals into existing society. Partly, no doubt, because of his specifically Italian concerns, his vision of societal health entailed a still-deeper cohesion to enable the society to act collectively, projecting into the future. The liberal parliamentary order could not be revitalized, as for Durkheim, but had to be transcended altogether—by a committed new elite, capable of violence, emerging from the outside.

Still, although he departed from Durkheim's equilibrium model, Pareto was positing neither a teleological nor a radically open-ended conception of history. In suggesting a natural tendency for even a new elite to decay, for lions to turn into foxes only to be overturned by a new revolution of lions, his notion was essentially cyclical. Solidarity and shared commitment can never be established once and for all. Even the proletariat, as a new elite, would gradually lose its "lion" qualities and govern through guile as it increasingly obviously pursued in its own interests. So whereas will and commitment were essential to Pareto's conception, a deeper structure limited what they could accomplish; the world was not open to will, to human shaping, on a long-term basis.

Pareto was obviously thinking on two different levels. What mattered for now was the emergence of agents with the necessary commitment and will to act, using force as necessary. They did not have to understand the wider contours of history; indeed, any such understanding would compromise their capacity to act. Although they could grasp the need to keep inculcating their values and even to replenish themselves, those with the necessary commitment would be unable even to conceive of losing that commitment and thus operating on some other basis. But Pareto himself grasped the larger historical contours; in the event of a revolution of the lions, he would understand as the agents would not. So although he found an antidote to the contemporary problem essential, Pareto retained a measure of distance, even a certain cynicism. In this sense, theory and practice remained distinct in his conception. Extrapolating, we might say that whereas Pareto could envision something like a totalitarian antidote to liberalism, he could not have become a full participant, a totalitarian agent himself. The actual totalitarian departure would entail a very particular way of bringing together theory and practice, a very particular combination of historical sense and collective action.

Pareto was sympathetic to early Fascism as potentially the revolutionary force needed, but he died in 1923, before the direction of Fascism was clear, and before an unequivocal choice was necessary. Still, his thinking directly influenced the creators of Italian Fascism and helped to establish the contours of the new historical-political terrain more generally. More fully to grasp his place, we must consider him alongside his almost exact contemporary Georges Sorel.

Unlike Pareto, Sorel embraced Marxism as a framework during the 1890s as he sought to conceive the present problem and the scope for a systematic alternative. However, he sensed from the start that a radical rethinking of this mainstream radical framework was necessary and almost immediately began claiming to spearhead a distinctive "New School." His quest for fresh thinking led to an unusually wide frame of intellectual reference, encompassing French thinkers from Durkheim to Henri Bergson. And virtually from the start, his thinking reflected interaction with the Italians Francesco Saverio Merlino, Antonio Labriola, and Benedetto Croce; indeed, he would correspond regularly with Croce from the mid-1890s until his death in 1922.

The direction that resulted proved parallel to Pareto's, despite the difference in initial framework. Although less overtly concerned with the role of elites, Sorel, too, thought he saw, for a while, the qualities for a systematic alternative developing among the workers through the moralizing effects of union membership and collective action. From within this framework, he also came to accent the importance of both violence and non-rational images in the process of maturation that could make the working class capable of such a regenerative role. The implications of his thinking pointed beyond the working-class experience to the general question of the scope, and the requisites, for the new forms of collective action that seemed to be bound up with societal health. His thinking about myth, will, and violence especially expanded ways of conceiving possibilities and helped to channel subsequent political departures in a particular anti-liberal direction. Sorel's significance in this regard, as both influential and symptomatic, has long been recognized. Yet despite the ongoing, deeply critical efforts of Zeev Sternhell, he has become known ever less directly over the last generation—even as certain of his categories have come to be taken for granted. Sorelian myth, especially, is widely invoked, but in almost stereotypical form, divorced from the context of Sorel's wider argument and the circumstances to which it responded.

Taking for granted Bernstein's revisionist understanding of the present capitalist economy, Sorel concluded that socialists needed to turn from the objective unfolding of capitalism to the other side of the coin, proletarian psychology, or consciousness, a dimension that had remained undeveloped in classical Marxism in light of Marx's mature preoccupation with the putatively contradictory logic of capitalism. But this imperative only reinforced Sorel's concern with the questions about values, the bases of societal commitment and effectiveness, that had made him disaffected with the present bourgeois order in the first place. Much like Pareto, he sensed that the underlying problem stemmed not from capitalism or from objective economic relationships but from deeper societal values and practices. The problem could be summed up as decadence, loss of commitment, manifested as cynicism and egotistical particularism. On the political level, it found expression in the premium on getting elected, maximizing power, doing favors, and lining pockets, which was provoking widespread disillusionment with the institutions and practices of parliamentary government.

Whereas Pareto sought a more nuanced understanding of the social role of what purported to be rational claims, Sorel found rationalism and positivism to be central to the contemporary problem and thus assaulted them directly. Especially in its present critical positivist guise, rationalism undercuts belief and commitment and thus engenders skepticism and cynicism—and ultimately egotism, particularism, and societal decadence. But there was no turning back to the old beliefs once society had begun to see through them rationally. Regeneration could come only from outside the mainstream rational order, even from below, through a species of non-rational primitivism.

As he was seeking to get deeper into proletarian psychology, Sorel was stimulated by Durkheim's accent on the social basis of morality and the potentially moralizing and integrative role of occupational groupings. In that light, he began to examine the actual practice of trade unions in England by the late 1890s, and he was struck with the new discipline and self-sacrifice, the new sense of collective power that seemed to be emerging from the ground up through trade union organization and activity. In a series of articles published as "Avenir socialiste des syndicats" (1898), Sorel insisted that, counter to Durkheim's paternalistic corporativism, new moralizing organizations could emerge spontaneously only from the outside.[24] The contemporary trade unions were valuable precisely because they had indeed emerged in this way, and they had to remain outside, and autonomous, if they were to fulfill their potential as moralizing agents. So although he had been influenced by Gustave Le Bon's widely discussed *The Crowd* (1895), which showed the scope for a kind of collective, supra-individual consciousness or mind, Sorel viewed the collective, non-rational sentiments that feed action from below not as menacing, like Le Bon, but as moralizing and positive. Although the non-rational newly emerging through the collective life of the working class would seem threatening to the bourgeoisie, the workers, insofar as they came together through trade union organization and activity, were *not* a mere "crowd" but potentially a precious source of new values, of wider societal commitment and renewal.

Understood from within the Marxian framework, the scope for a different, "socialist" kind of society depended, as Sorel saw it, on the industrial working class maturing and acting on its own, outside bourgeois political institutions. On that basis, Sorel became an advocate of revolutionary syndicalism, insisting that the possibility of revolutionary transformation rested not on political parties operating in parliament but on the *syndicats*, in the trade unions. As specifically proletarian institutions, they were cradles of the new values necessary for a qualitatively different order. Any association with political parties, any premium on parliamentary activity, could only compromise that potential.

But indispensable though they were, organizational membership and activity afforded only a first layer. A focus on unions as opposed to political parties might yield mere "economism," a premium on gains for the workers within the existing system. So in *Reflections on Violence* (1906), Sorel sought to probe more deeply the basis of the *revolutionary* potential that he continued to attribute to the organized workers. This was to show not only why they were capable of overcoming, rather than merely becoming part of, the present order but also why the nature of the process itself would entail a certain desirable post-bourgeois outcome. Although still seeking to interpret actual working-class practice, Sorel was now looking more to France and Italy than to Britain, and he was adding more of his own gloss, partly through encounter with Bergson.

The key trade union weapon was the strike, which often included the measured use of violence, reflecting not merely indiscipline or self-indulgence but a willingness to break the mold in light of the workers' dawning sense that they were developing the capacities to produce a superior, more committed order. A strike could encompass workers in more than one factory or even more than one locality or economic sector; thus the scope for a general strike, the very possibility of which gave the workers a sense of their own power. And that sense of power gradually engendered a collective image of the catastrophic general strike, encompassing images of all that the organized workers might accomplish, of a whole future order based on their values.

That collective image was an instance of "myth," which, as Sorel saw it, emerges spontaneously as a collective sense of power and commitment bound up with images of the future. What mattered about any such myth was not its literal truth but its effectiveness, which had nothing to do with the actual realization of any of those images. Buttressing belief and commitment, cementing solidarity, the myth galvanized disciplined and effective action, so it both expressed and reinforced the workers' determination to act together. In that sense, myth and the essential new values and capacities grew together. Although Sorel's thinking about the non-rationality of societal bonds bore some superficial similarity to Durkheim's, Sorel's thrust was very different: as Isaiah Berlin put it, the function of Sorelian myth was not to stabilize but to direct energies and inspire action.[25] By implication, for Sorel renewal through myth had driven history itself, much as had Pareto's lion-led revolutions. Sorel cited historical examples—the early Christians, the French Revolutionary armies, the Mazzinians with their seemingly impractical dreams of a new Italy—to suggest how a sublime, heroic mentality woven around myth had yielded notable transformations.

What Sorel envisioned, then, was anything but some elite—especially some *intellectual* elite—mobilizing the workers through myths. Misreadings that treat myth as manipulative, as consciously fostered to direct and control mass movements, remain widespread and keep us from grasping the more subtle, innovative thrust of Sorel's concept—and thus its subsequent place.[26] In Sorelian terms, it is crucial that myth wells up spontaneously, organically, from below—in this case from within the working-class experience and thus from outside the decadent bourgeois order. To be sure, the new values emerge not from undifferentiated masses but from those who have had a particular experience as organized industrial workers. And as an empirical fact, even some among the workers were currently more militant, committed, and disciplined than others. In that sense, the new values characterized a new elite, as for Pareto, but Sorel was not advocating "elitism" as usually understood, and certainly not the manipulative use of myths by those who see through them rationally. It is also true that such values were bound up with an accent on authority and discipline. But Sorel featured not some hierarchical control but the *self*-discipline and even individual initiative that result from trade union membership and the kind of collective action that it makes possible.[27]

The workers' new values would enable them not only to supplant the decadent bourgeoisie but to run the industrial system without masters in the new economic order, "the regime of free producers." Thanks to industrialization itself, but especially to their experience of collective struggle through the unions, the workers were accustomed to working together, eschewing egotistical individualism, exercising self-discipline yet taking initiative as necessary.

Sorel, like Pareto, stood in ambiguous relationship with the social transformation he envisioned. He too was a rational intellectual—and certainly no irrationalist. The question was what role a rational intellectual could play in light of his diagnosis and prescription. Intellectuals could offer theoretical clarification, explaining the value of myth and the process through which a new myth might emerge. They might even discern, from a distance, the actual emergence of a new myth. But they could not galvanize action or act themselves. Indeed, they had to keep their distance or they would compromise the value-creating potential of outsiders like the organized workers. Rather than presuming to prescribe a direction for the workers, Sorel sought to explain how significant change could take place, to explain the significance of autonomous trade union activity, and on that basis to call off other middle-class intellectuals and politicians, with their well-meaning or self-serving schemes to win working-class support for socialist parties in parliament, as if electing socialist deputies could create a new order. To create a superior order, the workers would have to act on their own, developing their own institutions, values, and commitments on the basis of class separation and struggle. In that sense, Sorel's direction was diametrically opposed to Bernstein's, although each had been impressed with British trade unionism.

Still, Sorel, like Bernstein, was pulling back from any clear specification of the socialist end. Although aspects of "the regime of free producers" could be extrapolated from the newly emerging values of the organized workers, Sorel was departing radically from any hint of developmentalist predictability.[28] Outcomes were inherently unforeseeable—not only by the workers, galvanized by myth, but also by rational intellectuals like Sorel himself. Although we cannot foresee where it will lead, the present energizing force is what matters because it is bound up with the moralization that alone can afford the basis for a systematic alternative to the liberal order.

However, such openness meant a new element of contingency. With the departure from any determination by objective economic factors, the scope for organized workers to spearhead systematic change depended on their continued maturation outside the bourgeois order. Sorel's vision had a measure of empirical basis in the practice of the unions in the first decade of the century, but by 1910, as French working-class militancy waned, he was losing confidence in the workers, who seemed merely to be pursuing immediate advantage, pulling back from the sublime, heroic, value-creating mentality bound up with myth.[29] The workers were no better or worse than their own "bourgeois" society; they were simply pursing their own particular interests like everyone else.

Such empirical conclusions opened a new universe of questions. First, did the proletariat have any privileged role in creating the systematic alternative that had been envisioned for a century? Quite apart from actual working-class priorities in practice, the new thinking about the purposes of revolution suggested that revolution might be conceived without the proletariat as the leading force. Indeed, if the psychology or values that defined any genuinely revolutionary force was not a function of objective economic circumstances but of experience, or perhaps simply will and commitment themselves, the alternative to the proletariat would not have to be defined in class terms at all. Energizing myth, bound up with new commitment, could emerge elsewhere, utterly beyond the Marxian frame that had led Sorel to focus on the proletariat as a potentially revolutionary force in the first place. Perhaps the whole mode of thinking in terms of class, objectifying people as in some sense determined by material forces, was part of the generally positivistic legacy to be overcome if a more appropriate radicalism was to be conceived. Insofar as class categories were indeed an obstacle, a genuinely modern radicalism might even have to oppose immediate proletarian aspirations insofar as they reflected the outmoded notion that the workers' pursuit of their particular interests had universal value.

Having grown disillusioned with the workers, Sorel himself began looking around for other sources of regeneration, even flirting briefly with Action Française on the eve of the First World War. He admired the Leninist revolution and regime in Russia, a fact that we can best consider after we have discussed Lenin below. However, we note immediately that Sorel's enthusiasm seems utterly incompatible with his earlier vision, for in prescribing a vanguard role for intellectuals Lenin was explicitly denying that the essential new consciousness could come from below, even from the working class. It might seem that in endorsing Leninism Sorel was simply grasping at straws, confirming the judgment of George Lichtheim, who dismissed him as a mere "romantic litterateur."[30] In fact, however, Sorel, in endorsing the Leninist experiment, was glimpsing, albeit haltingly, a deeper congruence with Leninism in light of his own earlier categories and ongoing concerns.

Robert (Roberto) Michels was another of those who tried to work from within Marxism but found it necessary, on the basis of the empirical evidence, to push beyond Marxist categories—and who helped to reorient thinking about the scope for political action in the process. Although he had been active in the Marxist German Social Democratic Party (SPD), he grew disillusioned as he studied the workings of his party from the inside. In his noted *Political Parties* (1911), Michels generalized his conclusions to suggest that oligarchical and conservative tendencies are inherent in all political parties, even those professing revolutionary aims, and indeed in all large organizations. So whereas organization seemed essential for effectiveness, it seemed necessarily to breed tendencies antithetical to democracy and even significant change. This was not a matter of villainy but simply an unforeseen tendency of the modern world, revealed by experience, now to be faced, its implications thought through.

Michels concluded that whereas leaders initially administer the collective will of the organization, they gradually become independent of rank-and-file control. As the organization grows, so does the internal gap between leaders and followers. The followers come to view the leaders—including, in the case of the SPD, the socialist parliamentary deputies—as heroes. Enjoying the prestige of celebrity, the deputies invariably get re-elected, even if they flagrantly violate the professed aims of the movement.

The party's need for expertise reinforces the separation of the party's leaders from the inexpert rank and file. At some point, as with the SPD between 1905 and 1909, the organization comes to rely on paid functionaries, whose livelihood and success depend on the present fortunes of the organization, whatever its professed *raison d'être* and long-term aims. Such functionaries stress membership increases and voting strength over revolutionary strategy or the party's role as the bearer of a new principle. And as bureaucratic experts focus on delimited problems within their particular areas of competence, the organization's original ends get lost. Because the leaders and the paid bureaucrats have a stake within the system, preservation of the organization becomes the highest aim, almost an end in itself. Even a self-proclaimed revolutionary party like the SPD undergoes such *embourgeoisement*. Increasingly, its priority is to avoid antagonism with the state, especially in a crisis, when government authorities might especially desire—and have an excuse—to crack down on the organization.

For Michels, even revolutionary syndicalism afforded no antidote, despite its effective criticism of the tendency of socialist political parties to become part of the existing system. The same forces producing oligarchy and conservatism are equally to be found in trade unions. Even if some group did manage to pull off a socialist revolution, the result would be a mere change of masters. The leaders will always seek to preserve their own position. Michels noted that in fact leaders with genuinely working-class backgrounds especially tended to take on lower middle-class lifestyles and attitudes, whereas bourgeois intellectuals were more likely to retain their original radical principles.

In contributing to the shift in diagnosis and prescription, Michels was offering another variation on the theme of elites, myths, and masses. The leaders continue to mouth the principles of the organization—and may really believe in them, after a fashion. But in fact those principles become myths—as they seemed to have become for many European socialist leaders on the eve of the First World War. These were not Sorelian myths that mobilize effective action but, rather, myths that hide, even from the agents themselves, what is really going on—the dissolution of the virtues necessary for post-bourgeois modes of action.

Although his findings as a dispassionate analyst were disillusioning, Michels as activist and would-be radical did not find the situation altogether hopeless. "The iron law of oligarchy" was not an answer but opened a new set of questions. The key was simply to face up to what experience had revealed, to get beyond the longstanding democratic and even socialist principles that experience had shown to be myths. There was less reason to insist on formal democracy or parliamentary government, and the challenge was to specify alternative forms of leadership, participation, and collective action. Even for the pursuit of a systematic alternative that would bear some relationship with socialism, objective class background was irrelevant. Indeed, the first key, Michels insisted, was to have leaders with genuine culture and learning.

Part Italian by birth, Michels gravitated to Italy and supported Fascism, assuming a position at the Fascist Faculty of Political Science at the University of Perugia, even as he maintained considerable intellectual independence. As we will see in Chapter 6, he was especially interested in charismatic leadership as a potentially more genuine expression of the popular will than parliamentary government could provide. But he also noted the pitfalls of any reliance on such leadership. Although there was scope for experiment with post-democratic political forms, the results could not be predicted.

The ideas of Pareto, Sorel, and Michels at once reflected and contributed to the deepening sense of the limits of liberalism and the generally positivist conception of society, based on rational, predictable, self-interested individuals. At issue especially were limits to the forms of collective action that liberalism and positivism seemed to warrant or make possible. And in their different ways, each thinker responded to and reinforced the sense that orthodox Marxism afforded no alternative to positivist liberalism. The interface of history and politics had to be reassessed on the basis of that empirical understanding. Sensing the scope for an alternative to both liberalism and orthodox Marxism, each sought to specify at least some of what any such alternative would have to involve. In doing so, all three helped to foster wider thinking about the place of commitment, will, spirit, discipline, and self-sacrifice in collective action. In some ways, the capacity for commitment was coming to seem itself the key to the necessary change. There need be no clear specification of ends insofar as the ongoing capacity for a post-liberal, post-positivist mode of collective action would itself constitute a systematic alternative to the mainstream.

Pareto and Sorel stressed the significance of non-rational sentiments and the positive potential even of violence, which was not a mere atavism; on the contrary, the willingness to use violence in a particular way manifested and reinforced commitment—and might even help to convince others of the seriousness of that commitment. They thereby helped to foster a new sense that violence was to be expected as a positive moment in the emergence of any systematic alternative.

Some variation on "myth" was central to all three thinkers, but their varied ways of using it indicated how polyvalent the category was. Within the array from genuine belief to foxy cynicism, there were intermediate possibilities, including the scope for myth to emerge as an inadvertent by-product, along the lines that Michels indicated.

In one sense, Pareto offered the most differentiated understanding of myth, which, on his account, can underpin genuine belief and solidarity or play a merely instrumental role, cementing the power of a cynical, self-interested elite. Thus myths, like elites, can be distinguished according to their societal function. Conversely, myth was more central for Sorel, who specified its nature and the galvanizing function in a now classic way. And although he elaborated his conception, linked to the trade union experience, from within a quasi-Marxist framework and with a particular role for it in mind, myth could be taken— consciously or unconsciously—from its original context and variously combined with other components once he had interjected it into the discussion.

The new prominence of the category could in itself stimulate others to use myth in a cynical, manipulative way, utterly different from what Sorel envisioned. But there was scope for a more nuanced, "intermediate" role for myth, defying any dichotomy of above and below, elites and masses, or even knowers and doers. Even if, on one level, the elite is privy, in a rational way, to the new thinking about myth and collective action, the relationships between the elite and myth, and between the elite and the masses, need not be merely cynical. In light of the changing sense of how history happens, or could be made to happen, the elite may believe in the power of myth and fully share in the new sense of what is possible that some particular myth encapsulates. From this perspective, the will and capacity to believe, to participate in mythical thinking, are central to the elite's self-understanding, manifesting and reinforcing its capacity to impose itself and to galvanize collective action. However, this is not merely to manipulate but to cement a certain kind of reciprocity. The capacity for shared belief proves to be the key to the superior effectiveness of the new order that the elite spearheads, but how the element of myth might affect the elite's performance over the longer term remained uncertain.

Sources and implications of the Leninist departure

Whereas the commitment of Sorel and Michels to Marxism was tenuous, V.I. Lenin sought resolutely to work within Marxism throughout his career. Although he fully grasped the questions that orthodox Marxism had encountered, and although he pondered the relevance of idiosyncratic Russian circumstances and traditions in light of them, he never questioned the overall Marxian framework. Yet without admitting it even to himself, Lenin necessarily grappled with what orthodoxy meant, could possibly mean, in light of the new directions that now seemed necessary. In fact, the Marxian framework proved ever less relevant as he sought the basis of a new kind of collective action.

Emerging from within the wider revision of Marxism, Leninism proved the bridge between the ongoing modern political experiment, at the point it had reached by the turn of the century, and the later Soviet regime. Efforts to understand that bridge have long centered on the interface within Leninism between Marxism, as a pre-existing ideology elaborated in the more modern West and positing a particular process of modernization, and the idiosyncrasies of the Russian context, encompassing both relative backwardness and distinctive revolutionary traditions. It is obviously crucial that Lenin not only embraced Marxism but also identified with the Russian subversive tradition. Starting with these two components, it is easy to factor in an ahistorical psychological propensity to fanaticism and to take some combination of the three elements as the key to Leninism—and the whole Soviet departure.

For Alain Besançon, the political and intellectual conditions that shaped Leninism existed together only in Russia, but as a human type, Lenin was beyond national specification.[31] Conversely, the particular fanaticism with which he embraced Marxist ideology stemmed from an ahistorical character type, with Russian admixtures accounting merely for the particular form of that ideological embrace. In Besançon's account, ideological fanaticism produced an utter lack of realism: "the key to Lenin . . . lies in total devotion to the demands of ideology, and complete subordination to the revolutionary practice dictated by it. In Lenin this absorption reached a pitch of perfection." As a result, "Lenin, blinded by ideology, perceived only a falsified version of the truth. He did not deceive the enemy, but he deceived himself."[32] From this perspective, the anomalous features of Soviet practice seem virtually inevitable. As confirmation of Lenin's ideological fanaticism, Besançon cites his superficial reliance on stock arguments, his unchanging tastes—he was stuck in the 1860s—his disinterest in modern art, and his active wariness of the literary *avant-garde*.[33] But although Marxist ideology, character type, and national context surely have their place, even in combination they do not make sense of the Leninist departure. We must also encompass supranational, historically specific elements growing from the new terrain emerging at the turn of the century.

It is surely no accident that among the several revisions of Marxism, this one—Leninism—came from Russia, but what did it mean that Lenin explicitly claimed kinship with the Russian revolutionary organizations of the 1870s? Was it mere nostalgia and chauvinism, or was he positing some particular relevance, in light of the uncertain overall circumstances of Marxism at this point? From within a framework encompassing the wider new terrain, the Leninist departure appears not as some throwback, reflecting Russia's relative backwardness, but as a "European" response intended to open the way to an alternative modernity. It required a particular personality and particular national traditions for this alternative to have emerged, but its direction and content reflect the wider historically specific situation.

Russian revolutionary traditions encompassed both a mode of directed action from above and a mode of subversive action from below. Robert Tucker was prominent among those featuring "Russian Jacobinism," the tradition of state-centered, top-down activism running from Peter the Great to Sergei Witte. Affording an image of how grandiose change had previously taken place in Russia, it could be grafted onto Marxism to suggest that in the event of a revolutionary seizure of power from below, the revolutionary party could then use its monopoly of political power to carry through the socialist transformation from above. This accounts for Tucker's own accents in his noted study of the subsequent Stalinist revolution.[34]

The distinctive subversive revolutionary ethos emerged in Russia from the 1850s to the 1880s, especially in those loosely labeled "populists" (*narodniki*). It afforded priority to action even at the expense of doctrine and fostered an array of images and conceptions, including the party as a sect of true believers, the scope for global, definitive solution, even palingenesis, and the revolutionary as meta-hero, sometimes in interaction with a crowd. Central was Nikolai Chernyshevsky's *What Is to Be Done?*, written in prison in 1862 and an inspiration to three generations of revolutionaries, including Lenin.[35]

Until the 1880s, this loosely populist revolutionary tradition was widely identified with pre-Marxist notions of a special Russian path to socialism, taking the *mir*, or rural peasant commune, as the nucleus and bypassing the evils of capitalism altogether. At first, even Russians claiming to embrace Marxism failed or refused to grasp the essential progressive role for capitalism that Marx had posited. But the Russian reception of Marx gradually matured as, during the last third of the nineteenth century, Russia found itself increasingly caught up in the wider capitalist economy and thus in convergence with the modern West.[36]

For all his identification with the earlier Russian revolutionary tradition, Lenin vehemently denied any special Russian path to socialism and insisted precisely that Russia was increasingly becoming part of the capitalist mainstream. He was so insistent, in fact, that in his early study of *The Development of Capitalism in Russia* (1899), written in Siberian exile, he surely overplayed the extent to which Russia was by then following the orthodox model of capitalist development.

But mere orthodoxy was hardly enough. That same year—1899—saw the publication of Bernstein's *Evolutionary Socialism* and the first instance of a socialist—Alexandre Millerand in France—actually joining a bourgeois government. The apparently growing lure of reformism and parliamentary politics brought home how pressing were the questions facing Marxism about strategy, priorities, and the relevance of orthodox premises. There was even the danger that the Marxian alternative would be dissolved into the liberal bourgeois mainstream. Thus Lenin, overtly echoing Chernyshevsky, offered his famous pamphlet of 1902, "What is to be done?" which launched Leninism as a distinctive, always controversial current within European Marxism.

Although he quickly fastened upon the importance of Russian conditions and traditions, Lenin began this tract with a hard-hitting attack on current tendencies within European social democracy. Indeed, he noted that the very scope for his own fresh thinking indicated the progress that the overall movement had made, for it was now genuinely international.[37] In writing his pamphlet, then, Lenin was seeking to contribute on the European level, not simply to adjust orthodox Marxism to idiosyncratic Russian circumstances, let alone to devise a distinctively Russian path to socialism.

Lenin turned his sights first on Bernstein and Millerand, charging opportunism, selling out to the bourgeoisie.[38] Then he attacked the recent emphasis on "spontaneity," especially in the Russian movement but reflecting another more general tendency then emerging within European Marxism. Spontaneity was bound up especially with "economism"—the notion that, with the fight for socialism itself premature, the priority for Marxists was to back the workers in their efforts to achieve immediate economic benefits. Although it was a tendency everywhere, this direction tempted especially in Russia, with its political limitations, its relative economic backwardness, and its still-fledgling proletariat. The Russians that Lenin was targeting had not developed a full revolutionary syndicalist alternative, but they too stressed the importance of autonomous working-class trade union activity, especially strikes, and played down the role for a Marxist party or for intellectual leadership.

Although orthodoxy, as Lenin saw it, certainly envisioned a process of proletarian maturation, it did not necessarily entail privilege and priority to whatever the working class did; to afford it such privilege could mean lapsing from Marxism's systematic historical understanding into something more fluid, flabby, and sentimental. To emphasize spontaneity was to play down the role of theory—and was thus to strengthen bourgeois ideology among the workers, for just as there were two classes, there were only two ideologies. There was no third alternative, no scope for workers to elaborate their own ideology through their own activity. Indeed, the slightest departure from socialist ideology necessarily strengthened bourgeois ideology. So Lenin warned that the present "*slavish cringing before spontaneity*" portended, just as surely as Bernstein's heresy, ideological subordination to the bourgeoisie, leading the workers to settle for mere trade unionism.[39]

Nevertheless, the Russian working class had moved well beyond mere revolt with the strikes of the 1890s, but as Lenin saw it, these were still spontaneous, based on immediate economic grievances, not informed by a genuinely socialist consciousness, which could only have come from without. Thus we have the famous empirical premise of Lenin's pamphlet: "the history of all countries shows that the working class, exclusively by its own effort, is able to develop only trade-union consciousness."[40] From Lenin's perspective, neither orthodox Marxism, stressing the workers' negative experience of the dehumanization of wage labor, nor syndicalism, emphasizing their positive experience of trade union membership and collective action, could be sufficient or even the key variable in the pivot to a post-bourgeois order. The theory of socialism, having grown from intellectuals, most notably Marx and Engels themselves, was distinguishable from the actual experience and practice of the working class. And theoretically sophisticated intellectuals, the bearers of a genuinely socialist consciousness, had to continue to lead.

So Lenin began to envision a certain mode of action with a particular kind of leadership role for a small, centralized party of disciplined revolutionaries defined not by class but by their socialist consciousness. Such a party would contrast, most prominently, with what the German Social Democratic Party seemed on its way to becoming—a mass party, placing a premium on quantity of membership, voting strength, and seats in parliament. Lenin's revolutionaries would understand themselves to be a vanguard—by definition, the vanguard of the proletariat, insofar as their socialist vision equated with the objective interests and the universal importance of the proletariat.

Despite the charges of critics then and thereafter, Lenin was not simply returning to Blanquism or palace coups. Whereas the party alone was the source of revolutionary consciousness, it could not make a revolution on its own; the active involvement of the proletariat and a particular relationship between vanguard and masses were both essential. Indeed, the masses would first take the initiative in a revolutionary situation; such initiative was itself the essential indication that historical circumstances had ripened. What defined the vanguard was the capacity to take advantage of the opportunity that such mass spontaneity afforded, shaping it in light of its privileged reading of the objective circumstances of the moment. Only the vanguard could decide whether this or that bread riot or expression of popular discontent had wider potential significance.

Despite the deference to mass spontaneity, the notion that the vanguard was following the masses on some level was a kind of myth. A genuinely novel relationship with the masses was indeed at issue, but it was more uncertain and open-ended than Lenin and his colleagues were admitting, even to themselves, in claiming to be the vanguard of the proletariat. To a considerable degree, the form of elite–mass interaction that Leninism portended could emerge only in practice. Even what would count as opportunism or adventurism was not clear at the outset.

The vanguard had to develop a certain relationship not only with the industrial working class but also with a broader array of social forces, especially because in autocratic Russia the peasantry and even the bourgeoisie itself were also central to the prospects for revolution. Thus questions about immediate priorities and strategy led to two intersecting debates, each of which remained quite intense until the revolution of 1917. The first concerned the respective roles of those social forces and thus the actual modes of interaction of the vanguard with them. The second concerned the scope for telescoping the bourgeois/liberal/capitalist and proletarian/socialist stages of the overall revolutionary transformation. Especially at issue was the scope for a "modern" Marxist, as opposed to an anarchist, populist, or socialist revolutionary, way of involving the peasantry. This modern variant would eschew any accent on the socialist potential of the *mir*. Such questions would prove to have major implications for the nature and meaning of the whole revolutionary process.

During the revolution of 1905, the bourgeoisie proved quick to cave in, making it clear that the strength of tsarism and the weakness of the Russian bourgeoisie were two sides of the same coin. However, this pointed up both the need and the opening for a new, more grandiose kind of action. Because the bourgeoisie on its own would not seek to overthrow tsarism, some sort of worker–peasant bloc was required to spark and shepherd the democratic revolution. Indeed, that bloc could fight for bourgeois democracy in its most radical form, even against the wishes of the bourgeoisie itself. Although in Leninist language this would entail the proletariat leading the peasantry, the key was the role for the vanguard party to shape such a bloc and engineer the necessary action.

At the same time, Lenin insisted that the final aim, beyond bourgeois revolution, be kept in mind. The point was not simply to entrust power to the bourgeoisie for some undetermined period, as orthodoxy might seem to suggest. In some sense, in fact, this revolution could lead directly to the socialist revolution. But the two revolutions could not be completely telescoped. Thus the proletariat must share power with the peasantry, not push to socialism, because a proletarian regime could not last without peasant support. So the first revolution was to yield not a single-handed conquest of power but, for an unspecified period, some sort of multi-party system. Still, it was not at all clear what would follow should the vanguard party carry out the bourgeois revolution. The key for now was the capacity to organize and act, to seize and maintain power.[41]

Lenin's "What is to be done?" immediately provoked controversy within both Russian social democracy and wider European Marxist circles. Although some saw Leninism as a realistic adaptation to Russian circumstances, others charged authoritarianism, Blanquism or excessive opportunism in the emphasis on following mass spontaneity. Leninism could easily seem a throwback to specifically Russian traditions that modern Marxism had left behind. Within Russian social democracy, the pamphlet precipitated the formation of the distinctive Bolshevik current, immediately opposed by the Mensheviks, who claimed to defend orthodoxy against Lenin's challenge. This *de facto* split persisted in the party until Lenin finally engineered a formal split in 1912.

The Mensheviks charged that Leninism entailed an anti-Marxist faith in subjective factors at the expense of objective conditions. Ever since 1883, Georgi Plekhanov, the respected "father of Russian Marxism," had been attacking populism and "Russian Jacobinism," insisting that any effort to force revolution from above would lead to authoritarianism. And as recently as 1898, he had taken on the whole issue of hero and crowd from the new, orthodox Marxist perspective, insisting that the extraordinary individual can merely accelerate, facilitate, the objective unfolding of history. So even as he sought at once to remain independent and to be a force for unity, Plekhanov was quick to charge that Leninism was a mere throwback. For Plekhanov and the Mensheviks, to embrace Marxism meant repudiating precisely the sorts of notions that Lenin seemed to be advocating.[42]

In response to the Bolshevik accent on the scope for crashing ahead, these guardians of orthodoxy continued to insist that revolution required two distinct stages. The present priority was a genuinely bourgeois democratic revolution against the tsarist autocracy; democracy had to be introduced by the liberal bourgeoisie, following the original script. The Mensheviks were quick to stress that they were not abandoning their overall revolutionary posture for reformism, and it was certainly true that to emphasize the present need for democracy was not to say that socialism could be created by parliamentary means. But the orthodox position was becoming slippery in light of the other forces at work in international Marxism. To catch up with the Western mainstream by achieving bourgeois democracy would mean, at the very least, getting caught up in the ambiguities that the orthodox mainstream, represented by Karl Kautsky and the so-called Erfurt synthesis, had encountered. It would then surely entail the temptations represented by Bernstein and Millerand as well. The whole two-stage notion rested on a deterministic conception of history that was coming more generally into question.

The degree to which Leninism was in fact a departure from Marxist orthodoxy has long been disputed. Obviously, Marxism assumed some scope for agency, bound up with correct consciousness, but what form it might take was not clear; nor was the scope for voluntarism in light of the implication of predetermined stages. Especially at issue was the place for a conscious vanguard *vis-à-vis* the workers themselves. Leszek Kolakowski noted that Marx had allowed a role for a vanguard when conditions were ripe—but he left no indication of the criteria for ripeness. Could conscious agency actually create such ripeness in some sense? In any case, Kolakowski insisted, it was surely a departure from orthodoxy to attribute the vanguard role not to a movement of workers but to a party defined by correct ideology, to suggest that its actual class composition was irrelevant to its class character, to assume that, conversely, the proletariat on its own could not formulate its own genuine class aims. Lenin's notion that the party would provide coordination and organization in response to spontaneous outbreaks by the workers and, more specifically, his vision of an alliance with the peasantry to promote a bourgeois revolution, were also of dubious orthodoxy. So for Kolakowski, whereas Marx had surely discussed the need to act and the role of will, he had just as surely not envisioned an elite vanguard like Lenin's playing the sort of role that Lenin envisioned.[43]

From these Leninist departures, further heterodoxies or distortions long seem to have followed. The idea of the dictatorship of a revolutionary party on behalf of the proletariat was surely foreign to Marx and Engels, as was the notion that the workers, once they had power, would need some distinguishable party as their teacher and guide in building socialism. Alfred G. Meyer noted that in orthodox terms it would be no less than criminal to make a revolution before the workers themselves had come to a socialist consciousness. Lenin did not explicitly disagree, but thus the crucial element of ambiguity in his thinking about the relationship between the vanguard and the workers and/or masses.[44]

In short, although we might argue about degrees, it is hard to deny that Leninism entailed forms of agency and modes of relationship between above and below that pointed beyond anything in orthodox Marxism, whatever its ambiguities. The challenge is to account for the measure of heterodoxy and to gauge its implications. No combination of prior ideology, national idiosyncrasy, and personal characteristics proves to be adequate to make sense of the novelty of Leninism. In its orthodox form, Marxism simply did not specify all that was necessary to respond to the uncertainties it had encountered in light of accumulating experience with capitalism and democracy by 1900. To respond effectively, a Marxist would eventually have to make choices, and whatever its direction, the choice would entail certain admixtures. In the case of Leninism, the choices and admixtures pointed beyond Marxism altogether.

Lenin claimed to derive his pivotal conclusion about the propensity of the workers, on their own, to develop a mere "trade-union consciousness" from "the history of all countries." But although that conclusion was genuinely empirical up to a point, Lenin was quick to jump to it, and it seems premature if we consider, for example, the intellectual trajectory of Georges Sorel and the timetable of revolutionary syndicalist activity in the labor movements of France and Italy. To some extent, the key was the other side of the coin; Lenin jumped to this conclusion in order to justify a lead role for intellectuals—not just as theoreticians but as agents of a particular sort. The key was the capacity to act collectively, a capacity that seemed to require a certain kind of leadership.

Insofar as forcing the empirical conclusion was bound up with the desire for action, we might be especially tempted to invoke the undoubted measure of personal, ahistorical fanaticism to explain it. In Besançon's account, fanatical commitment to the ideology explains Lenin's determination to act, to force the revolution, and would thus surely explain why he was so quick to jump to his negative conclusion about working-class capacities. But the "characteristic impatience" that Besançon cited in contrasting Lenin with Plekhanov and the Mensheviks suggests something very different from the hubris of ideological self-assurance.[45] There was something shrill in Lenin's emphasis on the scope for action, especially as he continued to insist on Marxist ideology even as his link to orthodoxy in fact grew tenuous. The shrillness suggests a very different sense of history and the scope for action than was implicit in the Marxian mainstream, which still included a reassuring element of determinism. Knowing better, Lenin mocked the quietism of the Mensheviks, their moderate faith in the dialectics of history.[46] Hence not only his impatient activism but also his determination to conceive and forge the new modes of action that seemed necessary. They required a new kind of leadership, entailing a new relationship between elite and masses.

In a long-admired work first published in 1957, Alfred G. Meyer suggested that Lenin was not an ideological fanatic, sustained by confident hubris, but a "secret doubter." Although he resisted facing the basis of his own doubts, Lenin was not at all sure about the direction of history:

> Marxism as adopted by Lenin was colored by an unstated but nonetheless persistent pessimism, perhaps even desperation, a feeling of doubt about the historical process in which Marx and Engels had expressed unbounded confidence. . . . The decided note of pessimism pervading Leninism is the seed from which his entire operational code grew: the spirit of manipulation, the belief in organization, the preoccupation with strategy and tactics, the willingness to apply any means, the flexibility as well as the ruthlessness

displayed in Lenin's attempt to bring about the revolution by trial and error. Pessimism is also related to the most characteristically Leninist trait, the stress laid on consciousness as the history-making force par excellence, by which the pre-eminence of the party is rationalized.[47]

Such "secret doubts" underlay Lenin's emphasis on vanguard leadership, and more generally, his characteristic combination of ideological rigidity and extreme operational flexibility. The innovative neo-Marxian scholar Alex Callinicos has similarly suggested that rejection of the inevitability of socialist revolution was central to the Bolshevik departure. Otherwise, he concluded, the doctrine of the vanguard party is unintelligible.[48]

Meyer traced Lenin's doubts to the wider revisionist context, suggesting, at least implicitly, that they reflected a still more general change in historical consciousness: "The typical Leninist impatience stems ... from a hidden pessimism, creeping doubts that history has not [*sic*] been going in the right direction, or perhaps, that the danger of its deviating into utter chaos is ever present."[49] So obviously Lenin doubted not simply the prospects for Russia but the wider scope for socialism in the West.

But despite the undoubted shrillness, for Lenin the corollary of the new doubt was not simply unrelieved pessimism, as some of Mayer's emphases suggested, but a new sense of openness that entailed contingency, to be sure, but also opportunity—and responsibility. It is in this light that we must understand Lenin's embrace of his Russian revolutionary predecessors. He conceived Russia's idiosyncrasies, both its backwardness and its revolutionary tradition, as crucially pertinent to the wider situation facing Marxism.

Lenin always thought in terms of the overall challenge, as opposed to the Russian case *per se*. Even insofar as the immediate task—overthrowing the tsarist autocracy—was idiosyncratically Russian, it had to be understood as a moment in a wider international struggle. From the orthodox Menshevik position, the enterprise of overthrowing the autocracy and establishing democracy had no wider significance; the point was simply to catch up. Lenin saw more grandiose possibilities. Precisely because of Russia's idiosyncrasies, Russians could best see what needed to be done and, on that basis, play a lead role in the wider international movement.

As Lenin saw it, Russia faced the most revolutionary immediate challenge of any country—destruction of the most powerful bulwark of reaction. "The fulfillment of this task," wrote Lenin in "What is to be done?" "would make the Russian proletariat the vanguard of the international revolutionary proletariat." But he also insisted "*that the role of vanguard fighter can be fulfilled only by a party that is guided by the most advanced theory.*"[50] And the Russians were positioned precisely to move to the theoretical forefront. It mattered, first, that forced emigration had made the Russian Marxists uniquely well informed about the world revolutionary movements by the end of the nineteenth century.[51] But, more importantly, because the immediate problem of autocracy was so pressing, the Russians could see that the theoretical question for the overall movement concerned precisely the question of action. Looked at from the opposite side, the challenge was to avoid being sucked into bourgeois ideology from any of the several directions that had opened. Because even addressing the immediate task required that the Russians act outside parliamentary institutions, their mode of action would necessarily afford an antidote to the bourgeois temptation.

At the same time, the Bolsheviks were heirs to the idiosyncratic Russian revolutionary experience, which suggested what such action would have to require.[52] But although "the most advanced theory" at this point could not be derived directly from Marxism, neither was it a matter of simply returning to earlier Russian traditions. Because the stakes and possibilities on the wider stage were now so different, the Bolsheviks had to frame in novel ways whatever they took from their Russian revolutionary predecessors. Transcending both Marxist orthodoxy and Russian idiosyncrasy, "the most advanced theory" entailed an understanding of the need and scope for new forms of collective action, including the place of leadership, will, consciousness, commitment, organization, discipline, and self-sacrifice. Such action would entail new forms of interaction between the vanguard and the masses, and it would be bound up with a sense of making history.

The belief that the Russians had a special insight into priorities on the wider level produced a sense of mission that was itself energizing. But it also produced shrillness. What Russia offered was unique and precious in light of wider tendencies and uncertainties; it was crucial for the wider possibility of a post-liberal alternative that Russia assume and maintain the vanguard role. The situation was such that the hope for a systematic alternative in the West had come to depend on Leninist action.

As central participants in the revision of Marxism, Bernstein, Sorel, and Lenin found themselves in the same new universe, facing questions, envisioning possibilities, that had never come up before. They came up as they did because of the wider change in the historical-political terrain at issue for us. Each thinker was backing off from determinism and, in his own way, accenting the scope and need for human agency.

At the same time, the need for revision forced each at least implicitly to back up to the field from within which Marxism and even the aspiration for "socialism" had emerged in the first place. And this was to reopen some fundamental questions. What was it about the mainstream bourgeois order that demanded systematic overcoming, an alternative modernity? What would constitute the desired alternative, and how could it come to be? Certain conceptions had settled out so far, but it was not clear what, if anything, had been settled definitively. Marxism had entailed a certain conception of the various "bourgeois" components—economy, political structure, modes of thought and self-understanding—as well as a certain conception of their relative significance and the intersections among them. But the whole agglomeration was open to question. The components on that layer had been assembled by intellectuals, as Lenin pointed out explicitly, and surely there was scope for intellectuals to rethink the issues and even reassemble the components, adding new ones as necessary.

Sharing in the newly more open-ended sense of history, Bernstein, Sorel, and Lenin all found the scope for specifying the end much diminished, but perhaps that was less damaging than it seemed. Action against the bourgeois order was still possible, but it required new thinking about how such action might take place. And for each, the results of that thinking had implications for the whole way of conceiving what it would mean, what was necessary, to have a systematic alternative to the bourgeois order. With the connections between the components loosening, values and modes of thought or consciousness were coming to seem more autonomous, irreducible—and even more significant than capitalism as the immediate problem to be overcome. A systematic alternative might be possible even as the end grew blurry, insofar as the key proved not some particular experience of the capitalist economy but a post-liberal consciousness that would at once underpin and be nurtured by new collective action. On the basis of that consciousness, the collective agent could respond to the other deleterious components of the bourgeois order, but action would be ongoing, for in an open-ended world with ends indeterminate, the key was not this or that concrete change but the capacity to act collectively itself.

From within this new framework, however, Bernstein, Sorel, and Lenin obviously responded very differently. In Besançon's account, what resulted from the impasse of Marxism around the turn of the century was a kind of Lenin—Bernstein fork. Whereas Lenin insisted fanatically on orthodoxy, Bernstein shifted to an altogether different, non-ideological mode, eschewing dogmatism and system while entailing freedom, pluralism, openness, flexibility, and experiment.[53] As Besançon saw it, Bernstein's alternative was essentially self-recommending. From Besançon's perspective, in fact, Lenin stood out even more as an ideological fanatic in light of the open-ended direction that Bernstein was indicating at the same time. But Besançon's framework was too limited to get at what Lenin was in fact offering and why he diverged from Bernstein. As Lenin saw it, bourgeois democracy, first because of its political forms, but ultimately because of the whole culture or ideology underlying it, had proved more insidious than even Marx had imagined. Eschewing and overcoming them was the immediate challenge.

In Russia, democracy had barely been tried even by 1917, but the asymmetry with the Western experience was not decisive. While in exile, Lenin and the Bolsheviks had seen how mainstream parliamentary democracy worked, and their priorities presupposed and responded to the wider Western political experience. It was partly because they had encountered both the temptations and the limits of parliamentary democracy that they became so determined to forge a post-parliamentary instrument for collective action. Lenin's strong aversion to formal democracy and parliamentary government is well known. Numerical majority was merely mechanical, and there was no reason to be beholden to it. He denounced the Mensheviks for making a fetish of democratic rules.[54] Despite the Mensheviks' own protestations, plausible in orthodox terms, that they were not reformists but remained revolutionaries, Lenin sensed that even to settle, in the Menshevik way, for democracy as the immediate goal entailed the danger that the scope for a systematic alternative would be swallowed up by reformism, mere liberal democracy.

But most deeply at issue, as Lenin saw it, were not the institutions themselves but the modes of thought, the sense of the world, underlying democratic practice. In "What is to be done?" he insisted that there were only two possibilities, two modes of thought, and the slightest departure from socialist ideology necessarily strengthened bourgeois ideology.[55] Even the workers themselves could not elaborate their own ideology on the basis of their own experience and activity. The correct ideology was the province of intellectuals; without it the workers would not grasp the wider framework and would fall into "bourgeois thought," becoming just another interest group.

We noted that Besançon found the key to Bernstein on this level and gave a decidedly positive spin to the free, open mode of thought that Bernstein's departure seemed to entail. But this mode, read with different valences, was what Lenin most feared—and sought to head off. "Bourgeois thought" was far more powerful than classical Marxism had grasped; it might even triumph definitively, dissolving any possibility of a systematic alternative. Thus Lenin inveighed against "freedom of criticism," which, he said, portended not simply the substitution of one ideology for another but the loss of any theoretical framework—and thus eclecticism and lack of principle.[56] The danger lay not so much in questioning Marxism in particular but in the spirit of critical questioning that undermined lack of belief and commitment and thus fostered cynicism and egotistical individualism.

Preoccupation with snares of "bourgeois ideology" fueled Lenin's effort to head off the whole array from Bernstein to Millerand to Menshevism to trade unionism. It was essential to specify an alternative not only to the mainstream but also to Bernstein's alternative to the mainstream, through modes of organization and action that would at once reflect and nurture genuinely post-bourgeois forms of consciousness, will, and values.

In his sense that "bourgeois thought" was the immediate problem, requiring systematic opposition in its own terms, Lenin converged with Sorel up to a point. Although more concerned with rationalism *per se*, Sorel, too, worried that liberal culture, with its openness and pluralism, entailed a premium on immediate selfish interests and a cynicism dissolving belief, commitment, and the scope for collective action. Yet on the immediate level, Lenin's emphasis on a vanguard role for an elite, essentially of intellectuals, seems to be diametrically opposed to Sorel, who associated intellectuals precisely with bourgeois thought. The new consciousness and resulting mode of action could emerge only from outside, even as a form of "primitivism" from below. And Sorel found that source for a while—encompassing the formative period of Leninism—in the trade unions, thanks to a reading of contemporary trade union activity diametrically opposed to Lenin's. The workers, on their own, were developing precisely a post-liberal consciousness and *not* the mere "trade-union consciousness" that Lenin attributed to them.

The difference was not only one of empirical assessment. From Lenin's perspective, Sorel's essentially tripartite way of apportioning reason, theoretical understanding, and the bases for commitment and collective action was inadequate as both diagnosis and prescription. Sorel's belief that autonomous working-class initiatives could assume a genuinely revolutionary character thanks to myth was too romantic and indeterminate. Conversely, Sorel's mistrust for intellectuals was excessive. We saw that Lenin was quick to insist that socialist theory was the product of intellectuals and could not have emerged "from below," from working-class experience alone; hence the need for intellectuals to update the understanding of contemporary prospects and priorities through "the most advanced theory." Whereas Sorel had assumed that "intellectual" conflated with rational and thus precluded the capacity for committed action, Lenin was implicitly suggesting that the tensions in bourgeois thought made it possible for some, at least, to think and to probe, but also to care, to will, to aspire, and to depart in a way transcending the dichotomy of myth and rational but corrosive analysis and understanding.

The possibilities within the new terrain proved such that Sorel himself came to agree. His tripartite apportionment in *Reflections on Violence* had not made sense of the requirements and possibilities. Most basically, he came implicitly to accept Lenin's notion that workers, by their own devices, were capable of no more than a "trade-union consciousness." In other words, they had been, and would continue to be, sucked into "bourgeois thought." Even as he remained on the lookout for some other outside regenerative force, Sorel implicitly adjusted his understanding of the components in light of further experience. And he did not hesitate to embrace the Leninist revolution as it transpired in fact.[57]

Although he compared Lenin to Peter the Great, finding each seeking to force history, the key was Sorel's sense of the audacity of the enterprise on which Lenin had embarked, of the effort to build a socialist economy in the face of Russian backwardness. As Sorel saw it, Lenin grasped the need for a nimble intelligence, free of prejudices, open to practical experience, if such a project was to be undertaken. Above all, the enterprise required a particular relationship between leaders and masses that drew Sorel's enthusiastic approval. The leaders had won the moral authority to get the masses to make sacrifices, to accept factory discipline and certain rules of production. Sorel particularly liked Lenin's notion that the workers would come freely to serve the state not just while at work in the factories but essentially all the time; they would thus, as Sorel saw it, be on the lookout for those who were incompetent or merely exploitative.[58] Sorel understood better than Lenin himself the core of the Leninist revolution, which seemed to entail the total commitment and capacity to act that Sorel had anticipated all along.

The Leninist mode of action was not precisely "from below" in the sense Sorel had originally envisioned, but neither did it entail mere elite mobilization through myths. The Leninist elite could galvanize the masses, nurturing the essential virtues, only on the basis of genuine belief and commitment. Sorel was implicitly admitting that he had been too rigid in positing a bifurcation between intellectuals with at best a theoretical grasp and the energizing force itself, which he had assumed could come only from below. It was simply necessary to be clearer on what a moralizing myth might entail, on the scope for differentiation within a movement inspired by myth, and on the ensuing modes of interaction between the new elite and the masses. With the precise end indeterminate, the key was the consciousness going in, and its measure was precisely the capacity to inspire others, to draw out unsuspected virtues and capacities, through mobilization, education, and even, on occasion, violence. In this case, the masses too become capable of the discipline, self-sacrifice, and heroic effort that had been the key to the Bolshevik mode of action in the first place. Indeed, Lenin accented the need and the scope for a new kind of leadership for the same reason that Sorel had insisted on agency exclusively from below. Central to its defining mode of consciousness, the vanguard was post-bourgeois, not paralyzed by the doubt that results from corrosive "freedom of thought" and thus capable of spearheading supra-individualist collective action.

But Lenin, in clinging to orthodoxy, was not facing up to certain implications of the new historical-political sense. Thus he was not conceiving his new mode of action in anything like such quasi-Sorelian terms. But whatever ahistorical psychological propensity was at work is not sufficient to account for his ideological rigidity and even fanaticism; he was caught up in a wider, historically specific interplay of new ideas and new opportunities for action, an interplay that brought the ahistorical dimension to bear in a very particular way. In that regard, even the crudeness, the intellectual limits, the unchanging tastes that critics like Besançon and Kolakowski had emphasized come to appear in a different light.[59]

Lenin not only insisted on the original ideology, even while sensing its inadequacy, but he deliberately eschewed any encounter with wider intellectual currents that might have illuminated the sources of his secret doubts and thus the basis of his insistence on a particular mode of action. Although they too continued to stress orthodoxy, more intellectually adventuresome Bolsheviks such as A.A. Bogdanov, Anatoly Lunacharsky, and Maxim Gorky reached out, hoping to find intellectual justification for Bolshevik departures. They did so not simply for rationalization or for propaganda purposes but so that they could better understand why they had come to feel those departures to be necessary and justified in the first place.[60]

Bogdanov sought to jettison what he took to be metaphysical leftovers—matter, subject, causality—and to see the world in fully anthropocentric terms, relating all of reality to human existence, as congruent with the Marxian emphasis on human beings as the creators of their world. However, to posit the human world as subject to self-creation in this way only opened a new set of questions—but those now seemed the important ones.[61] There was even a specifically Bolshevik interest in Nietzsche, including a kind of Nietzschean socialist religion within the left wing of Bolshevism from 1903 to 1913, as Gorky and Lunacharsky sought to conceive the revolution itself as an act of god building.[62]

However, such intellectual adventurousness simply confirmed Lenin in his rigidity, most notably when he engaged some of this new thinking, only to brush it aside, in his one philosophical work, *Materialism and Empirio-Criticism: Critical Comments on a Reactionary Philosophy* (1909). He found no need seriously to seek new answers to what were in fact new philosophical questions, for he assumed that all the important ones had been settled by Marx and Engels.[63] He was especially hostile to any engagement with Nietzsche.[64] Such wider questioning was indeed risky; in principle, it might have compromised not just commitment to Marxism but confidence in the scope for *any* radical alternative to the liberal mainstream. But it also might have illuminated the basis of the new sense of opportunity and responsibility and the implications of the mode of action being chosen.

In any case, Bolshevism as a departure within Marxism was not precisely rounded off but, even after the 1917 revolution, continued to betray loose ends on the underlying cultural level. Despite friction with Lenin, those like Bogdanov and Lunacharsky remained prominent. Even in 1926 Lunacharsky was embracing Nietzsche, endorsing, for example, his contempt for petty bourgeois morality.[65]

Yet Lenin, until his death early in 1924, remained for the Bolsheviks the embodiment of the will and capacity for the extraordinary, history-making action that seemed to have become possible. With the Russian Marxist movement on the defensive, even declining, from the aftermath of the revolution of 1905 to the outbreak of the Great War, the Bolshevik current held together thanks especially to Lenin's charisma, stemming from his belief, energy, faith, and will.[66] The Bolsheviks were already embarked on a novel and risky course, and partly thus Bolshevism came to be leader-centered virtually from the beginning, even though no one advocated any sort of Führer principle. Lenin's pamphlets, and even the polemical *Materialism and Empirio-Criticism*, "exerted," as Robert Tucker put it, "a hypnotic power over many others precisely *because* of the spirit of partisan practicality that permeated them."[67] He attracted those hoping that, despite the present difficulties within Russian social democracy, action might indeed be possible, defying the Menshevik insistence on the orthodox model and involving all strata against the tsarist autocracy.[68] In conveying the sense that revolution was possible, Lenin helped to make it possible. However, it would be a new and very particular kind of revolution in light of precisely the new mode of consciousness that made it possible.

Giovanni Gentile and the new Italian historicism

Precisely as Lenin was beginning to establish his distinctive direction, confrontation with Marxism was central to the young Italian philosopher Giovanni Gentile, who, as we noted briefly in Chapter 1, would go on to become the single most important Fascist ideologue.[69] Only 21 years old, Gentile intervened in 1896 in the developing interchange between Georges Sorel, Antonio Labriola, and Benedetto Croce over the center of gravity of Marxism. Then, in 1899, he published a book on Marx that also addressed his three contemporaries.[70] Although not explicitly concerned with politics at first, Gentile was caught up in the set of questions about history and agency that Marx had brought to the table but that seemed to require fresh answers in light of experience by the 1890s. In what sense is humanity the maker of history, and what was the scope for making it in a different way? What would it mean to unify theory and practice? Gentile was on his way to a non-Marxist but, in one sense, comparably radical conception of the scope for new forms of human action in history to overcome the liberal order. And he remained in spoken or unspoken dialogue with Marx throughout his career. In 1937, at the height of the Fascist period, he republished his youthful work on Marx, noting in the new preface that Lenin had numbered the book among the best non-Marxist works on Marxism.[71]

Indeed, Gentile proved a major articulator of the new historical-political terrain and a significant conduit to the actual practice of totalitarianism. Abbott Gleason was surely right in labeling him "the first philosopher of totalitarianism."[72] Indeed, he was groping toward a totalitarian vision from his first philosophical encounters in the later 1890s. His eventual commitment to Mussolini's regime, his aspirations for it, grew directly from his formal philosophy and his sense of the cultural role that philosophy could play.[73]

Gentile first came to prominence in Italy just after the turn of the century as Benedetto Croce's junior partner in a broad effort to renew Italian culture and public life in light of the outcome of the Italian Risorgimento thus far. But especially as they attacked the reigning positivism, the two thinkers sensed that they were caught up in a much wider intellectual revolution, responding to a broader challenge bound up with modernity and secularization. Civic renewal would enable Italy not merely to catch up to the modern mainstream but to point beyond it altogether. Even the term "renewal" is misleading; the wider challenge was novel, and the Italian response could only produce something entirely new.

Because, in their opposition to positivism, Croce and Gentile embraced some of the categories of German idealism, they were long characterized as neo-idealists or neo-Hegelians. But rather than simply doing philosophy from within an established tradition, they were engaged in a much broader effort of diagnosis and prescription that entailed a radically historicist departure from Hegel. And even as they found it crucial to engage with their German contemporaries, they found the basis of the necessary departure in idiosyncratic, even marginalized, Italian cultural traditions. Both were especially indebted to Giambattista Vico, who, two centuries earlier, had managed to recast the distinctive Italian humanistic tradition in response to the Cartesian challenge. By further recasting that earlier tradition, contemporary Italian thinkers might offer an innovative response in light of the waning of transcendent religion and the apparent limitations of the dominant liberal-positivist culture.

The contemporary challenge was to conceive, more consistently and radically than ever before, the place of human beings in a world without a transcendent god—indeed, without transcendence of any kind as usually understood.[74] At the same time, the death of the transcendent god did not necessarily undercut the spiritual conception that Christianity had posited, with human beings as free, responsible moral agents.[75] The challenge was to make sense of the central insights of Christianity for a secular world of radical immanence. That world was to be understood as an ongoing process, transcending subject/object dualism and bringing human beings and history together in a way never quite conceived before. There is only the concrete historical world that is forever coming to be through free, creative human response. The perpetual incompleteness of that world is a measure of our own freedom and responsibility. What the world next becomes results from all that we do—and thus is up to us.

Despite this accent on human freedom, the new orientation entailed little regard for the conventional understanding of liberal democracy, based on rights and the natural law tradition. Although Croce was the more explicit at first, together Croce and Gentile suggested that the current understanding of liberal democracy was sentimental and superficial, not at all congruent with the genuinely modern, rigorously secular thinking that they themselves claimed to offer. Among other things, their conception seemed to warrant not negative freedom *from* the state, not freedom as a private sphere, but freedom to act, to have a chance to affect what the world next becomes.

At the same time, Croce and Gentile were seeking to head off what seemed the irrationalist or aestheticist overreaction to the modern condition, evident in an array of recent or contemporary cultural innovators from Mallarmé and Nietzsche to D'Annunzio and Marinetti. The key was to nurture a sense of responsibility based on the defining human capacities. Vico had accented the interpenetration of historical knowing and making. We shape history as we understand it in a certain way because that particular understanding initiates an imperative for a certain direction in practice. And our ethical capacity, our sense of responsibility, our care for the world, underpins the entire relationship. As Gentile came to see it, it is precisely this care that feeds endless thinking and opens thinking to truth.[76]

On the basis of what they found it possible to establish from their distinctively Italian angle, Croce and Gentile gradually came to believe that they had moved to the forefront, that they constituted the cutting edge of modern thought in the West.[77] By the eve of the First World War, in fact, they took it for granted that their thinking *was* modern thought. And they had become central to the Italian culture of the period, which E.J. Hobsbawm aptly characterized as "both extremely sophisticated and relatively provincial."[78] The idiosyncratic, "provincial" dimension made it possible to raise some new questions, not posed in the same way elsewhere; it thus contributed to the sophisticated substance. And the sense that Croce and Gentile offered the ultimate in modern thought made them especially exciting to a number of their Italian contemporaries. But any such notion of leadership, especially as based, even in part, on reconnection with Italian traditions, could also breed myth making.

Although they continued to share a common framework, the accents of the two thinkers were a bit different from the start. They gradually split, first over rarefied philosophical issues in 1913, then over the cultural significance of the First World War, and finally, early in 1925, over Fascism, as Croce, after some initial acquiescence, finally turned to outright opposition.

Even before his encounter with Croce, Gentile had begun to develop his own understanding of the need and scope for civic renewal, including a particular way of conceiving the cultural interplay of history, philosophy, religion, and education. Philosophy was privileged, as human self-awareness, and, abstract though it might be, speculative philosophy had to play a practical role as the cornerstone of civic renewal. But crystallizing almost immediately was what proved to be Gentile's lifelong concern with the philosophy and practice of education. Its mission broadly religious, education could at once make sense of and instill the new sense of human freedom, creativity, and responsibility. Although initially we can conceive the package only in traditional religious terms, education affords us a philosophical understanding of our human role. So philosophy was at once the foundation and the capstone of education.[79]

Even as Gentile encountered Croce in the discussions about Marxism during the later 1890s, he differed from the older thinker in symptomatic ways in his reading of Marx. Whereas Croce, seeking to distinguish between what seemed the disparate components in Marxism, found historical materialism to be a mere canon of historical interpretation, relevant only sometimes, Gentile found it crucial that for Marx himself historical materialism had *always* been central. As the category underlying Marx's whole philosophy of history, it could not be separated from the rest, and it was bound up with what Gentile found the promising core of Marx, the idea of *praxis*, that we ourselves make history. Croce seemed to be sidestepping this dimension altogether. But Marxism, as Gentile saw it, was ambiguous or even contradictory about agency, about how materialism interplayed with praxis, understood as activity of spirit.[80] Gentile's way of understanding the challenge of Marx helped to lead him to emphases potentially more grandiose—and risky—than Croce's.

Gentile was more insistent than Croce on the value of reconnecting with the Italian tradition to address the wider modern challenge. Even as Croce sensed himself to be on the cutting edge, and even as he recognized a major debt to such earlier Italian thinkers as Vico and Francesco De Sanctis, he did not claim there was anything specifically Italian about his own thinking. On the contrary, he played up his wider European heritage, and he would remain one of the century's most cosmopolitan intellectuals. He refrained from any claim that Italy had a special role partly because he feared that any such preoccupation would lead to provincial excess. Gentile was more intrigued by what seemed the specifically Italian contribution to the alternative modern thought now emerging.[81]

During the 1890s, while preparing his college graduation thesis (*tesi di laurea*) on the nineteenth-century Italian philosophers Antonio Rosmini and Vincenzo Gioberti, Gentile became interested in Bertrando Spaventa's notion of the circulation of Italian ideas within European philosophy. By 1905, he was looking back not only on Vico and the nineteenth-century Neapolitan take on Hegel but even back to Marsilio Ficino, Giordano Bruno, and Renaissance humanism, which, as he saw it, had reacted against medieval transcendence to initiate a humanistic tradition that remained at the origins of the modern world.[82] But what had so far proved the modern mainstream, developing through Descartes to the Enlightenment and contemporary positivism, had grown from that foundation in a particular way, privileging the natural sciences and marginalizing aspects of the original Italian insight, which had persisted only as a kind of counter-tradition.

Whereas that mainstream tradition started with the natural world, as described ultimately in mathematics, the Italian tradition started with humanity, understood as self-creating through history. Gentile insisted in 1912 that we discern first in Bruno "the truly modern notion of the seriousness and importance of history, as the actuality of the spirit in its development." Even knowing must be understood as constructive activity. And as Bruno had been the first to discern, not only knowledge but the mind itself grows and develops and thereby makes itself over time, in history. What happens is not, as we assume from a dualistic perspective, mind developing through stimulus from without "but . . . auto-formation of mind itself, which makes of each step reached the basis for further steps beyond that would not otherwise have been possible."[83] The only telos is the recognition that in this sense human beings make history—and endlessly remake themselves as they do so. But rather than develop Bruno's notion that mind itself is transformed as knowledge expands, the subsequent mainstream of European thought conceived progress only in quantitative terms; human beings remain the same but accumulate ever more knowledge.[84]

By the eighteenth century, this anti-historical conception of human nature had clearly triumphed, although Vico, marginal to the mainstream, managed to give Bruno's insight more systematic elaboration.[85] The Italian tradition was then carried into the nineteenth century, especially by Vincenzo Cuoco. At the same time, Hegel encompassed some of the Italian insight, but his handling of spirit, nature, becoming, and the dialectic proved problematic. As the most innovative of the Neapolitan Hegelians of the 1860s and 1870s, Bertrando Spaventa had offered promising indications for a way out, especially by accenting thought in action and thereby deepening Hegel's way of conceiving "becoming." If, more radically than Hegel, we posit becoming as essential to spirit, or human being, there is no need to posit alienation or the objectification of nature as nature. By developing the leads he found in Spaventa, Gentile thought it possible to dissolve the problems left over from Hegel and to offer a consistent philosophy of immanence, avoiding any problematic subject/object dualism and positing spirit, or human being, as self-creating in history.[86]

After beginning tentatively to move in his own direction by 1910, Gentile gave a lecture in 1912 that provoked Croce's criticisms and led to a public divergence in 1913. Croce's response helped Gentile to clarify his emerging position and lay out his distinctive philosophy, labeled actual idealism or actualism, which he outlined systematically in 1916 in *Teoria generale dello spirito come atto puro*, soon translated as *The Theory of Mind as Pure Act*.[87]

Today even the title is enough to put off all but the most determined enthusiasts of philosophical idealism. And Gentile's central move, reducing the world to a continuous act of thought thinking, may seem simply vacuous on first encounter, at best a play in an empty intellectual game. But this notion proves to have significant implications once we understand what "thinking" and "continuous thought" entail and how they relate to Gentile's more tangible underlying concern—to respond to the perceived inadequacies of modern culture, revolving around liberalism and positivism.

Although Gentile's brand of philosophical idealism was highly abstract in one sense, no thinker has been more concerned to *deny* abstraction by connecting thinking to commitment, responsibility, and action. Even as he gave it systematic form, Gentile never conceived his philosophy apart from praxis or from the wider contemporary challenge, especially the civic program that was his central concern from the start. He was not suggesting that philosophical problems were somehow self-contained, that a formal solution to some technical problem left over from the idealist tradition was worth anything in itself. No one has been more contemptuous of any such notion than Gentile. He was seeking to show, in rigorous philosophical terms, that thinking is not merely reflective but is bound up with action. Indeed, as we have noted, Gentile envisioned his philosophy as itself a crucial form of practice, constituting both the foundation and the capstone of the new education.

Abstract though it was, even the 1913 philosophical dispute with Croce brought to the surface differences with broadly political implications. In response to tendencies toward conflation in Marxism, pragmatism, utilitarianism, and aestheticism, Croce insisted on distinctions—between imagination and cognition, politics and ethics, knowing and doing. But he also posited a kind of circular relationship between these differentiated attributes of human being, a relationship that underlies or generates history. Gentile, in contrast, kept trying to bring things together, to find deeper unities or identities. Croce charged that Gentile, by dissolving oppositions, was lapsing into "mysticism," reducing the world to an immobile present. And as Croce saw it, Gentile's reduction was merely arbitrary in any case; the "pure act" that he called thinking could as easily be called life, will, or sentiment.[88]

In response, Gentile insisted that a rigorous philosophy of immanence shows the mutual implication of the components that Croce sought to distinguish—and thus the unity or wholeness of the totality. It was distinction or separation, not unity, that produced abstraction. Gentile's way of unifying will and intellect was to transcend intellectualism *and* mysticism.[89] This was not immobilism but history; reality was not given but self-creating, as we come to understand human creativity as the other side of the self-creation of reality.

Although Croce never fully worked out the relationships between the human attributes even to his own satisfaction, he continued, partly in response to Gentile's challenge, to adjust the connections between the distinguishable formal categories, eventually affording a certain privilege to the ethical. In pondering how thought and action interpenetrate, moreover, he came to emphasize the role of thought, or historical understanding, in preparing action. Nevertheless, he continued to avoid Gentile's way of positing unity, which he found excessive—and ultimately dangerous. Gentile's later overt totalitarianism confirmed the worst.

Yet Gentile had been right to counter in 1913 that Croce's charge of mysticism and immobilism was a red herring. The two thinkers were simply coming to a different understanding of human prospects in the world of radical immanence that they had jointly posited. Responding to Croce's criticisms, Gentile called Croce's attention to "that sense of profound melancholy that pervades your whole contemplation of the world."[90] At issue was how the world gets made, or could and should get made, once we discern the human place in what now seems a purely historical world. Once we grasp Gentile's sense of the possibilities, we can understand why he found "melancholy" implications in Croce's denial of the sort of unity that Gentile himself posited—and claimed to be the key to addressing the contemporary challenge.

In reducing the world to a continuous act of thought thinking, Gentile was fastening upon thinking as the archetypal human activity. Thinking is the realm of openness, freedom of the spirit; only in thinking do we overcome determination by being—what already is. This was not to indulge in the extravagant notion that we can merely think away what we dislike, or that a mere vision, or wishful thinking, could change the world, or that we might escape from reality or action through fantasy. Rather, Gentile simply offered, on the most basic level, a way of characterizing the scope for human freedom and creativity, for always going beyond what is. If we did not think, we would indeed be determined by being.

In no sense, then, was Gentile accenting thinking *as opposed to* doing, thought as opposed to action. Rather, thinking is utterly bound up with action—each implies the other—and thus Gentile's insistence on unity in the face of Croce's distinctions. Thinking is the defining human activity only insofar as it is *not* mere passive reflection or contemplation but itself creative activity—indeed, the most fundamental such activity. Thus Gentile cast his key category in the active participial form—*pensiero pensante*, thought thinking. And to say "thought thinking" as opposed to "mind thinking" was to dissolve any suggestion of some physical basis or substratum, some *thing* that does the thinking. Thinking is "willful," in the sense that it wants to realize itself in the world, and action is genuinely human and not mere instinctual reflex only insofar as it is informed by thought. If we *really* think something, we act on that basis. Indeed, *only* insofar as we seek to translate some thought into action do we know we really think it. At the same time, thinking is continuous and even supra-individual in the sense that it is never *ex nihilo* but always a response to the resultants of earlier thinking.

To posit unity around the act of thought thinking was to say that to think something is to believe it, to commit oneself to it, to conform one's actions to it, to want others to believe it, to seek to shape the world in accordance with what one thinks. Because thinking wants to be true, universal—to convince others— the human ethical capacity is central to the indissoluble mix. Left stunted by natural law and contractualist conceptions, with their atomistic, materialistic notions of the individual, the ethical could now be nurtured, brought fully to the fore in a newly unified culture. Because we care for the world, we want our thinking to be true; our ethical capacity opens us to truth, which contrasts with fantasy or even the fictions of the novelist. Conversely, to posit thinking as a continuing act denies the fixity of truth but not truth itself, which rests on the enduring human ethical capacity.[91]

To grasp this fundamental unity of thinking, willing, and action is to take life seriously, to take responsibility for the world.[92] The alternative can be seen in the various modern tendencies, which we might discern even in ourselves, to "know" without acting, to embrace "ideals" without committing ourselves to anything, to experience the world as something separate that happens to us, and that is either more serious, or less serious, than we are.

As Gentile saw the contemporary problem, such tendencies were supranational, bound up with liberalism and positivism, but for historical reasons the problem was especially close to the surface in Italy. What he took to be the characteristic Italian vices going back to the Renaissance—rhetoric, most obviously, but ultimately the frivolously skeptical mode of life that spawned rhetoric—exacerbated the more general modern tendencies toward cynicism, indifference, and narcissism that stemmed most immediately from the liberal and positivist distinctions between subject and object, inner and outer, public and private.[93] Thus Italy had experienced with particular force the tensions in liberal individualism and parliamentary politics. The underlying problem was precisely the separation of words from actions, of ideals from commitments, of humanity from reality, which could too easily be talked about without genuine commitment and the action that follows from it. The antidote was to create Gentile's unified culture.

For Gentile, then, to grasp the new philosophy in its rigorous logic was to feel not some abiding structure but, as never before, the openness and incompleteness of the world. What philosophy gives us, from this perspective, is a hole, an opening, compelling a more radical understanding of human freedom and a deeper, potentially all-encompassing sense of responsibility. To understand the world philosophically is thus to be propelled beyond the present through action. And a form of education informed by this philosophy could bring this self-understanding to the fore in others.[94] Whereas the ethical capacity is a defining aspect of human being, it requires "social production," starting with a particular education conscious of its ethical mission. Such education was not merely, as for Durkheim, endlessly to renew the consensus, the sense of common belonging, in a stable society, but to prepare, even to mobilize, individuals for ongoing collective action.

Although he did not draw out the political implications until after the First World War, Gentile's conception suggested the scope for more concerted forms of action to exercise that responsibility through collective world making. As early as 1902, he had begun to adumbrate a post-Hegelian variant on the "ethical state" notion, which he would explicitly characterize as totalitarian in seeking to make it the core of Fascism in the mid-1920s.[95] Whereas Hegel had posited the ethical state as the focus for what now seemed static political obligation, the notion could now be recast for the dynamic and ever-provisional world that had opened up. Indeed, the ethical state was the vehicle needed to translate the newly all-encompassing sense of responsibility into collective action—in light of a historical framework that was more open, more genuinely immanent, than even Hegel had grasped.

In this light, Gentile's totalitarianism would require three intersecting, mutually dependent dimensions: education, to nurture and focus the ethical capacity; an expanded collective reach, so that more could be done; and a concentration of power, affording the capacity for collective action to match the expanded reach. Only the scope to participate in that power, in that collective exercise of positive freedom, could fully draw out the ethical capacity. In fact, to be fully ethical and human in the modern world we *require* a totalitarian state; we feel full responsibility insofar as the instrument to act is available. We will consider the obvious questions about quality of participation when we come to the level of practice in Chapter 6.

Gentile's alternative, in response to the more circumspect and "melancholy" Croce, was typical of totalitarian thinking in combining grandiose hubris with an underlying note of shrillness, suggesting his concern that other modern tendencies carried dangerous implications. In one sense, Gentile moved confidently beyond Croce, whose alternative, he felt, simply did not do justice to human possibilities in this world of radical immanence. With his emphasis on distinctions, Croce was not affording an adequate antidote to positivism, with its subject/object dualism, or even liberalism, with its public/private distinction. His distinctions left us with an element of blindness. Although the next moment results from what we do, we do not know what we are doing. Indeed, lacking a collective will, we do not know what we want to do. In this sense, Croce's notion was too passive, leaving world making too much the aggregate of private individual response and thus the world as something that happens to us. In denying the scope for a unified culture, Croce was missing the scope for marshalling our creative human capacities in such a way that, as we act collectively, we do indeed know what we are doing. Thus he would end up stressing humility as he offered a mere recasting of liberalism. In Gentile's terms, insofar as world making remains merely the resultant of a concatenation of individual decisions, we are not free in the same way, and human responsibility is not invited in the same way.

But whereas Gentile's vision in one sense reflected hubris, or at least confident humanistic assurance, he understood that "melancholy" did indeed lurk in a world without transcendence.[96] Although Croce claimed to offer a middle course sufficient to invite responsibility and to head off irrationalist excess, Gentile sensed that the Crocean alternative would not hold, that the culture would lapse into mere egotism or nihilism. Although a new world results from what we do, the degree of contingency and blindness breeds a sense of futility. We lapse into irony, cynicism, passivity, indifference. Or we become self-absorbed. Action becomes at best an irrational gesture of self-assertion, "authenticity." At the same time, although Croce stressed the role of historical understanding in preparing action, thinking, as he conceived it, threatened to become a mere exercise, irrelevant for practice. In light of these lurking possibilities in a mass secular age, Gentile found it essential to go beyond Croce's moderate humility and show the way to a unified culture. Indeed, it was essential to go all the way to totalitarianism to head off melancholy. At first, some would surely continue to insist on the bourgeois principle—the primacy of negative freedom and individual interests, the sanctity of the private sphere. If they could not be educated, they would have to be excluded.

Gentile found his way to this more grandiose alternative partly through the engagement with Marxism that, as we saw, began in the mid-1890s. The Marxian counter-tradition had already posited a way of unifying theory and practice, as "praxis," and a way of transcending the several dualisms that virtually defined liberalism. Marxism offered much that Gentile could appreciate, but it also entailed uncertainties and contradictions that, precisely as Gentile encountered it, were coming to the fore even for those seeking to work within the Marxist tradition. Marxism was shaky especially with respect to freedom, agency, and world making, all of which had implications for the whole set of diagnoses and prescriptions that it had made central to radicalism by the end of the nineteenth century. For Gentile, in a key sense, Marxism was simply not radical enough; it had to be criticized to show the way to a different alternative modernity.

It was hardly surprising, said Gentile, that Marx's disciples were not sure what to do, given the eclectic, contradictory quality of Marxism, and especially its tensions concerning agency.[97] And he pinpointed, in terms that precisely anticipated Bernard Yack's, the awkward amalgam of materialist and idealist themes, necessity and the scope for agency, that produced those tensions. Adumbrating his own emphasis on the scope for lucid collective world making, Gentile played up what is now taken as the Hegelian or idealist side of Marx, emphasizing praxis, the notion that man makes history and history makes man.[98] He also noted anticipations of Marx in Vico's insight that doing is the condition of knowing. But Marx had encountered problems in seeking to make Hegel concrete by linking praxis to matter and the sensible world—by substituting the economic factor for the idea. For although Marx usefully avoided earlier mechanistic and naturalistic ideas, he could not integrate the materialist dimension into the Hegelian understanding of the self-realization of spirit. And this was because materialism simply could not be made dynamic and historical; matter is inert and can be only transformed by spiritual or human activity. History is that spiritual realm of human beings changing the world through creative activity.[99] So although Marx had wanted to eschew transcendence, he had had to invoke transcendence to change the world; he thus ended by backing up from Hegel to Platonic dualism, a bifurcation of idea and reality.

Whatever our views on the long-vexed question of Marx's center of gravity, Gentile surely did not do justice to the force of the materialist side of Marxism, what it meant to say that humanity makes history under the compulsion of particular economic relations—currently those of capitalism.[100] From that perspective, the tension between freedom and necessity is precisely the point, and the key is to transcend the element of determination. As we do so, history as we have known it ends, and we are at last free to make it in a new mode. That mode does not entail some static fulfillment, but in a sense it cannot be conceived as history making at all, for the tension will have dropped away once a classless society has been reached.

However, it remains the case that Marx's conception of the present relationships among freedom, consciousness, and material necessity betrayed uncertainties, quite apart from how ends or goals might be conceived. On the one hand, he had accented class determination. Human freedom and ethical capacity were stunted in a particular way from within bourgeois culture, and only the proletariat, through its particular experience of industrial capitalism, was situated to develop the consciousness necessary for a systematic overcoming. Moreover, that consciousness would necessarily be a *universal* consciousness, and the overcoming it would yield would thus be the *final* overcoming. On the other hand, Marx recognized that even without that privileged experience, some individuals from within the present bourgeois order could develop a superior, post-bourgeois consciousness or understanding, although such understanding necessarily included grasping the essential role of the proletariat in any systematic overcoming.

Marx did not explain how that post-determined consciousness was possible under present circumstances; nor did he specify what differentiated those capable of it from those who apparently were not. Thus he was leaving a crease that might open to a different way of conceiving the scope for a radical alternative to the bourgeois order. For Gentile, that consciousness meant especially consciousness of human freedom and its place in history. Humanity determines circumstances. And that consciousness can be nurtured in others. Already in *La filosofia di Marx*, Gentile was accenting education as the central, continuous societal praxis through which our very capacity to educate and be educated grows.[101] The change in consciousness currently possible could carry beyond the separation and the specific forms of incompleteness of the bourgeois order.

We saw that Lenin, wrestling with questions about agency in light of what seemed to be the growing danger that bourgeois ideology would dissolve the possibility of a socialist alternative, stressed the role of an elite defined by consciousness. That consciousness included grasping the need for a new kind of interaction with the proletariat—or, more accurately, the masses—to achieve power. Although it was not what the original Leninist conception specified, it was an easy step to understand the vanguard as raising the proletariat or the masses to consciousness through education and mobilization from within the new framework. In that sense, a post-liberal order could be created before anything usefully characterized as "socialism," understood as a systematic *economic* alternative, although the image of "creating socialism" could surely galvanize energies and virtues.

From Gentile's perspective, the residual emphasis on class in the Leninist self-understanding as the vanguard *of the proletariat* was inconsistent with the transition envisioned. The educators would necessarily be the vanguard of the post-liberal sense of collective human capacity, which would entail above all a consciousness of the need and scope for collective action. They would concentrate power to universalize that consciousness of freedom, responsibility, and collective capacity—and thereby to forge the ongoing collective will. The "realm of freedom" is not negative—as it was even, to some extent, for Marx, as freedom from economic constraint—but rather "positive," as the capacity to act collectively to shape our world, including our economic relations, on into the future.

In banishing the dimension of materialist determinism, Gentile could claim to have overcome the second, more precise, contradiction that Yack found in the tradition of "longing for total revolution," culminating in Marx. But with his insistence on a unified culture, Gentile might seem to be retreating to the level of the first contradiction, based on the quest for some definitive overcoming of the fragmenting spirit of modernity. As we noted, the sense of the problem, and the image of what overcoming would mean, had remained vague in the tradition that Yack explored; his thinkers were the first to try to articulate the terms of a purely secular, immanent yet ever-changing world, yielding particular, finite cultures. Insofar as this "modernity" was experienced as sinking into mere historicity, it engendered a feeling of being trapped, of dehumanizing determination. These pioneers were right in inferring that this novel sensibility stemmed not merely from the rise of the bourgeoisie or some change in socio-economic or class relations but from something deeper, broader, in one sense precisely "the spirit of modernity" itself. Indeed, it was the wider modern dispensation, wound around a particular conception of humanity and history, that warranted the culture that, in turn, made possible the hegemony of the bourgeoisie. Conversely, that hegemony entailed a particular self-understanding, a particular set of assumptions, priorities, and desiderata, in response to what newly seemed an immanent world in motion. The bourgeoisie thus came to stand for a particular modern strand, hegemonic in the sense that it came to seem equivalent to modernity itself. Once bourgeoisie and modernity became contingently bound up during the nineteenth century, the target for those dissatisfied came to seem, and on the first level genuinely had to be, *bourgeois* modernity, with all that had come to entail.

Even if we find no scope for some qualitative break from "modernity" as a secular world of immanence, finitude, and change, we can perhaps achieve an alternative to *bourgeois* modernity. By separating what was essential from what was contingent in modern thinking so far, Gentile was seeking to specify an alternative that was more convincing and workable than Marxism. The sense of falling heir to the specifically Italian tradition from Bruno to Vico gave him the confidence that he was uniquely able to respond, because it was on this level, concerning the interface between humanity and history, that the Italian humanistic tradition, marginalized though it had become, remained at the very foundations of modernity.

The preoccupation with historical finitude or particularity among Yack's figures reflected a sense of incongruence between humanity, as free and creative, and the modern world, newly experienced as inherently finite, ever provisional. As we give up the demand for some total grasp or some liberation from history, we understand the scope for an alternative modern dispensation, affording the coherence that mainstream bourgeois modernity had frustrated yet truer to the endless incompleteness and finitude of the world *and* to our specifically human capacities. Rather than transcend history, we seek to mesh with history in a new way. That alternative was not only more coherent than Marxism but was realizable, as the orthodox Marxian vision was not, under present socio-economic circumstances. Grasping the sense in which we make history, now feeling the responsibility for making it, we can begin actually to do it in the radically new way now possible. We simply require the understanding, the will, and the power to create the collective instrument for the positive exercise of human freedom in ongoing collective action. There could be no more detailed specification in advance about what actually to do, about actual policies or choices; what would happen would depend on free, creative human response. The end, after all, was nothing.

Even before the First World War, especially as he began to distance himself from the more bland and circumspect Croce, Gentile began to attract a remarkable array of young intellectuals, offering what seemed to be a more hopeful, affirmative direction in his "relatively provincial but extremely sophisticated" culture.[102] More generally, his diagnoses and prescriptions help us better to grasp the possibilities of the new terrain, the scope for pursuing alternatives to both the liberal mainstream and the mainstream Marxist alternative. It remained to be seen how Gentile's overtly totalitarian alternative would actually work, what experience with it would tell us about human possibilities in a purely secular world in motion.

Science, will, and power

Precisely as Croce and Gentile were stressing a form of humanism, partly to counter the seeming cultural hegemony of positivism, naturalism, and science, others were advocating a new, more overtly political role for scientific expertise. Confidence in science had grown from the Enlightenment, but how science was to play its cultural role in interface with other cultural components was being worked out with experience, together with much else. Stephen Holmes, in his defense of liberalism and the Enlightenment tradition, was surely right to insist that critics had often overdone the charge of scientific hubris, that the Enlightenment understanding of science in fact entailed fallibility, modesty, corrigibility, and openness in reaction against the scholastic effort to penetrate essences.[103] But accents could vary considerably and, on the basis of both experience and further thinking about the scientific enterprise, there could be significant changes in self-understanding from within the original framework. By around 1900, several factors had converged to affect the place of science in the wider mix bound up with politics and history.

In a seminal paper presented in 1988, Detlev Peukert traced "the genesis of the 'final solution'" to a change in "the spirit of science" around the turn of the century. As he saw it, in fact, the intersection of science, politics, and the quest for post-religious sources of meaning yielded a whole new dynamic, riddled with tensions, at this point. Now "a scientific approach to the study of human beings and to the tackling of social problems had become a broadly practicable project for the first time," but "the switch from religion to science as the source of meaning-creating mythology for everyday life" meant that "science took on itself a burden of responsibility that it would find a heavy one to bear." Both expecting and expected to do more, the new social scientific and medical professions expanded their reach, coming together with the broadly political sphere, but their confidence in their capacity to perfect the social body, which sometimes bordered on fantasies of omnipotence, proved unrealistic.[104]

The key was precisely the changing *spirit* of science, as Peukert's title and overall argument suggested. But Peukert was vague on both the basis of the change and the novelty of the relationship that resulted. The spirit at issue was not merely hubris, as in Bauman's gardening vision, but was itself new, emerging from a deeper layer of possibility alongside other strands having comparable implications for political action. By relating Peukert's syndrome to the wider historical-political break emerging at this point, we can better grasp its implications.

Returning to Bauman's metaphor, the modern sense of the scope for gardening was not in itself an answer, as if it was enough simply to keep discovering and applying scientific knowledge. Rather, the scope for gardening opened a new universe of questions about how the gardening gets done, about modes of agency. Even assuming that the scientific enterprise could yield increasing mastery of both the physical and social worlds, it was not obvious how new knowledge was to get translated into such mastery in practice, how scientific expertise was to interface with the political realm, especially as the sphere of collective responsibility expanded. In that sense, questions about the interplay of science, politics, and history had been implicit in the Enlightenment deployment all along. And the actual public role of science that had resulted by the end of the nineteenth century was not simply the teleological unfolding of the Enlightenment possibility but a particular, contingent outcome that left room for further departures. A confluence of factors at the end of the nineteenth century then changed the relationship between scientific expertise and the political realm.

The age of positivism during the late nineteenth century is widely taken as the peak of confidence in scientific approaches, including the applicability of science to the human world. Now the conscious application of scientific knowledge to industrial processes and to medicine and public health began to result in significant improvements to everyday life. Medicine, especially, won new prestige—as scientific, as professional—thanks to its success in identifying the causes of diseases like tuberculosis and cholera by the end of the century. The application of science made progress seem almost automatic, so success fed the various developmentalisms, with their suggestions of determinism and predictability. Still, the tension between expertise and democratic imperatives that we noted in the last chapter became potentially more intrusive. Proto-technocratic ideas like those of Saint-Simon and Ferdinand Lassalle had surfaced throughout the nineteenth century and suggested possible new directions that in principle could include everything from eugenics to economic planning. Some maintained that continuing progress required, or would yield, a more grandiose role for experts—as with Auguste Comte's vision of a scientific understanding of politics and ethics binding on all. Even as the expanding reach of government increased the scope for political controversy and divisiveness, governments could hope to depoliticize potentially contentious issues by making them matters of apparently objective, value-neutral expertise.

Concerns with national strength and wealth, including even the size of the population, had been longstanding, but, as is also well known, by the end of the century, the confluence of imperial rivalry, social Darwinian thinking, and scientific achievement produced a new syndrome, stemming from a sense of the scope and the need for more active governmental intervention in the population sphere. Even in seemingly successful Britain and Germany, concerns about national competitiveness or "efficiency" were bound up with fears of declines in population quantity and quality. At the time of the Boer War in Britain, for example, the number of would-be volunteers for military service who had to be refused because of inadequate health or height produced consternation—and much discussion of policy implications.

In light of the new prestige of medicine, doctors began to feel responsible for addressing national health and, on that basis, to seek expanded public roles. Through much pioneering research, Paul Weindling showed that housing, work, nutrition, and sexuality were increasingly the objects of medical surveys and public health regulations by the first decade of the twentieth century.[105] Alliance with public authorities in the state expanded both the powers of the medical community and opportunities for individual doctors and allied professionals. The result was what Maria Sophia Quine has called "a new vision of the domain and scope of politics as experts called upon governments to regulate sex and reproduction in the nation's interest."[106] Pressures came from within the public sphere as well. Weindling noted that as the prospect of war heightened concern about the condition of the German population in 1914, army leaders called for direct state intervention to promote the health of mothers and children. Infant welfare was essential to maintain Germany as a world power.[107]

With population matters, as with public health not long before, it was coming to seem that government could not simply let nature take its course or rely on some *laissez-faire* concatenation of self-serving individual decisions. Indeed, there was no clear line between public health and population management, or between either and welfare policy. It was arguably the responsibility of government to shape society by actively managing population quantity and quality, although the enterprise seemed to require more direct involvement by scientific experts.

Under the circumstances, the professionalization newly at work was undoubtedly a significant supranational, historically specific factor, and professional ambition has lately been much in vogue as an explanatory category. Although mere careerism was part of it, professionalization could become significant in the case at hand only because of the new sense of opportunity and responsibility, of the need and scope for new forms of collective action that might centrally involve scientific expertise. The advent of professionalization was simply a reinforcing mechanism.

By the turn of the century, questions about the range and cultural place of science were also at issue on a theoretical or philosophical level. Even as its successes carried science to a peak of prestige in one sense, questions about the scientific enterprise and the status of the knowledge it produced led to a deepening understanding of the interface between science and human purpose or will. That relationship was more complex than had been recognized, even in terms of the categories that had so far emerged from Kantian and contemporary neo-Kantian ways of thinking beyond subject/object dualism. Raising such questions from within the positivist tradition, philosophically inclined scientists like Ernst Mach, Richard Avenarius, and Henri Poincaré stressed that science is a human tool, developed in response to human needs. Whereas no one suggested that will trumps scientific discovery, or that wishing can make it so, the new thinking suggested that scientific truth could not so easily be distinguished, as "objective," from the human realm of will, purpose, responsibility, even politics, as had been assumed. Whereas Comte, half a century before, had thought that even ethics and politics were on their way to being made rational and objective, it now seemed necessary to turn in the opposite direction and to explore how science meshed, or might better mesh, with the political sphere, with human will and purpose.

The sense that science might operate still more beneficially by coming together with the inflating governmental sphere—by, in a sense, acting politically—was itself energizing. But anxiety crept in at the same time as the sense that more *could* be done—to assure progress—slid into the sense that more *had* to be done—to avert depopulation or degeneration, for example. Thus the anxiety of heightened responsibility, but thus also the anxiety of contingency. And thus the element of shrillness that accompanied the energizing sense of expanding opportunity.

To exercise the new responsibility required new power through the state, in contingent interface with the political sphere. Scientific expertise meshed especially uneasily with *democratic* politics. Moreover, even assuming an effective alliance of political power and scientific exercise, interface with the wider cultural sphere was at issue as well, for the new mode of action seemed to require intervention in spheres in which, despite secularization, traditional religious and ethical conceptions had remained dominant. The need to act in new ways in these realms might require a departure from the *laissez-faire* form that secular modernity had so far assumed, which left these residuals to survive if they could or to die out on their own.

The population management immediately at issue could mean mere natalism, or efforts to promote population expansion, but most significant was the growing interest in eugenics at the turn of the century, fed by the concerns about national efficiency and "degeneration" that we noted above. Although the subject of a large and still-growing literature over the last twenty years, eugenics was long neglected—the archetypal instance, it seems, of the tendency that Mark Roseman featured to sidestep aspects of modernity that proved uncomfortable in the wake of Nazism. Eugenic thinking had been widespread and seemingly progressive, even quintessentially "modern," and was by no means confined to fanatics in Germany. It had even attracted many on the Left. Now that eugenics, as a historical phenomenon, is front and center, the challenge is to put it in proportion as we seek to think afresh about the origins of totalitarianism.

Francis Galton coined the term "eugenics" in 1883 to characterize the program that followed from the opportunity he saw for humanity, on the basis of the new insights into evolution and heredity, to take control of its own evolution.[108] Although a notably supranational movement, eugenics quickly became especially prominent in Britain, Germany, and the United States. In Germany, Alfred Ploetz coined the term "racial hygiene" in publishing his pioneering *Grundlinien einer Rassenhygiene* (Foundations of Race Hygiene) in 1895. Concerned about the counter-selective effects of war, welfare, and especially medical care for the weak, Ploetz quickly became the central figure in the German movement, founding the Society for Racial Hygiene in 1905.[109] His closest rival was Wilhelm Schallmayer, who came to prominence as the winner of the noted Krupp competition announced on January 1, 1900. Seeking to promote science as the basis for unifying progressive social forces, the prominent armaments firm offered a handsome prize for the best essay on the application of the laws of evolution to society. Schallmayer's winning entry, *Vererbung und Auslese* (Heredity and Selection), was promptly revised and published in 1903. Although much controversy surrounded its publication, it soon became the standard German eugenics textbook.[110] As an international movement, eugenics came of age with the first International Congress for Eugenics, held in London in 1912 with 300 participants, and with Leonard Darwin, one of Charles Darwin's sons, and the head of the British Eugenics Education Society, as presiding officer.

Already at that conference, certain national differences in accent were evident. Experts from Germany, Britain, and the United States were considerably more likely to favor negative selection to keep the "disgenic" from procreating, whereas those from France and Italy were more receptive to the environmentalist notion that improvements in health, education, and welfare could produce heritable benefits in the quality of individuals.[111] At the same time, the French and Italians tended to stress natalism, though for somewhat different reasons, in light of the different demographic situations facing the two countries. Even as overpopulation forced a growing wave of emigration, which reached a peak of 870,000 in 1913, Italian eugenicists tended to laud Italy's high birth rate, which they associated with sexual prowess, fecundity, and health. The challenge was to encourage an even higher birth rate. As Quine emphasized, frustrated imperial ambitions were clearly at work in such thinking.[112] Analogous arguments were made by Italian economists like Achille Loria, who associated a high birth rate with cheap labor, which would help Italy's industrialization effort.[113]

Eugenics offered the scope for both positive and negative intervention, although each would expand the sphere of collective action. What opened, in a sense, was a continuum from less to more extreme measures, from somehow promoting the fit to keeping those deemed unfit from reproducing to actively eliminating those deemed unfit through "euthanasia." When first discussed in the 1890s, "euthanasia" had genuinely meant "mercy killing," but even then it was recognized that such death might also be in the social interest.[114] After the turn of the century, the relatively moderate Schallmayer noted that "the rational management of population" might encompass actually killing the unfit, those deemed a burden, even against their wishes.[115] More aggressive was Ernst

Haeckel, who explicitly advocated killing the sick in *The Riddle of Life*, published in 1904.[116]

However, although it was bound up with the widespread sense that new action to shape society was necessary and possible, eugenics was always controversial. The noted German sociologist Ferdinand Tönnies attacked the whole direction on the grounds that there was no agreement even about criteria of fitness.[117] Another prominent critic was the Christian Socialist Friedrich Naumann. Although he saw the birth rate as a key index of vitality and long urged welfare measures to protect military prowess, he emphasized social integration as opposed to conflict—whether class struggle or survival of the fittest. He condemned eugenics and social Darwinism on those grounds even during the First World War.[118]

Partisans of eugenics disagreed sharply among themselves along several criss-crossing axes. Especially uncertain was the interface between eugenics and neo-Malthusianism, the movement for family planning through birth control. An advocate of eugenics could be pro-natalist, neo-Malthusian, or anti-neo-Malthusian without being especially natalist. French eugenics allied with pro-natalism, whereas leading Germans like Ploetz and Schallmayer strongly opposed neo-Malthusianism, especially the claim that family planning itself had eugenic consequences.[119] From their perspective, it was negative to have the most talented women limit births and take outside jobs while others stayed home and had children. From their perspective, a eugenic priority was to make motherhood socially desirable.

The interface between eugenics and racism or racialism was equally controversial. Although the distinction has become hard to grasp, even "race hygiene"—caring for the health of the race—need not presuppose the primacy of racial categories, let alone some hierarchy of races. But for many eugenics was interwoven with racism from the start. Galton in 1883 advocated scientifically improving the stock so that the superior races could prevail more quickly.[120] This was still to think in developmentalist terms; the superior could hasten the natural direction by applying their superior understanding. But others, like Schallmayer, deplored race thinking as a deleterious diversion; association with racism would give eugenics a bad name. Insisting that all population groups were open to eugenic improvement, Schallmayer advocated meritocracy and attacked notions of racial, and especially Aryan, superiority.[121]

But even when it was not concerned with racial hierarchy *per se*, early eugenic thinking often implicitly mixed categories or fell into inconsistency. Ploetz, for example, noted that there were no pure races anyway, and besides, racial mixing was a good source of variation. But he also took Aryan superiority for granted. Although emphases varied from one figure to another, eugenics took on racialist connotations especially as it became known through Ploetz's term as a movement for "race hygiene."[122] Indeed, ambiguous though it was, this association with eugenics as modern and scientific enhanced the pedigree of racialist thinking even as the argument continued about the meaning of what seemed to be racial differences.

Whatever the priorities, advocates of eugenics shared a sense of privileged, pioneering insight into the scope for using the new understanding of heredity to shape society. It was not only possible but necessary, in light of expanding societal responsibility and the need for collective effectiveness, for the society, spearheaded by scientific experts, to shape itself as never before. But traditional humanitarian, moral, and religious imperatives were likely to impede the requisite action. Schallmayer pointed to the doubly negative effects of humanitarianism—in protecting the insane, for example, or in treating those with tuberculosis.[123] Such measures were both counter-selective and a drain on resources. Accenting the significance of race consciousness to the medical profession at the London congress of 1912, the German physician and eugenicist Agnes Bluhm urged doctors to reconsider their ethical stance on, for example, the rights of the unborn. The imperative of racial health took precedence over outmoded moral precepts.[124]

However, the point was not simply to suppress the moral sense but to redirect it, even to inflate it. For surely it was a human responsibility to take advantage of the scientific expertise now acquired; it would be immoral not to do so. Even traditional humanitarian notions had to be reconsidered in light of the new scope for intervention. It could be more humane, even for those directly affected, to keep the unfit from being born in the first place. Both Schallmayer and Ploetz held explicitly that to control breeding, not leaving it to natural selection, was not only more efficient but also more humane.[125] But, as Leonard Darwin noted, the requisite new mode of action pointed sufficiently beyond conventional morality that *courage* was required for the action needed.[126]

Whatever the link of race or ethnicity to eugenics, the need for stepped-up collective action invited deeper scientific attention to manifest differences in mental and physical attributes. The Enlightenment emphasis on humanity and equality had come to seem abstract, but the scientific side of the Enlightenment tradition suggested the scope for rational differentiation along objective racial lines in the way that Zygmunt Bauman pinpointed.[127] Racial differences might loom more important as society sought to do more collectively.

Whatever the range, mere understanding and advocacy were obviously not sufficient; the necessary action required bringing those with the requisite expertise together with those who had the equally requisite political will and power. They would converge in an expanded state that claimed sovereignty over matters affecting the quantity or quality of population. Matters of quality encompassed family health and welfare as well as eugenics proper. In principle, expanding governmental sovereignty entailed denying any scope for purely private decisions in the whole broad population area.

But the move to action was hesitant prior to the First World War. On the one hand, the United States seemed like the bold pioneer: first Indiana, in 1907, and then ten other states had adopted sterilization laws by the end of 1913. American eugenics advocates were able to win financial support and influence legislation, but Germans like Schallmayer and Ploetz found too much *laissez-faire* looseness in the modes of state intervention in the United States and Britain and called for a more systematic approach.[128] Critics found U.S. laws not only haphazard in conception but also poorly enforced.[129]

Obviously, some of the science that resulted from this conjuncture is now easily derided as "pseudo-science," but even in terms of what counts as proper scientific approach and procedure, the science/pseudoscience dichotomy is not as neatly ahistorical as we like to assume. At any moment, part of what passes as science will later appear to have been pseudo-science—not simply mistaken in its results, and thus corrigible, but prejudicially delimited or mistaken in its assumptions, questions, and investigations as a result of some broadly political or ideological agenda. So it cannot be unequivocally clear what constitutes "real" science at any one time. Conversely, even some new, broadly political agenda may yield fruitful new questions and, eventually, results that are accepted as helpful, even true.

In one sense, the key is that these early twentieth-century agents were trying to be scientific, not to reject science and embrace some atavistic irrationalism. Insofar as it passed for science at the time, what they offered still had particular force *as* science. But the borders were becoming especially uncertain as the importance of "subjective" factors—will, purpose, responsibility, and values—intruded from several angles on thinking about science and its societal function. What counted as scientific, what role political purpose was bound to play, even ought to play, was on its way to being contested as never before.[130] Thus, for example, as early as 1918 some Germans were claiming that the Soviet insistence on a Lamarckian orientation, positing the inheritance of acquired characteristics, was an illegitimate intrusion of politics into science to discredit race hygiene.[131] Of course the Soviet leadership did have its own affirmative but still broadly political reasons to emphasize such an orientation. Science and politics were intertwining in new and dramatic ways for both sides, and what was reasonable, modern, and scientific was becoming central to the contest between Communists and anti-Communists. What was new was the mode of political–scientific interface that invited such contesting.

The totalitarian political regimes would go absurdly overboard in making science dependent on will or other subjective factors. We think first of the notorious Lysenko case in the Soviet Union or the Nazi proscription of "Jewish science." In retrospect, it is easy to see that ideology was dictating choices, determining which alternative would be credited as science. At the same time, however, we have recently come to recognize that the wider change in the cultural framework occasioned by these regimes stimulated some innovative questioning and pioneering achievement.[132] As remains true today, there was no clearly rational, universally accepted criterion at work, so assessing motivation, and the connection between motivation and results, is not as easy as it once seemed. Just as what detractors found politically motivated and even irrational at the time could yield what would later seem like scientifically sound results, directions that seem irrational in retrospect could have been experienced as boldly modern and responsible—even if, perhaps especially if, they pointed beyond what seemed conventional, unmodern, even irrational moral categories.

The significance of Nietzsche

Also beginning around the turn of the century was the infatuation with Nietzsche, who had no use for biologistic thinking but whose pioneering reading of the modern cultural situation in the 1870s and 1880s added some distinctive elements to the new thinking about problems, possibilities, and priorities. He explicitly posited a radical cleft, with himself as a kind of prophet; beginning in his own time, things were becoming possible that had not been possible before. And a link between Nietzsche and some subset of the subsequent troubling political departures, especially insofar as they have been understood as irrationalist and/or nihilistic, has long been assumed.[133] Yet the political implications of Nietzsche's thinking, and the sense in which he may have been symptomatic or influential, have been notoriously difficult to pin down.

We noted that whereas Lenin, clinging to orthodoxy, resisted mightily, even some Bolsheviks turned to Nietzsche as they sought to make sense of the new direction that they found necessary. Bernice Glatzer Rosenthal has recently shown how pervasive was Nietzsche's influence on Bolshevism, even into the Stalinist period, and even when Nietzsche was officially proscribed.[134] In Italy, Nietzsche was very much part of the mix as Mussolini and other heterogeneous figures, many also coming from the anti-bourgeois Left, reconsidered problems and the scope for solutions on their way to creating the first Fascism.[135] But the question of Nietzsche's place has always focused especially on Nazism. Certainly, the Nazis claimed Nietzsche as a precursor, and independent contemporary observers widely imputed a link. Still, in the face of such claims and assumptions, many since 1945 have insisted on radical disparity, both to defend Nietzsche and to avoid elevating the intellectual stature of Nazism. So eager was Walter Kaufmann to offer rescue, in his influential reinterpretation of 1950, that he tended to make Nietzsche an updated liberal humanist and individualist, a treatment that now seems one-sided at best.[136] Still, there remains an almost reflexive tendency to play down any link of Nietzsche to the Nazi departure. Typical is the confident insistence of one recent commentator that Nietzsche would surely have despised the "merely cruel monsters" of Nazism.[137]

It is pointed out again and again that Nietzsche valued superior individuals and was not concerned with races or evolutionary categories.[138] He was contemptuous of German chauvinism and all forms of mass politics, including political anti-Semitism. Indeed, he found the whole political sphere despicable in its contemporary liberal and/or German Bismarckian guises. Thus he is widely viewed as an anti-political thinker. Moreover, as he became newly central to humanistic scholarship in the 1980s, Nietzsche was treated primarily as a valued herald of postmodernism. The problems by then at issue seemed to require turning altogether from the old concern about Nietzsche's relationship with Nazism, whether it was to condemn or to defend him.

Although reaction against the earlier, too easy assimilation was surely appropriate, a limiting "either/or" tendency still lurks in the discussion, as if the choices are to take him as fundamentally a precursor of Nazism or to deny any link at all, as if it was crude and illegitimate even to raise the question. Our assumptions and preoccupations lead us to misconstrue the terms of the sort of relationship that might have been at work. Whether the Nazis read Nietzsche selectively, for their own purposes, or whether he would in fact have loathed them, is not really the issue. Certainly, the Third Reich was not merely implementing some prior Nietzschean blueprint, but a more subtle yet still crucial link remains possible.

Whereas most of those concerned with Nietzsche and postmodernism turned from any concern with Nietzsche's link to Nazism, Jacques Derrida denied that the question could be sidestepped: "if, within the still-open contours of an era, the only politics calling itself—proclaiming itself—Nietzschean will have been a Nazi one, then this is necessarily significant and must be questioned in all its consequences." But he cautioned that this does not mean rereading Nietzsche on the basis of what we think we know Nazism to have been. "I do not believe that we as yet know how to think what Nazism is. The task remains before us, and the political reading of the Nietzschean body or corpus is part of it."[139] Derrida was suggesting that we might begin more genuinely to understand the place of Nazism within our wider, "still-open" era if we find a way to treat Nietzsche and Nazism in tandem.

Bernard Yack noted that we cannot know whether Nietzsche would have been attracted or repelled by the particular forms of cruelty of the twentieth-century dictatorships. But that, he implied, is not the point, for "it is clear . . . that on many occasions [Nietzsche] expresses a longing for the reimposition of physical discipline and cruelty by a new ruling caste, and that he sometimes expects a cultural revolution to follow from this reimposition of discipline."[140] This is to suggest that Nietzsche's categories could genuinely have inspired and sustained those cruel dictatorships, whatever his own attitude toward them might have been. To carry the point a step further, probing those categories might enable us better to understand the novel and troubling content of those regimes.

To get at the sort of relationship that Derrida and Yack had in mind would not be to pin down some definitive meaning of Nietzsche, whose thinking was rich, multifaceted, and full of seemingly conflicting impulses. In his indispensable study of Nietzsche's impact in Germany, Steven Aschheim showed how protean was the Nietzschean legacy, how it helped to fuel the most disparate directions. So whereas it goes without saying that the Nazis read Nietzsche selectively, for their own purposes, in his case, more than most, *any* reading would be selective, *any* reading could be condemned as tendentious on some grounds. The Nazi appropriation, especially as articulated by genuine experts like Alfred Bäumler, cannot be dismissed as merely willful, arbitrary, and self-serving. Indeed, it was arguably less so than Kaufmann's, understandable and even laudable though his reading may have been in its time.

Virtually from the start some noted that, on one level or another, Nietzsche was genuinely important to the Nazis *even though* they read him selectively, in some ways even erroneously. Writing in 1937, Georges Bataille derided Nazi anti-Semitism and racism as a betrayal of Nietzsche but went on to recognize that "the teachings of Nietzsche 'mobilize' the will and the aggressive instincts" and "represent an incomparable seductive force."[141] Although as Bataille saw it, Nietzsche's thinking was self-contained and could not legitimately have been used to buttress some other doctrine, he also found it inevitable that politicians would seek to exploit it for their own purposes.

Writing in 1941, the *emigré* German scholar Karl Löwith disputed those claiming the Third Reich to be the fulfillment of Nietzsche, whose thinking, he noted, was alien to both the "'national' and the 'social' in National Socialism." It was also antithetical to Nazism in its treatment of Wagner, the Jews, and above all what was "German." But Löwith went on to insist that "this does not contradict the fact that Nietzsche became a catalyst of the [Nazi] 'movement' and determined its ideology in a decisive way.... 'Forerunners' have ever portrayed roads for others which they themselves did not travel."[142] Löwith carried the point further in his memoir of 1986: "A gulf separates [Nietzsche] from those who unscrupulously preach his message, yet he prepared the way for them that he himself did not follow. Even I cannot deny that the motto I wrote in my war diary, 'Have the courage to live dangerously,' leads in a roundabout and yet direct way from Nietzsche to Goebbels' heroic clichés about self-sacrifice."[143]

Franz Neumann similarly noted the gulf between Nietzschean individualism and Nazism or any form of authoritarianism. But stressing the importance of Nietzsche's hostility to Christianity, he concluded that "his reception in Germany favored the growth of National Socialism," providing it with "an intellectual father."[144]

More recently, Aschheim well articulated the need to get beyond the long-standing preoccupation with selectivity and distortion so that we can focus on strategies of transmutation and the extent of diffusion. Indeed, the Nietzschean admixture, he argued, proves to be indispensable for understanding the sources of what otherwise remains so anomalous in Nazism, its "attraction to the outmost limits, its arrival at a grotesque *novum* of human experience."[145] In other words, harping on the undoubted differences, deriding the Nazi embrace *a priori*, keeps us from understanding what the Nietzschean legacy contributed to the historically specific "frame of mind" from within which the extremes of Nazism became possible.

By now, in fact, what is arbitrary and tendentious is not to *posit* such a link but to deny or neglect it. The above indications help us to clarify what that link might entail, what we are and are not looking for. At issue is not some blueprint or faithful rendering but simply the difference it made to the direction and content of Nazism that Nietzsche had come before, articulating the terrain as he did, offering a particular understanding of the scope for novelty. And selectivity does not necessarily mean, as we tend to assume, taking this and not that in a conscious, manipulative way to serve some independent purpose already established and settled. The interplay between Nietzsche's categories and the Nazi self-understanding was more complex, dynamic, even dialectical, as those categories interacted with other factors to help to shape the Nazi sense of what needed to be done and what would be required to do it.

At the same time, what is at issue is not merely a matter of the unintended consequences of ideas, along the lines that Löwith suggested in the passages quoted above. To be sure, Nietzsche could not control the uses of his legacy, and, in any case, that legacy intersected, in the mix available to the Nazis, with concerns and ideas that he had not shared. But what Nietzsche was the first to find necessary and possible helped to shape the Nazi intention, which bore a certain relationship with Nietzsche's own. In this sense, again, the Nietzschean legacy directly affected Nazi vision and purpose; it was not an add-on chosen to buttress something already settled.

Grasping Nietzsche's place has been difficult partly because his critical response to the modern mainstream sometimes pointed in a proto-totalitarian direction but sometimes afforded a basis for denying or transcending that direction. However, it is not enough simply to pinpoint the contradiction, as if one could simply pick and choose. Rather, the particular terms of that contradiction illuminate the new possibilities and tensions that opened from within the wider new historical-political framework. And the relationship between Nietzsche and Nazism cannot be grasped without attention to that contradiction or tension.

To get deeper into the significance of Nazi selectivity, let us consider the treatment of Nietzsche by Alfred Bäumler, an ardent Nazi and professor of philosophy at the University of Berlin during the Nazi years, when he was recognized as Germany's leading Nietzsche scholar. In several influential works, most notably *Nietzsche, der Philosph und Politiker* (1931), he sought to construct a political Nietzscheanism congruent with Nazi purposes.[146] Even the critical Bataille noted that Bäumler brought genuine knowledge and theoretical rigor to the effort. If there was any way to make Nietzsche politically useful, said Bataille, Bäumler's conception, positing a people united by a common will to power, was surely it. But Bäumler explicitly marginalized Nietzsche's notion of eternal recurrence, thereby, as Bataille saw it, overtly violating Nietzsche's thought.[147] Although some have found the notion nonsensical, eternal recurrence was indeed central to Nietzsche's mature vision, yet its implications seem to be apolitical and even post-historical. But nuanced though his account was, Bataille did not do justice to the force of Bäumler's reading, in light of the wider frame of historical-political possibilities that Nietzsche had helped to articulate. At the same time, Bäumler, although he grasped better than Bataille a central tension in Nietzsche's thinking, was not quite getting at its basis.

Bäumler justified dismissing eternal recurrence by claiming that it had no connection with the central Nietzschean category of will to power; indeed, taken seriously, eternal recurrence would shatter the coherence of will to power.[148] Nietzsche, he insisted, was fundamentally a historical thinker—and anyone who thought historically as Nietzsche did could not be an individualist. Aschheim picked an appropriate quote from Nietzsche to show the side that Bäumler had in mind: "We are *more* than the individuals: we are the whole chain as well, with the tasks of all the futures of that chain."[149] Bäumler insisted that even the Nietzschean individual is part of such a chain of generations. Indeed, Nietzsche warranted the belief in something higher than the sovereignty of present individuals; the present must have reverence for the dead, whose sacrifices made possible our world, and must itself be prepared to sacrifice itself for the future.[150]

Bäumler was zeroing in on a symptomatic tension in Nietzsche's thinking revolving around will to power, eternal recurrence, politics, and history. But because he did not fully grasp its basis, Bäumler did not specify the stakes of opting for one Nietzschean direction to the exclusion of the other. At issue is, first, how the political and apolitical, historical and post-historical, impulses played against each other in Nietzsche and, second, how Bäumler's Nazi reading at once drew from and denied Nietzsche's diagnosis and prescription.

The first couple of steps in the Nietzschean reading of the situation, now that modernity had been loosed upon European civilization, are not in dispute. He was deeply opposed to both the liberal mainstream and the conventional socialist alternative. Only in his own time, he felt, was it becoming possible to grasp all that had fed into the dominant current orientations—and what would be necessary to oppose them and to offer a healthy, affirmative alternative at the same time. Modernity, it now seemed, had not been a new beginning but a particular kind of culmination of the whole Western tradition. Modernity entailed not merely secularization but the death of God, not merely "enlightenment" but the end of "the true world"—the end, in fact, of any sort of transcendent dimension or external, independent, objective world. Thus, critique had to encompass not simply "modernity" but the whole tradition that had yielded this particular modernity as its outcome.

As the implications of the death of God become clear, humanity seems first to be left with nothing but empty becoming. However, even without transcendence the world is not a formless heap but endlessly becomes some particular, although seemingly ever-provisional, way. For us, it is *this* particular way, encompassing all that we are capable of doing, thinking, seeing, and feeling. Still, the world becomes some particular way only because human beings *act* in some particular way. Only through the exercise of human "will to power" does empty becoming take on some particular content, does some particular world come to be. So Nietzsche offered, most basically, a radical voluntarism, a deeper sense of the scope for human agency or will. From this perspective, belief in "objectivity," "realism," and "the true world" are ways of eschewing responsibility, and "power" is the neutral glue that enables will to have impact and thus the world to take on some particular shape.

Even as the resultant of will to power, however, any particular world could only come to be through an unedifying historical process involving a contingent, even freakish concatenation of lies, errors, accidents, and self-serving actions. Although the aggregate outcome at each moment gives content to the otherwise empty becoming, there is no transcendent reason why it is as it is; there is no transcendent sanction for it. Historical accounts seemed to show up the sheer groundlessness of anything that has come to be through history.

In his early meditation *On the Uses and Disadvantages of History for Life*, Nietzsche expressed quite explicitly the sort of nausea he felt at this modern revelation of the nature of a world that comes to be through nothing but history. We moderns, he said, are caught up in "the tireless unspinning and historicizing of all there has ever been." History dissolves everything "that possesses life," just as it had, partly through the agency of David Friedrich Strauss, the Christianity in which Nietzsche himself had been raised. And this makes for the "dismantling of all foundations, their dissolution into a continual evolving that flows ceaselessly away." There may have been something great and noble about the founding of Christianity, but between Christianity's founding and its historical success "there lies a very dark and earthy stratum of passion, error, thirst for power and honor."[151] The mode of historical understanding that opens in a purely secular world is thus corrosive, for it "always brings to light so much that is false, crude, inhuman, absurd, violent that the mood of pious illusion in which alone anything that wants to live can live necessarily crumbles away."[152] So the modern hypertrophy of historical-mindedness threatened to undermine action, not by breeding complacency but by undermining the foothold for commitment.[153]

At that early point, Nietzsche was suggesting that we need the illusion of some better reason for things if we are to go on believing, committing, acting, recreating the world. And historical-mindedness was but one part of the wider modern package that portended a weakening of will—and thus nihilism. Despite what is still loosely assumed in some reaches of the culture, Nietzsche himself was no nihilist but cared deeply for the world, cared that there be value and meaning. However, we do not simply find value and meaning built in; they come to be only through the creative human response, stemming from will to power, that imposes some particular structure, makes the world some particular way, giving it whatever value and meaning it has.

Jerry-built and merely contingent though it is, the actual present world is in one sense precious, for it is all we have. But as the modern culmination of the Western tradition, the present in Nietzsche's own time was coming to appear in an especially problematic light, for two distinguishable but related reasons. Present culture was life-debasing, and it was not sustainable. Yet the present situation also seemed to portend a pivot into a healthier culture, even a superior mode of being. The new cultural self-awareness emerging first in Nietzsche himself was the beginning.

We come to understand that the present, including its assumptions about both objectivity and morality, rests on a particular, life-debasing form of will to power. As the culmination of the Western tradition, the liberal mainstream, with its characteristic egalitarianism and humanitarianism, was the outcome especially of Judeo-Christian moral categories, including, in Nietzsche's terms, a solicitude for the weak. We come to recognize at the same time that this entire package is merely contingent—and thus open to unearthing, deconstruction. To deconstruct the present was to open the way to action to impose an alternative, leaving behind conventional moral categories and the enervating notion that the world is objective, given independently of human will.

Before pondering the terms of Nietzsche's alternative, let us consider what such extravagant musings on the part of a one-time philology professor could have meant in light of the historical-political break around the turn of the century, when the vogue for Nietzsche began. Aschheim traced Nietzsche's impact on an entire generation of Germans to a "religious crisis," a crisis of Protestantism.[154] Nietzsche was not the source, but those affected embraced his thinking as they sought to respond, and his categories thus helped to shape the understanding of post-Christian alternatives. But much of his immediate impact was superficial: "Live dangerously" was a favored Nietzschean motto, as Löwith recalled in a passage quoted above. It is doubtful that any of those reading Nietzsche aspired to be part of "the herd." Insofar as the point was the scope for will, even an invitation to "hardness," the importance was more determinate, although various directions were still possible.

Nietzsche's most significant immediate impact was in adding a layer of justification to the new determination to address population questions that we discussed above. As Aschheim put it, Nietzsche's "masculine and militant prescriptions for regeneration" seemed especially relevant in light of "the perception of pervasive decadence and degeneration and the accompanying search for new sources of physical and mental health."[155] Although Nietzsche himself was not a eugenicist or even a social Darwinist, and although some eugenicists and social Darwinists explicitly rejected him, he seemed to provide a basis for distinguishing between vital and decadent forces, forces worthy and unworthy of propagation. So even an early Nietzsche scholar like Raoul Richter portrayed Nietzsche as the philosopher of biological anthropology and selective breeding.[156]

More generally, Nietzsche's categories helped both to reassure and to energize those who worried that conventional humanitarian principles, based largely on Christianity, were impeding what needed to be done. It was a human responsibility actually to carry out eugenics measures, even in the face of conventional moral strictures. For the relatively moderate Schallmayer, Nietzsche had contributed to a new morality conducive to the development of the highest community powers. The more rabid Alexander Tille invoked Nietzsche's dismissal of Christian ethics as he explicitly advocated "helping nature" by killing the unproductive.[157]

Although the juxtapositions were somewhat arbitrary, the Nietzschean admixture added essential fuel to the eugenicist direction, as we will see in Chapters 4 and 7. But Bäumler was positing a deeper relationship between Nietzsche and Nazism; as he saw it, the whole Nazi project, not just the willingness to go "beyond good and evil," was fundamentally Nietzschean. So we return to the question of Nietzsche's vision and its political implications.

In pondering the scope for new creation, Nietzsche offered a number of indications of what he thought had now become possible, likely, and/or desirable. They clustered as essentially two directions that were ultimately incompatible, although there was a crucial relationship between them. One was explicitly political and even anticipated something like totalitarianism. The other was apolitical, even post-historical, and entailed a premium on individual self-creation and innocent edification.

In some of his best-known passages, Nietzsche envisioned the first contours of a different politics based on a new form of collective action. The vision emerges, along with much else, in the oft-quoted, almost hysterical, opening of "Why I am destiny," the concluding section of his late retrospective work, *Ecce Homo*:

> I know my fate. One day my name will be associated with the memory of something tremendous—a crisis without equal on earth, the most profound collision of conscience, a decision that was conjured up *against* everything that had been believed, demanded, hallowed so far. . . . My truth is *terrible*, for so far one has called *lies* truth. . . .
>
> I contradict as has never been contradicted before and am nevertheless the opposite of a No-saying spirit. I am a bringer of glad tidings like no one before me; I know tasks of such elevation that any notion of them has been lacking so far; only beginning with me are there hopes again. For all that, I am necessarily also the man of calamity. For when truth enters into a fight with the lies of millennia, we shall have upheavals, a convulsion of earthquakes, a moving of mountains and valleys, the like of which has never been dreamed of. The concept of politics will have merged entirely with a war of spirits; all power structures of the old society will have been exploded—all of them are based on lies: there will be wars the like of which have never yet been seen on earth. It is only beginning with me that the earth knows *great politics*.[158]

Bäumler quoted the later portion of the above and was clearly fascinated with Nietzsche's proclamation of "great politics," linked to organization, unity, and ongoing struggle.[159] In other passages as well, Nietzsche associated the new politics with war and violence, which would manifest the essential upsurge in energy, vitality, and will to impose form. In this regard, he was fond of pitting Russia, as a kind of sleeping giant, against smug, self-satisfied "Europe":

> The strength to will, and to will something for a long time . . . is strongest and most amazing by far in that enormous empire . . . where Europe, as it were, flows back into Asia, in Russia. There the strength to will has long been accumulated and stored up, there the will—uncertain whether as a will to negate or as a will to affirm—is waiting menacingly to be discharged, to borrow a pet phrase from our physicists today.
>
> . . . [what I want is] such an increase in the menace of Russia that Europe would have to resolve to become menacing, too, namely, *to acquire one will* by means of a new caste that would rule Europe, a long terrible will of its own that would be able to cast its goals millennia hence—so the long-drawn-out comedy of its many splinter states as well as its dynastic and democratic splinter wills would come to an end. The time for petty politics is over: the very next century will bring the fight for the dominion of the earth—the *compulsion* to large-scale politics.[160]

Precisely in its sense of long-term historical responsibility, that politics would be resolutely opposed to liberal democracy. And it rested explicitly on the will and capacity for large-scale organization, not merely the superior self-consciousness of certain individuals. The potential of Russia was striking in this regard as well:

> Democracy has ever been the form of decline in organizing power. . . . In order that there may be institutions, there must be a kind of will, instinct or imperative, which is anti-liberal to the point of malice: the will to tradition, to authority, to responsibility for centuries to come, to the solidarity of chains of generations, forward and backward *ad infinitum*. When this will is present, something like the *Imperium Romanum* is founded; or like Russia, the *only* power today which has endurance, which can wait, which can still promise something—Russia, the concept that suggests the opposite of the wretched European nervousness and system of small states, which has entered a critical phase with the founding of the German *Reich*.[161]

The accent in these passages is on anything but individualism or edifying self-cultivation. Rather, Nietzsche envisioned a new politics resting, precisely as for Bäumler, on a strong sense of the history-making quality of collective enterprise; in acting, the present understands its debt to the past and its concomitant "responsibility for centuries to come." Such collective action to forge a world for the future required organizing power and collective will. The task fell neither to human beings in general nor to superior individuals *qua* individuals but to a new caste or elite, defined by its sense of the challenge, its refusal to make excuses, its capacity to organize, its willingness to act. Its immediate task would be to create the new political instrument—to galvanize a single collective will, overcoming the splintering of liberal democracy. And the new politics would obviously require toughness, especially the courage to transcend conventional moral categories and merely personal scruples. It would also entail the exercise of violence, which, much as for Sorel and Pareto, would at once reflect and reinforce the commitment that alone builds worlds. Such violence had nothing to do with mere resentment or nihilism, with self-indulgent sadism or cruelty.

But even as he anticipated and seemed to welcome a new great politics, Nietzsche sensed a downside to any such inflation of the political, so he also found it necessary to think beyond, to specify a kind of post-political alternative, even an antidote to the anticipated inflation of politics. The two strands can be found side by side, in tension, in his thinking. Still, insofar as the second was an antidote to aspects of the first, it can be taken as Nietzsche's own final position. What mattered, what gave the world value, was a particular mode of individual life revolving around the most problematic of Nietzsche's mature categories, *amor fati*, eternal recurrence, and the innocence of becoming. Together, they afforded antidotes to the combination of resentment and inflating responsibility that a rigorously modern historical sense proved to entail.[162]

To grasp, from within the new secular framework, the capriciousness through which our particular world has come to be, and the finitude of the range of modes of life that has thereby become possible for us as individuals, seemed to breed a kind of resentment against history itself. Overcoming this resentment of contingency and finitude required *amor fati,* loving one's fate, genuinely willing and affirming the whole totality of things, including all the "dreadful accident" that had produced this, our particular world. This orientation has nothing to do with inventing some fictional past, making it up to suit one's fancy or to serve some other purpose; on the contrary, it entails precisely affirmation of the actual, in its finitude and particularity. The point is not to imagine alternative pasts but fully to affirm the actual particular past, all of which was necessary for the present, my mode of living included, to be as it is. "My consolation," said Nietzsche, "is that everything that has been is eternal."[163]

However, the present moment is not only the resultant of the whole past but also the pivot into an undetermined future. Nietzsche suggested that just as "everything that has been is eternal," everything we do affects what the world becomes—and thus endures: "What I do or do not do now is as important for everything that is yet to come as is the greatest event of the past: in this tremendous perspective of effectiveness all actions appear equally great and small."[164] And because of this insight into the permanent weight of what we do, Nietzsche could write a few years later: "I myself am fate and have conditioned existence for all eternity."[165] Yet though, when attacking metaphysics and ideals of suprahistorical truth, Nietzsche consistently held that human beings create a world, as opposed to discovering a world already there, he increasingly found it necessary to deny the scope for novelty and creativity, the idea of the world as created— even through willed human action.[166] This tack stemmed from quite explicit anxieties about agency, responsibility, guilt, and judgment. As long as there is scope for novelty and creativity, endless, relentless responsibility for the future remained even to those who, through *amor fati,* managed to affirm the whole past that had produced their present.

Even after his proclamation of the death of God, Nietzsche found the shadow of the divine lurking in our notions of novelty and creativity. That shadow will "cease to darken our minds" only when we have managed fully to de-deify the world. The transcendent God had long seemed to be the creator of the world and the judge of human beings. With the death of that God, the idea of the world as created remained, but in the merely historical world, creation seemed to result from ongoing human activity. Having inherited or usurped God's creative attributes, we feel responsible for what the world becomes. This heightened sense of responsibility entails heightened anxiety about guilt and judgment, for in this purely historical world we do not know what will become of what we do, and there is only the capricious future to judge.[167]

So what mode of being and experience would afford an antidote not only to resentment of finitude and contingency but also to this inflating sense of responsibility? By adding eternal recurrence to *amor fati,* Nietzsche sought a mode of total affirmation encompassing not only the past but also the future, not only everything that produced the present moment but also everything that will result from it. Eternal recurrence, positing the world as "a circular movement of absolutely identical series," means that whatever the future holds, it will do no more than come back around to this, this moment, my me-ness now, in all its finitude.[168]

Rather than a stepping stone into a different future, every moment is at once a culmination and a microcosm of all that has ever been and ever will be. Although endlessly becoming, the world is complete as a finite particular; we experience reality as, for all time, this way—this particular closed system, and not some other. What is to be affirmed, then, is not simply the past that resulted in this present but the whole closed system of which this present moment is a necessary part. The experience of *amor fati* becomes total.

On the first level, this mode of eternal recurrence makes even more appalling the capriciousness of the coming to be of everything—my own life included. We know the sort of stuff that went into making this moment what it is, yet we find ourselves confined to this particular world for ever. For Nietzsche, the ultimate life-affirming mode is the capacity fully to face up to this fact and yet genuinely to say I would not have it otherwise. Every moment is experienced affirmatively, as an end in itself. Nietzsche could thereby envision a world, a mode of living, "without goal, unless the joy of the circle is itself a goal.[169]

This was to restore, as Nietzsche put it in a telling phrase, "the innocence of becoming": "Becoming has been deprived of its innocence when any being-such-and-such is traced back to will, to purposes, to acts of responsibility: the doctrine of the will has been invented essentially for the purpose of punishment, that is, because one wanted to impute guilt." But insofar as we live in the mode of eternal recurrence, we understand

> That no one gives man his qualities—neither God, nor society, nor his parents and ancestors, nor he himself. . . . No one is responsible for man's being there at all, for his being such-and-such, or for his being in these circumstances or in this environment. The fatality of his essence is not to be disentangled from the fatality of all that has been and will be. . . . One is necessary, one is a piece of fatefulness, one belongs to the whole, one is in the whole; there is nothing which could judge, measure, compare, or sentence our being, for that would mean judging, measuring, comparing, or sentencing the whole. But there is nothing besides the whole. That nobody is responsible any longer, that the mode of being may not be traced back to a *causa prima*, that the world does not form a unity either as a sensorium or as "spirit"—that alone is the great liberation: with this alone is the innocence of becoming restored.[170]

As the ultimate denial of novelty and creativity, eternal recurrence dissolves the imperative, resulting from an experience of tension with the resultant of history so far, to make a different future. With everything already "here," the world is complete at every moment, and we feel no call to relentless great politics. Because there is nothing that needs to be done, we are free not only from resentment of the past but also from the responsibility and guilt that remained as a shadow even in a purely secular world. Purposiveness itself drops out, and we experience ourselves not as creating the world but as happening with the world. Although action continues, it is experienced as innocent play, even "dance," as opposed to responsible, purposive, history-making creation. Thus Nietzsche's reference to "'play,' the useless—as the ideal of him who is overfull of strength, as 'childlike'."[171]

So whereas the future brings no redemption, we can have redemption now from the feeling of limitation, the anxiety of ongoing responsibility, the potential for guilt and judgment. "Heaven" is no longer something to come but a mode of present living and acting for every moment; "the kingdom" is now.[172]

Nietzschean play or dance might entail a premium on edifying *self*-creation, even "life as literature," as Alexander Nehamas put it in his indispensable exploration of this angle. And some such accent on individualism has been the rule for sympathetic observers seeking to distance Nietzsche from Nazism. But this playful, individualistic direction presupposed the post-political and post-historical mode of experience bound up with eternal recurrence. It is not to be understood in vulgar Nietzschean terms simply as the scope for imposing fictions, reinventing or edifying oneself, in light of the death of God and the waning of "the true world." The playful dance that Nietzsche envisioned is possible *only* in the post-political, post-historical mode that the embrace of eternal recurrence makes possible. From Nietzsche's perspective, the alternative to that post-political, post-historical mode at this pivotal moment is not some facile fictionalizing but a great political mode entailing inflated responsibility and increased weight, precisely as opposed to innocent play.

Only a few superior individuals, comprising a new aristocracy, would be capable of such a life-affirming orientation to the world; the weak would be unable even to fathom it.[173] But then what relationship was this elite to have to the rest, which Nietzsche so notoriously dismissed as "the herd"? We noted that the political mode, too, assumed differentiation and a special value-creating role for an elite. In that mode, the elite is functional; its members experience themselves *not* as their own justification but precisely as historically responsible—responsible for and to history. They thus must be capable of a particular relationship with the others, including mobilization and large-scale organization.

The post-political mode would entail the opposite: "a good and healthy aristocracy" must be able to experience itself as its own justification; its value is not based on some socio-historical function. And although its members must be willing to subordinate others as necessary, such subordination is not in itself essential to their value-creating role.[174] No dominant political role is required; indeed, no political role at all is necessary. Although in one sense this mode of life is also an instance of will to power, these hardy spirits experience no responsibility for doing anything in particular. They give the world value simply by living, experiencing the world, in the life-affirming mode of which they are uniquely capable.[175] Nothing could be further from Nazism or totalitarianism.[176]

But it remains crucial—and not just for his intellectual biography or posthumous reputation—that Nietzsche both affirmed and sought to transcend the new "great political" direction he anticipated. And to conceive his place in the overall intellectual mediation, we must avoid emphasizing either to the exclusion of the other. Instead, we must hold on to the tension, both sides of what the emerging inflation of politics seemed to portend.

Bäumler was on the right track in suggesting that the key tensions in Nietzsche revolved around the oppositions between eternal recurrence and will to power and between individualism and historical-mindedness. But he was characterizing the tensions prejudicially, even symptomatically suppressing aspects of Nietzsche, as he justified his Nazified reading. It is not, as Bäumler suggested, that eternal recurrence shatters will to power; we have seen that to live in the mode of eternal recurrence entails will to power and gives value to the world. But that mode does dissolve the sort of *political* will that for Bäumler characterized Nazism, and Bäumler was not prepared to ask why Nietzsche had pushed on in that direction. In the same way, in the last analysis it was not, as Bäumler contended, that a historical thinker could not be an individualist; we have seen that Nietzsche stressed a particular mode of individualism precisely in response to what his historical thinking had revealed. But that individualism did undermine the premium on history-making collective action that Bäumler found central, and here again, the student seems to have been reluctant to probe the reasons for the master's emphases.

The tension between Nietzsche's political and post-political directions manifested underlying tensions in the new terrain itself, which, even as it opened the way to a new great politics, included the shadow that Nietzsche had foreseen. And those embracing the new political direction would get the shadow as well, even though Bäumler sidestepped engagement with it. The relentlessness of the challenge, the demand for unity and total mobilization, and the embrace of grandiose, "thousand-year" tasks opened the way to, yet demanded the suppression of, modes of experience that could come to be imagined, and desired, only as the scope for political action became limitless. A longing for innocence and play would be paramount. Thus, in part, the shrillness, the restlessness, the sense that the pace must be accelerated to keep from backsliding, that proved characteristic of the totalitarian departure.

Although individualism and the scope for post-political "dance" surely seem more attractive today, the proto-totalitarian political direction followed just as logically from within the framework that Nietzsche had outlined. Stemming from a particular, and particularly innovative, reading of the wider new terrain, that framework reflected Nietzsche's sense, first, of the gaps, tensions, and blind spots in the modern mainstream and, second, of their increasing salience. Conversely, that sense enabled him to offer new categories that helped to structure and articulate the new terrain in a particular, extreme way. Had it not been based on insight into genuine creases and gaps, the response of this seething outsider could not have had the impact it did.

Nietzsche's vision could at once inspire those seeking a new radicalism and, in affecting their sense of the challenge, the possibilities, and the imperatives, help to channel their responses in certain directions. Above all, his way of blocking out the new space suggested the scope for transcending conventional moral categories, mainstream political alternatives, even the criteria that had long differentiated Left and Right.[177] The goal for action was less important than the overall orientation, the mode of action itself, involving will, commitment, and organization. To act effectively from within the new terrain would require a courageous sense of world-historical responsibility and hardness in the face of humanitarian imperatives. Having Nietzsche as part of the mix enhanced the likelihood of precisely the "great politics" he prophesied. Nietzsche was indeed "dangerous," just as he proclaimed himself to be, and for precisely the reasons that he understood himself to be.[178]

Intellectual innovation and new possibility

Because the intellectuals we have considered found themselves in the same new universe resulting from the late nineteenth-century historical-political break, their responses overlapped to yield a novel cluster that helped to shape the subsequent perception of problems, possibilities, and priorities. Nobody could have thought in these terms in 1830, or even 1860—not de Maistre or de Tocqueville, not even Mill or Marx. Still, what emerged at this point was only a cluster of new ideas in play, not some finished ideology, and certainly not "the ideology of totalitarianism." That cluster suggested some of the terms of a new political direction, but how those terms might intersect, and what sort of dynamic would result, was not at all clear.

Although the components could be shuffled in various ways, it seemed that some combination of will, commitment, courage, discipline, leadership, expertise, mobilization, and organization could afford the new mode of collective action necessary in light of the new sense of the human relationship to history. Hostile though it was to conventional parliamentary democracy, the new thinking obviously portended anything but passive authoritarianism or mere conservatism. Nor was it merely elitist, assuming that only the elites count, that their very being is a value in itself. Yet the new action demanded differentiation, which might encompass an array from new modes of leadership to new roles for technical expertise. Most importantly, action demanded *new* elites, defined by their capacity to play the role that seemed to open. That role required a new kind of relationship between elites and masses, including mobilization for the modes of involvement necessary. This would entail, on some level, nurturing and focusing the human ethical capacity. At the same time, the new forms of action might necessitate going beyond conventional morality, bound up with assumptions about the human place in the world that were coming to seem outmoded.

Such action might not be rational in a conventional means–ends sense, but conventionally calculative thinking was coming to seem part of the problem. Means and ends were not so easily separated, for with history more open-ended, ends were less foreseeable. In some ways, the willingness and capacity to act in the new mode were themselves decisive. This was not to warrant mere "blind activism" or "activity for its own sake"; it was simply better to conceive what a superior alternative to the mainstream had to entail in a world that now seemed less predictable and ever-provisional. At the same time, the new thinking seemed to suggest a positive role for non-rational collective images—myths—which might galvanize commitment, enthusiasm, and the essential capacity to act. Collective action could also entail violence, which might at once reflect and reinforce that essential commitment and capacity.

This cluster pointed not only beyond the liberal mainstream but also beyond the mainstream Marxist–socialist alternative. The socialist tradition had been essential in positing the need and the scope for a systematic alternative and in suggesting something of the new relationship between individual and society that any such alternative would involve. But experience with the modern liberal dispensation had made it clearer why an alternative might be desirable and what it would have to entail. In some respects, the socialist and mainstream Marxist traditions seemed to have misconstrued the underlying problems and the range of plausible responses. It became possible to argue that the key modern problem was not capitalism, however exploitative or dehumanizing it had so far proved, but the wider culture of bourgeois liberalism, fostering particularism, egotism, and cynicism. The problem was very different from, and certainly not reducible to, the conditions specifically affecting the working class, legitimate though working-class grievances might be. Thus the scope for the necessary alternative did not depend on the maturation of the proletariat through the experience to which it was uniquely subject under industrial capitalism. Rather, the alternative depended on a capacity to organize and act that stemmed from modes of consciousness, will, and commitment not reducible to class.

From this perspective, what modernity had come to entail so far was not so much "capitalism," too easily reified, taken as a coherent system, but a way of leaving private decisions ultimate, partly the result of an earlier, delimited understanding of freedom, of the public/private relationship, and of the scope for collective action. Capitalism was the aggregate of economic decisions made from within that delimited liberal framework. The key was to politicize or even spiritualize the economy on the basis of the new consciousness and ethical-political will. This might entail central planning from above or some sort of mandatory corporativist economic self-regulation from below.

Put more generally, the alternative to the mainstream was not to be some utopia created once and for all but a different orientation that would warrant and underpin ongoing collective action. Therefore, to address the problems of the modern economy was not a matter of replacing "capitalism" with some other system but to deal with them on an ongoing basis, recognizing the need for experiment in an open-ended world.

On a deeper level, the recasting entailed a rethinking of praxis, the interaction between consciousness or theoretical understanding and world-making action. Looking at what seemed an increasingly uncertain Marxism, Sorel and Pareto posited a kind of bifurcation that denied the unity of theory and practice that Marx had found possible. Intellectuals could understand and, at most, advocate, but it fell to others to commit, to act, to create a systematic alternative. In their very different ways, Lenin, Gentile, and Nietzsche insisted, like Marx, on the scope for a radical unity, although all three went beyond Marx to a different

sense in which knowing is doing—and arguably to a more consistent understanding of praxis. Whereas Marx had retained Hegel's *a priori* and teleological
frame, the new, post-Marxian way of bringing understanding and acting
together was necessarily bound up with the new sense of historical openness and
creativity. Insofar as understanding cannot encompass some overall structure or
final end, praxis, the unification of understanding and action, could not mean
what it did for Marx. It becomes bound up with grasping the need to act, with
the determination to act, with understanding the requirements for action. Again,
something like collective non-rational images might become part of the mix as
understanding and action, theory and practice, come together in a new way. But
in light of the number of variables and the uncertainty of the mix, the place that
myth might assume was not at all clear.

Indeed, the mix included lots of uncertain implications as well as some symptomatic tensions and contrasting priorities among the components. Still,
precisely because all the components were operating from within the same new
terrain, a certain common channeling proved to be operative even in the face of
manifest differences. One example will make the point clear.

Frustrated that his new eugenics was not affecting government policy,
Wilhelm Schallmayer attacked humanistic education as the underlying source of
the societal failure to grasp the new biological perspective and imperative. Those
humanistic lags were keeping modern humanity from addressing its essential
problems.[179] The manifest content of this argument could not be more opposed
to Gentile's, which called for a renewed emphasis on humanistic education to
nurture the ethical capacity and sought to counter growing demands for a
greater technical thrust in Italian education.

But this difference in the evaluation of humanistic education was less important than the fact that Schallmayer and Gentile both stressed the new centrality
of education in light of the new collective action to be undertaken. Each thinker
saw the need and scope for more grandiose collective action, and each saw
obstacles that, if not addressed, would not only undercut the positive possibility
but also make the present situation worse. So a sense of now or never, of impatience, of frustration, mixed with the sense of opportunity. It was necessary not
only to use the educational system more overtly, with broadly political ends in
mind, but to do so in a particular, delimited way.

Prior to the First World War, we have only the still-molten strands that these
intellectual responses engendered. Without the fortuitous, unforeseen length and
strain of the war, these ideas could never have had anything like the same political impact. But as it was, they intersected not just with the war but with
contingent national experiences of the war to yield potentially explosive new
political possibilities.

4 Innovative departures in the wake of the Great War

The Great War as crucible

Whatever the significance of earlier intellectual antecedents, it is widely recognized that the contingent occurrence of the First World War created the conditions of possibility for the later totalitarian regimes, with all their troubling outcomes.[1] The novel political departures in Russia, Italy, and Germany grew directly from the war, to some degree playing off each other as they did so. And the perceptions and priorities that fueled them stemmed in important measure from the new experiences that the war proved to entail as a result of its unforeseen length and difficulty. Thus, for example, Victor Chernin's comment that "the moral nature of the Bolshevik Revolution was inherited from the war in which it was born."[2] In the same vein, Ian Kershaw insisted that "the First World War made Hitler possible"; what happened under Hitler was not presaged by imperial Germany but by the experience of the war and its aftermath.[3]

The first challenge is to pinpoint the supranational, historically specific dimensions of the war that opened the way to totalitarianism, and scholars from Elie Halévy to Omer Bartov have established some of the essential connections. Writing in 1936, Halévy proposed a kind of baseline that has held up remarkably well. Finding the resulting new regimes characteristic of the era, he described them not as mere dictatorships but as *tyrannies*, connoting something provisional, an emergency expedient as opposed to a full-scale system of government:

> The era of tyrannies dates from August 1914, that is, from the time when the belligerent nations turned to a system which can be defined as follows:
>
> (a) In the economic sphere, greatly expanded state control of all means of production, distribution, and exchange;—and, at the same time, an appeal by the governments to the leaders of workers' organizations to help them in implementing this state control—hence syndicalism and corporatism along with *étatisme*.
> (b) In the intellectual sphere, state control of thought, in two forms: one negative, through the suppression of all expressions of opinion deemed unfavorable to the national interest; the other positive, through what we shall call the organization of enthusiasm.[4]

So the war proved to mean something like total mobilization, including coordination of the economy, most famously in Germany, first with Walther Rathenau's
Kriegsrohstoffabteilung (KRA), or war raw materials office. By the end of 1916,
Germany had developed a militarized economy, with all aspects of economic life
coordinated for the war effort. Under the supervision of the military leadership,
state agencies, big business, and the trade unions were brought into close collaboration. But as Halévy noted, drawing on earlier observers like Harold Lasswell,
the "totality" of this particular war also entailed a broader mobilization of
opinion—or enthusiasm—through propaganda.[5] Such mobilization suggested the
scope for a new relationship between government and people, or, from another
angle, between elites and masses, in response to an unforeseen need.

The unprecedented extent and scale, the level of killing and maiming, the
destruction of famous monuments, the damage to the countryside, the frightening
uses of advanced technology, all gave the war an apocalyptic aura that fundamentally affected wider notions of what the world could hold, for good or for ill,
thereafter. Some, crying "never again," sought to assure that this would indeed
prove to have been a war to end all wars. But in bringing home the potential for
war on a vastly expanded scale, the First World War also suggested very different
novel possibilities, including the scope for overcoming the national vulnerabilities it
had revealed. So others learned different lessons, which those seeking to end war
tended to view in conventionally moralistic terms and thus proved singularly ill-
prepared to grasp. For to seek seriously to come to terms with modern war did not
have to mean mere nihilism, or some cult of violence, reflecting the war's brutalizing effects. The reality revealed—or created—by the war suggested the need
even to adjust moral categories, including the understanding of violence in relation
to moral commitment, as older notions came to seem questionable or outmoded.

Everywhere the carnage enhanced the already prominent fears of degeneration—of this or that national community, of Western civilization itself. In the event
of war, the best are killed off as the shirkers and the handicapped survive. Many of
those seeking to draw lessons during the war concluded that such dilemmas and
trade-offs would have to be addressed in the aftermath.[6] As a result, the war intensified concerns with population policy, which now seemed bound up with national
survival and thus suggested expanded collective responsibility and the need for
expanded collective action. The notion that government should intervene in
matters of sexuality and reproduction won greater acceptance.[7]

Whereas most of those at the front came to hate the war, viewing it with irony
and sarcasm, the experience also entailed for many, as the other side of the coin,
a two-sided sense of comradeship and separation. In some, the sense of separation and differentiation yielded a corresponding sense of constituting the germ
of a new elite capable of spearheading fruitful innovation thanks precisely to its
wartime experience. In Omer Bartov's effective delineation, this new sense of
mission, stemming from the higher morality of the trenches, reflected the imper-
sonality and the recast ideas of heroism and sacrifice that the mechanization of
warfare had called forth, replacing the hollow, outmoded ideals that had accompanied the outbreak of fighting in 1914.[8]

More generally, Bartov noted that the war's apocalyptic aura combined with the seemingly endless resources of new technology to profoundly affect the European psyche, producing in some a fascination with extremity.[9] This syndrome was famously explored, and celebrated, by Ernst Jünger in his *Storm of Steel* (*Stahlgewittern*) of 1920, then developed further in such works as *Total Mobilization* (1930) and *Der Arbeiter* (1932). As Jünger saw it, "total mobilization" characterized a society that had genuinely grasped the meaning of the war, the wider global tendency that it had revealed.[10] Weapons and tools, soldiers and workers, were essentially equivalent, for war and industrial production equally demanded relentless organization, mechanization, and will. Abbott Gleason noted that a vision much like Jünger's informed Leon Trotsky's call for the militarization of labor in the Soviet Union in the early 1920s.[11] And certainly the notion that labor was a national task, that productive labor and military service were closely related, equally subject to mobilization, would be central to the overall totalitarian departure, even though Jünger himself found Nazism too plebeian to merit his endorsement.

Bartov also argued that from within the new apocalyptic framework, "the occurrence of industrial killing, inevitably accompanied by its representation, made its recurrence all the more likely"—even on a vaster scale. Indeed, Auschwitz would have been inconceivable without the precedent of the Great War, which not only entailed the advent of mechanized killing but also suggested the scope for an even greater moral remove. In light of the new elitist ethos, such industrial killing could be taken as a noble duty dictated by a more profound and relevant morality.[12] Although Bartov may force the argument in suggesting that the traumatic experience of war led to a determination to assure that, the next time, all the victims would be confined to the opposing side, his notion that the First World War produced a new, supranational range of possibility from within which the Holocaust itself became possible is surely convincing.[13]

It is well known that the war erupted as the mainstream socialism of the Second International faced increasing turmoil. In Germany, the SPD's success in the 1912 Reichstag elections paradoxically brought home the limits of the parliamentary strategy and led Rosa Luxemburg, for example, to press more aggressively for a radical alternative. In the Habsburg empire, the war erupted amid growing concerns about nationality questions and their interface with socialist aspirations. In Italy, the imperialist Libyan War occasioned a Socialist Party turn to the left that brought Benito Mussolini to prominence. The immediate questions of strategy at issue in every case had deeper implications for the condition of Marxism as a framework for transcending the bourgeois order.

And then the initial socialist support for war in most Western European countries profoundly shook assumptions. The reasons for this decision in Germany, France, and Austria, for example, were complex, and certainly not to be reduced to simple patriotic euphoria or nationalist sell-out. Although the socialists can be faulted for not having faced up to them earlier, at issue were genuine dilemmas in light of differential national development. As long as revolution was not yet at hand, support for the national war effort could be justified in orthodox terms as necessary to protect the longer-term prospects for socialism on the domestic level. But the self-understanding of international socialism, as leading the way to something superior, had rested to a considerable extent on the assumption that, in light of international proletarian solidarity, socialists and workers would not support such a war—indeed, would keep it from happening. The fact that it did happen further strained the pretense of a settled orthodoxy for the foreseeable future. But if socialist votes for war credits raised questions about the scope for an international Socialism, socialist support also afforded a new sense of the scope, under certain circumstances, for national solidarity transcending what had seemed irrevocably divisive issues.

The coming of war also occasioned some deeper socialist thinking, especially in light of the wider new historical-political frame, about the relationship between the war and socialism. In a more open-ended world, subject to human will, the war might prove to be in some sense revolutionary, although the precise contours could not be foreseen. Even before the war, Lenin and Mussolini had each been addressing the wider impasse of Marxism, and, although their reasons were diametrically opposed, each welcomed the war as a revolutionary opportunity.[14]

In establishing the conditions for totalitarianism that emerged from the war, Halévy did not address the layer of national differentiation, but he implied that only a thin line separated the tyrannies from the democracies after the First World War. Indeed, he warned that if, as had come to seem possible by 1936, Berlin and Rome provoked another war, the democracies would not be able to retain their liberal parliamentary institutions. More generally, "when the war begins again, it will consolidate the 'tyrannical' idea in Europe."[15] Yet the outcome, when war did return, was far from what Halévy had in mind. Whereas he thought the pressures of modern war were themselves sufficient to yield tyrannies, the departures after 1918, and the outcomes after 1939, make clear the need for differentiating elements. The experience of total war was necessary but not sufficient for the actual emergence of totalitarianism. Even Bartov's categories do not get at the place of idiosyncratic national factors in connecting the novel features of the war with the content of the subsequent totalitarian departures.

Although obviously all experienced the war's novel features, the war experience, and the way it played out in the aftermath, varied among the belligerents in important respects. Some of the national differences, which help to explain why some were especially quick to embrace new possibilities, are obvious. Russia and Germany suffered military defeat, and Italy, although sharing in the victory, went into war bitterly divided over the wisdom of intervention itself, then, as a fragile young country, was particularly strained by the long, difficult war. In the immediate aftermath, the Italian share in the Allied victory appeared to be denigrated, even "mutilated," by the outcome of the peace conference. In these three countries, the war yielded unprecedented situations—crisis and revolution—that not only exacerbated the strains of the war experience itself but also called forth further response that further differentiated these countries from the mainstream. So we must grasp a complex interplay of factors if we are to understand how the novel features of the war affected the direction and the content of the common departure toward what proved to be totalitarianism.

Just as idiosyncratic contextual dimensions affected the experience of the war's novel features in Russia, Italy, and Germany, that experience magnified the salience of familiar, longer-term contextual features, including a sense of being somewhat outside the Western mainstream. And in each case, the interface of national circumstances with the war's special features yielded a particular receptivity to, and a potentially explosive way of appropriating, new ideas that had emerged in light of the wider historical-political break. Indeed, in these three countries the general features of the war were experienced as they were, and yielded the responses they did, partly because of this interface with that prior intellectual layer. Innovators in those three countries, as nowhere else, were able to begin translating into practical terms some subset of the new oppositional possibilities that that layer entailed. The resulting ways of articulating the wider features—and lessons—of the war magnified existing contextual differences to further differentiate these particular nations.

Partly because of their place in the Great War, but also because of this mode of embrace of the new layer, Italy, Russia, and Germany each seemed, by the end of the war, to be caught up in history in an especially dramatic way. Although the war revealed, reinforced, or produced vulnerability and insecurity in each case, it also apparently afforded each country a special capacity to point beyond the mainstream in response to the challenges of the uncertain new era emerging from the war. Indeed, each seemed situated to leapfrog the smug, much-resented victorious democracies and to lead. But it was essential to seize the moment to act in new ways and to establish the basis for *continuing* action in such new ways. Each of the three countries was "major" enough—in terms of great power status, geographic–demographic potential, or intellectual standing and tradition—to claim such a vanguard role, taking on challenges that those in the mainstream would not and, on that basis, forging an alternative modernity. This sense of extraordinary possibility was itself energizing, but its reverse side was a sense of now or never, of the possibility of catastrophic failure. So the opportunity was precious but fragile, and thus shrillness accompanied confident self-assertion.

We could treat the three cases in any order; indeed, each has a plausible claim to be treated first. Germany quickly encountered a naval blockade, bringing home its vulnerability. In Italy, the question of intervention itself proved catalytic. However, we will treat Russia first, for its revolution, resulting from the strains of war, radically changed the wider political framework, the sense of what could happen, for good or ill, all over the Western world. Both Italian Fascism and Nazism defined themselves not only by their take on the war but also by their posture toward Russian Communism.

War and the occasion for revolutionary action in Russia

Lenin thought the war could be, had to be, revolutionary. His thinking stemmed from his desire for action and his intuition that war would make it possible, but on that basis he offered what was, up to a point, a plausible theoretical recasting, centering on a particular understanding of imperialism, that justified his insistence on the revolutionary potential of the war.[16] But the war would be revolutionary only if understood in those terms, and only if the implications for action were drawn out. So up to a point the prospects depended on consciousness and will.

Robert Service described Lenin as "astounded and appalled" at the news that the SPD had voted overwhelmingly for war credits, not least because he had shared the near-universal respect for the SPD, and especially its leading theoretician, Karl Kautsky.[17] But thus the mantle of "the most advanced theory" was even more up for grabs than Lenin had thought. And he promptly developed a distinctive reading of the war that brought him a higher level of international recognition. Whereas the great majority, at the two conferences of anti-war socialists in Switzerland during 1915–16, simply called for an end to the war, Lenin proposed that the war could afford the occasion for revolution by the soldier-workers.[18] With his "revolutionary defeatism," he was on the way to a distinctive revolutionary position based on two mutually reinforcing strands, his theory of imperialism and his deeper rethinking of historical change and the scope for a new mode of action.

Most immediately, Lenin based his sense of the war as revolution on a conception of imperialism that suggested the imminence of the crisis of Western capitalism. There was already a large Marxist literature on imperialism, with Rudolf Hilferding's study of 1910 especially central. Lenin adapted Hilferding and the earlier book by J.L. Hobson (1902), and he also responded to his Bolshevik colleague Nikolai Bukharin to develop his own interpretation, written during 1916 and published as *Imperialism, the Highest Stage of Capitalism*, early in 1917.[19]

Lenin followed Bukharin in stressing the significance of the manifestly uneven development of capitalism, but he found Bukharin too orthodox in his reading of the implications of that fact. In assuming that a single, unified capitalism was still gradually emerging, Bukharin was missing the necessity— and the revolutionary implications—of conflict between capitalist nations.[20] Imperialisms were bound to clash. Transposing the scramble to make up for falling profits to colonial and semi-colonial dependencies, imperialism necessarily led to international war. Because imperialism was the last stage of capitalism, war was the form that the revolutionary crisis of capitalism would take. The contradictions in the overall system would first come to the fore on the fringes of the capitalist world. Russia, as both the weakest of the exploiters and itself dependent on international capital, was ideally situated to become the spark for wider revolution.

Lenin also sought to view in orthodox terms the unprecedented socio-economic coordination that soon accompanied the war effort in Germany and elsewhere in the advanced capitalist West. As an outgrowth of imperialist rivalry, the war was proving revolutionary in accelerating the maturation and consolidation of the industrial economies. Impressed with the efficiency of the German war economy, Lenin expressed great admiration for Rathenau and the military mastermind Erich Ludendorff. The capacity for wartime coordination seemed to indicate that the advanced capitalist countries were fully mature, so the situation was ripe for a transition to socialism. If Germany could direct its economy, the same could be done by the non-propertied masses led by the class-conscious workers.[21] The key was to take over the means of such economic coordination and then operate it for the whole society, beyond particularistic concerns.

The war also led Lenin to begin rethinking his wider sense of how change happens—or could be made to happen. At issue was the relationship between action and consciousness, thinking, or knowing. Seeking to get at the root of Kautsky's error in voting for war credits, he read Hegel, then Aristotle, jotting down his thoughts in his 1916 *Philosophical Notebooks*.[22] Without admitting it, he was led to drop much of the epistemology of his *Materialism and Empiro-Criticism* of 1908.[23] Knowledge now seemed more complex, especially because it was apparently in some sense constructed by human beings as they respond to an eternally changing and developing nature. Whereas Neil Harding featured Lenin's continued emphasis on science and certainty, Service suggested that Lenin, with this rethinking,

> had at last found a rationale for the risky, exploratory approach to politics for which he was well known. Earlier he had claimed that his policies were based on predetermined scientific principles. Now he asserted that "practice" was the only true test of whether any policy was the right one. Flexibility was essential. . . . Nothing was permanent or absolutely definite. . . . Politics required experimentation and . . . would involve "leaps," "breaks" and interruptions of gradualness.[24]

Lenin's revolutionary defeatism had envisioned not passivity but extraordinary scope for action—the opening that the Bolsheviks had been contemplating all along. However, for Lenin's intuition to come to fruition, the war had to take a certain form, and the cataclysmic character of the war, as it dragged on, lent credence to Lenin's notion that the crisis of imperialist capitalism was at hand.[25] The fact that the circumstances seemed to justify telescoping the bourgeois and the proletarian revolutions in Russia afforded the opening for a seizure of power that would spark wider revolution.

Although the nature of the war indeed expanded the possibilities for extraordinary action, Lenin's new emphases further strained Marxist orthodoxy. Above all, action would require great tactical flexibility on the part of the coordinating vanguard. As Leszek Kolakowski noted, Lenin had long sensed that to wait for the contradictions of capitalism to mature was to abandon any hope for revolution, but now the scope for revolutionary action was becoming clearer. It required the support of non-proletarian social elements and links to other mass movements. In light of the centrality of imperialism, it even required links to the movements of non-Russian nationalities opposed to the tsarist empire. All over Europe, mass struggles had to encompass reactionary fantasies and feudal leftovers, but objectively even those components would be attacking capital. Kolakowski stressed that such thinking was a complete departure from orthodoxy—although the extent to which Lenin was facing up to his heterodoxy was not clear.[26] The deeper question concerns the basis and nature of what was beginning to emerge instead.

The energizing sense that the war opened revolutionary possibilities intersected with the Bolsheviks' prior sense that the key was to be able to act, guiding events, when the opportunity arose. Yet it is well known that Lenin's efforts to precipitate revolution in 1917, from his April theses to the October takeover itself, met with a good deal of incredulity and even some active opposition within his own party. As Robert Tucker put it, Lenin's "essential contribution was to *nerve* the Bolsheviks into making their decisive revolutionary move when the time came."[27] Now, in response to a spontaneous eruption from below, born of wartime hardship and impending defeat, the Bolsheviks' willingness and capacity to act could precipitate further events and then shape them. Moreover, the action that they alone could spearhead in Russia could trigger the wider European revolution that the wartime crisis had made possible.

Agreeing to an armistice with Germany in December 1917, the Bolsheviks expected Russia's withdrawal to speed the collapse of the war effort on all sides. The key symptom would be troop fraternization, which the new Bolshevik regime would actively foster by publishing the deposed tsarist government's copies of secret *entente* agreements, thereby demonstrating the imperialist nature of the war. At this point, the Russian Revolution was but a chapter in this larger story. As Lenin noted to Trotsky, "if it were necessary for us to go under to assure the success of the German revolution, we should have to do it. The German revolution is vastly more important than ours." Indeed, said Lenin to the Bolsheviks' party congress of March 1918, "It is an absolute truth that we will go under without the German revolution."[28] There was no thought of "socialism in one country."[29]

The Bolsheviks' sense of the scope for action, their willingness to act, and the measure of success they achieved were all bound up with the cataclysmic magnitude of the war, which had confirmed Lenin's intuition about the war's revolutionary potential.[30] But despite his emphasis on imperialist conflict, the sources and historical meaning of the war's revolutionary implications were not necessarily comprehensible in anything like orthodox Marxist terms. Even as he clung to a semblance of orthodoxy, Lenin stressed the scope for action in light of faith and will, especially against Bolshevik doubters on the eve of the Bolshevik takeover.[31] What was emerging was a new, post-Marxist sense of the scope for a certain mode of action. Even in his sense that wartime economic coordination itself indicated capitalist maturation, Lenin was envisioning the scope for transition to a systematic alternative that eluded orthodoxy. An elite defined by its faith, will, and capacity to organize, mobilize, and act could take over and run a modern economy even though the proletariat, even in the advanced countries, had not yet had the full experience of capitalist exploitation and alienation that was to have made it a universal class, capable of creating a post-capitalist order. As Martin Malia put it, the rational organization of the economy that resulted from total mobilization for war was itself the essence of socialism—or, we might say, the germ of a post-bourgeois order.[32]

The need to work with and coordinate broad social forces did not mean actually sharing power with those forces. As a self-conscious elite, contemptuous of mere "quantitative" democracy, the Bolsheviks' first priority, along with spreading revolution internationally, was to achieve a monopoly of power in Russia. After Lenin inveighed against "subordinating the interests of the people to formal democracy" in a December 1917 speech, the Bolsheviks dispersed the elected constituent assembly in January 1918. Responding to those who raised questions, Lenin did not hesitate, in a speech of July 31, 1919, to assert that, yes, this was the dictatorship of one party.[33] Confidence in the capacity to organize, mobilize, and lead from above was the first requisite of the new mode of action.

Successful though it had been on one level, the revolution did not follow the Leninist script and spark wider revolution, despite considerable revolutionary unrest elsewhere in the aftermath of the war. Moshe Lewin noted that whereas Grigory Zinoviev and Lev Kamenev had been wrong regarding the prospects for seizing power in 1917, they proved more accurate than Lenin about the international situation and the consequences of a Bolshevik takeover: "Rarely had a victory—a brilliant one as it happens—been won on so many false assumptions." Lewin went on to stress that the impact of the unexpected isolation of the revolution would be heavy indeed.[34]

Insofar as the expectation of wider revolution had been linked to war and the fraternization of armies, the armistice of November 1918 necessarily occasioned rethinking. But the disarray, misery, political uncertainty, and revolutionary or quasi-revolutionary agitation in much of Europe suggested that the situation remained open. In founding the Third International, or Comintern, in 1919, the Bolsheviks asserted their leadership of international socialism based on the international relevance of what they had accomplished in Russia. They stepped up control at the second Comintern congress during the summer of 1920, when they promulgated the famously strict twenty-one points, or conditions for membership in the new organization. This tough stance reflected growing frustration, although also a sense that the situation was still fluid enough to be mastered. Even as they settled into a period of more protracted struggle, once the scope for immediate revolution seemed to have passed by the end of 1920, the Bolsheviks continued to insist on the international relevance of the Russian experience.

The effort during 1918–20 to foster the spread of revolution intertwined with a brutal civil war, and with menacing though poorly coordinated and ultimately ineffectual foreign intervention against revolutionary Russia. By the end of 1920, the Bolsheviks had prevailed in the civil war, re-establishing or newly establishing their power in what remained of the old tsarist empire. But the wider revolution had fizzled. So by the beginning of 1921 they found themselves in unanticipated territory, the complex civil war experience having added a layer as the dynamic they had initiated gathered momentum. The long-term significance of that experience is clear up to a point, but there has long been controversy over its nature and extent.

Most obviously, the civil war emergency, in the context of active opposition from abroad, seemed to require ruthlessness and even violence. Thus the beginnings of a terror apparatus, including the camp system begun in 1918 with outposts along the White Sea. Still, the extent of continuity with the later Stalinist terror remains contested. Some see this early step as an emergency expedient, not decisive for subsequent departures, but the considerable new research since the fall of the Soviet regime has reinforced the case for continuity. In any case, a certain precedent was established from the need to respond to the unforeseen outcome of the new mode of action so far. Moreover, the emergency demanded militarization, especially of the economy. So even as the civil war, devastating in a country already seriously weakened by war, produced a context ever less congruent with orthodox prerequisites for socialism, the mode of action had established a power base for the new elite, as well as precedents for further action.[35]

The policy of "war communism" has been especially controversial. To what extent was it simply an *ad hoc* response to the civil war emergency, and to what extent did the leaders, from some combination of ideology, voluntarism, and utopian expectation, believe that these measures constituted the definitive transition to socialism?[36] Those critical of the whole Soviet experiment have tended to stress genuine belief, although the basis for any such belief has not been entirely clear. For Martin Malia, the leaders saw war communism as the path to socialism; ideological delirium changed what was in fact economic collapse into a radiant vision.[37] Yet even as he accented ideological thinking, Malia noted that this was to emphasize the voluntaristic and coercive aspects of class struggle while leaving the lockstep aspects of the formal logic of history to the Mensheviks and Western social democrats.

However, the extent to which the ideology warranted such emphasis on the voluntaristic and coercive aspects of class struggle is centrally at issue. Even insofar as war communism was more a matter of belief than an emergency expedient, did it stem from hyper-ideological thinking, or was that accent on coercive voluntarism a departure based on new experience and wider insight? Moshe Lewin's characterizations suggest the need to get at some novel element, beyond merely ideological thinking. After noting that war communism had been bound up with utopian illusions of the scope for instant communism through militarism, terror, and direction from above, he asked: "Was this still Marxism? In any event, Leninism, through certain of its attitudes and still more through impulses generated in it by the situation, encouraged voluntarist hopes of this kind."[38]

What was at work, from this perspective, was not so much Marxism but a still-evolving Leninism, bearing a complex relationship with the problematic prior ideology and thus itself ambiguous about the scope for voluntarism. But whatever faith that socialism was actually being created rested less on ideology than on confidence in the new mode of action. And the voluntarist departure and expectation at this point bred further voluntarism. Even as war communism proved almost ruinous in practice, alienating many, the effort itself, with the utopian expectations it stimulated, galvanized enthusiasm and, even in light of immediate frustration, contributed significantly to the subsequent momentum of the experiment now in progress.

That momentum was bound up with the wider excitement of being out in front. As hopes for the immediate spread of the revolution faded, the possibility of eventual wider revolution seemed to depend not on the workers or even vanguard communists elsewhere knowing what to do but on further *Bolshevik* agency, responding to yet another contingency by exercising the right kind of leadership. So the sense of Russian special opportunity, and responsibility, in this newly open world deepened, and the stakes of this particular episode, this *Russian* revolution, grew. All the hopes for an alternative modernity, for deeper human self-realization, embodied in the Marxian legacy now rested with this Bolshevik elite. Marxism was becoming *only* the receptacle of such hopes, no longer a guide to diagnosis and prescription. And although Bolshevik agency was not merely a spark, for now the Bolsheviks were doing it themselves, what it was they were doing was not at all clear.

Assessing the Bolsheviks' triumph in 1917, Steven Kotkin found more striking than opportunism "their reckless sense of a world-historical mission, which made possible such opportunism amid the mind-boggling swirl of events. As products of the nineteenth-century intelligentsia, the Bolsheviks were inclined to that tradition's obdurate sense of righteousness and paternalism."[39] Although convincing up to a point, this characterization does not do justice to the novelty of the situation and the mode of action developing in response. The Bolsheviks were becoming further differentiated on the basis of a particular voluntaristic historical-political sense that presupposed but transcended *both* nineteenth-century paternalism and nineteenth-century ideology. It was leading them into twentieth-century totalitarianism.

Virtually from the start, the Bolshevik venture encountered harsh criticism from socialists abroad, including some of the most authoritative, like Karl Kautsky, and some who were indisputably revolutionaries themselves, like Rosa Luxemburg. Charging that the Bolshevik mode of forcing things from the top down portended dictatorship and terror, such critics agreed that the continuing Bolshevik experiment could only yield a travesty of the Marxian revolution.[40] The need to respond to such criticisms led Lenin and his colleagues to draw out and articulate certain implications of the dynamic now in course. Addressing Kautsky's charges in *Terrorism and Communism*, his second volley in this particular polemic, Trotsky countered that the concern for the sacredness of human life that Kautsky had invoked was a shameful lie, serving oppression, as long as human labor power, and thus life itself, was bought and sold:

> If it is a question of seeking formal contradictions, then obviously we must do so on the side of the White Terror, which is the weapon of classes which consider themselves "Christian," patronize idealist philosophy, and are firmly convinced that the individuality (their own) is an end-in-itself. As for us, we were never concerned with the Kantian-priestly and vegetarian-

Quaker prattle about 'the sacredness of human life." We were revolutionaries in opposition, and we have remained revolutionaries in power. To
make the individual sacred we must destroy the social order which crucifies
him. And this problem can only be solved by blood and iron.[41]

At about the same time, Lenin sought to specify both the lessons so far and the
contours of the developing challenge in what was arguably his masterpiece, the
pamphlet "'Left-wing' communism—an infantile disorder," written in April
1920, published in May, and distributed to delegates to the pivotal Second
Congress of the Comintern in Moscow in July. Arguing most immediately
against those abroad, mostly in Germany and the Netherlands, who wanted to
be revolutionaries—even Bolsheviks—but who seemed to be misreading what
Bolshevism meant, Lenin offered, in no uncertain terms, a lesson in Bolshevik
tactics based on a review of the actual operations of his party as a self-conscious
vanguard.[42] In the process, he revealed his changing sense of the situation, the
prospects for the future, and the nature of the historical transition that the
October revolution had initiated.

The "infantile disorder" of the "Lefts" stemmed from two intertwined
concerns that had arisen in the context of the revolutionary situation in Europe
that the Bolshevik achievement had helped to precipitate. First, some held that
the dictatorship of the proletariat must be more genuinely "from below," with
greater scope for the workers to develop their own forms of organization, as
opposed to falling in behind the dictatorship of a party of leaders. Second, some
ruled out any compromise, such as working in parliaments or cooperating with
still craft-oriented trade unions.

In ridiculing such concerns and criticisms, and to justify the Russian claim to
leadership in international socialism, Lenin constantly referred to the actual
history of Bolshevism. Invoking essentially the combination we discussed in
Chapter 3, he insisted that special Russian circumstances had enabled the
Bolsheviks to take the measure of the international situation around the turn of
the century and to leapfrog those in the economically more advanced countries
who had seemed, and assumed themselves to be, positioned to set the pace.
Then, even before making a revolution, the Bolsheviks had undergone a practical experience under difficult conditions not remotely approached anywhere
else. Now they controlled a major country. And they were positioned to lead
those who had earlier seemed the most advanced because what mattered was not
the objective maturation of capitalism but the capacity to act—and to know how
to act further in response to the outcomes of such action.[43]

The Bolsheviks' success rested on the vanguard party role they had posited,
and now, by 1920, in light of the tests encountered in practice, it was clearer
that that role entailed a new historical consciousness, resulting from experience, and bound up with the capacity to learn from and react to experience.
To be sure, Lenin was still taking a certain orthodox frame as a given,
appealing to the authority of Marx and Engels on occasion and assuming
that the vanguard could discern the dialectic through its Marxist insight into

objective class antagonism.[44] But although the defining consciousness of the vanguard included a general sense of the scope, and the need, for a post-bourgeois alternative, linked to the abolition of classes, what defined the vanguard was not simply the capacity to interpret the ideology, as if it held the answers but required priestly interpretation. The key was the capacity not merely to "know"—or even to discern how to act. Rather, the key was the capacity to *determine* how to act.

Whatever Marx's ambiguities regarding the process of revolutionary transformation and the place of human agency, the earlier orthodoxy could help very little precisely because it was bound up with an earlier historical sense that envisioned simplification—the world shaking down to two classes, in ever more naked struggle, with the two sides clear. Lenin, in contrast, accented complexity. What required a response was not simply a matter of classes but masses, encompassing various strands and variable modes of involvement or potential involvement at all levels of the transformation. In light of that complexity, there could be no algorithms, no recipes, no cut-and-dried solutions; there was no rule about when—and with whom—a vanguard was or was not to compromise.[45] Reflecting the reading that fed his 1916 notebooks, Lenin remarked that those who conflated the Communists' willingness to compromise with opportunism were too naive to understand that "in nature and society *all* distinctions are fluid and up to a certain point conventional."[46] So the capacity, bound to be confined to a vanguard, to respond to provisional outcomes and experience by picking and choosing, making such distinctions, was central to the agency that the revolutionary process demanded. The ideology afforded only the most general guidance. Moreover, Lenin noted, specific features of capitalist development and class relations varied by country. So revolutionaries had to learn to apply general principles country by country.[47]

Such complexity was bound up with Lenin's changing sense of history, which had come to seem still more open-ended. It had become clear, Lenin noted, that the immediate sources of a revolutionary situation were not predictable and could vary considerably. In Britain, for example, the ice might be broken by a problem stemming from imperialism, or by a parliamentary crisis, "or perhaps by some third cause, etc." He cited the Dreyfus affair as an example of an unexpected concatenation—in one sense, petty, utterly contingent—that had led the relatively placid French Third Republic to the brink of civil war. He found lots of potential sparks in the present, crisis-ridden world situation—but no one could know which would prove an actual spark. Lenin still assumed that whatever the immediate cause, the crisis and transition would be objectively Marxist, but knowing that helped very little and was not really the point. The spark might not be immediately related to the capitalist economy, and the capacity to respond when the moment came had nothing to do with the economic situation.[48] So the vaunted ideology now proved to mean only that the longstanding hope for a systematic alternative to liberal capitalism rested on the capacity to act in a certain way in light of a new, post-Marxist historical-political sense having nothing to do with capitalist maturation.

Lenin went on to note that even in the revolutionary process itself, the essential mass, spontaneous dimension was bound to elude even the most lucid and
experienced vanguard, if only because of the sheer numbers involved: "History
as a whole, and the history of revolutions in particular, is always richer in
content, more varied, more multiform, more lively and ingenious than is imagined by even the best parties."[49] This valorization of spontaneity might seem a
"democratic" emphasis, but in fact it suggested a more complex interface
between elites and masses. Against the "Lefts," Lenin charged that to privilege
either above or below, *either* leaders or masses, was as ridiculous as insisting that
the right or left leg was more important.[50] Even as history came to seem more
open-ended, there was scope for the leaders to shape collective action, although
extraordinary vigilance and organization were required. The capacity to exercise
leadership when the occasion arose entailed not some Blanquist seizure of power
but a new mode of interaction with the masses—and, again, explicitly "masses"
as opposed to industrial workers exclusively.

Still, Lenin insisted, the masses remained mostly inert, habit-ridden—ridden
even with *bourgeois* habits. So, again counter to the "Lefts," leadership required
the capacity to work with—and to convince—such backward elements wherever
they were found, even in unions still betraying a craft orientation. In the same
way, by participating in even the most reactionary parliament, the vanguard
party helped to demonstrate to the masses the futility and obsolescence of the
parliamentary form.[51] The vanguard had to be prepared to exploit any rift, to
take advantage of any opportunity, to win over a mass ally, however vacillating
or unstable it might be.

The imperative, Lenin concluded, was not compromise *per se* but flexibility—
and the deeper imperative was to understand the difference. The key was
knowing when and how to adopt both legal and illegal means, sometimes in
combination, and when to eschew now the one, now the other. Above all, it was
crucial not to be doctrinaire, telling the enemy how you will fight—by repudiating compromise up front, for example. Flexibility also entailed a willingness to
admit mistakes and a capacity to learn from experience, as opposed to rigidly
invoking and relying on a prior ideology. And flexibility entailed being prepared
to take elusive action if some outcome proved disadvantageous. The history of
Bolshevism showed lots of examples of such flexibility.[52]

Although the conditions for a vanguard bid for power could not be specified
in advance, Lenin insisted, neither was it possible to take power at just any time
and create the alternative from there. Far from mere adventurism, the art of
politics lay in pinpointing the moment when the vanguard could *successfully*
assume power, which required gauging the scope for the longer-term construction of a new order. Success required not only support from a sufficiently broad
strata of the working masses, proletarian and non-proletarian alike, but also the
scope for training and educating ever larger numbers as part of the communist
reorganization of every sphere of life.[53]

Especially as Lenin contemplated what such success would require under
contemporary Russian circumstances, his characterization of the strategic challenge

came to implicate the nature and meaning of the transition itself, carrying ever further from anything that might be construed as "ideology," let alone Marxist orthodoxy. He noted that

> the abolition of classes means, not merely ousting the landowners and the capitalists—that is something we accomplished with comparative ease; it also means *abolishing the small commodity producers*, and they *cannot be ousted*, or crushed; we *must learn to live* with them. They can (and must) be transformed and re-educated only by means of very prolonged, slow, and cautious organizational work. They surround the proletariat on every side with a petty-bourgeois atmosphere, which permeates and corrupts the proletariat, and constantly causes among the proletariat relapses into petty-bourgeois spinelessness, disunity, individualism, and alternating moods of exaltation and dejection.

The strictest discipline was thus necessary so that the organizing role could be carried out correctly. And thus "the dictatorship of the proletariat means a persistent struggle—bloody and bloodless, violent and peaceful, military and economic, educational and administrative—against the forces and traditions of the old society. The force of habit in millions and tens of millions is a most formidable force." Such struggle required a party of iron, tempered in the struggle: "It is a thousand times easier to vanquish the centralized big bourgeoisie than to 'vanquish' the millions upon millions of petty proprietors; however, through their ordinary, everyday, imperceptible, elusive, and demoralizing activities, they produce the *very* results which the bourgeoisie need and which tend to *restore* the bourgeoisie."[54] The enemy, it seemed, was not the bourgeoisie as an objective class but a frame of mind, the bourgeois principle itself.

The transformation, Lenin observed, entailed working "not with abstract human material, or with human material specially prepared by us, but with the human material bequeathed to us by capitalism."[55] Although he did not make the point explicitly, this situation had arisen because capitalism, from an orthodox perspective, had not yet done its work, exhausting itself and giving rise, through its contradictions, to the alternative socialist consciousness in the vast majority. But it had come to seem that the essential change in consciousness was not going to happen on its own. On the contrary, the underlying bourgeois principle would remain at large, still powerful, for the foreseeable future. Although a difficult, long-term process would be required, the vanguard could bring about a "socialist" alternative through a certain mode of interaction and collective action.

At this point, in April 1920, Lenin was still seeking the immediate spread of revolution, but wider revolution was no longer essential to make possible a post-bourgeois transformation, now that what it could, and had to, entail was coming more clearly into focus. Even if the revolution was not to spread immediately, the Bolsheviks could simply proceed as before, studying each new situation, learning from experience, adapting, determining how to make the most of every situation as they began to build a post-bourgeois culture, above all though education and mobilization. The process would depend on the underlying virtues that had sustained them as a self-conscious vanguard from the start—will, passion, imagination, devotion, tenacity, flexibility, self-sacrifice, heroism, "iron discipline."[56] Forged in action, through actual historical experience, and stemming from a new sense of history—as open, contingent, but not merely chaotic and beyond human mastery—those virtues, not some privileged grasp of Marxist ideology, defined the vanguard and justified its role.

The new education would generalize the vanguard's post-bourgeois consciousness, thereby overcoming the tendency toward "petty-bourgeois spine-lessness, disunity, individualism, and alternating moods of exaltation and dejection." This would be to create a new human type, immune to "a petty-bourgeois atmosphere" and capable of acting collectively to create, first, a post-capitalist economy. The task might even be called "building socialism," but the transformation rested on the new values that would sustain ongoing collective action in the face of an open-ended history. Although Lenin and his colleagues would continue to insist on class terms, those terms had come to characterize the competing principles for contingent historical reasons that were no longer relevant. Even in 1920, the logic of Leninism suggested a departure from Marxism into the dynamic of great politics, of totalitarianism.[57]

War, crisis, and the birth of Fascism in Italy

Founded in March 1919, Italian Fascism emerged from the war as a quest for a third way beyond both liberalism and Marxism, including the Russian Bolshevism that was attracting socialists in Italy, as elsewhere. The erstwhile socialist leader Benito Mussolini came together with an array of those who, especially in light of the particular Italian experience of the war and its aftermath, deplored the mainstream traditions but envisioned the scope for some positive, even grandiose, alternative. He seemed a credible leader partly because he appeared to have the essential will, energy, and commitment to action, but also because he was seemingly radical yet overtly post-Marxist.

A talented journalist, Mussolini had risen to prominence in the Italian Socialist Party with the backlash against reformism that surrounded Italy's imperialist war with Turkey for Libya in 1911–12. He was made the editor of *Avanti!*, the party's national newspaper, at the age of 29 and was now recognized as the leader of its left-wing faction—even as the bright young face who might revitalize Italian socialism. Already attentive to wider intellectual currents, Mussolini sensed that Marxist socialism had reached an impasse, which even the innovative, anti-party Italian syndicalist current had not satisfactorily addressed. Having distilled something of Nietzsche, Sorel, Pareto, Gustave Le Bon, and other innovative thinkers, he began to suggest, even before the war, the scope for new forms of action that would respond to the impasse of orthodox Marxism.[58]

In fact, Mussolini was moving into post-ideological territory, and thus he was given to a certain extravagance, as if he really believed that faith could move mountains.[59] As a result, his aims, and his role, have always been extraordinarily hard to characterize. Although not a consistent ideologue, neither was he a mere opportunist. He sensed the scope for a radically new direction, and he sought, if sometimes haltingly, to forge the necessary instrument. But he seemed none too sure where that direction might lead on the level of institutional change or policy prescription.

Still, thanks partly to Mussolini's leadership, the fledging Fascist movement seemed promising enough that many from diverse antecedent movements, most notably nationalism, syndicalism, and Gentilian idealism, had joined forces with it by 1923. Yet each of these groups claimed to provide direction based on diagnoses and prescriptions worked out independently, and it was not clear how each would mesh with the new movement. Moreover, their priorities differed, although, in its own way, each of the proffered directions was totalitarian in implication. And young Fascist militants interfaced with these antecedents, on the one hand, and with Mussolini, on the other, from odd angles. So early Fascism constituted a particularly uncertain and volatile mix.

But we already sense that the totalitarian response to Italy's postwar crisis stemmed not simply from Mussolini's will, or some generic vision of national palingenesis, nationalization of the masses, sacralization of politics, or mobilization around ritual and spectacle. The totalitarian direction emerged from within, and reflected, a much thicker texture of discussion regarding the limits of mainstream liberalism and Marxist socialism and the scope for a radical alternative in light of the wider new historical-political framework that seemed to have emerged.

The sense of possibility that fed Fascism grew first from the Italian war experience, which seemed to bring to immediate political currency certain prewar intellectual responses and even longer-term Italian cultural traditions. At the same time, the Russian example demonstrated that revolution was possible, but the Bolsheviks seemed to the creators of Fascism to be embarked on a misguided course. As mainstream Italian Socialists promised a Bolshevik-style revolution just after the war, the early Fascists claimed that they could create a revolution more appropriate to both the Italian situation and the larger political-cultural moment in the West. Despite Fascist anti-Bolshevism, then, in Italy, as in Russia, the experience surrounding the war occasioned a confluence of ideas and contextual features that yielded a sense of unique opportunity to create an alternative modernity.

Whereas the outbreak of war in 1914 yielded unanticipated domestic unity in much of Europe, it bred symptomatic and ramifying division in Italy. The country could easily have remained neutral, and when the question of intervention arose once the fighting had begun in August, most Italian socialists and Catholics joined with the Giolittian political mainstream in calling for neutrality. But many, especially among educated elites, insisted that Italy could not stand idly by in a war that would surely decide the future of Europe for the foreseeable future—and in which vital national interests were at stake. Italy could hope to incorporate the Italian-speaking areas still within the Habsburg empire and gain a defensible strategic frontier at the Brenner Pass. Whatever the tangible gains now within reach, moreover, the war would afford an essential test, even necessitate a maturing process, for this "least of the great powers."

Mussolini followed many of the syndicalists and others from the heterodox Italian Left in coming out for intervention in November 1914. Although he had expected to carry the bulk of the socialists and socialist workers with him, his decision for interventionism cut him off from his former constituency, which remained neutralist and which considered him nothing less than a traitor. However, he encountered another constituency as, especially through his new newspaper *Il popolo d'Italia*, he quickly emerged as a leader among those interventionists who thought the war could trigger radical change in Italy. Mussolini had assumed that the war would reveal, or actually create, new, unforeseen possibilities. And it was already happening. By no means all of those pushing for intervention would end up Fascists, but it was above all belief in the value of the war that bound together those who did.

Whereas Lenin, in claiming to show why the war could be revolutionary, was seeking to update and save Marxism, Mussolini was clearly abandoning Marxism altogether—and seemingly falling into a kind of adventurism. But in sensing that the war could be revolutionary, Mussolini and Lenin converged in crucial respects. And despite the element of adventurism in each case, we must recognize how much each got right in comparison with the vast majority of their contemporaries. They were right that the war would be sufficiently apocalyptic to open a new era, entailing the scope for radically new forms of political action that would require involving large numbers of people in new ways. Each could anticipate this direction because each shared in the wider new sense, emerging from within the new terrain, of how history happens, or could be made to happen. Those with the appropriate historical-political sense and the essential will, faith, and discipline could take advantage of unforeseen circumstances and mold events. The fact that their wider intuition about the revolutionary nature of the war proved to be correct reinforced, in each of the two leaders, the sense that he had precisely the attributes necessary.

In Italy, controversy over intervention continued for almost ten months before Italian troops commenced hostilities during "radiant May" 1915. Committing Italy to intervene with the secret Treaty of London a month before, King Victor Emanuel III, prime minister Antonio Salandra, and foreign minister Sidney Sonnino had been guided by "*sacro egoismo*," the scope for concrete territorial gains, not some vague notion of renewal. Even with intervention, the political leadership remained cautious, declaring war only against Austria–Hungary; war against Germany followed only in 1916. And although none of the belligerents had adequately prepared for the war that in fact developed, the Italian political and military leadership proved particularly ill-equipped. The rout of Italian forces at Caporetto in October 1917 stemmed primarily from innovative German tactics, but it seemed to suggest that Italy had failed this test of its nationhood. Occasioning much soul searching among educated Italians, Caporetto raised the stakes of the war even for those without grandiose expectations at the outset. However, Italian forces managed to hold off the enemy assault at the Piave

River, then contributed to the Allied victory by defeating the Austrians at Vittorio Veneto in 1918. But was it a genuine Italian victory, or merely the collapse of the Austrian army as the wider war was ending?

The war's unanticipated hardships inevitably deepened the divisions over the wisdom of intervention in the first place. Yet despite those hardships, or partly because of them, the war galvanized some genuine idealism at the same time. Much is familiar. Among the junior officers, especially, the front experience, separating them from those at home, gradually produced a sense of constituting a new elite, a new aristocracy from the trenches, a *trincerocrazia*. Yet the war also seemed to suggest the scope for deeper national unity in what had been an especially fragmented nation. The idealism of the trenches meshed with the wider form of idealism that developed especially with the recovery after the traumatic defeat at Caporetto.

Giovanni Gentile and others within the Croce–Gentile circle were especially influential, helping to shape the understanding of the wider meaning of the war among educated Italians.[60] Some of what they offered is hard to swallow today, but if we are to begin to understand their impact, we do well to heed a cautionary note from the distinguished historian of philosophy Eugenio Garin. While no partisan of Croce and Gentile, he emphasized that if we refuse to take seriously the cluster of wartime ideas at issue, "we risk not understanding the position of so many young people who, at the time of the First World War, found in Croce and Gentile two incomparable teachers" whose ideas seemed to show these young Italians "how the course of history might converge with their ideals."[61]

Especially in light of the anomalies of Italy's voluntary intervention, the war brought sensitive questions about Italian cultural identity to the fore. With the intervention debate and the possibility that Italy would switch to the Entente side, some were eager to portray the war as a pro-democratic crusade, alongside Latin sister France, against aggressive Germany.[62] Croce and Gentile, long seen as vehicles for German cultural influence in Italy, inevitably became central to discussions about the wider meaning of Italy's voluntary participation in an anti-German war. The backdrop for those discussions was the wider cultural debate about the cultural meaning of the war that developed all over Europe, as French and German intellectuals, especially, began denigrating the culture of the other.

Although he sought especially to keep the war from contaminating cultural relations, Croce particularly disliked the pro-French wartime propaganda that trumpeted conventional democratic ideas. Throughout the war, he criticized— even ridiculed—the assaults on German culture by both French and Italian intellectuals, reminding Italians that German culture had been of vital importance for Italy but also stressing that there was no connection between German culture and specific German wartime actions. As Croce saw it, the key for now was to turn from cultural stereotyping and to follow the more austere conception of the war that he himself was drawing from his developing historicism. People should say simply that since the course of events has led Europe into war, we Frenchmen or Italians or whoever will do our best to win it, making every sacrifice. But each side should respect the other as they both responded to this moment of tension, the outcome of which would simply be a new, unforeseeable phase in the common European civilization.[63]

Still, Croce found the Latin countries, with their Masonic traditions and their democratic ideals, especially unable to see the war, the political sphere, and ultimately life itself in terms of this more severe conception; they were thus especially prone to assign an artificial cultural meaning to the war.[64] Although he occasionally suggested that the Italians might seek to spread his own more austere conception to the European level, a wariness of chauvinistic myth-making made Croce reluctant to address Italy's uncertain role in the war or to specify any positive meaning. The key for Italy was to fight without illusions or myths.[65] But thus Croce seemed disappointingly circumspect to Italians who looked to him for insight into the meaning of Italy's unnecessary war.

Gentile agreed about austerity up to a point, but virtually from the outset he found it necessary to say more about the potential cultural significance of Allied victory and German defeat. By the last year of the war, he was going beyond Croce to propose that Italy's capacity to fight without myths reflected a new maturity, which suggested the scope for Italy to play a distinctive cultural role in Europe. In his inaugural lecture upon assuming a chair at the University of Rome in January 1918, Gentile charged that in philosophy, the cornerstone of any national culture, the Italians had for too long remained passive spectators, concentrating on absorbing the innovations of others.[66] It was still essential to avoid any cult of the Italian past; earlier in the war, he had condemned not only the German Fichte but also the Italian Gioberti for their artificial theories of national superiority.[67] But thanks to the austerity of the war experience itself, Italy could now come to terms with its tradition in a healthy, creative way, building on it to make a distinctive contribution to contemporary European culture.

As Gentile saw it, a task of redefinition and synthesis fell to Italy—and especially to those Italians who had most fully come to terms with the Germans. Contemporary Italian culture was uniquely positioned between the relatively superficial culture of France, based on positivism and liberalism, and the once deeper culture of Germany, recently grown arrogant and complacent. At present, Gentile claimed, the German philosophical tradition was better understood among foreigners—and it went without saying that the Italians were in the forefront. Just as Hegel and the Germans had forged a new European synthesis a century before, it was now Italy that was situated to play a special role, taking advantage of German culture but developing it in such a way as to offer something new even to the Germans themselves.[68]

Gentile's sense of the scope for synthesis seemed to have political implications, although they remained highly abstract in his wartime writings and speeches. While Croce repeatedly defended the German conception of the state against the attacks of democrats, Gentile stressed the limits of both the French emphasis on abstract rights and the German emphasis on power and authority.[69] With its abstract individualism, French thinking undervalued the role of the state in constituting the individual; with its crude realism, German thinking undervalued the power of ethical ideals. Italy could transcend both partly because of its own marginalized traditions. Whereas for Croce the nineteenth-century nationalist Giuseppe Mazzini, with his dreams of a third Rome, remained something of an embarrassment, Gentile felt that Italy had matured sufficiently to reconnect with this earlier figure, developing the viable parts of his conception while avoiding the chauvinistic excesses.[70]

In invoking Mazzini late in the war, Gentile pointed to the radical populist who had trumpeted the duties of man in opposition to the liberal accent on rights.[71] Mazzini suggested how the moral legacy of the Italian war effort might take political form. More generally, Mazzini's vision gave more overtly political coloration to Gentile's conception of the serious, committed, responsible mode of life, standing opposed to notions of fulfillment as private satisfaction or utility. And the Mazzinian populist angle suggested that political virtue was not to be confined to some bourgeois elite, as old-fashioned liberals envisioned, but could and should be infused throughout society in this mass age. Meshing with Italian intellectual traditions, the austere, responsible conception of the world that the Italian war experience had nurtured could point the way to a new politics, beyond anything that France or Germany could offer. Conversely, the Italian war experience had been a vital intermediate step between the prewar cultural renewal, to which Gentile and Croce had been central, and new political forms.

Among those influenced by the wartime writings of Croce and Gentile was the young Luigi Russo, who would go on to become one of Italy's best-known literary scholars. After a year and a half as a soldier at the front, Russo joined the faculty at the Military School of Caserta in October 1916. The next year, he outlined his sense of the meaning of the war in a series of lectures there that, promptly published, proved especially influential, drawing high praise from both Croce and Gentile.

Russo insisted that the war experience could be the elevating moral experience that Italy needed—to overcome the "spiritual poverty of skepticism"—only insofar as it was surrounded by Crocean austerity.[72] Neither cultural chauvinism nor denigration of the enemy was compatible with the appropriate experience of the war, which was not a crusade of right against wrong but, as for Croce, a moment of tension in the ongoing, apparently endless evolution of a single European culture. For the moment, one could have faith that the war, by overcoming problems dividing Italians from some of their fellow Europeans, would foster cultural growth and enrichment, although the exact result could not be foreseen. Still, Russo deemed it appropriate for people to react morally against the enemy in a war, as long as the responses were genuine and not the result of manipulative propaganda. It was precisely in this way that Gentile and his followers had gone beyond Croce, specifying what they had against Germany but keeping their balance, never losing sight of the ultimate reconciliation with the enemy that the war would make possible. Russo insisted that lies and illusions cannot be effective in the long term anyway; the moral force that makes lasting victory possible requires austere lucidity.[73]

Nowadays, this whole set of ideas seems quaintly archaic; indeed, it can easily be vilified or parodied in light of the war's grim features. However, recalling

Garin's warning, let us note, first, that whereas these ideas are surely unfamiliar, we need to be open to differences that defy our assumptions, which, reflecting subsequent experience, may be too cynical to enable us to grasp the force that such ideas could have had at the time. Whatever its realism, this line of thinking did not entail the vitalism, the cult of violence, the chauvinistic nationalism, or the idea of war as hygienic that we have come to associate with pro-war ideas. Indeed, thinkers from Gentile to Russo proved that it was possible to assert the value of Italy's war effort and to seek to dampen the chauvinistic excesses of others at the same time. And although Russo had experienced two seasons of front-line battle, his response was a kind of idealism, not disillusionment, cynicism, or skeptical irony.

However, not all of the impulses that grew from the Italian war experience were as elevated as these; even the interface between Italian tradition and the lessons of the war could also be read in a very different way. Alfredo Rocco, the leading spokesman for the Italian Nationalist Association, appealed to some of the same Italian traditions as he, too, suggested a special postwar role for Italy. The doctrine of the state as force, he contended, was erroneously taken to be Prussian and German when in fact it derived from Roman and Italian sources, as carried into the modern world by Machiavelli, Vico, and early nineteenth-century southern Italian writers reacting against the Enlightenment. Precisely because the Germans had not fully grasped that doctrine, they had botched it, and thus it now fell to the Italians to reclaim that legacy and translate it into action.[74] For Rocco, that would mean a stronger, more intrusive state capable of spearheading an effective Italian imperialism.

Still, it is crucial that the new mix included Russo's idealistic sense that the war had been of special ethical significance for Italy, pointing beyond both particularism and skepticism. Precisely because of their anomalous, voluntary role, this line of thinking went, the Italians had been uniquely positioned to experience the war in the appropriately austere way, boxing out the facile, chauvinistic excesses found elsewhere.

Gentile, especially, emerged as a singularly influential civic educator as the war was ending. Gabriele Turi has shown how surprisingly widely his thinking reached in this "relatively provincial" but "extremely sophisticated" culture.[75] With his accent on the centrality of education, Gentile developed an especially significant following among teachers. His account of the meaning of the Italian war experience enhanced the appeal of his wider vision of a newly unified culture, beyond positivism and liberalism. Moreover, Gentile excited because he especially seemed to show the wider contemporary value of neglected Italian traditions. The sense that, by updating the lineage from Giordano Bruno through Vico and Mazzini to Bertrando Spaventa, Gentile had overcome the problems left open even in the best German thinking, including Marxism, suggested that he was indeed at the forefront of modern thought. But heady though it was, Gentile's conception was abstract, its political implications uncertain. And for all its accent on austere lucidity, its accent on Italian cultural contributions could breed myth making.

The seeming denigration, at the Paris peace conference, of the Italian contribution to the Allied victory inevitably exacerbated the effects of the ambiguities surrounding the Italian war effort—the contested intervention, the questionable military victory, and the easily inflated sense of cultural meaning. In fact, in gaining most of what had been promised in the Treaty of London, Italy did not fare badly. But the break-up of the Austro-Hungarian empire, not foreseen in 1915, complicated the situation, whetting Italian appetites even as it also led to the creation of Yugoslavia, with a seemingly legitimate claim to some of the territories earlier promised to Italy. So Italy did not get everything it wanted, and the sense of mutilated victory produced resentment not only against the victorious Allies but also against the governing elite, which seemed to be unable to deliver the prizes that many found necessary to redeem the sacrifices the war had necessitated.

The resulting frustration led to a pivotal episode in September 1919 revolving around the disputed port city of Fiume (now Rijeka, Croatia) on the Adriatic coast. When Prime Minister Francesco Saverio Nitti, seeking economic aid, acquiesced in Woodrow Wilson's decision that the city go to Yugoslavia, the noted writer-adventurer Gabriele D'Annunzio defied the government by leading a band of "legionnaires" of the front generation in a quasi-insurrectionary march on the city. The outlaw "regency" he established lasted until December 1920, when D'Annunzio's legions were finally dispersed by Italian troops. The Fiume venture assumed almost mythical proportions partly because, in the late summer of 1920, the regency adopted a neo-syndicalist constitution, the *Carta del Carnaro*, which, as we will soon see, suggested to a number of young war veterans a direction for political change congruent with their ideals.

Although Italy had ended up sharing in the victory, those sensing the promise of renewal felt that the established political elite, lacking confidence in the nation, had not really wanted war in the first place, had been unnecessarily cautious in waging it, and was now failing to realize its fruits. Above all, the liberal establishment did not grasp the scope for renewal that the war experience offered. To be sure, the electoral reform of 1919, by introducing proportional representation, pointed beyond *trasformismo* toward mass-party politics. But the new system quickly encountered problems of its own, thanks especially to the relatively rigid stances adopted by the two mass parties, the Socialists and the new Catholic Popular Party (*Popolari*). The return of Giovanni Giolitti, now 78, for yet another term as prime minister during 1920–21 epitomized the crisis of the old liberalism. He was still able and energetic, but the transformist methods he had perfected before the war were singularly ill-suited to the crisis that was coming to face the Italian liberal order.

At the same time, the liberal regime had seemed ill-equipped to deal with the postwar challenge from the Left during the *biennio rosso*, the "red biennium" of 1919–20. As the trade unions, their membership soaring, grew more militant, the Socialist Party, infatuated with the Bolshevik example, claimed to be pointing the way to revolution. In light of the Russian precedent, the wave of strikes that culminated in a series of factory occupations in September 1920 seemed seriously to suggest that a Marxist revolution was in the offing. But having remained aloof from the war effort, the Socialists did not reach out to politically discontented but pro-war young veterans; on the contrary, they continued to denigrate the war, thereby provoking hostility even among many who were also seeking radical change. Although the Socialists proved at once too doctrinaire and too hesitant to pull off a revolution, they had posed what seemed a genuine threat, exposing the weakness of the liberal state.

At the same time, certain industrial sectors found themselves especially vulnerable in light of the rapid, in some ways unsustainable, economic expansion that Italy had experienced during the war. In that context, the newly endemic labor unrest seemed especially threatening. Yet in Italy, as elsewhere, wartime industrial expansion had fostered new links between government and business leaders that had seemed to foster productive development, especially because they bypassed the parliamentary political process. Such links might afford the basis for a more competitive Italian role in the postwar international economy.[76]

So balancing the sense of expectation and new possibility in immediate postwar Italy was a volatile mix of trade union particularism, proto-revolutionary unrest, economic vulnerability, and a seemingly ineffectual parliamentary state. Apparently defying mainstream liberal and socialist ideas, the situation nourished a particularly rich discussion revolving around the role of expertise, the interface of economics and politics, the place of class and class interests, and the scope for political virtue. Also at issue were the scope for a more equitable international order that might benefit this over-populated, under-resourced country, and, conversely, the scope for a more successful Italian imperialism.

As we saw in Chapters 2 and 3, the trade union phenomenon, whether as opportunity or threat, was much discussed before the war, but the circumstances of the war and its aftermath brought it particularly to center stage in Italy. Questions about the actual and potential role of trade unions, and economically based groupings more generally, proved central to considerations of Italy's postwar crisis and its possible solutions. Were the unions a particularist threat to the sovereignty of the state, a healthy expression of new societal energies that might serve a revitalized, pluralistic liberalism, or potentially the vehicle for a more intense politicization—even the germ of a new, post-liberal state? From several angles, there seemed to be scope for radical change in response to the threat and/or opportunity that the unions constituted.

It was especially this issue that brought together syndicalism and Nationalism, two of the most important antecedent currents that sought to give Fascism direction. But although the element of overlap was important, crucial and instructive differences remained between them even as they converged within Fascism. They had different reasons for rejecting parliamentary democracy in favor of a new state based on occupational groupings.[77]

The Italian Nationalist Association, founded in 1910, was the institutional outcome of the renewed nationalism that emerged in Italy after the turn of the century, spearheaded especially by Enrico Corradini. Merging with the Fascist Party in March 1923, the Nationalists provided Mussolini's regime with a number of major functionaries and ideologues, including the jurist Rocco, who, as minister of justice from 1925 to 1932, was arguably the single most important architect of the new Fascist state.

Nationalist thinking about the place, and potential place, of the unions reflected the changing socio-economic context during the war and its immediate aftermath. Significant links between the Nationalist Association and big business developed during the war, as heavy industry expanded but faced an uncertain future with the return to a peacetime economy. Nationalists like Corradini, Rocco, and Luigi Federzoni called increasingly for economic coordination, even as they sensed that the existing liberal state, revolving around parliamentary government, could not be adequate to the task. New modes of collaboration and discipline would be necessary for the era of more intense international economic competition and imperialist struggle that would surely follow the war.[78] Corradini advocated a new "national democracy," with productive, energetic business leaders playing a more active political role and with the lower classes fully participating, although in a well-coordinated form as, explicitly, "the base of the pyramid."[79] More generally, Nationalist thinking reflected a sense of Italy's special vulnerability as a new, fragmented nation, in contrast, for example, with England, where longstanding traditions of national unity compensated to some extent for liberalism's particularist tendencies. Rocco insisted that the nation must be conceived as a living, historical organism, with government in the hands of those capable of transcending immediate concerns and satisfactions to pursue the nation's long-term interests.[80]

From the evolving Nationalist perspective, the trade union phenomenon posed an immediate threat but also afforded a longer-term opportunity. Rocco had called for a new system of Nationalist unions as early as 1914. When, in March 1919, the Nationalist Association met for the first time since the end of the war, amid the widespread discussion of impending socio-political change, the scope for trade unions to play a nationalist role proved the dominant theme. As Rocco saw it, the welcome concentration of industry that the war had brought about in firms like Ansaldo and Fiat had to be extended further by taking advantage of the trade union phenomenon. Such associations, emerging from the industrial system, characterized the era, but they could not be encompassed, politically or juridically, within the liberal framework, based on individualism and a particular demarcation of public and private. Yet the unions had already proved valuable in providing structure to a mass society of atomized individuals. The present challenge—and opportunity—was to encompass them, even to make them the basis of political life. Properly directed, they could become vehicles to mobilize, to coordinate, to foster productive values and class collaboration.[81] Only thus could the necessary collective action become possible as the Italian state expanded its reach.

By late 1920, Rocco's emphases were becoming more shrill as the socialist threat grew, with public service strikes paralyzing parts of Italy for days at a time, and as the liberal state seemed unable to respond effectively. In a noted inaugural lecture at the University of Padua in November, responding partly to what seemed the inadequacy of the liberal Oreste Ranelletti's prescription, Rocco insisted that although the threat of trade union particularism, exacerbated by the weakness of the liberal state, was proving especially intense in postwar Italy, the crisis was more generally modern. With the unions increasingly effective as vehicles of particular interests, their power portended, from within the liberal framework, a return to the Middle Ages, the anarchy of private force. But if there could be no liberal antidote, neither was the solution simply to suppress the unions by returning to mere authoritarianism. Even as the need for a post-liberal framework seemed more urgent, Rocco continued to insist that the unions, as products of modern industrial capitalism, were potentially valuable as vehicles of mass mobilization, coordination, and education.

To take advantage of the opportunity, Rocco called for state unions in every economic sector, with membership obligatory. At the same time, he advocated extension of state sovereignty over labor relations, which could no longer remain private in the modern world of economic interdependence and global competition, a world in which ever more had to be done collectively. The first step was a magistracy of labor through which the state would adjudicate labor conflicts, setting salaries in the national interest. This meant that technical experts would exercise expanded state sovereignty, doing what had previously been left to private bargaining—or often conflict, resolved by mere force as opposed to law.[82]

So Rocco was advocating moving beyond liberalism from two directions, to mobilize, coordinate, and channel mass energies but also to extend state sovereignty. Although the term had not yet been coined, the direction of each—and especially in combination—was totalitarianism, understood as appropriate to modern problems that Italy was now, thanks to the war, experiencing with particular force. Italy could show the way; Italy *had to* show the way.

Rocco's sense of the fragility of modern society in some ways recalls Joseph de Maistre, whom Isaiah Berlin found at the origins of fascism.[83] Of all the major Fascist ideologues, Rocco was certainly the closest to de Maistre—and to a threatened conservatism more generally. In the same way, Rocco was closest to rejecting democracy on the basis of the fear of the masses that Zeev Sternhell emphasized, and he explicitly advocated a new governing elite as the antidote to mass-based parliamentary government, with its premium on short-term interests. But in his sense of the challenge and opportunity, even Rocco was more innovative than Sternhell allowed, and he departed from de Maistre in what proved a totalitarian direction.[84]

Moreover, Rocco constituted but one pole of the proto-totalitarian spectrum in Italy, and his categories cannot account for the appeal of Fascism to those who rejected parliamentary democracy on a basis quite different from fear of the masses. Some sensed that the potential of ordinary people for deeper political involvement, even political virtue, had not been, and could not be, realized through the mechanisms of parliamentary liberalism. Sternhell argued that democracy had been an object of disdain for the French and Italian syndicalist intellectuals, who "had always been extremely doubtful about the capacity of people to govern themselves."[85] Certainly, the Italian syndicalists were hostile to parliamentary democracy, but it seemed possible to pinpoint the sources of its apparent inadequacies and, on that basis, to devise other ways for "people to govern themselves." The trade unions were a potentially valuable source of political capacity and commitment. The Nationalist accent on permanent elitism and hierarchy reflected no such confidence in the potential political capacity of ordinary working people.

Those in the syndicalist current had gradually developed ideas for a neo-syndicalist or proto-corporativist reconstruction of the state as, starting well before the war, they gradually jettisoned Marxism as the framework for the pursuit of a radical alternative. In Italy, at least, the liberal political system itself seemed to be impeding the development of modern capitalism according to the orthodox script. The revolution that mattered for now pitted not workers against capitalists but producers against the parasites clustered around the parliamentary state, seeking and dispensing favors. By 1918, the leading syndicalists were offering proto-corporativism as the basis for the essential third way, explicitly disputing the post-liberal terrain with the Bolsheviks on that basis.[86] We noted that D'Annunzio's venture in Fiume assumed almost mythical proportions partly because his regime adopted a neo-syndicalist constitution, the *Carta del Carnaro*, in the summer of 1920. Drafted by the veteran syndicalists Alceste De Ambris and A.O. Olivetti, the document distilled neo-syndicalist ideas to offer a post-liberal conception of politics based on economic groupings, to politicize production and involve the nation's producers in public life in a more constant and direct way.

Although the proto-corporativist proposals of the Nationalists and the syndicalists reflected somewhat different priorities, the fact that each current got caught up in polemics with liberal critics over the issue helped to draw the two together. Such prominent liberals as the philosopher Guido De Ruggiero, the jurist and former prime minister Vittorio Emanuele Orlando, the economist Umberto Ricci, and the newspaper editor Luigi Albertini all addressed the proto-corporativist ideas being offered. Even as he ridiculed as unrealistic the grandiose claims emerging from the neo-syndicalist current, Domenico Settembrini, writing in 1991, stressed the seriousness of these debates, which, he noted, reflected both the disquiet and the anticipation that characterized the era throughout much of Europe. Thus the international interest that the eventual outcome, the Fascist effort to construct a corporativist state, would elicit.[87]

The fact that liberal spokesmen did not address the trade union phenomenon with much imagination surely enhanced the appeal of the various proto-fascist corporativist proposals. The liberals tended to view the unions merely as a threat, not a welcome manifestation of new societal energies that might even portend a deeper, more pluralistic liberalism. From the liberal perspective, to make an expanded trade union system the basis of political life would be simply to give in to particularism, degrading the political sphere to the material level. The state would be reduced to a collection of monopolies, each protecting its own narrow interests. But insofar as the unions constituted a threat to the sovereignty of the state, what did the liberals propose instead? Conversely, how did they conceive, in the dawning mass age, the political virtue that would stand opposed to the particularism they deplored?

We noted that Gaetano Mosca had been concerned with the issue even before the war, but especially in the wake of the *biennio rosso* he stressed the danger of intermediate bodies to the sovereignty of the state and, in light of increasing economic interdependence, to the whole social fabric. But his antidote was merely to call for national loyalty; the trade unionists had to put the nation first, to look to government leaders before union leaders.[88] In 1923, he closed the second edition of his *Elementi di scienza politica* with an appeal to Italian youth not to give up on but "to restore and conserve" the liberal parliamentary system in the face of the germs of dissolution facing it. However, he admitted that although the war had increased their virulence, those germs were inherent in the system itself.[89]

In Mosca's terms, some form of elitism was inevitable, but could any *liberal* elite, accenting pluralism and tending toward particularism, afford the integration, the consensus, the sense of community that he found essential? Certainly the Italian liberal effort, including Mosca's patriotic exhortations, rang hollow to the unionized workers during Italy's postwar crisis. A new, post-liberal elite might go beyond mere patriotic exhortation to forge a deeper consensus, based on a deeper sense of the possibilities of modern mass politics. By dealing with the unions more radically, actually integrating them into the state, this elite could discipline these sometimes unruly particularist organizations and, at the same time, focus their energies to enhance the state's capacity to act.

If Mosca at least thought exhortation worthwhile, another respected but aging liberal, the long-time *meridionalista* (advocate for the South) Giustino Fortunato tended toward gloomy resignation.[90] Although embittered over what seemed the short-sighted particularism of the unions, he found only the same particularist mentality in the various proto-corporativist proposals. To those on their way to fascism, liberals like Mosca and Fortunato seemed too old-fashioned to grasp the dramatically new postwar situation, which seemed to invite new thinking about economic and political relationships, about production and the societal interest, about political virtue and technical competence. Those who proposed systematic change in a corporativist direction seemed at once more hopeful and more modern.

Responding to the liberal Orlando's concerns in a lecture at the University of Ferrara in November 1922, just after Mussolini had become prime minister, the veteran syndicalist Sergio Panunzio insisted that the modern development of unions outside the state was a symptom not of pathology but of health, energy, and renewal. The phenomenon now afforded the key to creating a new, radically popular state based on the organized, productive society. The traditional liberal state had remained aloof, leaving much of the society politically inept or indifferent because it had been based on abstract individuals, not the concrete, living society, now finding expression in the new economically based organizations. The liberal state was exhausted, unable to contain the social content now overflowing it, so it fell to the dynamic society to constitute a new state. Even within liberal society, Panunzio pointed out, the new organizations tended to federate and confederate, thereby creating in embryo the syndical state of the future.[91]

Taking up the challenge the following month, the noted liberal philosopher and historian Guido De Ruggiero vehemently criticized the syndicalist–fascist emphasis on economic roles and technical expertise even as he recognized that the older liberal understanding of politics was in crisis. As De Ruggiero saw it, Panunzio remained within the tradition of historical materialism, taking the political sphere as some merely reducible superstructure, whereas in fact it was, or could be, the sphere of freedom achieved by rising above particular material interests. Some human beings, at least, were capable of discerning and pursuing the wider collective interest. The challenge, in light of all the undeniable negatives of Italian political life, was not to replace parliament but to develop a worthier form of political education.[92]

In response, Panunzio claimed that De Ruggiero had it backwards: what neo-syndicalism, and now Fascism, envisioned was not degradation of the political to the economic or particularist level but promotion of the economic to the political level—to politicize the sphere of production and thereby extend a genuinely political perspective to all producers. After all, why had the liberal regime failed? In insisting on the separation of the political and economic spheres, De Ruggiero's liberal state was too abstract; there was too much it did not encompass—labor conflicts, the whole sphere of production. It was time to try an alternative based on an expanded system of unions, now obligatory, which would educate through new forms of participation. By drawing on Mazzini's vision, updated through Sorel and the syndicalist ethic of association, and by expanding the sovereignty of the state, Italy was poised to create a whole new form of democracy.[93]

In fact, even in its liberal form the state had been taking on ever more functions, especially as it had expanded during the war. Such expansion had happened partly through decree laws—legislation bypassing parliament—and this, in turn, had produced widespread concern about the hypertrophy of bureaucracy that seemed to result. Whereas De Ruggiero charged that to bring economic groupings into the state would simply add a layer, thereby exacerbating the bureaucratic tendency, Panunzio insisted that basing the state on economic groupings was precisely the antidote. The war had merely accelerated the irreversible modern expansion of the state into the socio-economic sphere. The question was by whom, and in what way, that ongoing expansion was to be carried out from this point on. Devolving legislative capacity into the occupational groupings, now made the basis of the state, would directly involve those with hands-on expertise. The productive society could govern itself in a way that was less bureaucratic, yet also more constant and thoroughgoing.

As the Fascist regime began to commit itself to this general direction, Luigi Albertini, the distinguished editor of the Milanese *Corriere della sera*, Italy's leading newspaper, charged that the outcome could only be a narrow, selfish system, "in which the day-to-day content would be low-grade bargaining over the division of the common spoils among the corporations strongest at the outset." To give existing economic interests political power would only freeze present economic patterns, excluding new interests and ideas. The optimum was still liberalism, with parties competing in parliamentary elections and alternating in power. And liberalism offered the best way for the minority of individuals with character and high ideals to emerge to lead the disoriented, sluggish society.[94]

Responding in unsigned articles in *Il popolo d'Italia*, the long-time syndicalist A.O. Olivetti insisted that such particularism was a problem only from within the abstract liberal framework. Linked to the Mazzinian legacy and the war experience, the advent of trade unions afforded the scope for novelty beyond Albertini's grasp, a post-liberal organic state encompassing the whole effort of production and affording the more constant political education necessary to raise the people to political competence.[95]

Although they differed over elitism, hierarchy, political educability, and the scope for initiative from below, the Nationalists and the syndicalists both found in the spontaneous emergence of economically based organizations the basis for mobilizing producers, politicizing the economy, and expanding the sovereignty of the state. The first key for each was to dissociate the modern organizational tendency from liberalism, with its particular understanding of the public/private relationship, and to move in a direction that would soon be termed totalitarian. Each seemed to have something more affirmative and innovative to say than the old-fashioned liberals, who merely lamented the short-sighted egotism of parliamentary politics and the particularism of the unions. Yet in privileging economic roles and productivism, was corporativism congruent with the deeper political virtue that Gentile envisioned? Although Panunzio insisted against De Ruggiero that Fascism was promoting the economic to the higher level of political virtue and commitment, there were potential tensions among the most explicit early Fascist ideas, despite their common totalitarian implications.

Although it was not clear how a totalitarian corporativist system was to work, it was certainly possible to move in the envisioned direction, and the Fascists would emphasize trial and error as opposed to rigid blueprints. But the grandiose images in their emerging post-liberal vision were based on arbitrary juxtapositions betraying an element of myth making. At the least, it would require faith and will for the new, war-hardened elite to forge a Mazzinian nation of politically virtuous producers.

In any case, Nationalism, syndicalism, and Gentilian idealism were but three components in the generally messy mixture of Fascist ideas and aspirations. As a quest for a third way, early Fascism was bound to attract a disparate array, some more educated, experienced, and sophisticated than others.[96] And the fissures, even Left/Right differences, between them were quickly evident. Still, all Fascists shared a hostility to parliamentary democracy as corrupting and ineffectual, breeding political cynicism and indifference; all found Marxist socialism inadequate, even counterproductive, in its diagnoses and prescriptions; and all sensed that the germs of an alternative to both had emerged through the Italian war experience. A new elite, embodying the legacy of the war, grasping the extraordinary present challenge and willing to act, even to use violence, could seize the opportunity for Italians to point the way to a mass-based, alternative modernity.

More specifically, all saw the scope for a radical departure that, under present circumstances, would have to be overtly anti-Marxist. The wartime industrial push, with the new relations between government and business that it occasioned, had suggested that the contrast between producers and parasites was more relevant for the foreseeable future than orthodox Marxist class conflict. Moreover, Marxist materialism had kept the Italian socialists from grasping the meaning and potential significance of the war. The sense of having worked through and beyond Marxism, as an outmoded nineteenth-century conception of problems and solutions, was a major aspect of the Fascist self-understanding and claim to leadership. Thus, for example, Mussolini would review the earlier impasse of socialism while invoking Sorel and prewar Italian syndicalism in his noted article on Fascism of 1932 for the new Italian Encyclopedia.[97] It was especially as the limits of Marxism became evident that Mazzini, long-marginalized within the wider European radical tradition, might at last come into his own.

Insofar as we view Fascism as "revolutionary in its own right" and, more generally, pull back from the master narrative of modernization, we no longer rely on the stereotypical categories and reductionist tendencies—counterrevolution, petty bourgeois resentment, "military desperadoes" unable to readjust to civilian life—in our approach to early Fascist aspirations. But the shadow of those earlier categories continues to impede engagement with Fascist aspirations and to produce a certain myopia in treatments of the Fascist trajectory. Thus we may tend to find this or that as a definitive defeat for Fascist radicalism when in fact much remained fluid and uncertain.

Noting explicitly that it falls to the historian to restore original Fascist ideas to light, Renzo De Felice sought to open the way, but he still framed the Fascist departure in the language of class. Against the standard interpretation going back to Luigi Salvatorelli's *Nazionalfascismo* of 1923, he noted that *declassé* bourgeois types were to be found only on the fringes. The key was that the Great War had mobilized sectors that had been excluded politically and that now challenged the legitimacy of the traditional ruling class:

> Fascism as a movement was in large part the expression of an emerging middle class, of bourgeois elements who, having become an important social force, attempted to participate and acquire political power. . . . Fascism was therefore the attempt of the petit bourgeoisie in its ascendancy—not in crisis—to assert itself as a new class, a new force. What produced Fascism as a movement was an attempt to put forward new "modern" solutions and "more adequate" methods.[98]

A generation later, Emilio Gentile pinpointed the ambiguities that resulted from De Felice's way of tracing aspirations to social background even as he sought to get beyond the earlier reductionism.[99] Perhaps, writing as he was in the mid-1970s, De Felice had had to remain within the expected framework and repair to some variation on "class" even to undercut the stereotypical "declining petty bourgeoisie" notion. However, as Gentile implied, to force class even in De Felice's

way only obscures the relevant axis, which was, first, experiential and generational but which also reflected irreducible differences in conceptions of political
possibilities and priorities. Industrial workers were doubly underrepresented, in
light of their embrace of Marxist socialist categories and their denigration of the
war. But the under-representation of workers tells us nothing about Fascist motivation or content; anti-Marxism and anti-Bolshevism did not necessarily mean
anti-worker.

Still, it is well known that Fascism gathered force in reaction against the
socialist working class in light of the revolutionary wave of the *biennio rosso*. During
1920 and into 1921, bands of Fascists, the *squadristi*, broke up Socialist unions,
attacked Socialist newspapers and meeting halls, and beat up workers, especially
the organized agricultural workers in the Po valley. Not surprisingly, in light of
the immediate threat from the socialist left, the anti-Bolshevik stance of the
fledgling Fascist movement attracted merely conservative or counterrevolutionary
elements who were more than willing to pay the bills.

Perhaps this immediate counterrevolutionary role fatally compromised
whatever revolutionary potential Fascism had, but its longer-term implications
could not have been clear at the time. And the central issue is not who paid the
bills but the basis of the Fascist claim to offer an alternative revolution that
would, among other things, more genuinely integrate the working class into the
nation. In light of the uncertainties within Marxism, the claim to be seeking an
alternative revolution was not implausible on the face of it. Indeed, it was not
clear what was radical, revolutionary, conservative, or counterrevolutionary at
this point. Conventional notions of Left and Right had become especially
uncertain. The notion that the war experience itself had forged the essential
new capacities was vague, but perhaps not vacuous insofar as it connected with
the layer of earlier intellectual articulation. Aging though he was, Pareto enjoyed
considerable currency as, converging explicitly with the Italian neo-syndicalists
up to a point, he discussed the scope for a new elite to emerge from war characterized by austerity, self-sacrifice, and the other virtues once expected of the
proletariat.[100]

Although Mussolini was Fascism's most plausible leader, he, unlike Hitler, did not
fall heir to a Führer principle already established among his country's discontented.[101] To be sure, Hitler encountered several challenges to his authority from
within the Nazi movement as he rose to power, but the Italian situation was more
volatile and open-ended. In light of the heterogeneity of Fascism, Mussolini, up to a
point, had to be a balancer or juggler, and virtually from the start he was forced
to devote much of his energy to taming and controlling Fascism itself.[102] Indeed,
as his movement grew, he found himself tangling over priorities with other
Fascists who were more impatient, perhaps even more radical or committed,
than he. But confusion resulting from conventional categories, especially criteria
of "radicalism," have made it difficult to sort out the stakes of those disputes.

The Fascist radicals were often young local leaders coming straight from the
war, quick to use violence in pursuit of their aims. From Mussolini's perspective,
their recklessness could compromise Fascism's longer-term prospects. From their

perspective, in contrast, Mussolini was too quick to compromise with pre-Fascist elites seeking merely to exploit Fascism and too prone to use the movement as a mere instrument for his own maneuvering within the parliamentary game.

By 1921, Mussolini found himself trying to operate between these militant young Fascists and established elites, afraid of socialism, increasingly disillusioned with liberal democratic institutions, but nervous about Fascist radicalism at the same time. By some reckonings, he made a definitive turn to the Right, selling out to the establishment and taming radical Fascism, as he first agreed to a government-sponsored "pacification pact" with the Socialists and the unions in August 1921, then transformed the fascist movement into a party at the Fascist congress at Rome that November. Finding Mussolini too willing to compromise, the young militants Dino Grandi, Italo Balbo, and Piero Marsich rejected the pacification pact and mounted a serious challenge to Mussolini's leadership between August and November. Stressing the scope for a new, implicitly totalitarian state based on occupational groupings, they embraced especially the neo-syndicalist *Carta del Carnaro* elaborated for D'Annunzio's regime at Fiume. In an article on "l'uomo più grande" (the larger individual) in July 1920, Grandi had invoked the *Carta del Carnaro* in arguing that the advent of modern social organization afforded the key to transcending both liberalism and Bolshevism.[103] Hence his emphasis, in opposing Mussolini in 1921, on the need to continue the assault on the Socialist unions while developing new Fascist unions.[104] The *Carta del Carnaro* continued to generate much excitement among the young Fascist war veterans seeking a third way.[105] Grandi and several of his fellow militants even approached D'Annunzio himself about leading an insurrectionary march on Rome.

It is increasingly recognized that the outcome of the infighting of 1921 was not, as was long assumed, a definitive defeat for radical Fascism but was rather a compromise that left much open.[106] The divisions over the role of the movement/party were overcome only superficially, and the militants got some of what they wanted, especially repudiation of the pacification pact. This meant the chance further to foster the nascent Fascist trade union movement, through which they envisioned reorganizing the workers in the wake of the forcible break-up of much of the Socialist union network. And Fascist radicalism remained, although where it might lead was not at all clear, partly because of its problematic links to the violent legacy of early *squadrismo*.[107]

However, Italian elites seeking to exploit Fascist anti-Marxism did not envision an alternative revolution, although some, in response to Italy's postwar crisis hoped to shore up the existing state, even at the expense of parliament, through government by a traditional conservative like Antonio Salandra.[108] But by 1922 even some major liberal intellectuals were coming to sense that the old liberal elite was exhausted and needed at least a breather, if not wholesale renewal or replacement. Although the wider Fascist movement had been violent and claimed a more grandiose role, some among the established elites came to support Mussolini as the one leader who could return the country to normal—

not least because he alone seemed capable of checking the radicals in his own movement.

So it was not obvious what Mussolini's appointment as prime minister in October 1922 was to mean. Although it was accompanied by the choreographed march on Rome, it could seem more the final stage of Italy's postwar unrest than the beginning of a new, post-liberal regime. Perhaps it portended renewal from within the system, a circulation of elites revitalizing the political class through new elements from below—young lions, tempered by the war experience and willing to use force. They had the energy to revitalize the existing government, making the trains run on time. In January 1923, Mussolini seemed to justify the hopes of his establishment supporters by channeling the violent *squadristi* into a Fascist militia clearly subordinate to Mussolini himself as head of government.

But even that taming was not definitive. The apparently bland, legalitarian outcome so far produced frustration among the many Fascists expecting more in light of the grandiose visions that had accompanied the end of the war. Such frustration produced a second wave of Fascist violence, intended to force Mussolini's hand. It culminated, in June 1924, in the murder of the democratic socialist and outspokenly anti-Fascist deputy Giacomo Matteotti, which produced a genuine crisis for Mussolini, who seemed unwilling or unable to control Fascist radicalism after all. The resulting public outcry almost forced Mussolini to resign. If Fascism was to continue in power, it seemed to require a clearer historical *raison d'être*. Thus Mussolini became more open than ever to the suggestions—or demands—of Fascists seeking systematic institutional change.

Pressures for Fascism finally to commit itself focused on the meeting of the party's National Council, which brought together Fascist parliamentary deputies and local party leaders in August 1924. The veteran syndicalist Sergio Panunzio and the young militant Curzio Suckert were prominent in focusing the discussion on neo-syndicalist proposals, but more right-leaning Fascists like Carlo Costamagna forced a compromise. Still, the outcome of this meeting proved to be the beginning of the process that eventually led to new corporativist institutions.[109] However, the immediate outcome was merely a commission to study and offer proposals, and that in itself hardly constituted the decisive step that the militants had wanted. Late in December, thirty-five of them called on Mussolini to insist that he commit himself unequivocally to a radical break with the liberal order.

Just days later, on January 3, 1925, Mussolini addressed the Chamber of Deputies with a defiant speech that may well have been patterned on Lenin's of July 1919, asserting the dictatorship of one party. Now Mussolini took responsibility for the whole new direction that had emerged in Italy since the struggle for intervention, including all the violence, and he essentially declared the advent of a specifically Fascist regime based on a Fascist monopoly of power.[110] Several months later, in June, he began to invoke the term "totalitarian," now in general use by the opposition, to characterize his regime's direction. But the term was new, and what it meant, in terms of both institutional development and the wider Fascist self-understanding, was by no means clear.

War, vulnerability, and the quest for an alternative modernity in Germany

Coming at a time of increasing social tension in Germany, the outbreak of war in 1914 yielded an experience, and an enduring image, of deeper unity that seemed to portend an enhanced capacity to act collectively. But the war ended up exacerbating divisions, which seemed all the more disappointing and obstructive—and anomalous—in light of that earlier experience of unity.[111] Although specialists differ on its extent and significance, a sense that Germany was especially vulnerable, even facing growing encirclement, balanced the new Germany's assertiveness on the eve of the war. Russia, especially, loomed as a long-term threat. Then the war experience itself greatly exacerbated the sense of vulnerability. In peacetime, Germany had depended on imports of food, fats, oils, and chemicals, including the nitrates needed for explosives. With the onset of war, these goods were immediately in short supply. Thus Britain's naval blockade, which made no distinction between military and non-military goods, was quickly effective, forcing Germany to adopt especially stringent economic coordination and control. Quite apart from the military effort, shortages produced massive malnutrition among German civilians.[112] As Woodruff Smith put it, "extreme, autarkic versions of economic imperialism that had gained only limited currency before the war seemed more plausible under circumstances of blockade, shortages, and rationing."[113]

The shape of the current war made Germany's special vulnerability in any long war clear to the country's top officials. And as it dragged on, the war seemed likely to prove only the beginning of a new era of intense international competition in which the old rules would no longer apply. Vulnerable Germany especially had to reassess its geopolitical situation and access to raw materials, to examine its capacity to act, to question and perhaps to jettison conventional moral and legal strictures if it was to compete in the new era. In the immediate term, Germany seemed forced to take economic advantage of its preliminary conquests. In exploiting the economy of occupied Belgium, for example, the Germans compelled 62,000 Belgians to work in German factories under conditions of virtual slave labor. By the time this practice was stopped in February 1917, nearly a thousand Belgian workers had died in German labor camps. And the Germans had requisitioned foodstuffs even to the point of causing starvation among the Belgians themselves.

Under these circumstances, the longstanding tension between *Weltpolitik*, seeking overseas expansion, and *Lebensraum*, envisioning expansion on the European continent, became still more salient, even as the emphases of each evolved at the same time. As *Weltpolitiker* envisioned rational economic management and moderate political reform, the ascendancy of the military leaders Paul von Hindenburg and Erich Ludendorff by 1917 meant the ascendancy of a more focused *Lebensraum* orientation—and the denial of any scope for a negotiated peace.[114] From this latter perspective, the present war had come to afford a precious opportunity to conquer the territorial basis to fight the next war on a more favorable footing. Responding in February 1918 to calls for a white peace,

Ludendorff stressed that "if Germany makes peace without profit, it has lost the war." Germany, he insisted, must win the military and economic basis for future security—to "enable us to contemplate confidently some future defensive war."[115] Many officials believed that Germany could achieve parity with Britain, and thus the basis for security and peace, only if it maintained control of the Belgian coast. German expansion into Russian Poland and up the Baltic coast of Lithuania and Latvia also seemed essential.

The Treaty of Brest-Litovsk imposed on defeated Russia in March 1918 made clear how radically annexationist German war aims had become. European Russia was to be largely dismembered, leaving Germany in direct or indirect control of nearly half of Russia's European territory, with 75 percent of its iron and coal. In the wake of Brest-Litovsk, planning for German resettlement in what had been Russia's European empire, directed first at the Baltic states, expanded greatly.[116] Smith noted that whereas wartime circumstances encouraged visions of economic imperialism and autarky everywhere, the onset of peace entailed normalization in countries like Britain and France facing the practical task of developing long-range policies for newly acquired territories. But in defeated Germany, which was not forced to face realities in the same way, such visions continued to grow.[117] And they grew in a very particular way, in light of defeat, political change, and the ongoing volatility of the Weimar Republic. Although *Lebensraum*, associated with the insistence on total victory—but thus also with the total defeat that resulted—was to some extent discredited, the experience of defeat did not occasion a fundamental reassessment on the part of either party.[118] But with *Weltpolitik* linked to reform, and with earlier reformist *Weltpolitiker* like Friedrich Naumann and Max Weber prominent in the creation of the Weimar Republic, anti-Weimar *Lebensraum* ideas found scope for wide diffusion on the German Right, becoming linked to biological racism for the first time.[119]

In this context, the geopolitics of Karl Haushofer, whose students at the University of Munich included the future Nazi Rudolf Hess, was an effort at synthesis.[120] The key was to overcome the vacillation about priorities that had weakened Germany prior to and during the First World War. Adapting the ideas of Rudolf Kjellen and Halford J. Mackinder, Haushofer envisioned eastward expansion on the Eurasian land mass as the appropriate direction for Germany. The more general key, Haushofer insisted, was to decide, to forge a consensus and the means to act. Yet the Weimar Republic, the regime produced by moderate political reform, found consensus especially difficult.

Smith concluded that only the Nazis managed to fuse the *Weltpolitik* and *Lebensraum* strands as a means of forging such a national consensus. However, as he saw it, the two strands were incompatible.[121] Thus, in part, the incoherence of Nazi policy during the Second World War—a contention to which we will return in Chapter 8. The question for now is what differentiated the Nazi departure. Why did the Nazis believe that they uniquely could forge the deeper consensus essential for more effective collective action? According to Smith, they thought that new modes of opinion manipulation would enable them to exploit the changes in attitude that accompanied the war. But something deeper was crucially at work as well. It was only on the basis of the wider new historical-political sense that the Nazis could have envisioned the particular combination of will, concentration of power, and mobilization that would make the new mode of action possible. Moreover, it matters that in conceiving action as collective history making, they were seeking not merely to fuse interests, as for Smith, but to transcend interest-based thinking altogether.

Although the effort to overcome the debilitating confusions in German imperialist traditions was also at work, it was especially Weimar welfare and population policy that raised new questions about consensus and action. At issue in this area was immediate experience, not merely dreams for the future. Although the war intensified concern with population policy everywhere, the matter seemed especially pressing for Germany in light of its newly evident vulnerabilities and its eventual defeat.[122] Without condemning the war, Wilhelm Schallmayer lamented its population costs and worried that the potential threat from Russia, better able to absorb them, would only increase.[123] Natalist concerns interfaced with territorial demands: resettling families in new territories could yield the larger population that Germany seemed to need.[124] There was also much concern over population quality in light of the seemingly counter-selective effects of war. On all these grounds, eugenics advocates stepped up calls for the government to assume an active population policy.

During the war, some German government officials began to make the same argument for the first time. As early as March 1915, Chancellor Bethmann-Hollweg called for vigorous state intervention to defend the quantity and the health of future generations. Although also addressing the birthrate, he and others were increasingly concerned to lower infant mortality rates to compensate for falling birthrates. Thus they favored positive measures like maternity benefits to foster family welfare. Paul Weindling's pioneering research indicated the emergence of a new pro-natalist consensus, bound up with a shared organicist ideology that viewed the family as the cell of the state organism. And because medical policy was becoming so intertwined with nationalist concerns, he found that "statistics and commentaries on health conditions were more ideological constructs than reflections of actual conditions."[125]

But though the state became somewhat more interventionist, extending the responsibilities of doctors and public health officials, government policy during the war remained resistant to anything beyond natalism.[126] So even as eugenic or "race hygiene" ideas spread, their actual influence on German legislation remained limited during the war. Moreover, squabbles between ministries, reflecting both administrative divisions and differences in expertise, compromised the effectiveness even of the delimited attempts at state intervention that developed. Thus new questions emerged not only about the range but also about the capacity of the modern state—even in its bureaucratic as opposed to its parliamentary guise—to handle the expanded range of action that some proposed.[127]

Whatever its immediate impact on actual policy, the German war experience intensified, and radicalized, wider eugenic thinking, even making discussion of "euthanasia" more respectable.[128] Michael Burleigh showed that in light of scarce resources, negative selection was practiced in an actively passive way in German psychiatric asylums, quite apart from government policy. Almost 72,000 people, or about 30 percent of the prewar population in such asylums, died of hunger, disease, or neglect during the First World War.[129] Reflecting back in his opening address to the annual conference of the German Psychiatric Association in May 1920, chairman Karl Bonhoeffer observed:

> It could almost seem as if we have witnessed a change in the concept of humanity. I mean simply that we were forced by the terrible exigencies of war to ascribe a different value to the life of the individual than was the case before, and that in the years of starvation during the war we had to get used to watching our patients die of malnutrition in vast numbers, almost approving of this, in the knowledge that perhaps the healthy could be kept alive through these sacrifices.[130]

The political outcome of Germany's defeat was the new Weimar Republic, which sought to consolidate democracy in the context of seemingly anomalous defeat, harsh peace terms, economic uncertainty, and the threat of wider revolution. Obviously Nazism was a revolt against Weimar democracy, and it was long held that Nazism was, more deeply, a revolt against modernity, fed by "Germany's new conservatism" or a "politics of cultural despair" that, while growing from earlier counter-traditions, came to the fore especially during the unsettled Weimar years.[131] But a more nuanced conception of the novel features and discontents of the Weimar period, in relationship to both German wartime traumas and the content of the Nazi alternative, has emerged over the past generation. Jeffrey Herf's *Reactionary Modernism* (1984) fostered reconceptualization by showing how even those opposed to conventional democracy could embrace modern and modernizing technology.

The Weimar period was characterized by the complex interplay between a "catastrophic" sense, wrapped in Spenglerian pessimism and including even fears of German extinction, and a sense of unprecedented scope for expanded collective action. Germany, having lost 10 percent of its territory and all its overseas colonies, had to close ranks, applying expertise more rigorously to both production and population matters. It seemed possible to reconfigure industrial relations through some form of *Berufsstaat*, or vocational state, while also addressing population matters and even sex and gender roles in a more active way.[132] Biological expertise and the rationalization of industry converged as experts assumed responsibility for inspection and certification of workplace health and safety.[133]

In general, then, the challenge for Germans was not merely to catch up with those with a fuller experience of parliamentary government; they had to create something new, democracy with a difference. Indeed, Weimar leaders were claiming to redefine modernity itself. And although some measure of continuity with Prussian or German statist traditions is clear, Richard Bessel insisted convincingly that the relationship of the German people to the state changed in the aftermath of the war—and yielded a particular dilemma: "Popular expectations of what the state could and should provide for its citizens outstripped what the Weimar system was able to deliver."[134] Developing this overall line of argument with particular force, Detlev Peukert contended that the republic's difficult quest for legitimacy led it to seek a new consensus by expanding governmental roles, thereby becoming the first thoroughgoing modern welfare state. Against those who insisted that welfare remain a matter of private philanthropy, the Weimar constitution provided for the protection of the health of the family and of future generations.[135] At the state level, a new welfare ministry was established in Prussia, for example, in 1919.

Peukert emphasized that with this new welfare commitment, Weimar Germany was seeking to become *more* modern than Britain and France, each of which had traditions legitimizing established institutions and values—and thus continuity. And for Peukert, the promise of a welfare state was a reasonable compromise for postwar Germany in light of the revolutionary pressures and conservative resentments that surrounded the birth of the new regime. The question was whether the German economy would enable the republic actually to deliver on its new commitments.[136]

Intersecting with the economic issue were complex demographic trends, producing contradictory pressures. The German birthrate had reached a standstill by the 1880s, then actually began to decrease by 1900. The net reproduction rate had reached an all-time low by the mid-1920s. Wartime losses only exacerbated concerns about this decline in births and the concomitant aging of the population. By 1925, married fertility rates were but half what they had been in 1900. Those concerned that Germany was becoming "a nation without young people" tended to blame contraception—and ultimately the state itself, which, having expanded its reach, inevitably became a lightning rod for discontents concerning population.[137] Yet members of "the virtually redundant generation" born around 1900 found themselves especially vulnerable when, as young adults during the 1920s, they faced an exceptionally crowded labor market. Both Nazis and Communists appealed to such superfluous young. Thus Peukert admitted "a certain specious plausibility" to the notion that Germany was a *Volk ohne Raum*, a people without space.[138] In any case, Germany experienced concerns about overpopulation and depopulation simultaneously—an especially explosive combination.

In accounting for the fate of the Weimar experiment, Peukert drew heavily on the pioneering researches of Weindling, Gisela Bock, and others who had recently probed the changing place of science, expertise, and eugenics. The new welfare commitment itself reflected growing confidence in the scope for social engineering and amelioration through an objective, scientific population policy. Weindling noted that the attitudes of both officials and interest groups changed after 1918 as the voluntary, ethical, humanitarian, Christian slant long associated

especially with Friedrich Naumann gave way to reliance on newly professional-
ized experts. Careers in areas like social work opened for such experts, who
gained access to the power of the state as the government accepted expanded
responsibility. Most basically, with population quantity and quality a national
concern, the government sought to promote nutrition, the health of mothers
and children, and improved infant mortality rates. Through health education
in the schools and exhibitions on personal health and social hygiene, the
government tried to educate people about healthy lifestyles and the need to
increase the birthrate.[139] Although it marked a major change in state and expert
roles, the government's embrace of scientific expertise as it expanded its reach in
the population realm won widespread agreement across the political spectrum.

At the same time, the wider, ambiguous mix of race hygiene, social hygiene,
and eugenics was more broadly institutionalized during the 1920s through
university appointments and curricula, as well as through wider institutes and
programs. One milestone was the publication, in 1923, of the definitive edition
of Erwin Baur, Eugen Fischer, and Fritz Lenz's *Grundriss der menschlichen
Erblichkeitslehre und Rassenhygiene* (Outline of Human Heredity and Race Hygiene),
a highly influential textbook that included an overtly prescriptive dimension.
Robert Proctor noted that this was one of the most esteemed scientific works of
the age, much praised when the English translation, entitled simply *Human
Heredity*, appeared in 1931.[140] One of the co-authors, Lenz, became Germany's
first professor of race hygiene at the University of Munich in 1923 before
moving to the University of Berlin in 1933. He proved to be Germany's premier
racial hygienist during both the Weimar and the Nazi periods.[141]

The apocalyptic dimension growing from the German war experience
pointed scientific thinking about population matters well beyond the quest for a
new consensus to underpin the Weimar Republic. As even government officials
expressed concerns about the extermination of the German race, expertise in
population and welfare matters was coming to seem a means of national salvation. Some positive eugenic measures enjoyed widespread agreement—for
example, marriage counseling and certification to minimize putatively degenerate children and the accompanying burdens on the state. Even this relatively
mild measure afforded doctors growing authority over marriage and procreation
in the name of promoting, or enforcing, what seemed to be the collective
interest. Alfred Grotjahn, a leading expert in social hygiene who, in stressing
social, was a moderate on the eugenics axis, estimated that one-third of the population was degenerate and, on that basis, called for the institutionalization of
those unfit to reproduce. Such notions were introduced into the prescribed
training course for doctors, nurses, and social workers. Weindling noted that
Germany was moving well beyond even the wartime position: "The biological
nationalism that had been decisively rejected during the war was to provide
authoritative guidelines for social policies that were to save the nation from
destruction."[142]

From within this framework, discussion of "euthanasia" took on a still sharper
tone. Especially influential was Karl Binding and Alfred Hoche's *Die Freigabe der*

Vernichtung Lebensunwerten Lebens (Permission for the Destruction of Life Unworthy of Life), published in 1920. Following up on the difficult choices made necessary during the war, this tract calculated the actual costs of keeping mental patients alive and suggested that certain forms of life were actually negative for society. The experience of war, which demanded great sacrifices among the healthy, seemed to have suggested that even such hallowed notions as the sanctity of human life were historically specific, not given for all time. However, the authors recognized that it would take time to develop the new ethical perspective needed to address the issue.

Not surprisingly, the sharper key surrounding the discussion of race hygiene and "euthanasia" was bound up with the continuing appropriation of Nietzsche, whose thinking, especially in light of the wider new apocalyptic sense, seemed to open the way to the post-Christian ethical perspective that some found necessary. In Ernst Bertram's *Nietzsche*, reissued seven times between 1918 and 1925, Nietzsche, "the climactic German," became both agent and metaphor for German redemption.[143] Nietzsche's legacy seemed to buttress the notion that the capacity to exterminate the weak and the sick was essential to a healthy society.[144]

But if certain directions were clear, there was no consensus on how extensive a more active policy was to be or on what it should encompass. Indeed, the overall Weimar effort to move to the modern forefront entailed myriad tensions, ambiguities, uncertainties, and disagreements. Peukert noted how hard it was for contemporaries—and remains for us—to distinguish forward-looking from reactionary impulses in the ideas and responses at work.[145] On the institutional level, the Weimar constitution was unclear regarding the respective roles of state and municipality. Professional and bureaucratic rivalries inevitably developed as the state's role expanded.[146] And with the increasing extra-governmental interest in population policy, various private advocacy groups emerged, often in complex interplay with governments and official policies.[147] The role of such private bodies was sometimes quasi-institutionalized—but *only* quasi-institutionalized. So there were sometimes tensions between experts and officials.

Still, prior to the Depression, advocates of the more extreme forms of positive eugenics were marginalized from policy making as activist forms of welfare policy won out. Although both sterilization and "euthanasia" continued to be discussed, judicial officials, supporting liberal individual rights, remained opposed, and even within the eugenics community, most resisted even compulsory sterilization, not to mention "euthanasia."[148] The wide debate that surrounded the 1920 book by Binding and Hoche included considerable humanitarian opposition to "euthanasia," which, critics charged, would poison doctor–patient relations, open the way to irreparable mistakes, and fundamentally compromise the medical/ethical imperative to care and to cure.[149] Even Lenz saw "euthanasia" as irrelevant; the key was family welfare, which could, however, include sterilization as well as marriage certification.[150] Regardless of official policy, however, some doctors simply proceeded with sterilization on their own, viewing it as at once humane and cost-effective.

Already before the Depression, some were growing frustrated that so little seemed to be getting done on the governmental level. The Kaiser Wilhelm Institute for Anthropology, Human Heredity and Eugenics, established in 1927, produced research—and publicity—that yielded a new threshold of confidence in eugenics, which now seemed sufficiently mature as a science to be made to work, so that population matters could be subordinated to scientific laws, benefiting both the political and the economic realms. By 1928, eugenicists like Lenz and Otmar von Verschuer were actively calling for eugenic alternatives as they attacked the welfare state for preserving the weak and the work-shy.[151]

The advent of the Depression, threatening the economic basis for welfare measures, led to intensified charges that Weimar's "burgeoning" welfare state, including its measures for the aged, the insane, and the incurably ill, had outstripped national resources. Those who had been seeking a stronger eugenic component grew ever more frustrated, so the Depression deepened the rift between eugenicists and the government. Charging that governmental responses to the Depression were neglecting the implications for health and population matters, eugenicists increasingly called for negative eugenics measures, including sterilization and other modes of differentiation to sustain child-rich families and channel benefits to quality individuals.[152] By the early 1930s, the *Deutsche Ärztevereinsbund* (German Physicians League) was demanding forced sterilization partly to ease the burden on the treasury.[153]

Some of those actually delivering welfare services were coming to agree that welfare was not a universal right, that society had a duty to differentiate, excluding those who had least to contribute in order properly to provide for the remainder. As such thinking grew even in government circles, Prussia was poised to adopt a compulsory sterilization law by January 1933, when Hitler came to power. But all the uncertainties, tensions, and fits and starts suggested to many that a whole new relationship between such social engineering and the political order was necessary.

For most of the 1920s, both state officials and the eugenics community had resisted certain political conflations. Officials and welfare experts had taken great care to separate medical- and welfare-oriented eugenics from ideologies of national or racial purity. At the same time, even those like Alfred Ploetz, prominent in the "racial hygiene" wing of eugenics, were concerned to uphold scientific standards against any association with *völkisch* racism and anti-Semitism. And although some early links developed between Hitler and the eugenicists, the scientists generally remained aloof, seeing the Nazi leader as a mere demagogue, if not a psychopath.[154]

The frustrations surrounding the Depression opened new possibilities for interaction. Although the race link remained controversial, the distinction between eugenics and racism now blurred further. Notions of Aryan superiority gained currency, and researchers began examining blood type as the key to race. There was even an effort, spearheaded by Eugen Fischer, to correlate all health records in order to produce an anthropological survey of Germany, a total map of the biological characteristics of the population.[155]

Meanwhile, those frustrated had foreign models to study. As state roles expanded and confidence in scientific expertise grew, eugenics was becoming institutionalized in Britain, the United States, Austria, and the Scandinavian countries. Sterilization legislation was the central issue.[156] Although Fascist Italy did not emphasize such negative selection, its seemingly concerted population policy—from a bachelor tax to measures to ensure the economic viability of rural populations—attracted Germans disappointed with the performance of the Weimar Republic. Lenz was greatly interested in Mussolini's natalism, encouraged through taxation policy, even as he was pessimistic about the prospects for eugenics. Both Lenz and Eugen Fischer assessed the Italian situation at first hand while attending the meeting of the International Federation of Eugenics Organizations in Rome in 1929.[157] In general, international comparisons enhanced the sense that Germany, in light of its special vulnerability, had to address population and welfare matters in a more thoroughgoing and rigorously scientific way.

At the same time, many eugenicists began to conclude that a more authoritarian political framework was necessary if science was to play the public roles that seemed ever more essential. This emphasis meshed easily with their concurrent denunciations of democracy, egalitarianism, humanitarianism, and individualism as threats to the long-term health of the race. And although the need for some degree of eugenics was widely accepted across much of the political spectrum, it was the Nazis who used the population issue most explicitly and effectively. Hitler renewed calls for sterilization of the hereditarily ill in 1931. The Nazis stressed the need for action on a large scale, getting beyond sentimentalist obstacles.[158]

Writing in Ploetz's *Archiv für Rassen und Gesellschaftsbiologie* in 1931, Lenz expressed his admiration for the Nazis as the first political party to make racial hygiene central. He noted that Hitler had borrowed from the noted textbook that he, Baur, and Fischer had published in 1923. But although he liked the Nazi treatment of sterilization and rural settlement, Lenz was put off by what he found the Nazis' exaggerated fears of racial inbreeding and their demagoguery in appealing to the lower classes, where psychopathy was prevalent. Nor did he approve of the Nazis' anti-Semitism. Even the Nazi form of political authoritarianism gave him pause; whereas biology, as science, should be supreme, the Nazis seemed to claim infallibility. So Lenz's enthusiasm was selective; he joined the Nazi Party only in 1937. Indeed, most racial hygienists still remained independent of Nazism by January 1933, although government by the Nazis seemed to afford them the best chance to pursue their policy agendas.[159]

The tension-ridden relationship between scientific expertise and political power had lurked in discussions throughout the Weimar period. Even as he lauded Nietzsche in a 1926 article, E. Kirchner criticized Nietzsche's accent on will, which seemed to conflict with the modern, strictly biological approach that Kirchner himself favored.[160] Yet it could not be sufficient merely to understand the biology, or simply to wait for nature to take its course. Indeed, the natural biological tendency seemed negative unless human beings took hold and acted in new ways. The key was to find a relationship between scientific expertise and political power that would make possible the new form of action—the more systematic application of eugenics—that was necessary. Political will and scientific expertise had to come together. And because of the issues that Germany's wartime and postwar experience had brought to the fore, Germans had to take the lead.

Peukert stressed that although the Depression obviously worsened the situation dramatically, the foundations of the welfare state were collapsing even before the Depression began.[161] Except during the unsustainable inflationary boom of 1920–21, the new regime never had the economic basis to deliver on its overall welfare promise. Structural factors combined with chronic agricultural depression and other cyclical factors to produce high unemployment, which reached one peak even in 1926, in the midst of the stabilization period. But although the republic proved unable to deliver, it mattered crucially that it had tried what it did. As Weimar encountered an impasse, the agents did not simply return to the *status quo ante* or turn in a completely different direction. Rather, for many the imperative was to adjust in light of what the novel Weimar experiment had revealed—and thus to move to another layer of innovative action. In that sense, the frustrated Weimar effort itself opened new possibilities that would not have opened otherwise.

For Peukert, totalitarianism had come to seem the only viable response to the modern tensions that had come uniquely to the surface in Germany.[162] However, totalitarianism was not a system or blueprint but simply a post-liberal direction entailing, most immediately, a more systematic confrontation with the population issues that the Weimar experiment had brought to the fore. And we must beware of overemphasizing the continuity between Weimar and Nazism. While recognizing that Weimar discussions and initiatives lent legitimacy to the Nazi departure, Atina Grossmann stressed the radicalism of that departure. In assuming power, the Nazis themselves were well aware that their vision of race hygiene differed from that of many of those in the relevant reaches of the governmental bureaucracy. Thus she sharply disputed any implication "that Weimar sex reformers, softened up by years of eugenic discourse and faith in state intervention, paved the way for, or were easily seduced into, support for Nazi population policy. Quite the contrary: their pioneering institutions were systematically liquidated. Weimar sex reformers had to be silenced, fired, arrested (often on abortion charges), killed, driven to suicide, or forced into exile."[163]

It is surely true that we must avoid any implication that the Weimar effort involved merely apolitical experts who seized the chance to act on the new basis that the Nazis offered. Although the particulars had been much contested, population policy activism had drawn from across the political spectrum, and the political divide certainly did not disappear when the Nazis came to power. Leftist population activists remained leftists. But the Weimar experience suggested to the Nazis themselves that a particular new mode of action would be necessary to address population issues more effectively. And although we must not overdo continuity, those like Peukert, Weindling, and Proctor make it clear that a degree of continuity there surely was. The Nazi determination to act in a more concerted way drew the support of some, like Lenz and Ploetz, who had not otherwise been attracted to Nazism.

The debilitating effects of Weimar's multi-party system have long been recognized, but we have increasingly noted a propensity to form single-issue interest groups that tended to undermine the major parties and further fragment the polity.[164] Dieter Langewiesche showed that even the "centrist" DDP (German Democratic Party) and DVP (German People's Party) proved to be coalitions of interest groups that did not succeed in reconciling their conflicting aims through generic appeals to state and nation. By 1929, leading spokesmen for these parties, including DVP chief Gustav Stresemann, were lamenting not just the difficulties of coalition politics but also the lack of party discipline in coalition member parties.[165] It may be true, as Langewiesche suggests, that DVP deputy Otto Most lapsed into caricature in a Reichstag speech blaming economic interest-group particularism, linked to the party system itself, for dissolving the German sense of community, but such laments reflected genuinely increasing particularism that produced deepening concerns about the bases of consensus in Germany.

Langewiesche noted, more particularly, that "the liberals were denied the recourse to material interests as a basis for a policy of social reform, since the middle classes disintegrated into many mutually competing interest groups."[166] So Weimar came to manifest, in extreme form, a peculiar combination: on the one hand, the scope for, and promise of, an expanded state role; on the other, a tendency toward interest-group particularism that compromised the capacity for the necessary collective action. The alternative to Weimar democracy would have the shape and content it did partly as a result. More particularly, it would insist on a seemingly deeper—ethnic—basis for the homogeneity that was apparently necessary to form a collective will and act. As it became clear that the Weimar expansion of the state raised new issues in political and judicial theory, the young Carl Schmitt emerged as an innovative and influential jurist. He became known for advocating stronger presidential government in light of the weakness of the Weimar democracy and its difficulty in coming to collective decisions.[167] But he first came to prominence in departing from traditional, still-prevalent German legal thinking by taking more seriously the fact of change, in light of the Weimar experience and the tendencies of modernity more generally. Societal needs and expectations, and even the political order itself, had become too fluid to be encompassed by abstract norms and static codified law, even by traditional notions of sovereignty. People disagree about societal values and priorities, and only the political clash of concrete human groupings can decide, making collective action possible.[168] Conservatives charged Schmitt with relativism because he seemed to privilege change and history in this sense.[169]

Schmitt welcomed the advent of Nazism as an antidote to what seemed the chaotic, excessively pluralistic expansion of the state in response to growing societal demands during the Weimar period. In this light, the top-down coordination—*Gleichschaltung*—that marked the first stage of the Nazi revolution could be understood, up to a point, as a welcome restoration of state sovereignty and authority.[170] But as a response to the Weimar crisis and all it had revealed about modern politics, the Nazi revolution had to be more innovative than that. In his *Staat, Bewegung, Volk* (State, Movement, People) of 1933, Schmitt offered what he took to be a new synthesis, pointing beyond the liberal dualism of state and society, to show how the state could encompass the expanded societal content. In doing so, he thought he was doing justice to the novelty—and primacy—of Nazism at the same time. The state was no longer a sphere of fixed law that determines the political element but was now determined by it—by the movement and its leadership.[171]

But Schmitt proved symptomatically ambiguous in treating the interface of restoration and novelty, of static and dynamic, of society, politics, and state. To a considerable extent, he was still stressing the state's conventional role of maintaining order by adjudicating conflicts and harmonizing contending social forces.[172] At the Nazi Party Congress of September 1934, his conservative notion that the people were to be ruled aroused protest and was rejected.[173] From the Nazi perspective, the people, spearheaded by the movement, were the agents. Although he had departed from the conservative traditionalists up to a point, Schmitt's thinking remained too conventional and static to grasp why the Nazis insisted on the "movement," as opposed to a new state, as the vehicle for the essential modern dynamism.

By implication, the point for the Nazis was not merely to order a newly more active and demanding society, although, in light of the chaotic tendencies of Weimar, a new discipline did seem necessary. Such discipline, however, served the deeper aim of making society—the people—into a dynamic instrument for ongoing action. In comparison, Schmitt's conception remained "pre-totalitarian": individual moral response fuels socio-political antagonism, and politics simply orders the conflicting forces, as opposed to mobilizing, nurturing, and channeling societal energies for dynamic collective ends. Thus the Nazi charge that Schmitt was a neo-Hegelian positing the primacy of the state *vis-à-vis* the *Volk*.[174] Although he sought mightily to make himself the dominant Nazi jurist, Schmitt found himself largely marginalized by 1935. The Nazis had come to more radical conclusions about what was necessary, and possible, in light of all that had resulted from the war and its outcomes in Germany.

The new scope for experiment with great politics

Their idiosyncratic experiences of the war and its immediate aftermath, against the backdrop of longer-term national idiosyncrasies, differentiated Russia, Italy, and Germany from the victorious democracies, which could more readily return to normal as they continued to define the modern mainstream. In light of that differentiating experience, Russia, Italy, and Germany were especially positioned to connect with, and draw sustenance from, the layer of antecedent intellectual articulation that we discussed in the preceding chapter. Conversely, the inchoate sense of new political possibilities that had earlier emerged among intellectual elites became more concrete with the response to the war and its aftermath in these three countries.

The atmosphere of drama, of violence, even of potential catastrophe evident especially in Russia, Italy, and Germany enhanced the sense of the need and the scope for new modes of collective action. From the perspective of the emerging counter-elites in those countries, Britain and France were old, tired, decadent, lacking the fresh ideas and the will needed to address the challenges and to seize the opportunities that had opened. In contrast, the new counter-elites in Russia, Italy, and Germany could claim to have derived, partly from the cataclysmic experience of the era, the toughness, courage, will, vision, and commitment required to match the challenge, to take advantage of the opportunity, and to spearhead an unprecedented great politics.

Although it is arguable that the situations in Italy and Russia, at least, were potentially explosive even before the war, an explosion at that earlier point could not have entailed the grandiose sense of alternative modern innovation that became possible once the war had revealed and stimulated all it did. Radically opposed on the immediate level, Soviet Communism and Italian Fascism both emerged to assault the bourgeois order and, soon enough, to dispute what the terrain beyond was to entail. Germany entered the equation from a very different angle partly because its socialist spectrum, from Friedrich Ebert to Rosa Luxemburg, had largely *defined* the wider mainstream alternative that innovative radicals in Russia and Italy felt it necessary to transcend. So in Germany the developing sense of the scope for a different systematic alternative, especially in light of the war and its immediate aftermath, did not emerge directly from within the impasse of orthodox Marxism.

Under semi-duress, Germany tried democracy, and from within that new democratic framework tackled tasks that were in one sense unprecedented in their advanced modernity. The outcome of this experience brought home further the limits of parliamentary democracy, especially as a mode of response to the new possibilities and necessities that seemed to have emerged from the war. So Germany, too, proved to be especially positioned to discern the need and the scope for a grandiose, post-liberal alternative. Even as immediate priorities differed, the three departures manifested certain common features in diagnosis and prescription, in the modes of action adopted, and in the dynamic that resulted. The implication of the overall package was "totalitarian." This was not to conform to some pre-existing form, model, or ideal; only with the practice itself would totalitarianism come to be.

5   The totalitarian dynamics of Leninism–Stalinism

Ongoing questions about the Soviet experience

The new Bolshevik regime faced an unforeseen situation at the beginning of 1921 when, having maintained its power in Russia by winning the country's civil war, it found itself isolated on what had seemed the crucial international level. Despite the Russian revolutionary spark, Socialists elsewhere had not grasped the opportunity offered by the war, so the revolution had not spread as expected. Thus the situation facing the Bolsheviks, and the stakes of whatever they might now do, had changed dramatically since 1917.

On one level, the Bolsheviks, newly styling themselves "Communists" in 1918, expressed bafflement and confusion in light of the unanticipated outcome by early 1921.[1] Lenin clearly grasped the Communists' isolation not only on the international level but even in their own country.[2] Yet the civil war victory made it clear that the revolution was to stick, despite the initial assumption of many abroad that it would quickly dissipate. And although the expected wider revolution had not been forthcoming, the "spark" notion could be adjusted to maintain the link to orthodoxy; even as "socialism in one country," the new Soviet Union, as constituted from the Russian empire in 1922, could be the socialist homeland and, as such, the base for further revolution over the longer term. Sparking wider revolution would take longer, and take a different form than anticipated, but the fact that the Bolsheviks had made their revolution, and made it stick, could still prove decisive in the quest for socialism.

However, we noted in the last chapter that Lenin's emphasis changed as the expectation of wider revolution met frustration, and as an array of Marxists elsewhere criticized the Bolshevik departure, denying it any wider relevance. Even more sympathetic observers lacked the terms to make sense of what had resulted from the revolution by 1921. Under the circumstances, the Communists' sense of their own role, the significance of what they had done, and were doing, was bound to change—and in a way that mixed renewed self-assertion with shrillness and doubt. They could not be certain about the wider relevance of what they were doing. Perhaps it mattered only to backward Russia after all, despite the earlier assumptions and claims. Or worse: on what basis could it be denied that this was just an isolated gang of adventurers on the verge of wrecking their country?

Especially in light of the undeniable element of Russian backwardness, the Communist departure had to retain its link to universal Marxism to convey the universal significance of what was being done. This was also important as Fascism emerged to dispute the post-liberal terrain. So Leninism would continue to entail an embrace of Marxism, most obviously in positing a Manichean world of class bifurcation and struggle. As we have seen, however, Lenin understood that it would be necessary for the foreseeable future to operate in a world that did not conform to such Manichean terms. And as the Communists proceeded, following a certain mode of action, they diverged ever further from orthodoxy into a new realm of their own.

Under Russian circumstances, this unprecedented combination of achievement, isolation, and criticism was especially likely to rekindle a sense of national pride, even mission.[3] Indeed, the situation invited a modern renewal of the earlier tendency, going back at least to Alexander Herzen, to identify liberalism with the West and the scope for a superior socialist alternative with Russia.[4] Yet we noted that even as Lenin claimed a link to the Russian revolutionary tradition, he denied that his strategy was a mere throwback; rather, he was reconnecting with that national idiosyncrasy in a creative, modern way that enabled Russia to indicate the route for the European socialist movement overall. From the Leninist perspective, then, the point was not simply that a party claiming to be Marxist had come to power first in backward Russia. The success of the revolution so far rested not on the validity of Marxism but on the effectiveness of Leninism itself, based on a willingness and capacity to act in a certain mode. The course from here might rest less on Marxism than on the logic of this particular mode of action.

Whatever the possibilities in 1921, the outcome of the entire Soviet experiment would arguably rest on the sequence of events that transpired under Stalin from about 1927 to early 1939. If the regime emerging from the Russian Revolution had dissolved with the New Economic Policy (NEP), as Vladimir Brovkin, for example, claimed was imminent by 1927, it would have proved a mere blip resulting from war strains in a backward country, an unorthodox bridge to normal development. Thus the relationship—the connection or disconnection—of Stalinism to Leninism, as it had evolved by the early 1920s, is central to any assessment of the overall Soviet experiment. Are we to understand Stalinism as merely the logical development of Leninism, or are we to take Stalinism as a phenomenon in its own right, thus positing a discontinuity or rupture that must be explained, along with the novel Stalinist features that emerged?

The question of continuity is famously complex, with most of the answers open to positive or negative readings. But although myriad ways of shuffling this set of cards remain, and although each of the familiar cards, including ideology, Russian idiosyncrasy, and ahistorical psychological factors, surely remains part of the mix, the deck has been incomplete. At issue is the scope for a deeper way of understanding continuity, beyond ideological fanaticism, Russian contextual features, or coercive methods.

Stressing a mode of positive continuity, E.H. Carr and Isaac Deutscher each deemed Stalinism a plausible, even logical and necessary way of carrying the revolution forward. Stalin was doing essentially what any Leninist would have done under the difficult, unforeseen circumstances facing the new regime. Facing genuinely dangerous foreign enemies, the Soviet Union required a developmental dictatorship to mobilize for rapid industrialization and modernization. So even insofar as the first priority was to continue the revolution, something of a rupture was necessary to make it work, or to carry it to the next phase, as the situation changed. For Carr the Leninist revolution, without Stalin, would have "run in the sand."[5]

Those most critical of the whole Soviet experiment have been the most likely to stress continuity in a negative key. Leszek Kolakowski insisted that the despotic and totalitarian Communist system was prefigured by Lenin's doctrine over many years. Indeed, there was nothing in the worst of Stalinism that could not be justified by Leninist principles. But whereas Lenin called things by their real names, Stalin lied to legitimize a regime based on such Leninist principles.[6]

But from Leon Trotsky to Hannah Arendt to Nikita Khrushchev to Stephen F. Cohen to Giuseppe Boffa, an array of prominent critics have stressed not continuity but rupture. At issue is a matter of degree; few would deny any relationship between Leninism and Stalinism. The key from this perspective, as nicely pinpointed by Cohen, is that Bolshevism afforded the seeds for other outcomes besides Stalinism, while Stalinism had other sources besides Bolshevism. The bottom line is the distinctiveness of Stalinism, which is *not* to be understood as the logical outgrowth of Leninism, let alone Marxism.[7] Many, but not all, of those featuring discontinuity found something hopeful not only in Marxism in general but also in its Leninist form. By recognizing the negative outcomes of Stalinism while accounting for Stalinism as a contingent deviation, they could suggest the scope for more positive outcomes from within the Russian Communist framework. In the wake of de-Stalinization in the Soviet Union, Leninists like Roy Medvedev argued that if the experiment had been led by Nikolai Bukharin instead of Stalin after Lenin's death, Soviet practice would have entailed neither forced collectivization nor terror. Cohen was especially influential in arguing the scope for a far more benign Bukharinist alternative growing from the NEP.[8]

Lenin's moderation and pragmatism between the civil war and his death in January 1924 were long taken as evidence against any strong continuity argument. Even Hannah Arendt, who ended up emphasizing the prior totalist ideology, and who was by no means featuring the scope for positive outcomes from within Marxism or Leninism, found Stalin's way of embracing that prior ideology quite different from Lenin's. Insisting that Stalinist totalitarianism was *not* inherent in Leninism, she noted that in the purely practical matters at issue by the early 1920s, Lenin followed pragmatic instincts of statesmanship rather than his Marxist convictions. Even the Communist Party's monopoly of power at the expense of the soviets could have led to a mere one-party dictatorship as opposed to full-blown totalitarianism. Thus Arendt's emphasis that the regime's direction—in agricultural policy, for example—was still open on Lenin's death.[9]

Those stressing discontinuity differed widely over how to account for and characterize Stalinism as a negative deviation and phenomenon unto itself, although they tended to rely on some combination of ahistorical psychological propensities and national idiosyncrasies. Especially familiar is reduction to paranoia. Such ahistorical propensities surely played some role, but the key questions about the interface with other factors, about proportions and implications, remain. Most basically, it would be hard to deny that the presence of genuine foreign enemies was to some extent responsible for bringing any paranoid propensity to the fore. Indeed, there may have been something about Stalin's whole mode of action that nurtured a certain self-understanding with concomitant paranoid propensities, so to invoke paranoia is simply to open another set of questions.

The other dominant accent was on the significance of the Russian context, its relative backwardness and idiosyncratic traditions, as the underlying source of the Stalinist deviation. From this perspective, the break or rupture might be understood as a turn, within Bolshevism, from "Westerners" like Lenin, who had considerable experience abroad, and "natives" like Stalin, who did not. Stalin's apparently anomalous course was thus traceable to the Russian context. This tack is congruent with reversion to Russian traditions of revolution from above or, more loosely, with an emphasis on developmental dictatorship, which might include some embrace of nationalism.

In Robert Tucker's well-known account, Stalin turned from the Leninist course and reverted to earlier Russian models of revolution from above; the familiar state-building and/or economic development tradition from Peter the Great to Sergei Witte offered both precedent and legitimation. The remaining trappings of Marxism led the resulting system to be characterized as socialist. Still, Tucker played down the significance of nationalism *per se*, insisting that it had not been a rallying point but had produced conflict within Bolshevism.[10]

Plausibly sensing that reliance on ahistorical or idiosyncratic Russian factors was to miss certain essential origins of the Stalinist departure, Giuseppe Boffa argued not only that Stalinism was a phenomenon in its own right but also that it was specifically modern as totalitarian. Even as Stalin manipulated Marxist theory as one tool at his disposal, he had his own ideas, antithetical to both Marxism and Leninism, which he forced on society. But even as Boffa found the earlier "totalitarian school" insufficiently flexible to grasp the change and novelty that developed from within the Stalinist framework, Stalin's ideas, in Boffa's account, proved to be essentially the conventional litany of totalitarianism.[11] The difference was simply that now that litany stemmed from "Stalin's ideas" as opposed to Marxism, Leninism, or the logic of some reified totalitarian system.[12] But it was not quite clear, in Boffa's account, what factors, beyond the ahistorical psychological or idiosyncratic Russian, would explain the emergence or embrace of the ideas at issue. Although he judged Stalinism to be "modern," Boffa did not consider in what sense this novel, modern Stalinism might have been part of a wider supranational, historically specific phenomenon.

For Hannah Arendt, in contrast, Stalinism had to be understood precisely as part of a wider supranational, historically specific dynamic that also involved Nazism, although even in her case the mix of elements remained uncertain. Her account rested heavily on the putative embrace, by Stalin and Hitler, of a prior totalist ideology, although, as we have seen, she found it at least as important that neither was simply following the ideological blueprint but found it necessary to force reality to conform to the ideology. In each the ideology, denying free human creativity, was unrealistic, but why adopt such an ideology in the first place and then try to force it? We have suggested that some historically specific admixture must have been operative. Even as she denied that either Stalin or Hitler was merely seeking power for its own sake, her account seemed implicitly to rest on ahistorical psychological type, and thus the essence of Stalinist practice proved to be merely the quest for top-down domination.

Since Arendt, various ways of locating the Stalinist departure in terms of wider supranational, historically specific trends and possibilities have emerged. Their emphases have differed, so we have a thick web of possibilities. But partly because of dualistic, either/or tendencies, we have tended to miss, even to preclude, the particular mode of connection, and thus the particular mode of continuity from Leninism to Stalinism, that the great political temptation entailed.

We can best grasp what has been missing if we consider briefly a few of the major voices, and the axes of differentiation between them, in discussions of the place of Stalinism since the decay of the earlier totalitarianism model. In introducing his study of Magnitogorsk, a new steel town in the Urals, Steven Kotkin positioned himself counter to Moshe Lewin and Sheila Fitzpatrick, each of whom, he said, saw Stalinism as an end to the revolution and a return, although under conditions of great stress, to non-revolutionary traditions.[13] In contrast, Kotkin emphasized the revolutionary enthusiasm, the sense of drama and openness, bound up with the energizing sense of actually living a new civilization that marked the Stalinist 1930s. At the same time, he charged that neither Lewin nor Fitzpatrick had made clear whether the society that had emerged by the end of that decade was new and socialist or traditionally Russian with a socialist veneer.

In using Fitzpatrick and Lewin as foils, Kotkin was exaggerating his departure from them to some extent. In her recent work, especially, Fitzpatrick has had plenty of room for the revolutionary enthusiasm that Kotkin emphasized, and Lewin certainly recognized that something novel, even strange, happened during the 1930s. Neither was claiming that the course of things was clear in 1932. Rather, each pinpointed unexpected, heretofore underestimated forces in play that would eventually produce a particular, and arguably decisive, outcome by the end of the decade of upheaval. And each pinpointed aspects of the narrowing that would be central to the regime's evolution thereafter. Yet Kotkin was right that certain of their emphases tended to restrict the discussion, leading us to miss some of what happened during those years and even the place of the narrowing in the overall trajectory.

In their different ways, Lewin and Fitzpatrick helped to undermine the classic top-down totalitarian model by charging that an overemphasis on ideology had produced a corresponding neglect of Soviet society, which, they showed, was not merely putty to be molded from above. But whereas Fitzpatrick suggested something like "normalizing" convergence with the modern Western mainstream, Lewin saw the Soviet trajectory as anomalous, yielding ongoing difference from that mainstream, although the difference had nothing to do with socialism.

Reacting plausibly against the earlier concentration on coercion from above, Fitzpatrick showed how a new elite began to emerge with the cultural revolution of the late 1920s, as higher education was thrown open to the children of workers and peasants. But the process ended in 1932, when, as she saw it, the momentum of the revolution was checked. Now the new middle class, technically literate but culturally conservative, began to establish routine, thereby checking further revolution.[14] Whereas for those like Deutscher who found the socialist quest still central, the point of Stalinist modernization was to make the now isolated Soviet Union a viable base for wider revolution, Fitzpatrick found the ideology fading as its limits were reached in practice, and as getting onto the normal developmentalist escalator came to seem what mattered. What was happening, in the last analysis, was not the achievement of socialism but the achievement of modernity itself. Despite its excesses and errors, Stalin's developmental dictatorship laid the foundations for essentially the same modernity that the more advanced countries of the West had achieved.[15] Even at the height of the terror of the later 1930s, there were supporters and beneficiaries; there was societal interplay, upward mobility, and the scope for negotiation between interest groups. To stress some different agenda, from whatever combination of totalitarianism or ideology or socialism, could only inhibit understanding of the actual societal experience during the Stalinist period and the longer-term trajectory that followed from it.

By the 1960s, it seemed, the Soviet Union was becoming a normal society, now more obviously marked by upward mobility and societal negotiation. The Soviet system proved its capacity to evolve as the coerciveness and other dimensions featured in the classic totalitarian model gradually dissipated; they had been anomalies that responded to special circumstances. From this perspective, the ideological difference with the West diminished in importance. Whatever the gloss, the Soviet experiment had ended up *only* an idiosyncratic but ultimately successful effort at modernization as the quest for socialism, and all it had come to represent, fell away.

Although Fitzpatrick nuanced her argument in her more recent work, paying deeper attention to the terror and placing greater emphasis on ongoing "ideological" idealism, her overall emphasis remained on *embourgeoisment*, the dissipation of the earlier revolutionary enthusiasm. And in the last analysis, the terror of the later 1930s was simply the process through which Stalin got rid of enemies, not an anomaly suggesting the need for an expanded range of categories.[16]

Lewin similarly charged that the classic totalitarianism model had missed the actual dynamic by overemphasizing coherence, top-down intention, and control to the neglect of the societal dimension, starting with the capacity for agency among the peasantry. At the same time, he insisted that in the unanticipated situation by 1921, virtually *nothing* was left of Marxist ideology that could make sense of events or guide subsequent practice. This was to depart even from original Leninism, for which "voluntarism and idealism were . . . built on a sense of historical process that gave the indispensable backing to conscious intervention and ensured that the revolution was not a leap into the unknown but was to some extent a continuation of previous trends." By the end of the civil war, Lenin and his colleagues recognized that the situation defied such expectations. No social forces or discernible trends in Russia could be counted on to generate a dynamic in a socialist direction "except," as Lewin put it, "the pure political will of the leadership." A Marxist was "thus on entirely unfamiliar ground where there was no visible backing 'of a process' for the party's long-term ideological aims. On the contrary, the party found itself in a rarefied atmosphere of unpredictability and contingency, generated by chaotic, hostile petit bourgeois tides." And those hostile forces seemed to the Bolsheviks to be pushing the country in frightening directions.[17]

So from Lewin's perspective little was left even of Leninism insofar as it rested on the assumed value of the ideology and especially the Bolsheviks' privileged capacity to interpret it in order to understand concrete possibilities and thus to guide practice. Whatever the utopianism of the civil war period, Lewin found decisive the moderation of Lenin's testament, which emphasized cultural transformation, alliance with the peasantry, and the capacity to proceed gradually as the supreme virtue. Indeed, against those Bolsheviks who wanted to rush by means of voluntarism and violence, Lenin advocated adapting to the unforeseen present circumstances in order not to jeopardize the longer-term vision.[18] He did not mention the dictatorship of the proletariat, let alone call for revolutionary terror to transform the society, so whatever the possibilities by early 1921, Lenin was leaving open the key questions for longer-term practice.[19]

From Lewin's perspective, the Bolsheviks were essentially starting over in 1921, improvising, so what resulted was necessarily unanticipated and unprecedented. Under the unforeseen situation of the early 1920s, party membership was often raw, opportunistic, and not fully reliable. So with "the pure political will of the leadership" the only force for a socialist direction, the result proved an unforeseen kind of statism, which had not been implicit in original Leninism, although it had begun to develop from the civil war emergency. By 1925, Lewin noted, the state, with or without the proletariat, had come to seem the embodiment of the ongoing revolutionary purpose. This was to overturn Marx's famous reversal of Hegel and to restore primacy to the "superstructure"—with consequences that Lewin found fateful for the whole course of the Soviet experiment.[20] The primacy of the state meant the centrality of bureaucracy, which was not the social basis the Communists expected or wanted. And although bureaucracy was quickly an issue, the Bolsheviks were not equipped to understand or confront it.

At the same time, Lewin stressed the constant narrowing of the apex where decisions were made. The party could have exercised leadership as long as it had a supra-bureaucratic, political role, but it lost that possibility when it turned from democratic procedures, which were dwindling fast by the late 1920s.[21] With the ban on factions, each group tended to deny the legitimacy of the other, yet the outcome of the ensuing political struggles was essentially a matter of chance. The system would soon revolve around the relationship between a single leader, emerging in this contingent way, and the bureaucracy, increasingly a class apart concerned to preserve its privileges.

Lewin concluded that whereas the term "Leninism" continued in use, the ideological changes accompanying the metamorphoses of the regime after 1918 were so profound that even Leninism lost its meaning. By the Stalinist 1930s, Marxism–Leninism had become a harmless catechism, or simply a set of counters to be manipulated in a political experiment that the original ideology could not guide or understand. Although not as the result of some manipulative intention, the ideology served simply to justify whatever the leaders were doing at that moment. Class explanations were pushed aside, and the leaders used conflicting rationales even in public.[22] As a departure from original Leninism, Stalinism entailed not only a changed strategy but altogether different objectives—from creating a situation leading to the disappearance of classes and the state to creating a state to preserve the classes that had emerged with the transformation surrounding crash industrialization.[23]

Lewin certainly recognized that the process entailed a sort of modernization, but it was an archaic form, stemming from backwardness, and thus the characteristic jerky rhythms, the sense of permanent crisis. Lewin found none of the tendency toward normalization and convergence that Fitzpatrick discerned in Soviet-style modernization. Yet, as different, the resulting Soviet system had nothing to do with socialism either.[24] On the contrary, for Lewin, "the more the Stalinist system rushed ahead with its economic development and socialist transformations, the deeper it sank into the quite traditional values of authority, hierarchy, and conservatism."[25] So neither did the Soviet experiment yield a genuinely modern alternative to socialism as the mainstream alternative to Western modernity. Rather, Lewin was suggesting, what the Soviets produced was *sui generis*, an unfortunate anomaly stemming from backwardness, illusion, misapplication, and degeneration into banality.

Giuseppe Boffa similarly contended that although the Communists created a new order, it had little to do with socialism as envisioned by Marx and Lenin. Far from a state that might gradually wither away, they produced the opposite—a powerful state, with a strong and permanent repressive apparatus and growing privileges for a new ruling class. For Boffa, this was not socialism, above all because it precluded the effective participation of the workers in management, a criterion to which we will return below.[26]

Although their contributions remain indispensable, Fitzpatrick and Lewin were using criteria of revolution and conservatism that, just as Kotkin suggested, made them too quick to see the "end of the revolution" by 1932. Fitzpatrick's criteria of revolution, reflecting especially the "cultural revolution" of the late 1920s, were unnecessarily delimited, as if rapid social change and a certain form of egalitarianism were what ultimately mattered. In the same way, Lewin was foreclosing too much in invoking the narrowing of the 1920s, the bureau-cracy syndrome, and the return to conservatism. The anomalous modes of agency that emerged with the effort at post-liberal mobilization and collective action during the 1930s, even the role that bureaucracy ended up playing, cannot be understood in terms of the mere banality of pursuing and preserving privileges.

Kotkin insisted convincingly against both Lewin and Fitzpatrick that to those who lived the Stalinist 1930s, especially in the vortex, at a place like Magnitogorsk, there was no sense of normalization or retreat; on the contrary, the revolution was at last proceeding at full speed. And it was all the more exhila-rating in light of the Depression context and the rise of fascism, the combination of which enhanced the drama of the Soviet experiment for the participants and its appeal for many foreigners. As the antidote to quasi-reductionist variations on the "end of the revolution," Kotkin assumed the centrality of ideology, variable though it was in application. To follow those like Lewin and Fitzpatrick in playing it down was to render incomprehensible the behavior and thinking of the participants.[27] For what crystallized during the 1930s was nothing less than a new and revolutionary civilization. In concluding, Kotkin went on to insist that the Soviet Union needs to be reincorporated into European history, especially because "Stalinism constituted a quintessential Enlightenment utopia." And he characterized the process at work as "the realization of socialism."[28]

Kotkin was convincing in contending that something new and revolutionary had developed and that, in that light, the Soviet experience needed to be under-stood within the wider contours of European history. And his way of taking ideology seriously usefully countered the ongoing tendency to reduce it all to cynical manipulation to serve power and privilege. But Kotkin's determination to feature the experience of revolution during the 1930s led him to untenable—and unnecessary—claims. His argument that "Stalinism constituted a quintessential Enlightenment utopia" is surely questionable. The question is how, on what basis, we are both to encompass that revolutionary experience in our under-standing of the Soviet trajectory and to reincorporate the Soviet experience into European history. Kotkin's tendency was simply to fall back on the Marxist ideology that Lewin and Fitzpatrick had played down. But Lewin, especially, had had good reason to suggest that Marxism and even Leninism had been left behind. Yet more may have been left of them than he allowed. To make sense of the insights on all sides, we need a wider supranational frame than Kotkin provided.

Central to any assessment of the Stalinist 1930s was the place of terror, partic-ularly the Great Terror of 1937–38, more widely known as the *Ezhovshchina* after police chief Narkom Ezhov. What was known of the terror, and what was made of it, has its own complex history.[29] Terror had been central to the whole top-down model of totalitarianism, and from this perspective, it had been randomly universal and, as such, intended by the leadership as a means to atomize society, producing submissive puppets. To create totalitarian rule, said Arendt in a passage we have already encountered, "Stalin had first to create artificially that atomized society which had been prepared for the Nazis in Germany by historical circumstances."[30] The point, she assumed, was to create the conditions for total domination necessary to do the work of history, as specified by the totalist ideology. But as we noted in Chapter 1, this was essentially to rely on the reified totalitarian model to account for the sources of the terror.

The anti-Cold War assault on that model, including the growing emphasis on societal initiative and the capacity of the system to evolve, demanded a rethinking of the place of the terror. But revisionists assaulting the classic model sometimes disagreed sharply. From his negative discontinuity perspective, Cohen charged that Fitzpatrick's way of emphasizing society was to play down both the symptomatic nature and the long-term significance of the Stalinist terror.[31]

As the assault on the classic model proceeded, some found reason to focus on aspects of the 1930s apart from the terror, while others focused on the terror in a more single-minded way, without relying on reified totalitarianism as an explanation.[32] The result was a curious incongruence in emphasis by the 1970s, as well as renewed bite to questions about continuity and Russian specificity.

Even as it suggested the inadequacy of the rigid totalitarian model, the de-Stalinization that began in the 1950s made it possible to assess the terror in a new, more genuinely historical way. Khrushchev hinted at its magnitude in his secret speech of 1956, then authorized publication of Alexander Solzhenitsyn's *One Day in the Life of Ivan Denisovich* in 1962. Deeper study of the phenomenon during the 1960s led to contrasting assessments of its meaning. Roy Medvedev's pioneering, systematic study *Let History Judge*, first published in 1967, served his wider purpose of separating Stalinism as a deviation from the Leninist mainstream, which, as for Cohen, had offered, and still offered, other possibilities. Medvedev was a major source for Robert Conquest's highly influential *The Great Terror*, although Conquest was more hostile to the Soviet experiment as a whole.[33] Then Solzhenitsyn in *The Gulag Archipelago* of 1973–75 offered a still-different reading, portraying the terror as the outgrowth of an alien Western import—Marxism itself.

Even as the "from below" revision was challenging the top-down model, Conquest became the new orthodoxy for some. Without positing some reified totalitarian system, he portrayed the terror as intended, planned, and orchestrated by Stalin, who aimed, most immediately, to eliminate actual or potential enemies, to consolidate power, and to foster a new loyal elite. But the longer-term aim was to secure absolute power by atomizing society through fear, induced through essentially random, arbitrary arrest and punishment.

Beginning in the 1980s, a new revisionist wave emerged as J. Arch Getty, Gabor Rittersporn, and Robert Thurston, despite important differences, even incompatibilities, among them, offered partly overlapping arguments as each reacted against Conquest's account of the terror. None questioned Stalin's centrality; indeed, each explicitly stressed his participation and responsibility.[34] At issue, rather, were the roles and relative importance of state and society, above and below, as well as the actual mechanisms and thus the scale and impact of the terror. For these revisionists, Stalin, though central, was but one player among others, caught up in a complex dynamic that was often out of control, producing unintended outcomes. Although fear surely played a role, there were also areas of autonomy and differences of opinion as the terror proceeded. The party line was often unclear or contradictory. At the same time, the mechanism was not merely top-down but entailed a particular mode of interaction between above and below, with agency from below fed by genuine belief, commitment, and enthusiasm.

Thus this revision showed that to emphasize "society," the scope for agency from below, was not necessarily to play down the centrality of the terror, but some of these revisionist emphases provoked objection even from those who by no means held to the Conquest orthodoxy.[35] Finding the revisionist emphasis on "out of control" excessive, Kotkin sought to outline the logic of the terror from within the framework that had emerged by the mid-1930s.[36] But that logic was not to be understood in terms of the older totalitarianism model, and there were questions to be raised about Kotkin's alternative, which emphasized the ongoing importance of ideology. The challenge is still to find a framework adequate to integrate the convincing features of the revisionist view of the terror with the other convincing themes in the mix, in light of the dynamic in course by that point.

More systematically than Kotkin himself, Martin Malia offered a way of relating the whole Soviet experiment, including Stalinism and the terror, to the wider framework of European history. Indeed, he explicitly tackled the interplay of suprahistorical, national, and supranational, historically specific factors, bound up with modernity and the Enlightenment deployment, in the Soviet trajectory. Like Kotkin, Malia insisted on the importance of socialism and ideology against those who found something else in operation by the 1930s. Again like Kotkin, he insisted that Stalinism could not be separated from the dynamic at work, in opposition to those who sought to marginalize Stalinism as an idiosyncratic wider revolutionary deviation. But Malia went much further than Kotkin in insisting not simply that "socialism" was an energizing and experiential ideal but that the socialist utopia had actually been realized in the Soviet Union by the mid-1930s. However, in light of problems inherent in the socialist idea itself, realization had entailed unexpected consequences that had had to be denied.[37]

Although he was highly respected, not to be dismissed as a mere Cold War ideologue, Malia had been a long-time critic of Soviet Communism, thanks partly to the influence of Raymond Aron.[38] In seeking to assess the Communist experiment in light of the unforeseen collapse of the Soviet regime by 1991, Malia explicitly criticized the varied modes of revision represented by Cohen, Lewin, Fitzpatrick, and Getty, each of whom seemed to have missed, almost willfully, the actual dynamic that had developed. For Malia, the whole Soviet dynamic stemmed from the effort to create ideological socialism from above through political action. Although fueled partly by ahistorical "privation and suffering," socialism was still historically specific, modern, stemming from the demand for equality that became possible with the Enlightenment sense of secular possibility.[39] The socialist aspiration took Marxian form, but ultimately at issue in the Soviet experiment was any conceivable form of socialism. Whatever the circumstances, socialism could have been implemented *only* in a top-down way, starting with something like Leninism, which was thus not simply an admixture responding to backwardness but the essential practical corollary of Marxist socialism itself.

Moreover, Malia went on, Leninism could reach its socialist objective only by Stalinist methods. Stalin's decision for the primacy of militarized politics was quite in accord with basic Leninism, which was never a particular economic program but a way of conceiving the party as history's unique vehicle for achieving socialism.[40] Although the transition from war communism to the NEP established an alternating pattern of "hard" and "soft" approaches, and although the NEP legacy suggested the ongoing possibility of a gentler approach, Bukharin's alternative was too narrowly economic to have succeeded. Once the Leninist choice had been made with the 1917 revolution, the only viable long-term option was essentially what Stalin did—to push on politically. To be sure, some watering down followed Stalin's death, but there was no qualitative departure. For Malia, seriously to have pushed the soft, quasi-Menshevik, "Bukharinist" alternative could only have yielded dissolution—precisely what resulted from Mikhail Gorbachev's neo-Bukharinism after 1985.[41] That outcome confirmed that Stalinism was the only way in which socialism could have been implemented—and even made to work, for a while. For Malia, then, what those Stalinist methods produced by the later 1930s was precisely *socialism*.

Although Marxist socialism had had considerable political and intellectual impact in more advanced countries, Malia insisted that relatively backward Russia offered the *only* sort of conditions where not only Marxism but the socialist idea itself could actually have been tried. Moreover, precisely as the implementation of socialism, the enterprise could not be understood as some mere modernizing revolution from above, in the tradition of Ivan the Terrible and Peter the Great. For Malia, the oft-cited parallels with earlier phases of Russian history were essentially accidental and irrelevant; at most, they constituted analogous contextual reflections but were in no sense determinant.[42] The core content and the ensuing dynamic stemmed exclusively from the socialist ideology.

On the first level, the revolution took place in Russia not from the logic of that country's internal development but from the contingent, exogenous factor of war—and, we might add again, the fortuitous factor of its length, from the unforeseen stalemate. But, for Malia, it was no accident that the experiment grew from this particular war, because Marxism could only have come to power, affording the idea a test in practice, in an especially weak civil society, pulverized by war, fed partly by "privation and suffering," lacking the antibodies to resist. Thus, Malia insisted, war-weakened Russia's role was not to pervert Marxism but to provide precisely the *tabula rasa* necessary for a Leninist party actually to try to realize its fantasy. It happened in Russia, in other words, because there, almost uniquely, could be found a social void that allowed ideological politicians actually to try it, to push it through.[43]

So, as Malia saw it, Russian circumstances mattered only in helping to provide the opening. The specific Soviet programs—nationalization, collectivization, planning—were not idiosyncratic products of Russian backwardness but prime corollaries of the socialist idea itself. Conversely, the chaotic, tension-

ridden Russian situation by itself could have yielded but a national authoritarianism of merely regional significance. Only ideological socialism could have
yielded the world-historical Soviet tragedy.[44]

Malia, then, would have no part of the longstanding objection, or excuse, that
backward Russia could not have provided a fair test of the socialist aspiration.
The socialist failure, he insisted, stemmed not from having been tried in the
wrong place but from flaws in the idea itself. Conversely, the Soviet outcome
stemmed neither from Russian idiosyncrasies nor from some betrayal of
socialism but from the effort actually to implement the impossibly utopian
Marxist fantasy.[45]

For Malia, the result of this effort was bound to end up *totalitarian*, now understood as historical and dynamic, not as conforming to some static model.
Totalitarianism denoted not the actual realization of total control over society but
the totalist claims of the state.[46] Its utopian pretensions made the Communist
ideology totalitarian in implication, but, more specifically, the process of implementing socialism entailed the systematic suppression of capitalism—private
property, profit, and the market—which required the extermination of civil society
and the "statization" of all aspects of life. Such an unnatural order could come
into being only through institutionalized coercion by the party, so the Soviet experiment turned totalitarian not in spite of its socialist objective but precisely because
of that objective. As Malia saw it, democratic socialism was an oxymoron.[47]

Although he recognized the value of the recent emphasis on initiative from
below in undermining the earlier totalitarian model, Malia found fault with both
Lewin and Cohen for playing down the continuity in worldview and party role.[48]
And he had no sympathy for Getty's revisionist account of the terror, which he
found symptomatic of a reluctance in the West even by the 1980s to face up to
the terror's dimensions and significance.[49] By implication, Getty had simply
misconstrued the state–society interaction.

But Malia especially derided those like Fitzpatrick, who, he felt, had gone
too far in emphasizing societal agency, thereby playing down the autonomous
role of ideological politics that he found essential to the actual dynamic. The
party–state was an overwhelming presence with which there could be no genuine
"negotiation." Thus those like Fitzpatrick had been unprepared for the collapse
of Soviet Communism by 1991 and the societal weakness revealed in the
aftermath. Their failure reflected the wider, longstanding scholarly tendency to
privilege modernization theory, social science, reductive social class categories,
and, more recently, agency "from below," all of which precluded understanding
of the autonomy—and in this case the primacy—of politics and ideology.[50]
As Malia put it, characteristically eschewing any ambiguity, in confronting
what resulted from the Russian Revolution, we are never dealing first with a
society but always with a particular, absolutely novel political regime, an "ideo-
cratic partocracy."[51]

The problem, as Malia saw it, was that modernization theory had led
Western Sovietology to foist on the Soviet case categories derived from a very
different Western experience. The Soviet Union had to be like—or, we might

add, becoming like—other modern countries as opposed to being unique or *sui generis*, but the collapse of the Communist regime, and the societal disarray that followed, made it clear that assumptions about modernization and convergence had led us to miss how different the Soviet Union had become as a result of its own trajectory. Malia was surely right to suggest that the widespread misreading of the Soviet situation at the end indicated a systematic limitation in our questions and categories.

The key is that the Soviet Union was, or became, genuinely *different* in ways that we were not prepared to grasp. The question is the basis and wider meaning of that difference. Malia's implication was that even though socialism could have been tried only in a place like Russia, the trajectory of the Soviet experiment was of wider significance precisely because it stemmed from the "universal" socialist idea and, more specifically, from Marxism, which had been central to Western political culture, even if did not come to power on its own in any more advanced country. By affording a *tabula rasa*, Russia offered a near-pure laboratory test of the socialist idea and ended up showing how fundamentally misguided it was. So Malia was not saying that, because modernization is not the appropriate category, the Soviet experience was merely *sui generis*. That was Lewin's position. On the contrary, for Malia the Soviet experience was a test of the wider socialist/Marxian possibility, *as modern*. The Bolsheviks succeeded in creating a genuinely different, anti-bourgeois, modernity—and the result was a tragedy.

But even as he made valuable points about difference, ideology, and the possible autonomy or primacy of politics, Malia was too eager to insist that the Soviet experiment was about socialism. At issue is the scope for an alternative mode of *modern difference*. We have seen that in light of the earlier historical-political break, socialism did not exhaust the space for a supranational, historically specific alternative to the mainstream. But are we prepared to recognize and characterize whatever else might have been at work? Although he convincingly downplayed Russian idiosyncrasy and usefully highlighted Leninist voluntarism, Malia found it sufficient to attribute the Soviet dynamic to the logic of Marxism without considering the scope for breaking out the sources and implications of some distinguishable Leninism. Thus he featured the Soviet link to the Enlightenment break without attention to the changing historical-political sense within the Enlightenment deployment by around 1900.

Whereas for Malia the creation of socialism by the end of the 1930s had proved to entail unwelcome dimensions that had to be denied, Alain Besançon, writing before the collapse of the Soviet regime, took a step further in characterizing the novelty that had emerged. The key was the gap between the language and the reality, which was not really about building socialism at all. Yet all the liturgical language that surrounded "the fictional building of socialism" produced a simulacrum—and thus a myth.[52] The lack of correspondence between what was said and the reality served the regime up to a point, but the leaders themselves were caught up in the unreality and could not see that the core reality was simply their own power; thus their increasing ineffectiveness, even impotence.[53] But, as Besançon saw it, the whole syndrome resulted because they were blinded by ideology. Yet we have seen that Lewin had good reason to suggest that whatever the echoes, essentially nothing had been left of the ideology by 1921.

The various ways of conceiving, and factoring in, ideology, socialism, difference, modernization, backwardness, and banality have afforded a number of possibilities in conceiving the Soviet trajectory. But the combination of factors has invited dualistic thinking, based on an assumption of two alternatives and an illusion of exhaustiveness that leads us to settle for an unnecessarily restricted array of possibilities. If, for example, we find limits in Fitzpatrick or Lewin and insist on the primacy of ideas and politics, we assume that socialism and pre-existing ideology must be our focus. If we do not seem to find consistent ideological commitment, it must all have been about banal power, or perhaps Russian modernizing revolution from above. A dualistic assumption lurks in Kotkin's charge that Lewin and Fitzpatrick left open whether the Soviet society that had emerged by the 1930s was new and socialist or traditionally Russian with a socialist veneer. Even as Cohen noted that Stalinism had its own dynamic, beyond socialism, Marxism, and Leninism, he tended to take Russian context and Westernizing modernization as the two ways of accounting for it.[54] If we grant that the Soviet experiment produced something at once different and modern, it must have been socialism, which seems to exhaust alternative modernity. But even as it proclaimed itself to be socialism, the Soviet departure could have ended up something else—yet still modern and different—requiring further categories if its place in wider European history is to be understood.

In expanding the framework, we can better align each of the angles we have considered. And certainly we must do justice both to Fitzpatrick and Lewin *and* to Kotkin to grasp how even after 1932 the experiment could at once galvanize enthusiasm and produce terroristic excess yet yield, as the outcome, a certain kind of ossification. That outcome was "conservative" in one sense, but it was not merely a return to an older conservatism; nor was it attributable to the enduring power of Russian traditions. Yet neither did it mean convergence with the Western mainstream. It was not a mere continuation of a situation already discernible in 1932, because it took the unforeseeable upheaval of the later 1930s for the forces that Lewin and Fitzpatrick found in operation to settle out as they did, in an alignment with certain implications. Yet the mechanisms that Fitzpatrick and Lewin featured are crucial to understanding the place, and the proportions, of the idealistic enthusiasm that Kotkin got at so well.

Rethinking the place of Marxism and Leninism

Even as he emphasized the irrelevance of the prior ideology by 1921, Lewin took for granted that the Communist Party had long-term ideological aims. The problem was simply that history afforded no support; it was not clear how to get there from here. Those aims were still generally Marxist, entailing the creation of socialism, but the loss of any "visible backing 'of a process'" had implications for those aims themselves. So the first question is what "their ideological aims" entailed.

After having become the dominant framework for seeking a systematic post-bourgeois alternative, Marxism had been unraveling for a generation by 1921 in light of the tensions that we encountered in Chapters 2 and 3. Especially in light of the changes in the economic framework by the turn of the century, classical Marxism, always unspecific with respect to action, proved still more radically incomplete. As leading non-Marxist intellectuals began to point out during the 1890s, Marxism offered an approach to history, a critique of capitalism, an image of fulfillment, a call to and an inspiration for action, but it did not provide an actual blueprint for action or even a reading of history from which principles of action could readily be derived.

By the turn of the century, the most innovative of those seeking a systematic alternative from within the Marxist framework began to understand that the mode of action had to come from elsewhere. There had to be *some* admixture, some hyphenated form like Marxism–Leninism, even if the nature and implications of the extra dimension were not fully faced. No admixture could have been merely a neutral, logically necessary corollary of the original doctrine, so to embrace some particular admixture carried beyond strategy and tactics to affect content, and the sense of problems and solutions. Because the crisis of classical Marxism was bound up with the new historical-political sense, the new content was certain to concern the scope for collective action and the making or happening of history.

Quite apart from its lack of specificity on the level of practice, Marxism was itself an amalgam, and indeed so was the broader socialist aspiration that had fed Marxism in the first place. The practical admixture, necessarily reflecting experience beyond original Marxism, could loosen, destabilize, even begin to break apart the components that had gone first into socialism and then into Marxism. But the earlier elements, reflecting all the aspirations and expectations that had come to rest in Marxist socialism, did not dissolve and disappear. They remained as components, although now in uncertain interaction with the newer admixtures. So in the gap between original Marxism and *any* blueprint for action much was uncertain, potentially contested.

As one possible mode of implementation, Leninism entailed its own particular admixture with its own uncertain implications. The key is to grasp the implications of the Leninist elements in their interaction with the elements that had fed Marxism.

As we noted in Chapter 2, the quest for an alternative to the mainstream necessarily had started with a particular understanding of that mainstream, but we must take care not to take as given the dominant categories that had settled out by about 1900. What had been most deeply at issue all along was more general even than "socialism" versus "capitalism" or "bourgeoisie" versus "proletariat." Moreover, those categories and oppositions were imprecise and unstable, and they begged essential questions. So it is best, when on the most general level, to refer to neutral "modern mainstream" and "alternative modernity" rather than immediately adopt more specific and thus more freighted categories.

Driving Bernard Yack's protagonists was a sense of the dehumanizing spirit of modernity itself, seemingly bound up with some systematic obstacle to overcoming social sources of dissatisfaction. What *was* the obstacle to a world without social sources of dissatisfaction, overcoming the dehumanizing spirit of modernity? Many nineteenth-century critics found "capitalism" central, but on what basis? Among the possible targets were private property, inequality, alienating modes of production, unfair and exploitative distribution, inattention to social ends, and the anarchy of the market, all of which might be variously bound up with more general bourgeois tendencies, from short-sighted egotism to the atomizing and mechanical qualities of liberal democracy. What, then, would a systematic alternative have to involve? Although Malia featured an underlying aspiration for equality, the Marxian accent was more on human self-realization, overcoming separation and alienation. Certainly, the ultimate aim was not a particular economic system but a new mode of being, of consciousness and experience.

The Marxist framework afforded a particular meaning to the array of impulses that had fed the quest for a systematic alternative to the modern mainstream. Indeed, a certain set of images, categories, and relationships came to be taken for granted by those seeking to understand the scope for an alternative from within that framework. But as the revisionist challenge loosened the Marxist assemblage, the uncertainty of some of the components and their relationships, the contingency of some of the juxtapositions, began to dawn. Although they might still be essential, the bits and pieces perhaps needed to be recombined and perhaps even embedded in some other framework to provide coherence. These included such matters as class and the place of the proletariat; the relationship between the economic and political spheres; the importance of private ownership of the means of production; the place of egalitarianism and differentiation; and the criteria of fuller individual self-realization.

Although the Communists were still seeking an alternative modernity, and although, clinging to ideology, they claimed to be building socialism, the notion could only be largely a myth in light of the disaggregation and recombination of elements at work. Crucially, however, this did not have to be some merely manipulative myth, used by the leaders to extend their power over the others. Rather, the myth might entail a cluster of images that, for a while, bound leaders and led together in genuine solidarity, that fired genuine enthusiasm, and that nurtured a capacity to tackle great tasks.

What was really involved, in all that Kotkin insisted must be taken seriously during the Stalinist 1930s, was not the pre-existing ideology but the experience itself, the sense of involvement in a grandiose enterprise of world-historical significance. As Fitzpatrick noted, although the transformation was called "building socialism," that notion had little specificity.[55] Criteria became scrambled partly because of the tension between "socialism" itself and the process of "building socialism." The new accent on qualitative differentiation and even heroism that fed Stakhanovism, for example, was in no sense the realization of socialism, although it could be portrayed, understood, and experienced as contributing centrally to the building of socialism.

The ongoing embrace of Marxist ideology meant an emphasis on class categories, an emphasis with real consequences, especially until the early 1930s. As the self-proclaimed vanguard of the proletariat, the Bolsheviks had ceaselessly proclaimed theirs to be a proletarian revolution, and they sometimes sought to bring actual industrial workers to the forefront through a form of "affirmative action." But although periodically important, that effort proved sporadic—and it dissipated during the 1930s. Yet this rhythm, too, proved more complex and symptomatic than a mere oscillation between idealism and cynicism—or even between idealism and functional requirements, in light of the modernization task at hand.

Characterizing the initial priority, Kotkin noted that for the Bolsheviks a proletarian revolution required a real proletariat.[56] Essentially, this meant that the conscious elite was to raise the workers to fitness to rule. But the relationship between that process and socialism, and especially *Marxist* socialism, was dubious in the extreme. A "proletariat" brought to the fore or even created in this way could not be Marx's proletariat, because it was not undergoing the particular experience that Marx had proposed would yield a post-bourgeois, even "universal," consciousness.

In classical Marxism, that subjective transformation, privileging the proletariat, was to result from the objective logic of capitalism. The workers were so situated in the industrial system that they, like no one else, would fully experience capitalist exploitation and dehumanization and thus be propelled beyond the bourgeois order, with its particular sense of the world and its possibilities. And the logic of capitalism ensured that most people—even, in some readings, the vast majority—would be proletarianized and thus actually undergo that universalizing experience. Non-proletarian intellectuals like Marx and Lenin might themselves grasp the issues, break off from the bourgeoisie, and join with the proletariat, but the very coherence of Marxism—crucial as to why the alternative to liberal capitalism would be "socialism"—rested on the relationship between consciousness and the proletarian experience of capitalism. There was no basis for privileging the proletariat if it had not undergone that experience.

Underlying the revision of Marxism were doubts about whether that process could ever take place in an orthodox way, hence all the rethinking about what was necessary to a post-bourgeois consciousness. The place of the proletariat remained uncertain in the wake of Bernstein, Lenin, and Sorel. But whatever the implications of the revision, the fledgling Russian working class certainly had not had the orthodox universalizing experience, and once capitalism had been eliminated in Russia, there was no possibility that it ever could. Simply giving the workers privileged access to leading roles was not in itself going to give them the appropriate consciousness, so, despite appearances, to privilege the industrial workers under Soviet circumstances did not in fact maintain orthodoxy.

At issue were principles that had no real class basis. The key was consciousness, which did not rest on the level of capitalist development or experience of the capitalist economy but was *sui generis* in the elite, then could be generalized through education. As we saw, Lenin decided that, if anything, working within capitalism tended to foster a petty bourgeois mentality, a mere trade union consciousness, that would apparently recur endlessly. Thus his warning in 1920 that the "small proprietor mentality" was likely to keep coming back—and to corrupt the proletariat. But although some might prove irredeemably bourgeois, in principle all could be educated into the essential post-bourgeois consciousness, especially through participation in great collective action.

As the core of their education, the workers would learn to operate within the post-capitalist Soviet economy as the Soviet regime took on the great task of industrialization. And although that could not give the workers the orthodox universalizing experience that Marx had envisioned, it could make them conscious of their essential societal roles, and responsibilities, as producers in a modern economy. They would thus be full participants, but not privileged leaders, in a society of producers. But that society might still be superior to the modern capitalist mainstream because of the modes of participation involved and the virtues elicited.

In light of all the rhetoric about class, it is not surprising that the actual Soviet dynamic during the first generation was highly uncertain, or that the leadership was not consistent. Even as class categories remained central, their use was variable, then blurred. As Fitzpatrick has emphasized, proletarian and Communist became hopelessly entangled, and "bourgeois" came to mean opposition or deviation.[57] That opposition or deviance was "bourgeois" became true *a priori*. The variable factor had nothing to do with the differentiated socio-economic roles that had led Marx to posit class as determinant; rather, it was a matter of consciousness, belief, commitment, and will.

As a link of the Soviet experiment to Marxist orthodoxy, the sense of collectively creating socialism was more important than the use of class categories and the assumption of proletarian privilege. Throughout his study of Magnitogorsk, Kotkin emphasized that socialism was conceived and above all experienced as the antithesis of, and antidote to, capitalism. It was this that afforded a sense of coherence, despite the endless improvisation. The wider context of Depression and fascism seemed to magnify the drama and grandeur of the enterprise.

As Kotkin saw it, the participants understood socialism as a commitment to social justice "grounded in putatively nonexploitative property relations."[58] Thus it included such concrete measures as the provision of food, schooling, employment, and medical care for all. But as Kotkin's characterization implied, what constituted "nonexploitative property relations" was not so clear. Moreover, the competing fascist regimes also moved in the same welfarist direction, similarly providing health care and paid vacations for those included in the community. Implicitly recognizing competition from these novel post-liberal regimes, Stalin insisted that neither Italy nor Germany was in fact comparable, precisely because in each private property had remained untouched.[59]

It is certainly true—and some still assume decisive—that the Communists eliminated most forms of private property, while the fascists and Nazis did not. But even if eliminating private property overcomes capitalism, the alternative was not necessarily called socialism—unless, of course, there were only two possibilities, so that anything post-capitalist was "socialist" by definition. Otherwise, at issue was simply a difference in economic forms, and how decisive that difference might be, from within the wider effort to create a post-bourgeois order, was itself subject to dispute—and was in fact central to the contest in progress among the post-liberal experiments by the 1930s.

To be sure, "socialism," having become the core of the mainstream quest for an alternative, carried all sorts of resonance. But the criteria of socialism were themselves uncertain. We noted that for Giuseppe Boffa, for example, there could be no socialism without the effective participation of the workers in management—surely a plausible criterion. But this was a question of broadly political decision making, participation, power—not a matter of the economic system *per se*, even including ownership, the profit mechanism, or any particular allocation of resources. If the workers had not had the universalizing experience that Marx had posited, who could say that they would not use their managerial power to maximize their own advantage at the expense of consumers, competitors, the environment, or the long-term well-being of society?

As we emphasized in Chapters 2 and 3, part of what was at issue within the evolving quest for an alternative to the liberal mainstream was the interrelationship between economic activity, the political sphere, and the scope for human self-realization. And there were various ways of shuffling the economic–political relationship, various ways of rethinking the place of economic relationships within the aspiration for an alternative modernity. Marx came to insist on a particular way of arranging the components that necessarily marginalized other possibilities. But as Marxism began to unravel, and as the relationships between the components became uncertain, it could seem that the immediate target was not capitalism or private property but the wider liberal-positivist culture, that what was most objectionable about capitalism stemmed from the inadequacies of that culture. A change in political culture might yield a qualitatively superior relationship between the political and economic spheres even if major aspects of private property remained.

To grasp the place of what the Soviet leadership in fact ended up doing, we must think through the logic of Leninism, pondering the continuity it afforded as a mode of the new great politics that became possible with the wider historical-political break. Besançon might seem to be on the right track in insisting precisely that the dynamic of the Soviet regime derived logically not from Marxism but from Leninism. However, the question concerns what Leninism entailed and how it played out, shaping practice even under Stalin. For Besançon, the key was fanaticism. Having embraced the ideology as a privileged, even infallible, guide to practice, Lenin was, logically enough, quite willing and eager to force history to conform to it.[60] Thus, even in the face of unforeseen situations, Leninism entailed invariability, monotony: "The Leninist regime has remained immobile, fixed in the ideology which preceded it, shaped it and maintained it."[61] Because Soviet practice resulted from the imposition of the given, stable ideology, there was no need to consider differentiated stages or to grasp how various steps constituted a particular, unforeseeable dynamic. For Besançon, Stalinism, entailing especially the arbitrariness of repression, followed directly from Leninism.[62]

Those like Cohen and Lewin came to something like the opposite view. Cohen stressed that Bolshevik ideology had been far less cohesive and fixed in the first place than the standard interpretation had suggested. The ideology had subsequently been affected by events like the civil war and then had changed radically under Stalin.[63] As we noted, Lewin implied that with virtually nothing left of Marxist ideology by 1921, there was nothing left of Leninism either, since Leninism had rested on the claim to a superior grasp of the ideology. Finding themselves "in a rarefied atmosphere of unpredictability and contingency," the Communists were on their own.

Any such emphasis on the variability or even dissipation of the original ideology usefully counters any tendencies toward ideological reduction or inflation, but it is possible to overemphasize variability, contingency, or sheer capriciousness at the same time. To grasp the enduring importance of Leninism we must navigate between these contrasting positions, taking advantage of the insights of each. To do so, we must be more attentive to what has passed as "ideological" continuity even as we also attend to the unforeseen dynamic of the situation, with its *ad hoc* adjustments. Contrary to Besançon, Leninist practice was *essentially*, not merely incidentally, *ad hoc* and improvised, and thus, precisely as Lewin showed, yielded unintended outcomes, including the hypertrophy of bureaucracy and the reduction of the original Marxian ideology to a mere set of instrumental tools. But this was not, as Lewin suggested, because the agents found themselves cut off from some stable Marxist ideology but because, having started on a Leninist path, they were already caught up in the unforeseeable logic of great politics. For although it is surely true that Marxism had little substantive to tell them, it does not follow that nothing was left of Leninism either, for Leninism entailed more than simply a putatively superior grasp of the ideology. And more was left in 1921 of that Leninism, as a distinctive departure from within the revision of Marxism, than Lewin's characterization of the situation suggested.

In recognizing that the Communists still had long-term ideological aims in 1921, Lewin was positing a kind of bifurcation. The Communists could not immediately realize socialism, which would have to be put off for the foreseeable future, but then the central imperative was somehow to preserve their regime as the foundation for a superior future down the road. With the disaggregation of the original ideology, however, the scope for a different, in some ways more grandiose, self-understanding emerged. And the Communists clearly conceived their own role, what they were doing, the opportunity and responsibility before them, in that more grandiose way.

We have seen that although Russia was idiosyncratic, even backward, Lenin plausibly insisted that Russians were best positioned to grasp the scope and requirements for the new action necessary to address the wider impasse of Marxism. Such new action was essential if the movement for a systematic alternative to liberalism was not to get absorbed by parliamentary democracy. And the essential Leninist admixture cannot be attributed simply to Russian backwardness, precisely because it reflected the wider new *modern* historical-political sense emerging as Lenin began to rethink the choices for Marxists.

Whereas Lenin had always denied the possibility of achieving *socialism* in Russia alone, by April 1920 he was thinking through what happens in the first country to make a revolution, acting on its own for a while.[64] Even at that point, his characterizations pointed beyond merely holding the situation open until the German Marxists, for example, did their job. Although the Russians would not be achieving *socialism*, they might achieve something else, more congruent with the new historical-political sense and thus more coherent as a modern alternative to the mainstream than nineteenth-century Marxism afforded.

We noted that Lewin, in stressing that the dissipation of the ideology left only "the pure political will of the leadership" to generate a dynamic in a socialist direction, also held that an earlier historical consciousness, affording a sense of continuity and predictability, was dissipating. Central to what must be understood is the relationship between that changing historical consciousness and the "political will of the leadership," which, for Lewin, was all that remained. The question is what was lost and what was left—and the implications of whatever was left.

For Lewin, the earlier historical consciousness had afforded assurance and underpinned political action in a certain confident mode. Without that consciousness, there was nothing left but "the pure political will of the leadership." But this dualism is too limiting. To the agents, losing the backing of a putatively built-in process did not have to be experienced as a leap into the unknown. It depended on their sense of how history gets made—and now could get made by those who had found the appropriate mode of action.

Recalling our theme from Chapter 3, Leninism from the start had entailed a departure from an earlier, reassuring "sense of historical process" toward a different understanding of the human relationship with history. To be sure, the departure was halting, especially because Lenin sought to cling to ideology, but it entailed a particular voluntaristic combination that was at least implicit from the start, including the centrality of will, sacrifice, and discipline, but also the need for flexibility and pragmatism, including the capacity to learn from experience, even to retreat, and to develop new modes of interaction between elite and masses. Lenin sought to fold what he learned back into the ideological frame-work, but as new situations elicited new responses, the dynamic generated was less linear, more angular, more open and contingent than Besançon had suggested in emphasizing the imposition of a prior, apparently stable and determining ideology.

Through a particular mode of action, it was possible to make things happen, even, to some extent, to shape history. There were no unvarying principles other than the scope for acting, trying out, adapting—on the basis of one's own privileged consciousness. And the basis of that privilege was not some grasp of Marxism but the historical-political sense that afforded the capacity to act in a post-liberal way. What Lenin's success in securing and maintaining power seemed to confirm was not, as for Besançon, the original, orthodox ideology, but rather the differentiated Leninist mode of action.[65]

It obviously made a difference that by 1921 the agents had acted from within a Leninist frame already. The measure of success that they had achieved, in one sense astonishing, was a source of solidarity, pride, determination—and confidence in the mode of action adopted. What sustained them was thus the historical-political sense underpinning their willingness to act in a certain mode. There was no turning back—and there need be no turning back. Years later, Lev Kopelev noted how insulting had seemed any suggestion that those who had made the revolution and won the civil war could not build "socialism in one country."[66]

Whereas Leninism was a continuing orientation and set of virtues in one sense, it was by its very nature evolving at the same time as the agents responded to each new stage, each set of unforeseen circumstances. The difficulties of action led to the use of military metaphors—and even self-understanding in military terms. Central among the essential virtues required were toughness and pitilessness.[67] Moreover, because what was required was ongoing improvised response, Leninist action generated a characteristic dynamic, a herky-jerky dialectic of control and unforeseen, ever-new situations, calling forth new responses—but from within the same framework of ongoing action. Although Lewin noted something like that rhythm, he traced it to backwardness; it is better seen as a corollary of the new, great political mode of action itself.

Even the moderation, pragmatism, and flexibility that Lenin demonstrated in 1921, with the onset of the NEP, is easily misread. We noted that Arendt, in arguing that Lenin, in contrast to Stalin, was not a totalitarian ideological fanatic, stressed that he followed his pragmatic instincts of statesmanship rather than his Marxist convictions. However, such pragmatism is not to be taken in this dualistic way but must be embedded in a framework of ongoing response over a broader timeframe. Compromise and pragmatism do not mean that the overall dynamic was not totalitarian. Although Lenin himself, by the time of his death, seemed to embrace an apparently more moderate and pragmatic course than Stalin's later, he was responding to the particular situation of the early 1920s. The Stalinist departure was a response to a different situation, but one that had resulted from the outcome of Leninism so far. And Stalin's was a Leninist response, a step within a continuing dynamic reflecting the Leninist legacy.

We noted that, as Lewin saw it, to be left with sheer political will, embodied in the state, was a reversal of Marx's reversal of Hegel. However, this "statism" resulted not, as Lewin implied, from crazy contingencies but from the logic of Leninism itself. It followed naturally from the vanguard notion once the vanguard had conquered a state but found itself isolated in a society that had not undergone, and now could not undergo, the orthodox consciousness-transforming experience posited in classical Marxism. And this was not simply some dualistic return to Hegel but pointed well beyond, precisely because the agents were in the new world that became possible only with the wider historical-political break. The new Communist state was not simply the sphere of power, or the guarantor of rights, or the focus for the "positive freedom" of individuals internalizing its norms as rational. Rather, it was an entirely new kind of state as the instrument for the unprecedented continuing collective action that the situation demanded. It was a dynamic state, capable of a certain kind of action based on a new kind of interaction with society. It was to be a *totalitarian* state because of the education, mobilization, and interaction necessary in light of the scope of the ongoing action required.

The state's expanded function, starting with mobilization and education, made bureaucracy especially necessary. But although Lewin's understanding of the implications of bureaucratization remains indispensable, his way of accounting for its source is to overdo the rupture as the Communists responded to the unforeseen situation by 1921. Statism and bureaucracy followed from the whole mode of action once an elite defined by its virtues had taken power.

None of this is to suggest smooth continuity in 1921. The situation was indeed unforeseen, and the Bolsheviks began to grasp, for the first time, some of the implications of the mode of action that they had adopted. As Lewin suggested, the deepening sense that they were on their own meant a still-greater party spirit. At the time of his initial defeat in 1924, Trotsky observed that one could not be right against the party, as the sole instrument for ongoing revolutionary creation. Malia noted that for the Communists by this point, the party spirit—more than any particular economic policy—was crucial; it was precisely this spirit that the party sought to extend to the population at large during the 1920s.[68]

The Communist Party was precious precisely because Marxist ideology was *not* adequate, and although the Bolsheviks had a crucial basis for a claim to privilege, it rested not on some unique grasp of Marxism but on their capacity to organize and act in the appropriate new way. The party was explicitly the unique and precious vehicle for history-making action because it *embodied* the post-bourgeois virtues. And what it sought to diffuse to the wider population was not Marxism but those post-ideological, Leninist virtues, which, in fact, were themselves coming to seem the keys to the post-bourgeois alternative desired in the first place. The new politics of spirit would itself produce the systematic alternative that now, in light of the historical-political break, seemed uniquely desirable and possible.

To be sure, myths of "creating socialism" and of ideological privilege thanks to Marxism would remain crucial to the mix. But single-minded though it surely was, the action that developed was not simply to force the prior Marxian ideology. Conversely, it was not the logic of Marxism that produced the momentum, including the Stalinist break of 1927–30 and all that resulted from it. Contrary to Malia, Russia was positioned not to test Marxism or socialism but something else now at work in the wider experience of the West, the great political mode of collective action as the basis for an alternative modernity.

This is to recognize, with Besançon, that Leninism was in some sense determinant, that subsequent steps emerged from within the frame that Lenin had established. Conversely, it is also to deny the degree of rupture posited by Cohen, Boffa, and all who portray Stalinism as a deviation. Yet it is also to posit a weaker mode of continuity between Lenin and Stalin than ideological determinists like Malia and Besançon portrayed. At the same time, it is to accept Lewin's point that the outcome by the 1930s was more *sui generis* than any emphasis on prior ideology could explain, yet also to posit a continuing momentum that Lewin could not account for.

With the new situation of the early 1920s, then, Russia was positioned not merely to provide a spark, which would have entailed almost immediate subservience to others. What opened was a far more grandiose relationship with the West; the new Communist regime was now uniquely positioned to lead, to create something new, to show the way beyond the liberal order, whether or not that direction entailed "creating socialism."[69] Longer-term hopes for a systematic alternative rested on the Russian Communists, and in light of what they had already accomplished, surely they could do whatever proved to be necessary. But as the sense of opportunity inflated, so did the sense of responsibility—and risk. Claims of orthodoxy masked only superficially the sources of the self-doubt, the sense of vertigo, that the Communist venture entailed. Yet even if they were more radically departing from Marxism than they wanted to recognize, the opportunity to spearhead a post-bourgeois order was genuine. The question was what would develop from an effort to sustain the Leninist mode of collective action.

Rekindling the revolution in the wake of the NEP

With the Communists isolated and the country exhausted, the immediate concern in 1921 had to be the economy, and Lenin announced the New Economic Policy at the Tenth Party Congress in March 1921. Offering a delim- ited return to market mechanisms, this was a strategic retreat that reflected a recognition of the mistakes of war communism.[70] But what it portended for the future was uncertain. Within months of Lenin's death in January 1924, Stalin and Bukharin were beginning to suggest that the Communists might actually build socialism from within the new framework. From their perspective, Trotsky's ongoing insistence on wider revolution as a prerequisite was but a variation on Menshevist determinism, expressing a lack of faith in Soviet potential. But the notion of "socialism in one country" did not have to mean grandiose adven- turism. Meshing with Bukharin's economic thinking, it seemed at this point to be compatible with cautious pragmatism and gradualism.[71]

The NEP was successful as an immediate response to the economic emer- gency, but despite Bukharin's gloss, the new dispensation soon seemed to portend not the gradual construction of socialism but "Thermidorean" degeneration. The NEP seemed to invite semi-corrupt alliances of officials and merchants or producers, precisely the "bourgeois" patterns to be transcended.

By 1925–26, the course of the NEP was producing fierce squabbles in the party leadership that inevitably interfaced with the struggle over the leadership itself in the wake of Lenin's death. In retrospect, Stalin appears to have cynically played both ends against the middle, merely exploiting the situation for his own ends, but all the parties to the dispute faced a complex and evolving mix of genuine issues. Differences in assessment and priority were plausible. Sparring between those more aggressive and those more moderate had marked the Bolshevik regime from the start, as the "Left" tended to denounce calls for prudence as "Menshevik." Lenin navigated between the two sides, maintaining his freedom of maneuver—even viewing abrupt reversals as salutary.[72] And

Leninism mandated the capacity to change directions as circumstances warranted, so it is arbitrary to reduce Stalin to cynical power hunger in contrast with a more principled Lenin. As restiveness with the cultural implications of the NEP neared breaking point by 1927, the next step was bound to be some form of intensification, despite the successes of the NEP—or because of them.

In the fateful radicalization that followed, agency from both above and below was at work, and there has been much controversy over the bases, the roles, and the relative importance of each. In fact, entirely new forms of interaction were emerging as the great political dynamic developed.

In a recent study based on much new research, Vladimir Brovkin played down pressures from below in insisting that a narrow stratum on top rekindled the revolution during the late 1920s, essentially to preserve its own power. Probing the unforeseen forces that resulted from the success of the NEP, Brovkin showed how local party leaders in both the countryside and the cities developed profitable links with market-producing peasants or emerging leaders of private enterprise. The local party was being co-opted as it became intertwined with new economic forces against the center. Such people advocated continuing the NEP not because they knew about or agreed with Bukharin's moderate proposals but simply because they liked the current arrangements.

In short, from Brovkin's perspective, the NEP was generating a healthy, normal society incompatible with Communist Party dictatorship.[73] Stalin sought to reverse the process at work through a pre-emptive strike by the central party–state apparatus against NEP winners, including party officials with NEP ties as well as the more prosperous peasants. Seeking to strengthen the center's control, the new policy "was an admission of failure to generate voluntary social support. It was a new war on society to preserve the dictatorship."[74]

For all his debunking, Brovkin allowed some role for ideas and ideals, but he claimed to find a crisis of confidence, even a deeper intellectual crisis, among the leaders by the later 1920s. They sensed that even though they had followed the Leninist script, they were facing "the bankruptcy of the socialist construction project in Russia." The socialist sector of the economy was not proving more productive; indeed, the reverse was true. Although it had been proletarianized, the party was proving a mere vehicle to compete for power and privilege. If most continued along, it was because, having come to accept the central Communist line as their own, they could see no other way to make sense of what they had already done.[75]

However, we noted that the utopianism and heroism of the civil war period had deepened the revolutionary legacy, adding images and a layer of expectation, all of which made it still harder for some, at least, to settle for the NEP or even Bukharinist gradualism. In several earlier studies, Sheila Fitzpatrick showed how nostalgia for the earlier heroic struggle fed the growing malaise, the fear that the revolution might be fatally compromised, that marked the NEP period. In response, renewed revolutionary enthusiasm, even a new premium on proletarian identity, welled up from below to become the basis for the Stalinist departure from the NEP. As Fitzpatrick saw it, the party—especially its younger members—was hungry for achievement by 1929, and by that point Stalin was offering more than did those on the Right.[76] From the perspective of these enthusiasts, obviously, Brovkin's mutually advantageous patterns could only have seemed like mere corruption.

Brovkin countered that those like Fitzpatrick who stressed pressures from below were merely accepting the official rhetoric. In fact, those who had joined the party were not the idealistic best and brightest but the least desirable, joining for material advantage—and the leaders knew it. The break with the NEP stemmed not from idealistic pressures from below but simply from the effort by the central leadership to re-establish control and preserve the dictatorship.[77]

Malia, too, disputed Fitzpatrick's implication that the initiative came from below, but with his emphasis on socialism and ideology, he was willing to credit idealism—both above and below. Whereas Brovkin stressed the dilution of the party, Malia insisted that the party had matured enough during the NEP era to seek to complete the revolutionary conquest interrupted with the retreat of 1921. By this point, in fact, the alternative was not Bukharin but the fatal dissipation of the party's ideological momentum. Conversely, the next step stemmed not from Stalin's caprice but from the logic of the ideological commitment to Marxist socialism. So Malia was not so different from Fitzpatrick when he stressed that during 1928, urgency fused with exhilaration at the prospect of a new socialist offensive that would end the compromises and humiliations of the NEP.[78]

At issue, then, is the basis of the response of both the leadership and the rank and file, and the interaction between them, that rekindled the revolution in the late 1920s. Surely the center was concerned about the tendencies that Brovkin outlines. And the banal, ahistorical factors that Brovkin features on both levels—power, position, place seeking, resentment, mere rebelliousness—figure to some extent. But so does a galvanizing idealism; Brovkin's debunking reductionism was surely one-sided. And although the precise proportions are undecidable, the key is to understand the interplay of idealism and banality, and of above and below, in the responses at work.

That interplay entailed a kind of reciprocity, with above and below responding to and/or anticipating each other in a way that intensified the overall level of energy. This next step in an ongoing minority revolution entailed coercing those who were prepared to settle for the NEP, but although those pushing for change were still a decided minority, the push by now involved, in addition to the original vanguard, newly energized participants who were determined *not* to settle for Brovkin's version of a normal, healthy society.

In that light, Brovkin was surely premature in characterizing the revolutionary construction project in the Soviet Union as "bankrupt." Although naive expectations had abounded, short-term economic productivity was not the decisive test of the effort to build an alternative; it was not even the decisive test of socialism. And insofar as the expanded party was degenerating into competition for privilege and power, it was settling into precisely the bourgeois modes that an alternative was to overcome. The antidote was more extensive galvanizing action to bring out the virtues that would constitute the real antidote to bourgeois culture. Ronald Suny noted that

> the Bolsheviks required more than passive acquiescence in the new order; they wanted active support that could be mobilised toward heroic goals. One of the central dilemmas of the Communists in the first two decades of their rule was to move from an exercise of power through force toward creating a base of support through the construction of a widely accepted, hegemonic understanding of the historical moment.[79]

The sense of the scope for mobilizing virtues, in other words, was crucially bound up with the new historical-political sense, now to be generalized throughout the society.

By 1927, deepening difficulties over grain collection were straining Stalin's alliance with Bukharin and even portended a crisis of the whole system, although the source of the problem has been controversial. There is much evidence that the economic crisis was less a cause than an immediate outcome of a political decision to rekindle the revolution.[80] According to Malia, the crisis stemmed from choices to favor industrialization by adjusting prices, thereby leaving the peasants less incentive to deliver grain. But the crisis would require further political decision as the momentum grew. The determination for new, more grandiose action produced three mutually reinforcing measures prior to the break into forced collectivization and crash industrialization at the end of 1929.

By the later NEP, the free market in agriculture had proved to be the key sphere of unpredictability and contingency, so a priority for the leadership was to gain control over the agricultural surplus. Without it, they were not really in control at all; they lacked the power to act. In this sense, to seize control over the surplus was not to force history but to grasp the means to make it, to take responsibility for it, rather than settling for the mainstream tendency to rely on market outcomes. So although the shortfall in grain procurements by December 1927 stemmed at least partly from decisions to favor industry, the leadership could have responded by simply readjusting prices to right the balance. But they choose to intensify their political effort instead. As Suny put it, following T.H. Rigby, Stalin changed almost overnight from the soul of caution and moderation to intransigence itself.[81] In January 1928, Stalin and his lieutenants set out personally to force grain collections. This improvised coercion worked—and emboldened Stalin to try full collectivization.[82]

Meanwhile, a surge of leftist activism, especially among Komsomol members and shock workers, also began in 1928. Although this is widely known as the "cultural revolution," Malia objected that scholars had adapted that term to make it seem that it was not intervention from above but initiative from below that launched the next phase—that the next phase had thus been democratic in origin.[83] But to approach the next step in an oppositional, dualistic way, reflecting exogenous preoccupations, is to miss the significance of the characteristic reciprocity. In this case, the sense of an impending response to NEP dilemmas energized the initiative from below, but growing restiveness from below had helped to stimulate the new directions from above in the first place. Moreover, any opposition between above and below does not turn on democracy; initiative from below may be minoritarian and/or coercive. Even as he stressed the initiative of Stalin and the leaders, Malia agreed that the initiative from above tapped into and galvanized wider militant leftist energies endemic since 1918, albeit marginalized during the NEP. The militant phase that resulted from this radicalizing reciprocity continued at least into 1931, but the interplay would prove to be complex as new initiatives produced unanticipated outcomes and the leadership found it hard to control the momentum that had been unleashed.

Prominent among the initial fruits of the new militancy was a crackdown on bourgeois specialists, fed especially by worker suspicion of engineers of bourgeois origin. Indeed, the new militancy largely commenced in May–June 1928 with the "Shakhty trial," a show trial of fifty engineers accused of sabotage, or "wrecking," and espionage in the Ukrainian mining region of Shakhty. All confessed; five were executed. Because such specialists were still much needed, the overall campaign significantly damaged the Soviet economy.[84]

Yet the regime pushed ahead, launching the First Five-Year Plan in April 1929, even backdating it to October 1, 1928. The decision for systematic planning emerged not directly from Stalin and his group but from a wider technocratic momentum that had developed during the 1920s, feeding especially into the left-wing current. As initiated, however, the First Five-Year Plan went far beyond what the Left had proposed. The effort took on the trappings of a military campaign, partly because it consciously followed the German model that had so intrigued Lenin during the First World War. Despite that precedent, however, this was a novel enterprise, unprecedented in magnitude and ambition. The advent of planning elicited much enthusiasm in the party and in urban society; not only would Russia be propelled out of backwardness at last, but it would show the world, for the first time, the scope for human mastery of the economy. And the planning enterprise indeed attracted widespread attention abroad at that time.[85]

Malia emphasized that the classical Marxist critique of capitalism had not focused on the irrational anarchy of the market in allocating resources, so there had been little thought about what would replace the market in a post-capitalist economy.[86] The socialist tradition had included a technocratic Saint-Simonian strain, growing from the Enlightenment interest in the scope for social engineering by rational, scientific experts, but that strain had not been central to Marxism. Only now, as the Soviet regime began to act in a more determined way, did the planning impulse become centrally associated with the quest for a systematic alternative to the bourgeois mainstream.

This Leninist experiment could have wider impact, even as its connection to an uncertain Marxism grew tenuous, because it sought to act in this new way, taking on the great task of economic planning to modernize the Soviet Union. Partly at issue was precisely the scope for technical expertise, in light of the wider questions concerning the requirements for an expanded range of collective action. But expertise and planning were not remotely sufficient in themselves to the task of modernization being undertaken; the whole society had to be actively involved. And that involvement required not simply rational self-interest but enthusiasm, the sense of world-historical innovation. As a genuinely novel alternative modernity, planning fueled a sense of pride, even exhilaration—and a determination to make it work that was itself energizing. Planning was the cornerstone of a great collective enterprise that would give the world a full-scale alternative modernity based on the capacity to make history as never before. It would entail an entirely new relationship between the political and economic spheres. But only when coupled with the industrialization effort of the early 1930s would the magnitude, the stakes, and the real content of the transformation become clear.

The great politics of crash industrialization

With planning as the cornerstone, late in 1929 the regime embarked on an entirely new mode of socio-economic development, crash industrialization built on forced collectivization in agriculture.[87] An overtly totalitarian coordination of culture, including a renewed attack on religion, accompanied the new direction.[88] Even as the enterprise seemed to nurture the desired virtues and feed a sense of world-historical magnitude, at least among some, it also yielded anomalies, excesses, and unforeseen consequences, from inflated bureaucracy to renewed social stratification.[89]

Although forced collectivization was in one sense simply a means to extract the agricultural surplus to finance industrialization, the two prongs of the new direction were equally important. Each side required the other once the leaders had decided to proceed in this more grandiose way, so forced collectivization and crash industrialization proceeded in tandem. On the one hand, the leaders decided to accelerate industrialization radically at the end of 1929—five-year targets were to be achieved in four—and forcing collectivization seemed to be essential to make it work. On the other hand, once the decision for full collectivization was made late in 1929, the leaders had to accelerate industrialization in order to mechanize the collective farms. Thus the decision to complete the First Five-Year Plan in four.[90]

Whatever the economic justification for forced collectivization, the new direction entailed another dimension that was in one sense gratuitous, although symptomatic. Whereas the process required expropriation of the kulaks, it did not have to entail the class war against them that proved to be bound up with the process from the start. In his speech of December 1929 announcing the policy shift in agriculture, Stalin indicated that the kulaks were to be liquidated as a class, so rather than merely having their property expropriated, the kulaks were often killed or sent to forced labor camps.[91] Now the camp system—the Gulag—reached gigantic proportions, gradually assuming a major role in the economy.[92]

Having succeeded and profited under the provisional NEP dispensation, the kulaks personified the bourgeois patterns that had emerged with a vengeance once the regime had been forced, with the NEP, to turn from what had seemed serious revolutionary implementation during the civil war. Rekindling the revolution seemed especially to require eradicating these tangible embodiments of the power of the bourgeois principle.

Seeking to justify the assault on the kulaks in orthodox ideological terms, Stalin proposed that the class struggle could be expected to intensify as the revolution approached its culmination.[93] Although this notion served as psychological mobilization for the struggle, it manifested the wider tendency to manipulate the bits and pieces that were left as the original ideology came apart. Although still serving the quest for an alternative modernity, the choice of when and how to invoke class was by this point part of the new dynamic that stemmed not from the logic of Marxism but from the new mode of action being attempted.

The new offensive quickly took on a momentum of its own, even began to spin out of control, unleashing what proved to be a characteristically jerky dynamic as unanticipated results called forth new responses. The leadership gave no detailed instructions for the collectivization drive; indeed, local officials requesting instructions were rebuked. Thus Fitzpatrick found the winter of 1929–30 "a time of frenzy, when the party's apocalyptic mood and wildly revolutionary rhetoric" recalled the climax of the civil war and war communism.[94] At the same time, a combination of peasant resistance and local excesses in forcing through collectivization produced violence and anarchy in the countryside. The excesses stemmed from genuine zeal but also from a fear of being branded "rightist" if not zealous enough. But after just a few months, the tendency to spin out of control prompted Stalin to call a temporary halt to the process with his famous "Dizziness from Success" speech and a concomitant Central Committee decree in March 1930.[95]

However, the retreat proved temporary in light of the reciprocal interplay of above and below now in course. Many local activists were furious with Stalin for going soft, and the offensive resumed late in 1930. Although it was now under somewhat better control from the center, it was no less repressive. And although this wave of enthusiasm from below was largely exhausted by 1932, forced collectivization reached its tragic culmination only with the terror famine of 1932–33, which claimed three to six million lives.[96]

Another pull-back to relative moderation followed in 1933, including a second, more realistic five-year plan. Notable economic successes during 1934–36 made it seem that the transition had been made, that the period of upheaval was over. In the slogan adapted from Stalin's speech to combine drivers in December 1935, and widely cited for the rest of the decade: "Life has become better, comrades; life has become more cheerful."[97] But the unprecedented dynamic in course by this point had not played out. The step in 1929–30, stemming from the situation by 1927, had upped the stakes, thus stimulating energies hard to fathom from a liberal perspective, but also unanticipated outcomes that then called for further response. The "Stalinist system" that gradually crystallized stemmed less from intended policies than from improvised, sometimes desperate attempts to cope with the crises created by the new direction of 1929–33.[98]

An array of memorialists and scholars have stressed the energizing sense of epic enterprise and grandiose achievement that developed as the experiment proceeded, from the cultural revolution and the First Five-Year Plan to the crash industrialization program.[99] Writing decades after the fact, Lev Kopelev recalled the idealistic mindset, the sense of revolutionary duty, that had enabled him, as a young activist, to participate in the exactions of grain from the peasants.[100] But it was especially the industrialization effort that galvanized enthusiasm as it mobilized millions. Ronald Suny noted that as the regime embarked on "the most mammoth building project in modern times, . . . a romance of dams and power-stations, new cities on the steppe and in Siberia, created enthusiasts among the new workers and managers." Moreover, "the sheer scale of the transformation and its construction as a human epic engendered the broad social support that the regime had sought for two decades."[101] Even Malia stressed that the transformation of the 1930s was unprecedented in scope, the means "unique in their mixture of the insane and the criminal with—it must be admitted—the grandiose and the epic." He went on to note that whereas collectivization proved far more problematic, even disastrous, Soviet industrialization—despite its brutality and waste—was a significant historical accomplishment and a source of genuine pride for much of the urban population.[102]

Noting how hard it has become, in our skeptical age, to recapture the utopian enthusiasm, prominent especially among the young, Sheila Fitzpatrick warned that this sense of participating in a world-historical transformation cannot be dismissed as deception and camouflage. Still, she could not resist adding that the rhetoric served precisely those purposes for the Stalinist regime.[103] This was to suggest that, despite the genuineness of the enthusiasm, what was ultimately at work was the familiar syndrome of elites using deception and camouflage to maximize their own power and advantage. But during the course of the 1930s a richer interplay between what the leadership proclaimed and many participants experienced was at work.

In his study of Magnitogorsk, Kotkin showed that this bizarre showplace epitomized the wider enthusiasm that accompanied the rekindling of revolution after the NEP.[104] And although much propaganda surrounded the grandiose effort at Magnitogorsk, he cautioned against any suggestion that the enthusiasm stemmed simply from coercion or manipulation. Coercion there was, but it did not preclude genuine and deep commitment, even as tempered by elements of cynical realism.[105] As Kotkin put it, ordinary people believed the story they were being told because it captured their imagination and seemed to conform to the very ideals it stimulated. It was, as it had to be, a story that people could express in their own words. In this light, Kotkin stressed the widespread sense of living the revolution on the everyday level, of participating in a genuinely new culture, with new attitudes, language, even forms of dress. Thus his book's subtitle: "Stalinism as a civilization."

For Kotkin, this was "participation in the grand crusade of building socialism," and certainly it was thus trumpeted and even experienced.[106] The sense of "building socialism" was essential to the energizing sense of wider mission, of making history by showing the world a morally superior model of modern society, without exploitation, based on planning, and spreading benefits from health care to paid vacations. The Soviet Union, and Magnitogorsk itself, saw a parade of foreigners who denounced capitalism and praised this socialism in the making, thereby reinforcing the sense that "building socialism" was indeed what was happening.[107] And, as we have emphasized, the sense of competition with fascism, linked to capitalist interests, was central to the whole energizing experience during the 1930s.

Kotkin's insistence on irreducible enthusiasm and idealism is compelling, but how we are to understand and place them within the overall dynamic is not so clear. Even as we recognize that it is too easy to refer to mere manipulation from above, we still must understand the tension between what the participants thought was happening and what proved to have been happening in fact. For all the enthusiasm, the regime proved, in important respects, to be unable to handle the great task undertaken.[108] Thus the effort continued to produce unforeseen consequences, which interpenetrated with the ongoing enthusiasm and idealism to force the regime in a particular direction, both radicalizing and narrowing.

To create a new order, the vanguard leadership obviously required administrative cadres, yet, as Moshe Lewin emphasized, the Bolsheviks viewed bureaucracy with deep ambivalence virtually from the start. Lenin in his last years was explicitly concerned with the potential for distortion that the need to rely on bureaucracy, even a nominally socialist bureaucracy, entailed. The antidote seemed to be education—which demanded another layer of bureaucracy to supervise the educators.[109]

Whatever the suspicions, bureaucracy was inevitable, especially as state powers expanded with the First Five-Year Plan and the subsequent acceleration of the industrialization effort. Lewin argued convincingly that the essential characteristics of the resulting Soviet bureaucracy stemmed not from Russian traditions but from the Soviet enterprise itself, the effort to tackle an avalanche of increasingly complex tasks like economic planning.[110]

Especially as it expanded, bureaucracy inevitably got caught up in the complex interaction of above and below. "Above/below" is relative, of course, because the cadres were often segmented hierarchically themselves. Moreover, bureaucracy encompassed an array of offices and functions. Local party officials, factory managers, and police members, to choose the most obvious examples, played different roles and were caught up in the dynamic in different ways. Yet each was central to what proved a common dynamic.

As it took on expanded tasks, the regime was bound to encounter the more general paradoxes of modern bureaucracy pinpointed by observers from Robert Michels to Zygmunt Bauman. These intertwined with the special problems of preparation and commitment, stemming from the ambitiousness and hurriedness of the Soviet effort, to produce an unprecedented syndrome. That the new bureaucrats were often unprepared has been widely emphasized, but the problem had several dimensions. Although there was opportunism and dubious commitment, even the committed were often poorly trained. The affirmative action dimension during the cultural revolution and the rapid promotion during the purges of the mid to late 1930s exacerbated the problem, with lasting impact.[111] Yet bureaucratic managers were expected to take on tasks that would have required unprecedented training, experience, and dedication even under the most favorable circumstances. No wonder factory managers, especially, found it difficult to master their jobs.[112]

The dysfunctional results were legion. The incompetence resulting from unpreparedness invited compensating corruption, drunkenness, or heavy-handedness in dealing with workers. Lewin concluded that the perennial bureaucratic bargaining and infighting "actually blocked the system's capacity to act."[113] Laments of drowning in paper became widely heard. Planning was to mean the triumph of human rationality, but almost immediately it produced its own unforeseen forms of anarchy, together with doctored production figures and inflated rhetoric.[114]

Under the circumstances, Gabor Rittersporn found it hardly surprising that obscure machinations now became inseparable from the actual policies of the regime: "Officials routinely misused their powers in order to make a show of success, and in many cases they hardly had a choice, confronted as they were by the indifference or hostility of the masses, by inadequate resources, and by the prospect of censure, dismissal, or penal sanctions if they could not produce at least the semblance of results or find scapegoats for failures."[115] Managers had always to request more than was needed.[116] Yet because achievements were exaggerated, expectations were raised. Fitzpatrick noted the extraordinary boost-erism and self-congratulation, buttressed by a barrage of statistics intended for both foreign and domestic consumption, that accompanied the measure of undeniable achievement.[117] But thus the tendency was to blame deliberate wrecking when unrealistic expectations were not met.

At the same time, Kotkin noted that the confused organizational structure made authority perpetually contested and ultimately produced a vacuum of responsibility.[118] Reflecting the often uncertain relations between center and periphery, local officials often became "little Stalins," tough guys operating on their own, establishing local centers of power, not performing the intended function of mediation between the vanguard and the people.[119] Meanwhile, crash industrialization also produced what Lewin termed a "quicksand society," with rapid changes in class relations and individual roles.[120] Such openness meant upward mobility, which afforded support for Stalin up to a point, even as it also helped to fuel excess by inviting resentment and the settling of scores.

Not surprisingly, the whole chaotic syndrome produced a sense of increasing powerlessness at the top but then also various attempts to master the situation, some of them arbitrary and despotic.[121] Indeed, the complex interplay between the leadership and the bureaucracy proved fundamental to the rhythm of the regime.

Although Lenin had always played a special role, Bolshevism had posited collective leadership, in keeping with the vanguard notion. By the early 1920s, Lenin was expressing strong displeasure, even horror, at the cult of personality growing up around him.[122] It is well known that his widow, Nadezhda

Krupskaya, did her best to prevent the quasi-deification of Lenin that took place after his death, So although the potential for a leadership cult was apparently inherent in Bolshevism, the sort of leadership that Stalin came to exercise was clearly a departure to some extent. The question is how the development of Stalin's role fitted into the wider dynamic following from Leninism. Although it was partly a matter of sheer contingency that an individual with Stalin's particular personal qualities, including his (surely very low) threshold of paranoia, ended up in charge, it was no accident that the regime developed as it did, or that Stalin ended up playing the role he did, despite Lenin's own repudiation of any cult of personality.

Malia pinpointed two key dimensions of the relationship between leadership and the wider dynamic. Each is worth considering in detail. First, Malia insisted that the logic of the system made for a single leader; the cult of Stalin was an expression of the system, not a self-serving creation of Stalin himself. Stalin personified the infallibility of the party.[123] In this light, Malia found the ban on factions, which, as Lewin emphasized, was central to the narrowing of decision making that favored reliance on a single leader, to have been a resultant, not a cause.

Whereas for Malia, some such outcome followed from the logic of socialist implementation, for Lewin, that outcome was much more contingent. At issue is the strength of the contingency in light of the wider dynamic, and again we must find our way between contrasting positions to grasp the strong contingency of Leninism. We cannot simply attribute the narrowing and personification to the logic of socialist implementation, because the process at work entailed something more complex, as we have emphasized. At the same time, we cannot trace the outcome to the mere contingencies of ahistorical power struggles, because the logic of that process shaped the direction in particular ways. Having tied the future of the revolution to improvisation, trial and error, and the force of will, the leadership had to act in a certain mode. The party was not really infallible in the sense of having a blueprint or script; it had *only* that mode of action, a capacity to act to shape circumstances. In that light, the image of Bolshevik toughness that Stalin presented was crucial. As Suny put it, the position of the ruling elite depended on enforcing decisions from above "with determination, even ruthlessness."[124]

Malia made his second point in addressing the interface of psychological propensities, which we tend to view as both ahistorical and determining, with the wider dynamic in course. Stalin, said Malia, proved cruel to the point of sadism, suspicious to the point of paranoia, but those personality traits had not been evident even in 1929. It thus seems likely that "his character was not a constant, but . . . evolved under the pressure of the unprecedented tasks of the offensive."[125]

In other words, we cannot start with Stalin, his being as he was, in some ahistorical sense, to explain the process; indeed, the truth is closer to the reverse. Although certain psychological propensities were given beforehand, and although proportions are indeterminate, Stalin came to be the individual he was, with certain possibilities of character coming to the fore, because of the pressures that resulted from the historically specific dynamic in which he was caught up. In short, "Stalin" was himself historically specific in this crucial sense. Whatever the proportions, we cannot explain the "Stalinist" outcome as a deviation resulting from some combination of ahistorical psychology and the contingent outcomes of power struggles. Rather, we must grasp the interplay between character or personality and the Leninist dynamic.

Because Stalin, in contrast to the more freewheeling, seemingly *sui generis* dictators Hitler and Mussolini, was more the creature of the ongoing party, he has sometimes been portrayed as the "chief bureaucrat." But although it usefully resists any reduction to mere personality, this characterization is surely too simple regarding the dynamic in course. Stephen Cohen, endorsed by Giuseppe Boffa, deemed the "chief bureaucrat" notion incongruous while also denying that the bureaucracy had become in itself a class capable of animating events in the 1930s. If anything, Cohen insisted, Stalin saw the bureaucracy as a conservative obstacle as he embarked on such risky, dangerous tasks as forced collectivization. "Indeed," Cohen concluded, "Stalin's repeated campaigns to radicalize and spur on officialdom in the years 1929–30 and after suggest a fearful, recalcitrant party–state bureaucracy, not an event-making one."[126] In the same way, Lewin stressed that Stalin was not, like Lenin before him, merely restive with bureaucracy but worried that a bureaucratic regime was already emerging, that the bureaucrats wanted to contain the leader and implement normal rule.[127] The key is that from the great political perspective by then in place, any such normalization was intolerable; only great, extraordinary politics could galvanize the energies and virtues for a superior order.

The logic of the effort to counter bureaucratic inertia or ineptitude led to further radicalization through the mutually reinforcing interaction of energies from above and below that we have already seen at work. Even during the collectivization drive, proudly militant Komsomol activists from the towns sought to serve as watchdogs and, when necessary, critics of any tendencies toward bureaucratic inertia, a role the wider population appreciated.[128] But such interaction interfaced at an odd angle with questions about functional differentiation in light of the industrialization drive.

Initially, the regime fostered egalitarianism, or even working-class privilege, on ideological grounds, an impulse that was reanimated with the cultural revolution beginning in 1928. The chronic labor shortages that accompanied crash industrialization gave ordinary workers added leverage, but among the unintended consequences of the new dynamic was a growing problem of worker discipline by the early 1930s.[129] The industrialization drive produced what Lewin called the "ruralization of the cities," which included a breakdown in labor discipline, evident, for example, in absenteeism and alcoholism.[130] But thus, as the importance of labor quality became clearer, Stalin began to stress the significance of "the human factor," most famously in a speech of July 1931.[131] The concomitant emphasis on quality and differentiation meshed uneasily with ideals of classlessness or equality as the original ideology continued to come apart.

With labor quality emphasized, the workers were encouraged to compete for rewards.[132] This was implicit recognition that, for the present at least, the point was not to live socialism but to act, to do something else, called "*building* socialism," requiring galvanizing virtues that were entirely different from, even antithetical to, egalitarianism. In another sense, all were indeed equal now, as participants, but from within that framework, differentiation was legitimate because it was functional, essential to the great task that all were carrying out together.

The accent on differentiation fed a wider glorification of heroism, as heroic pilots or polar explorers were featured in the media.[133] Maxim Gorky offered a quasi-Nietzschean understanding: Soviet man was becoming "Man," pitting the force of human will against nature in grandiose, tragic struggle.[134] But in light of the great task of crash industrialization, even ordinary workers could become heroes.

In this context, the coal miner Alexei Stakhanov mined fourteen times his quota in August 1935, initiating Stakhanovism as a movement of labor heroism. Through comparably prodigious feats, 22 percent of industrial workers had achieved Stakhanovite status by September 1936, and another 23 percent had become "shock workers," the next step down. A kind of mania for setting production records swept the country during late 1935, with another wave emerging during the second half of 1936.[135] Although it was encouraged from above, Stakhanovism was not merely the product of cynical manipulation but rather grew spontaneously from the enthusiasm of workers caught up in the idealism of the heroic collective task in progress.[136] Yet this phenomenon, feeding into the already complex interaction between workers, managers, and the political leadership, ended up adding another layer of confusion and unintended consequences. In this sense, Stakhanovism proved at once symptomatic of and essential to the great political dynamic in course.

Lewis Siegelbaum stressed that Stakhanovism gave the leadership both less and more than expected.[137] On the one hand, it served, as intended, to encourage workers to master new technologies and thus to increase their own productivity. And although it meant not egalitarianism but differentiation, leading workers found new opportunities to help to set norms and, as they gathered confidence, to speak for their laboring comrades in conveying grievances and criticisms. The leadership, in turn, expected managers to pay close attention to demands and suggestions from below.

For the workers themselves, having enjoyed some bargaining power in light of labor shortage, Stakhanovism meant more intense politicization, but also differentiation and resentment. Kotkin noted that whereas some workers looked for opportunities to ingratiate themselves, others avoided the highly charged rituals.[138] But there was nowhere to hide, especially as Stakhanovism intensified the politicization of economic roles. So the movement ended up reinforcing resentments and antagonisms within an already factionalized workforce, and the competition, leading to strongly differential rewards between workers, ended up sapping the enthusiasm that it initially inspired.

Lewin noted that whereas Stalin and the leadership, in encouraging Stakhanovism, were seeking to shake up the bureaucrats by drawing on the pride and initiative of the workers, the bureaucrats ended up clipping the wings of the campaign.[139] However, at work was not just bureaucratic conservatism, self-interest, or incompetence, but particular, unforeseen tensions unleashed by the mode of action being attempted.

The productive changes in work methods stimulated by the early Stakhanovites required changes in the division of labor—and thus the concurrence of supervisors. Initially, managers tended to cooperate, even affording individual workers the opportunity to set records. But increasingly managers resisted Stakhanovite pressures from both above and below, partly from mere resentment but especially from plausible concerns about efficiency, safety, and fairness.[140] Solicitude for individual achievement did not mesh with the orderly procedure and predictability necessary for any generalized, sustainable increases in productivity. Thus, as Siegelbaum showed, Stakhanovism produced bottlenecks, disruptions, distortions, unanticipated confusion, and new dilemmas for managers who were already having to scramble and bend rules.

But the resistance of managers led to stepped-up criticism and even demands, both from below and from the national leadership, to expand Stakhanovite opportunities. Pressures for sometimes unrealistic upward adjustment in production targets especially intensified the difficulties for local managers. Even as the movement was declining by late 1936, workers were accusing such managers of holding back or even sabotaging production.[141] At the same time, the rash of worker complaints and the increasing factory tensions made national leaders suspicious of managers. So the Stakhanovite movement sharpened tensions between workers and managers, increased labor turnover, and left a legacy of animosity.[142]

The encouragement of denunciations from below, the intensified suspicion, and the accusations of sabotage helped to nurture the next phase, which was beginning by late 1936. In light of the enthusiasm, the inflating rhetoric, and the sense of grandiose achievement, seemingly *only* the machinations of saboteurs, enemies, and wreckers could explain the anomalies and failures, the unexpected turmoil.[143]

The long moment of terror, 1936–39

What followed was the Great Terror or *Ezhovshchina*, which began to develop late in 1936 and reached its peak in 1937–38. Although it is surely central to any assessment of the overall dynamic, its sources, nature, and even key aspects of the immediate outcome remain especially controversial.[144]

Any revolution will provoke opposition and make enemies, and any revolutionary regime must be vigilant as a condition of survival. In the Soviet case, the Communists were claiming an ongoing international role in a world that remained largely suspicious or hostile. But with the Japanese turn to a more aggressive orientation and the advent of Hitler's regime in Germany, the Soviet Union by the mid-1930s faced a genuinely menacing international situation that was bound to cause serious alarm. Moreover, the power struggles of the 1920s, especially the fate of Trotsky, had obviously produced the potential for opposition to the Stalinist regime. The problems of the industrialization/collectivization drive, with its unforeseen excesses and incredible loss of life, exacerbated that potential. Trotskyites constituted a genuine opposition, linking disaffected elements in exile to those in the Soviet Union. And it was certainly conceivable that such opponents might work with hostile powers to overthrow Stalin or wreck the regime, even through sabotage in the economy. Although the evidence suggests that Stalin's Communist opponents did not in fact use terrorism or work with foreign agents, the nature and extent of the danger could not have been clear at the time.[145]

Overt opposition to the Stalinist direction, including forced collectivization, began to surface in 1932. That summer, a group centered around M.N. Ryutin circulated a 200-page tract among party leaders calling for a retreat from Stalin's economic program and a return to democracy within the party. It advocated readmitting those who had been expelled—including Trotsky. Moreover, the document strongly condemned Stalin personally, describing him as "the evil genius of the Russian Revolution, who, motivated by a personal desire for power and revenge, brought the Revolution to the verge of ruin."[146] Although eighteen signers of this "Ryutin platform" were expelled from the party, the Central Committee vetoed Stalin's proposal that Ryutin himself be executed.

Stalin's wife, Nadezhda Allilueva, also expressed opposition to Stalin's policies, drawing a public rebuke from Stalin in response. She then committed suicide in November 1932.[147] The worst of the famine that accompanied collectivization took place during the winter of 1932–33. That same winter, in January 1933, Hitler came to power. To be sure, the official Comintern line had proclaimed Nazism a lesser evil than the "social fascism" of the SPD; Nazi power would swell the Communist opposition and possibly revoke revolution. However, it quickly became clear how devastating the advent of Nazism was to the Communists' international situation.

Still, the trend after the winter of 1932–33 was seemingly toward moderation, thanks partly to the economic improvement noted above. An effort, clear by January 1934, to enhance individual rights, to overcome police arbitrariness, and to establish due process, continued even into 1936.[148]

At the same time, however, the sense that extraordinary machinations were at work, calling for an extraordinary response, was intensifying. Central was the murder of the popular Leningrad party chief Sergei Kirov on December 1, 1934. Extreme intentionalists like Conquest have sought to demonstrate Stalin's responsibility; Kirov, the argument goes, was a potential rival, and his murder afforded Stalin, as the Ryutin platform had not, the needed excuse for a systematic crackdown. But although opinion remains divided, the consensus is that Stalin was not responsible for Kirov's murder. And if he was not, it surely could have frightened him.[149]

As Roberta Manning has emphasized, Stalin and the leadership expected great economic breakthroughs and new miracles based on the achievements of 1934–35, but for mostly endogenous reasons a slowdown began in 1936, when the double-digit industrial growth rates of the early 1930s suddenly declined sharply. Even with a notably good harvest in 1937, the downturn would last until 1940 or 1941, having been intensified and prolonged by the political upheavals that it had itself helped to occasion.[150] In light of the inflated expectations and the danger of active opposition, it was easy to attribute any such disappointing results not to the inherent difficulties of the unprecedented task at hand but to ineptitude and indifference, if not deliberate wrecking. The fact that the "little Stalins" on the periphery were proving hard to manage added to the sense that somehow, anomalously, the regime was unable to act as expected.

As J. Arch Getty emphasized, purges of the Communist Party had been more or less routine, to eliminate those who proved incompetent or uncommitted, corrupt or abusive, or prone to drunkenness. There was ongoing and plausible disagreement between Communist leaders over how broadly based as opposed to restrictively elitist the party was to be now that its task was not to spearhead a revolution but to build socialism. And thus there was disagreement over how frequently and extensively it needed to be purged.[151] The purging process was not inherently arbitrary, let alone violent. It initially allowed the member being examined to make a personal statement and to respond to questions from the purge commission, even from the audience.[152]

In light of the accumulating frustrations as the regime stepped up its activity, more careful admission and supervision of cadres seemed essential. Thus the periodic purging of the party became more frequent during the 1930s, focusing first on incompetence or abusiveness, not so much on wrecking or active sabotage. Three major party cleansings in 1933, 1935, and 1936 reduced the membership by 750,000–800,000, or more than one-third, to 1,450,000. Despite this intensification, those expelled were not automatically arrested; indeed, they could appeal, and some were in fact reinstated.[153]

So, as Getty, especially, made clear, the mere fact of purging is not to be conflated with "terror"—the familiar syndrome encompassing the often arbitrary arrest of large numbers of people, followed by interrogations, forced confessions, then execution or confinement to the Gulag. Indeed, there is no logical or necessary connection between the two. One could be purged from party—as insufficiently committed or sober, for example—without being sent to the Gulag or shot. And purges targeted the party membership, a small elite sector, not the citizenry in general. Robert Thurston argued that even the party purges of 1935–36, although "intensely political," were not the beginning of a planned assault on the party, let alone the nation as a whole.[154]

But with the wider great political dynamic in course, even the purging process tended to spin out of control, producing unforeseen extremes. Experts disagree even on the point at which purging of the party began to snowball into the Great Terror. But the most intense phase began with Stalin's frightening report on capitalist encirclement and wreckers to the plenary meeting of the party's Central Committee on March 3, 1937.[155] With the accent shifting from re-education to arrest, the additional 500,000 purged from the party during 1937 were more likely than those previously to be shot or sent to the Gulag.[156]

Just as purges do not necessarily entail terror, neither are they to be conflated with the show trials that also had an important role in the wider dynamic. Such trials can be traced back to the extemporaneous local theater of the civil war period, but they became important especially as the Shakhty trial of bourgeois specialists in 1928 initiated a series of highly publicized show trials that continued into 1931. These local trials had a genuinely populist aspect and sometimes, at least, stemmed from plausible charges.[157]

But the three famous Moscow trials of August 1936, January 1937, and March 1938 were particularly spectacular, especially the last, which brought Bukharin, Alexei Rykov, and Genrikh Yagoda to the dock. Thurston controversially challenged the longstanding presumption that these trials were based entirely on trumped-up charges and intended for cynical propaganda purposes, and he may go overboard in shading certain particulars.[158] But his overall point is convincing and important. The criteria of rationality and plausibility were becoming blurred indeed, in light of the dynamic in course. As Thurston had it, Bukharin had in fact lied repeatedly to Stalin and the Central Committee, and Stalin had serious reason to distrust him. Even as Bukharin himself denied many key charges, he believed the charges against others. Thurston concluded that although most were clearly innocent, there was always a grain of truth to the accusations.[159] Ordinary people could not be sure, and up to a point, at least, it was not irrational to believe that findings of guilt were justified. The show trials, then, fed the tendency to believe that systematic wrecking was going on. But thus it also fed the developing surreality of the regime, for whatever the grain of truth in each case, the larger point remains that not only were the accused confessing to crimes they had not committed, they were confessing, for the most part, to crimes that had not been committed at all. Yet their confessions could only suggest to many that such crimes were indeed taking place.

In assessing the intentions and mechanisms that fed the terror, it is essential to recognize, first, that everyone from Stalin to the police to ordinary people tended to believe that a vast network of opposition and wrecking really was at work; Stalin and the leadership were not simply manipulating fear and resentment for conventional power reasons.[160] But although some level of concern was surely plausible, the agents at all levels seem anomalously to have overplayed the threat, at least its domestic component (for it would be hard to argue that they overplayed the potential threats from Germany and Japan). And the process seems to have carried beyond any plausible effort to root out actual enemies, so the mere fact of belief takes us only so far. To account for and to place the extremes that in fact resulted, we must account for whatever measure of implausibility. Insofar as the belief was not credible, why did they believe it? What frame of mind would have made such incredible belief possible, even likely?

Assessing grounds for belief at the time is tricky partly because of differential access to information, so starting with what Stalin might plausibly have believed, we must proceed through the hierarchy to ordinary people, asking what *they* might plausibly have believed in light of what Stalin and the leadership told them. And whatever it is, beyond immediate plausibility, that explains the several responses may differ considerably for Stalin, his intimates, party and police functionaries, and ordinary people.

For Stalin, the mere fact of belief does not preclude either of the two lines of argument that, in one combination or another, have long seemed to explain the terror. Whatever the degree of genuine belief, Stalin and his henchmen might knowingly have *overplayed* the threat in order to provide scapegoats, cement control, settle scores, foster a new loyal elite, and/or produce a submissive populace readily subjected to "total domination." Indeed, whatever the belief at the outset of the process, the leadership could *react* even to unintended events with cynical manipulation, and the eventual *outcomes* could conform to the traditional view, which took the terror as random and atomizing in its effects. So we must be open to the scope for disjunction between initial intentions and effects in light of the wider dynamic in course.

Whether stemming from cynicism at the outset or cynicism in response, any such direction would seem to bear some relationship to Stalin's personal psychology, combining an ahistorical power drive with idiosyncratic paranoia. Even the major revisionists accept crucial parts of this now familiar line of explanation. Thurston referred to Stalin's "deep suspiciousness bordering on hysteria" and, following Dimitri Volkogonov, who enjoyed special access to Stalin's files, noted that Stalin repeatedly ordered police investigations in the wake of denunciations and always believed the resulting reports.[161] In the same way, Getty observed that Stalin was cruel and vindictive—once he had made up his mind.[162]

But if no one denies the significance of Stalin and his idiosyncratic psychology, it is clear that a more complex dynamic was at work. Thurston's way of meshing several of the key variables offers a useful start: "With some justification, Stalin saw dangerous opposition developing around him. He was almost certainly mentally disturbed in some way and therefore blew the dissent out of proportion. But he was not plotting a campaign against the nation." Nor, Thurston added elsewhere, was he using extraordinary means in an effort to bend the party to his will.[163] But how do we understand what he *was* doing, and how did it lead to the excesses it did?

This terroristic phase of the dynamic revolved around the interplay of the three layers at work all along in the effort to carry out this revolution: at the top, Stalin and the leadership; in the middle, party cadres, local officials, plant managers, political police; and acting from below, ordinary people, including especially factory workers. And, once again, the particular, complex reciprocity among the three proved mutually reinforcing, producing radicalization.

Central though Stalin was, the evidence indicates not coherent direction but confusion, indecision, mixed signals, and retreats throughout the process. Getty emphasized Stalin's strange zigs and zags on the eve of the *Ezhovshchina* and suggested that his mode of response reflected the same patchwork, reactive quality evident in his decisions in other policy areas. Indecision in the face of chaotic events produced what Getty found the contradictory evolution of the repression until mid-1937.[164] Even during the worst of the terror thereafter, Stalin was unwilling or unable to guide events firmly. Genuine fear and a sense that things were going too far appear to have mixed in his mind. He seems even to have sought to expand the process and to moderate it at the same time. Stalin's top lieutenants were divided, with Vyacheslav Molotov favoring a hard line, Andrei Zhdanov a more moderate course. As Thurston put it, although Stalin and his close associates had "helped create a tense and ugly atmosphere," they "repeatedly reacted to events they had not planned or foreseen."[165] And this was because they were caught up in the wider three-way interaction indicated above.

In introducing his argument, Thurston did well to note that "a crucial, unresolved issue is why, between 1935 and 1939, so many people supported violence by the state and even participated in it willingly." But in concluding, he attributed the essential measure of popular participation to a generic societal tendency toward panic, as with McCarthyism or the various witch crazes.[166] But though such an ahistorical dimension was surely at work, Thurston was too quick to take it as a sufficient explanation, to the neglect of the implications of the wider historically specific dynamic in process, especially as it involved ordinary workers.

As an aspect of the purges, the leadership had encouraged workers to criticize their superiors as a way to invite more citizen involvement, to improve the economy by rooting out corruption, and to identify active wreckers all at the same time.[167] And such encouragement was central to the process through which normal purging became extraordinary terror. Indeed, radical populism proved to be a powerful force as industrial workers, especially, proved more the agents of the terror than its victims.[168] Not feeling personally vulnerable, the workers tended to support Stalin's effort and eagerly denounced their "wrecking" superiors, sometimes even demanding that they be shot.[169] In doing so, such workers were sometimes settling scores against those they resented for whatever reason, but they also acted out of genuine commitment to the great task of "building socialism." It was their duty to sniff out "enemies of the people," the wreckers responsible for, most immediately, the hardships in working and living conditions.

As we have seen, the level of incompetence and heavy-handedness on the part of the new, mid-level elites was relatively high.[170] The intensified criticism from below then created an image of the middle cadres as especially incompetent, dishonest, and indifferent to the welfare of the workers. That image, in turn, made charges of wrecking more plausible, which then contributed to the expanding scrutiny and soon the widespread arrest of managers and engineers during 1937–38.[171]

The managers and other mid-level officials found themselves on a tightrope as they sought to survive scrutiny from above and below. They had to head off denunciations from their employees but also take care that there were no wreckers under them. Officials might have to purge the institution under their jurisdiction in order to prove their political trustworthiness, but if they went too far they themselves could seem to be wrecking. Nobody knew—there was no way to know—where the line would be drawn.[172]

Also central were the political police, called the People's Commissariat for Internal Affairs (NKVD) from 1934. Responsible for the arrests and interrogations, the police, like the managers, were caught up in a reciprocal relationship with both above and below as part of the overall dynamic. Under the circumstances, the police almost had to proceed on their own initiative, to prove they were sufficiently vigilant, to avoid falling under suspicion themselves. As Getty emphasized, there is room for disagreement about the significance of police chief Narkom Ezhov's own agenda, but he seems to have been ahead of Stalin on occasion, contributing on his own to the momentum of the terror. Partly because he had himself been a factory worker for eight years, Ezhov tended to heed worker complaints as indications of genuine wrecking. At the same time, the NKVD more generally fed on and reinforced the sense among ordinary peoples, that extraordinary vigilance and punishment were necessary in light of the wrecking going on.[173]

To recognize an important measure of autonomy for Ezhov and the NKVD is certainly not to absolve Stalin, who approved NKVD lists of those to be arrested. Not only did he always believe reports of wrecking, but he then pressed the police for even more arrests, worsening the vicious cycle in which the NKVD was already caught up. And of course the exponential progression of denunciations, confessions, and incriminations produced ever-widening circles of vulnerability. With the police a power unto itself on the local level, the process acquired a momentum that even Stalin found difficult to brake.[174]

Under the circumstances, police methods became increasingly extreme, including torture to force confessions even from those the police knew might well be innocent. Such behavior has long been central to our image of totalitarianism, and placing such excess, in light of the wider process at work, is central to the deeper overall understanding we seek. In this regard, too, it is tempting to settle for ahistorical impulses, such as sadism, or some "authority situation," the desire to please superiors, the duty to obey orders, to explain the excesses. Certainly Ezhov selected investigators who, because they had sins in their pasts, were likely to be especially eager to appear conscientious and vigilant to their superiors.[175] Such mechanisms are all part of the mix, but recent research has suggested a more complex interplay, which is also best understood in terms of the great political dynamic. Even sadism was especially likely to come to the fore in this historically specific situation, which was not just any "authority situation."

Even when indulging in brutality at the height of the terror, the police were surprisingly attentive to evidence and procedure.[176] They, too, believed that real crimes had been committed; they targeted those genuinely suspected to be criminals, not the population at large. Although in this regard, especially, Thurston's characterizations sometimes seem forced, he rings true in insisting that *even* when they forced confessions from suspects they knew might be innocent, the police were seeking information about real crimes. Kotkin similarly emphasized the NKVD's belief in its righteous duty.[177] But in order to do their duty fully, the police needed not merely to eliminate those arrested but to wrest confessions and incriminations from them. In this sense, the terror mushroomed not from randomness but from following specific connections in light of suggestions of guilt at some point along the chain.

Meanwhile, the terroristic process was yielding unintended, distinctly counter-productive consequences as it proceeded. At the height of the terror, people sensed the greater vulnerability of those in the upper reaches of society and thus became reluctant to accept promotion. The sense that many innocent people were being arrested produced confusion and avoidance, as opposed to the mere fear and conformity of the standard "anyone could be next" syndrome.[178]

By early 1938, officials on both the local and national levels were complaining about the implications of the persecutions for the quality of the remaining cadres.[179] Widespread public discussion, even in the press, stressed the need to curb excesses, to take greater care in denunciations. National leaders warned that local and provincial cadres were trying to "overinsure" themselves through excess denunciations. But although efforts to reign in the terror began as early as January 1938, the effort to control the process proved lengthy and difficult, marked by inconsistent and conflicting patterns as the momentum continued. Gradually, however, the process was brought under control. Local Communist organizations even began to reinstate some of those who had been purged and arrested. By October 1938, the judiciary, no longer betraying a panicky sense of the need to act quickly, had switched from facilitating terror to opposing it by proscribing torture and insisting on proper procedure and standards of evidence. Yet even after the Central Committee had ousted Ezhov as police chief, replacing him with Lavrenti Beria in November 1938, executions proceeded at, if anything, a stepped-up pace.[180]

We noted that despite—or partly because of—the widespread departure from the earlier totalitarian model, the meaning of the Stalinist terror of the late 1930s is arguably more controversial than ever. Although the toll in human suffering and death proved incredible—surely inconceivable before it happened and hard to grasp even now—there has been dispute even over the numbers of victims, accompanied by some unfortunate moralizing, all of which has blurred the discussion to some extent.[181]

Typical of the revisionists, Thurston insisted that neither the beginning of the terror, the process itself, nor the end suggests a master planner. Rather, "events spun out of control" as the hunt for perceived enemies produced unexpected twists and turns. During 1938, the leadership was beginning to admit grotesque mistakes. And, for Thurston, the changes beginning late that year especially belie any notion that the public was to stay terrorized. The NKVD was purged and, although some reversal followed the German invasion in 1941, its powers were checked through reorganization. Police torturers underwent open trials, and police misbehavior under Ezhov received broad public notice.[182]

Getty argued effectively, in response to moralistic criticisms, that to accent "indecision and chaos" is by no means to exonerate. Indeed, on the contrary, making Stalin into an omniscient and omnipotent demon diminishes the real horror of the period. Stressing that Stalin's colossal felonies were unplanned and erratic, Getty concluded that "his evil, like Eichmann's, was ordinary and of this world; it was banally human and is more horrifying for being so."[183]

But such prominent scholars as Fitzpatrick and Suny distanced themselves from the revisionist account of the terror, even as they recognized the importance of agency from below and the difficulties of controlling the periphery. While admitting that there was no consensus about the underlying motives, Suny stressed Stalin's personal involvement in the details of the process and concluded that Stalin's will and ambition remain the keys. It was no accident that the outcome was a younger, more loyal political and economic elite.[184]

Although she had been a pioneer in emphasizing agency from below, and although she continued to emphasize the importance of upward mobility, Fitzpatrick similarly came around to an overtly conventional view of the terror's sources. While recognizing that the process could not have snowballed as it did without popular participation, she stressed the differences from revolutionary terror stemming from spontaneous popular violence. What happened in the Soviet Union resembled Jacobin state terror—directed mostly against the revolutionaries themselves. And in the key documents of the period—the transcripts of the show trials, even the speeches of Stalin and Molotov, repudiating mass purging and admitting excess, at the Eighteenth Party Congress early in 1939—she found a staginess, a lack of real emotion. "One feels," she concluded, "the hand of a director, if not an *auteur*." From her perspective, Stalin's purpose was relatively straightforward—to kill political enemies—although perhaps also to refute Trotsky's charge of Thermidor. Terror showed that the revolution was still in progress, but it was by now all contrived.[185]

The revisionists' accounts produce uneasiness insofar as they imply that chaos and "out of control" constitute a sufficient alternative to intention. We sense that it is not enough simply to disembed the process from the earlier totalitarian frame, which had afforded one way of explaining intentions and effects. At the same time, although an element of ahistorical banality was part of the mix, Getty was quick to jump from one ahistorical accent—power—to another—banality—as he responded to moralistic objections. Although banal evil can indeed be troubling, Getty's dualism does not seem adequate to get at Stalin's role in a situation that was not ordinary but quite extraordinary—and extraordinary in a very particular way. Thus, perhaps, the determination of those like Suny and Fitzpatrick to keep their distance from the revisionists. But Suny and Fitzpatrick were quick to resort to conventional notions as the alternative. Fitzpatrick's conclusion that we feel the hand of an "*auteur*" seems arbitrary, almost as if she was seeking to atone for having apparently played down the terror in the past. The key point is that the alternatives offered by the revisionists, on the one hand, and quasi-traditionalists like Suny and Fitzpatrick, on the other, do not exhaust the options.

To characterize Stalin's role in the terror, we need greater attention to the wider Leninist dynamic, with the various forces it had already set loose, with the characteristic modes of interaction it invited, with the characteristic emphasis on decisiveness and ruthlessness that it entailed, and with its capacity to trigger latent potentials of personality, thereby producing a certain kind of Stalin. Rather than setting out to atomize and control in light of whatever combination of ahistorical propensities, the leadership had to respond to the concatenation of forces, now spinning out of control, that had been set in play by the effort to tackle an unprecedented task through an unprecedented form of collective action. That response then led to a further out-of-control dimension. So although the terror played out in ways that no one could have foreseen, let alone orchestrated, it was not merely an accident. Contingent though it was, it was strongly contingent, a likely outcome of the great political process in course. In that light, we recognize that whereas chaos and "out of control" do not afford a sufficient alternative to the standard model, they were characteristic provisional outcomes from within a wider historically specific dynamic that, properly understood, provides the essential alternative to the standard model.

Whatever his threshold of paranoia, Stalin certainly had some good reason to be concerned—but why was that? By the 1930s, it was not simply the danger of counterrevolution that any revolutionary regime faces for a while. In initiating a great political dynamic, the Bolshevik Revolution had produced or helped to produce an array of unanticipated but not merely fortuitous consequences, from the advent of Fascism and Nazism to the isolation of the Soviet Union to the dispute over direction that exacerbated the succession struggle and led to the exile of, and subsequent danger from, Trotsky. Together, these outcomes had produced an unprecedented, especially troublesome framework from within which to undertake the great task of planned, rapid industrialization. At the same time, the forced collectivization that had seemed to be necessary for that industrialization had produced unforeseen negative consequences that provoked further opposition.

Thurston noted that Stalin and the leadership had created a mood in which every accident had to have had a wrecker.[186] But the creation of that mood was not *sui generis*, the starting point. That mood was bound up, in ways that no one had foreseen, with the reckless decision for crash industrialization, which itself stemmed from a wider mood, or "frame of mind," bound up with great political collective action.

Even as he, too, stressed that Stalin and company really believed that wreckers were at work, Rittersporn was more attuned to the wider anomaly of the situation. He noted that "the monstrous accusations of 'subversion,' 'high treason,' or 'conspiracy' against leading officials were not necessarily incredible in the 1930s." In fact, there was *not* a wrecker behind every accident, so how could such monstrous charges be credible? For Rittersporn, the "perceptions of omnipresent conspiracy" seemed to be credible only from within the framework created by "the unpredictable, incomprehensible, and treacherous daily reality of the system."[187] However, we achieve a measure of understanding only when we grasp how that "surreal" daily reality had resulted from the particular new mode of collective action being attempted.

Roberta Manning got at the reverse of the coin as she noted that other factors besides the economic downturn, her immediate frame, were needed for the terror—including, as she put it, "a leadership that expected 'miracles' and refused to accept economic constraints."[188] The leadership really did expect miracles, but, again, such expectation is not merely an unproblematic given, and the "frame of mind" underlying such anomalously inflated expectations obviously intersects, in a mutually reinforcing way, with the assumption of a wrecker behind every accident. Crucially, however, the expectation of miracles did *not* stem from Marxism or ideology but, again, from the historically specific attempt at great politics.

In expecting miracles and seeking wreckers, Stalin was responding in part to pressures from ordinary people, but those pressures, too, were historically specific, stemming from the dynamic in progress, which entailed a new reciprocity of above and below. And that reciprocity was sufficiently realized to help to fuel the momentum as each side fed, and fed on, the other. Despite grumbling, ordinary workers had been mobilized sufficiently to feel a sense of common participation in the grandiose enterprise, as opposed to mere disaffection or cynicism. Their denunciations from below then played into radicalization and excess. So to account for the out-of-control dynamic that resulted from popular involvement, we cannot merely invoke an ahistorical tendency toward popular hysteria; we must grasp the implications of the historically specific mode of collective action being attempted.

We noted that although the issue of intention is crucial for one set of questions, it does not determine the answer to the question of outcomes and effects. Especially insofar as the terror got out of hand, it obviously could have had unintended consequences. Even if it was not orchestrated, with atomization and control in mind, the process could have had something approximating the atomizing effects long attributed to intention.

The question of outcomes and effects is bound up with the question of magnitude. Although some, like Conquest and Walter Laqueur, claimed that new evidence, available with the collapse of the Communist regime, supports the earlier notion of random, generalized terror to produce frightened submission, the preponderance of recent research suggests something else—but it has been hard to characterize whatever it is and to place it in the longer-term course of the Soviet experiment.[189]

Seeking to head off the moralizing that the subject has invited, Thurston took care to note that the toll was incredible and tragic. But the numbers, he went on to stress, are important for our understanding of how the regime ruled and how people responded.[190] And not only does new evidence indicate that the number of arrests and deaths was considerably lower than conquests and others had argued, but the terror, whatever its sources, was simply not sufficiently extensive to have atomized society. In fact, Thurston concluded, life went on.[191] Even Fitzpatrick noted that the second half of the 1930s was the great age of Soviet musical comedy.[192]

The preponderance of recent research suggests that the terror targeted specific cohorts, so vulnerability varied considerably across the population. To identify who suffered disproportionately and why is obviously crucial to both intentions and outcomes. Although no correlation was very strong, the key variable was not overall biography but position in 1936. Thus, contrary to the longstanding belief that Stalin set out to destroy the old Bolsheviks because they seemed a particular threat, long-time Bolsheviks were not overrepresented among the victims. Rather, the terror targeted senior party and government officials and especially industrial leaders. But it was unpredictable and chaotic within those limits, so even as it targeted certain elites disproportionately, it included an important but unintended random element.[193]

At the same time, we have come to recognize that responses among Soviet citizens varied considerably along an unstable continuum from active approval, including admiration of Stalin for taking the tough steps necessary, to lamenting the methods and the resulting excesses, to a sense that something had gone fundamentally wrong.[194] The young, especially among workers, students, and intellectuals, long more prone to idealism and less concerned with immediate economic hardship, remained overwhelmingly loyal to the regime and tended to see the terror as justified.[195] Most had not felt personally threatened. To be arrested oneself, or to have a family member tabbed, could change perceptions, but such arrests seem often to have been understood as simply isolated mistakes, not indications of a systematic problem. Even years later, some purged army officers still believed that the overall purge of the army had been necessary—that their own fate resulted simply from a local mistake.[196]

Conversely, as we have noted, many Soviet citizens benefited through enhanced upward mobility, which meant a measure of rejuvenation for the regime at the same time. Even Cohen conceded Stalin's popularity on these grounds. Whether or not it was intended, an upsurge in membership in 1938 followed the nadir of 1937 and served to replenish the party.[197]

Thurston went further to claim that the process fed a limited but positive political role for those who were not victims and, more particularly, enhanced the workers' identification with the regime by the eve of the war. By no means martyrs or puppets, they had played significant roles not only in the achievements of industrialization but also in the state-sponsored violence apparently needed to preserve those achievements. The terror had enhanced their sense of participation and, more particularly, their scope for genuinely influencing practice through complaints, criticisms, and suggestions, all of which flowed constantly upward.[198] And, for Thurston, this experience was not merely a one-shot anomaly, confined to the late 1930s. Enhanced confidence in the right to criticize endured, helping to produce the energetic civil society that accompanied *glasnost* under Mikhail Gorbachev during the late 1980s.[199]

But just as it is possible to overemphasize atomizing effects, Thurston, at the other end of the spectrum, seemed too quick to emphasize the positive implications of the terror in the regime's overall trajectory. So how did the outcomes of the terror affect the subsequent dynamic?

Narrowing and the dissipation of idealism after the terror

The worst was surely over by early 1939. There would be sporadic terror again after the war, but not on the massive scale of 1937–38.[200] And the "system" could and did evolve, contrary to the earlier totalitarian model. Surely the outcome of the Soviet experiment was not determined once and for all as a result of the terror. Still, the terror was not some fortuitous moment of excess, as if a nightmare from which one might awaken. Once this unforeseen phenomenon had occurred, as one provisional outcome from within the totalitarian dynamic in course, it remained as a layer, delimiting the range of possibilities thereafter. So although the regime surely evolved, it did so within a more restricted range, with certain directions now more likely than others. In this sense, the terror proved to be a tipping point, decisive for the fate of the overall Soviet experiment.

In ending the terror, the leaders restored their control, but necessarily on a new basis, with certain unforeseen but mutually reinforcing implications. "Normalization" entailed a kind of narrowing in the Communist self-understanding. The original energizing idealism, based on the sense of creating a systematic alternative, diminished, eventually to dissipate almost entirely.[201]

Despite the upward mobility and the efforts to reign in the police, Soviet citizens could not come to terms with what had happened in the terror. Yet the fact that it had happened, and the fact that they could not come to terms with it, affected everything thereafter. Fitzpatrick noted that despite the admission by 1939 that many had been wrongly accused, few were released at that point—or for years thereafter. Many remained confined to the Gulag until the period of de-Stalinization that followed Khrushchev's secret speech of 1956. In short, terror scarred the society partly because it remained taboo.[202] And it remained taboo because of what it said not about socialism but about the mode of collective action that had been attempted. That mode was not being abandoned, but the dynamic it fueled was necessarily moving to a new phase.

Experience of the terror exacerbated special features of the bureaucratic tendency already in place. Cohen noted that whereas the Soviet bureaucracy had status and power, it lacked security, in light of Stalin's demonstrated willingness to purge, even to terrorize. Thus the bureaucracy became especially conservative, seeking security and predictability.[203] Yet the dynamic was such that the regime did not get the advantages—the regularity and predictability, the even-handed procedure, the impersonal legality—that modern bureaucracy purportedly entails. On the contrary, the system functioned through privilege, patronage, and personal relations. At the same time, the need for managers to take risks to secure raw materials, for example, and thereby to function effectively produced a gambling mentality antithetical to rational planning.[204] So the system proved to entail the worst of both worlds; although rigid, it was arbitrary and unpredictable.

In the same way, Cohen noted the insecurity of the new middle classes that emerged from the upheavals of the Stalinist 1930s.[205] Such insecurity not only fostered cautiousness but contributed to the overall narrowing of purpose as nationalism and the cult of Stalin came increasingly to set the tone.

We noted that, virtually from the start, the Communist leadership's disdain for bureaucracy helped to feed the reciprocal, energizing interaction of above and below. Indeed, as Fitzpatrick put it, the leaders longed for direct communication with the people without intermediaries. This, they assumed, would tap into the spirit of the revolution as opposed to the dead letter of the law.[206] Leninism from the start had envisioned not some static hierarchy or mere manipulation from above but genuine interaction and reciprocity. The regime conceived itself as having a popular and historically sanctioned mandate—to work, first through education and propaganda, to increase support, to get everyone pulling in the same history-making direction.

In that light, the Communists had fostered new, post-liberal forms of participation that were taken seriously, experienced seriously, by both leaders and led during the 1930s. After a long period of Cold War dismissal, we have come to recognize the genuineness and significance of the broad national discussions encouraged over, for example, the constitution and the new abortion law during 1936.[207] Especially significant were the letters registering complaints against bureaucratic officials that ordinary people were encouraged to write by the 1930s—and that the leaders themselves took very seriously. Both leaders and led saw this interaction as a new form of participation from below with no equivalent in bourgeois democracy.[208] Thurston noted explicitly that the system afforded modes of worker involvement not to be found in the United States, a fact that itself helped to inspire Soviet workers.[209] It is certainly true that the liberal system affords no such chance to denounce, for example, the incompetent among our economic superiors. The market is to do the weeding—firm by firm—and individuals simply lose their jobs if the firm fails. In politicizing the economy, the Soviet totalitarian experiment increased the scope for popular involvement in decisions vitally affecting individual prospects.

In the same way, Kotkin showed how ordinary people could influence the regime's direction through everyday decisions that sometimes circumvented official structures altogether. On the shop floor, in housing choices, in denouncing the store manager, daily life was "a constant negotiation of the political terrain constituted by the totalizing revolutionary crusade. Living socialism was a pioneering adventure."[210] Such everyday negotiation could be experienced as meaningfully political precisely because, with the totalitarian direction of the Soviet regime, the political, and the scope for participation, expanded to encompass, by definition, all aspects of life. In negotiating and deciding, ordinary people were participating in the ongoing great task rather than merely protesting, pursuing private advantage, or opting out. Obviously, such modes of participation carried only so far, but they were not merely illusory or sham, and they helped to sustain genuine enthusiasm—for a while.

The problem was that such alternative participation soon proved too wild, even dysfunctional, as it yielded various excesses, from labor indiscipline to terror. It was not sustainable even from within the framework of great politics, so a narrowing of participation proved to be a key outcome of the intense experimental phase of the 1930s. Although shortages during the winter of 1939–40, stemming largely from a poor harvest, prompted a new wave of letters to officials urging that the wreckers be found and punished, the end of the terror entailed a new accent on hierarchy and enhanced discipline from the top. With the terror subsiding by early 1939, the managers found their authority enhanced, while the workers faced increasing discipline and tighter labor laws. Fitzpatrick stressed that this direction had a greater impact on the workers than the purges—and was greatly resented.[211]

Meanwhile, James Van Geldern showed that even as the regime's focus expanded to the whole people after the sectarianism of the cultural revolution, citizenship roles were increasingly circumscribed during the 1930s. Indeed, they gradually flattened into mere rituals of participation as ordinary people were encouraged to observe political spectacles and identify with great projects from the outside: thus, for example, the show trials, the glorification of the Moscow subway, and the celebration of the Pushkin centennial in 1937. The myth of direct contact was maintained in Red Square demonstrations, seen through newsreels. Although the emphasis on the heroic effort of the people in meeting the unprecedented challenge continued, for a while, to galvanize pride and enthusiasm, "the people" was becoming hypostatized; ordinary individuals were to take pride in achievements in which they were ever less directly involved.[212] This tendency toward static hierarchy, with participation as passive spectatorship, was central to the narrowing in process.

This was not the relationship between leaders and led that the Bolsheviks had intended in making the revolution. To be sure, they had envisioned replacing traditional religion with new forms of ritual and ceremony, but these were not incompatible with genuine education to make full, authentic participation possible. However, by the late 1930s the leadership increasingly had to settle for ritual wrapped in manipulation and propaganda in light of the functional needs and the tendencies to excess revealed by the effort at post-liberal collective action thus far. And the focus of the ritualized ceremonies narrowed as they came to include a quasi-cult of the secular state underpinned by the cult of Stalin himself.[213]

Increasingly left as passive spectators, increasingly resentful of the privileges of their superiors, ordinary people came to experience themselves especially as recipients of welfare-state benefits, even if the system could not consistently deliver them.[214] This new mode of involvement—as passive recipients—entailed a further pulling back from active participation as ordinary citizens came to understand the historical meaning of the Soviet experiment in narrower terms.

All the elements of the cluster—leader, party, bureaucracy, even the now delimited interaction of above and below—remained in play after Stalin's death in 1953, but that event inevitably led to a turn of the kaleidoscope. On the one hand, Stalin's successors managed to restore the party to primacy, not least in order to keep any such leader from emerging again.[215] Yet personality inevitably continued to matter, especially as it played against the particular bureaucratic mentality that had emerged. Although he sought to revitalize the regime after Stalin, Khrushchev was himself erratic. In light of his personality, his efforts to foster quasi-populist elements, bypassing the bureaucracy, especially provoked bureaucratic resistance. But, unlike Stalin, Khrushchev was unable or unwilling to foment terror against the party and the bureaucracy. He ended up ousted by the now more deeply entrenched bureaucracy in 1964, after a relatively short period of leadership. The system was still jerking back and forth even as the space for such oscillation grew more restricted.

Lewin's way of characterizing the larger contours and implications of the process remains indispensable. Whereas Stalin had been powerful enough to prevent a full takeover by the bureaucracy, the key features of personal despotism were dismantled after his death. Now the bureaucracy blossomed into a full fledged ruling class, taking over the system even as it also effectively emancipated itself from the party.[216] The outcome was an unprecedented bureaucratic abso-lutism. But the bureaucratic ruling class, ideologically vacuous, increasingly corrupt and demoralized, was not able to act in a dynamic, history-making way. Rather than being the vehicle for wider collective action, its *raison d'être* was increas-ingly to protect its own privileges. The advent of Leonid Brezhnev, emerging as the alternative to Khrushchev by the end of the 1960s, portended virtually lifetime tenure for the bureaucracy. The resulting aging of Soviet elites helped to precipi-tate the crisis of the regime that was becoming evident by the late 1970s.[217]

Such differentiation and privilege stood in obvious tension with the egalitarian ideal that Malia, for example, found central to the whole socialist aspiration and that had underpinned all the concern with class and property.[218] In the same way, Suny noted the irresolvable tension between the desire to extend the egalitarian participatory impulses of 1917 and the tendency to resurrect stratification and authority.[219] The tendency toward renewed differentiation, hierarchy, and privi-lege sapped idealism and proved to be deeply debilitating over the long term. Although not irrelevant, the familiar banal, ahistorical impulses do not suffice to explain it. They were not constants but came increasingly to the fore as the histor-ically specific dynamic proved to lead in a certain direction.

The sense that the bourgeois mainstream rested on and continued to breed illegitimate inequalities, that there was scope for greater equality and *thus* self-realization, had fed the original aspiration for a systematic alternative, helping that aspiration to settle out as "socialism." But equality was and is notoriously ambiguous—not an answer but a new universe of questions. In seeking to act in the new way, the Soviet regime encountered tensions latent in the ideal of equality, especially as it mixed with some of the other aspirations that had fed the quest for an alternative modernity. How, for example, did egalitarianism relate to self-realization and even justice?

Although it meant especially affirmative action for industrial workers, a genuinely egalitarian impulse was central to the early idealism of the Soviet experiment. Even this impulse bumped up against functional differentiation, but Leninism had allowed for such differentiation and hierarchy up to a point. Once the experiment focused on crash industrialization, equality meant common participation in the collective action, in the great task of "building socialism." In that sense, all the participants had become equals. In light of the task at hand, functional differentiation, serving community needs, could seem consistent with genuine solidarity. Still, any such emphasis on functional difference was inher-ently tension-ridden. And in light of the extraordinariness of the task, the Leninist legacy reinforced the differentiation tendency and exacerbated the tensions. The accent on heroic effort and self-sacrifice that had been central to the elite's confident self-understanding made it harder to distinguish the banal pursuit of privilege from functional differentiation. With the party still in principle the energizing embodiment of ongoing revolutionary construction, it was difficult to grasp the degree to which it was becoming a vehicle for mere careerism and place seeking. Hence in part the ambiguity, myth making, and even surrealism that were coming to mark the whole experiment.

Even as the effort itself seemed to call forth the virtues essential to a superior order, the expansion of the political gave rise to a class of functionaries who came to exercise *de facto* ownership over state property. Moreover, those distinguishing themselves tended toward *embourgeoisment*, even adopting distinctions modeled on the old regime. It seemed a triumph of the revolution that new people were now assuming such distinctions, but this was to narrow the revolution to a mere circulation of elites.[220]

Some saw differentiation as legitimate because, with class having been transcended, it was now based solely on "culture." Fitzpatrick noted that convinced Communists saw nothing wrong with having servants. An emancipated female teacher felt it entirely appropriate that someone less educated should do the housework. In the same way, the leaders did not question that they deserved their privileges. From their perspective, it was essential that their amenities were state-owned, not personal property. And such privilege was seen as temporary, a corollary of scarcity.[221] Whereas some denounced the tendency toward privilege, others, for a while, continued to stress the significance of the overall departure.

But such differentiation and privilege proved to be incompatible over the long term with the energizing idealism that had initially sustained the experiment. Although everyone could participate and contribute, worker grumbling about the privileges of the Stakhanovites and wider resentment of privileged officialdom fed the tendency to excess and loss of control that then required a pulling back. The unforeseeable result was a combination of differentiation, hierarchy, and privilege, on the one hand, and resentment, cynicism, and passivity, on the other. Jeffrey Goldfarb noted that after Stalin the system came to function through what he called legitimation through disbelief; the language of idealism and difference was used only officially, or for distancing, obfuscation.[222]

All these tendencies served to narrow the sense of what the whole Soviet enterprise was about. Economic development, which started as merely a means to create a post-liberal, alternative modernity, still called "socialism," became increasingly an end in itself. As the gloss dissipated, increasingly the regime was just a modernizing developmental dictatorship, to be assessed, as some leading Western scholars came to insist, not as an alternative modernity but as an economic system seeking to catch up to, and in competition with, the capitalist mainstream. The great task, and whatever hope the Soviet regime might still have to leapfrog the West, increasingly boiled down to such essentially material terms.[223]

To be sure, the planning model, which had elicited such enthusiasm early on, remained genuinely different. But it had become dependent on precisely the bureaucracy, which proved much better at preserving and enhancing its own privileges than at delivering the goods, let alone creating an alternative modernity. The bureaucracy could not even sustain, let alone carry forward, the project that had earlier elicited such enthusiasm.

With its victory in the Second World War, the Soviet Union spread Communism to a band of satellite states and rose to superpower status, but Leszek Kolakowski convincingly depicted this outcome as a kind of consolation prize. As nicely summarized by Abbott Gleason, Kolakowski referred to "an unarticulated ideology conveyed to people between the lines, a 'subtext' calculated to assuage the Russian sense of inferiority: that the current regime had at least brought Russians the glories of superpower status."[224] In this light, we might note especially the pioneering Soviet achievements in space travel, beginning with the launching of *Sputnik I* in 1957. The Soviet Union led the ensuing "space race" with the United States well into the 1960s. While such achievements elicited enthusiasm of a sort, they did not invite active participation. Moreover, being a "superpower" is an entirely different mode of self-understanding *vis-à-vis* the modern West than spearheading an alternative modernity. As the Communist experiment narrowed to this more limited self-understanding, the difference with the West became ever less energizing.

As it happened, the Soviet regime could neither deliver as a "normal" consumer society nor keep up as a superpower. And a widely noted decay of belief and commitment accompanied those failures. Gleason noted that by the 1970s many Western scholars had recognized that the confidence of the Soviet rulers in their own ideology had long been declining—and thus, as he saw it, the loss of dynamism by that point. For those becoming dissidents, especially in Poland but then also in Czechoslovakia, the ideological sphere had shrunk irreversibly: "Bureaucratic socialism has lost its ideological base." Hence the scope for opposition, for hollowing out from below, and hence the emergence of the wholly unforeseen notions of "de-totalitarianization" and "post-totalitarianism."[225]

Seeking to account for the growing cynicism that led to the collapse of Soviet-style Communism, Malia noted that a permanent revolution from above cannot be sustained indefinitely. After the initial burst of economic expansion, the effort netted progressively diminishing returns. And the brutal results belied the original moral aspiration that had gotten attached to the aspiration for socialism. The assumption that socialism would be superior, even fulfilling the moral aspiration, had informed the whole Soviet enterprise. But once socialism had been built in the 1930s, the results proved otherwise, and the myth, said Malia, was transformed into the lie. As a lie, the notion that this was *superior* as socialist became merely cynical, and from that point the whole effort could simply dissipate. The party's will to coerce eroded along with the credibility of the ideology. Under Gorbachev, this erosion permitted the nascent civil society to challenge the party's hegemony.[226]

Although some such progression from idealism to cynicism was surely at work, the process, even the cause and effect relationship, is trickier than Malia's characterization suggests, for what, exactly, had dissipated? It is too simple to say that the ideology had lost its force, for, as we have seen, it had not been ideology that had driven this particular experiment. At the same time, it was not simply belief in the regime's effectiveness as a welfare state or a superpower that had decayed. We can understand the outcome only if we understand the content of the idealism, the nature of the commitment, and what it meant to have *those* dissipate. The erosion of idealism stemmed not, as for Malia, from forcing socialism—and encountering certain unpalatable consequences of actually succeeding, after a fashion. Rather, they could not act collectively as envisioned, in a way that nurtured and sustained commitment, but encountered one unforeseen outcome after another.

Kolakowski got closer than Malia in noting that by the end virtually no one believed any longer that Marxism–Leninism could be used to mobilize the population. So it was not a matter of the original ideology *per se* but the capacity to mobilize, to form a collective will, to get people to act in concert.[227] Gleason, too, observed that "even many who were unwilling to give up altogether the term *totalitarian* recognized that the Soviet Union was losing its appetite for mobilizing its population or drastically reshaping their inherited individualities."[228] That was not socialism or "the ideology" but, again, the great political enterprise that involved ideology and "socialism" in the very special ways we have discussed. "Totalitarian" was indeed the operative category; the surprise was that it denoted something that could dissipate in this way.

In recognizing that the Soviet experiment had included an element of "the grandiose and the epic," Malia himself noted that "it was the supreme feat of Bolshevik voluntarism."[229] But in portraying that voluntarism as merely a practical corollary of the prior Marxism, he was missing what most needed to be explained. The peculiar rhythms at work, including the sense of enthusiasm and grandiose challenge, resulted not primarily from the quest for socialism, stemming from "suffering" or some Enlightenment ideal of equality, yet neither were they reducible to some combination of Russian idiosyncrasy or ahistorical banality. Rather, they reflected a historically specific syndrome, newer than the modern socialist aspiration and centering on precisely that voluntarism. Great politics must be understood on its own terms; having had its own sources, it produced its particular rhythms, galvanizing its particular form of enthusiasm, and leading to its own characteristic forms of crisis and dissolution. In light of that trajectory, we can better grasp the interconnections between the individual episodes and dimensions of the Soviet experience, so many of them anomalous on their own.

Although the point was never fully articulated, the Communists themselves began to realize that they were not really implementing Marxism, yet neither were they simply trying to catch up with the Western mainstream through neo-Jacobin revolution from above. Although the task they set themselves—industrialization, development—was indeed supposed to catch them up, the deeper meaning of what they were doing lay elsewhere. They were not simply overcoming backwardness but doing it through a new mode of collective action that elicited the essential post-bourgeois virtues and mode of consciousness, that even made possible a new mode of individual fulfillment through participation in history-making collective action. This was to respond to liberal inadequacies on both the macro-political and micro-individual levels.

That new mode of action engendered the energizing sense of difference, of already being caught up in something new and superior, that gave the otherwise mundane task of catch-up modernization a galvanizing gloss of world-historical meaning. The task's very magnitude, calling forth those virtues, was beyond what liberal detractors, with their petty individualism and their merely negative conception of human freedom, could envision. And although "building socialism" was a myth, the experiment in great politics galvanized genuine belief and enthusiasm and yielded real achievement—but also what proved to be a characteristic trajectory toward narrowing and dissipation.

The novel mode of action portended not some utopia but an endless succession of history-making tasks—tasks that might themselves be open-ended, as with planning in the economy. The end was nothing, the means everything. And the enterprise carried no guarantee of success. Indeed, the combination of enthusiastic achievement and loss of control soon produced a further change in the historical sense, although its place in the process is especially hard to characterize. Kotkin noted, for example, "their obsession with outracing time," their sense even that time was an enemy, to be fought, assaulted.[230] As we noted in Chapter 1, Lewin similarly featured the peculiar haste, the sense of urgency, that characterized the upheavals of the early Stalinist years. Those responsible seemed to feel caught up in "a race against time," even that "they were running out of history."[231] Like Kotkin, Lewin was implicitly suggesting anything but some sort of secure ideological mindset, but Lewin was clearer than Kotkin that something new and extra was at work and that, whatever it was, it was not a mere corollary of the creation of socialism. Yet, as we noted, he found it baffling.

In fact, that element reflected the deepening shrillness that resulted as the effort actually to practise great politics revealed hitherto unrecognized aspects of the human relationship with history. Although it was clear that collective action entailed uncertainty and risk, the faith had been that it would be possible to make history in a more concerted way through will, commitment, even audacity, all combined with a measure of trial and error. But the effort to act on that basis seemed to encounter an unforeseen uncanniness about history making itself. The resulting self-doubt could produce a deepening of the heroic spirit for a while, but the essential virtues proved to be unsustainable in the face of other aspects of the unforeseen dynamic that resulted from the effort to act in this new way.

Virtually from the start, the attempt at great politics produced oscillation and self-defeating paradox. Kotkin noted that in the life of the party, a sense of omnipotence alternated with deep uncertainty. The party was deadly serious about its role, but the more it tried to live up to that role, the more strident and brittle the effort became.[232] Although the unprecedented nature of the tasks being undertaken generated excitement at all levels, the fact that the cadres were especially ill-prepared in this case elicited a particular mode of above-and-below interaction that tended to unforeseen extremes. That fact also fed the tendency—indeed, the determination—to find wreckers behind every accident. And determined to find them, they did, thereby feeding the "perceptions of omnipresent conspiracy" that Rittersporn noted.[233]

In short, whereas we sometimes take this or that—the narrowing of leadership, the dominance of bureaucracy, the return to differentiation and hierarchy, the expectation of miracles, the belief in wreckers, the denunciations from below, the activism of the police—as definitive, each must be understood in terms of an overarching trajectory that became possible with the earlier historical-political break. It was that whole trajectory that produced these outcomes—the specific anomalies and excesses, the tendency to zigzag, and the final dissipation of commitment and belief. Even insofar as a banal concern with power and privilege seems to be predominant by the end, it was an outcome from within that overall trajectory.

The energizing idealism long kept the Soviet leaders from facing up to the nature of the dynamic that was resulting from their ongoing action. What "had to be denied" was not, as for Malia, that socialism, now put into practice, did not live up to its promise, but rather that they could not act as envisioned. To recognize that uncontrollability and excess and abuse were corollaries of great politics would have compromised their claim to an extraordinary role. It was precisely their shrill confidence in the history-making mode of action that dissipated by the end, in light of what experience had revealed.

The overall experience, including the surreal Stalinist provisional outcome, has fundamentally expanded our sense of what the modern world can hold. Thus, even as it continued to inspire some outsiders, the resultants of the Soviet experiment proved frightening to many precisely as totalitarian, quite apart from any fear of socialism. What had become clear were the previously unsuspected dangers inherent in the mode of action itself.

6   Conflicted totalitarianism in Fascist Italy

Questions emerging from the practice of the Fascist regime

As we noted in Chapter 1, the place of Italian fascism in any discussion of totalitarianism has proved to be especially tricky. Although Mussolini's regime attracted much interest abroad at the time, its outcomes not only discredited it but even suggested that, whatever its pretenses, it was not really totalitarian.[1] Still, reductionism, teleological thinking, and uncertainties over how to locate and characterize whatever radical or totalitarian thrust it contained have made it especially difficult to get a handle on this, the first fascism—its origins and the shape of the ensuing regime. Whatever the potential at the outset, one step after another has long been taken as the definitive defeat for radical or totalitarian Fascism.[2]

However, recent studies, most prominently those of Emilio Gentile, have pointed the way to a more flexible and ultimately deeper understanding of the Italian case that suggests how it might illuminate the wider departure of the era. Not only do many such studies view Fascism as in some sense "revolutionary in its own right," but they take seriously its totalitarian thrust. Still, much of the argument has rested on a particular subset of the evidence—the Fascists' pioneering use of ritual, spectacle, commemoration, and myth—which raises new questions about the center of gravity of Fascism and its trajectory in practice. This broadly culturalist approach may be too quick to privilege what proves to be a *restricted* subset. And whereas earlier studies surely overemphasized definitive defeats, the newer ones may err in the opposite direction in positing a relatively homogeneous and continuous radical thrust. This may be to miss changes in the meaning of the elements, even in the nature of the dynamic itself, that occurred once the regime had begun to seek to act as it did.

In any case, not all have been convinced by the recent cultural turn, and innovation has yielded new uncertainties and axes of contest. Even taking "culture" seriously, as totalitarian, may suggest not some autonomous revolutionary thrust but deeper ways of understanding Fascism as reactionary or anti-modern. And some worry that to take Fascism seriously as revolutionary and totalitarian is simply to accept its own pretenses at face value and even to invite relativistic acceptance.

We have seen that although Mussolini became prime minister in October 1922, Fascism began to commit itself to construct a specifically post-liberal state only late in 1924, in the wake of the Matteotti murder that June. Pressured by Fascist radicals, Mussolini essentially announced the advent of a new regime on January 3, 1925, in his speech to the Chamber of Deputies affirming his responsibility for all that Fascism had become, including all its violent excesses. Fascism was no longer to brook any opposition. By June, Mussolini was characterizing the new direction as "totalitarian." Although the term had been coined by the opposition in 1923, the Fascists now embraced it with pride as it quickly became central to their self-understanding.[3]

Some uses of the category were relatively bland; it referred to Fascism's new monopoly of power, even to Mussolini's assertion of authority over the Fascist movement. But it also expressed the regime's determination to mold a new Italian, to shape a new society, to make Italy great and powerful. And quite explicitly, it meant that there was no room for political indifference; anyone who was not actively for Fascism was against it.[4] More specifically, it meant the expansion of the state's sovereignty—in principle to infinity. Speaking in Milan in October 1925, Mussolini offered perhaps his best-known dictum: "Our formula is this: everything within the state, nothing outside the state, no one against the state."[5]

By this point, Giovanni Gentile had become a major Fascist ideologue, proclaiming that the new regime was constructing a totalitarian ethical state. Especially during Fascism's first decade in power, he assumed a number of major cultural roles, spearheading the first Fascist education reform as minister of education in 1923–24, serving as founding president of the *Istituto Nazionale Fascista di Cultura*, and writing the theoretical portion of Mussolini's well-known encyclopedia article on Fascism of 1932, the closest thing to an official statement of Fascist ideology that the regime was to produce.[6] But some disputed his authority virtually from the start, and whether Gentile's doctrinal statements actually reveal the Fascist self-understanding, in its novelty and difference, or whether they merely provided instrumental window dressing, is surely not obvious.

Still, by 1925, the regime seemed to be moving decisively in a totalitarian direction on the institutional level. Seeking to establish Fascism's ongoing *raison d'être* in light of the Matteotti crisis, Mussolini appointed a Commission of Fifteen under the aegis of the Fascist Party late in 1924. These "Solons," as they were quickly dubbed, were to propose changes in the institutional and legal framework that would create a post-liberal, specifically Fascist state. The commission was made a state organ and expanded to eighteen members in January 1925, shortly after Mussolini's speech to the chamber. Typically, Mussolini carefully balanced the commission's composition. Chaired by Gentile, it also included veteran syndicalists and Nationalists as well as such luminaries as the legal scholar Santi Romano, the economist and demographer Corrado Gini, and the independent corporativist theorist Gino Arias.

Although some of its members were traditionalist conservatives concerned primarily to strengthen the executive *vis-à-vis* parliament, the commission's proposals led promptly to the beginnings of systematic, sustained institutional change with corporativism as the centerpiece.[7] That this was the direction chosen is not surprising in light of all the proto-corporativist ideas under discussion with the sense that the liberal state was in crisis after the war. Renzo De Felice emphasized that Mussolini genuinely supported corporativism as the deeper content of the Fascist revolution—and as a third way for the West.[8] In principle, the corporativist direction was at once to expand the sovereignty of the state, politicizing the economy, and to mobilize people more constantly and directly through their roles as producers. Yet from the beginning there were ambiguities over how the corporativist system was to function, even over its basic purposes.

Although corporativist institutions were erected only in a piecemeal way, the corporativist direction led to significant legislation and institutional change throughout the course of the regime. Starting with the Law for the Judicial Regulation of Labor Disputes of 1926, a series of measures established one association for workers and one for employers in each branch of production, made collective labor contracts a matter of public law, to be enforced by the state, and outlawed strikes and lockouts. Labor disputes were to be settled by a system of labor courts. To coordinate these changes, a Ministry of Corporations was established in 1926, and the much-trumpeted Labor Charter of 1927 specified the new relationship between labor and the state that Fascism was to entail. The National Council of Corporations, a sort of economic parliament, was instituted in 1930, followed in 1934 by the formation of actual corporations, one for each of twenty-two economic sectors. In 1939, a new Chamber of Fasces and Corporations replaced the Chamber of Deputies. Amid discussions of the need for a whole new constitution to replace the 1848 *Statuto*, which the new Italy had inherited from Piedmont, a corporativist reform of the legal codes followed in 1942.

This ongoing corporativist development was central to the Fascist sense of assuming the forefront in constructing, in an appropriately gradual, *ad hoc* way, a wholly new type of state. And the effort attracted much interest abroad at the time. Yet practice did not live up to the surrounding rhetoric, and the meaning and significance of Fascist corporativism are especially hard to pin down. Certainly, its place *vis-à-vis* other dimensions in the Fascist mix, from ritual to population policy to imperialism, is not obvious. In light of certain outcomes, in fact, it may be tempting to understand the whole corporativist thrust in reductionist terms.

At the same time, virtually from the start, the Fascists began mobilizing the population in other ways, beyond the sphere of production. Indeed, although they learned from socialist examples, they quickly pushed mobilization and organization to unprecedented levels, partly through the pioneering use of new media. As early as 1923, Mussolini proclaimed cinema to be Fascism's strongest weapon.[9] Although ritual and commemoration were significant from the start, commemorative exhibitions and various forms of spectacle became still more central during the 1930s. At the same time, the Fascists began to mobilize and politicize Italians through organizations for women, for youth, for university students, and, with the *Opera Nazionale Dopolavoro*, for leisure time. And they insisted that such mobilization had to be continuous, because the task was ongoing, never to be completed once and for all.

Although the basic aim was to politicize the society more broadly and intensely, thereby fostering a deeper identification with the nation, it was not clear what such mobilization was to mean for individuals or how deeply ordinary people were to be involved. Nor was it clear for what broader societal purposes the Italians might be called upon to participate. As reflected in the early corporativist thrust, much revolved at first around the demand and seeming scope for enhanced production, but to make Italy a stronger and more respected nation could easily mean imperialism and war.

Mussolini famously boasted in 1927 that Fascism would "make Italy unrecognizable to itself and to foreigners in ten years."[10] This was to be the basic totalitarian project, and it meant that in principle Fascism was prepared to take on anything and everything. In that spirit, the regime embraced an array of mobilizing great tasks, often characterized by military metaphors, from the reconstruction of the Italian infrastructure to the battles for grain, on the one hand, and for births, on the other. As in the Soviet Union, the sense of being caught up in grand and unprecedented collective action seems to have captured the imaginations of ordinary people up to a point. Mabel Berezin noted the "civic enthusiasm" generated by the massive rebuilding and restoration program in Verona.[11] But the mere fact of mobilization, grandiose initiative, and "civic enthusiasm" does not answer the central questions about the nature of the participation that the regime was to make possible—and made possible in fact.

The "battle for births" was central to Fascist demographic policy, an area that, in light of the Nazi experience, requires particular scrutiny if we are to assess Italian Fascism as totalitarian. Because its demographic policy was less radical in certain respects, Fascist Italy has sometimes been judged less totalitarian, or less than totalitarian. But in Italy, as in Germany, the determination to shape the future through expanded collective action led to a more aggressive and interventionist effort at population engineering. Indeed, it was self-evident in each that such engineering was a major responsibility of the new regime. In Italy, a new Central Institute of Statistics (ISTAT) was established under the noted demographer Corrado Gini to manage the national population. This included transferring people to reclamation sites but also the wider use of demographic measures to equip Italy for a leading role in Europe.[12]

Still, Fascist priorities differed in important respects from those of the Nazis, who emphasized negative selection and the centrality of race. Moreover, the place of population policy in the overall Fascist dynamic, and its significance in assessing the Italian case for the totalitarian question, are not so clear. The Nazi example and certain current concerns may lead us to misconstrue the significance and place of demographic themes, even to miss what was specifically Fascist and essential to the totalitarian dynamic in the Italian case.

In Italy, demographic concerns and ideas about expansion had gone hand in hand for decades, and in the aftermath of the First World War it was not merely plausible but imperative to focus on the combination anew. With the United

States and other countries severely restricting Italian immigration, the regime sought, especially with the concerted new population policy of 1927, to tackle a genuine national issue. Colonialist expansion was obviously a possibility, but the immediate result was a curious mix of natalism, ruralization, and even, for a while, the embrace of emigrant Italians. The implications of the mix, the proportions among the elements, and the overall direction were not clear during the 1920s.

Considering the uncertain meaning of "expansion" during that period, Luca de Caprariis made it especially clear that ruralization emerged as a priority "only after a wave of restrictive measures had closed almost all outlets for Italian expatriates."[13] So "ruralization" was not some "revolt against modernity" but an effort at totalitarian social engineering in light of a problematic demographic situation. But the centerpiece of Fascist policy was natalism, which today seems bizarre indeed as a response to overpopulation. But the very notion of "overpopulation" proves to be problematic, even prejudicial. Too many Italians? Who had the right to say so, and according to what criteria?

Maria Sophia Quine stressed that natalist thinking had become popular in Italy well before Fascism.[14] What was specifically Fascist, then, was not natalism *per se* but the newly concerted effort, as one aspect of the new, grandiose politics, actually to implement the new ideas about population that had emerged earlier. What differentiated Fascism, in other words, was not some dramatic change in content or direction but the determination and willingness to act. Indeed, Fascism, precisely because of its grasp of the place of spirit and will, could translate a demographic situation that liberals would consider "overpopulation" into an asset, thereby changing history by affording the basis for a healthy expansion of Italian influence. Conversely, such expansion was healthy especially because Italy, thanks to Fascism, with its idealism, spirit, and will, had something universal to offer the modern world.

In the battle for births, some measures, like the bachelor tax of December 1926, were modeled on French precedent, a reminder that even measures expanding state sovereignty through a more intrusive demographic policy were possible from within a liberal democratic frame.[15] But precisely as totalitarian, the Fascist regime pursued such measures more systematically as it mobilized the population and sought to politicize what had been private decisions. To get married and have children was now inherently political, indeed, a form of political participation.

A good deal of public health and welfare legislation accompanied the "battle for births," including the establishment of the National Agency for the Protection of Mothers and Children in 1925. Indeed, the regime claimed to have moved to the forefront in recognizing that women needed substantial social support for bearing and rearing children.[16]

This welfarist dimension reflected the national differences in emphasis that we found emerging as the scope for population management drew attention in the years before the First World War. Whereas German, British, and American experts had been more likely to stress negative selection, to keep the "unfit" from procreating, their French and Italian counterparts tended to embrace the environmentalist notion that improvements in health, education, and welfare could produce heritable benefits in the quality of individuals.[17] Moreover, the most influential Italian natalist, Corrado Gini, linked fecundity to class and, in a quasi-Paretan way, the scope for renewal from below. Any natalist policy would especially influence the working class, but that was desirable because the upper classes tended to lose their drive, becoming senile and sterile.[18] The natalist–environmentalist emphasis differentiating Italy from Germany, Britain, and the United States persisted well into the Fascist period. Although Gini's institute sponsored eugenics research, Gini himself continued to favor a natalist direction, and few Italian experts advocated selection or elimination. Indeed, the softer, more moderate environmentalist emphasis of the French and Italians led in 1935 to the founding of a separate international eugenics federation, headed by Gini and including representatives from other Catholic and Latin nations.[19]

Despite the differences from Nazi Germany, the Fascist direction in the paradigmatic area of population policy was clearly totalitarian. But to grasp that fact, in the face of what have seemed the reasons for skepticism, may lead us to inflate the importance of population policy in the overall totalitarian trajectory of Fascist Italy. Partly because Fascist population policy was milder than the Nazi equivalent, it was not as central to the departure, the sense of moving to the forefront in tackling unprecedented tasks, so it did not have the energizing force that it had in Germany. Thus any inquiry into totalitarianism in Fascist Italy must take care to put population policy in proportion, not allowing it to overshadow other dimensions central to the Fascists' totalitarian self-understanding.

Questions about institutional focus remained despite the taming of the *squadristi* through the organization of the militia in 1923. The second wave of violence, associated with unruly provincial Fascism, had seemingly proved decisive in 1924, and the place of the party *vis-à-vis* the new Fascist state was not at all clear. After Mussolini's decisive speech to the chamber in January 1925, it seemed a further turn toward radicalism when he selected Roberto Farinacci, the "Ras" or party chieftain of Cremona, to be the national party's secretary the next month. Farinacci wanted a small elite party, hierarchically organized, as the guarantor of ongoing revolutionary development to supplant liberal elites and institutions. Although his longer-term vision was vague, the key for now was that the party, as the vanguard of the ongoing revolution, was to remain autonomous, at least the equal of the inherently more mundane government. And Farinacci had the stature and ability to bring the party under control, establishing centralized discipline.[20]

But Mussolini, typically playing both sides, envisioned subordinating the newly disciplined party to his government, and Farinacci's tenure proved quite limited, lasting just over a year, until March 1926. And in a sense the party was certainly checked, and even depoliticized, after he was forced out—a result long viewed as a definitive defeat for Fascist radicalism. A circular to the local prefects in January 1927 specified that the party leader was subordinate to the state apparatus on the local level. A law of 1928 made the Fascist Grand Council, founded as a party organization in 1923, a state institution, and a new party statute of

1929 further checked its autonomy. Especially during the long tenure of Achille Starace as party secretary from 1931 until 1939, the party was reduced to what long seemed an essentially choreographic role, revolving around ritual and the cult of the Duce. From this perspective, the movement–party, as the embodiment of Fascist radicalism, was made the mere servant of Mussolini's dictatorship.

Yet as Emilio Gentile has insisted, even the 1927 circular to the prefects, subordinating the party to the state, was not necessarily to check Fascist radicalism; in principle, at least, the state in question was the new fascist, totalitarian state, and to subordinate the party to the *Fascist* state, the *Fascist* perfect, was itself a totalitarian measure.[21] Still, the minister of the interior to whom the prefects were to report was initially Luigi Federzoni, who had come to Fascism from the conservative monarchist wing of Nationalism. So the meaning of the outcome by this point was uncertain. Nor was it clear whether making the Fascist Grand Council a state institution was to tame the party or revolutionize the state. However we might assess any such specific measure, we certainly cannot understand the changing party—state relationship if we take depoliticization and mere Mussolinianism or authoritarianism as the only alternatives to Farinaccian radicalism.

Other leading Fascists like Augusto Turati, who followed Farinacci as party secretary, and Dino Grandi worked with Mussolini to tame and subordinate the party. Giuseppe Bottai, quickly a spearhead of corporativist development, was dubious not only of Farinacci but of party pretensions of any sort. Such Fascists were more moderate or legalitarian on the level of tactics, but for none of them did a more subordinate role for the party mean ending the revolution and returning to normal. The longstanding tendency to associate the radical, revolutionary, and/or totalitarian potential of Fascism with provincial radicals like Farinacci severely restricted understanding of the elements in the play and the dynamic that resulted from their interaction.

Turati, who had been the local Fascist leader in Brescia, was comparable to Farinacci in background and had betrayed many of the excesses of early provincial Fascism. But although he ended up less rebellious, he sought to make the party the instrument of a wider, more coherently totalitarian vision for Fascism than Farinacci's. And as party secretary from 1926 to 1930, he played a key role in developing the practices that Emilio Gentile, for example, found essential to Fascist totalitarian implementation. Yet Mussolini dumped Turati in 1930, finding him a bit too fervent and independent.[22] Still, even the ouster of Turati did not mean normalization of some sort. Again and again, the meaning of the components and changes as the regime evolved prove hard to pin down.

The meaning of party–state interaction depended in part on a number of ancillary factors in light of the institutional innovations being attempted. What of the new Fascist trade union network so important to the young militants who had dared to challenge Mussolini's authority in 1921? We noted in Chapter 4 that although the "pacification pact" and the transformation of the movement into a party were long seen as one of the definitive defeats, the outcome in 1921 was a compromise that allowed further development for the Fascist trade union network as an alternative to the mostly socialist unions that the Fascists were destroying. A full-blown confederation of Fascist unions, led by the veteran syndicalist labor organizer Edmondo Rossoni, took shape in January 1922, and some Fascists envisioned it playing a strong independent role within the broader ongoing Fascist movement.

But Rossoni's confederation was broken up with the *sbloccamento* in 1928, which also has long been seen as a definitive defeat for radical fascism, even the regime's capitulation to business interests, which certainly welcomed the move. However, maintenance of a strong, class-based confederation and capitulation to business were not the only alternatives. Lots of committed corporativists did not view the *sbloccamento* in such delimited, either/or terms.[23] Precisely as totalitarian, Fascism had to create a mode of organization more radically transcending class division. That was corporativism, which would encompass the unions as they were reconfigured in the wake of the *sbloccamento*. As we noted, however, the basis and meaning of corporativism are especially hard to pin down. What it would mean, even for the workers, was not at all certain in 1928.

The Concordat and the Lateran Pacts of 1929 have long seemed the archetypal indication that any radical and/or totalitarian thrust in Fascism bogged down in compromise with existing elites and institutions. Certainly, the Concordat, in giving the Catholic Church a role in education and in marriage and divorce law, seems utterly untotalitarian on the face of it. These measures greatly displeased those Fascists—Giovanni Gentile, for example—who sought a more consistently totalitarian policy.[24]

Still, even Gentile did not immediately view the outcome in 1929 as a defeat. In ending the separation of Church and state, the compromise was a departure from liberal agnosticism—and thus was not all bad. The situation remained open, with much to depend on implementation. Mussolini seemed reassuring.[25] Conversely, the Church remained wary of the regime's pretensions; the compromise of 1929 was no guarantee against future difficulties. Friction between the regime and the Church continued and even intensified thereafter, most immediately over youth organization and family and welfare policy.

Partly in response to the dissatisfactions with the measures of 1929, Mussolini turned back toward militancy with the crackdown on the Church's youth organization, Catholic Action, in 1931, prompting a new crisis in relations with the Church. Although Catholic Action was preserved, its activities were circumscribed, limited to religion and recreation. De Felice stressed that monopoly over the formation of Italian youth was a "constant preoccupation" for Mussolini and the leading Fascists. And, as he saw it, the outcome of the crisis of 1931 suggested that the Catholic sector was becoming de-Catholicized and nationalized.[26] Meanwhile, Pope Pius XI issued encyclicals in 1930 and 1931 criticizing Fascist family and welfare policy, especially the Fascist effort to politicize marriage and childrearing and to secularize ecclesiastical and lay Catholic organizations helping the poor and sick.[27] Another encyclical, *Non abbiamo bisogno*, issued in June 1931 at the height of the controversy over Catholic Action, went further to denounce, as pagan idolatry, the very notion of the totalitarian state.

Although there was a significant measure of continuity in religious identities, there is increasing agreement that the Church was indeed being enveloped by the wider totalitarian effort by the eve of the Second World War.[28] Although the regime avoided direct confrontation, it competed constantly through a war of symbols.[29] And perhaps Catholic identities did not have to be eliminated, only subordinated to the wider totalitarianism. The Fascist tendency was to portray Catholicism as a central component of Italian tradition, created by the Italians in historical time, as opposed to divine and universal. Up to a point, the argument was even congruent with Giovanni Gentile's longstanding argument that Catholicism remained essential as the historically specific basis for Italian spirituality.[30] Although Gentile himself saw Catholicism as merely a step to be transcended on the way to a mature self-consciousness, others came to suggest that it was fine for a Fascist to be a Catholic, with Italian Catholicism merely serving the wider Fascist revolution.

Despite the compromise of 1929, then, the regime was, on balance, expanding its reach at the expense of the Church by the later 1930s. Still, in light of the overall question of totalitarianism, the deeper question concerns the purposes and stakes of this direction. Was the regime merely establishing a monopoly of power for its own sake? At issue is content, the modes of identity and participation, the sense of purpose and meaning that seemed to compel Fascism toward this totalitarian subordination of the Church.

Whatever the direction of relations with the Church, a sense that Fascism was in danger of bogging down in compromise and infighting helped to fuel a turn to foreign affairs by 1933, which led to the imperialist conquest of Ethiopia (Abyssinia) in 1935–36, then to intervention in the Spanish Civil War, to the Axis with Nazi Germany, and to intervention in the Second World War. Even those otherwise skeptical that Fascism was totalitarian have tended to recognize a developing totalitarian thrust surrounding this turn, which also led to militarization, an anti-bourgeois "reform of custom," and anti-Semitic legislation on the domestic level. But whether all this was somehow the revelation of original purposes, even of an original essence, or a more contingent outcome is still in dispute. Moreover, the meaning of these departures and the criteria of totalitarianism are themselves at issue as we assess the place of this cultural turn in the overall trajectory of Italian Fascism.

In short, Fascism remained an uncertain and volatile mix even as the regime embarked on a novel, self-proclaimed totalitarian direction in 1925, necessarily bumping up against pre-Fascist elites and institutions in the process. Assessing the various steps and stages, their relative significance, their interrelationships, and their implications for the overall trajectory, is tricky indeed. Again and again, to take any one measure as decisive proves too simple, leading us to miss the fluidity and ongoing contesting. What we can discern in retrospect is a continuing dynamic with a characteristic shape in light of the originating aspirations and the resulting effort to do "great politics."

Axes of debate in light of some recent studies

After initially endorsing Hannah Arendt on the limits to the totalitarian thrust in the Fascist regime, Renzo De Felice came to stress a totalitarian departure around the turn to overt imperialism in 1935–36. Seeking to overcome the pre-Fascist elites who seemed to have ensnared him, Mussolini was seeking not merely to divert the public or to glorify himself but more deeply to fulfill the fascist vision of a new society.[31] And although the vision was never realized, the regime moved in that direction thereafter. De Felice stressed that the regime had already achieved a monopoly of power, excluding the old ruling class almost entirely. Although the remaining institutions—crown, army, judiciary—had so far been dominated only marginally, would have encountered ever graver difficulties, and Fascism would slowly have absorbed even the Catholic world had not war and defeat abruptly ended the experiment.[32]

But what was the vision at issue, and what would have been entailed in realizing it? De Felice was still taking as fundamental the dichotomy between movement and regime that he had posited earlier, and that had quickly come to frame the discussion. Explicitly embracing J.L. Talmon, he found the Fascist *movement*, although it included *squadristi* violence, to be radical, even leftist, modernizing in a sense, yet also totalitarian in wanting to create a new state, a new moral community, a new kind of human being. In contrast to the recent Greek and Chilean regimes seeking demobilization and exclusion, the movement envisioned mobilizing the masses, engendering active participation and enthusiasm, first through intensified use of the mass media and the educational system.[33]

Although for De Felice the radical thrust was clearest at the outset, prior to the March on Rome, the Fascist Party continued to embody the original revolutionary aspiration.[34] But the aspiration itself became blunted as the regime evolved, concentrating power in Mussolini's hands while also leaving much of the traditional state apparatus intact. So even as he came to stress a totalitarian turn, De Felice essentially endorsed the negative verdict on the Starace era; indeed, he found the direction under Starace symptomatic of the contradictions that mark all totalitarian regimes.[35] Starace intensified mobilization around new cultural accents, but they corresponded only superficially to the originating aspirations of the Fascist movement.

Offering a double challenge to De Felice, Emilio Gentile has found a more sustained and significant totalitarian thrust in Italian Fascism. First, for Gentile, Fascist totalitarianism was not simply a departure of the 1930s in light of an impasse to that point; rather, the measures of the mid-1930s constituted a phase in an ongoing effort of totalitarian implementation that had already begun to accelerate by the early 1930s. But this difference reflected a much deeper difference over the meaning and criteria of totalitarianism itself. Gentile found significance in precisely the stylistic dimensions that, for De Felice, were symptoms of depoliticization and impending crisis.[36]

Although he was indebted to George L. Mosse's work on Nazism and generic fascism, Gentile insisted that the level at issue is not generic fascism, even as revolutionary in its own right, but precisely *totalitarianism*. Warning against measuring the Italian case against some Hollywood version or abstract standard, he argued that Fascism represented simply "the Italian way to totalitarianism"; it was not qualitatively different from the Nazi and Stalinist regimes.[37] And Gentile's revisionist case gained plausibility from the many studies of Stalinism and Nazism showing how little the Hollywood image applies even to them. Gentile stressed that although Mussolini continued to play personnel and institutions against each other, Fascist Italy never settled into authoritarian routine, mere state control—in contrast to Franco's Spain, for example.[38]

For Gentile, totalitarianism in Fascist Italy as elsewhere was not a static reality, defined once and for all, but a process, a continuous construction through the complex interplay of Duce, party, and state.[39] Even more than De Felice, he stressed that Mussolini, whatever his ultimate aims, grasped that his link to the party remained indispensable, especially in light of the regime's compromises with traditional elites. Because his own extraordinary role derived from the party, Mussolini could not eliminate or depoliticize the party altogether without compromising his own legitimacy and jeopardizing his own power.[40] Moreover, as we noted above, Gentile showed that insofar as the party was indeed subordinated to the state, it was not to the established, traditional state but to the new *Fascist* state, itself under construction, at least putatively totalitarian, and itself caught up in the ongoing dynamic.

For Gentile, the regime ended up a kind of "totalitarian caesarism," which was not a mere reduction to personal dictatorship, for the Duce's role made sense only in light of the rest—especially the single party and the modes of mass mobilization it undertook.[41] A comparable symbiosis of leader and single party characterized the other two new regimes. In none of the three could the party operate apart from the leader, yet in each the personalization of power derived from the revolutionary single party.[42] But even as he took care to portray the ongoing dynamic in terms of the interaction of leader, party, and *Fascist* state, Gentile featured the continuing role of the Fascist Party, showing that, contrary to the longstanding assumption, it had not been marginalized with Mussolini's triumph and/or compromise with pre-Fascist elites.[43]

As Gentile saw it, Italian Fascism was totalitarian in seeking to remake its society through a new form of mass politics revolving around an "internal symbolic universe" of liturgy, ritual, ceremony, symbol, myth, and commemoration, all serving what he came to call "the sacralization of politics." The effort grew from the determination of the front generation to embody the values of the war in a new national religion, to be imposed on all Italians.[44] Against those who found mere "depoliticization" in the symbolic/religious side of Fascism, Gentile insisted that we must start by considering this politicization "*in a Fascist sense*" and participation "*in a totalitarian sense.*"[45] Although some rituals bordered on the ridiculous, the Fascists sought seriously to educate and convert on the basis of a genuine faith. From that perspective, Starace's effort to use the Fascist Party to promote sacralization through permanent mobilization was authentically totalitarian. While recognizing that the Fascist Party was caught up in the infighting among Fascist oligarchs, concerned with their own turf, Gentile stressed the overall coherence of the party's effort and its success in expanding its role during the 1930s. Thus, for example, the party secured a monopoly over the formation of youth with the creation of the Gioventù Italiano del Littorio (GIL) 1937. As channeled by Starace, the omnipresent party was able to condition the experience of millions as the only vehicle for participation in the life of the state.[46]

Gentile's work on Italian Fascism was central to his still-developing inquiry into the wider phenomenon of modern political religion. In his view, it was especially as a new form of political religion that all three of the new interwar regimes were totalitarian. On that level, Fascist Italy was a full participant, even a pioneer.[47] As a political religion, totalitarianism was not a regime or form of rule but an ongoing experiment, animated by the will of the single party, using the state as its instrument. With its characteristic set of beliefs, dogmas, myths, rites and symbols, the party sought at once to create a "new man" and to shape the masses into a single body dedicated to realizing the party's revolutionary and imperialist aims, which revolved around the creation of a new supranational civilization.[48]

Other innovative scholars, especially in the United States, shared some of Gentile's emphases as they, too, focused on the Fascists' pioneering use of ritual, commemoration, and spectacle, taking these dimensions not as merely superficial diversion or extrinsic form but as the core of Fascism *as* totalitarian.[49] Like Gentile, moreover, they tended to posit a greater measure of success in producing a sense of belonging and participation than had been recognized on the basis of earlier criteria.

Still, many of those adopting this generally culturalist approach invoked this stylistic or aesthetic dimension explicitly in opposition to ideological coherence or ideational content. Coherence lay at the level of style in the face of ideological confusion, as for Jeffrey Schnapp, or in light of a contextually appropriate de-emphasis on ideas or texts, as for Mabel Berezin. As Berezin saw it, relative backwardness had left even the Italian middle classes "quasi-educated."[50] Italy was thus "a culture that rejected text in favor of gesture or performance."[51] In response to this culture, "Italian fascism rejected discursive prose or linearity. It repudiated the word and the text. Argumentation, explanation, the scientific method were all aspects of modernity and rational discourse that fascism replaced with the primacy of feeling and emotion."[52] Berezin concluded that ritual action, performance as opposed to text, therefore affords an excellent way of analyzing the Fascist project.[53]

Gentile, in contrast, warned that "the theme of fascist religion is not to be summed up merely by its liturgical displays. . . . To take its symbols and rituals only in their aesthetic and propagandistic aspects, disregarding the system of beliefs and values, the theological politics that inspired them and that these represented, would give a partial and distorted view of the rituals themselves and would lead to a misrepresentation of their historical significance."[54] For Gentile, then, if we stick to the symbolic universe we miss something, apparently deeper, about both the source and the content of that educational impulse. He started his career with a study of Fascist ideology, and he subsequently sought to account for the longer-term sources of the totalitarian aspiration in terms of both the well-known limitations of Italy's nineteenth-century Risorgimento and the wider religious dimensions of modern politics since the French Revolution.[55]

In noting with approval that Fascism was increasingly viewed as revolutionary in its own right, Stanley Payne similarly mentioned that fascism had its own ideology.[56] So whereas culturalists like Schnapp and Berezin suggested that coherence and meaning lay on the level of style, both Payne and Gentile insisted on ideology or some substance "deeper" than mere liturgical display. Culturalists who played down intellectual substance tended to posit a measure of success as totalitarian, although in a sort of postmodern sense, taking style as substance, the medium as the message. What had seemed to be deeper substance either was not really deeper but just play on a flattened-out surface, or was unstable, affording no bedrock. Insofar as we pull back from positing some deeper, and thus more stable, ideology or substance, it becomes possible to conceive style as in some sense sufficient. But the outcomes in the Italian case may especially invite the teleological fallacy, leading us to take some combination of ritual, spectacle, style, rhetoric, and myth as sufficient and to eschew any engagement with originating ideas. We may thereby misconstrue the place, the perhaps changing place, of those aesthetic or stylistic dimensions. At issue is how we are to understand "revolutionary in its own right," the content or substance of the Fascist revolutionary aspiration, *even* in a situation in which ritual, spectacle, style, rhetoric, and myth were of undoubted importance.

Such substance could encompass a conscious emphasis on the importance of style and/or myth, so at issue is not necessarily "ideational" substance *as opposed to* myth or style. Zeev Sternhell, insisting on the overall coherence of Fascist ideology, concluded that "faith in the power of myth . . . is the key to the Fascist view of the world."[57] Influenced by Sternhell, Roger Griffin similarly featured myth, linked to palingenetic renewal, in showing that generic fascism must be taken seriously as revolutionary in its own right.[58] Myth has long been central to Gentile's way of characterizing the totalitarian aspiration and the sacralized politics of Italian Fascism.[59]

At the same time, both myth and style are polyvalent notions, and as the Fascist regime developed either or both could come into play in ways beyond those originally foreseen by those who created Fascism in the first place. Innovative substance could have fed an energizing sense of moving to the modern forefront—a sense that, in turn, could become intertwined with myth making in a less lucid sense. Any such belief in the scope for innovation was perhaps especially likely to get bound up with myth making in Italy, where a long, idiosyncratic history had bred a dialectic of grand expectation and pessimistic self-denigration by the late nineteenth century.[60]

Whatever the significance of their differences over "ideology," Gentile and the American culturalists were taking Fascism newly seriously, as totalitarian, on the basis of criteria that some found inappropriate. Particularly critical was the Australian scholar R.J.B. Bosworth, who worried that the culturalist approach, emerging against a postmodern backdrop, led to a trivialization of Fascism. He associated the cultural turn with a combination of "end of history" liberal hegemony and "anything goes" relativism voiding history of its cultural significance and moral import. Fascism becomes merely the latest "other," one culture among others, to be taken on its own terms.[61] In this complacent, postmodern mode, we forget that the Fascist regime was vicious, cruel—and a failure.[62] More generally, Bosworth charged that the culturalists were prone to take the Fascists at face value, credulously reporting what they said. As he saw it, even Emilio Gentile was taking Fascist texts too literally, failing to distinguish between word and deed. We must read between the lines instead.[63]

At the same time, Bosworth questioned the applicability of "totalitarianism" to the Fascist regime, citing recent research showing continuities, and thus the limits of the regime's impact, in such areas as religion, education, family life, and gender roles.[64] In addition, the longer-term structural factors that had made Italy the least of great powers continued to shape foreign policy even under Fascism.[65] Moreover, aspects of the modern consumer society emerging in Italy as elsewhere at the time conflicted with the totalitarian aims of Fascism.[66]

Bosworth had reason to worry about certain implications of the culturalist emphasis on style, but he himself seemed to invite only a limited and conventional way of reading between the lines, encompassing class-based counterrevolution and the familiar "revelation" argument attributing Fascism to enduring Italian weaknesses, many of which, he suggested, were then sidestepped in the aftermath. Any opening to a wider array of possibilities seems to invite his moralistic charge of naively taking the Fascists on their own terms. As Bosworth had it, even Roger Griffin's ambitious, widely admired study of European fascism merely replicated the accustomed liberal view, essentially because Griffin played down class and played up the genuine radicalism of fascism, its real distance from the establishment.[67]

Bosworth's determination to maintain his particular critical focus led him to miss the element of force in the arguments of Gentile, Griffin, and the culturalists more generally. Moreover, his reading of postmodernism, which clearly affected his sense of present historiographical priorities, was surely one-sided. Still, the elements of uncertainty and incompleteness in some expressions of the culturalist argument no doubt contributed to Bosworth's sense that we had better stick to his relatively conventional orientation. And his concerns about postmodernist relativism and the contemporary uses of historical understanding were surely plausible.[68] So it is worth pondering how we navigate the terrain in light of his concerns.

Although we need considerably more research on the regime's societal impact, no one claims that Fascism achieved totalitarianism, in the sense of fundamentally reshaping Italian life in whatever direction. Mussolini himself admitted as much on a number of occasions, despite all the grandiose Fascist rhetoric to the contrary.[69] And we saw that Emilio Gentile, the most forceful advocate of the applicability of the category, portrayed totalitarianism as an aspiration and direction, with practical effects we have tended to miss, without claiming that some total coordination or transformation was achieved. In any case, whereas the issue of effectiveness—the actual impact on the lives of Italians—is obviously crucial for some questions, we also need to understand the sources and content of any novel totalitarian aspirations at work, whatever the measure of realization they achieved in practice.

"Meaning" is of course what we are after, and we must read between the lines to get it. But before reading between the lines, we have to engage the lines themselves with a greater measure of openness than Bosworth himself seems prepared to countenance. To back up and allow more openness, more room for experiment and difference, is not to fall into "anything goes" relativism but to enable us to learn more deeply from historical experience, including what may be *unintended* outcomes. At present, the moralism, presentism, reductionism, and teleological assumptions that preclude reading the Fascists with sufficient openness constitute a greater obstacle to understanding than "taking them at face value."

As we noted in Chapter 1, the "modern" perspective entailed a master narrative that enabled us to trace the troubling departures of the interwar period to backwardness or wayward divergence from putatively normal modern development. In the Italian context of insufficient national integration, Fascism seemed, from this perspective, to have stemmed from some combination of counterrevolution by an especially insecure, vulnerable establishment and revolt against modernity by an especially threatened petty bourgeoisie. Or, turning the tables from within the same "modern" framework, Italian Fascism was an effort at developmental dictatorship, adopting the extraordinary means that seemed necessary to overcome relative backwardness and catch up. In a postmodern mode, we recognize that the modern triumphalist master narrative, warranting various reductionisms, restricted questioning and thus what we were prepared to hear, even as we *thought* we were reading between the lines.

Insofar as we get beyond such familiar modern readings, the responses at issue stand by definition in more complex interaction with national contextual idiosyncrasies than the modern master narrative would lead us to assume. From this postmodern perspective, Italy was not so much backward or wayward as simply different, with idiosyncratic traditions, a unique modern experience, and thus a distinctive take on wider modern problems and possibilities. Whereas Berezin featured backwardness in accounting for Fascism's putative premium on style, we noted that E.J. Hobsbawm, writing a generation earlier, characterized the Italian culture of the pre-Fascist period as "both extremely sophisticated and relatively provincial."[70] At the same time, the new conditions of possibility that had been articulated, in halting ways, prior to the war seemed especially germane in light of Italy's experience of the war and its immediate aftermath. Thus Italians might have been positioned to offer idiosyncratic, but genuinely innovative diagnosis and prescription in response to creases in the modern mainstream to that point. Insofar as we approach the Fascists in "modern" ways, warranting easy reductionism, we are likely to miss the substantive dimension in their responses. We must be prepared to account in non-reductionist, more deeply historical terms for the emergence of a reading of modern priorities and possibilities that was simply different—from that of the mainstream at the time, and from our own.

Quite apart from modernist reductionism, the particular outcomes in the Italian case especially seem to warrant a cynical orientation that reinforces the teleological temptations always present in historiography. Fascist aspirations invite sarcastic put-down, and thus it becomes especially difficult to grasp any such deeper difference in substance. But in inviting a deeper reflexivity and a greater attention to contingency, the postmodern turn prepares us better to grasp the terms of the initial idealism, the sense of excitement and possibility, that fueled the Fascist departure. Indeed, we may find something more substantial than a diffuse longing for "renewal." But as we noted in more general terms in Chapter 1, just as the ideals or aspirations at work may have been deeper than usually recognized, they may also have been flawed, risky, and dangerous in ways not recognized as well.

In the Italian case, particularly, the longstanding confusions about theory, ideology, and the possible significance of antecedent ideas have kept us from the approach necessary—and thus from the essential expansion of categories. Fascist Italy was long assumed to lack an ideology or consistent worldview—a major difference, it seemed, from Nazism and Soviet Communism. And thus Fascism was often reduced to some combination of opportunism, activism, and irrationalism. Yet even as many continue to downplay "fascist ideology," others assume that categories from antecedent thinkers like Nietzsche, Sorel, LeBon, and Pareto illuminate the Fascist departure on some level. And during the Fascist period itself, non-Italians seeking insight into the Fascist departure took the authority of Fascist ideologues like Giovanni Gentile, Sergio Panunzio, and Alfredo Rocco seriously indeed.[71] But the significance of all such ideas for actual practice is notoriously hard to pin down. Indeed, any ideas in evidence are often taken as mere theory, irrelevant for practice, or as merely instrumental, lending an illusory aura of legitimacy, unity, and purpose to a hodge-podge personal dictatorship.[72]

As we noted, culturalists like Schnapp and Berezin insist on emotion, aesthetics, spectacle, ritual, and rhetoric, as opposed to ideology or articulated ideas, on the grounds that Fascist ideology was either contradictory, confused, or malleable, not the real key to whatever substance or coherence Fascism managed—or to the trajectory of Fascist practice. But such arguments betray tensions. Even as she played down "text" and ideological coherence, Berezin could not avoid positing "ideology," although she assumed that it played up emotion at the expense of reason: "Rituals were vehicles of solidarity—communities of feeling—in an ideological project. Rituals multiplied in Fascist Italy because they served as public dramatizations of the merging of the public/private self that characterized non-liberal ideology in an age of large nation-states. They were also particularly suited to a political ideology and Italian culture that eschewed text in favor of emotion."[73] Devoid of cognitive content, rituals were displays of emotion to generate a feeling of solidarity.[74] But can there be an "ideology" with no texts, no antecedent ideas to be engaged? On the face of it, we surely must come to terms with the discursive, "ideological" side of the assault on liberal democracy that, even in Berezin's own account, underpinned the Fascist turn to emotion and ritual. The dichotomy of cognitive content and emotion or feeling is surely too simple. Berezin could not do justice to the issues because, contemptuous of discursive evidence, she had not read what the Fascists said about the role of spirit and will in the construction of a post-liberal politics. Hence the categories that she brought to bear in assessing Fascist purposes proved to be limited. Those focusing on spectacle, ritual, and rhetoric have illuminated important dimensions of Fascism, but they generally have been so quick to eschew encounter with ideas that they cannot do justice to the sources of these dimensions or their place in the overall trajectory of Fascist practice.

The anti-culturalist Bosworth, seeking to be hard-headed, errs symptomatically from the opposite direction. At one point, he casually refers to the gap between theory and practice, when what is in fact at issue, in the point under discussion, is the gap between intentions and effects, or outcomes.[75] The difference is crucial. Insofar as we conflate originating aspirations with "theory," we infer from the limited impact of this or that initiative that it was not serious in the first place. From this perspective, even to probe such aspirations is fallaciously to take them as if they had actually had the intended effect. In fact, the point is not that they were not serious, or that "theory," as some merely instrumental smokescreen, can be distinguished from hard-headed practice. Rather, the point is that once they began seeking to act on the basis of their originating aspirations, they failed.

Usefully challenging the longstanding tendency to deny any "ideology of Fascism," A. James Gregor and Zeev Sternhell each claimed to find a coherent and significant Fascist ideology encompassing some of the ideas—of Sorel, Pareto, and Michels, for example—that we discussed in Chapter 3. However, reflecting delimited "modern" premises in a double sense, each tended to restrict the focus in spite of himself. Each posited an ideology as unified and stable. And although their respective readings of the content differed radically, each reflected the modernist master narrative. Gregor posited backwardness and catch-up through developmental dictatorship, whereas Sternhell posited the negative reversal of a smooth, unified, rational and humanizing Enlightenment tradition.[76]

Eschewing generally modernist assumptions and approaches, we find in Italian Fascism not a systematic ideology but a looser mix of serious, sometimes challenging ideas that articulated and helped to shape aspirations. What characterized Italian Fascism, in fact, was not a dearth of ideas but a plethora, for books and journals proliferated, as Herbert Schneider noted in 1928.[77] But rather than forming a neat synthesis, the various intellectual strands betrayed symptomatic—and debilitating—tensions. Although Gentile, Rocco, and Panunzio each offered a forceful and innovative reading of the situation that demonstrably affected practice, and although the approach of each was overtly totalitarian, some of their emphases clashed, and none of the three was definitive.[78]

But such fissures do not mean mere confusion, or irrationalism, or that this or that particular strand can be dismissed as mere theory, or that we must focus on style as the basis of coherence. Fascism included a common energizing insight and aspiration sufficiently coherent to inspire enthusiasm and indicate the general direction for practice. But it proved subject to contest along various axes from within that common framework. A rich debate, based on articulated, published ideas, took place over direction and priorities throughout the history of the Fascist regime. Thus in part the regime developed a characteristic dynamic in which the meaning and relative significance of the original components changed.

Obviously, Mussolini's role was crucial under these circumstances, but its nature is hard to characterize. Although intelligent, and reasonably well read as political leaders go, he is often viewed as more a talented journalist, a gifted actor and propagandist, than an ideologue.[79] On occasion, certainly, he seems to have been more a balancer or juggler than an ideologue providing direction. Well into the 1930s, he allowed a significant measure of cultural freedom, even encouraged diverse currents to compete, as long as they accepted his leadership and remained within the broad framework of the Fascist revolution.[80]

Gregor, in contrast, insisted that Mussolini, starting from within the prewar revision of Marxism, synthesized the various strands that made up "the ideology of Fascism." Also featuring Mussolini as ideologue, up to a point, was MacGregor Knox, who convincingly criticized longstanding assumptions that Fascist ideologies must have been expressions of particular social groups or classes. On the contrary, he insisted, those ideologies were the products of individuals, and only Hitler and Mussolini ultimately mattered: "the dictators were the doctrine, the word made flesh."[81] The key in Mussolini's case was the drive toward radicalization and war, which amounted to "Mussolini unleashed" during the 1930s.[82] Yet Knox denied any implication that this drive stemmed from the views of "just one man." Rather, Mussolini's doctrine brought to extreme culmination longstanding perceptions and aspirations of Italian elites. Insofar as those aspirations were not merely *sui generis*, they presumably reflected Italy's latecomer status and relative weakness.[83]

Yet even as he took seriously not only Mussolini as ideologue but also Fascism as totalitarian, Knox found a major source of Fascist weakness in "the absence . . . of anything resembling the powerful ideological mechanisms that gave Marxism–Leninism and National Socialism their fanatical élites and masses." The Fascist vision of a new civilization, a new Rome, recalling the Giobertian and Mazzinian myths of the Risorgimento, "lacked the credible world-revolutionary dimensions of Mussolini's principal ideological rivals, Hitler and Stalin. It also, even more damagingly, lacked the pseudo-scientific links between the regime's goals and the historical process found in Marxism and National Socialism."[84]

Certainly, Mussolini was no mere opportunist, and he, like Hitler, operated on the basis of a worldview, even if it was neither composed of fanatical *idées fixes* to the extent that Knox sometimes suggested nor as unified and systematic as Gregor claimed. It reflected the wider innovative sense of how history happens, or could and should be made to happen through new forms of collective action. In that regard, however, Mussolini was by no means unique among the creators of Fascism, and in light of the new sense of the world at issue, even his own role as leader could only be part of a fluid and uncertain mix.

Reflecting the prewar layer of intellectual articulation, the cauldron of Fascist ideas included accents on will, spirit, myth, and action at the expense of rationalism or intellectualism. But none of these categories is straightforward; none can be grasped in a simple dualistic way. Even "anti-intellectualism" depends on the meaning of the "intellectualism" being opposed. In fact, Fascist "anti-intellectualism" pointed in two contrasting but quite coherent directions. On the one hand, the Fascist emphasis on will and action was to oppose the sort of intellectualism, linked to "positivism" and "materialism," that seemed to warrant passivity through this or that mode of determinism. We have seen that by the time of the First World War Giovanni Gentile was seeking to show how thinking, willing, and doing might come together in a unified, post-liberal culture. What he posited, and the basis of his appeal, cannot remotely be grasped in terms of a simple dualism of activism versus intellectualism. On the other hand, Fascism was "anti-intellectual" insofar as intellectualism suggested the need and the scope for some dogma, some finished ideology, some rational blueprint. The Fascists agreed that there could be no such thing precisely because history was open-ended in ways only now being fully grasped. Under the circumstances, the key was to create the instrument for ongoing *action*—action that was itself open-ended—as opposed to laying out some intellectualistic blueprint. Mussolini often boasted that Fascism was modern in precisely that sense of eschewing doctrinal baggage, the better to keep up with the grand and mutable reality of life. And he took delight in turning the tables on liberal critics; skeptics had said that Fascism was ephemeral because it lacked doctrine, "as if they themselves had doctrines and not instead some fragments adding up to an impossible mixture of the most disparate elements."[85]

But whereas the Fascists generally agreed that we cannot specify everything in advance, there was room for disagreement concerning how much could and should be specified. Although he was by no means proffering a blueprint, Gentile, as a systematic philosopher, was bound to be suspect to some, whatever the content of his ideas. Although his thinking was more easily grasped in his own culture than in the Anglophone world today, and although he offered a philosophy of openness, even human creativity and freedom, he could seem to be claiming to codify things through abstract philosophical formulas. Hence in part the controversy he encountered within Fascism even as he assumed a leading cultural role.

But the key for now is that whereas the Fascist hostility to fixing dogma means the irrelevance of finished blueprints, it does not mean the irrelevance of antecedent ideas or of intellectual debate within the regime itself, not least because the Fascists wrote down and debated ideas about precisely these matters—historical openness, the irrelevance of fixed dogmas, and the uses of myth, will, and spirit for collective action.

In insisting that we consider politicization "*in a Fascist sense*" and participation "*in a totalitarian sense*," Emilio Gentile was opening precisely to the scope for experiment, for genuine difference, as opposed to dismissing out of hand anything departing from the familiar forms of representative democracy.[86] So we ask on what basis the Fascists rejected the mainstream and found totalitarianism the appropriate response to the possibilities of mass politics? Moreover, in treating the impulse toward political sacralization in its interface with the Italian problem of relatively weak political integration, Gentile was backing up appropriately, seeking to account for the emergence of totalitarianism in terms of the ongoing political experiment since the Enlightenment.

But "masses" and "mass politics" are merely shorthand terms masking ambi-guities and variations, and Gentile's sense of the novel substance proved to be limited. Although he was not, as Bosworth claimed, merely applying Mosse's insights to the Italian case, Gentile's debt to Mosse was clear.[87] As we noted in Chapter 2, Mosse was indispensable in showing the centrality of modes of polit-ical involvement long marginalized in mainstream discussion, but his categories, starting with "the nationalization of the masses," were not sufficient to encom-pass the alternatives to the modern mainstream that became possible around the turn of the century.[88]

Even "the sacralization of politics" and the effort to create a "new man," both emphasized by Gentile, are too simple and undifferentiated to get at the source and meaning of the impulses at work. In the same way, Gentile's use of such categories as freedom, irrationalism, and even myth was too conventional to encompass the novel substance and its interface with the liturgical themes he emphasized. For example, his reference to the Fascist propensity to abolish liberty rested on a too-conventional understanding of liberty, contrasted with such contraries as authority, discipline, and hierarchy.[89] If we back up a step, thereby better grasping the instability even of so essential a category as liberty, we also better grasp the scope for novelty, for innovative "substance," bound up in this case with a sense of the scope to enhance positive liberty, the collective freedom to act, through totalitarianism. In the same vein, although he usefully highlighted the Fascist embrace of the populist Mazzini—so surprising in light of earlier assumptions about Fascism—Gentile did not probe the Mazzinian theme deeply enough to convey its significance to the Fascist sense of spearheading a modern departure from both liberalism and socialism.[90] More generally, Gentile's understanding of the interface between idiosyncratic Italian factors and the wider supranational, historically specific dimension proved too conventional to get at the basis of the Fascist claim to have moved to the forefront in estab-lishing a systematic alternative to the modern mainstream.

In assessing the originating aspiration, the first question is whether, in prin-ciple, the Fascist sacralization of politics, wound around ritual, commemoration, symbolism, and myth, was intended to produce a new mode of action or a new mode of being and experience, perhaps best understood as a new sense of belonging, an end in itself. Insofar as the latter, are we to take the experience as genuinely meaningful in religious terms, or as bogus—boiling down to forms of spectatorship and ritual that afforded only the *illusion* of participation? Involvement could be more constant, direct, and intense yet still remain rela-tively superficial, as an essentially *de*politicized mode of experience, despite all the talk of politicization.

Even as it stresses the seriousness and effectiveness of the Fascist accent on ritual, spectacle, and the like, much of the new cultural approach sidesteps deeper purposes as it suggests that mere belonging through relatively superficial forms of participation was what Fascism was all about. This seems to be even Emilio Gentile's implication on occasion, but in emphasizing that the Fascists sought to shape the mass of "new men" into a single body dedicated to realizing the party's revolutionary and imperialist aims, Gentile suggested that the point was precisely a new mode of *action*, as opposed to a new mode of being or experience. Yet though this "new man" was not merely a spectator, he was still a mere automaton "available" for the ends of the leadership. As Gentile saw it, in fact, the aim of the Fascist effort of mobilization and socialization was not to foster individuality but to void the new man of individuality, thereby absorbing him into the collective, disciplined and obedient, ready to serve.[91] At the same time, Gentile noted that "the fascist conception excluded prejudicially the possibility that the masses could come to govern themselves and to acquire an autonomous awareness and self-consciousness."[92]

Such characterizations of Fascist assumptions obviously offend our individualist and democratic sentiments. Especially in light of Fascist outcomes, any such submerging of individuality into the collective seems self-evidently negative, whereas the notion of the masses governing themselves seems self-recommending. And those outcomes, together with the longstanding image of totalitarianism, lead us to assume that the only alternative to mere belonging was to produce automatons. In principle, however, these do not exhaust the alternatives to the liberal mainstream that became possible with the historical-political break we have emphasized. Even in the face of Gentile's laudable effort to understand participation "*in a totalitarian sense*," our liberal individualist assumptions make it difficult to distinguish between various modes of participation that may plausibly be deemed totalitarian. In this especially fluid moment of the ongoing modern political experiment, there was more room for experimentation than Gentile's categories suggest, and it was not obvious where departures might lead in practice. So to make sense of the actual Fascist departure, we must get beyond the dualism of individual autonomy and mass self-government, on the one hand, and the production of automatons, on the other.

At issue, let us remember, is originating aspirations, not yet practical outcomes—let alone desirability. No matter how well the new Fascist institutions worked, no matter the quality of participation they actually entailed, we may well find undesirable the politicization, the more constant and direct participation, that they were supposed to make possible. But there was scope for individuals to be politicized in a genuinely totalitarian sense that actually engaged ethical capacities and expanded the scope for significant, even fulfilling participation that encompassed initiative, decision making, and collective activity as the reach of the state expanded. Yet there was also the scope for subordination, leaving ordinary people with mere spectatorship, with superficial forms of ritualistic involvement. If we blur the essential distinctions, we may miss not only the originating aspirations but also the scope for changes in emphasis and meaning within the developing dynamic of Fascist practice.

But even if the production of automatons is not the only alternative to liberal individualism, we obviously still face lots of questions about the nature and quality of participation that the Fascist alternative could have made possible even in principle. Whether we are to view the Fascist "new man" primarily as a spectator, as an automaton "available" for the ends of the leadership, or as a

participant genuinely politicized in a deeper, but still totalitarian sense depends
on the modes of education to be provided, on the roles to be afforded, on the
forms of interaction between elites and masses, on what the collectivity was actually to do and how it was to do it.

Everyone was to be involved in the newly totalitarian system, but in light of
their different backgrounds, Fascists often disagreed over the shape of the collective will, the role that ordinary people should play, the modes of participation, the
measure of control from above, and the scope for initiative from below. In *The
Sacralization of Politics*, Gentile invoked such widely disparate Fascists as Alfredo
Rocco, Giuseppe Bottai, Giovanni Gentile, Achille Starace, and Paolo Orano as if
they all spoke with the same voice, when in fact rather different purposes fueled
their embrace of the new totalitarian politics. Insofar as we make the totalitarian
thrust of fascism too homogeneous in this way, we miss the actual dynamic, with
changes in proportions, including the place of the ritual dimension itself.

Like Gentile, Simonetta Falasca-Zamponi and Ruth Ben-Ghiat took fascism
seriously as totalitarian in sophisticated recent studies. But each sought to
pinpoint a tension or contradiction in the originating aspirations that seemed to
account for anomalies in the actual dynamic that Gentile, with his emphasis on a
relatively homogeneous totalitarian thrust, seemed to gloss over. But the accents of
Falasca-Zamponi and Ben-Ghiat differed, however, and their accounts raise further
questions about the range of possibilities that we are prepared to encompass.

Charging explicitly that Gentile's sacralization theme did not account for the
underlying ambiguities and tensions, Falasca-Zamponi argued that a kind of
sensory alienation made possible the totalitarian mobilization in Fascist Italy.[93]
By exciting the senses yet denying sensual pleasure, private enjoyment, and the
body, the regime desensitized individuals, leaving them disembodied, part of a
mass, significant only in their subordination—as raw material to be molded by
the Duce as artist-politician.[94] Linked to a denial of consumption, the productivist thrust of Fascist corporativism was central to the sensory alienation that, in
Falasca-Zamponi's account, underpinned the regime.[95] In the final analysis,
then, it was the *lack* of aesthetic satisfaction, the *denial* of the senses, that made
Fascism totalitarian.[96] So although she, too, featured aesthetics, even style as
substance, Falasca-Zamponi differed both from Gentile and from those
American culturalists who found a measure of sensual *realization* on the aesthetic
level. She was suggesting, in a deeper, more innovative way than Bosworth, that
the level of aesthetic satisfaction was superficial, even bogus.

Indeed, Falasca-Zamponi's characterizations of particular Fascist practices
were often especially illuminating. But although she sought to do justice, as even
Gentile's recent work did not, to the centrality of corporativism, and although
she featured the significance of generally idealist categories, appropriately
linking them to Fascist productivism, she was quick to account for the whole
syndrome in terms of an extrinsic theoretical discussion, from Walter Benjamin
to Terry Eagleton, centering on aestheticism. Indeed, her way of opposing the
Fascist emphasis on self-sacrifice, for example, to the satisfactions of
consumerism reflects the mode of postmodernism that has seemed to warrant

new forms of presentist imposition based on categories taken as privileged *a priori*, thereby precluding the scope for deeper difference. Falasca-Zamponi sometimes seemed to suggest that the underlying purpose was to give Mussolini, as Nietzschean artist-creator shaping the "womanish masses," a sensual high, with the other leading Fascists apparently to be understood as mere groupies or voyeurs. Yet on a deeper level it all seems to have served bourgeois capitalist interests in some sense.[97]

Even as she featured snippets from Mussolini on the basis of her aestheticist framework, Falasca-Zamponi did not seriously measure her understanding of corporativism or anti-materialism against the arguments of Fascist corporativists and idealists, assessing the scope for a non-reductionist reading in light of tensions and openings in the mainstream tradition.[98] In light of her framework, any opposing "idealism" could only have entailed a denial of the consumerist/sensory/aesthetic satisfaction, not an autonomous effort to focus the human ethical capacity in ways not possible under liberal individualism, let alone the emerging consumerism. The place of consumption, desire, and the body are surely worth considering in the Italian case, but Falasca-Zamponi was too quick to impose them *a priori* rather than first trying to enter into the thinking of those who shaped the actual debate over Fascism's direction. We cannot assess an explanation in terms of repressed consumption without also considering what else might be at work in the Fascist effort, so unfamiliar on first encounter, to "spiritualize" the economy and make production a collective ethical act. More specifically, Falasca-Zamponi could not convincingly make the disconnection between Marxian materialism and the Fascist emphasis on "spirit" fit her thesis without a deeper sense of the Gentilian dimension, especially in light of the overall revision of Marxism.[99]

Although Ruth Ben-Ghiat, in her *Fascist Modernities*, focused especially on second-generation Fascists and the dynamic from the early 1930s, she offered a more convincingly historical treatment than Falasca-Zamponi. Comparably taking seriously the totalitarian aspiration of Fascism, she effectively featured the overall centrality of *bonifica*, reclamation or remaking, in characterizing the overall impulse.[100] However, her way of accounting for this departure proved conventional and limited in symptomatic respects, partly because she did not seek to back up even as Emilio Gentile did.

For Ben-Ghiat, Fascism was a Janus-faced response to the challenges of modernity immediately after the First World War. Although in some respects Fascism pointed beyond mere reaction or resentment to the quest for an *alternative* modernity, it won the support of most intellectuals because it seemed to address longstanding Italian and supranational *anxieties* about modernity that were escalating in the postwar world. On this level, Ben-Ghiat concluded, Fascism stemmed from concerns to preserve order, comforting continuities, and master narratives of privilege and domination. Thus it sought to reinforce class boundaries and gender hierarchies, to forestall further social emancipation, and to defend national traditions in the face of the homogenizing tendencies of modernity.[101]

To suggest that Fascism stemmed from a mixture of sometimes incompatible impulses is surely convincing, and some of them can indeed be understood in such relatively familiar terms. But insofar as we eschew the master narrative of modernization, it may be hard to distinguish, in the Fascist accents that Ben-Ghiat featured, anxious defense from a quest for an alternative modernity. The criteria were themselves at issue, and thus we cannot be sure what counts as what.[102] Even impulses that seem most obviously to suggest anxious defense—"ruralization," for example—require a deeper look once we open to a wider array of possibilities.

In terms of the modern master narrative, any emphasis on rural, local, or regional values suggests conservative defense; the alternative is bound up with the self-recommending "emancipation" of individuals. But in light of all that "modernization" has wrought—overcrowded edge cities, for example, or the much-lamented homogenization of culture and even the landscape itself—an effort to enhance the viability of rural life and to preserve some modicum of local culture did not necessarily stem from a desire to preserve privilege and forestall emancipation. Stanley Payne noted precisely that the Fascist effort to control urbanization by keeping a percentage of the rural population in the countryside, long derided as anti-modern, paralleled directions lauded as ecologically sound by the 1980s; yet because of a kind of double standard, Fascism was not taken as prescient.[103] The efforts of the visionary engineer Gaetano Ciocca suggest that rural concerns within Fascism could be anything but traditionalist and "anti-modern." Viewing even the countryside in terms of the totalitarian corporativist thrust of the Fascist revolution, he sought to address the quality of rural housing and patterns of life, even including the rationalization of pig farming, through initiatives to overcome tradition and bring the agricultural population into the modern Fascist mainstream.[104]

On occasion, Ben-Ghiat's own evidence seems to elude such categories as anxiety and defense, suggesting that she may have been too quick to resort to conventional reductionist explanations because her sense of the possibilities was not sufficiently open to innovation and difference. At issue, in part, is the timeframe necessary to assess the meaning of the Fascist responses in question. In focusing on the immediate postwar period, Ben-Ghiat was not backing up far enough to grasp the basis for the Fascist claim to lead in response to tensions in the wider modern deployment. She makes it clear that those criticizing corporativist performance during the 1930s were serious, but how, then, are we to account for the whole corporativist direction in light of her stress on the Fascists' tension-ridden response to modernity? Her own evidence does not suggest that corporativism was simply about preserving hierarchies or forestalling social emancipation.[105] But she does not consider the outcomes of parliamentary democracy and Marxist socialism to that point, so she was not opening broadly enough to encompass the sources of the corporativist impulse in the first place. In the same way, Ben-Ghiat's emphasis on the defense of threatened national traditions does not make sense of Giovanni Gentile's highly selective embrace and specifically modern recasting of the Italian intellectual tradition, including the marginalized Mazzini. Mussolini's boast that Fascism would "make Italy unrecognizable" and other such expressions of the

Fascist aspiration suggest that what fueled the Fascist departure, as a response to modernity, was less fear and defense than a new, energizing sense of opportunity and responsibility to show the way beyond the modern mainstream.

As we have emphasized, the sense of opportunity betrayed an edge of shrill-ness, but what does it tell us about the Fascist response to modernity? Ben-Ghiat noted convincingly that modernity seemed to include a new sense both of the malleability of history and of the scope for new, technocratic forms of action. However, invoking Omer Bartov's accents on the place of expertise and the modern therapeutic or engineering mentality in Germany, she was quick to suggest that this sense of new possibility "offered comfort and an illusion of control to those racked by fears of Europe's imminent decline."[106] To assess whether the departure can be reduced to such fears, we would need to back up from the immediate conjuncture resulting from the First World War—with "modernity" now bound up with "mass society"—to the thick texture of longer-term challenges that we found to have been emerging. Doing so suggests the scope for a more complex sense of the historical moment, affording a more confident sensibility within Fascism—although still with an edge of shrillness. The open-endedness of the challenge was daunting, and it was not obvious how to forge the collective means necessary to meet it—to go on meeting it. Despite the energizing sense of opportunity, the departure entailed the potential for degeneration, for trivialization in light of frustrations occasioned by the difficulty of actually doing great politics.

MacGregor Knox, too, sought to pinpoint an underlying contradiction that compromised the overall Fascist effort. Even as he noted the lack of ideological foundations comparable to those of Nazism and Stalinism, he found ideological keys in the cult of the Duce, the myth of the new state, and the ideal of living dangerously. But he went on to note, convincingly enough, that these three themes were mutually antagonistic.[107] Still, even as he eschewed direct appeal to the modernist master narrative, Knox fell into a "modern" teleological essen-tialism that precluded probing Fascism's ideological substance with the openness necessary to understand *either* its range and force or its potential for weakness and narrowing. Dismissive of everything that did not fit the essentialist telos of impe-rialism and war, he privileged a restricted subset of the evidence, thereby precluding any openness to Fascist ideas that stemmed from an innovative response to modernity. Above all, he conveyed no sense of the deeper meaning of the totalitarian state idea. In the Gentilian portions of Mussolini's "Doctrine of Fascism," he found only "platitudes." From his perspective, apart from its emphasis on war as the test of nationhood, that whole "pompous" document did not reflect the real Fascist ideology but merely Mussolini's intermittent quest for a veneer of intellectual respectability.[108]

Elsewhere, Knox noted that "fascist corporativism, which the regime touted as the answer to the social needs of the age, remained a sickly plant in which Mussolini himself took little interest."[109] But if Mussolini had little interest in corporativism, and if only Mussolini's ideas mattered, it is curious that the regime devoted such energy to the corporativist experiment into the 1940s. In fact, De

Felice found Mussolini's commitment to corporativism "beyond doubt and amply documented."[110] But the wider point is that although Mussolini's role was unique and indispensable, he was caught up, precisely as Emilio Gentile emphasized, in a complex web that included ideas and pressures from others within the Fascist mix. Moreover, Knox's suggestion, so symptomatic of his teleological tendency, that corporativism does not really matter because it remained a sickly plant, is to miss its place in an overall dynamic in which provisional outcomes yielded responses that then changed proportions. That dynamic cannot be understood either as a single abiding thrust, as Knox generally has sought to do or in terms the cluster of mutually incompatible ideological elements mentioned above.

At the same time, the absence of "the pseudo-scientific links," as found in Marxism and National Socialism, "between the regime's goals and the historical process" was not necessarily, as for Knox, a source of weakness for Italian Fascism but could nourish a sense of superiority, based precisely on the recognition that those nineteenth-century ideologies were merely *pseudo*-scientific, that Italian Fascism rested on a wider modern humanism that featured not exclusion but positive construction, education, and the scope for inclusion based on culture, spirit, and freedom. Fascist ideologues did not envy what they themselves perceived to be the bogus certainties of their post-liberal rivals; quite the contrary. It remains true that such bogus certainties could help to galvanize enthusiasm, and that was much of Knox's point. But he was too quick to leave the matter there, with "ideological" strength bound up with pseudo-scientific certainty. To understand the actual dynamic, we must grasp what the Italians believed they had *instead of* such pseudo-scientific certainties, and how it fed a particular kind of enthusiasm with a particular place in the trajectory of the regime.

The totalitarian aspiration in Italian Fascism

Although Italy since unification had seemed to face a particular problem of "bringing the masses into the state," underlying the Fascist departure were more general questions about the modern liberal–positivist mainstream that, for historical reasons, were simply closer to the surface in Italy. By the immediate postwar period, dissident Italians could claim special purchase on intellectual antecedents that seemed to provide a privileged sense of the new direction that now seemed desirable and possible. They pointed to the legacy of Mazzini, the pioneering diagnoses and prescriptions of Mosca and Pareto, the sustained interaction with Sorel, and the modern Italian update of the idealist tradition, all against the backdrop of the growing uncertainties about nineteenth-century Marxism as the framework for a systematic alternative to the liberal mainstream. In light of those intellectual antecedents, the idiosyncratic Italian war experience seemed to open the way to a transformation that would address the longstanding aspiration for an alternative modernity, thereby producing a more effective nation and a deeper self-realization for individuals.

Although the new direction obviously required a monopoly of power to check socialism and restrict the role of parliament, the energizing key was a positive program in which reconstructing political institutions, mobilizing Italians, shaping minds, and expanding the range of collective action were to proceed together. To characterize the new direction as "totalitarian" is not to reduce the impulse to some ahistorical will to power but to suggest, most basically, the limit-lessness of the collective responsibility and reach that seemed to be required.

From the emerging Fascist perspective, neither liberalism nor Marxism had grasped the centrality of ongoing collective history making because neither had a sufficiently radical historical sense.[111] Liberal democracy had produced a merely quantitative, mechanical aggregate of individuals, leaving the masses either insufficiently politicized—indifferent, outside, easily exploited—or *wrongly* politicized through the embrace of particularism and materialism, whether in liberal individualist or Marxist class form. Those grasping what seemed to be the scope for the essential new mode of action constituted a new elite whose first task was to forge the necessary collective instrument, most basically through a new education, including widespread mobilization, to marshal comparable virtues in others.[112] More constant and direct participation was essential to the expansion of the capacity for collective action.

In light of all that Mosca, Pareto, and Michels had articulated about contem-porary democratic experience, it was essential to face up to the importance of differentiation and leadership. But how those stood with communitarian and even egalitarian impulses was not obvious, and there was room for significant differ-ences of emphasis among totalitarian Fascists. Moreover, if there is inevitably some form of political elite, there were questions, as with the other two regimes, about its basis, about how open it was to be, and how it was to be replenished.

Still more centrally at issue was the mode of relationship between elite and masses. The point was not mere elitism as an end in itself, let alone to preserve some traditional or hereditary elite. Nor did the departure stem from some merely conservative fear of the masses. Even for the Nationalist Alfredo Rocco, the aim was more actively to involve the masses through a new reciprocity between leaders and led.

It is possible to find in Mussolini statements suggesting a certain conception of the limits of the masses, confining them to a certain level of involvement. As we noted, Simonetta Falasca-Zamponi sometimes seemed to suggest that Fascism boiled down to satisfying Mussolini's wondrous sexual appetites while giving the womanish masses the seduction/gratification they sought. But voyeurism does not explain the interest, even excitement, of the many Fascists who addressed the issue in terms having nothing to do with some merely aesthetic-sensualist reduction.

"Mass" stands opposed to "individualism" in two contrasting directions. Insofar as individualism means anonymous, atomized, mechanical, short-sighted, egotistical, politically indifferent monads, to organize them and thereby create a mass, collective instrument might be conceived as positive—even for individual self-realization as an ethical being. Thus, for example, the original syndicalist emphasis on the moralizing effects of trade union organization. But insofar as "mass" refers to the *aggregate* of those anonymous, atomized individuals, the point is to make them individuals in a new sense.

In terms of the front direction, the Fascist aim was to *create* a genuinely mass politics for the first time, a new instrument for new collective action. The premise was that modern politics, in its liberal democratic form, had proved inadequate both for individuals and for the collective. From the second perspective, the point of Fascist mobilization and education was to take mere "masses" and transform them into active, committed participants. Although the immediate aim was enhanced collective effectiveness, not enhanced participation as an end in itself, and certainly not the individual self-realization central to some versions of liberalism, neither was the point to sacrifice individuality, submerging it into the collective/nation, making the masses cogs in a machine. By expanding the reach of the state, Fascist totalitarianism would afford, as liberalism did not, the scope for the masses to participate more meaningfully as appropriate, congruent with individual capacities. And sharing in expanded collective responsibility would make possible a deeper mode of individual self-realization than had liberalism, with its bifurcation of public and private and delimited state. In this sense, mass potential was bound up with the ethical capacity that pertained to free human beings, who were neither automatons nor subject to materialistic, mechanical limits based on class or race. But it was not clear what this overall direction would mean in practice—either in terms of the actual top-down implementation by the new elite or in terms of how ordinary people would actually experience it.

The sense of the scope for intensified mobilization and education was bound up with the Fascist embrace of generally idealist or voluntarist categories like will, spirit, even "life as a mission." It is well known that Mussolini liked to suggest that anything might be possible through the exercise of will.[113] Endorsing Sorel in 1912, he asked, "Is socialism reducible to a theorem? We want to believe in it, we must believe in it; humanity needs a credo. It is faith that moves mountains by producing the illusion that mountains move. Illusion is perhaps the only reality of life."[114] This was vintage Mussolini, pithy, even insightful, but an overstated, "journalistic" translation of the new historical-political sense. Such accents were bound up with the overall Fascist insistence, beyond both mechanical democracy and materialistic socialism, on the scope for action, whatever the obstacles, if the elite has the will and spirit to forge the necessary instrument. It is striking to find the notion that Fascism constituted a "spiritual" revolution, that it was superior to "materialist" Communism and liberal capitalism on that basis, prominent even in an engineer like Gaetano Ciocca.[115]

Grandiose achievement seemed to be fueled or enabled by something like myth, a category the Fascists embraced explicitly. Indeed, Sternhell was close to the mark in concluding that "faith in the power of myth . . . is the key to the Fascist view of the world."[116] But myth is a slippery and overloaded category that must be used with particular care. Because not only myth but also the elites–masses distinction was essential to the Fascist sense of the new scope for collective, history-making action, the Fascist embrace of myth may seem to suggest mystification, cynical manipulation from above—to serve power, for example, or the interests of the elite, diverting the masses from *their* real interests. In the context of Sternhell's overall argument, the centrality of myth suggests precisely the lucid manipulation of masses by elites, as well as the irrationalist revolt, to which he found Sorel central, against Enlightenment tradition. In the same vein, Abbott Gleason suggested that the methods of Giovanni Gentile's activist state included the mystification and social myths that Sorel had made famous.[117]

In fact, myth was implicated in Italian Fascism on several levels, with proportions and even meanings changing over time. But as embraced by the creators of Fascism, myth was not a matter of mystification but part of a different syndrome—equally familiar up to a point, but more complex, less obviously susceptible to reductionist readings. Writing in 1934, Giuseppe Bottai noted that Fascism was widely seen abroad as a doctrine of myths, but, turning the tables, he insisted that the liberal mainstream had come to venerate liberty and the individual precisely as idols, "myths."[118] However, the point was not simply that two can play this game. The Fascists claimed a more lucid grasp of the place of myth as central to the new historical-political sense that could itself *change* how history happens, or gets made. Along with commitment, audacity, will, solidarity, faith, discipline, sacrifice, and mission, that syndrome encompassed the capacity to project heroic collective goals wound around images of collective accomplishment. Determined action in itself helps to make new achievement possible, although with history open-ended, outcomes are not precisely foreseeable.[119] Still, action is not a mere shot in the dark insofar as the elite forges the appropriate instrument for collective action by mobilizing human virtues and capacities in a more thoroughgoing way.

The myths at issue did not differentiate elites from masses but bound them together, for even the new Fascist elite knew itself to be caught up in an overall myth as it pursued ongoing Fascist creation. In that sense the Fascist embrace of myth not only eluded Sorel, whose primitivism precluded any such lucidity, but also pointed beyond Sternhell, with his implication that, in the last analysis, myth was merely manipulative.[120]

The Fascists often claimed that Italy had a particular grasp of these generally idealist categories in light of its idiosyncratic traditions, from Renaissance humanism to Vico to Mazzini to the recent recasting of historicism and philosophical idealism by Benedetto Croce and Giovanni Gentile. Standing opposed to both historical materialism and biological naturalism, Italian humanistic idealism emphasized spirit, culture, and thus the scope for enhanced education to nurture and focus the human ethical capacity. Fascism claimed superiority to materialistic Communism and racist Nazism especially on that basis. Still, such idealist or voluntarist categories made for a volatile and multivalent mix. Although they expressed insights central to the Fascist claim to novelty, some are likely to seem, if not merely manipulative, simply vacuous from our present perspective. To probe them in a more open way suggests both deeper substance and the scope for excess, with the lines unclear, subject to contest in practice.

The effort to place this set of impulses must encompass Giovanni Gentile, who, we noted, was among the innovators who began to articulate new possibilities around the turn of the century, then emerged as a major civic educator in Italy as the war was ending. Although he provoked opposition, he was surely the single most important Fascist ideologue and organizer of culture, especially during the pivotal period of self-definition and institutional change from 1924 to 1932. Although by no means all of his immediate disciples followed him into Fascism, many did, including Ugo Spirito, Arnaldo Volpicelli, Armando Carlini, Ernesto Codignola, and Delio Cantimori. A number of the *gentiliani* played significant roles in their own right, helping to spearhead educational reform, corporativist development, and the assault on the Catholic Church, and probing the bases of Nazism and the scope for cultural ties between the Italian and German regimes.[121] However, growing doubts about the Fascist regime led some to drift away, one by one. Several of the most eminent, including Spirito, Cantimori, and Galvano della Volpe, eventually found their way to Communism. Yet Gentile himself hung on to the bitter end, even embracing Mussolini's late *Repubblica di Salò* before being assassinated by a partisan in 1944.

Although his influence was considerable, Gentile was always controversial within Fascism, and he attracted criticism especially during the early 1930s as frustration grew over the pace of change in Fascist Italy.[122] Some deemed him too intellectual; others, too "liberal"; still others, insufficiently Catholic. Plausible differences in priorities were at work, as were institutional rivalries and generational rebellion. Gentile was prominent among those playing down any privileged role for the Fascist Party; he even came to view the party as expendable.[123] So he drew the ire of those claiming a special ongoing revolutionary role for the party as the embodiment of the totalitarian ideal.[124]

Gentile encountered not only opposition but also frustration as the regime evolved. The fortunes of his educational reform effort proved to be mixed, and after a long interplay with leading Catholics during the 1920s, he bitterly opposed the 1929 Concordat, especially because of the role it allotted the Church in education. Still, as Gabriele Turi emphasized, Gentile in the aftermath simply intensified his exaltation of the totalitarian state, which, he claimed, was being realized in other spheres, most notably through the advent of corporativist institutions. As the Soviet experiment turned toward Stalinism at about the same time, Gentile more than ever saw Fascism as the best hope for a post-liberal alternative. Although less immediately active in Fascist politics after 1932, he remained a powerful voice, with direct access to Mussolini and major roles in the regime.[125] The categories he had developed in his earlier writings remained essential to Fascist self-understanding and continued to frame discussion. And Gentile was not alone in encountering ups and downs within the Fascist mixture. So did everyone else, and defeats were not necessarily definitive.

Throughout the Fascist years, Gentile was widely recognized abroad as the leading Fascist theorist. The influential American journal *Foreign Affairs* published a translation of one of his key essays as "The philosophic basis of fascism" in 1928.[126] But even then, Gentile was widely misconstrued. Whereas some, like Georges Bataille and Franz Neumann, stressed conservative Hegelianism, others, like George Boas and Herbert Marcuse, found irrational activism—although obviously the two angles meshed uneasily at best.[127] When treated at all during the decades after Fascism, Gentile's ideas were generally viewed as having played a merely instrumental role.[128] But his influence and wider symptomatic significance have been increasingly recognized over the past twenty-five years.

For Emilio Gentile, Gentile was central to the effort to establish a specifically Fascist culture that, by the late 1920s, had produced an intellectual consensus and a particular self-understanding: Fascism was translating the best of modern thought, brought to fruition by Gentile himself, into the post-liberal political form that the modern world needed, the new totalitarian state.[129] As Emilio Gentile saw it in 1993:

> The decisive contribution to Fascism's political theology was that of Giovanni Gentile and many of his followers. Viewing Fascism as a revival of the moral revolution of which Mazzini had dreamed, they gave the primitive religious feelings of early fascism a much stronger cultural underpinning. . . . Gentile was, at least until the 1930s, the chief theologian of the new state. Even when his cultural leadership within the régime began to decline, his mark on the Fascist vision of the state remained strong and clear.[130]

Still, Gentile's ideas and their significance have remained devilishly difficult to grasp. Even as he found Gentile archetypal, Abbott Gleason fell into commonplaces in conflating Gentile's thinking with both "conservative Hegelianism" and "George Orwell's demonic visions."[131] Even in Emilio Gentile's work, it was not quite clear how Gentilian themes, with their changing but still essential place, meshed with the abiding effort to sacralize politics that he emphasized overall. Although his vision was totalitarian to the core, Giovanni Gentile envisioned anything but individuals stripped of their autonomy, reduced to a mass, rendered available for the ends of the regime. Conversely, some of his argument especially invited a form of myth making that stands in problematic relationship with Emilio Gentile's way of accenting myth as one component in Fascism's "internal symbolic universe."

Even if we manage to penetrate to the core of Gentile's vision, his categories are easily ridiculed today. For Domenico Settembrini, his departure from liberal democratic mechanisms could only have led to a concentration of power in the charismatic leader, leaving ordinary people as mere spectators.[132] But this is certainly not what Gentile envisioned or advocated. To grasp what he had in mind, we must recognize that our cynicism stems partly from the outcome of the totalitarian experiments, which not only discredited Fascism but marginalized ways of conceiving human possibilities within the larger political experiment. Insofar as we are open to innovation and difference, Gentile can stretch the categories, from activism to freedom, that we bring to bear as we assess what the creators of Fascism found to be the possibilities and priorities. We open to a different way of understanding ethical-political action, a different relationship between individuals and the state, and we better grasp how such difference could have galvanized enthusiasm and confidence at the outset. Even for those who dissented in part, Gentile framed the discussion of what Fascism was all about and why it was of world-historical significance as a pioneering response to the perceived limitations of the liberal-positivist mainstream. At the same time, taking Gentile's ideas seriously enables us better to recognize the dangerous implications, the scope for excess, that they surely entailed.

We noted in Chapter 3 that as Croce and Gentile diverged in 1913, Croce found "mysticism" in Gentile's way of unifying thinking, willing, and acting, whereas Gentile called Croce's attention to "that sense of profound melancholy that pervades your whole contemplation of the world."[133] Although Croce claimed to offer an orientation sufficient to invite individual responsibility, Gentile sensed that a mass secular age is likely to fall into irony, cynicism, indifference, at best a premium on self-cultivation, but perhaps mere consumerism or some mindless popular culture—anything but the sense of collective history making that breeds responsibility for the whole and for the future. The antidote was the unified culture, bringing together thinking, willing, and acting, that Gentile had begun to discuss in philosophical terms even before the birth of Fascism.

As Gentile explained in his numerous speeches and writings, Fascism was replacing the liberalism and positivism still dominant in the West with the alternative foreshadowed by Mazzini and given rigorous philosophical underpinnings by Gentile himself. What the modern secular world required was not a socioeconomic revolution against capitalism but a cultural-political revolution with two mutually reinforcing dimensions. On the one hand, that revolution was to be socio-cultural, using more broadly encompassing forms of education to marshal and focus the human ethical capacity, so that everyone would come to share in the sense of total ongoing responsibility for the future. On the other hand, the revolution was to be political and institutional, expanding the reach of the state to begin shaping the world in a new way, more lucidly as making history. In inviting, even demanding, more constant and direct participation, such expanded collective action would itself marshal and focus the human ethical capacity.[134]

Within the delimited personal sphere, individuals may respond freely and ethically, and even affect what the world becomes through personal decision—as with raising children well. And the political sphere afforded a vehicle for collective ethical response to some extent even under the liberal dispensation. But as, with the waning of transcendence, the world comes to seem a human responsibility as never before, our personal sense of responsibility grows, and we are further drawn to the public, political sphere, for it is there that we have built institutions concentrating power in such a way that the nation, as a historically given community, may act collectively and thereby affect the world more directly and widely. So, in response to the question of how the world could and should get made, Gentile specified a new mode of collective action through what he termed explicitly a totalitarian ethical state.[135] Although it surely seems oxymoronic on first encounter, this category entailed an innovative reconceptualization of the relationships among power, freedom, responsibility, and participation.

Put simply, as our sense of responsibility grows, we need to expand our capacity to act, to shape what the world becomes. In concentrating and extending power through the state, we expand our collective freedom to act. Indeed, freedom requires that the state's reach be potentially limitless, totalitarian. So to make the state totalitarian does not limit our freedom, as would seem the case from a liberal perspective, but enables us to exercise it more extensively, effectively, and responsibly.

In that sense, the totalitarian state does not stand opposed to the freedom of differentiated individuals, as we tend to assume it must. On the contrary, it values individuation and presupposes anything but a lifeless uniformity.[136] Indeed, for Gentile as much as for any liberal, individuals differ, and each individual is a precious fount of human ethical capacity.[137] It is essential, then, that the free, ethical capacity of individuals be nurtured and respected within the totalitarian ethical state. Wide participation and free discussion remained essential—not, however, because individual self-expression is somehow an end in itself but because only thus can the state reflect the ethical responses of the whole community and change and grow as it does so.[138] Gentile himself allowed open debate in the periodicals he directed, and we have noted that Mussolini, too, stressed the scope for, even the value of, free discussion within the overarching Fascist framework—at least until the mid-1930s.[139]

Still, although our commitments will differ, we are to live lives of total public commitment, total responsibility. All are to be involved, all the time. There is no place for contemplative withdrawal, or self-cultivation, or mere alienation—let alone for some challenge to the overall vision. Self-cultivation is merely narcissistic; alienation is merely frivolous. So Gentile's totalitarian vision stands opposed not to individuation, not to debate within the state, but to what had come to seem the passive indifference, the selfish egotism, the corrosive cynicism of the merely "private" person. The alternative—freedom *from* the public world; personal, private freedom in withdrawal from the world—might make sense in terms of a transcendent dimension, but in a post-Christian world, the individual's free moral agency can realize itself only "horizontally," by becoming one with the public world. There can be freedom only *in* the world, with the world—only insofar as we feel at home in a world that is forever coming to be. And this means not passive acceptance of a world that comes to us from outside, about which we have no choice, but a sense of full involvement with a continuously growing world, the collective making of a world that, precisely in its openness, invites our sense of full responsibility.

So totalitarian involvement is essential to human self-realization in a flattened-out, historical world. Individuals are free, and part of the community, only insofar as they experience an identity between their lives as responsible moral agents and the expanded collective action that the totalitarian state makes possible. Thus they are *not* free to reject the whole vision and the sense of responsibility and involvement that follows from it. To do so would be to deny their own humanity.

Since history is open-ended and outcomes are ever provisional, the sense of responsibility is continuous and limitless, and thus so is the involvement. Although some have assumed Gentilian statism to be conservative in comparison with an accent on the dynamic movement-party, Gentile's totalitarian ethical state was an ideal direction or regulative principle; it could never be fully realized in some tangible, empirical institution.[140] As totalitarian, even the new Fascist state could only be constantly under construction, ceaselessly recreated, as history generates new challenges and as the ethical capacity of individuals is called forth.

In this sense, especially, Gentile was not simply recasting the familiar notion, associated variously with Rousseau and Hegel, that individual freedom lies in obeying the state as the incarnation of rational will, or in internalizing the law as the expression of one's own rational will. His conception was more dynamic and open-ended in light of the break in historical consciousness around 1900. As totalitarian, the new state is not merely a rational juridical institution that disciplines individual wills but a collective actor that mobilizes and draws on individual wills precisely for that collective action. Rather than fold into the existing state, individuals endlessly recreate the state as, exercising their freedom, they participate in such collective, history-making action.

At the same time, Gentile's vision differentiated him in principle from the Nationalist Alfredo Rocco, with whom he is often lumped.[141] Although each was a totalitarian envisioning a limitless expansion of the state's sovereignty, each posited a different relationship between the individual and the state, based on a different reason for rejecting liberal democracy. Although he advocated more intense forms of mass mobilization, Rocco was responding in part to what he found the appalling vulnerability of governmental institutions in the liberal order in light of the rise of the masses and the growth of powerful private associations like trade unions. Gentile was more attuned to what seemed the positive opportunity to nurture the human ethical capacity and to exercise collective responsibility. We noted that he had come to embrace Mazzini as the war was ending, and he was a major source of the notion that Fascism could address wider mainstream creases thanks to the heretofore unrealized Mazzinian legacy.[142] Embrace of the populist Mazzini expressed Gentile's sense, so different from the rigidly elitist Rocco's, that the scope for political virtue was universally human. Whereas Rocco envisioned subordinating individuals to a state imposing itself from above, Gentile posited a more reciprocal relationship in which individuals are unified with the state, recreating it through their participation.[143]

Rather than conservative statism, Gentile's conception more plausibly suggests the activism and ongoing dynamism that have long been associated with Italian Fascism. But his thinking forces us beyond longstanding assumptions and conflations—the notion, for example, that Fascism entailed some blind worship of "activity for its own sake." As we noted in Chapters 3 and 4, what Gentile had offered even before Fascism was precisely a *philosophy* of ongoing action. He believed his philosophy to be the modern cutting edge, and to grasp its logic was to feel not some abiding structure but, as never before, the absence, the incompleteness of the world. Thus his insistence that "the world is no longer what there is but what there ought to be; not what we find, but what we leave—what is born insofar as we, with the energy of our spirit, cause it to be born."[144] In other words, the world is forever incomplete, forever in the process of being (provisionally) realized through human moral response.

To understand the world philosophically is thus to be propelled beyond the present through action. But that ongoing action stems from an ongoing sense of responsibility, not from irrationalism or some blind worship of "activity for its own sake."

Whatever its plausibility, this vision cannot be understood in terms of the widely held dualistic conception that takes Fascism as a reaction against the progressive Enlightenment mainstream. In a lecture inaugurating the academic year at the University of Pisa in 1930, Giuseppe Bottai admitted that in their youthful impetuousness, he and his Fascist cohorts had not always been clear enough about the relationship between fascism and the French revolutionary tradition, the ideas of 1789. And their enemies, especially abroad, had been able to exploit the ambiguity, portraying the Fascists as merely reactionary. In fact, insisted Bottai, Fascism was not a mere negation but a dialectical overcoming of the liberal democratic tradition that had issued from the French Revolution. That revolution had been one of the notable events in human history, yielding much that remained essential, including denial of hereditary privilege, equality before the law, and the freedom to hold and communicate ideas.[145] But for Bottai, echoing Gentile, the underlying key was the emergence of the human spiritual self-awareness essential to modernity. With the French Revolution, spirit, or humanity, began to grasp its liberty, its creative power, its capacity to construct its own history.

But whereas liberalism had perhaps been a necessary stage, it could not, Bottai insisted, realize the potential of the principles of 1789, most basically because, in resistance to absolutism, it embraced the natural law tradition and thus developed a particular delimited conception of the individual–state relationship. The first line of Bottai's critique is familiar. Liberalism was abstract in positing the individual as prior to the state or any mode of social organization and then, as a corollary, in conceiving freedom in negative terms as *freedom from* the state.[146] But in this lecture, and throughout his mature writings, Bottai was not simply echoing the romantic reaction, or Hegel, or even Durkheim, but adding a dimension, derived especially from Gentile's way of linking individual freedom and ethical self-realization to the new sense of collective world making in history. The liberal idea of freedom as private, as the capacity of the individual to act at his own pleasure, could not realize the moral personality, and the liberal state could not fulfill the potential for freely constructing our own history that also came into the world with the French Revolution. The alternative was not simply to ground individuality in the state but to unify individualism with the state *as history-making*. It is that sense of future projection, that sense of ongoing struggle to construct what ought to be, that, overcoming particular egotisms and interests, draws out the human ethical capacity. So the Fascist totalitarian state, as the concentration of ethical capacity for collective history making, was not the repudiation but the fulfillment of the deepest ideas of 1789.[147]

Whatever the implications for practice would prove to be, the notion that totalitarianism expands collective freedom, congruent with ethical capacity, by creating the instrument for expanded collective action is coherent in principle, unfamiliar though it is. But even insofar as we admit that self-realization need not be the end, we still ask about the nature and quality of the involvement that totalitarianism, with its expanded exercise of power, was supposed to make possible.

For many Fascist totalitarians, including Gentile and Bottai, it was especially the development of corporativist institutions that gave a measure of concreteness to the ethereal notion of the totalitarian ethical state. Gentile portrayed corporativist development as confirmation of his ideas, and several of his most prominent followers, such as Ugo Spirito and Arnaldo Volpicelli, became leading corporativist publicists.[148] Corporativist leaders like Bottai embraced Gentile's categories as they explained the significance of the corporativist direction. And we have noted that De Felice found Mussolini's commitment to corporativism "beyond doubt and amply documented."[149] Corporativism was intended at once to expand the reach of collective action by encompassing the economy within the political realm and to involve people more constantly and directly in public life as, through groupings based on the workplace, they shared in the expanded range of decisions to be made politically. Its corporativist dimension, especially, was to make the totalitarian state the instrument for ongoing collective action as opposed to merely ritualistic participation or spectatorship.

We noted that Fascism settled on the corporativist direction in the wake of the Matteotti crisis. And although it was not quite clear what it would mean— open-ended experiment was emphasized from the start—that direction was widely welcomed, galvanizing enthusiasm. Indeed, the corporativist state, with an idealist gloss, was consistently featured as Fascism's institutional centerpiece. And it was corporativism, not imperialism, population policy, or the sacralization of politics that most confirmed the notion that Fascism was out front, innovatively addressing concrete contemporary issues.

As De Felice emphasized, the corporativist aspiration was not some nostalgic throwback to medieval guilds or Catholic traditions.[150] This was a *modern* corporativism, responding to problems that had emerged with the advent of industrial society and that, the Fascists claimed, continued to elude both liberalism and Marxism. On that basis, Fascist corporativism was much discussed abroad at the time.[151] Yet it gets only cursory treatment at best in much innovative recent scholarship that purports to take Fascist totalitarianism seriously. Even Emilio Gentile hardly mentioned corporativism when discussing the radical, totalitarian aspiration.

The Fascists measured themselves against the Bolsheviks virtually from the beginning, recognizing a significant kinship, even borrowing certain Soviet techniques but claiming superiority at the same time.[152] Most emphasized that the Soviet Communist experiment was proving negative, confirming the need for the Fascist third way, which opposed corporativism to bureaucratic statism and idealism to materialism. Giuseppe Bottai charged that the socialist idea in Soviet Russia was in the process of yielding an enormous, clumsy, bureaucratic state capitalism.[153] Even those more sympathetic suggested that Stalinism inevitably tended toward Fascism, the only viable alternative to the liberal mainstream. In *Il trionfo del fascismo nell'U.R.S.S.* (The Triumph of Fascism in the U.S.S.R.), published in 1934, Renzo Bertoni stressed that the antithesis between Communism and Fascism, stemming from the materialist/idealist dichotomy, could only be temporary, in light of their common enemy, liberal individualism with its attendant capitalist exploitation, and especially in light of the wider economic crisis. But as an effort at socialism, the Soviet regime had definitively failed, producing forced collectivization and terror and thereby demonstrating the absurdity of Communist principles; it could only abandon Marxism and move toward the Fascist mode of organizing production and regulating class relations.[154]

Although Fascist corporativism attracted much interest abroad, many non-Italians continued to see Fascism, and thus corporativism, either as reactionary, serving employers' interests, or as a mere dictatorship, suffocating individual liberties and initiatives. Ben-Ghiat noted that Indro Montanelli, the young editor of *L'Universale*, was irritated and surprised that some French participants at the Italian–French Conference on Corporativist Studies in Rome in May 1935 viewed Fascism as a nationalistic movement of the extreme Right.[155] Partly because they felt that Fascism was being misrepresented abroad in this way, Bottai and his colleagues took every opportunity to respond to questions and spread the corporativist word.[156] The conferences and other activities of the International Labor Office at Geneva, created by Section 13 of the Treaty of Versailles, were major occasions for taking the measure of the competition, both liberal and post-liberal, and for trumpeting the pioneering achievements of Fascist corporativism.[157] Still, the Fascists had encountered skepticism in this venue from the outset. In light of the early Fascist assault on the socialist labor movement, the veteran French trade union leader Léon Jouhaux spearheaded objections even to seating the Italians—as Fascists.

Although there was surely room, in principle, to seek a non-Marxist way of politicizing the workplace and a post-liberal way of handling economic conflict, the corporativist direction is easily read in reductionist terms, especially in light of the ongoing effort by pre-Fascist economic elites to exploit Fascism. Indeed, the tendency for decades after the fall of Mussolini was to dismiss corporativism as a sham, even to suggest that it was intended from the start to serve business interests by regimenting the working class.[158] Although it would seem that we must listen to the corporativists themselves, the various confusions about theory and practice and taking the Fascists at face value have come into play especially with this issue, affording an excuse to avoid actually reading them.

With his attention to the nationalist and syndicalist origins of Fascism, Zeev Sternhell at least recognized the significance of proto-corporativist ideas, and he correctly pinpointed the Nationalist–syndicalist synthesis as the basis for the corporativist direction chosen. But when he actually treated Fascist corporativism, it was not in its Italian genesis but simply as an aspect of the overall anti-Enlightenment, Sorelian culture that he found to be all too widespread in much of Europe by the 1930s.[159] So, rather than consider major Italian corporativists like Rocco, Panunzio, Bottai, Spirito, and Volpicelli,

Sternhell fell back on such figures as Henri De Man and Marcel Déat. Whatever their wider interest, such people are not the keys to understanding the Italian embrace of corporativism. Because of the generality of his inquiry, Sternhell could not possibly have found any features in Italian corporativist thinking that pointed away from his *a priori* syndrome encompassing elitism, anti-humanism, and free-market economics.[160]

In his most pointed characterization, Sternhell found corporativism to have been one manifestation of an overall Fascist reduction of socio-economic problems to matters of psychology; corporativism produced the *feeling* of change, of participation, without any real change in socio-economic structures.[161] This conventional reading of corporativism as a conservative subterfuge is surely worth considering in light of the eventual outcome, but precisely because he started by taking ideology seriously, Sternhell had access to evidence that challenges any such narrowly reductionist interpretation of origins and purposes.

Whatever their background, Fascist corporativists agreed that the modern class struggle reflected genuine issues that liberalism had proved ill-equipped to handle. Industrial capitalism had entailed a heightened sense of class and differential interests, yet the liberal state, agnostic and short-sighted, had left the clash of particular interests uncoordinated, unharmonized, to be worked out in private, despite the wider public stake in the outcomes. Up to a point, the emergence of the socialist movement had usefully forced the meaning of class and class differences to the forefront and, at the same time, made clearer the significance of labor and production as collective tasks. But the mainstream Marxist alternative, reflecting an outmoded materialist and teleological reading of history, entailed a conception of present possibilities and priorities that seemed ever more misguided. Although differences in class interests were real and unavoidable, they did not simply pit proletariat against bourgeoisie but were much more diverse and complex. Thus, as Bottai put it, the appropriate modern response was not Marxist class struggle but corporativist recognition and synthesis.[162] The priority at present, when nothing like the orthodox crisis of capitalism was on the horizon, was to manage class differences in a way that best served the longer-term public interest.

Moreover, industrial development in Italy had been blunted by political favoritism, fostered by the parliamentary system, so it was essential to refashion the relationship between the political and economic spheres. But if political revolution against liberalism was one priority, a broader cultural revolution was essential as well. Although Robert Wohl proposed "more and better-paid jobs" as a more realistic priority than the "spiritual revolution" so favored by the European generation of 1914, what must be grasped, from the Fascist perspective, is why the two went hand in hand.[163] "Spiritualizing" the economy, making production a collective ethical act, was the key—an idealist, post-materialist key—to improved economic well-being.

It is too simple, then, to dismiss Fascist corporativism as merely reactionary, intended to head off "emancipation" or to serve business interests. The Fascist state was to rest on a new relationship with sometimes conflicting social interests, recognizing their legitimacy as modern, built into the industrial system, and potentially productive. But to harmonize them for the collective interest required a post-liberal framework in which their conflicts would no longer be settled in private but by labor judges within the state, as a matter of law. Collective labor contracts, left as merely private arrangements under liberalism, would become legally binding, enforced by the state. This arrangement would better protect the workers, who, under the agnostic liberal dispensation, had often seen newly won gains eroded as employers violated labor accords as soon as they felt strong enough.[164]

At the same time, the workers were to be organized into mandatory Fascist unions that were then to be brought into the state as public institutions. With the turn to full-scale corporativism, all factors of production were to be organized into comparable bodies that would exercise the expanded sovereignty of the state in governing the economy. Political representation itself would have a corporativist basis, and indeed the Chamber of Fasces and Corporations replaced the old Chamber of Deputies early in 1939. Meanwhile, the new economically based groupings would play the same broadly politicizing role that had attracted the earlier syndicalists to the trade unions. Now within the framework of a post-liberal, totalitarian state, such organizations could still nurture post-bourgeois virtues, even the human ethical capacity trumpeted by Gentile, and channel those virtues for collective action. Economic activity was a social function, and production, now not merely politicized but "spiritualized" through infusion with ethical capacity, was the central collective task.

Although up to a point it is fair to speak of a Nationalist–syndicalist synthesis at the root of Fascist corporativism, we must beware of the assumption of homogeneity that we find in Sternhell and to a lesser extent even in Emilio Gentile. The syndicalists and the Nationalists had each stressed the significance of trade unions as products of industrial society that potentially, at least, could nurture a new ethical-political consciousness through the economic roles of individuals. But in Chapter 4 we noted, in a preliminary way, certain differences in Nationalist and syndicalist perspectives, and even as they shared a totalitarian corporativist direction, they differed in conceiving the purpose and functioning of the new institutions. Although both envisioned expanding the sovereignty of the state to encompass the unions and the whole sphere of production, and although both had long advocated, for example, a labor magistracy to settle labor conflicts, the two currents differed over the nature of the participation that would become possible through the newly politicized economy.

For the Nationalist Rocco, corporativism was, most obviously, a means of disciplining the unions, but ultimately also of mobilizing and regimenting Italians for production—and eventually imperialism. Important younger Fascists like Carlo Costamagna similarly emphasized authority, discipline, hierarchy, and coordination from above, but the direction suggested by the *Carta del Carnaro*, the proto-corporativist constitution that the veteran syndicalists De Ambris and Olivetti had drafted in 1920 for D'Annunzio's regime at Fiume, insisted on the scope for participation and initiative from below. As Fascists, veteran syndicalists like Panunzio and Olivetti portrayed corporativism as a system for enhancing popular political capacity through more constant and direct involvement in public life. Mosca and Pareto had shown that, despite the rhetoric of popular sovereignty, politics had remained elitist and exploitative under the liberal parliamentary system. But it was possible to do better by politicizing the workplace and expanding state sovereignty, diffusing political decision making into economically based groupings developed from the trade unions that had attracted the syndicalists in the first place. For the syndicalists, then, corporativism afforded at once an alternative venue for political participation and a new institutional framework for addressing concrete socio-economic problems.

Although this "leftist" understanding of corporativism was overtly totalitarian, bound up with expanded state sovereignty and the mandatory politicization of economic roles, the conception did not entail Rocco's rigidly authoritarian top-down coordination. The system demanded the participation of all producers in institutions that would enjoy greater autonomy than Rocco envisioned and that would make substantive decisions as, exercising the expanded power of the state, they carried out this self-regulation of the economy. Rather than producing automatons, totalitarian corporativism would invite and expect autonomous individual decision and initiative, just as had the unions in the original syndicalist vision. But the overall accent was on *collective* action; individuals were to experience their initiative and participation as serving the nation's productive enterprise.

Differences in conceptions of Fascist corporativism, reflecting especially the disparity in the Nationalist and syndicalist origins, suggested the scope for tensions in practice. And significant debates in print, such as the notable exchange between Panunzio and Costamagna in 1926, made the underlying tensions clear.[165] Even among those who did not share Rocco's top-down vision, differences over what politicization could and should entail introduced some further tensions and ambiguities. Although the syndicalists consistently spoke of promoting the economic sphere to the political level, their emphasis on technical competence meshed uncertainly with the Gentilian accent on ethical capacity.[166] What was to be the respective role of each in practice was not clear.

Yet Bottai, the most authoritative corporativist spokesman, sought mightily to synthesize Gentilian and neo-syndicalist themes. Bottai came from a republican family, was wounded and decorated as a member of the elite *arditi* during the war, then was active in republican circles before turning to Fascism in 1919, helping to organize the Rome *fascio*.[167] He rose quickly to become minister of corporations, and even after he was removed as part of wider shake-up in the top Fascist leadership in 1932, he remained the leading corporativist advocate. Indeed, he continued to influence the self-understanding and direction of Fascism in a variety of roles, from editor of *Critica fascista* to minister of education. In De Felice's judgment, he proved second only to Mussolini in his impact on the substance of Fascism over the long term.[168]

As corporativist spokesman, Bottai periodically criticized the International Labor Office in Geneva for its sometimes skeptical, if not hostile, attitude to the Fascist social experiment. In 1929, for example, he charged that the Geneva body, with its international labor charter, was proving the merely "conservative" tool of the liberal democracies; it was thus unable to grasp the significance of Italian innovations in the realm of labor relations. Nevertheless, Bottai deemed it worthwhile for the Italians to go to Geneva to make their case. With its social and trade union experience now the most advanced in the world, Italy, he claimed, was prepared to make a unique contribution to the office's international conferences.[169] Indeed, with its own new Labor Charter and its emerging corporative state, Fascist Italy was out in front in the new, multinational effort to secure workers' rights. Making explicit comparisons, Bottai went into great detail to show how Italian corporativism best served the needs of workers.[170]

In his many speeches and writings, Bottai also stressed the wider significance of corporativism in light of the sense, evident in the vogue of Spengler, for example, that Europe was suffering an unprecedented spiritual crisis, reflecting corrosive doubt about the old truths, especially the notions of liberty and the individual that had grown from the French Revolution.[171] Fascism, especially through corporativism, provided the essential new idea force for the world because, with the values of spirit now determining material forces, it was developing the essential fresh approaches to concrete economic and political matters. In this context, Bottai offered the standard corporativist mantra: Fascism was at once elevating the economic to the political level and making the political concrete by expanding its socio-economic content.[172] So for all his emphasis on spirit, Bottai consistently insisted on the concreteness of the participation that corporativism, as opposed to liberal capitalism, made possible. Within the expanded state, the workers were no longer passive but were being educated for active collaboration with the employers in confronting concrete socio-economic issues, from the organization of single branches of production to international tariff policy.[173]

For Bottai, corporativism was the natural extension of the trade unionism that had emerged in reaction to the atomizing individualism of liberalism. The unions manifested the wider modern tendency through which associations were replacing individuals as the basis of society.[174] In embracing this tendency, Fascism was not denying individuality but treating the individual more realistically, as part of a complex of social relations and as performing a social role, bound up with the collective action, encompassing production most fundamentally, through which the society goes on recreating itself in history. Labor was not merely material activity but moral, a social duty, and the most basic mode through which the individual participates in the great and endless task of constructing the collective life. That effort obviously transcends the individual, who brings his contribution and then disappears. In a sense, then, to move from liberalism to Fascism was to move from "economic man" to "historical man," who helps to create the collective future as he brings his moral-communitarian potential to bear through participation in the politicized economy.[175]

Although Bottai proclaimed corporativism to be universal in the same sense that liberalism had been, it had to be adapted to particular contexts.[176] Reflecting the new historical sense, allowing no scope for logical blueprints or pure science, he stressed that even the pioneering Italian departure was an open-ended experiment. Thus the relationships between the individual firm, the union (*sindacato*), the corporation, and the state could not be fixed definitively. And thus he stressed the need for ongoing debate over these issues. And such debate was indeed forthcoming, as during the much discussed Second Conference on Corporativism held in Ferrara in May 1932. To credit Bottai's statement to the conference, as part of his insistence on the need for free debate, that there had been no prior pressure on the speakers may betray the dreaded pitfall of taking Fascism at face value. But this conference undeniably saw a lively discussion, with genuine disagreements over substantive issues.[177] More specifically, the centrality of the Gentilian Ugo Spirito's proposal for proprietary corporations, to be discussed below, indicates the scope for offering novel and controversial ideas—as long as a certain common framework was accepted.

That framework was the unquestioned assumption that Fascism was in the process of grandiose achievement through the construction of the totalitarian corporativist state. But, as we will see, the disagreements that surfaced in 1932 reflected tensions, uncertainties, frustrations, and a wider fissuring tendency in light of the effort actually to implement corporativist ideas. And the need to surround any idea with ritualistic praise of grandiose corporativist achievement soon bred myth making. Moreover, although corporativism was to make the totalitarian ideal concrete, even "the corporative state" might prove more an ideal direction than a set of institutions, in light of the stress on openness and experiment. So before considering the place of corporativism in the actual dynamic of the regime, we must revisit the Fascist use of myth.

Even if the intent was not mere manipulation from above to serve power and interests, what mode of participation becomes possible if collective action is shot through with myth? Although even Emilio Gentile occasionally implied that myth was a consciously chosen tool, he went well beyond Sternhell in recognizing its more complex place in a wider, more innovative totalitarian mix.[178] And whereas for Sternhell myth was integral to the finished "ideology of Fascism" in place by 1922 but then blunted through compromise with existing elites, Gentile found myth to be central to practice as the regime, in its open-ended, experimental way, actually sought to begin to realize the totalitarian myth by more fully integrating the masses into the state.

For Gentile, the "new state," as totalitarian, was itself the dominant myth of Fascism after 1922—a notion that surely makes sense up to a point.[179] But how did that myth mesh with the effort to realize the new state by actually building new institutions, especially corporativist institutions, putatively the core of the new state? Even as they talked explicitly in terms of myths, early Fascists like Dino Grandi made it clear that the new mode of action at issue had to entail concrete institutional change, that mere mobilization through myth was not suffi-cient.[180] To be sure, the Fascists eschewed blueprints and emphasized experiment, but in light of myth's connotation of unreality or a-rationalism, and in light of longstanding assumptions about Fascist irrational activism, Gentile's repeated reference to Fascist goals or even images as "myths" breeds confusion about content.[181] Partly because he devoted so little attention to corporativism, his emphasis suggested that Fascism could cohere as myth and succeed on the level of sacralization even if the new state remained a mere image and the new participation proved merely ritualistic. But the effort actually to construct a new state reflected substance, and it mattered—it mattered decisively—what resulted on the level of concrete institutions and procedures. In fact, outcomes on that level stimulated further response that fundamentally affected the overall trajectory of the regime, including the place of myth within it.

Trumpeting Fascism in 1924, Camillo Pellizzi offered an especially telling example of the early Fascist embrace of myth, linked precisely to the quest for a new state. He was seeking to articulate a new vision of things that he clearly shared, including the scope for grandiose, unprecedented accomplishment as Fascism forged a mode of collective action for open-ended history making. That instrument was the new Fascist state, and although the term was not yet in wide use, it could only be "totalitarian." When we work for history and not for ourselves, said Pellizzi, there is no end of the discipline, no limit to what we may be called upon to do.[182]

At the same time, Pellizzi recognized a tension in the Fascist effort to reconceive the *state* as the instrument for the action required. Precisely because of their privileged sense of open-endedness, he said, the Fascists were loath to have Fascism institutionalized in the state, understood as a static juridical-bureaucratic entity. However, this danger did not lead Pellizzi to privilege the party as the embodiment of the essential ongoing dynamism. Rather, the key was to reconceive the state in a certain way. Although the bourgeois mentality would not be able to grasp it, the Fascist state was constantly transcending the static juridical-bureaucratic mode because, precisely as the instrument of collective history making, the Fascist state was a creative dynamism without preset limits—and thus forever incomplete.[183] Echoing Giovanni Gentile, Pellizzi insisted that the new state was constantly being recreated as collective ethical response welled up in response to historically specific challenges.[184] In our purely historical world, said Pellizzi, even laws are mere hieroglyphs in the sand.

In this sense, the Fascist ethical state could only be a myth and thus, Pellizzi admitted, difficult to describe. But it was still "a concrete principle of action in action, of action historically valid and vast."[185] To claim that it was "historically valid" was to insist that the direction was not just adventurist activism but was based precisely on a new, rational and empirically grounded understanding of the human place in history. The Italian idealist tradition had shown the way beyond the mentalities of Marxism and liberalism, which Pellizzi deemed comparable in reducing the state to the economic level, to the interests of individual monads. As heir to the idealist tradition, Fascism was overcoming liberalism in constituting itself precisely as the instrument, the form of state, necessary for the endless, ethically grounded collective remaking of the world in history.[186] In light of openness, the new state could never be fully realized as an empirical institution but was a kind of ideal, or myth—but myth as operative in a particular way.

Pellizzi's testimony suggests that the Fascists were not merely manipulating the masses on a "rational," means–ends basis but knew themselves to be caught up in precisely the myths they sought to foster. Myth was central to the essential new modes of interaction and collective action. As the regime evolved, however, this sense of the positive role of myth proved to invite further, and quite different, modes of myth making—modes that the Fascists themselves were especially unlikely to recognize precisely because they had lucidly embraced myth in a different sense earlier on.

Underlying this whole combination of impulses was the sense that Italy, through Fascism, was uniquely marshalling the will and power for ongoing innovation—and thereby assuming the modern lead. In fostering a sense of new possibility, the Fascist context itself encouraged modernizing aspiration. Thus, for example, the engineer Ciocca was clearly energized by the kind of innovation the regime seemed to be spearheading, although his diverse projects did not always win political support. As he wrote in 1937, "the true miracle is that of fascist Italy, which has gathered together all the nation's active energies. . . . No one who cares deeply about the nation's greatness finds himself isolated. His voice is echoed by other voices in other domains; his energy is fed by their energy. . . . This is the true innovation that today's Italy represents."[187]

The attempt at totalitarian collective action

Although the extent is obviously difficult to gauge and impossible to quantify, and although there is much further research to be done, we increasingly recognize that the Fascist enterprise, with its claim to world-historical importance, succeeded in winning some measure of identification among ordinary Italians.[188] A number of them seem genuinely to have experienced mass politics in "sacralized" terms as never before. The *Mostra della rivoluzione fascista* (Exhibition of the Fascist Revolution) of 1932, commemorating the tenth anniversary of the coming of Fascism to power, elicited pride and enthusiasm. A number of soldiers' letters home during the Second World War suggest a genuine sense of commitment to duty based on the Fascist sense that "life is a mission." Even in the face of defeat, some died on the battlefield with their Fascist faith intact.[189]

But on the level that ultimately mattered, Fascism surely failed, and not only in immediate military terms. As Mussolini admitted in a well-known lament to an old leftist colleague, Ottavio Dinale, in 1943, the regime had not created a totalitarian order or a Fascist nation.[190] Even by the early 1930s the overall effort was encountering frustration, a sense of blunting and impasse. Achievement constantly fell short of the grandiose rhetoric that surrounded every initiative. Partly because of funding limitations, even the new welfare legislation was generally poorly implemented or enforced; thus its actual impact proved limited.[191] At the same time, the regime recognized by 1938 the failure of the demographic campaign; birth and marriage rates had continued to fall over the decade.[192] However, most problematic was not the outcome of this or that initiative as the state expanded its reach but the new mode of collective action itself.

We noted that even as the Fascists agreed about the third-way totalitarian direction, certain emphases differed from the start, and those differences intensified especially as, moving into the effort of positive reconstruction, Fascism encountered questions about differentiation, hierarchy, individuation, and the scope for initiative from below. So quite apart from the inevitable personal rivalries and careerism, the very effort to act added layers of fissuring and scapegoating in light of unanticipated difficulties and unintended outcomes.

This phenomenon was central to the dynamic that resulted from the fascist effort at great politics. To place Italian Fascism in light of the experience of the other two interwar regimes, the key is to get at the nature of that dynamic, assessing its "totalitarian" quality. Although Emilio Gentile's accent on the ongoing three-way interaction between Duce, party, and Fascist state was an essential advance over earlier approaches, and although it still affords a useful start, his way of actually using this framework leaves questions about the meaning of the phenomena at issue and does not always seem to make the best sense of the evidence. Certainly, the totalitarian effort remained ongoing, just as Gentile insisted, but despite his stress on the three-way interaction, he tended to leave the thrust too static and homogeneous. To cut deeper, we must be prepared to recognize that as the Fascists encountered frustration in practice, the very nature of the process changed, as did the proportions of the elements at issue, so that an effort that began as one kind of thing ended up as another.

In the same way, Ben-Ghiat's delineation of the frustrations among youthful enthusiasts and the fissures and uncertainties that opened as they criticized the practice of the regime by the early 1930s remains invaluable, but even her own evidence suggests that these debilitating outcomes stemmed less from ambivalence about modernity than from the difficulties encountered in this new effort at collective action. So we require greater attention to the dynamic that resulted from the effort to act in light of the originating totalitarian aspirations.

To emphasize fissuring on the level of substance may seem to confirm culturalists like Schnapp and Berezin, who suggest that totalitarian coherence lay on the level of style. Up to a point, their emphases convince. In light of the tensions emerging from the "underlying" layer of substance, the combination of style, symbol, and ritual afforded some measure of coherence within the wider dynamic. But it is precisely that wider dynamic that these culturalists tend to miss, because, having neglected "ideology" and ideas, they eschewed serious engagement with the originating substance. Thus they could not make sense of the changing meaning of the stylistic elements they emphasized.

Committed Fascists agreed on the centrality of a new education, with the state not agnostic but responsible for using the educational system to promote Fascist values. But starting with Gentile's reform bill of 1923, the effort to create the appropriate system provoked endless controversy over the specifics—the role of religion, for example, or how traditionally humanistic, as opposed to newly technical, a Fascist education should be. Stressing humanistic training, with philosophy as the capstone, the Gentilians traced the technical emphases of some of their opponents to the aims of big business, which needed to be headed off.[193] However, others found the technical direction needed to move from empty liberal politics into concrete productivism. Each had a point, but the tension was obvious—and debilitating. During 1935–36, precisely the period of the Ethiopian turn, Gentile was highly critical of new education minister Cesare Maria De Vecchi's emphasis on authority and discipline at the expense of freedom of thought in the Italian educational system.[194]

Also at issue was how restricted or open a specifically Fascist educational system was to be. The Gentile reform of 1923 had made higher education more demanding and meritocratic—and thus, some charged, more elitist. This direction has even been explained away in reductionist terms, as if the purpose was to respond to professional unemployment by reducing the number qualified for jobs in government or the professions.[195] Certainly, aspiring university students and their parents disliked the emphasis on more rigorous selection.[196] At issue was simply a dilemma that was bound to produce controversy and resentment as the regime sought to maximize the nation's potential by at once educating a new governing class and educating all Italians to participate in the new totalitarian state.

Some of the more restrictive features of Gentile's reform began to be jettisoned almost immediately. As education minister from 1936 to 1943, Giuseppe Bottai, himself a Gentilian in important respects, engineered further changes, as codified in his educational charter (*Carta della Scuola*) of 1939. Although it left the classical core of the Gentile system intact, this document sought to break with the apparently elitist elements of the Gentile reform by adding even an element of manual labor to the curriculum. Yet the new program also sought to enhance peasant attachment to the land, and it too sought to shift students into technical training institutes to ease pressures on white-collar employment.

The dilemmas of education reform contributed to wider frustration among educated young people as a new generation came of age by the early 1930s. Committed veteran Fascists like Camillo Pellizzi and Massimo Bontempelli were warning that the gap between rhetoric and reality threatened to alienate the brightest of the new generation.[197] Seeking to keep alive Fascism's revolutionary and totalitarian aim, and still allowing a modicum of free discussion and criticism from within the Fascist framework, the government authorized publication of an array of new independent reviews during the early 1930s, including *Saggiatore* (1930–33), *Orpheus* (1932–34), and *L'Universale* (1931–35). As Ben-Ghiat has shown, the young intellectuals around these journals took seriously the radicalism of Fascist claims and ideals, but they found the regime too beholden to compromise and normalizing imperatives in practice.[198] Such frustration grew especially as the Depression and the anomalies of the Stalinist departure in the Soviet Union reinforced the sense that Fascist Italy had the potential to create something of universal value.

But under the circumstances, even normal generational rebellion proved particularly debilitating as younger Fascists vented their frustration with the halting outcomes of the revolution so far.[199] Some, like Gastone Silvano Spinetti and Enzo Paci, began denouncing Gentile's continuing predominance and called for a cultural revolution to curtail the influence of all those with ties to the liberal era.[200] Although he remained active, even intensifying his efforts at cultural hegemony, Gentile found himself forced onto the defensive.[201] A number of critics found Gentilian idealism too far removed from Italy's Catholic traditions. But in accusing Gentile of abstraction and metaphysics, in insisting that Fascism was about action as opposed to principles, younger intellectuals often misconstrued Gentile's thinking, which arguably remained essential to the Fascist self-understanding as "spiritual," even as "totalitarian" in a way superior to the two competing regimes. Insofar as the quest for renewal seemed to require assault on Gentile, the young dissidents were diluting an important part of the original fuel. Still, for all the anti-Gentilian reaction of the early 1930s, Gentilian themes remained central to many of those seeking to reanimate the revolution even into the early 1940s.

So it was not as if the generational differentiation proved decisive. Rather, it simply added another axis of fissuring as young Fascists seeking revitalization disagreed, for example, over internationalism versus autarky and over whether the depersonalization of mass society was to be fostered or resisted.[202] Ben-Ghiat concluded that most continued to value individual agency and humanistic traditions in opposition to modern tendencies toward leveling, but the effort to combine individuality, differentiation, group action, productivism, and selected humanistic traditions was bound to produce uncertainty and disagreement.

Surrounded by both internal criticism and much grandiose rhetoric, concrete corporativist development continued into the 1940s, and it was not just the theory but also the practice that attracted the interest of outsiders. A good example was the British economist Paul Einzig, who offered a book on fascist corporativism shortly after a trip to Italy late in 1932 for an international conference on monetary policy and currency reform. While in Italy, he had occasion to meet and discuss corporativism with both Mussolini and Bottai. Introducing his book, published just after Hitler became chancellor early in 1933, Einzig stressed that as an apolitical expert on monetary policy, he had gone to Italy with an open mind.[203] But he came away full of admiration for the discipline and cooperation that Fascist corporativism seemed to have produced. As he saw it, corporativism uniquely opened the way to a modern economic system combining scientific management with individual initiative. Under the postliberal corporativist framework, class differences would gradually diminish in importance. On the immediate level, Einzig found corporativism to promise precisely the economic planning and coordination that were essential before international currency reforms could work.

Even as he lauded corporativism, Einzig vehemently denigrated Nazi Germany, which, he insisted, had so far proved merely barbarous, with nothing of the constructive spirit of Italian Fascism. Unfortunately, the Nazi departure in Germany had tended to discredit fascism in general in British public opinion. Italian Fascist corporativism needed to be examined on its own terms.

Quite apart from the views of such outsiders looking in, there is evidence that even younger workers, who might have been particularly skeptical or hostile, developed some confidence in the system during the 1930s. De Felice noted that the trade union layer experienced a measure of revitalization during the first half of the decade, after the *sbloccamento* of 1928 had seemed to compromise the capacity of the Fascist unions to defend immediate working-class interests. By the late 1930s, in fact, identification with the regime more generally was growing on the part of younger workers, who tended to believe its pro-labor and anti-capitalist proclamations.[204] Still, this issue remains particularly sensitive and controversial. Others, like Tobias Abse, stress ongoing diffidence among the workers, reflecting at least tacit opposition and resistance.[205]

But although the Fascist claim to offer a third way through corporativism retained a measure of plausibility into the 1930s, in the last analysis, no one claims that corporativism succeeded in its aim of fostering a new mode of participation while politicizing the workplace. By the early 1930s, an array of committed Fascists, including the second generation featured by Ben-Ghiat, had become sharply and openly critical of the developing corporativist institutions, which tended to function in a top-down way, precluding autonomy and initiative.[206] Although it politicized the workplace in a superficial sense, the new system afforded little scope for substantive, deliberative discussion, so it proved limited at best as a vehicle of participation. Even the workers' representatives were not genuinely representative. Although the wider Fascist context of experiment surely facilitated them, some of Fascism's major economic innovations of the 1930s, such as the creation of the Istituto per la ricostruzione industriale (Institute for Industrial Reconstruction, or IRI), were pragmatic responses to the Depression, not specifically corporativist.[207]

So whereas Fascist corporativists plausibly stressed open-endedness and experiment, their effort proved unsuccessful. They encountered four levels of difficulty. First, and most basically, the regime's wider compromise with pre-Fascist elites maintained the influence of both the business leadership and the traditional bureaucracy, each of which sought to preserve its prerogatives in the face of corporativist aspirations. Although business was forced into a cat-and-mouse game with the regime, the business community generally managed to avoid the political coordination that totalitarian corporativists envisioned. And certainly business could flex its muscle on occasion; business lobbying got Bottai removed as minister of corporations in 1932—although, typically, Bottai was not out of favor for long, and corporativist development continued.[208]

But, reaching the second level of difficulty, even insofar as we focus exclusively on committed Fascists and what was putatively totalitarian implementation, practice brought institutional ambiguities and rivalries to the fore. In principle, corporativist development did not have to be antagonistic to the party's role; the two could be complementary. As party leader, Augusto Turati had fully supported corporativism as essential to bringing the masses, including especially the workers, into the state, not least because working-class support seemed to be essential if the regime was to break from compromise with traditional elites.[209] But rivalry and antagonism inevitably developed as the grandiose new mode of action met frustration. Seeking to cement and expand its influence, the party interfered with the corporativist institutions, compromising their autonomy and initiative. Writing shortly after the fall of the regime, Bottai charged that the party, with its lack of vigor and elephantine bureaucracy, had suffocated the innovative spirit and potential of the new corporativist institutions, serving the transformation of Fascism into mere Mussolinianism.[210]

But Bottai was merely scapegoating in one sense, because it is not clear how well those institutions could have worked in any case, in light of tensions we noted in the original corporativist vision. The third problem was that Fascists had different, even incompatible reasons for embracing corporativism, as some stressed discipline and hierarchy, others, genuine collaboration and initiative from below. Thus, especially, the debilitating ambiguity and pulling and tugging as corporativist institutions developed. Seeking to avoid exclusive identification with any one faction, Mussolini tended to balance both personnel and innovations in order to foster a façade of consensus and openness.[211] During the formative period beginning in 1925, Rocco was made minister of justice, and he put his particular stamp on the legislation constructing the new state. Giovanni Gentile was bitter that Rocco seemed to determine the immediate outcome of the corporativist direction.[212] But Bottai immediately became the dominant figure in the ministry of corporations, and the Labor Charter of 1927 was an effort at compromise in which Bottai and Rocco each had a hand. In the preparation of the document, Mussolini himself was instrumental in seeking to placate veteran syndicalists and to check Rocco's influence.[213] Although there was much shifting of personnel thereafter, there were no definitive victors, but the underlying ambiguity and fluidity inevitably blunted the corporativist thrust.

But, reaching the fourth level of difficulty, the effort to implement the corporativist vision made it clear that even those who disliked the Nationalist emphasis on discipline and hierarchy were not all on the same page. Symptomatic was the controversy over Ugo Spirito's proposal for "proprietary corporations," offered at the second conference of syndical and corporative studies, held in Ferrara under Ministry of Corporations sponsorship in May 1932.[214]

Spirito wanted the corporations actually to own and operate businesses, thereby, among other things, rendering the class-based syndical or trade union layer of the corporativist system superfluous. Yet Panunzio, endorsed by the union leader Mario Racheli—like Panunzio a veteran syndicalist—accused Spirito of falling into economic reductionism. The corporation was a political entity that was to order the economic sphere through law, not carry out economic activity. The issue of ownership was secondary. Criticizing from a different angle, Bottai insisted that the class-based syndical layer, which had a fundamental, ongoing value in moralizing and thereby disciplining the individual, remained an essential aspect of corporativism.[215] Spirito, in contrast, envisioned jump-starting the semi-stalled corporativist vehicle by transcending class altogether from within the totalitarian corporativist framework.

More generally, with the issue of quality of participation very much on the table, the Spirito controversy reflected the deeper ambiguity regarding the relationship between technical-economic and ethical-political capacities that we have encountered at several points. As we noted, Bottai insisted that both came into play as the producers themselves came to determine the direction of economic life, but the oft-repeated formula—that Fascism, through corporativism, was at once elevating the material sphere and making the political concrete—glossed over tensions, ambiguities, and differences in accent that proved increasingly debilitating in practice.

Fascist corporativism retained some of the earlier syndicalist anti-political vision of a society of producers governing itself without "politics," understood in the parliamentary sense and taken as inherently self-serving and short-sighted. In the new Fascist state, based on economically based groupings, political participation was to grow from economic roles as producers. When Bottai claimed in Geneva in 1932 that thanks to Fascist corporativism Italian workers were fully involved in the resolution of the great problems of the day, the examples he cited, such as tariff policy, reflected a wider sense that political issues were on some level technical—or at least that such socio-economic problems were the central ones the polity had to address at present. Yet Giovanni Gentile, even as he embraced corporativism, criticized any emphasis on technical expertise or economic interest at the expense of the primary ethical capacity of individuals, to be realized in and through the totalitarian state. So whereas it was surely possible to transcend both liberal and Marxist thinking about the political–economic relationship, the element of ambiguity and potential tension produced a tendency even among Fascists with relatively "populist" leanings to rely on generalities, glossing over uncertainties about participation.

Although there was some waning of enthusiasm as corporativism seemed to bog down, the struggle continued, as did the institutional innovations. But even as the whole array from old syndicalists to second-generation enthusiasts criticized actual practice, frustration itself fed inflated rhetoric, which, in turn, impeded sober evaluation. At the same time, the tendency toward scapegoating, evident, for example, in Bottai's way of blaming the party, was bound to weaken the whole ongoing Fascist experiment.

The most significant of the fissures within Fascism stemmed from disagreement over the place of the Fascist Party in an ongoing revolution still putatively centered on the totalitarian corporative state. To grasp the nature and significance of this fissure requires that we back up to our wider frame, for, as we have seen, uncertainty about the criteria and the institutional locus of Fascist radicalism has long complicated efforts to understand the fascist dynamic, just as it earlier proved debilitating for the Fascists themselves. First, the longstanding tendency to link radicalism to the legacy of *squadrismo* and early provincial Fascism continues to throw us off. Even as they insisted on the enduring significance of the Italian war experience, some who had been *squadrisiti* did not find *squadrismo* the core of radical, totalitarian Fascism. Some who endorsed or indulged in violence early on found it counterproductive later.[216] Those pushing for radical tactics or what seemed a radical direction at various times are not readily differentiated with reference to a single axis. For example, Curzio Suckert was among the most vociferous of those who demanded, in light of the Matteotti crisis, a decisive step beyond legalitarian compromise. Writing in December

1924, he stressed that Mussolini was no more than a servant of the revolution like every other Fascist.[217] But looking back with satisfaction a year later, when Fascism seemed to have turned the revolutionary corner, he found the outcome the triumph not of the *squadristi* or the party but of proto-corporativism, as advocated by Panunzio.[218] Despite his heroic war record, Giuseppe Bottai was "moderate" according to some criteria, although in several major roles he pushed for ongoing revolution.

As in the Soviet and Nazi regimes, there was room on the first level for disagreement, and experiment, over how new tasks were to be apportioned between state and party. Despite the claims of various proponents at the time, the answer was not in itself the determining criterion of "totalitarianism." And in all three regimes there were personal and institutional rivalries, careers to make, but the Italian case was especially complex and fluid. At various points, some suggested that, with the framework of the new Fascist state now in place, the party had completed its task and was expendable. As early as 1923, the former syndicalist Massimo Rocca foresaw the rapid dissolution of the party as the Fascist revolution found its institutional outcome in productivist *gruppi di competenza*, groups based on technical expertise.

Emilio Gentile noted a constant tension between authoritarian Fascism, seeing the system realized during 1925–29, and totalitarian Fascism, insisting that the revolutionary process was ongoing, having so far reached only its first stage in this period necessitated by compromise. Some such differentiation between authoritarian and totalitarian Fascism was surely at work, but drawing the lines and characterizing the interface is tricky. Gentile was too quick to conflate those playing down the role of the party with those who were merely authoritarian and who thought the revolution essentially finished. Although for decades some students of the interwar regimes have assumed that to emphasize the state at the expense of the party was to favor static, authoritarian institutions as opposed to an ongoing revolutionary dynamic, those Fascists who downplayed the role of the party were not necessarily less radical or totalitarian.

Assessing Giovanni Gentile's willingness to dispense with the party by 1928, Emilio Gentile found him to be converging with the Nationalists, despite certain ongoing ideological differences. The key at this point was that each, believing that Fascism as a movement and party had exhausted its function, was settling for generic patriotism within the new authoritarian state.[219] But this suggestion meshed uneasily with Emilio Gentile's accent on the ongoing significance of the categories that Giovanni Gentile had elaborated as the "first theologian" of Fascism's totalitarian religion.

However, this is not to suggest that Giovanni Gentile adequately assessed the significance of the factors in play in the ongoing totalitarian effort. Especially in light of the pre-Fascist holdovers in Italy, it was surely plausible to believe that an active, autonomous role for the Fascist Party remained essential if a fully post-liberal order was to be to created. As Emilio Gentile emphasized, the party did not have to take over the state on the immediate level as long as it had the substantive educational and mobilizing role that would enable it to create a new culture—and thus the foundation for new institutions in the future. The priority was to endure, to keep up the pressure, and thereby gradually to proceed toward, in Emilio Gentile's terms, the realization of the totalitarian myth.[220] And, as we noted above, Gentile showed that the party expanded its role in significant ways as the regime developed.

Although any assessment of the scope for ongoing revolution must encompass the actual and potential role of the party, Gentile was prone to overreact against the longstanding denigration of the party and to associate ongoing totalitarian radicalism with the fortunes of the party *as opposed to* the state. But not only could the party itself not embody totalitarian fulfillment, it could not be totalitarian against the state; it could only claim to embody the totalitarian ideal, to be realized in the totalitarian state. Even as he stressed appropriately that this was a *Fascist* state, and even as the "myth of the new state" remained central to his account, Gentile did not do justice to the "state" part of the Duce–party–state trinity. To characterize the dynamic requires a deeper sense of what was to have made this a *Fascist* state, but also a clearer sense of what was or was not being realized, in light of the underlying totalitarian aspiration. These in turn require a fuller grasp of Giovanni Gentilian categories and a greater attention to corporativism than we find in Emilio Gentile's account.

In positing his influential movement/regime distinction, De Felice had assigned corporativism, which in its early "D'Annunzian" guise he found potentially revolutionary, to the movement. But as the movement was marginalized with the triumph of the regime, corporativism was reduced to a mere administrative instrument lacking the importance that the movement had given it.[221] Gentile convincingly challenged De Felice's marginalization of the movement–party, but somehow that challenge did not lead him to reassess the place of corporativism, which, as we have noted, received very little attention in his later works.

In fact, De Felice's dualistic distinction can only mislead with respect to the place of the corporativist thrust. We saw that the proto-corporativism of the D'Annunzian Carta del Carnaro was crucial for young provincial Fascist leaders like Dino Grandi, Piero Marsich, and Italo Balbo as they spearheaded the challenge to Mussolini in 1921, but it was not associated with Farinacci-style fascism—and certainly was not marginalized because of the direction of the leader–party relationship with, for example, the ouster of Farinacci as chief leader in 1926. On the contrary, with the partial subordination of the party, corporativism became central to the effort to build a post-liberal state. So insofar as the party was being subordinated to the state, it was a state being reconstituted not just on a Fascist basis, as Gentile emphasized, but on a corporativist basis.

Gentile's accent on the party reinforced his tendency to portray the revolutionary totalitarian thrust as relatively homogeneous, unified, and stable and to gloss over the sources and implications of certain ongoing differences of emphasis. To be sure, the *regime*, developing through the three-way interaction, was anything but homogeneous in Gentile's account, and he had plenty of room for ongoing controversy and contest, even over what continuing revolution might mean. But as Gentile had it, the dynamic stemming from the effort of totalitarian implementation was homogeneous in the sense that, given the logic of the Fascist religious vision, the same kind of thing kept happening throughout the course of the experiment.[222]

In fact, the party's claim to embody the innovative substance of Fascism made it enemies not only among those who thought the revolution complete or who wanted to return to normal. Corporativists like Bottai and many of those around his journal *Critica fascista* had long been hostile to or dubious about the *squadristi* legacy and the pretensions of the party. We noted that Bottai tended to blame party interference for the deficiencies of corporativism in practice. In the eyes of such critics, the party had come to represent not revolutionary vigor but careerist conformity and superficial, outward forms.

We also noted Camillo Pellizzi's insistence that Fascism could not be crystallized definitively in some static state. But this was not to play down the state and to play up the party instead as somehow the embodiment of Fascism's ongoing dynamism. Rather, the key was the construction of a new kind of state, understood in Giovanni Gentilian terms as itself dynamic, constantly to be recreated as opposed to fulfilled in some set of empirical institutions. The question is what the new state was to do, how it might continually be reanimated, how it would involve people, what modes of education, mobilization, and participation it was in fact to entail. In that light, Emilio Gentile was not sufficiently concerned with how the party's educational and mobilizing activity was to serve the construction of this sort of state. Indeed, his assertion that the party won the role it had wanted for itself after Farinacci, a role that afforded participation in the only way possible—entailing, by implication, a significant measure of "politicization *in a fascist sense* and . . . participation *in a totalitarian sense*"—proves slippery; it simply begs the essential questions about what was happening overall.

The party's role was necessarily bound up with wider changes in the regime's priorities during the 1930s. Although imperialist war was obviously a possible direction for Fascism, it was not inevitable, and the regime did not turn definitively toward it until the mid-1930s. As with corporativist policy, the initial fascist conception of international relations was bifurcated, similarly reflecting, most basically, generally Left/Right differences among the diverse Fascist components. The common assumption was the need for revision on the international level in light of differential population pressures and the differential distribution of colonial territories among the Western powers. The status quo was not just or sacrosanct.

Up to a point, such thinking was based on the "proletarian nation" argument pioneered by the Nationalist Enrico Corradini; it seemed especially germane after the First World War in light of Italian resentment of Britain and France as grand imperial powers who seemed hypocritically to be seeking to preserve or even extend their advantages while mouthing platitudes about international justice. But in light of their historical sense, the Fascists believed that the situation remained dynamic—or could be made dynamic through new action. Those coming from the syndicalist Left initially challenged the League of Nations to address Italian disadvantages by devising a more equitable allocation

324 *Conflicted totalitarianism in Fascist Italy*

of territories and resources.[223] To make Italy a more effective nation surely entailed an enhanced capacity to fight wars, but an accent on such capacity did not necessarily entail war as an ideal, essential to galvanize virtues; it did not necessarily entail a vision of perpetual antagonism between nations.

Especially as opportunities for emigration were being severely restricted during the 1920s, the Fascists were bound to rethink population policy priorities, although, as Luca de Caprariis has shown, even the meaning of "expansion" remained vague throughout the 1920s.[224] Insofar as imperialism was bound to be considered, it was widely held that the Italian Fascist version would be different, attuned to human values, partly because Italy, unlike Britain and France, would be seeking not simply to exploit colonial territories but to find land and work for emigrants.[225] But it was not clear during the 1920s what place a radically revisionist foreign policy might come to play in the Fascist mix. De Felice referred to "the Western foreign policy, which Mussolini followed at least until 1934, and which appeared to be a peaceful one."[226]

From that point, however, Mussolini began not only to emphasize international affairs but also to pursue a more aggressive policy, leading to imperial conquest in Ethiopia, intervention in the Spanish Civil War, alliance with Nazi Germany, and intervention in the Second World War. This fateful turn stemmed from the contingent interaction of two disparate provisional outcomes. On the one hand, Mussolini genuinely resented the pre-Fascist elites, who seemed to have ensnared him in a web of compromises on the domestic level. He worried that his regime was in danger of wearing down; it would not survive him.[227] So whereas Mussolini had been quite serious about corporativism as the core of the Fascist revolution, he was coming to recognize that the corporativist vision could only be realized down the road, by generations formed by Fascism. The immediate prerequisite was more seriously to fascistize society, which seemingly could best be done in tandem with a more aggressive foreign policy.[228] But what mode of fascistization was now possible?

In light of longer-term Italian territorial concerns and imperialist ambitions, the turn to foreign affairs raises wider questions about continuity and discontinuity. As we noted in Chapter 4, the war intensified concerns about "expansion," which was obviously one possible priority for Fascism. In probing the possibilities for expansion in the Adriatic and the Balkans, and in seeking to delimit the pre-Fascist diplomatic community, Mussolini, by the late 1920s, was already departing from tradition to some extent.[229] Yet on balance this was but one thrust as domestic reconstruction took center stage. And in light of the breadth of the Fascist enterprise, reflecting the overall sense of challenge and opportunity, it is too simple, too reductive and teleological, to view the turn to a certain mode of expansion, more clearly focused on living space (*spazio vitale*), as the revelation of some abiding essence, as if Mussolini was just waiting for the right opportunity. Conversely, it is surely not coincidental that this turn took place from within Fascism, with its accent on the scope for grandiose collective action.[230] But even as it radicalized Fascism in one sense, the new direction proved to narrow the overall Fascist enterprise, with its claim to offer a third way, an alternative modernity.

The turn toward imperialism took place from within a wider dynamic, already in progress under Fascist Party secretary Achille Starace, that included an increasing emphasis on style, ritual, spectacle, commemoration, and the cult of the Duce. Certain new cultural accents, as well as the intensification of others, attended the conquest of Ethiopia in 1935–36. Now the regime sought to root out the bourgeois mentality, including, for example, the "bourgeois" use of irony. At the same time, there was still-greater emphasis on ritual, increasingly bound up with military trappings, the cult of the Duce, and *Romanità*, the preoccupation with ancient Rome. War was a school of what now became the essential Fascist virtues; indeed, the Italians were learning to become hard-edged conquerors, masters.[231]

Much like Emilio Gentile, Mabel Berezin found something too facile about the longstanding tendency to delimit the cultural accents of the Starace era to a particular phase within Fascism, even to Starace personally, and thus to take them as less than totalitarian. Such accents were central to the whole Fascist project. Yet she also noted that it was only in the late 1930s that all the absurdities and cruelties that have contributed to the popular image of Fascism came to the fore.[232] But not having grasped what else was in the mix, Berezin could not make sense of the changing place of ritual and other stylistic dimensions. We need deeper distinctions between types of ritual and between the roles that ritual played at different points in the regime's evolution.

Even Emilio Gentile's treatment of the Starace era presents a contradictory pattern that leaves us uncertain regarding the place of the new cultural themes in the ongoing dynamic. That the party won the desired monopoly on commemoration and celebration indicated the success of Starace's effort, but Gentile recognized that the party tended to overuse them, compromising their seriousness. Rather than developing new energies, Fascist participation became more formal and mechanical, sometimes even ridiculous, reflecting the declining vitality not just of the party but of the whole regime. Gentile went on to note that Starace's dismissal in 1939 was widely applauded; Italians had grown tired of the rituals, the militaresque formalism, the petty party presence everywhere.[233] Recognizing, in 1941, that the regime had yet to form a totalitarian morality, Camillo Pellizzi insisted that its error had been precisely in relying on mere spectacle and propaganda as opposed to genuine education.[234]

So even as he insisted that we consider the new modes of politicization "*in a fascist sense*," Gentile's own researches suggested that Starace produced politicization only in a very particular "fascist sense," one that did not maintain, let alone realize, the potential of the originating vision. Despite his important insistence that "the theme of fascist religion is not to be summed up merely by its liturgical displays," and despite his reference to the production of "new men" ready to do the regime's bidding, Gentile tended to leave the "religious" experience merely in belonging, participating in more or less empty rituals. Indeed, he seemed to shift his ground, even to lapse into circularity, when he noted that "fascism's self-portrayal as a religion was not confined to its symbolism, to ritual and mythology; it was also useful as a means by which its institutions and its totalitarian ambitions could be made real."[235] This was to suggest that they could be made real precisely through its "self-portrayal as a religion," but that was a very limited and superficial realization of the original totalitarian aspiration.

Although ritual, spectacle, and rhetoric were important from the start, such dimensions could be more or less empty, depending on the wider purposes, on what else was in the mix, and in what proportions. When the construction of a specifically Fascist state began in earnest, the ritualistic dimension quickly wound around that grandiose project, which, with its idealist and corporativist core, seemed to entail real venture and experiment. As this thrust blunted, the stylistic dimension became more central, even tended to take on a life of its own, as if ritual and spectacle sufficed as post-liberal participation. At best, politicization tended to become mere subordination of the individual to the regime, producing a certain mode of availability, as opposed to focusing ethical capacities through the actual exercise of expanded responsibility. So whatever the effectiveness of the party's effort under Starace, it could only have been superficial because the content, considered in light of the earlier aspirations and possibilities, had by now been considerably diluted. Whereas there might have been, for example, a serious Giovanni Gentilian underpinning to, for example, the theme of avoiding irony as "bourgeois," it was merely trivializing without a wider framework of Gentilian education. In insisting on the measure of ongoing totalitarian implementation through the party's expanded role, Emilio Gentile was not recognizing the narrowing of the possibilities, the deeper trivialization at work from within the unforeseen dynamic.

The cult of the Duce of the 1930s was an aspect of that process of narrowing and trivialization. Fascism was not about Mussolini in the first place, as some were quick to remind him at several points during the earlier 1920s. And the Duce remained part of the wider dynamic; even the myth of the Duce evolved with the trajectory of the regime.[236] But the reaction against parliamentary government and the accent on will and spirit invited a reliance on charismatic leadership, as Roberto Michels explained with reference to the Italian case as early as 1926.[237] The point, he stressed, was not power for its own sake, with masses mobilized through manipulation, but a new mode of extraordinary action in pursuit of lofty, supra-individual goals. But such leadership entailed dangers stemming from the reverse side of its special strengths; most basically, the masses were likely to expect too much of the leader.

The actual dynamic in Italy, with so much fractiousness compromising the capacity to act, was bound to intensify that reliance. Each competing faction could only entrust its hopes to the Duce even as each also sought, not implausibly, and not without successes, to influence the Duce's direction. But the deepening reliance on the leader occasioned further trivialization and narrowing, summed up in the fatuous slogan "Mussolini is always right." Precisely as Michels had anticipated, such reliance invited capriciousness as the Duce grew increasingly mistrustful and isolated. Unable to delegate, he sought to juggle too many functions and ended up making decisions impulsively, without adequate preparation.[238]

De Felice found it typical—yet one of Mussolini's gravest errors—that the Ethiopian campaign entailed a clampdown on the internal debate among youth that Mussolini had encouraged to that point: "When the war began, everything was reduced to 'believe, obey, fight.' This was principally a question of face, to give the impression of a monolithic country. But it was also that Mussolini had a charismatic vision of his own power. . . . only his myth was capable of holding things intact in the difficult moments."[239] So although, as Ben-Ghiat showed, the Ethiopian turn produced fissuring among second-generation Fascists who had sought revitalization on a different basis, most continued to invest their hopes in Mussolini even if they disliked aspects of his policy, including the eventual German alliance.[240]

With Italian intervention in the Second World War, many began calling for an anti-bourgeois and anti-bureaucratic "third wave" finally to realize the Fascist revolution.[241] So although what had emerged as "Fascism" by this point seemed but a preliminary sketch, the ideal remained. But how well would committed Fascists diagnose and prescribe? And what scope for a more satisfying outcome was there by this point?

Encouraged by established spokesmen like Bottai, many youth saw this as a war against international finance and thus as a chance to defeat the plutocrats who had frustrated the Fascist revolution. Yet Ben-Ghiat noted that increased political fragmentation from internecine rivalries left many youths unsure about Fascism's ideological identity and impeded formation of a united fighting front. Was the war to defend Italy or to transform it? Was it for the nation or to transcend the nation?[242]

As featured by Emilio Gentile, the pivotal phase in the wartime quest for renewal proved to be the brief, long-neglected but intense period of Adelchi Serena as party secretary, from October 1940 to December 1941. Serena enlisted the help of major ideologues like Costamagna, Panunzio, and the economics professor and former Fascist finance minister Alberto De Stefani, each critical of the outcome of Fascism so far, in identifying the measures needed to enable the party better to promote totalitarian ideals.[243]

Although Gentile had found Starace a credible chapter in the ongoing totalitarian effort, it is striking that for Serena the first imperative was to break the Starace mold. So Serena set out to reform the party itself, first by drastically reducing its numbers to overcome the careerism that had come to the fore during the 1930s. Party membership was to entail genuine faith and commitment. And he sought to deepen participation through a more genuine education, partly through renewed links with the cultural world that Starace had scorned— and that had come to scorn Starace and the party in turn.[244] But Serena continued and even intensified Starace's effort to establish the autonomy of the party *vis-à-vis* the state.

Gentile showed convincingly that many, even in the cultural realm, openly approved of the party's new direction, including this insistence on the autonomy, even the primacy, of the party. Those seeking revitalization looked to the party because the existing state seemed so removed from the ideal of the new Fascist state; a stronger party role was essential to counter the tendency of the state bureaucracy to take on a life of its own and to dominate.[245] In an especially influential analysis, De Stefani insisted that the core problem had been the degeneration of the putatively totalitarian state into mere administration with full powers. Although De Stefani was still propounding an essentially Gentilian vision of a totalitarian ethical state standing opposed to liberal-capitalist materialism, the Fascist state had failed in its ethical-political and religious function, so it fell to the party to spearhead renewal.[246]

But even as he stressed that De Stefani's reflections attracted much consideration, Gentile recognized that De Stefani lacked concrete proposals to offer.[247] And whereas certain measures to revitalize the party were surely possible, Serena's effort to solidify the party's institutional and even constitutional role brought longstanding tensions back to the fore, as major Fascists like Bottai, Pellizzi, and Dino Grandi, who, though *not* associated with the party, were also dissatisfied with the present outcome, expressed reservations about Serena's effort and continued to oppose the party's pretensions. Thus, for example, Bottai and those around *Critica fascista* insisted explicitly that the state—in its new syndical, corporativist, and educative guise—had to remain the key, that the party could usefully operate only in dialectic with this *new* state.[248] Pellizzi, now director of the National Institute of Fascist Culture, reflected the Giovanni Gentilian vision more explicitly in denying the implication of party advocates that the state was somehow inert and needed to be energized constantly by the revolutionary impulse of the party. The party had its specific educational function—but not its own ideology.[249] It did not uniquely embody the Fascist revolutionary spirit, and it did not play its role through more or less permanent opposition to the state.

Certainly, Emilio Gentile recognized that Pellizzi and Bottai also believed in continuing totalitarian revolution; they simply had a different idea of totalitarian politics and the means to realize it.[250] But he was glossing over the significance of the tension, its implications for the overall totalitarian dynamic, and how debilitating this difference had by now become. More particularly, Gentile neglected the content of the countervailing accent on the state, which was still to feature corporativism, education, and idealist themes—and not merely the primacy of the state over the party. It was not clear how a renewed party enterprise could serve the deeper realization of totalitarian state ideals by this point.[251]

Even in Serena's relatively coherent effort, much energy was devoted to the institutional prerogatives of the party—in winning recognition of party hierarchs as public officials, for example. In light of the obstacles to genuinely transforming the state, this pursuit of party prerogatives *seemed* to keep the revolution alive, but those prerogatives tended to become ends in themselves as, despite the appearance of radicalization, the revolution narrowed. The renewed insistence on the party could only deflect from the deeper problems that the effort of revolutionary implementation had revealed.

Serena conflicted with top state officials like justice minister Grandi, and Gentile himself stressed that the renewed party–state tensions came to constitute a significant problem for the regime as it faced the difficult wartime challenge.[252] Mussolini finally replaced Serena in December 1941. As Gentile saw it, Serena had proved too independent for Mussolini's liking.[253] But although they obviously did not help, the mere obtuseness and vanity of the Duce do not seem to have been decisive. Rather, Serena's effort had exacerbated the longstanding party–state tension and thus made it harder to prosecute the Fascist war. Although the ongoing attempt to deepen and radicalize surely merits attention, what strikes us by this point is how futile, even self-defeating, the effort had become.

With each step along the way, unintended outcomes occasioned further steps that proved to entail narrowing and trivialization even as the Fascists sought, and claimed, revitalization and radicalization. Gentile and, in a different way, the American culturalists tend to miss the sense in which "success," whether on the level of party prerogatives or on the level of style and symbol, entailed such trivialization, as opposed to realization.[254] And whatever success was achieved on either of those levels did not arrest but furthered the negative dynamic in course.

Meanwhile, the Nazi regime afforded an image of greater success and suggested some practical steps that might serve revitalization. But the relationship with Nazi Germany, in this situation of frustration, proved to be complex, although it eventually occasioned another layer of fragmentation and furthered the narrowing in course. Such leading Fascists as Italo Balbo greatly disliked the turn toward Nazi Germany.[255] And interaction with Nazism led Mussolini himself to an erratic but single-minded and ultimately reckless policy that eventually distanced him from much of his movement.

Aristotle Kallis usefully features the idiosyncratic interaction between Mussolini and Hitler as a distinct factor that helped to radicalize the expansionist policies of both regimes, beyond rationality or what either initially had envisioned. But the impact became asymmetrical as Italy's relative weakness came to light, first after the two regimes intervened in the Spanish Civil War. That surprising weakness suggested that Italy was on the verge of losing its status, seemingly its birthright into 1936, as the senior representative of fascism. Kallis noted that even as Mussolini, in response to uncertainties in the wider international framework, oscillated between aggressiveness and peaceful diplomacy from 1938 to 1940, his increasing sense of inferiority and jealousy produced inflating international ambitions and a concomitant determination to regain the initiative.[256]

The opportunity seemed to arise in the early fall of 1940, in light of Germany's moves into Romania and the modest initial successes of Italian forces in North Africa. Rather than, as before, promoting a separate peace with Britain, Italy would now lead the assault on Britain. Acting in defiance of his military experts, whom he accused of failing to grasp the spirit of Fascism, Mussolini relied on his own charismatic authority and proceeded without strategic planning. The result was first confusion, then defeat.[257] So the epochal interaction between Hitler and Mussolini led the fascist regime to a narrowing mode of radicalization, to myth making and lack of realism, and soon to ruin.

Meanwhile, even as Fascist spokesmen stressed the common totalitarianism of the two regimes, the Nazi regime was coming to seem better focused and more dynamic, leading those seeking revitalization to try to pinpoint the bases of the difference.[258] Somehow, Nazism seemed to have more successfully overcome egotism and class distinctions, opened careers to talent, and even, up to a point, nurtured the moral-religious basis for the essential new civic consciousness. Although such views were especially prevalent among younger Fascists, the veteran Pellizzi had occasion to visit an *Ordensburg*, one of the centers for educating future Nazi leaders, in 1941, and he returned full of admiration for the new political–religious mentality and communitarian life it seemed to be nurturing.[259]

But contact also brought home differences and led some to play up still further the significance of Italian humanistic traditions and to anticipate, on that basis, Fascist Italy's civilizing role in the new Europe. Introducing an Italian translation of several of Carl Schmitt's major writings in 1935, the Gentilian corporativist Arnaldo Volpicelli sharply criticized Schmitt's now famous friend/foe dichotomy. Fascism, Volpicelli insisted, understood "the political," of which the substance and ideal is the ethical itself, as the ceaseless overcoming of separation or hostility. Our need to include others in the circle of our humanity leads us toward a common spiritual life and thus a regime of peace. Although this was simply an ideal direction, not an actual end to be reached, it meant that the goal of politics is not nationalism but internationalism, the linking of peoples in an organic humanity. Here, insisted Volpicelli, lay the categorical superiority of corporativist Fascism over National Socialism.[260]

Unfamiliar though it is, Volpicelli's underlying notion—that Italian humanistic values, especially as institutionalized in corporativism, uniquely equipped Fascism to address modern needs—remained an essential component of the overall Fascist self-understanding. But Volpicelli's conception did not preclude—indeed, it could even invite—a more aggressive foreign policy under certain circumstances, and that policy could then produce tensions with the original self-understanding.

Even the conquest of Ethiopia was accompanied by the notion that an expansionist Fascist Italy would not merely exploit, that Ethiopia, as the site for corporativist experiment, pointed beyond individual greed and capitalist speculation.[261] The engineer Gaetano Ciocca viewed Italian East Africa as an ideal laboratory for such experiment and, on that basis, for a state-induced leap into the ultra-modern.[262] The corporativist idea itself was becoming ever more elastic and mythical as it continued in rhetoric even as corporativist institution building bogged down.[263] The sense of epochal competition with Nazism fed the Fascist tendency to exaggerate achievements, to misconstrue possibilities, and to gloss over deficiencies.[264] Although the sense of Italian difference and leadership continued to inspire, its inflating mythical dimension was increasingly blinding Fascists to reality as practice defied the ideal.

From within this framework, we must consider the official turn, in the late 1930s, to anti-Semitism, heretofore essentially absent in Italian Fascism. Although long marginalized as stemming from German pressures or an extremist fringe, this new direction has recently come to seem more deeply symptomatic.[265] Much of the Fascist elite, including Bottai, for example, eagerly embraced anti-Semitism.[266] But granting that the anti-Semitic turn was more endogenous and more widely welcomed than we had recognized, what do we make of it?

The presence of Italy's small Jewish community had simply not been an issue for Fascism until the mid-1930s. So thoroughgoing was Jewish assimilation during the liberal period that the Jews seemed to be moving toward self-extinction as a separate community.[267] It was not news when Italian Jews embraced Fascism in proportionate or perhaps even slightly greater numbers.[268] As Nazism came to prominence in the 1930s, Mussolini and other Fascists proclaimed that there was no Jewish problem, and thus no anti-Semitism, in Italy. Indeed, Nazism, with its biological racism, was crude and vulgar, diametrically opposed to Italian idealism, accenting culture and human freedom. Even when fascists traced international criticism of the Ethiopian venture to the international Jewish plutocracy, they called for stepped-up assimilation of Italian Jews through intermarriage, not expulsion or elimination.[269]

Despite the emphasis on population policy, race thinking in general remained almost incidental to Italian Fascism before 1936. The favored term was "*stirpe*," or "stock," but even when "*razza*" was used, it had the usual Fascist idealist connotations of culture, spirit, and mentality—of shared sentiments expressed in Fascist values—as opposed to biological race. But usages and connotations began to change as, with the conquest of Ethiopia in 1936, matters of race became seemingly more germane. Overtly racial emphases, including anti-miscegenation laws, followed, although they were not unusual in the West for the time.[270]

The new salience of race was no doubt a prerequisite for the subsequent adoption of anti-Semitic measures, although the anti-bourgeois campaign that accompanied the conquest of Ethiopia also fed into it. The Fascists began conflating Jews with the bourgeoisie as bearers of corruption.[271] But official policy changed only in July 1938, when the "Manifesto of the Race," declaring Jews to be unassimilable aliens, opened the way to a series of laws, approximating those already implemented in Germany, that began stripping Jews of their rights.[272] Still, the place of this anti-Semitic turn within the wider, ongoing dynamic remains hard to pin down. Even the factors so far discussed do not seem adequate to explain why the presence of the Jews became an issue when it did, in the later 1930s, or what the new anti-Semitism meant in light of the problems and possibilities in the Fascist experiment by that point. So what does this step say about the nature of the totalitarian implementation in Fascist Italy? Was it radicalization or trivialization to focus on the Jewish presence?

Ben-Ghiat suggested that even with the adoption of the race laws, the aim was not to eliminate the Jews but to force changes in customs and behavior to fulfill long-frustrated Italian and Catholic fantasies of total Jewish assimilation.[273] But granting her premises about *longstanding* fantasies, obviously the turn to anti-Semitism at this point was not merely Italian and Catholic; rather, it was a moment from within the totalitarian dynamic in course. And in light of when it happened, well into that dynamic, it is hard to argue that Italians turned to totalitarianism *in order* to act at last on such fantasies; on the contrary, even insofar as such longstanding fantasies were at work, they now became operative only because of the totalitarian course of action in progress.

In the earlier phase of the Fascist totalitarian experiment, the demand for homogeneity had not led to concern about the Jews, who seemed as Italian as anyone. Linking the anti-Semitic turn explicitly to the logic of totalitarianism, Emilio Gentile found this step to be simply part of the totalitarian radicalization in process by the later 1930s. As early as 1927, he noted, the Fascists claimed the right to legislate against "those who persist in maintaining their separateness from the fundamental aims of Fascist life."[274] And surely it is true that, reprehensible though we find it, to demand complete assimilation, allowing no diversity or pluralism, no sense of separate community or identity, was entirely consistent from a totalitarian perspective. But to insist on this step in 1938 was to follow the logic of totalitarianism in a very particular way.

As the attempt at totalitarian action encountered frustration in practice, various measures to rekindle the revolution were attempted. Although in principle the logic of totalitarian practice suggested eliminating Jewish separateness altogether, the question was whether the presence of the Jews as still a somewhat distinct community had anything to do with the difficulties of acting in the totalitarian way envisioned. And once the question is posed, the answer is surely beyond controversy. Even crediting concerns about Zionism in light of Fascist Italy's aspirations in the eastern Mediterranean, the threat from the measure of Jewish distinctiveness to the deeper realization of Fascism at this point was nil. Yet it seemed to be essential to do something to tighten up, and in light of the very real obstacles, the internal fragmentation and ambiguity, the Fascists could do no better than to fasten onto this bogus issue. It was as if the putative insufficiency of Jewish assimilation explained the incapacity to act collectively as envisioned. To focus the effort of creating a post-bourgeois alternative on eliminating "Jewishness" reflected and reinforced the trivialization in progress.[275]

Moreover, although it occasioned a deeper consensus than was long recognized or admitted, the new accent occasioned some further fragmentation among committed Fascists. After the "Manifesto of the Race" was published, those like Pellizzi who were uncomfortable with the new direction scrambled to deny any imitation of Nazi Germany. Bottai's embrace of anti-Semitism left some of the younger Fascists who had looked to him for leadership feeling bitter and betrayed.[276]

The actual implementation of the race laws turned out to be contradictory, although the primacy of culture over biology generally remained, despite the letter of the law. Thus there were exceptions for "Aryanized" Jews, exceptional Jews, and proven patriots, and thus the Fascists continued to emphasize stepped-up assimilation through intermarriage, even though this was diametrically opposed to Nazi policy. This difference enabled even Fascists who were less than enthusiastic about anti-Semitism to reaffirm the "spiritual" basis of Italian policy and thus Fascism's superiority over Nazism, with its crude biological categories.[277] Indeed, some may have embraced the issue partly as a way of confirming that Italian Fascism was still out in front, in light of its putative basis in idealism and humanism. The claim to be out in front, at least potentially, had not been without substance at first, but as the effort to act bogged down, the Fascists could only fasten upon this narrow, even trivial, basis for the claim to superiority.

As the Italian military effort foundered during the Second World War, the accent on cultural superiority became still more central to the Fascist self-understanding. To position Italy for spiritual leadership within the new order, Bottai launched the journal *Primato* in 1941—to reanimate Fascist culture and to represent Fascism abroad as modern, out front, open to fresh ideas. Among the contributors was Galvano Della Volpe, reared a Gentilian and eventually a major Communist thinker. He took it for granted that mainstream Franco-British culture was collapsing; the question was what would take its place.[278] And as he saw it, the Italians remained poised to assume the leadership. By this point, the new layer of myth was leading the Fascists into a world of fantasy.

We have noted that although myth was central to Italian Fascism, it operated in different ways on several levels. It was important to the new Fascist thinking about how history might be made collectively in a more concerted way. At the same time, the sense of the scope for leadership in Italy after the war, although it could have developed only in tandem with a measure of innovative substance, was surely overblown—a myth in that familiar, less lucid sense. It was fed by intellectuals like Giovanni Gentile who, exaggerating the significance of indigenous Italian traditions, began to overstate the cultural significance of the Italian war effort and to posit a special cultural mission for Italy in the aftermath. But the place of myth changed decisively as the quest for substantive innovation bogged down.

To be sure, even as the possibility of actual realization shrank toward zero, the Fascists could make rational arguments about the superiority of Fascism not only to the liberal democratic mainstream but to Nazism and Soviet Communism as competitors for the post-liberal space. In that sense, the initial substantive core remained an abiding source of energy; Fascism never reduced to mere fantasy or wishful thinking—or to the faith that faith moves mountains. But although they grumbled and criticized at the same time, the Fascists' self-understanding became ever more mythical as they faced competition from Nazism and as even radicalization yielded narrowing and trivialization. Thus they overstated both actual achievements and continued prospects. Increasingly, in fact, the Fascist revolution itself became a myth. That revolution continued to celebrate and commemorate itself, to be sure, but with the substance narrowing, celebration and commemoration became ever more ends in themselves, as the regime celebrated commemoration and commemorated celebration. This was not to realize or even to move toward the originating vision.[279]

In support of Serena's revitalization effort, Emilio Gentile noted a strong faith in the myth of the party as both the locus of the revolutionary ideal and the ongoing agent of the revolution. Indeed, that myth was bound up with a sense that the two competing totalitarian regimes had proved more radical because, early on, they had solved the party–state question, as was logical, in favor of the party.[280] Thus, the disaffected assumed, Fascism might dramatically transform itself through a comparable victory of the party. Yet Gentile also noted that the sustaining faith was still "directed toward the same objective of completing the totalitarian state" based on the conviction that "the totalitarian state was the state form of the 'new civilization'."[281]

The Fascist *belief* that to increase party prerogatives was to continue the revolution, even though the revolution was about realizing the totalitarian state, is surely an important datum, but partly because of Gentile's overuse of myth, we miss in his account the place of that belief in the changing dynamic. Myth in the literal sense became more central as the conquest of party prerogatives came to seem itself revolutionary, and as the scope for translating the ideal into a genuinely totalitarian state became ever more tenuous. At the same time, in attributing the seemingly greater totalitarian success elsewhere to the triumph of party over state, which suggested the scope for dramatically changing what Italian Fascism had become, Fascist enthusiasts were indulging in mere wishful thinking, fastening upon a diagnosis that did not seriously address the complex impasse at hand.

Whereas it helped to cover over inadequacies and to maintain enthusiasm, myth bred posturing and rhetoric that masked the narrowing and trivialization, that impeded serious discussion of the lessons of the experiment and the prospects for the future. So the tendency toward myth making undercut whatever chance there might still have been for a more substantive outcome. And surely the place of myth in the original vision made self-criticism at this point especially unlikely. Indeed, it made the Fascists more likely to continue, as if willing and believing would indeed make it so.

As Arnaldo Volpicelli's account of international relations suggests, aspects of the enduring but ever more mythical idealist–corporativist self-understanding were incompatible with the new style proclaimed by the later 1930s—the accent on "believe, obey, fight," on becoming hard-edged conquerors. Such discordance was at once symptomatic and debilitating. Even Bottai, who deplored the superficiality of many of the latter accents, embraced the pathetic, ultimately tragic notion that the Jews were a problem, even *the* immediate problem, and still envisioned the scope for cultural primacy in 1941.

The Italian road to totalitarian failure

Focusing on the Fascist program in East Africa after the conquest of Ethiopia, R.J.B. Bosworth emphasized the irregularity of Mussolini's policy and the trivial bickering that resulted. There was no plan as to how the area should be run. Various rivalries thus came into play, and it was finally up to the Duce himself to decide. Bosworth concluded:

> If this vignette of imperial government has meaning, Fascist Italy was not a regime possessed of a simple and reliable system of command, nor one in which its leading figures thought only of how best they might serve their ideology and nation. . . . For all its pretensions to totalitarian uniformity, was the fascist system in practice riven by personal, practical, and ideological conflicts which the Duce was powerless to end (and which he may have fostered for utterly cynical reasons having to do with the protection of his own 'authority')?

This latter passage is central to a series of rhetorical questions, the answer to which is obviously yes, *yes*, *YES!* What surprises is not that all this characterized the Fascist regime but that Bosworth takes this syndrome as somehow undermining any notion of "totalitarianism."[282]

To be sure, even if we take the Fascist aspiration to be genuinely totalitarian, the resulting Fascist regime seems anything but—from a "modern" perspective. But we noted that postmodernism entails a changing sense of how history happens, how things come to be through history. Insofar as we conceive Italian Fascism not as some essence but as a dynamic, an event, from within which meanings and proportions changed, we can discern a totalitarian trajectory, stemming from the effort to do great politics. The slovenliness that Bosworth pinpointed, the improvisation in light of inadequate preparation, were also evident in the Nazi and Stalinist revolutions. In each, much was unintended, out of control, so practice was anything but "totalitarian" in the earlier sense. The Italian case shows that the totalitarian dynamic could lead to a kind of trivialization and impasse that contrasts with the still more tragic outcomes of Nazism and Stalinism at about the same time.

Recognizing the scope for unintended outcomes helps to undercut the teleological temptation that leads us to misconstrue origins. Classic studies by Roland Sarti and Charles Maier showed that in practice the regime yielded the expansion of private power, as "flankers" managed to exploit the situation that Fascism created.[283] But we are better able today to understand that fact as an unintended consequence, an aspect of failure, rather than as a warrant for assuming that it was all to serve capitalist interests in the first place. Rather than create an effective new collective instrument, Fascism so weakened the political order that, as one of many unintended outcomes, it did indeed yield the expansion of private power in certain respects. And this outcome frustrated wave upon wave of committed Fascists who had intended anything but that.

Understood as the whole trajectory, totalitarianism proves stranger, more layered and complex, than an ongoing attempt to implement the initial quasi-religious vision. Whereas Emilio Gentile, eschewing reification and teleology, usefully focused on radicalization within an ongoing, open-ended process, we must be alert to change in the nature of the dynamic itself as the effort to act proceeded, producing unforeseen tensions that elude even Gentile's three-way interaction of Duce, party, and state. That change was bound up with changes in the meaning of the substantive, stylistic, and mythical elements and in the proportions and relationships between them.

It only seems paradoxical to insist that the outcomes of Italian Fascism were quintessentially totalitarian even as, precisely as, they made a mockery of the regime's totalitarian pretenses. As the effort to act collectively encountered frustration, the energy tilted from idealist education and corporativist participation toward spectatorship, buttressed by inflating rhetoric. Realization on this more superficial level did not satisfy, but the further effort that resulted led to additional fissuring and trivialization, but then also to a thickening surround of myth. As a result, the regime *ended up* with a superficial focus on style, with an absurd cult of the Duce, with a pathetic accent on anti-Semitism, and with debilitating confusion and rivalry over institutional focus. These were the wages of trying to transcend the modern framework by acting collectively through the new great politics.

7 The hollow triumph of the will in Nazi Germany

Nazism as a radical departure

Opening to the supranational, historically specific dimension

In German Nazism, as in the other two cases, the significance of idiosyncrati-cally personal, ahistorically banal, and national contextual factors is not in dispute. But a supranational, historically specific dimension, made possible by the earlier historical-political break, interfaced with those more familiar dimen-sions to fuel the action we seek to understand. And in the German case, too, pulling back from the master narrative prepares us better to recognize a novel content that did not merely serve the interests of existing elites or respond to the traumas of petty bourgeois losers. Even the Nazi departure must be considered a quest for a post-Marxist alternative to the liberal mainstream, and we must be prepared to recognize irreducible and unanticipated difference as an outcome of the attempt, which proved to reveal further possibilities of totalitarian great poli-tics. It goes without saying that we find much about that attempt undesirable in the first place and that, whatever the plausibility of the originating aspiration, it led to tragedy and disaster.

It is not hard to understand why people voted for the Nazis in response to the impasse of the Weimar Republic, or why they were enthusiastic about Hitler's apparent successes on the political, economic, and international levels after he came to power in January 1933. Up to a point, we can even agree with George L. Mosse that Nazism was fueled by a desire to return to secure, conventional bour-geois morality in the face of newly prominent features of modernity widely associated with Weimar, from "the new woman" to simplified, "impersonal" archi-tecture and design. Mosse saw Nazism as an attempt not to overturn respectable bourgeois morality but to preserve it against deviant and outsider groups.[1]

The concerns that Mosse featured help us to understand the immediate appeal of Nazism and especially the extent of acquiescence—the sense on the part of so many ordinary Germans that, despite something a little troubling, the Nazi departure was all right after all. However, the Nazis' developing assault on Christianity and the churches, for example, suggests anything but a defense of tradition, respectability, and conventional morality, as does their unprecedented, radically interventionist population policy. Indeed, even as it developed in this very brief twelve-year Reich, Nazism proved as radical as any political departure we have known. And we increasingly recognize that whatever their reasons for going along in the first place, large numbers of ordinary Germans got caught up in the radical Nazi project in surprising ways.

Responding explicitly to Mosse, Steven Aschheim noted that "what requires explanation is the galvanizing motor that, translated into the bureaucratic, murderous impulse, enabled Nazism to transcend middle-class morality while embodying it." Although Mosse's emphases are not to be denied, Aschheim went on, we sense that the historical significance of Nazism "resided in its emphases on destruction and violent regeneration, health and disease." In this sense, he concluded, that galvanizing motor of Nazism entailed politics in a "great" Nietzschean mode, however debased and mediated.[2]

At the same time, there is by now widespread agreement that we cannot attribute Nazism simply to the dregs of society or to criminals or "gangsters" who freakishly got a chance at power. Rather, we recognize the essential roles played by the educated, even by experts, whose participation cannot remotely be attributed to coercion.[3] On the contrary, they embraced Nazism precisely because it seemed to promise the chance to act in the unprecedented ways they had come to believe necessary.

Nazism emerged as a self-proclaimed new elite demanded a monopoly of power on the basis of its claim to be uniquely qualified to spearhead the post-democratic forms of collective action necessary to respond to a seemingly extraordinary yet transitory opportunity. This paralleled what was happening in Russia and Italy, but the energizing sense of moving to the forefront had special force in Germany because, as we have seen, the country had already been out in front with the Weimar effort to create a welfare democracy. The impasse of that effort helped to warrant a second step and thus intensified the sense of leapfrogging, of doing something grandiose and extraordinary.

The wider epochal conjuncture had made clear the scope for transcending the forms of mass politics that had emerged during the nineteenth century.[4] First came the Russian Revolution, and then Italian Fascism, responding to the First World War and picking up on the Leninist precedent, claimed to establish a third way as it devised new forms of mass mobilization. Mussolini's level of aspiration, his willingness to move decisively beyond liberal expectations, enhanced the sense of openness and possibility and especially inspired the Nazis.[5] As the Weimar Republic neared its final impasse, there was much German interest in the seeming parallels between the developing Italian and Soviet experiments, each of which seemed to be forging something new and unforeseen from aspects of modernity.[6]

The challenge in light of the Weimar experiment

The new Nazi regime drew its momentum and legitimacy partly from the sense that it was responding more courageously than the democratic politicians to the impasse that the Weimar experiment had produced. But it was not simply that the Nazi regime, as dictatorial, was prepared to do what Weimar could not. What defined the departure was a deeper break involving the Nazi sense of the scope for a whole new mode of collective action, the mode necessary to *expand* such action in a way appropriate to the historical moment.

Following Detlev Peukert, we noted in Chapter 4 that although the Weimar welfare state failed, it mattered crucially that it had been tried. The fact that there had been such faith in social engineering exacerbated the sense of crisis but also underpinned a sense that there was scope to push forward once the diffi-culties of acting from within the democratic framework had come to light. Michael Burleigh noted, for example, that well before 1933 some German psychologists were advocating killing seemingly incurable mental patients, espe-cially in view of the economic constraints that had become evident but also to reaffirm their own therapeutic capacities in light of the political limits they had encountered. Indeed, said Burleigh, the outlines of most Nazi policies were already discernible in the Janus-faced and crisis-ridden health and welfare poli-cies of the Weimar Republic; in that sense, 1933 was not the decisive break it has seemed.[7] It was surely a break on some level, however; we simply need a deeper understanding of what the break entailed—the mode of action that now dawned, and why it was especially energizing as it intertwined with the particular policies at issue.

For many experts, Weimar democracy had remained too hesitant, with much discussion but too little policy determination and action. To resolve the modern tensions that seemed to have come to the fore especially in Weimar Germany, it seemed necessary to combine technical efficiency with a more authoritarian form of social control. Thus, as we noted, Peukert deemed totalitarianism to be the only alternative to democracy.[8] Those moving in that direction, he insisted, were seeking a modern alternative to democracy; their quest did not betray some *Sonderweg*, some failure of the German bourgeoisie to accommodate to moder-nity and progress. The elites turning against Weimar were attuned to modern trends and often saw themselves as "modern" in the sense of wanting rule by scientific experts.[9]

Sketchy though they were, Peukert's indications were especially suggestive. But he was quick to invoke totalitarianism almost as if it was ready-made, available to be taken off the shelf once the Weimar experiment in advanced modernity had reached an impasse. The failure of Weimar is not in itself sufficient to explain the availability of a movement capable of the particular mode of action that seemed necessary. Nor does it explain why that mode of action would lead in directions parallel to those in Italy and the Soviet Union at roughly the same time.

While stressing, up to a point, the value of Peukert's accent on modern conti-nuity, Mark Roseman suggested that three areas are needed to supplement Peukert's argument. First, totalitarianism had to be linked not simply to moder-nity *per se* but to the specific epoch of war and Russian Revolution, including the Nazi interplay with Bolshevism. Roseman noted that modernity and moderniza-tion are so slippery as to be virtually useless; what would not count? Second, the old *Sonderweg* notion had indeed been flawed insofar as its implication had been that only Germany had had an idiosyncratic path to modernity. But if there is no master narrative, if every nation has had its special path, then idiosyncratic longer-term national traditions may still have been crucial in the German case. Third, Peukert's argument had too little room for the role of more general cultural and intellectual traditions in shaping perceptions and responses. Roseman invited a deeper consideration of such longer-term factors even as he warned that the narrow old *Geistesgeschichte* would not do.[10]

It is certainly true, as Roseman argued, that the German cultural matrix was not a *tabula rasa* in 1918, and each of his three directions indicated elements for the wider framework necessary. But we must pin down and weave together the three strands that Roseman pinpointed and then get at the intersection between that whole package and the essential but incomplete Peukert syndrome. In other words, the point is not to distinguish the epoch of war and revolution from Peukert's modernity but to grasp their relationship, which yielded a new and unforeseeable dynamic. And we must focus not simply on distinguishable German intellectual and cultural traditions but especially on the idiosyncratic German take on the wider intellectual and cultural moment. For although the epoch at issue was indeed wound around war and revolution, we have seen that it had supranational, historically specific intellectual antecedents that responded to longer-term tensions in the Western mainstream. Without assuming some single modern or progressive standard, we can recognize that idiosyncratic German traditions helped to mediate that more recent supranational intellectual and cultural layer to afford a particular understanding of the challenges and possibilities crystallizing by the time of the Weimar crisis.

Although the fate of the Weimar attempt to build a welfare state seemed especially revelatory, the interest in forging an alternative modernity that Peukert noted among those turning to Nazism was not simply a response to the impasse of this particular effort. That impasse seemed to be symptomatic of a generic problem with liberal democratic procedures and, indeed, with the whole liberal model of society, especially in light of the situation created or revealed by the war. Yet that situation, too, was symptomatic of more general change, challenge, and opportunity. With the crisis of Weimar seemingly a distillation of this whole experience, the challenge was not simply to restore equilibrium, or to produce an organic community as a mode of being, but to forge the capacity for the dramatically expanded history-making collective action that seemed to be necessary. It was the inadequacy of parliamentary democracy for that role that seemed most obviously to have been revealed.

To create the essential new instrument for expanded action, a revolution seemed necessary—not socio-economic but political-cultural, to overcome an array of seemingly outmoded assumptions, priorities, and procedures loosely bound up with liberalism and "positivism." This seemed to require a deeper measure of societal homogeneity even as leader, elite, and experts had to play newly differentiated roles at the same time. And under these circumstances, the creeping assumption of collective welfare responsibility, brought dramatically to the fore with the Weimar experiment, quickly led to further, more specific questions. As society accepted a new level of responsibility for itself in the aggregate, the issue of who belonged, and on the basis of what criteria, was bound to become more insistent. Did "modernity" mean an open-ended state responsibility for "society," encompassing anyone who happened to be born? Although there were problems first on economic grounds, more general uncertainties about societal quality, glossed over by the modern mainstream, had to be confronted as well. At the very least, government increasingly seemed responsible not simply for individuals, to enable them to develop their individuality as a right or an end in itself, but for society in the aggregate, as a collective instrument.

Nazism could be the beneficiary of the crisis of Weimar because it seemed to be uniquely capable of the new form of collective action now required. Eugenicists like Fritz Lenz, co-author of the internationally respected 1923 treatise on heredity, turned to the Nazis as the only political party capable of translating eugenicist rhetoric into action. As we noted in Chapter 4, he was put off by Nazi anti-Semitism, but he lauded Hitler as early as 1930 as the first politician prepared to make race hygiene a serious element of state policy.[11] Although he did not join the Nazi Party until 1937, Lenz served on such governmental bodies as the Committee on Population and Racial Policy, which drew up the 1933 sterilization law, initiating the Nazi regime's venture into radical population engineering. Even many of those, like Alfred Ploetz, concerned primarily with eugenic meritocracy were willing to compromise, catering to Aryan enthusiasts in order to have a chance to begin actually implementing their ideas.[12] Conversely, the Nazis, as they came to power, claimed Ploetz as a precursor and made him a hero. With its promise to medicalize or biologize social problems, Nazism appealed to scientists and especially physicians, drawing them into the state policy apparatus on an unprecedented scale. At the same time, to medicalize or biologize these problems was to depoliticize them, so the enhanced role for scientific expertise served the quest for the deeper unity that seemed necessary.[13]

In the same vein, Jeffrey Herf noted that "Nazism's appeal for the engineers was not an antimodernist attack on technology but a promise to *unleash* modern technology from the constraints the Social Democrats had placed on it."[14] More generally, in Herf's influential argument, Nazism could embrace technology, yet, by incorporating it within a wider new political frame, also claim to discipline it even while making it "spiritual," no longer "soulless," through "the infusion of will into labor power."[15] Although idiosyncratic German traditions were obviously at work in these Nazi accents, the emerging framework also stemmed from the wider great political departure, with its emphasis on will and spirit. For Herf, that frame was reactionary and ultimately irrational, but although aspects of it would indeed prove irrational, thereby contributing to the failure of the whole project, it was initially experienced not as reactionary but as central to the quest for an alternative modernity.

Although the new mode of action was to entail an enhanced role for scientific expertise, it was not simply a matter of giving political power to scientists and doctors. Rather, establishing a new place for science was part of the wider political-cultural change, for even the more rigorous application of science required a new determination to act, reflecting will, courage, even hardness or toughness. And whereas scientists and doctors were often flattered by the opportunity and eager to participate in Nazi programs, their involvement cannot be reduced simply to banal careerism. Nor do coercion and fear seem to have been central, for those few physicians, for example, who declined to participate do not seem to have suffered for it.[16] The key was the chance, as the Nazi revolution changed the framework, to act in grandiose, world-historical—and distinctly post-liberal—ways.

More generally, we increasingly recognize the sense in which scientific expertise tended to trump ideology in the Nazi regime. Thus, for example, Alfred Rosenberg, as chief ideological functionary, was often frustrated in his efforts to determine appointments and research agendas.[17] But if this fact suggests the limited importance of ideology as usually understood, it does not suggest the triumph of some pure, modern technocracy. The scientific experts were falling in behind a regime with a particular, great political direction—a direction with its own sources. Antecedent ideas were among those sources, but the ideas did not derive from some particular ideology.

A new mode of action

The place of Hitler

In Germany, the leadership principle had been far more central than in Italy to anti-liberal thinking, and the Nazi movement was more focused on the particular attributes of its leader from an early stage. The more committed, single-minded leadership Hitler proved to offer then helped to differentiate the Nazi regime from Italian Fascism. Eventually, the Führer's will even assumed the force of law.[18] With both the will of the leader and the bond to the leader so central, it is not surprising that "explaining Hitler" sometimes appears to be the key to the whole problem of Nazism.[19] Against the backdrop of the familiar German contextual problems, Hitler as idiosyncratic, even *sui generis*, might seem to have afforded the content to be understood. Insofar as it seems too simple to reduce him to an ahistorical, opportunistic will to power, he might seem to have embodied a historically specific nihilism, symptomatic of this or that dimension of "the modern crisis."

Even for major scholars seeking to encompass wider dimensions in the face of reductionist tendencies, Hitlerism has remained a kind of default setting. When J.P. Stern, writing in the mid-1970s, sought to resist the reductive tendencies then prevalent, he found it necessary to emphasize Hitler's autonomy. Hitler was not merely the instrument of socio-economic elites, and the character of the Nazi state could not be explained in terms of class interests. Indeed, Hitler's "ability to use every institution and power-group for his own purpose" was essential to the regime's cohesion.[20]

At a time when reduction to class interests restricted discussion, to insist on Hitler's autonomy was a useful step, but Stern ended up by implying that insofar as we grasp the limits of class reductionism, we need only focus on Hitler, whose diabolical skill at political manipulation served his own ends—apparently power for its own sake, taken as self-explanatory. But it has become clear that reducing Nazism to idiosyncratic Hitlerism is too convenient, too exculpatory. The effort to make sense of Hitler's role within the overall Nazi revolution fueled the long debate between "intentionalists" and "functionalists," which helped to set the research agenda for a generation. As a way of widening the focus, heading off any easy reduction to "Hitlerism," the functionalist challenge was invaluable. We came to understand better not only the limits to Hitler's power and the infighting that marked the regime but also the importance of bureaucratic momentum, of agency from below, and of *ad hoc* adjustments to unforeseen situations.

But it is now clear that the functionalist challenge to the earlier intention-alism, stressing Hitler's agency, invited overreaction. Just as we cannot dismiss Hitler as a tool of the established elites, we cannot understand the overall dynamic apart from him to the extent the functionalists sometimes seemed to suggest. Even if he got up at noon and spent his evenings watching movies, he and his deeper purposes, reflecting his sense of opportunity and responsibility, were central to the particular dynamic of Nazism. So the more recent challenge has been to transcend the intention/function dualism by showing how Hitler interacted with other components from within a more complex dynamic.[21]

It is also clear that Hitler was neither a mere opportunist, seeking power for its own sake, nor a mere nihilist. Indeed, it is widely accepted that he operated on the basis of a *Weltanschauung*, or worldview, that not only specified the direc-tion for practice but that also gave him a measure of energizing confidence. That confidence, in turn, inspired others at various levels.[22] Yet, as has often been noted, the components of that worldview—social Darwinism, eugenics, racism, anti-Semitism, geopolitics—were found widely throughout the Western world. Even in combination they would not necessarily have yielded what we find most troubling about Nazism. So what Hitler grasped, and offered, was more than the sum of those parts—and was more complex than an ideology or worldview as usually understood.

Hitler's ideological obsession, centering on anti-Semitism, was not shared by most Germans, even many Nazis. Despite the sensationalist arguments of Daniel Jonah Goldhagen, to be considered below, there is a strong scholarly consensus that even with its undoubted upswing during the unsettled Weimar period, anti-Semitism was not particularly widespread or virulent in Germany; nor was it central to Hitler's appeal and electoral successes during the Weimar crisis.[23] Even lieutenants like Heinrich Himmler, Reinhard Heydrich, and Adolf Eichmann, who played crucial roles in the extermination of the Jews, were not especially anti-Semitic, so invoking anti-Semitism tells us little about the dynamic that developed.[24]

Conversely, Hitler himself, despite his fanatical hatred of the Jews, was not always the source of the radicalizing anti-Semitism in the Nazi regime. In fact, key measures against the Jews were often formulated without his direct involve-ment. He intervened in policy making unsystematically, in response to pressures from below, always with an eye to wider public and even international opinion. When he had to decide, he tended toward caution, favoring bureaucratic regu-larity over party zealotry.[25] So even on this level, involving seemingly the most obsessive ideological dimension, Hitler's anti-Semitism proves to be but one factor in a wider dynamic.

It was crucial that Hitler had experienced war, including the battles of Ypres and the Somme, that he was twice wounded and three times decorated for bravery. Thus, as Stern put it, "[Hitler's] endlessly repeated claim to have shared to the full the life of the front-line soldier, and by the same token to be the spokesman of his generation, was no idle boast. . . . The war experience provides him with a pattern and legitimization of the demands he will make on his followers and, eventually, on the German nation."[26] But lots of others had had a comparable wartime experience, and what matters is what exactly Hitler drew from it, and how what he drew from it interfaced with his sense of the wider challenge. In the same way, to grasp the content and direction of Nazism, it is not enough to invoke his well-known bitterness at defeat, the Versailles settlement, and the Weimar Republic, all comparably shared by others. Conversely, Hitler's discovery that he could move people through his oratorical skills could not in itself have been decisive; deeper was his sense that people needed to be and could be moved, mobilized, in new ways and for new reasons in Germany by the early 1920s.

Hitler's belief that he could and should play a special role in light of Germany's postwar situation stemmed less from his familiar worldview than from his wider sense of the historical-political conjuncture, reflecting the post-developmentalist turn we discussed in Chapters 2 and 3. And the role he in fact played, and the interaction with German society it entailed, stemmed from the great political mode of action that became possible in light of that turn. Like the Leninists in Russia, Hitler sensed that a new mode of practice was necessary precisely because ideology could carry only so far. Grasping the principles of racism and social Darwinism afforded not reassurance, as if understanding in itself was sufficient or the direction of history could be counted on. Rather, extraordinary action was necessary—but also possible, it seemed, for those with post-ideological insights into politics and history. So it is misleading to suggest that the ideology remained primary but that, because the ideology was unrealistic, totalitarianism was necessary to force it. In the German case, too, the mode of action had its own sources and implications that must be understood on their own terms, independently of the ideological content.

Against the earlier tendency to dismiss Hitler as a guttersnipe, Stern argued convincingly that the sense of challenge and opportunity that led Hitler to radical political decision reflected a sense of history based on wider reading than had usually been recognized—and that could not be dismissed as superficial.[27] Ian Kershaw's authoritative recent biography confirms that Hitler read widely, if unsystematically, and that his reading was important to his confident self-understanding.[28] Thus, in part, Hitler's sense of privileged insight into the historical moment, the unprecedented combination of opportunity and vulnerability that it entailed, the responsibilities that followed, and the scope for a new mode of collective action in response.

Hitler's sense of the challenge was historically specific, as was his sense of the scope for the new politics, based on will and new forms of mobilization, necessary to respond to that challenge.[29] Even before experiencing the war and the Weimar Republic, he had found deeply alienating the squabbling and paralysis of parliamentary government in Austria–Hungary by 1909.[30] A sense of the requirements for a post-liberal politics informed *Mein Kampf*, in which he discussed at length how will from above could interact with energies from below through new forms of mass mobilization and organization. Thus, obsessive though he surely was, we cannot understand Hitler as merely idiosyncratically maniacal in some ahistorical sense. And precisely in its historical specificity, his idealism and commitment energized others, who were attracted not so much to some particular policy or ideological theme but to the more effective mode of collective action, transcending the divisions of bourgeois politics and society, that he seemed first to promise, then to spearhead.[31]

Even Hitler's own will, although undeniably a kind of psychological substratum up to a point, cannot be understood as exclusively psychological in an ahistorical sense. Rather, it entailed a particular historically specific content and became possible only from within the new historical-political framework. Far from seeking mere self-aggrandizement, Hitler understood himself as an instrument of something higher; thus his sense of political responsibility and destiny. But thus too the characteristic shrillness, stemming most immediately from his sense that time was working against Germany, especially with the emergence of the United States and the Soviet Union as potential superpowers.[32] Christopher Browning noted Hitler's "increasing sense of himself as a man of destiny who must do all in his own lifetime, and the pervasive and ceaseless activism that possessed his own psyche as well as the Nazi movement."[33] We recall Moshe Lewin's emphasis on the analogous Soviet sense of "running out of history."

As George Mosse emphasized, Hitler even played down personal charisma and sought to head off any personality cult—precisely because he saw himself as an instrument of the movement, the servant of a wider struggle. Rather than an indispensable charismatic figure, he was to be integral to a new ritual or liturgy that would survive him in a new order not dependent on the personal qualities of any single individual.[34] But Mosse's emphasis on liturgy and ritual did not get at the wider dimension we most need to understand.

Stern cut deeper in suggesting that the Hitlerian language of hardness and absolute will proved appealing "because it and apparently it alone satisfied, albeit in a monstrous fashion, a religious need." For Stern, in fact, fascism in general understood will in terms of cosmic law that drew on and fused scientific confidence and religious faith. On the one hand, will "acts in the social and political sphere with the same absolute validity as the principle of natural selection does among the species of animals." On the other hand, "'the Will' becomes a pseudo-*religious* concept: in speaking of himself as one sent by History, or again as the agent of cosmic forces or natural laws," Hitler came close to Christ's affirmation that he was merely the instrument of a higher will.[35] But suggestive though it was, this formulation missed the element of shrillness, the awareness of contingency, and thus overstated the degree of assurance in Hitler's self-understanding. The agent of post-developmentalist history is very different from *either* the neutral instrument of scientific law *or* the deputy of a benign, possibly providential God. For even insofar as will could be compared to natural law, the only test of its sufficiency or superiority was action itself, which required mobilizing others to seek to shape a capricious, often recalcitrant history.

Stern usefully added a further dimension in linking Hitler to the "catastrophe-mindedness of the age," the "crisis" atmosphere of his culture.[36] Hitler's historical-political sense did indeed draw from that atmosphere—and his mode of action reinforced it. Thus the sense of great historical enterprise that many, at the time and thereafter, have noted in his sense of his own role. But "catas-trophe-mindedness" enhanced the sense of vulnerability that surrounded Hitler's sense of opportunity. In *Mein Kampf*, he expressed clearly, if crudely, his sense of the contingency of the whole human enterprise as this planet moves "through the ether." We come to recognize that we operate within a wider context of utter indifference or—worse—of dimly glimpsed forces toward chaos.[37] Without the ongoing exercise of human responsibility, we find ourselves back in the jungle.

Despite appearances, then, Hitler was not simply reducing the human world to nature; on the contrary, he was seeking to grasp the requirements for sustaining the human-historical world in light of the lessons of the war and the wider challenges of modernity. For if our situation were indeed reduced to the jungle, there would be no scope, and no need, for human beings to think it through and decide how to respond. Although in his crudeness Hitler sometimes seemed to suggest as much, the imperative was not simply to peel away human-istic illusions to get back to the jungle—and thereby prove that humans are animals after all. Rather, the point was the scope, and the need, for the exercise of collective human will through unprecedented forms of action in response to historically specific challenges so that we may go on creating the human world in history. Hitler's cockiness stemmed from his sense of having uniquely grasped the challenge and opportunity on precisely this level. But the outcomes were by no means guaranteed, and thus the shrillness.

This is not to contend that Hitler had a consistent, systematic philosophy of history. Sometimes he seemed to suggest that he was simply following laws of development, or even serving "providence." But the laws of development at issue were in fact no more helpful than those that Lenin and Stalin continued to claim to derive from Marxism. Even while referring to such laws in a telling passage in *Mein Kampf*, Hitler expressed his sense of the fragility of things—but also the scope for giving order to the universe through will, strength, and organization.[38] Whatever the lip service to a residual developmentalism, history making depended on contingent human response. And in referring to "providence," Hitler was merely expressing the sense in which the world is sufficiently coherent for history to be made to respond to and mesh with human will—if the appropriate means are found.

At some points, as when, in a notorious passage on the "Jewish virus" in his *Table Talk*, Hitler invoked comparison with Koch and Pasteur, he seemed to strut the confidence of science, as if all that was necessary was fully to apply science for the first time.[39] But although science was crucial, Hitler understood that mere scientific expertise not in itself sufficient, any more than was the mere operation of Darwinian mechanisms. As we noted in Chapter 4, it had increasingly dawned, especially in light of the war, that a new interface of science with political will and organization was necessary to make the requisite action possible. The application of scientific expertise would take place from within the wider framework of collective action that Hitler found imperative.

The overall key was the capacity to act, which, much as for Lenin and Mussolini, required flexibility as opposed to some fixed, consistent program. For Hitler, it was essential not to get caught up in divisive points of dogma.[40] And Kershaw makes it clear that it was not ideology that distinguished Nazism from other parties and groups on the right: "What set Hitler's movement apart was above all its image of activism, dynamism, élan, youthfulness, vigor."[41]

For Hitler himself, the Jews constituted the obstacle; they would continue to keep the community from coming together to do what needed to be done. So future success required isolating and eliminating the Jews. The vast majority of Germans, when encountering such thinking, found any such preoccupation with the Jews excessive, if not pathological—until they bought into the wider enterprise of great collective action.

The question of Hitler's role, then, is very much bound up with the question of Nazi ideology, but our ways of conceiving the alternatives can throw us off. Geoff Eley points us in the right direction in noting that functionalists like Hans Mommsen tended to pit political and bureaucratic mechanisms dichotomously against ideological factors. In doing so, said Eley, they were missing

> the insidiousness of Nazism's discursive power. For it's all very well to express skepticism about "Nazi ideology" in the narrower, formalistic sense of that term, and to doubt the penetration into everyday life of Nazism's programmatic propaganda. But as soon as we focus on the issue of complicity at all levels of German society after 1933, we immediately need an *extended* understanding of ideology, as being embedded in cultural practices, institutional sites, and social relations—in what people do and the structured contexts where they do it, rather than just the ideas they consciously think. . . . Reconstituting society as the *Volksgemeinschaft* was an ineluctably ideological process.[42]

Even this formulation may be too dichotomous in contrasting practice with thinking, but it specifies clearly that an ideological project was crucially at work *even though* it cannot be characterized in formulaic terms. And we have seen that that project, including a special role for leadership and will, had sources broader than the combination of ideological elements usually associated with Hitler and Nazism.

Modes of energizing interaction in the Nazi revolution

Until it collapsed at the end, the Nazi experiment achieved a degree of success that seems surprising in light of its radicalism. Such success was possible because of the energizing mode of interaction that developed between the leader and those who, on several distinguishable layers, got caught up in the Nazi project. Quite apart from Hitler's immediate collaborators and those in the Nazi hierarchy, this gradually came to include a wider array of Germans, from expert professionals to those who reported this or that to the Gestapo, to ordinary middle-aged policemen called for auxiliary duty in the hinterlands of the East. Such agents assumed essential, if segmented and delimited roles even in the most troubling aspects of Nazi practice. Because responses on the several levels proved mutually reinforcing, we must look beyond the familiar dualistic distinctions between leaders and followers, center and periphery, above and below, visionaries and bureaucrats to get at the complexity and the dynamic implications of the overall interaction. Although Hitler's sense of destiny helped to energize the whole array, and although the wider Nazi movement, as a new elite, had to spearhead the overall process, radicalizing initiatives from those lower in the hierarchy or on the periphery sometimes created new situations to which the leaders had to respond.

It is well known that the situation, on one level, was institutional chaos— "government without administration," a "Darwinian struggle" between traditional state entities and parallel Nazi institutions that often squabbled among themselves. The lack of system enhanced Hitler's role as arbiter.[43] Committed Nazis took the initiative by "working toward the Führer," in the illuminating contemporary phrase that Ian Kershaw has used to particularly good effect. As Kershaw made clear, the category reflects precisely the mutually reinforcing interaction of above and below that fed the regime's radicalizing momentum. Hitler suggested a certain direction, and others did on their own what they assumed the Führer would want done, what the further development of the Nazi revolution seemed to require. Such actions stemmed from an undecidable mix of revolutionary enthusiasm and banal ambitions and rivalries. But the initiative from the party rank and file or local leaders served both to pressure and to energize Hitler, leading, for example, to the escalation of anti-Semitic measures in 1935 and 1938. At the same time, Kershaw showed again and again how working toward the Führer produced not radicalization but chaos.[44]

When we come to ordinary Germans outside the Nazi hierarchy, we note that a certain mode of distancing from the magnitude of the Nazi project, as opposed to deepening involvement, was operative up to a point, especially at first. As Kershaw showed, the regime deliberately fostered "the Hitler myth," crediting Hitler with the regime's accomplishments, even making Hitler the embodiment of all that was positive in Nazism while leaving the widely unpopular party to bear the responsibility for the perceived excesses.[45] This enabled ordinary Germans to play down the radicalism of the break in progress, for anything that seemed untoward could be blamed on extremists or provincial party officials. The sense that the departure was legitimate and desirable, that the Führer was opposing any excesses, afforded Hitler and the Nazi elite the space they needed to begin what proved to be a revolution.

It seemed like normalization when, admittedly through extreme methods, Hitler cracked down on one relatively superficial brand of Nazi militancy by taming the

SA in 1934. In fact, however, this measure proved to facilitate the emergence of the SS as the new elite within the Nazi movement, necessary especially as careerists crowded the party. And as it was brought together under Himmler, the SS–Gestapo complex was entrusted with the regime's most sensitive tasks. It operated to some extent behind the scenes, reflecting the recognition by Hitler and the leadership that public opinion would not necessarily be sympathetic. But it has become clear that we can only go so far in attributing the most radical outcomes to the SS and to secrecy, for the barrier was breached again and again. The leadership proceeded both as if, on the one hand, the enterprise was elitist and secret and, on the other, as if it required the whole community as the collective agent. And the effort, initiated almost at once, of expanding and replenishing the Nazi elite drew widely from within society, enhancing upward mobility. Thus, for example, the *Ordensburgen*, new institutions to educate the next generation of Nazi leaders, were to go beyond traditional higher education, which the regime believed to be still too class-bound and specialized.[46]

Robert Gellately, focusing on the Gestapo, pinpointed two illuminating mechanisms at work as ordinary Germans got caught up in the Nazi project. First, he accented the surprising continuity of personnel in the political police; the transition from Weimar to the Third Reich entailed no purge or wholesale Nazification. Yet these police welcomed the enhanced scope for action, now with less restraint, that Nazism afforded them.[47] Although not subject to ideological fervor *per se*, they came to agree that it was desirable to "cleanse" those deemed opponents, even to accept in general terms the wider political aims of the regime. So the scope for higher-stakes, even history-making action that the Nazi project entailed was itself commitment-engendering and energizing.

Gellately showed at the same time that, in light of the central and expanding tasks that the political police were assigned, its numbers remained surprisingly limited. So the police effort depended on the willingness of the wider citizenry to cooperate, to volunteer information, to offer denunciations from below. Gellately's primary concern was not why such people stepped forward but how their doing so served the functioning of the police state. Still, he suggested that whereas petty score settling and other self-serving impulses played a role, as did ordinary fear in light of Nazi brutality, such mechanisms were not sufficient to account for the extent of the cooperation that took place; yet neither did that cooperation necessarily suggest conversion to ideological racism and anti-Semitism.[48] As with the police themselves, what mattered most seems to have been the energizing sense of contributing to the collective task of forging a more effective nation.

Whereas Gellately did not explicitly assess the import of ahistorical categories, Omer Bartov, studying the army, stressed the limits of ahistorical mechanisms, especially the primary group solidarity often adduced to explain the cohesion of military units in wartime.[49] Against the long-held view that the surprising loyalty of German troops on the eastern front, even in the face of extreme hardship late in the war, stemmed from such solidarity or even generic, supra-ideological patriotism, Bartov underscored the actual ideological penetration. Those troops had internalized a new and different sense of the world, and especially of the present war, precisely as unprecedented and ideological.

It is clear that such involvement from below, by those who had not been committed Nazis when the new action began, was essential to the change that the regime brought about. The question is the basis on which the regime gradually managed, at least up to a certain point, to foster and draw upon the new frame of mind at issue. Following the leader was obviously important, as was the enhanced sense of belonging on the level of ritual and liturgy, of weekend hikes and *Volksgemeinschaft*.[50] But in the last analysis Nazism, like Fascism and Leninism–Stalinism, was to be less a mode of collective experience than a mode of collective action. And although there was some internalization of overt ideological principles, Germans did not have to embrace all the extremes of racism and anti-Semitism to get caught up in the unprecedented dynamic as the regime set out to re-engineer German society and create a new order in Europe.

Wound around this complex interplay, the Nazi dynamic included both direction from above and initiative from below, both secrecy and mass participation, both bureaucratic routine and the capacity to foster and tap into extraordinary enthusiasm, both the zealotry of insiders and the capacity to co-opt outsiders—from experts to "ordinary men." In light of the set of tasks that seemed to open, the resulting dynamic itself affected the interaction between the components to produce what proved to be a particular kind of radicalization.

The Nietzschean frame of mind

Nazism was to respond, most immediately, to the Weimar crisis, although also to the situation at once revealed and created by the war. The key issues on both levels manifested creases within the modern Enlightenment deployment that suggested the need to transcend conventional humanitarianism and morality. We saw that, although it did not warrant them directly, Nietzsche's thinking long seemed to afford a kind of authority for the most radical population measures, including eliminating the unworthy altogether. And the Nietzschean legacy undergirded the sense of radical new possibility as the Nazis came to power and quickly initiated a new course of action. Their selective embrace of that legacy then proved central to the frame of mind that made possible the most troubling dimensions of Nazi action.

That the Nazis claimed Nietzsche is clear, but as we discussed in Chapter 3, the nature and significance of the link remain much disputed, partly because so many modes of relationship with the complex, protean Nietzschean legacy were possible. Even if we grant that that legacy was genuinely central to the Nazi self-understanding, and not merely instrumental window dressing, we may fasten onto Nietzsche's accent on the scope for willful shaping and fall into a kind of aestheticist reductionism. Even J.P. Stern, almost anticipating Simonetta Falasca-Zamponi's treatment of Mussolini, sometimes suggested that Nazism boiled down to the voluptuous aesthetic satisfaction of Hitler as leader-artist: "One is struck by the fantastic malleability, the disposability of the world and everything in it in the hands of this *artiste manqué*. His work and his 'creative Will' seem to be co-extensive." Whether or not this was what Nietzsche had in mind, Stern continued, it was clear that for Hitler, "this artist-politician, self-fulfillment and authenticity are one and the same thing."[51] Hitler was indeed an *artiste manqué*, as a matter of biographical fact, and "will" was obviously central, but the point was not merely aesthetic self-creation or self-realization as an end in itself. Rather, the scope for will was bound up with the need and the scope for history-making action, transcending the conventional morality that had emerged from within the Judeo-Christian tradition and taking new, more overtly humanitarian form with the Enlightenment break.

Steven Aschheim showed how extensively the Nietzschean legacy had penetrated the culture of Nazism. As he stressed, the question of Hitler's first-hand acquaintance with Nietzsche is secondary; Hitler espoused a popularized Nietzscheanism.[52] In any case, Kershaw's authoritative biography showed that Hitler read Nietzsche while imprisoned at Landsberg.[53] Moreover, Hitler even conveyed to Mussolini the collected works of Nietzsche as a sixtieth birthday present.[54] The Nazis had claimed Nietzsche as their own long before coming to power in 1933, and thereafter it seemed self-evident that Nietzsche had been a central forerunner. Indeed, they claimed that only now, with the war and the advent of Nazism, was Nietzsche's meaning becoming clear. During the years of the regime, Nietzsche's works—often edited or expurgated, to be sure—were published at a rapid pace, even integrated into the German school system. Aschheim found that a Nazified Nietzscheanism had spread into broad spectra of German society, well beyond official intellectuals like Alfred Rosenberg and Nietzsche scholars like Alfred Bäumler.[55] Through this "dense and broad diffusion," Aschheim concluded, suitably adapted Nietzschean notions became essential to the Nazi self-understanding. However, just as some Fascists disputed Gentile's authority in Fascist Italy, there were Nazis who denied, or nuanced, Nietzsche's intellectual patrimony. Still, as Aschheim put it, these responses, too, *"demonstrate the normative nature and centrality of that thinker as definitive of the Nazi order."*[56]

Although their embrace was selective, the Nazis' implication that their mode of selection was not only legitimate but privileged was not implausible on the face of it. Coming later than Nietzsche himself, they could claim a superior historical sense, including a superior grasp of the historical moment, and on that basis to be cutting through the undoubted tensions to the core of Nietzsche's thinking. And the sense that they, uniquely, were beginning to act on the new basis toward which he had pointed was deeply energizing. Those clinging to Christian humanitarianism, or to liberal individualism and democratic ideals deriving from the eighteenth century, were the ones who could not respond to modernity.

George Lichtheim pinpointed the basic relationship four decades ago: "Whatever Nietzsche may have *intended* it is clear what his work *portended*: namely the spread of attitudes which were wholly incompatible with the Judeo-Christian inheritance, including its humanist off-shoots. . . . Nietzsche was . . . the most radically anti-Christian writer known to history. . . . It is not too much to say that but for Nietzsche the SS–Hitler's shock troops and the core of the whole movement—would have lacked the inspiration that enabled them to carry out their programme of mass murder in Eastern Europe."[57]

With its accent on the scope for both human self-creation and a new great politics beyond conventional good and evil, the Nietzschean legacy was widely invoked to justify Nazi population measures.[58] Indeed, actually implementing a radical population policy in defiance of conventional morality not only drew on the Nietzschean strands in the culture but deepened the Nietzschean frame of mind, the sense of involvement in a grandiose, unprecedented world-historical enterprise requiring, and drawing forth, special qualities of will, courage, and hardness. J.P. Stern's remark that "the hallmark of the age of Hitler—its historicity—is hardness" rings true even though his aestheticist understanding of Hitler's will proved wayward, as we noted above.[59] Raul Hilberg noted the significance of the hard/soft distinction to Holocaust perpetrators.[60] Interior Minister Wilhelm Frick invoked "courage" when he told a meeting of population planners in June 1933 that "we must have the courage again to grade our people according to its genetic values."[61] Auschwitz commandant Rudolf Höss feared being thought weak and stressed the importance of not showing emotion as he carried out his difficult task.[62]

We often remark that Nazi population policy deprived individuals of "their status as human beings,"[63] but from a Nietzschean perspective, simply being a human being is not a value unto itself, certainly not the ultimate value. *What* status as human beings? Based on what? Self-recommending though we may now find it, the implied imperative is not necessarily privileged *even* as morality, understood as care for the world, especially if we start with the human place in a fundamentally *historical* world. Although much of Nietzsche's thinking suggests that the suprahistorical self-realization of superior individuals is the highest end, when anticipating the new "great politics" that would follow in his wake, he suggested a premium precisely on collective, history-making action instead. The aim was not just to cure or purify the social body so that the higher types could realize themselves but first to create the collective instrument and then willfully to tackle that ongoing world making. From this perspective, one's status as a human being depended on one's role in that ongoing collective project.

So different are these notions from our own that students of Nazism are often reluctant to credit any "idealism" in the Nazi embrace of Nietzsche, even as they recognize, implicitly or almost explicitly, its centrality. Thus, for example, Michael Burleigh observed that "talk of the 'idealism' of a Brandt, Catel or Schneider ignores both their lack of pity (never a quality much prized in German intellectual circles since Nietzsche), and the cold ruthless way they went about starving or gassing their own patients for the basest careerist, economic or political motives."[64] We share Burleigh's moral outrage, and banal careerist and economic motives were surely at work in this instance and in others, as we have taken pains to emphasize throughout. But they are not sufficient to explain the responses at issue, as Burleigh himself seems to recognize elsewhere, and to some extent implicitly even here, despite the seemingly cultivated ambiguity. Lumping "political" with these overtly banal motives, all taken as opposed to "idealism," obviously begs the essential question about the place of *political* idealism.

It neither exculpates the agents nor fatally compromises the term to admit that "idealism" of a sort was at work. Indeed, only thus can we account for the extraordinary lack of pity, precisely as Burleigh's reference to Nietzsche suggests. Idealism does not necessarily entail pity or preclude ruthlessness. On the contrary, idealism in a Nietzschean mode obviously may entail ruthlessness and preclude pity. That is the sense in which, distasteful as it surely is, we need precisely the Nietzschean mode, understood as "idealism," to understand the inner dynamic of Nazism. This genuine difference from the liberal humanitarian tradition stemmed not merely from ahistorical banality or evil but from precisely what we seek to understand overall, a historically specific departure from within the modern Western tradition.

The totalitarian direction

The Nazi direction was overtly totalitarian, whatever the Nazis' hesitations about the term itself in light of its presumed link to mere Hegelian statism in its Italian usage. That direction obviously entailed not only a monopoly of political power and new modes of mass mobilization but also an expanded reach for the public sphere itself, requiring, most symptomatically, a new conception of law, an assault on the Christian churches, and a more active, interventionist population policy.

As he played down Darwinian struggle as a source of radicalization, Burleigh found "the demise of the rule of law" to be central to the totalitarian practice of Nazism. The most basic parallels with the Soviet experience were especially evident on this level, but it was not as if law was simply to be jettisoned through some turn to anarchy or the law of the jungle. Law was being redirected, and although the new direction was surely totalitarian, the question concerns the source, basis, and purpose of the particular redirection in the Nazi case. As Burleigh had it, law was being subordinated to ideological ends; it was to serve "the urgent desire to achieve utopia at any cost." This meant, most basically, that law was now to protect and serve the community, not the individual. It followed that the scope for law and state intrusiveness was limitless, in light of all that could be construed as affecting the community interest. In principle, however, even such totalitarian expansion could have entailed codified law and rigorous, consistent procedure. As it happened in the Nazi case, however, the direction entailed arbitrariness and police intrusiveness. The reason is that for the Nazis a healthy community instinct was to be the basis of law, and Hitler's role was to interpret that community instinct. At the same time, a sense of the Nazi mission was to inform the decisions of the judiciary and the police.[65]

Insofar as such categories as ideology and utopia are not as valuable as is usually assumed to account for the Nazis' totalitarian mode of action, we obviously need something further. Conversely, an accent on ideological utopianism does not in itself explain the Nazi emphasis on instinct as opposed to codified law. We can best wait until Chapter 8, and a wider comparison with Fascist Italy, to make sense of the Nazi approach to law, the scope for arbitrariness that it entailed, and its implications for the meaning of totalitarianism.[66] But in light of all we have seen so far, the Nazi approach was clearly less about realizing some utopia than about assuring the capacity for ongoing collective action in an open-ended world.

The Nazi regime's anti-Christian thrust is increasingly recognized as fundamental, despite the short-term compromises with the churches, the eagerness of the Protestant "German Christians" to cooperate, and Hitler's opposition to the overt neo-pagan tendencies within the Nazi movement.[67] The regime faced opposition from the dissident Protestant Confessing Church and, despite the Concordat of 1933, friction with the Catholic Church, especially as an assault on confessional schools, starting in 1934, provoked bitter Catholic opposition.[68] Still, Hitler hoped to win the support of the churches for anti-Semitism, and until 1937–38 the regime sought not to eliminate the churches but simply to limit their influence. However, although Hitler sought to check them, anti-church pressures from Nazi activists, reflecting a widespread sense that Christianity was incompatible with Nazism, reached a new peak in 1937.[69] By that point, Hitler had gradually come to believe that the churches were part of the problem and began moving toward a more radical policy. At the same time, Pope Pius XI's encyclical of April 1937, *Mit brennender Sorge* (With Burning Concern), seemed like an overt rejection of Hitler's worldview by the Catholic Church. In December 1940, Pope Pius XII unequivocally condemned the sort of "euthanasia," the systematic killing of mental patients, the handicapped, and the terminally ill, that the regime was by then practising secretly.[70] And egregious though the German Christian response generally was, especially in treating the Jewish Christians in their own ranks, their refusal to give in to the Nazis on the sacredness of the Old Testament or the Jewishness of Jesus gradually separated them from the regime.[71]

By 1938, Hitler was giving a free hand in church relations to Martin Bormann, a zealot whom he especially trusted in this sphere. Typically, the deeper thrust of Nazi totalitarianism became clear first not in Germany proper but in newly acquired territories, where there seemed to be greater scope for experiment. After the incorporation of first Austria and then the Sudetenland in 1938, legislation deprived the churches in each area of their status under public law, and this proved a prelude to the overt oppression of and control over the churches in the Warthegau, part of the Polish territory annexed directly by Germany after the conquest of Poland in 1939. Months before, in his notorious speech of January 30, 1939, Hitler had suggested that development along these lines could be expected in Germany in the event of war.[72]

Although the war necessitated caution even as it also opened possibilities, Hitler was basically resolved to eliminate the churches and Christianity after the victory.[73] In his *Table Talk* of 1941–42, he articulated the terms of the developing conflict with both Christian denominations; the problem was not simply that these powerful traditional institutions constituted a check on Nazi power but that the whole orientation and value system of Christianity was antithetical to Nazism.[74] Writing in 1942, Bormann stressed the incompatibility of Nazi principles, based, as he saw it, on science, with Christianity, charging that the churches had an interest in perpetuating ignorance. In this vast universe, with lots of planets, there was no basis for belief in a God who cares about every individual. Determined to keep to the laws of life, the Nazis had to eliminate Christianity if Nazi principles were to have full sway over the German people.[75]

As we noted above, this developing assault on Christianity and the churches belies any notion that Nazism was conservative, or the servant of established elites. For Nazism, as for the post-liberal regimes in Italy and the Soviet Union, it was crucial actively to oppose Christianity as an obstacle not just to totalitarian power in the abstract but to the whole new self-understanding around collective world making. Christian principles compromised the capacity to seize collective responsibility. Indeed, as Bormann's appeal to "science" suggested, Nazism thought itself to be more radically modern insofar as its direction was post-Christian, carrying modern secularization to its logical next step. Conversely, insofar as Christian moral categories still impeded the requisite action, the situation was not fully modern.

It was necessary to defy Christianity to begin actively managing population, which was essential to forge the instrument for collective action on the most basic level. The effort surely transcended any simple dichotomy of rational/irrational or humanism/science just as it challenged the conventional understanding of moral/immoral. The Nazis assumed that we human beings need not—must not—simply let nature take its course, but neither can we leave the quality and quantity of population to the aggregate of individual decisions, understood as private, especially when a societal obligation for those individuals is increasingly assumed. Only insofar as a society takes responsibility for shaping itself as a collective instrument in a new, conscious and willed way can it seize responsibility for shaping the world.

Stressing, in *Mein Kampf*, that it had become necessary to differentiate between individuals more systematically, Hitler explicitly included even the right of individuals to have children.[76] Addressing a group of SS leaders in 1937, Himmler noted that in light of Germany's war losses, most immediately, but also in light of the longer-term geopolitical frame, sexual practices—including homosexuality, for example—could no longer be considered private: "All things which take place in the sexual sphere are not the private affair of the individual, but signify the life and death of the nation, signify world power or 'swissification'. . . . A people of good race which has too few children has a one-way ticket to the grave."[77]

Although Himmler's immediate concern in this passage was only quantitative and thus pointed to mere natalism, he made explicit the most basic totalitarian imperative. No private/public distinction was possible in the population sphere, in which the public implications of private decisions concern the community's very capacity to act successfully over the long term. More generally, all private decisions had public implications, so there could be no limit on either public intervention or individual responsibility. Thus the proclamation of labor front chief Robert Ley that "the private citizen has ceased to exist."[78] Only sleep, said Ley, was private, and individuals were not free even to sleep whenever they wanted. Conversely, the implication was that as the public/private distinction fell away, all were essentially participating all the time as they experienced the public weight of decisions once considered private.

The actual population policy of Nazi Germany was unprecedented, especially in its departure from conventional morality, so the agents had sometimes to be sensitive to public opinion as they initiated difficult measures from above. As each step suggested the scope for a further, more radical step, they had to control even language—generally through the language of distancing—to help to make the necessary measures possible.[79] But even language, it seemed, could be shaped through the unprecedented exercise of will and spirit.

Although some assume that the Nazis envisioned creating a sort of racial utopia, achieving "race hygiene" once and for all, the Nazis' own utterances suggest otherwise.[80] In light of the human place in history, there was no scope simply to breed a master race, create a perfect society, and then relax. The unprecedented Nazi effort of population management could be experienced as grandiose and even courageous, but it had to be ongoing, as part of the never-ending struggle to shape what the world becomes.

Engineering the population

Conceiving the intersecting layers

The assumption of some measure of governmental responsibility for population management had become widespread throughout the Western world by the early 1920s, although accents differed considerably. France and Italy featured natalism; interest in eugenics was considerably more widespread in Britain, the United States, and Germany. After much debate in pre-Communist and early Communist Russia, the Soviet Union settled on a natalist course while also stressing the scope for improving population quality through "environmental" change as opposed to eugenics. At the same time, a measure of race thinking and anti-Semitism, and a concomitant belief in the importance of ethnic homogeneity, could be found throughout the Western world at this point. So in probing the Nazi effort at population engineering, we start with a baseline not remotely unique to Germany. What made Nazi Germany different, producing outcomes not seen anywhere else, was a sequence of steps from that baseline, and we must distinguish those steps, probing the relationships between them, if we are to understand those outcomes. The essential distinctions may seem distasteful at first, in light of the manifest conflations in the thinking of many Nazis.

In light of the plausible concern with Nazi racism and anti-Semitism, students of Nazism were slow to research eugenics and the wider reaches of Nazi population policy, but over the last generation or so, starting with the pioneering efforts of such scholars as Ernst Klee, Gisela Bock, and Paul Weindling, we have come better to grasp that even racism and anti-Semitism must be understood in terms of a wider concern with population management that was itself central to the Nazi enterprise.[81]

Nazi population policy combined five distinguishable but intersecting elements, starting with the merely quantitative dimension, natalism, promoting births. Obviously distinguishable was the second, qualitative, dimension, eugenics, which, understood in terms of the ambiguous notion of "race hygiene," seemed to suggest that population quality could be, had to be, understood partly in racial terms. And thus the third point, that the degree of homogeneity essential for collective effectiveness needed to be understood in racial or ethnic terms as well. Fourth was territorial expansion to provide the spatial basis both for an expanded population and for the self-sufficiency necessary for, above all, the capacity to wage war. Fifth was the resettlement of ethnic Germans living abroad and even the selection of those deemed racially valuable from among those not otherwise defined as ethnic Germans in conquered territories. The outcome would be a massive country, unified around ethnic homogeneity, encompassing more and better Germans, the defective having been prohibited from procreating or eliminated altogether. This would be an effective political community, capable of the necessary ongoing collective action in the emerging modern world.

These concerns and aims did not always mesh perfectly, partly because diagnoses sometimes conflicted. Thus, for example, Robert Proctor noted the apparent contradiction in the sense of both population decline and overpopulation that carried from before the war into the Nazi period.[82] But, in addition, the relationships between the several dimensions of Nazi policy can be difficult to grasp, especially because of the Nazis' own conflations but also because of their complex interaction in practice. Certainly, many during the Nazi period were both eugenicist and racist, and even recent specialists sometimes lump the two categories together.[83] Yet only if we keep the distinctions in mind and proceed step by step can we grasp the synergy and the radicalizing momentum created by the interplay, even the conflations, among the several strands.

The determination to tackle eugenics lent credence to wider claims about the determinants of "racial health" and thus about the qualitative improvement possible and necessary. So the apparent plausibility and legitimacy of the eugenics steps seemed to enhance the plausibility and legitimacy of the racialist steps. The reverse also proved to be true. At the same time, the effort to tackle the whole universe of population issues, drawing on modern technocratic expertise, produced an unprecedented spate of studies in preparation for expansion.[84] The whole thus became greater than the sum of its parts, thereby enhancing the credibility of the overall package, making it easier for those not immediately involved at first to play essential roles—*even as* such conflation made that package seem irrational, criminal, or evil to some looking in from the outside. This was a measure of the emerging *difference*.

The Nazis' sense of their relationship with the democracies on population questions cut in contrasting directions, yet the combination proved particularly energizing. Their newly interventionist direction seemed plausible, even progressive, partly because of the element of perceived kinship with other advanced countries, especially the United States and Britain. The United States had come to seem the embodiment of modernity for many Germans by the 1920s, so

American examples, from racial segregation and immigration restriction to sterilization and anti-miscegenation laws, offered a measure of legitimation.

Although Proctor made some of the same argument, Stefan Kühl, who studied
under Gisela Bock, especially showed the thickness and significance of the
German–American interaction on eugenics, in its tricky interface with racism,
leading up to and into the Nazi break. Kühl explicitly challenged the longstanding tendency to play down these links by exaggerating early differences and
by invoking categories like "pseudo-science" or the political pressures assumed to
have been particularly at work in the Nazi context. In the controversies among
eugenicists about Nazi policy, Kühl showed, there was international distinction
on both sides, so the "pseudo-science" argument is facile. And political considerations intruded on both sides as well.[85]

After a hiatus surrounding the war, renewed and deeper contacts between
Germany and the United States on population matters developed by the late
1920s. American books were quickly translated into German, and the Rockefeller
Foundation became prominent among U.S. foundations supporting eugenics
research in Germany. Hitler read and even developed personal contacts with
American eugenicists.[86]

At the same time, the institutionalized and seemingly expanding racism of the
United States afforded a major precedent. Hitler joined a number of German
racial hygienists in applauding the American turn toward immigration restriction
on a racial basis during the early 1920s.[87] More generally, the Nazis cited with
approval the segregation of African Americans as well as the anti-miscegenation
laws in force in thirty American states—while periodically claiming German superiority in eschewing lynching. The influential American racist thinker Lothrop
Stoddard, praised by Herbert Hoover in testimony before the House Immigration
Committee in 1924, developed high-level contacts in Germany, even meeting
Hitler personally. His writings would eventually be featured in Nazi school books.[88]

In the modern, progressive United States, thirty-two states, starting with
Indiana in 1907, had adopted some form of sterilization law by the early 1930s.
California, where almost half of the 11,000 sterilizations performed in the
U.S.A. between 1907 and 1930 took place, proved to be the most important.[89]
Oliver Wendell Holmes and the U.S. Supreme Court upheld the constitutionality
of compulsory sterilization in 1927.

So it could seem that what the Nazis were doing was not so different—simply
more consistent and thoroughgoing. Yet, on the other hand, the difference was
not merely quantitative but qualitative, and the Nazis took pride in having the
courage and toughness to push beyond the hesitant democracies to the radical
forefront. The fact that many in the Western mainstream did not like what the
Nazis were doing reinforced the pride, the energizing sense of difference.

From natalism to eugenics

Nazi population policy shared many of the natalist presuppositions to be found
in Fascist Italy and to some extent even in the Soviet Union at the same time. Up

to a point, in fact, Nazi natalist policies paralleled those to be found even in the contemporary democracies, especially France, from which some of the new German measures were borrowed directly.[90] A high birthrate manifested vitality, and an effective modern society requires lots of bodies, most obviously to fight wars. Thus the Nazi regime's progressive maternity leave policies, pronatal maternity benefits, and manipulation of marriage, divorce, and abortion laws. But a concern for population quality was central to Nazi policy from the start. Only those considered racially valuable were eligible for the marriage loans and child allowances that were supposed to encourage large families.[91]

More generally, the concern with quality meant, as a fundamental aspect of the blurring of public and private, that personal health was central to the national interest. Even fighting wars requires not just cannon fodder but *healthy* bodies. Individuals had no right to dispose of their own bodies—rather, they had an obligation to be healthy.[92] And as specified in a Reich decree late in 1935, the German medical profession had a duty to protect the health of both individuals and the German people in the aggregate.[93]

In this guise, as Proctor has shown, Nazi health officials pioneered much that would gradually come to seem innovative and progressive in the Western mainstream.[94] They promoted research on the ill-effects of alcohol and tobacco, restricted the sale of alcohol to minors, and campaigned against smoking by pregnant women. Hitler would not allow smoking in his presence. At the same time, the Nazis promoted holistic, preventive medicine, midwifery, natural childbirth, and breastfeeding. They favored natural herbs and teas as well as whole-grain bread, explicitly in opposition to the recent shift to white bread, which they viewed as an artificial, chemical product. They sought to uncover problems with environmental toxins and radiation and the possible negative effects of artificial coloring and preservatives. They were out in front on cancer research and, sensing the importance of biodiversity, even adapted measures to protect rare species.

But the question of population quality pointed beyond health and nutrition to the scope for eugenic measures, encompassing both positive and negative selection. The positive direction simply entailed encouraging those deemed superior to have more children. Thus, for example, it was the duty of SS members, having been subjected to particularly rigorous racial screening and selection, to have as many children as possible.[95] Negative selection required a still-deeper departure from the mainstream, and the regime promptly initiated compulsory sterilization. Although they understood the measure as "race hygiene," improving the race or "stock," it generally had no basis in racial differentiation at first. The surreptitious sterilization in 1937 of the "Rhineland bastards," the approximately 500 offspring of German women and occupying troops from French Africa, was a notable exception.[96]

In June 1933, just months after the Nazis came to power, Interior Minister Wilhelm Frick established a Committee of Experts for Population and Racial Policy to prepare a sterilization law. The result was the Law for the Prevention of Progeny with Hereditary Diseases, issued on July 14, 1933, and effective from

January 1, 1934. Whereas, as we noted, 11,000 people in the United States were sterilized from 1907 to 1930, Nazi Germany had sterilized about 320,000, or 0.5 percent of the population, by the outbreak of the war in 1939.[97]

Late in 1932, the Prussian government had prepared a draft law permitting sterilization of those considered to have a hereditary illness, but the procedure required the consent of the person or a guardian. The Nazis' new national law went well beyond the Prussian precedent to establish compulsion and expand the range of conditions taken to warrant sterilization. Such categories as "congenital feeble-mindedness," "manic depression," and "serious physical deformities" obviously left much discretion to those actually implementing the law.[98]

Another key law in July 1934 created a centralized network of state health offices with departments for gene and race care, staffed by 12,000 medical officials by 1943. In addition to processing sterilization proposals and marriage approvals, this office began compiling an index of the hereditary value of every German, to be the basis for all state decisions concerning the professional and family life of individuals.[99]

Through several follow-up measures, compulsory sterilization was extended to "the asocial," from criminals to vagrants to the "work-shy"—those who, for whatever reason, had dropped out. "Social feeble-mindedness" was deemed adequate to justify sterilizing even individuals who could pass the prescribed intelligence tests.[100] A Himmler decree in 1937 added a further measure of legal sanction for the sterilization of criminals. However, there was controversy about where lines should be drawn, and Himmler did not always get his way. Conflict between his police empire and the Ministry of Justice impeded passage of the community aliens law that was debated from 1940.[101]

Still, the overall direction was clearly to preclude any scope for dropping out. Although the Nazis themselves, using the umbrella of race hygiene, tended to portray the relevant distinctions in racial terms, at work was a changing relationship—a change in mutual obligations—between society and individual that in fact had nothing to do with racial criteria. Most basic was obviously the expectation that everyone was to play a useful societal role. But a negative concern surely also lurked, in light of the Weimar extension of societal responsibility, which meant that some forms of dropping out could mean not "out of sight" but an expanded claim on society. Rather than provide some "safety net" for such people, it seemed that the rational, progressive course was to prevent them from reproducing.

Although the 1933 sterilization law was strongly influenced by U.S. precedents, some Germans had criticized American practice for arbitrary enforcement, even the use of sterilization as punishment. And with the implementation of the German law of 1933, the Nazis stressed the superiority of their own elaborate decision making process, including the role of special courts. And the German law was widely admired in the United States; American supporters found it so well conceived, with its clear definitions of hereditary illness and careful legal and bureaucratic procedures, that it made abuse nearly impossible.[102] Such positive reinforcement surely buttressed the conviction among ordinary Germans that, with this modern, rational, efficient, and fair-minded measure to protect both individual and society, the Nazi departure was moving Germany to the forefront.

The German sterilization law could gain such support in the United States partly because it had no racial provisions. Indeed, in the face of rumors that the law was intended precisely to eliminate Jews, American supporters were able to charge that anti-Nazis were betraying an untoward bias by tendentiously linking the Nazi departure to racism and anti-Semitism.[103] The fact that such false charges could indeed be refuted enhanced the apparent legitimacy of the German measure. Still, as the distinguishable anti-Semitic strand of Nazi population policy was radicalized during the 1930s, contacts with America diminished sharply. But international and especially American support had helped to persuade Germans of the legitimacy of compulsory sterilization, which proved to be a crucial first step in an ever more radical experiment in population engineering.[104]

We can appreciate the widely heard argument that compulsory sterilization, compromising the inviolability of the body and even the inherent worth of human life, began the moral descent that would lead to all the horrors that followed.[105] But the sterilization of 11,000 people in the United States, reprehensible though we now find it, did not start the same moral descent. Sterilization does not *necessarily* lead to "euthanasia." Thus the significance of the wider Nazi departure, which, as we have emphasized, grew from a sense that the human situation had changed with the war, which had in itself challenged traditional notions of the sanctity of human life and the inviolability of the body and thereby forced new questions about individual rights and societal responsibilities onto the table. In light of the war experience, sterilization was a turning point in one sense but not in another.

Although not the inevitable next step, the actual killing of those deemed unfit that began in 1939 surely required forced sterilization as a prerequisite. But in commencing this so-called "euthanasia" program, there was no formal legislation or public discussion, and the regime made every effort to keep the operation secret. Still, as the leading authority, Michael Burleigh, has shown in detail, widespread propaganda, especially through films, sought to build support for the overall direction. Although these films were used partly to initiate those who became directly involved in the "euthanasia" program, their major aim was not to recruit agents but merely to foster a new frame of mind in the German public. "Euthanasia," they suggested, could be legitimate, even a higher duty, restoring the law of the creator against the sinful human effort to preserve "life unworthy of life."[106] The film *Drei Menschen* (Three People), produced as popular discontent about the "euthanasia" program began to surface, started with an epigraph from Nietzsche: "What causes more suffering in the world than the stupidity of the compassionate?"[107] Although the vast majority of Germans were not directly involved at that point, the whole society needed the new frame of mind. The extraordinary action of great politics required potential involvement at all levels, whatever the differentiation of function in any particular instance and the expediency of secrecy at present.

Burleigh noted that the origins of the "euthanasia" program are complex— and that there are several versions of how it started. Moreover, there were separate programs for children and adults. The program targeting children began with the Knauer case, which surfaced late in the fall of 1938. Encouraged by a grandmother, a parental petition to Hitler asked if an infant in a Leipzig clinic who was born blind, retarded, and without a leg and part of an arm could be granted a merciful death.[108] Although the program targeting children was in one sense *ad hoc*, in a deeper sense it was central to a wider intended policy, with the timing bound up with preparations for war.[109] Indeed, Hitler had long envisioned something like the "euthanasia" program and, during the discussions of forced sterilization in 1933, had contemplated beginning to kill mental patients at once. But he decided that this would be too much too soon, that "euthanasia" was better attempted as part of concerted preparations for war, when objections from the churches might be more muted.[110] So Burleigh stressed that when finally implemented in 1939, the program targeting adults resulted not from some mere bureaucratic momentum; rather, it was a well-considered aspect of the preparations for war, intended to save money and, more immediately, to free hospital beds for war casualties and ethnic German repatriates.[111]

Sometime before July 1939, Hitler instructed Leonardo Conti, working for Bormann, to initiate a program for killing "useless" adults. Eventually taking the name "Aktion T-4" from the address of the headquarters villa, Tiergartenstrasse 4, in a Berlin suburb, the T-4 program was attached to the Chancellery of the Führer so that it could be implemented outside the regular state bureaucracy.[112] Under this program, the more systematic killing began as the military campaign in Poland proceeded during the fall of 1939. At first, the medical personnel might simply withhold food, but soon experts devised methods for killing mental patients in large numbers with carbon monoxide. By August 1941, when the T-4 program, at least in its then current form, was halted, over 90,000 adults had been killed.[113]

Growing rumors and protests from church leaders, culminating in the noted sermon of August 3, 1941, by the aristocratic bishop of Münster, Clemens August Graf von Galen, denouncing the "euthanasia" program, have long been taken as instrumental in forcing its ending. But even while recognizing the power of Galen's sermon, Burleigh concluded that it was merely "wishful thinking" to see it as decisive. T-4 ended at that point primarily because the regime had already slightly exceeded its target for the numbers of beds to be released—but also because of the crucial interface, which we will encounter shortly, with the evolution of Nazi Jewish policy.[114] Moreover, even after the official, centrally directed "euthanasia" program ended that August, the killing of both adults and children continued in a more decentralized way. Indeed, the program was broadened to include the healthy children of unwanted races in 1943.[115] Patients were still being killed in mental institutions as a matter of hospital routine until the last days of the war.

Pivotal to Nazi radicalization, the "euthanasia" program entailed, in almost archetypal form, the energizing interaction of layers that we discussed in the abstract above. As Burleigh noted, whereas plans for implementation were entrusted to others, "Hitler gave the decision to go ahead, and had already established both the approximate timetable and what one might loosely call the moral–political framework."[116] On the first level, the interaction was with insiders. Burleigh stressed that those like Christian Wirth who were most directly involved in the killing "were carefully selected for their proven brutality and ideological dedication." Indeed, all down the T-4 hierarchy, people were chosen for political fanaticism already demonstrated. These, Burleigh insisted explicitly, were not "ordinary men."[117] And their doings were to be kept secret.

Yet, crucially, others became involved in other ways, drawn, it would seem, by the unprecedented action that Hitler and the Nazi elite had initiated. Hitler's memo of October 1939 did not order but simply empowered doctors to kill mental patients and handicapped children. Although a few doctors opted out, and seem not to have suffered for having done so, the vast majority willingly proceeded through the opening that Hitler had afforded them.[118] And quite apart from the complicity of many members of the medical community, initiative from lower levels also seems to have played a role.

Burleigh speculated that the family initiative in the Knauer case "was probably not an isolated incident. In such a political climate, understandable human anxieties about severely disabled infants, terminal illness and severe incapacity were compounded by grass-roots ideological fanaticism."[119] Indeed, even as he stressed intention from the top and thus the limits of the countervailing functionalist–bureaucratic emphasis, Burleigh took pains to deflate any misty-eyed reverence for "ordinary people." Some ordinary Germans, he suggested, were not ill-disposed to having the state kill sick relatives. Having apparently gotten caught up in the overall Nazi enterprise, they facilitated the program through silent collusion. To be sure, parents were deceived about what was happening to their children—but some may have wanted to be deceived. The regime neutralized doubts partly by the promise of special treatment, so parents could believe that they had done everything possible.[120] Surely much the same dynamic was at work in the families of adults as well.

Noting, in a general way, what this measure of grass-roots agreement seems necessarily to have entailed, Burleigh went on to pose the central question about how it could have developed: "The gradual hardening of a particular moral climate . . . and the slow seepage of a post-Christian and illiberal ideology into the thoughts and actions of the generality are equally striking. Why did many plain people abandon concern for the 'weak', in favor of a vulgar Social Darwinist ideology which entailed a reversion to the laws of the farmyard or jungle?"[121] In leaving the question open, Burleigh's characterization recalls Moshe Lewin's "bafflement" about aspects of the Soviet historical sense that we noted in Chapters 1 and 5. To come closer, at least, to answering Burleigh's question requires recognizing that although we now find such acquiescence unconscionable, it cannot be characterized simply as a "reversion to the laws of the farmyard or jungle."

In assessing the set of responses at issue, it is especially hard to sort out banal ahistorical impulses—the desire to be relieved of a burden—from historically specific factors, and the answer is indeterminate in individual cases. But the key is precisely to get at the historically specific dimension that seems to have changed the threshold of response in this case. The Nazi "atmosphere" to which Burleigh referred had altered that threshold—to some extent, at least, not by undermining or blurring morality but by redirecting it. In acquiescing in the deaths of members of their families, individuals might even have felt a sense of enhanced participation in offering personal sacrifice for the higher cause of national effectiveness. At work was precisely the new "great political" frame of mind, entailing a sense of extraordinary collective responsibility and action transcending conventional "bourgeois" scruples. Active acquiescence or even initiative from below at once reflected and reinforced the new atmosphere that the Nazis had created.

It was a major radicalization actually to kill "life unworthy of life." And once the Nazis had done so, not only the precedent but the very availability of methods and personnel would affect, possibly decisively, the outcome of the parallel strand of Nazi population policy revolving around racism and anti-Semitism.

Societal homogeneity, race thinking, and the demonization of the Jews

As Sheila Faith Weiss noted, the "euthanasia" program, however morally perverse we judge it today, had a certain logic in terms of national efficiency.[122] Although some have posited at least a modicum of such rationality in the late stages of the process leading to the Holocaust, the evidence is overwhelming that the Nazi treatment of the Jews had no such logic.[123] Yet the momentum that led to that terrible outcome developed in close interface with the "euthanasia" program. Moreover, that momentum has increasingly seemed to be bound up in some measure with modernity, science, expertise, and the Enlightenment tradition. We cannot simply invoke some irrational atavism to account for it.

As we noted briefly above, whereas Hitler was obsessively racist and anti-Semitic, and whereas such sentiments were overrepresented although not universal in the Nazi movement, even in 1933 Germany was not qualitatively different from other modern countries, including France and the United States, in the extent or virulence of its anti-Semitism. No less a symbol of American modernity than Henry Ford had produced *The International Jew*, which Hitler and the Nazis read and circulated in an effort to credit their own anti-Semitism.[124] Conversely, for most Germans who voted for the Nazis or even joined the party, anti-Semitism was not the originating impulse, although it was an urgent priority for a minority of party activists.[125]

The pioneering, highly respected local study by William Sheridan Allen, first published in 1965, found that although ordinary Germans in 1933, much like ordinary Americans at the same time, held to a generic, abstract anti-Semitism, relations with Jews were not much at issue, and there was much integration by class on the local level. Most Germans ignored or rationalized Nazi anti-Semitism, which the Nazis themselves did not feature in their push for support. Thus, Allen suggested, in a point endorsed and generalized by Christopher Browning, that Germans were drawn to anti-Semitism because they were drawn

364 The hollow triumph of the will in Nazi Germany

to Nazism, not the other way around.[126] The 1936 report of the Socialist Party in exile on German public opinion (SOPADE), which is widely considered reliable, confirmed such a *change* in the German attitudes toward Jews: although anti-Semitism had not been especially pronounced before, it was growing now that the Nazis had come to power.[127]

So the measure of prior anti-Semitism in Germany was not remotely sufficient to yield the particular genocidal outcome, an outcome that required the active involvement of a significant part of the nation. The question is what mode of interface between Nazism and the wider society made that outcome possible. Just as we cannot invoke some merely German idiosyncrasy, neither do such ahistorical categories as fear, hate, and careerist banality get us to the key relationship. Precisely as Allen implied, the Nazi departure itself was decisive, producing a "frame of mind" more different from our own than we have wanted to recognize.

To understand the difference that Nazism made, and *how* Nazism made that difference, we must again distinguish certain layers or steps in the abstract, as neutrally as possible. Only thus can we discern how the distinguishable layers at work could intersect to change thresholds—even for the many Germans who were not abnormally racist or anti-Semitic in the first place—and then feed radicalization once the Nazi project had begun.

In Chapter 2, we found the first layers settling out even during the nineteenth century, as certain tensions in the Enlightenment deployment came to the fore, intersecting with the new historical-political sense that was emerging at the same time. Standing opposed to liberal individualism was not simply the longstanding concern for community as a mode of being but for community as a mode of action projected into the future. But it is one thing to end up insisting that collective effectiveness requires a measure of homogeneity, thus denying the liberal premium on individualism and pluralism. That was the position of Italian Fascism. It is quite another to conceive the essential homogeneity in racial or ethnic terms. By the early twentieth century, the Germans were prone to understand the scope for inclusion, or full citizenship, in racial or ethnic terms as the French, for example, did not. The German citizenship law of 1913, reflecting concerns over increasing immigration and especially the status of Polish workers already resident in Germany, restricted the scope for citizenship even as it also liberalized citizenship for ethnic Germans living abroad.[128] But its major purpose was precisely to restrict access to citizenship, not to exclude physically those already resident, let alone those already considered citizens. The degree of homogeneity later demanded did not yet seem to be an imperative. At the same time, even as exclusionist, a demand for racial homogeneity did not have to entail rac*ism*, a belief not merely in racial difference but in differences in value—and thus racial hierarchy. And even to posit some racial hierarchy would not have to entail singling out and even demonizing the Jews in particular. Why, then, did the Nazis, in their quest for collective effectiveness, insist on these further steps, and what were the implications of doing so?

Omer Bartov argued that racism becomes central only via legitimation by legal and scientific communities, "the most representative establishments of the modern state."[129] But Bartov tended to reduce the process to the arrogance of professionalization itself, as if it were all self-explanatory once the modern state had emerged. We noted in Chapter 2, following Berel Lang and Zygmunt Bauman, that tensions or hidden possibilities in the Enlightenment tradition invited the use of racial categories to establish the distinctions and classifications seemingly necessary to shape the world. That would help us to understand why any such enterprise, calling on professional expertise, could have seemed important in the first place. But as we also noted in Chapter 2, even Lang and Bauman left vague the conditions likely to bring that Enlightenment potential to the fore. We simply need to distinguish—and account for—some additional historical steps. And in our terms, it was only with the turn to a certain new mode of collective action that the racialist potential of the Enlightenment break could become central—and much more dangerous. Only as a deeper homogeneity came to seem necessary could experts come to play the legitimizing role that Bartov pinpointed; they seemed to know how to draw the essential lines on an objective basis.

If we take the potential for racist hatred to be differentiated across populations on the basis of ahistorical personality or psychological type, what is to be understood in the German case is a change in thresholds, so that the potential, at whatever level, became more actual. Even for Hitler and the others who manifested pathological levels of racist hatred, the ahistorical psychological propensity was necessary but not sufficient. And what changed thresholds and brought that propensity to bear was not generic crisis or insecurity but the sense that homogeneity was essential for deeper collective effectiveness. Such homogeneity seemed to be particularly imperative for Germany, deeply wounded and shown up as especially vulnerable by defeat in the First World War. The vision of the newly necessary homogeneity made the presence of the Jews not merely undesirable but intolerable. So only in the context of the new supranational, historically specific layer could the ahistorical element have become operative as it did. The point was not to devise a new mode of action in order to be able to get rid of the Jews but to get rid of the Jews in order to make a new mode of action possible.

Even Germans whose potential for such hate was not unusual seemed ever more willing to accept as necessary the isolation and exclusion of the Jews, and this seeming anomaly is central to all we seek to understand. What made anti-Semitism more widely salient, opening the way to dehumanization and even hate, was the sense that the regime fostered of at once forging the essential homogeneity and acting in the newly grandiose way. Once the new action was in process, the Nazi claim that the essential collective will could only rest on common "blood" could convince even those who had not been especially racist, especially as Bartov's apparently rational, modern, scientific experts seemed able to draw meaningful racial lines, and as other credible experts pursued the newly aggressive eugenics policy—distinguishable, but lumped together as "race hygiene." The isolation and then exclusion of those deemed non-German or non-Aryan could come to seem as credible as forced sterilization.

Proctor noted that study of the racial correlation of disease became a priority during the Nazi period.[130] It was not unscientific or inherently racist to ask such questions, which do not in themselves assume that some such correlation indicates clear racial differentiation, let alone inferiority. Indeed, it can be unscientific and ideological to eschew such questioning. Although Nazi research prejudicially presupposed the centrality of race, the very scope for such research on a scientific basis surely contributed to the sense that the Nazi project was legitimate, even producing the essential alternative modernity.[131]

Although the antecedent anti-Semitism in Germany was not unusually extensive or virulent, there, as elsewhere, a long tradition of stereotyping had produced particular ways of conceiving Jewishness. In light of the wider Nazi departure and aim, these garden-variety stereotypes seemed precisely congruent, in a negative way, with the imperative of deeper collective effectiveness. Now allegedly Jewish traits formerly viewed as merely objectionable appeared dangerous, even fatal. The Jews were not only unassimilable but were particularly divisive, most basically as "commercial," preoccupied with immediate material interests.[132] But in light of what seemed to be the requirements for the new mode of action, the notion that the Jews were a special problem took on added nuances, transcending garden-variety anti-Semitism. The Jews came to seem the source and embodiment of humanitarianism, even conscience—all that impeded the essential Nietzschean hardness.[133] So once the effort to act in the new great political way began, it was especially important to rid Germany of *them*. Although this mode of scapegoating obviously contradicts the notion of Jewish selfishness in the more familiar stereotype, the two could coexist because both pointed to the need for exclusion.

So what differentiated Nazi Germany from its democratic contemporaries was not modern expertise, or racism and anti-Semitism, or even the broad, ambiguous imperative of "race hygiene." Rather, it was the determination to act in unprecedented ways and the mode of action itself, buttressed by the broadly Nietzschean frame of mind. Once the Nazi elite had begun to act to forge the instrument for history-making action, singling out the Jews as the key obstacle to be overcome, other Germans, from leading eugenicists who had disliked racism to ordinary people who had not been especially anti-Semitic, acquiesced, grew indifferent to the fate of the Jews, even came to agree that Germany would be better off without them. These Germans were being drawn into a wider Nazi project that seemed to require homogenization and *thus* the isolation and exclusion of Jews.

Only because of the historically specific dynamic, with its mutually reinforcing strands, did the biologistic ideas being discussed in many countries find their most radical implementation in Germany. And only because of that dynamic did a country that was not atypically anti-Semitic produce the Holocaust. This is the difference that Nazism made.

From homogeneity to extermination

The twistedness of the road to Auschwitz

Obviously, even exclusion to produce homogeneity does not require extermination, although the distinction sometimes gets blurred in discussions of Nazism.[134] Reprehensible though we find it today, an insistence on homogeneity leading even to "ethnic cleansing," the forced emigration of minorities, is quite different from the genocide that the Nazis perpetrated. Although other countries were also expelling minorities at the time, and although other countries collaborated all too willingly in the Nazi genocide, only Nazi Germany set a genocidal process in motion; only Nazi Germany determined independently to act in a genocidal way.[135] Difficult and sometimes tedious though it is, we must follow the steps that led beyond mere exclusion, grasping the incremental nature of the process but also the underlying connective tissue, to understand how the Holocaust became possible, then actual, from within the overall dynamic that the Nazi project had set in motion.

Hitler sometimes seemed to envision extermination, most notoriously when he warned in his speech of January 30, 1939, that if international Jewish finance were again to plunge the nations into war, the result would not be the victory of Bolshevism and thus Jewry but "the annihilation of the Jewish race in Europe!"[136] He surely intended to find some "final solution" to Germany's "Jewish problem," but the term "final solution" was not a euphemism for extermination but a generality, suggesting definitive and complete. Despite Hitler's sometimes reckless rhetoric, and brutal though he and the other Nazi leaders could be, the evidence is overwhelming that they did not contemplate physically exterminating the Jews as a matter of policy prior to 1941.[137] And the magnitude and even character of the project changed even after the decision to begin killing Jews as a matter of policy was made. Even when, with the invasion of the Soviet Union in June 1941, the Nazis extended killing beyond Jews assumed or alleged to be Communists to women and children who were killed solely as Jews, the killing was not systematic, factory-like—not yet what we know as the Holocaust. Conversely, even the commencement of outright killing did not necessitate, or make inevitable, the turn to factory-like mass extermination. And although the distinctions dissolve on one level, the very form of the eventual outcome—gassing in specially constructed factory-like camps—has long seemed especially troubling, as bound up with all we had thought was "modern," progressive, rational. What is to be understood overall is neither a single event nor an abiding intention but a complex, layered process—"the twisted road to Auschwitz," as so aptly characterized by Karl Schleunes in his pioneering book of that title.[138]

It is striking that even Berel Lang, who ended up emphasizing intended evil, recognized that the genocidal outcome required stages, a process. Whether or not we take genocide as specific to the twentieth century, he said:

> it was even for the Nazis sufficiently alien (and even for them, one infers, sufficiently terrible) that they did not set out with the goal of genocide clearly fixed before them. They came at it, at the levels both of idea and of

practice, by a succession of steps, each opening onto further historical possibilities and only later, by this cumulative progression, affirming the intention for genocide.[139]

Here Lang nicely characterized the strong contingency of the process, but he was quick to infer an implicit, underlying intention. Conversely, we have been prone to resort to intention—even, with Lang, intended *evil*—partly because of the apparent difficulty of making sense of the progression of steps in some alternative way. Certainly "radicalizing momentum," for example, is not self-explanatory. *Whence* that momentum, and what did it consist of?

The Holocaust was an unintended but strongly contingent outcome of the characteristic dynamic that resulted from the Nazi effort at great politics. As in the previous two chapters, we must attend to *both* the contingency of the process and the strength of the momentum toward the radical outcome that resulted. Although the hints of future extermination in Hitler's writings and speeches are better seen as fantasy than as evidence of some abiding intention, his "catastrophe-minded" capacity to imagine in that direction was itself an aspect of the new frame of mind—and may well have been decisive when Hitler found himself facing a certain practical conjuncture in 1941.

Segregation and semi-forced emigration

Nazi policy toward German Jews during the first years of the regime was neither consistent nor merely random and contradictory. Germany had only a small minority of Jews—500,000, or 0.8 percent of the population—when Hitler became chancellor in 1933. The regime quickly found the German public more prone to accept forced sterilization than aggressive anti-Semitism. The boycott of Jewish businesses that the Nazis organized almost immediately, in April 1933, was widely ignored.[140] Still, discriminatory measures during 1933 and 1934, to counter allegedly inordinate Jewish influence, began to drive Jews out of the civil and military services, the professions, and cultural life.

The long-term goal, explicit by 1934, was Jewish emigration, which Reinhard Heydrich's SD (*Sicherheitsdienst*), the security service of the SS, was charged with encouraging. Grasping the need to foster a separate Jewish identity as a preliminary, the regime encouraged Zionist organizations and Hebrew schools and sporting clubs, as well as retraining geared for emigration to Palestine. One of the Nuremberg Laws of 1935 prohibited Jews from displaying the swastika but expressly authorized their display of the Zionist flag with the star of David.[141] At this point, however, Jewish policy was not a priority even for Hitler and the Nazi leadership, who were concerned with anti-Communism, anti-parliamentarianism, economic recovery, and rearmament.[142] But the radicalizing momentum of great politics was already at work.

As happened in Italy and the Soviet Union at pivotal junctures, party activists who were dissatisfied with the apparently conservative drift of Hitler's government seized the initiative in 1935 with unsanctioned "wild" terror directed at

Jews. This had the desired effect of forcing the regime to step up its anti-Semitic measures.[143] The Nuremberg Laws of September 15, 1935, included restrictions on marriage and sexual relations between Jewish and non-Jewish Germans. Moreover, Jews could no longer employ non-Jews under the age of 45 as household servants.

This set of measures has long seemed pivotal in the crucial interplay between the Nazis and the wider German populace on the Jewish question. Now, it is often said, Jews were excluded from the body politic by their very nature. As they were removed from proximity and personal interchange, the Jews became "abstract," Jewishness a metaphysical category, and thus there were no limits in principle to the steps that might be initiated against them.[144] But the longer-term significance of the Nuremberg Laws was not clear and would depend on what happened next.

Although aspects of the new legislation—exclusion from the civil service, for example—were overtly discriminatory by any measure, some of these provisions established segregation but not discrimination in the same sense. The key measures governing "blood" comparably restricted the freedoms of non-Jewish Germans, who were no longer free, for example, to marry Jews or enter domestic service in Jewish households. Moreover, the "racial" divide between the two groups could be uncertain, and the Nazis pointed out that anti-miscegenation laws targeting blacks in the United States were stricter.[145] At the same time, even some Jewish leaders welcomed the Nuremberg Laws as a step toward legal clarification of the status of the Jews in Germany, which might include recognition as a protected "national minority."[146] Although the leadership promulgated them partly to defuse the pressures from below, these laws did not seem to be a victory for anti-Semitic radicals at the time; on the contrary, the activists who were promoting radicalization viewed the Nuremberg Laws as a defeat.

But the increasingly explicit objective was not merely to segregate, and certainly not to confer "national minority" status, but rather to achieve ethnic homogeneity by encouraging or forcing Jews to emigrate.[147] Still, the effort was halting, and, typically, Nazi actions often proved at cross-purposes. Three-quarters of the Jews in Germany in 1933 remained in October 1938. Although external obstacles to Jewish emigration were mounting, the Nazi aim at that point was to force the emigration of all German Jews within eight to ten years. With the *Anschluss* of March 1938, the emigration policy was pursued with greater purpose and consistency as Reinhard Heydrich and Adolf Eichmann worked actively with Zionist groups to encourage Jews to leave Austria.[148]

Renewed pressures from below, which drew the support of some but the opposition of others within the squabbling Nazi elite, produced further escalation with *Kristallnacht*, the "Crystal Night" pogrom on November 9, 1938.[149] Featuring wanton destruction of Jewish property, it was orchestrated in full public view in response to the assassination of a German diplomat in Paris. Although there seemed to be no scope for active protest, even Germans who had acquiesced in restrictions on civil rights disapproved of the hooliganism and senseless destruction that *Kristallnacht* entailed. The combination of activist excess and popular opposition convinced the government that both greater discipline and greater secrecy were essential; both concerns led to an enhanced role for the SS. At the same time, Hitler, dubious about the pogrom in the first place, and sensitive to wider political implications both inside and outside Germany, actively protected Jews from the still more threatening pressures coming from below—by vetoing, for example, any provision for special identification. With some local Nazi leaders eager to exploit the crackdown by stealing the property of Jews, he understood that the Jewish community had to retain a modicum of economic viability if it was not to become a burden on the state.[150]

Whereas forced emigration became still more explicitly the priority in the aftermath of *Kristallnacht*, it was bound up in bizarre, even fanciful ways with growing international tensions, immediate relations with the democracies, and the contradictory pressures from within Nazism. At first, Himmler and Heydrich energetically condemned *Kristallnacht* as detrimental to their emigration policy, but they managed to turn it to their advantage by taking into custody and confiscating the property of 20,000 wealthy Jews to help to finance the emigration of others. There was even a sense that rich Jews would buy territory—anywhere from Canada to Madagascar—for the resettlement of much larger numbers.[151]

At the same time, partly to serve the effort to force emigration, a series of decrees in the aftermath of *Kristallnacht* far more radically restricted Jewish rights and activities. Jews could no longer own businesses, land, stocks, jewels, or works of art; they could no longer practice paramedical and health-related professions such as veterinary medicine, dentistry, or pharmacy. The "Aryanization" of Jewish property that had begun spontaneously was given legal sanction. The Jewish press was banned. Jewish children still in the public schools were expelled. Jews were excluded from the welfare system, and their right to be in public places was severely restricted. Discrimination extended to absurdities like prohibiting Jews from keeping carrier pigeons.[152]

So the measures of late 1938 to early 1939 severely limited the capacity of Jews to earn a living and produced almost complete social ostracism. Yet Germans who had deplored the hooliganism of *Kristallnacht* often welcomed the new legal measures, which, by regularizing the situation, seemed thereby to curb violence and head off worse outcomes. While stressing that the Jewish question was not a high priority for ordinary people during the Nazi era overall, Kershaw noted that the issue came to center stage during periods of violence—1933, 1935, and especially 1938.[153] At such times, ordinary Germans tended to accept legal discrimination, partly because it seemed to entail restoring law and order.

Whereas Nazi leaders seriously pushed Jewish emigration, restrictions on the financial resources that Jews could take, stemming partly from greed on the part of Nazi officials but also from illusions about Jewish wealth and connections abroad, reinforced the wider international obstacles to such emigration. By the late 1930s, a dearth of foreign exchange was combining with restrictions in potential receiving countries to make Jewish emigration ever more difficult.[154] Even as the extremes of Nazi Jewish policy became clear, such countries as Switzerland, Sweden, Britain, Canada, and the United States were admitting as few refugees as possible, especially if they were poor and lacked connections. Although over half the German Jews had managed to emigrate by 1939, the figure could have been far higher.[155]

Typical of totalitarian implementation, the effort to foster Jewish emigration was improvised, often incoherent, and mixed uneasily with other impulses, including the most banal greed. Rather than fully achieving homogeneity, Nazi policy by the eve of the war had produced a segregated, isolated remnant of the Jewish community, now forced by discriminatory measures into extreme, difficult conditions. Kershaw found that whereas the Jewish question remained a low priority for most Germans, attitudes had hardened. As a result of diminished social contact, combined with Nazi propaganda associating the Jews with foreign policy tensions and the threat of war, more ordinary Germans came to believe that there was a Jewish problem, that measures to curb "excessive" Jewish influence were warranted, even that it might indeed be better to exclude the Jews altogether.[156]

Nazis concerned with "the Jewish problem" were still seeking, in a typically helter-skelter way, to engineer emigration when the outbreak and subsequent course of the war radically changed the situation. But this was hardly an occasion for the Nazis to start over; rather, it meant building, in ways that could not have been foreseen, on what had already resulted from their venture into radical population policy to that point. Now they fell still deeper into the characteristic interplay of step-by-step logic and out-of-control outcomes in the actual deployment of their great political project.

After the conquest of Poland

The war occasioned precisely the sort of acceleration that Hitler had long envisioned, with population engineering central. But pursuit of that enterprise set in motion a process that quickly spun out of control, with unanticipated consequences.

On the basis of much pioneering research, Christopher Browning brought home how much remained unsettled after the Nazi conquest of Poland in September–October 1939. And he insisted compellingly on the need to avoid hindsight if, in light of the unprecedented situation that opened, we are to place the ensuing steps in proportion and grasp the larger dynamic in course. It is crucial, as he put it, that even in 1940 "Nazi Jewish policy was part of a wider demographic project that aimed at a racial restructuring of eastern Europe. But within this wider demographic project, Jewish policy did not *yet* have the priority or centrality in the Nazis' own sense of historical mission that has been argued for on the basis of what happened later."[157]

Prior to the outbreak of war in 1939, Hitler had been concerned with immediate diplomatic and military issues, so the Nazis began to formulate specific plans for Poland only with the euphoria of victory. Still, although much was *ad hoc*, the overall priority to German resettlement followed from the longstanding preoccupation with *Lebensraum*.[158] Central to the overall population project, the Nazi regime was to populate former Polish territories with ethnic Germans, thereby expanding spatially the ethnically homogeneous community. Himmler was in overall charge, with the *Reichscommissariat für die Festigung des deutschen Volkstums* (Reich Commissariat for the Strengthening of Germandom), or RKFDV, created to coordinate the relocation of ethnic Germans from Eastern Europe. According to the provisions of the German–Soviet non-aggression pact of August 1939, German minorities in the Soviet Union were to be repatriated as well. To secure territory and to cement the permanent subjugation of Poland, the Nazis set out, in a marked escalation of violence, to kill off the Polish elite in an effort to eliminate carriers of Polish national identity.

In September 1939, Poland had the largest concentration of Jews in Europe, about 3,250,000, or almost 10 percent of the population, whereas only about 240,000 Jews remained in Germany at that point.[159] So there were now far more Jews in the Nazi orbit. Whatever was to happen to the bulk of the Polish population, the Jews, for the Nazis, constituted a distinguishable problem. But in this initial stage, which focused on ethnic German resettlement, the Jews were merely a nuisance, their eventual fate secondary—and genuinely uncertain. Indeed, their fate would remain uncertain for almost two years, even as late as the pivotal summer of 1941.[160]

With the conquest of Poland, the great numbers involved precluded the earlier reliance on forcing the emigration of Jews as individuals or families, so Nazi policy makers began to consider a Jewish reservation somewhere in the conquered territories. But at that point it was still uncertain how extensive German settlement was to be and which Polish territories were to be Germanized. Hitler told Alfred Rosenberg at the end of September 1939 that only time could tell whether German settlement might push still further east in ensuing decades. Still, for now at least, the Nazis began to apportion populations in the former Poland into three belts from west to east, with Jews apparently to be concentrated in a reservation in the farthest east, the Lublin district, with Heydrich's Reich Security Main Office (RSHA) handling their expulsion eastward. Hitler, however, doubted that the Lublin district was big enough to serve as the reservation envisioned.[161]

But, as Browning showed, consolidating *Lebensraum* through German resettlement and solving the "Jewish problem" through expulsion proved to be competing, not complementary, tasks—and the former took precedence. Eichmann, seeking full-scale Jewish deportations from October 1939 into the summer of 1940, was consistently frustrated as priority went to the repatriation and resettlement of ethnic Germans.[162] At this point, moreover, Hitler himself was concentrating on the war in the west, leaving eastern policy to the "Darwinian" infighting of his subordinates, which especially pitted the more pragmatic Hans Frank and Hermann Göring against the more zealous Himmler, who was being forced to scale back his ethnic resettlement schemes by spring 1940. But with the brilliant successes in the west that May, Himmler drafted a memorandum, "Some thoughts on the treatment of alien populations in the east," outlining the contours of a radical program for Poland.[163] Seeking Hitler's approval, he submitted it to the Führer on May 25.

This now notorious memo is one of the most telling documents of Nazism, first in conveying the sense of grandiose enterprise, with its demand for hardness. And Himmler's way of articulating the Nazi sense of superiority makes clear how energizing it was to be involved in the project. Himmler's immediate concern was the ethnic re-engineering of the German share of the former Poland. Taking the liquidation of the Polish elite for granted, he advocated closing schools and churches and restricting education for ordinary Poles, who were to be left essentially as "drones" to do heavy and seasonal labor—while looking up in perpetuity to their German masters.

At the same time, there had been great ethnic mixing over the centuries in the territories at issue, and thus Himmler stressed the scope for selecting and re-assimilating racially valuable stock from what he called "the ethnic mishmash" in Poland, even among those who would not ordinarily be deemed German on the basis of surname, background, or language. To reabsorb such elements would require taking children from their parents, but it was on balance the best way of carrying out the world-historical task of ethnic re-engineering. The relevant comparison was not with the liberal democracies, which could not even imagine action on this scale, but with the Soviet Union: "However cruel and tragic each individual case may be, if one rejects the Bolshevik method of physically exterminating a people as fundamentally un-German and impossible, then this method is the mildest and best one."[164]

With such matters as these dominating discussion of how best to reconfigure the conquered space, it is not surprsing that the question of the Jews as a distinguishable group seemed secondary. Although the category "Jew" would disappear from the new greater Germany, Himmler envisioned "a colony in Africa or elsewhere" for the Jews. Hitler made it known that he approved Himmler's overall plan for the former Poland as a guideline, with the specific implementation up to Himmler himself. Browning noted Himmler's impeccable timing and great triumph.[165]

The defeat of France in June 1940 opened the way to serious consideration of making Madagascar, to be seized from the defeated French, a Jewish reservation. This "Madagascar plan," one of the possibilities that had been batted back and forth for several years, was attractive especially because of the bottlenecks that demographic engineering had begun to encounter in Poland. Eichmann strongly supported the Madagascar plan. Hitler told Mussolini on June 18, 1940, that he intended to use Madagascar as a Jewish reservation, and during that summer the Madagascar plan was taken seriously enough to affect patterns of population transfer in the former Poland. Indeed, the deportation of Jews to the General Government was canceled entirely in favor of the Madagascar plan. But the plan had faded by the fall as it became clear that the defeat of Britain, and thus the requisite control of the sea routes, was not imminent.[166] Yet Hitler still seems to have envisioned sending these concentrated Jews overseas even as late as June 1941.[167] However, the assault on the Soviet Union that month opened new possibilities. With victory expected by September, an SS memo of July 1941 on the thirty-year German settlement of Soviet territories envisioned concentrating the Jews, along with other deportees, east of the Urals.[168]

But some shorter-term way of dealing with the Polish Jews was essential as ethnic resettlement in Poland proceeded. The initial response had been "ghettoization," which was not, Browning argued convincingly, a conscious step to facilitate mass murder, or even a way of decimating the Jewish population, but "an improvised response by local authorities to the failure of the expulsion plans." Local German overlords initially viewed the Lodz ghetto, for example, as a venue for extracting Jewish wealth prior to deportation to the east. Even the sealing of the ghettoes happened for different reasons at different times, on the initiative of local authorities.[169]

The continuing transportation bottlenecks and the fading of the Madagascar plan meant that the ghettoes remained in place longer than anyone had expected at the outset. Thus new problems, and new questions, were gradually emerging by late summer 1940. With Berlin refusing to acknowledge that the official policy of deportation was becoming unworkable, those responsible for day-to-day decisions in Poland, especially the ghetto commanders, were left to cope as best they could for long periods. Under the circumstances, local initiatives became paramount—a situation that initially seems to invite a "functionalist" reading of the outcome. But Browning showed that cumulative radicalization did not result from the situation on the local level alone. Indeed, although there was much debate among officials in Poland, most of the leaders on the ground tended toward the "moderate," relatively rational course of exploiting the labor potential of the Jews—which required "normalizing" the increasingly chaotic situation in the ghettoes. By October, those at Lodz had come to recognize that they would have to make their ghetto self-sustaining; surely, they felt, they would be given the wherewithal to do so, in light of the wider German concern for economic productivity during wartime.[170]

At the same time, however, the rapidly evolving situation by early 1941 was beginning to present local leaders with a stark choice not conceivable before. Rather than a source of labor that had to be fed for economic viability, the ghettoes could be a venue for actually liquidating Jews. Debate ensued between proponents of economic exploitation ("productivists") and those who proposed letting the Jews simply die out ("attritionists").[171]

Adding fuel to the eliminationist argument was a consequence of ghettoization itself that, although not intended, was surely strongly contingent. Conditions in the ghettoes reinforced the anti-Jewish stereotypes that the Nazis had sought to foster from the start. The Jews contracted the spotted fever the doctors assumed they were especially likely to carry, and this prompted medical officials to advocate more widespread and stricter ghettoization in response. By the summer of 1941, ghetto conditions were so appalling that some were suggesting that it would be more humane to kill the Jews systematically than to let them die from hunger and disease. It was also argued that the Jews had to be killed now to head off the spread of epidemics beyond the ghettoes.[172] The threat of disease was genuine, but it was not the reason the Jews had been confined to ghettoes in the first place; rather, it had resulted from the regime's improvised response to a secondary aspect of forcing the grandiose resettlement program. Characteristically, in light of the dynamic in course, an unintended consequence changed the threshold, enhancing the likelihood of a still more radical response not foreseen to this point.

Even as some were advocating maintaining the ghettoes in self-sustaining productivism, the decision came from above to exterminate these Jews instead.[173] That decision might seem to confirm an abiding intention stemming from an ideological fanaticism that trumped productivist considerations. But the scope for economic viability in the ghettoes was simply not clear at the time the key decisions were made. The evidence in this instance, and the wider pattern of Nazi response, suggests a far more complex confluence of factors, typical of the great political dynamic. The forces unleashed by the Polish population project interfaced to produce unforeseen problems and possibilities—and thus the need for further improvised responses as the process tended to spin out of control. What fed radicalization under those circumstances was not simply intent from above but rather the characteristic interplay between the leadership and initiatives and pressures from below in response to unintended but not accidental consequences of the grandiose action so far.

The invasion of the Soviet Union

The decisive steps toward the liquidation of the ghettoes in Poland took place in interface with the Nazi invasion of the Soviet Union that began on June 22, 1941. In preparing for the invasion, Hitler made it clear that this was to be an escalation, a war not only of territorial conquest but of race, ideology—and extermination. Although abiding anti-Communism was also central, decisions about how the Soviet campaign was to be waged reflected the experience with the conquest of living space so far, which had led to unanticipated problems that were still very much on the table.

Whereas *Einsatzgruppen*, SS "task units" or "intervention squads," had been charged with liquidating the Polish elite after the German conquest, such units were specially selected and, for two months *prior* to the Nazi assault on the Soviet Union, trained to kill local Communist leaders. Recent research has shown that members of the regular army also received orders to kill such leaders on the spot. In March 1941, addressing 250 senior military officers on the nature of the forthcoming war, Hitler recognized that the task of killing Communist officials would not be easy: "The leaders must make the sacrifice of overcoming their scruples." Toughness now would mean mildness later. At the same time, ordinary troops must not be allowed to get out of hand in banal self-indulgence. Despite grumbling on the part of a few army leaders, the officer corps was substantially in agreement with Hitler's aims in invading the Soviet Union.[174]

Although the intent for escalation is clear, there has been much controversy over what, more precisely, Hitler and the Nazi leadership intended at this point, even over the exact parameters of the charge to the *Einsatzgruppen* and army officials. Especially at issue has been the extent to which the systematic killing of Jews was in some sense implicit from the start. Browning admitted that there is room for disagreement over the meaning of particular steps. Whereas it is likely that the *Einsatzgruppen* were told of future plans to make conquered Soviet territories *Judenfrei* through wholesale killing, there was probably no timetable, and certainly no pre-invasion order for the total extermination of Soviet Jews. The first task was to shoot Communist officials, and Heydrich's memo of July 2 included Jews in state and party positions among those to be liquidated at once. But although the *Einsatzgruppen* initially killed adult male Jews, especially those in leadership positions, there was no program of total extermination, and the vast majority of Soviet Jews remained alive even with the Nazi invasion.[175]

In that sense, even the overt turn to murder with the invasion of the Soviet Union cannot be taken as the decisive step toward the physical extermination of all Jews under Nazi control. Yet under the overall circumstances, to begin to kill Jews systematically as a matter of policy was almost bound to have radicalizing consequences. Indeed, in light of the interface between the difficult conditions in the ghettoes and the wider, long-term aim of German resettlement, this step opened the way to—even invited—a more radical response on *both* the Soviet and the Polish fronts. The conquered Soviet territories, like the Polish, would need to be free of Jews eventually. So although it was not the policy at the time of the invasion, within months the Nazis had decided simply to kill the Jews they encountered rather than having to round them up later. This would head off the problems that ghettoization had produced in Poland.

Although this step is especially contested, Browning insisted convincingly that some such escalation took place in July 1941, just weeks after the Soviet invasion began, in the context of euphoria over the impending triumph. Believing victory to be at hand, Hitler began to specify the basic goals for the east in a conversation of July 16. Even with Communism destroyed, Germany would never withdraw from this "Garden of Eden." Whereas cleansing the area had formerly been seen as a future task, it was now to be done immediately. Himmler responded with a massive build-up of killing forces behind the lines and personally visited a number of units in the east, offering exhortation and encouragement. During one such visit, in August 1941, he assured his men that he and Hitler were responsible for this difficult task; his underlings began to include women and children regularly in their mass shootings thereafter. By mid-August, the killing of Soviet Jews was in full swing.[176]

Meanwhile, the Soviet response to the German invasion fed the German radicalization. Most basically, Stalin's declaration of partisan warfare gave the Nazis a welcome excuse for systematic killing. But more significantly, reflecting the wider epochal dimension of the radicalization in progress, the Soviet NKVD, in the aftermath of the invasion, began shooting ethnic Germans already in camps and deporting as many as 700,000 others to Siberia or Kazakhstan. At the same time, the Nazis were killing Soviet prisoners of war—two million during the first nine months.[177]

The adoption of systematic killing as policy in the Soviet Union had obvious implications for the situation in Poland. Presumably after some sort of green light from Hitler, Heydrich secured formal authorization on July 31, 1941, to prepare a plan for "a complete solution of the Jewish question within the German sphere of influence."[178] This was to "supplement" the policy of emigration officially charged to Heydrich in January 1939. Vague though it was, under the circumstances this new charge was almost certain to lead to a more systematic form of physical extermination. Browning concluded that in the euphoria of impending victory, with labor considerations no longer an issue, Hitler had decided to eliminate not just Soviet but all European Jews; the decisions were made essentially concurrently.[179]

For Browning, this key decision was part of a larger pattern: "Nazi racial policy was radicalized in quantum jumps that coincided with the peaks of German military success, as the euphoria of victory emboldened and tempted an elated Hitler to dare ever more drastic policies."[180] Thus the key departures seem to correlate with the successes in Poland, France, and the initial phase in the Soviet Union. And such radicalizing elation was surely an essential dimension of the characteristic dynamic in progress. Only the feeling of involvement in an unprecedented enterprise, of being out in front and on the edge, could yield such euphoria—and thus that radicalizing momentum.

But even as Heydrich began to plan for a more systematic response, the situation remained fluid for months thereafter. In mid-August, leading Nazi experts, including Eichmann, were still assuming exportation to some reservation to be the official policy. Jewish emigration continued to be encouraged at the same time. Indeed, Germans Jews were still allowed to emigrate until October. General Government head Hans Frank was still trying to find a place to resettle the ghettoized Jews somewhere in the Soviet Union as late as mid-October, when he discussed the issue with Alfred Rosenberg, recently appointed minister for occupied eastern territories.[181]

Fits and starts continued in Poland especially in light of complex labor and supply considerations as the war continued. Although the decision for forced Russian labor seemed to render Jewish labor potential irrelevant, objections from both the army and the civil administration led Himmler to allow some Jewish work groups to be developed. Surely it made sense, from within the framework by now established, to use the Jews for labor, even if it meant working them to death.[182] At the same time, however, the need for resources to support the Soviet invasion had had an unforeseen negative impact on the quest for a "moderate," productivist course for the ghettoes. Although the Lodz and Warsaw ghettoes had been promised increased rations just weeks before the invasion, ghetto leaders found it ever more difficult to get the resources, especially the food supplies, necessary to make the ghettoes productive or even self-sufficient. Yet in September Himmler notified officials at Lodz that they could expect the arrival of even more Jews and Gypsies—news that prompted vociferous complaints from Lodz officials.[183] By this point, the strands at work were interweaving to produce a concerted program of systematic killing.

Whatever the July 31 authorization to Heydrich portended, and quite apart from the ongoing problem of the ghettoes, the policy of mass shooting in the Soviet Union produced unforeseen consequences that reinforced the radicalization in progress. Shooting Jews individually proved not only costly and inefficient but also psychologically difficult, even for the specially selected and trained killers of the *Einsatzgruppen*. In August 1941, on one of his visits to the killing units in the east, Himmler was himself shaken as he witnessed the shooting of 100 prisoners in a Minsk prison. Faced with complaints about the psychological burden, he ordered the search for less brutalizing methods.[184] So upping the ante in the Soviet Union yielded further unanticipated problems, the solution to which was a radicalization that opened further vistas of what might be done—but also suggested certain practical opportunities in light of the strongly contingent availability of means that invited the scope for a more systematic, indeed total, "solution."

We noted that the major phase of the "euthanasia" program was completed precisely at this critical juncture, in August 1941. Soon thereafter, gassing facilities that had been constructed in a number of German psychiatric institutions were dismantled and shipped east to be reinstalled at new killing centers during the fall. Doctors, nurses, and technicians who had been instrumental to the "euthanasia" program often followed the equipment.[185]

Thus when Lodz officials balked at the news in September that they would be getting even more Jews and Gypsies, the leadership sent Herbert Lange, who had been killing the mentally ill, with a mobile gas van.[186] Browning noted that this would surely have made it clear to Lodz officials what Berlin's policy now was, but, again, the outcome was not merely a *Diktat* from above but the outcome of a process of interaction of above and below. The pressure from below, responding to the worsening impasse that the center had created through its poorly coordinated action, had helped to crystallize and focus thinking at the top, speeding determination for a more radical course. And, more generally, the contingent interface with the course of the Soviet campaign promoted the decision to liquidate the ghettoized Jews in Poland rather than try to make the ghettoes self-sustaining or productive.

Construction of the first permanent camp installation, at Belzec, began in October, with gassing experts from the "euthanasia" program sent there. Even now, the purpose was simply to liquidate Lublin Jews incapable of work. The idea of killing all the Polish Jews emerged gradually thereafter, and extermination camps at Sobibor and Treblinka had joined Belzec for that purpose by spring 1942. But the first group of exterminations began at the gas-van station at Chelmno, in the southern Warthegau, during the first week of December.[187]

The developing extermination process was to have been coordinated at a high-level conference in the Berlin suburb of Wannsee early in December.[188] As it happened, however, the conference had to be put off until January 1942, when the momentum toward mass extermination was already well advanced. With large-scale gassing having begun at Chelmno in December, the preparations already in progress by January would enable Auschwitz–Birkenau and Belzec to commence much larger operations within the next three months. But Wannsee was important in establishing bureaucratic coordination even while also cementing SS leadership. Moreover, there it was made official that all European Jews were to be killed.[189]

It is clear, then, that the Nazi leadership came to a decision for mass death in factory-like gassing camps only in stages, from July to October 1941. In an especially effective passage, Browning sought to recapture the sense of uncertainty in the unprecedented situation that had resulted from Nazi action to that point. Hindsight, he noted, may lead us to read the documents *too* closely, and thereby to assume that the Nazis had a clear end in view when they began to contemplate the next step, into more systematic killing. But in fact they were tentative and groping. A coherent conception of how they would actually carry out mass extermination—special camps, factories, poison gas—emerged only gradually: "The extermination camp equipped with gassing facilities was not, after all, an obvious invention, immediately self-evident the moment Hitler decided to kill the Jews. . . . Only at the end of this journey of innovation did the Final Solution take on an air of obviousness and inevitability that could not have been apparent to the perpetrators at the time."[190] Thus, again, the dynamic, even the mode of action itself, had yielded a further departure that then produced something unforeseen—and opened still further vistas.

By the early fall of 1941, murderous precedents had accumulated—the victims of the "euthanasia" program, the Polish elite, Soviet officials, and Soviet prisoners of war had all been killed systematically, as a matter of policy.[191] The Nazi great politicians had become at once hardened and exhilarated by unprecedented murder, so the fact that mass murder was next directed at the Jews is in one sense not surprising. Nor, in light of yet another layer of unanticipated difficulties and the strongly contingent availability of means, is the impersonal, factory-like extermination in gas chambers that was eventually chosen. Although the process was tentative and groping on one level, the key is the strength of the contingency toward this chilling outcome once the Nazis had embarked upon the grandiose project of population engineering.

The changing place of the extermination process

Even well into 1941, the Nazis had favored German Jews, most notably by prohibiting the emigration of non-German Jews to keep slots abroad open for Germans. But a series of measures in September and October 1941 specified that even the 150,000 Jews remaining in Germany were to be deported to the east, to share the fate of the Jews already in Poland. First came the labeling of Jews that Hitler himself had explicitly rejected after *Kristallnacht*. As of September 1, 1941, German Jews had to wear the yellow Star of David imprinted with the word *Jude* in black. Within weeks, on September 18, Himmler announced the deportation of German Jews eastward and then, on October 18, prohibited further Jewish emigration from the Reich.

Although the yellow star and the deportations provoked a higher level of opposition than the regime had expected, this opposition was sporadic and did not affect policy. Overall, with the difficulties of the wartime context—including, by early 1942, the massive terror bombing of German cities, the sense of possible defeat, and fears of retribution—ordinary Germans were becoming still more insensitive to the plight of the Jews. Even as it became ever clearer what Jews faced in the east, the evidence suggests that despite some initial restiveness, most Germans looked on with a kind of malign indifference, seeking primarily to avoid personal involvement.[192]

The fact that Jewish emigration from Germany was permitted until October suggests that Hitler had not yet determined to exterminate all the Jews within the Nazi orbit.[193] So even the radicalization in July had not reflected a decision to kill as many Jews as possible. Thus the October decree, switching the policy on Jewish emigration, was yet another escalation, even, in one sense, more decisive than the decision for mass gassing. For only from this point did the Nazis seek to kill all the Jews within their grasp. But thus we encounter a further set of questions concerning the interface of the radicalization of Jewish policy with the fortunes of war.

Michael Marrus noted that whereas a consensus had come to posit a definite Hitler extermination order, linked to the fortunes of the Soviet campaign, there was no consensus about the context—whether the order reflected euphoria or disappointment.[194] Browning linked the further key decisions of early fall 1941, like the escalation that July, to the euphoria of military success.[195] Perhaps once they had a handle on how mass killing could actually be done, as they seemingly did by October, the Nazis became less concerned about the logistical difficulties of killing on the scale required even to clear the ghettos and, still anticipating victory, began to imagine the still more grandiose project of killing all the Jews they could. However, some have traced the decisive steps toward factory-like mass extermination to a *downturn* in military fortunes and expectations. By October, the Nazis might well have come to recognize that defeat was at least possible.

Philippe Burrin was especially persuasive among those linking the Holocaust to a sense of impending defeat. He stressed the seriousness of the earlier forced emigration policy and the Madagascar plan. He accepted Browning's account of the resettlement and ghettoization in Poland and even the quasi-functionalist argument that Jews were not included in the pre-invasion extermination charge to the *Einsatzgruppen* in 1941. But he also supposed that Hitler harbored the intention of exterminating the Jews should certain circumstances arise. And Hitler made the key decision, as Burrin saw it, at some point from mid-September to the beginning of October in a state not of euphoria but of murderous frustration and rage, stemming from his sense that the Soviet campaign might fail, and with it the whole Nazi project. Although Hitler did not think defeat inevitable at this point, he knew it was likely. If defeat was somehow to be avoided, he felt an extraordinary escalation to be required. As the perceived defeatism of the German Jews now especially exacerbated his hatred, he determined to kill the Jews both to exact pre-emptive revenge and to demonstrate his will to fight to the end: "By means of the somehow sacrificial death of the Jews, he was fanatically steeling himself to achieve victory, or fight on to destruction." Much of the Nazi elite similarly found appalling the image of the Jews surviving, as victors, a German defeat; thus the wider appeal of pre-emptive revenge. And, as Burrin put it, Hitler "would conduct this exercise of vengeance . . . with mounting determination as the situation worsened, and he advanced toward an apocalyptic end."[196]

The interface between the Nazis' genocidal decisions and the wider war has invited disagreement partly because it depends less on objective factors than on German *perceptions* of military fortunes. Certainly, the first couple of months confirmed the widespread sense, among officials in the democracies as well as in Germany, that the Soviet campaign was a mismatch, to be concluded with a decisive German victory by September. But at some point, surely, Hitler and the Nazi leadership began to experience doubts, then a sense of the likelihood and at some point even the certainty of defeat. But for a while, at least, growing doubts could coexist with hope, or alternate with periods of renewed confidence as faith in will and Nazi spiritual superiority sustained the German cause.[197] And even within the Nazi elite, the pattern of change in perception varied from one individual to the next.

So it seems unlikely that Hitler experienced some moment of definitive, rational realization that defeat was certain. Browning found little during the period Burrin emphasized—even taking it at its most inclusive, from mid-September to mid-October—that would have decisively undermined Hitler's confidence. And against Arno Mayer's effort to link the key decisions to a sense of impending defeat, Browning pointed out that, by December 1942, one month before the end of Stalingrad and six months before permanently losing the initiative on the eastern front at Kursk, the Nazis had already killed perhaps 75 percent of all Holocaust victims.[198]

But even if what we now know as the Holocaust did not start because of defeat, and even if the timetable is indeterminate, the Nazis no doubt began to experience differently the ongoing process as the possibility or even likelihood of defeat dawned. So whereas there was surely a moment of exhilaration that fueled radicalization, the frustrations that Burrin emphasized just as surely factored in at some point, whatever the exact timetable. And Burrin's characterization of what lay on the other side, once euphoria gave way, offered a useful insight into the next stage. Still, his suggestions were sketchy, seemingly based on mere *ad hoc* speculation. So how can we understand both the exhilaration and the apocalyptic revenge in light of the particular momentum in course?

Whatever the Nazis' sporadic faith in some weapons breakthrough, by 1944, if not earlier, the extermination of the Jews had become almost an end in itself, almost the major reason for continuing the war. Although in one sense the victims at this point still died simply because they were Jews, they were killed for an utterly different reason than those who had been first confined to ghettoes in Poland early in 1940, or those who found themselves in the path of the Nazi assault on the Soviet Union in the summer of 1941. And even if we accept Browning's implication that three-quarters of the victims died in the euphoric stage, the fact that, even after the war was lost, the regime insisted on prolonging the killing and thereby managed to kill the other quarter of the eventual total—and bent every effort to achieve a still higher percentage and total—is itself appalling and another step in the overall dynamic to be understood. Whenever it began, this stage of revenge and apocalypse entailed something different than did the earlier stage of mass killing.

In linking Hitler to "the catastrophe-mindedness of the age," J.P. Stern also noted the age's "bitter delight in apocalyptic visions" and found the whole syndrome evident especially in Hitler's wartime *Table Talk*.[199] Stern went on to suggest that only some attraction to the prospect of universal annihilation, consistent with Hermann Rauschning's noted emphasis on Hitler's nihilism, can account for Hitler's determination to prolong the war, his indulgence in an ever more reckless strategy.[200] Concluding his study, Stern insisted that Hitler "knew the truth about himself—the truth that not conquest but indiscriminate annihilation was his aim. This, rather than any heroic self-assertion or the prospect of material gain, emerges as the secret that bound his followers to him; and not his followers only. On this dark understanding his whole career is based."[201]

On the one hand, Stern's formulation is surely overstated; such annihilation *ended up* the aim only as a result of the unintended outcomes so far. But on the other hand, the point helps us to grasp the strong contingency of the stages in the process leading to this orientation—the *possibility* of which, we can see in retrospect, was surely present from the start of Hitler's departure. And the sense of risk, of danger, of being on the edge, did indeed energize his followers. Whatever the timetable, the overall dynamic could breed *both* euphoria and "bitter delight in apocalyptic visions." Moreover, as we will discuss below, Hitler seems to have given up all hope of turning the war around only at the very end. What sustained him was his enduring faith in will, starting with his own. In that sense, a key dimension of the mode of action endured, even as it increasingly mixed with other impulses during the later phases of the war.

The focus on killing Jews, as the great political project was winding down, was the archetypically tragic instance of the radicalizing narrowing, bound up with myth making, that resulted from all three of the interwar departures. The whole grandiose Nazi project, wound around race hygiene, ethnic homogeneity, and the re-engineering of whole territories, now boiled down to this—killing as many Jews as possible. In this sense, the Holocaust, though not intended and not a telos in the usual sense, was indeed the privileged outcome, and the Jews were indeed the privileged victims, even as we must recognize that the Holocaust could only have occurred as one phase within a wider project so grandiose that killing became almost routine—and thus claimed the lives of so many others as well.

Totalitarian great politics and the Holocaust

The radicalizing momentum

Now that we have followed the sequence of steps that led to the Holocaust, we can better grasp the nature of the connective tissue in its historical specificity. And we can better see how the responses necessary to sustain this bizarre and tragic dynamic emerged from within the ongoing Nazi effort at great political action.

As we noted in Chapter 4, Omer Bartov plausibly argued that mass killing on the scale of the Holocaust, carried out in a mechanized way in a factory-like setting, could not even have been imagined without the prior experience of the First World War. Modern warfare afforded the mentality and the imagery but also the tools for genocide, which now became practicable thanks to the advent of industrial killing on the battlefield. So the scope for such mass killing is modern; its occurrence is not some atavism. Nor, insisted Bartov, is modern genocide "the product of racism, which merely determines the identity of the victims."[202]

Bartov was seeking to pinpoint the supranational, historically specific conditions of possibility for the Holocaust and, more specifically, to specify the sense in which the war itself had been essential. But although that precedent, as modern, was surely a necessary condition, the war experience and the availability of the means for industrial killing obviously are not in themselves sufficient for understanding. Many beyond Germany shared the image and the means resulting from the war, just as they had comparably racist or anti-Semitic tendencies. Addressing Bartov's point in a generally appreciative mode, Burleigh agreed that the war altered moral parameters and lowered the threshold of what seemed possible in ways still barely investigated. But he went on to insist that a few superficially similar features do not explain the Holocaust, that the argument needs to be developed with more evidence.[203]

In short, the war was necessary but not sufficient, so we seek the differentiating mechanism, but also, from there, a deeper understanding of how the war precedent actually came into play. Although the particular German experience of the war, including defeat, was obviously central to the triggering mechanism, it does not suffice simply to invoke the familiar German contextual features. As we have seen, what such historically specific national factors triggered was a wider modern layer, encompassing, but not limited to, the experience of the First World War and revolving around a new sense of historical-political possibility. In Germany, that sense was given urgency, and a particular direction, from the problems of Weimar modernity. What seemed to be necessary was not genocide but a new mode of action that focused especially on radical population engineering. So whereas showing the significance of the precedent of industrial killing is surely useful, we need to account for a much thicker connection between the war and the Holocaust by grasping how the war fed a wider novel mode of action from within which the Holocaust became possible, even likely.

With their concerted effort actually to reshape society as a collective instrument for history-making action, Hitler and the Nazi elite initiated the momentum. Once the process was in motion, each effort to address a population "problem" in a "great," radically activist way prepared the way for, even invited, a comparable approach to the next such "problem." The connection between the "euthanasia" program and the extermination of the Jews affords the most telling instance. But although they have been widely noted, the links tend to be portrayed as merely *ad hoc*, as opposed to stemming from, and furthering, the particular, historically specific dynamic in course.

We have also seen how the interplay of components—most basically Hitler's leadership and initiatives from below—helped to fuel the dynamic. In the Polish campaign, the *Einsatzgruppen* were charged to kill the Polish intelligentsia only. But after some killed Jews on their own, Hitler quashed army attempts to court-martial those responsible. Indeed, he issued an amnesty on October 4, 1939, and two weeks later removed SS units from the jurisdiction of the military courts.[204] Such radicalization then proceeded further in the Soviet Union as some quickly went beyond their charge and began killing Jews, soon including women and children, on their own. And such further initiative from below surely emboldened Hitler in the decisions that led to the effort at systematic extermination. In the same way, Browning, in considering the changes in ghetto policy, pinpointed the energizing combination of decision from the top at decisive moments and accommodating response from below.[205] Again and again, the new mode of action and the grandiose project itself yielded an energizing reciprocity that, in turn, fueled an unforeseen but characteristic momentum. The capacity to tackle that project in the requisite Nietzschean terms, entailing a premium on the "hard" response to any situation, helped to radicalize that momentum. Indeed, the more difficult any such step in the conventional sense, the more exhilarating it was. This was anything but bureaucratic routine, a point to which we will return shortly.

The dynamic was such that even moderation, on the one hand, and internal division, on the other, fed radicalization. Considering what happened during the 1930s, Hans Mommsen noted that any effort to implement extreme policies all at once, affecting more Jews, and affecting them more deeply, would have provoked protest—indeed, would have shaken the social structure of the regime. By resisting the efforts of party zealots, the moderating initiatives of the bureaucracy, less Nazified overall, kept the overall anti-Jewish initiative within sustainable bounds—and thus enabled it to continue, step by step. Yet because the various state ministries, weakening in the system overall, sought to retain some measure of control, they also adopted more radical measures than they otherwise would have, thereby furthering the action in progress. More generally, Mommsen showed how intra-party and party–state rivalries contributed to radicalizing momentum that led to the Holocaust. Each step enhancing the domain of the party, for example, reinforced pressures for further steps from competing entities like the SS or Hermann Göring's Four-Year Plan.[206]

Many have noted that the radicalizing dynamic entailed something like "progressive brutalization," although the category tends to be invoked as if it were an explanation in itself. At work, however, was not some ahistorical psychological tendency that might turn up anywhere; nor was it idiosyncratically German. Rather, it emerged as one aspect of the dynamic that followed from the attempt to act in the Nietzschean, great political way. Only in those terms can we account for the tendency in Nazi Germany that Burleigh labeled "a general brutalization of thought and feeling" and that led, for example, to a particular crassness among youth toward the elderly and infirm.[207] And the same syndrome seems to underlie "the progressive brutalization of members of mass-killing institutions," which, for Ruth Bettina Birn, might explain the parties at "euthanasia" facilities celebrating "milestones" like the 10,000th killing.[208]

The tensions and unintended consequences that resulted from the new mode of action mandated further improvisation, and much ended up hodge-podge, out of control. Although they envisioned the conquest of living space, the Nazis invaded Poland without systematically planning the organization of the new territory. As they then rushed into their grandiose resettlement project, unforeseen problems ensued. The attempt to deal with them, even the decision to confine the Jews to ghettoes, soon led to another layer of problems. Determined to avoid the same mistakes in preparing for the invasion of the Soviet Union, Hitler was clearer about the wider aims of the enterprise and how they were to be pursued. So the radicalizing next step, declaring this to be a racial-ideological war of annihilation, responded to what had happened, and was still happening, in Poland.

In the Soviet Union, the Nazis were newly willing to kill—or sought to be. But when actually faced with the task, even those specially selected and trained proved not entirely up to the face-to-face murder required; it was not clear that they would be able to continue, despite the premium on hardness and the exhilaration of involvement in this grandiose project. Meanwhile, those responsible for the ghettoes in Poland, having to deal with a bizarre by-product of the grandiose Nazi effort so far, were tending toward the "moderate" immediate course of productivism. In both venues, the immediate outcome so far seemed to advise going slowly or even pulling back, but instead the Nazi elite pushed on to a still more extreme step.

They did so partly *because*, in light of their justifying self-understanding, the response needed to be grandiose, flying in the face of conventional morality, to be energizing, to sustain the sense of being out in front. And the "euthanasia" precedent, especially, afforded the "hard" but grandiose solution that seemed necessary. Because the "euthanasia" program had already been enacted, a particular radical "solution" to the Jewish problem was not just possible but likely to be adopted once the Nazis had encountered the unanticipated problems that resulted from their grandiose effort at population engineering by the late summer of 1941. The very availability of experts and procedures from that program was a major and perhaps the decisive factor in the decision to extend physical extermination to the Jews in the ghettoes.[209] And although less tangible, the precedent itself, the fact of having actually done the "euthanasia" program, was perhaps even more important. In light of what they had already done, they knew they could tackle the next step; they were out in front, and there was no turning back.

Obviously, the "euthanasia" program had not been initiated *in order to* develop techniques that could subsequently be used for a particular radical solution to the "Jewish problem." But neither was the connection an accident, for this was not merely a sequence of segmented tasks. Rather, the chain of relationships exhibits the strong contingency of the overall radicalizing process. In light of the initiating aspiration and mode of action, it was no accident, once the Nazis had done sterilization and begun preparing for war, that they had embarked on "euthanasia" in the first place. And thus it was no accident that the techniques and personnel were available, or that the precedent was on the table, all feeding the particular radical extreme outcome of the double crisis that Nazi Jewish policy encountered in 1941. Yet the magnitude and stakes of that next step had surely not even been imagined with the break into forced sterilization in 1933, or with the Nuremberg Laws of 1935, or even with the launching of war in 1939. Factory-like genocide became possible only from within the momentum in course, itself stemming from the mode of action chosen and the grandiose project initiated.

Segmentation, distancing—and elation

Energizing reciprocity or synergy initially seems to be the opposite of the bureaucratic segmentation that many have found indispensable to the Holocaust. Yet such segmentation and the distancing that it produces were surely at work as well, playing a role at all levels—not just on the part of under-lings distinguishable from the "visionaries" who initiated the process and made the key decisions. For no one saw, or did, the whole thing. Even Himmler did not pull any triggers, drop any gas pellets, or kill any Jews. Camp commandants Rudolf Höss and Franz Stangl did not have to watch—and they sought to avoid doing so. Even the SS played a surprisingly delimited role in the actual killing in the camps. The regime lured Ukrainians, Latvians, and others to serve as auxil-iaries and Jewish Kommandos to do much of the dirty work. Such segmentation and distancing fostered moral indifference, making participation easier all along the line.

In one sense, it was not "the Holocaust," as we now understand it, that such distancing enabled the agents to avoid seeing. Browning noted that it took us four decades to begin viewing the Holocaust as a monumental turning point in history; it is thus not surprising that its magnitude was lost on many of the perpetrators themselves. With their prior commitments to movement and career intertwining, they adjusted to the process through incremental steps; there was no awareness of crossing a threshold.[210] So the bureaucratic dimension and the genuine difficulty of grasping the magnitude were mutually reinforcing.

The importance of such mechanisms is undeniable, but their place in the overall process, especially as they interfaced with other dimensions, is not so clear. The oft-noted reliance on euphemism—the Jews as "cargo," individual Jews as "pieces"—might seem like an aspect of such distancing, but it cannot be understood merely as a by-product of modern bureaucracy *per se*.[211] Although the official line, prevalent even in conversations among leaders, that the extermi-nation camps were labor camps, stemmed partly from the premium on secrecy, it too seems to betray a need to hide, to avoiding facing the magnitude of the event in which they were caught up.[212] Yet for some at least, some of the time, the magnitude was clear—and itself energizing. Thus the "extraordinary exhilara-tion" or elation (*Rausch*) that Saul Friedländer noted among the perpetrators. Yet it seems very nearly the opposite of bureaucratic routine or distancing. So how could these seeming incompatible elements have been at work in the particular dynamic at issue?

The most influential and probing analysis of the relationship between distinctively modern instrumental rationality and the Holocaust is surely Zygmunt Bauman's, which we have encountered at several points. Bauman recognized that such rationality could not have initiated the Holocaust, which required the "gardening" aspiration of "visionaries," a related but distinguishable side of the modern Enlightenment break. Coming to the fore in situations of crisis, that aspiration required a more specific contextual triggering. Bauman implicitly took the sources in this case to be postwar German problems too well known to require analysis. So the key mechanism was the working of modern instrumental reason in the case at hand. It would have been "well-nigh impossible," said Bauman, even to conceive of exterminating a people apart from an engineering approach to society, entailing expertise, scientific management, and bureaucracy—all characteristic of an advanced state of modernity.[213] Three dimensions of that modern syndrome were at work in the Holocaust.

First, bureaucracy entails segmentation—splitting up action, with stages delineated by subordination, hierarchy of authority, functional specialization, and distancing, including reduction to quantification. In the Nazi case, the mechanism served to obliterate responsibility; each saw himself as not responsible for the whole enterprise, even as everyone was convinced that responsibility lay with some proper authority.[214] At the same time, modern bureaucracy eliminates contingent personal motives and emotions and redirects moral impulses that, in response to the suffering being caused in this case, would otherwise have impeded the process. On this level, in other words, the Holocaust came not from mobilizing dormant, implicitly malevolent personal inclinations but from neutralizing ahistorical moral impulses, isolating them from the machinery of action.[215] The first key for Bauman, then, was the capacity of modern industrial society to produce distance at which the normal moral claim becomes inaudible. Some, at least, of the human moral impulse certainly remains, but it is redirected, and boils down to doing efficiently the delimited task at hand, as defined by superiors.[216] Banal ambition and careerism may reinforce this response, but the mere desire to do the task well generally suffices.

Bauman buttressed his argument by recasting the results of the well-known experiments led by Stanley Milgram in 1973. Partly to counter the once-noted study of "the authoritarian personality" by T.W. Adorno and associates, Milgram tested the capacity of people to resist authority that is taken to be legitimate but not backed by external threat. He found that a substantial majority, not merely some delimited subset defined by personality type, obeyed even to the point of inflicting extreme pain. Having been told that the experiment was to discover ways of making learning more efficient, Milgram's subjects accepted that the authority was an expert and that the process, although it required inflicting pain—by administering what seemed ever more intense electric shocks—served the worthwhile purpose of learning improvement.[217]

At issue, then, was an abiding, widespread human possibility, and the question was under what circumstances it comes to the fore. For Bauman, the propensity did not depend simply on the contingent fact of some particular cause or authority figure; rather, it comes into play especially from within the framework of modern bureaucratic segmentation: "The meaning of Milgram's discovery is that, immanently and irretrievably, the process of rationalization facilitates behaviour that is inhuman and cruel in its consequences, if not in its intentions. *The more rational is the organization of action, the easier it is to cause suffering*—and remain at peace with oneself." Indeed, Milgram's findings suggested to Bauman that such cruelty stems more from the social matrix than from personality or character—and the capacity to produce such inhumanity increases with the increase in rationality and technique.[218]

Second, Bauman held that bureaucracy is not merely a neutral tool but entails its own self-propelling momentum, which will carry the action beyond what the initiators envisioned and render some outcomes more probable than others. So whereas it took visionaries to initiate the Holocaust, bureaucracy picked up the project and made the Holocaust in its own image. Although bureaucratic momentum is distinguishable from expertise and careerism, they are obviously mutually reinforcing. Bureaucratic experts with specific tasks take further initiatives, thereby continuously expanding on the original purposes. Especially as Nazi Germany was nearing defeat, the experts created the objects for their own expertise; the skills had to be used simply because they were there.[219] In the same vein, Burleigh and Wippermann noted how the very existence of bureaucratic experts helped to give momentum to discrimination against Jews; the pettiness of the later discriminatory measures "indicates the self-propelling momentum of bureaucrats whose jobs and professional expertise were inextricably bound up with solving the 'Jewish question'."[220]

Third, Bauman contended that modern means–ends rationality may obscure wider direction or meaning. As we have seen, there was no single decision for what we now know as the Holocaust, and the eventual outcome was not anticipated at the early stages of what proved to be the process toward extermination. Once that process had begun, each in the sequence of steps had a certain rationality as the agents responded to problematic aspects of each present situation, each a provisional resultant of previous responses. In that sense, the overall outcome, although not intended or foreseen, was still the result of a logical sequence. For Bauman, "the most shattering of the lessons" of the Holocaust is that the choice of physical extermination resulted from such routine, bureaucratic means–ends calculation, the most efficient solution to a delimited immediate problem, with no thought of where the whole process was heading.[221]

All three of these generally bureaucratic dimensions were surely part of the mix, but it is possible to overemphasize their aggregate significance and thereby to miss other essential mechanisms at work, even to miss *how* this generic modern bureaucratic syndrome became part of the larger momentum in the Nazi case. Most basically, what difference did it make that this was a *Nazi* bureaucracy? Was the Nazi action at issue simply a variation *within* the modern bureaucratic deployment, or was the Nazi departure deeper, thus more radically *determining* the bureaucratic deployment than Bauman recognized?

Although Bauman generally seemed to suggest that the bureaucratic syndrome, the gardening vision, and some national triggering moment exhausted the field, he indicated something of the difference that Nazism itself made as he characterized the changing German response to Nazi Jewish policy. He found the normal human moral capacity to be still operative at first, leading ordinary Germans to ignore the Nazi boycott of Jewish shops in 1933. But the capacity for such response was increasingly blocked by the modern premium on rational efficiency, which compromises face-to-face morality.[222] So whereas the mainstream German response to Jews was still morally saturated in 1933, it gradually became abstract and morally neutral thereafter. This was a significant change and, Bauman noted explicitly, an important accomplishment for the regime. He understood that such increasing indifference was conceivable only insofar as the Germans, through the Nazi revolution, were being caught up not simply in anti-Semitism but in something else involving the Jews from an indirect angle. In other words, he was suggesting something about Nazism's historically specific content. But because he attributed the supranational, historically specific fuel for the overall Nazi project to the generic gardening syndrome, he could not be sufficiently specific about the source, the nature, and the implications even of the element of content he indicated.

The Nazi departure opened the way to, and seemed to require, a mode of collective action more specific than generic gardening, with its aim of creating order. Indeed, Bauman's formulaic gardening metaphor barely hinted at the mode of idealism that fueled the novel dynamism in the Nazi case. We noted in Chapter 2 that, attractive though it is to us today, his conception of morality—as bound up with human fellow-feeling, finding archetypal form in face-to-face response to human suffering—is too limited to encompass the possibilities that opened as the new historical-political sense emerged late in the nineteenth century. And in tracing the blunting of normal moral scruples to the modern bureaucratic syndrome, he was sidestepping the content of the Nazi revolution and its implications for the moral capacity. Difficult though it is, if we are to grasp the nature of the momentum in course, we must consider the possibility that humanitarian notions of morality like Bauman's were not fundamentally human but merely historically specific, precisely as Nietzsche had argued, and that care for the world could lead in other directions as conceptions of the human challenge and responsibility changed. We have seen that the new historical-political sense made possible an alternative, "great political" morality, requiring overcoming at least certain aspects of conventional morality, which, from the new perspective, seemed outmoded. So it is not enough simply to posit amoral distance in light of modern rationality and bureaucracy. And because he did not adequately characterize the actual dynamic of Nazi practice, Bauman could not convincingly place the bureaucratic syndrome within it. Thus his account was not merely incomplete but a bit misleading.

Saul Friedländer's accent on *Rausch*, or elation, suggests that, contrary to Bauman, the Nazis experienced their overall enterprise *not* as normal, routine—but as extraordinary, world-historical, even apocalyptic. And it *was* extraordinary: thus, in part, the force of the momentum. Friedländer's way of accounting for the mode of elation offers a useful first step as we seek to understand how the undoubted measure of bureaucratic routine, with its self-propelling mechanisms, could have combined with an exhilarating sense of hardness.

Friedländer suggested that we have tended to miss something in our long-standing concern with ideological motives like anti-Semitism, on the one hand, and institutional and bureaucratic dynamics, on the other. Even after we have encompassed both, "an independent psychological residue" seems to remain, defying understanding. When recognized at all, Friedländer continued, that dimension was usually reduced to a vague reference to the banality of evil, which did not in fact encompass the residue in question. Friedländer found espe-cially telling the seemingly uncanny juxtapositions in Himmler's speeches as the extermination process was proceeding.[223] Hans Mommsen similarly noted that those speeches made unusually explicit the symptomatic double morality charac-teristic of Nazi rule.[224]

Most revealing was Himmler's oft-quoted speech of October 4, 1943, to a group of SS leaders in Posen:

> Most of you will know what it means when a hundred corpses are lying side by side, or five hundred or a thousand are lying there. To have stuck it out and—apart from a few exceptions due to human weakness—to have remained decent, that is what has made us tough. This is a glorious page in our history, and one that has never been written and can never be written.[225]

The human weakness, Himmler went on to note, had included disappointing instances of SS looting; such petty transgressions as stealing from the victims were to be ruthlessly extirpated. Anyone taking even a mark for himself would be shot. But although there had been temptations, Himmler could claim that the SS were performing their world-historical role, exterminating Jews, with only a minimum of moral damage. Yet even as he conveyed a sense of glory, Himmler insisted that this was a never-to-be-written page in German history.

What do we make of these odd and troubling juxtapositions? Friedländer noted that unlike Hitler himself, Himmler and the SS were not driven by some anti-Jewish obsession. Their bond or identification with the leader was obviously essential, but for Friedländer the key that has eluded us was precisely *Rausch*, elation, possibly resulting from repetition, from the ever larger numbers, the sheer magnitude of the undertaking. From this perspective, he insisted, "the perpetrators do not appear anymore as bureaucratic automata, but rather as beings seized by a compelling lust for killing on an immense scale, driven by some kind of extraordinary elation in repeating the killing of ever-huger masses of people (notwithstanding Himmler's words about the difficulty of the duty)."[226] Evidence of such pride in numbers could be found in Auschwitz commandant Rudolf Höss's autobiography, for example.

Although Friedlander, in focusing on such elation, was pointing toward precisely the frame of mind to be understood, he left questions about its source and place. He noted that the Führer-bond explains the elation up to a point; the more killed, the greater Hitler's will was fulfilled. But Friedländer concluded that the elation entailed something more, which he characterized as "psychological." However, what was at work was not simply another ahistorical psychological mechanism; rather, it could only have emerged from within the historically specific great political dynamic. The elation grew in tandem with precisely the sense of *both* the magnitude and the difficulty of the enterprise that Himmler noted.[227] The elation itself then crucially reinforced the overall dynamic.

From the outset of the Nazi regime, the determination to implement a radical population policy had mandated unprecedented action requiring a particular kind of moral response. The steps that produced the Holocaust seemed in some sense to be routine only from within that framework, central to the accelerating Nazi revolution. The determination to deal definitively with "the Jewish question," as an aspect of the wider re-engineering of the population, was precisely what that revolution had come to entail. Reflecting on the course of the genocide in his speech of October 1943, Himmler noted that they had all said in effect "It's clear, it's in our program . . . we'll do it," but it had proved difficult to carry out consistently, without flinching, without occasional "weakness"—petty corruption, surely, but also no doubt the sadistic cruelty that the nature of the process itself invited. So in light of the genuine difficulty of the task, pride in having the hardness, the moral self-control to do it "decently," reinforced the energizing sense of world-historical mission. In his pre-execution memoir, Höss stressed the intense self-control required to carry out his "monstrous" work as commandant of Auschwitz.[228] In the same way, Treblinka commandant Franz Stangl, interviewed by Gitta Sereny over twenty-five years after the fact, expressed pride in having done his work well.[229] And it mattered how the work was done partly because the virtues that the process thereby elicited were crucial for the action necessary to go on shaping the future in a post-liberal way. Thus the feeling of superiority, even elation, at carrying out the difficult task with ruthless consistency and hardness, and thus Himmler's stern proscription of the "human weakness" that would demean the grandiose enterprise.[230]

Even bureaucrats who were "just doing their jobs" were doing so within a framework of extraordinary Nazi action that, by the early 1940s, had produced a particular state of mind—and a particular atmosphere permeated by mass murder. Careerism within that framework was not a merely routine banality that can be separated from the energizing sense of hardness. This was *not*, in other words, just a job like any other in normal times. Thus "euthanasia" specialist Friedrich Mennecke, in his letters to his wife, sought to chronicle for posterity this, "the greatest of times" in which he was privileged to be a significant participant.[231] This was the sort of response that Burleigh and Wippermann had in mind in specifying as central to the Holocaust "the group intoxication with violence and the prospect of going outside the limits of received moral norms."[232] And thus the scope for even the bureaucrats at their desks to experience a quiet but energizing exhilaration, bound up with a sense of partaking of a new morality, appropriately historically specific, transcending *both* conventional face-to-face morality and the modern, banally redirected morality of simply doing one's segmented job well.

In this light, we can usefully ponder certain tensions in Hannah Arendt's treatment of Adolf Eichmann in her noted report on his trial in Jerusalem in 1961. Without anticipating Bauman's terminology, Arendt probed the implications of the distancing that enabled Eichmann to play an essential role in the Holocaust, seemingly without grasping the wider implications of what he was doing. As Arendt saw it, the crime—genocide, beyond murder—was new and thus so must be our approach if we are to understand "this new type of criminal" who "commits his crimes under circumstances that make it well-nigh impossible for him to know or feel that he is doing wrong."[233] Far from being some Iago, inherently evil, Eichmann was ordinary, normal—indeed, in light of the novel role he played, "terribly and terrifyingly normal."[234] And he has come to seem the Holocaust's archetypal career bureaucrat.

Yet Arendt found something uncanny, anything but commonplace, in Eichmann's "remoteness from reality," his "sheer thoughtlessness." Lacking imagination, surrounding himself with clichés, he simply *"never realized what he was doing."*[235] She recognized that a kind of elation was at work, even for the bureaucratic Eichmann, but she viewed it as just another mode of thoughtlessness: "Whenever, during the cross-examination, the judges tried to appeal to his conscience, they were met with 'elation,' and they were outraged as well as disconcerted when they learned that the accused had at his disposal a different elating cliché for each period of his life and each of his activities." To be sure, Arendt went on, the elating clichés consistently gave Eichmann a lift, but they made it hard to take him seriously. Yet she recognized that to consider him merely a clever, calculating liar would have been too easy.[236]

For this particular, now isolated perpetrator, years after the fact, the earlier elation had indeed degenerated into mere clichés, but probing beneath them suggests that Arendt was too quick in accusing Eichmann of "sheer thoughtlessness" and "remoteness from reality." To understand how someone who was no Iago, who would probably not have been capable of ordinary murder, came to play a central role in an extraordinary genocide, we must better grasp how normality or banality came together with historically specific extraordinariness.

On trial, seeking to save his neck, Eichmann notoriously indulged in selective memory, bifurcating the responsible leaders and those like himself, who, he tried to suggest, had simply been a law-abiding citizen with a job, trying to do his duty.[237] But this defense does not square with the self-understanding that he also conveyed as one of the tough, high-minded idealists in the Nazi enterprise.[238] Although he was indeed normal, ordinary, the developing situation had been extraordinary, as he had understood full well. After his mediocre beginnings as a traveling salesman, it had taken something in particular to inspire him, galvanizing his talents. It was not so much Nazi ideology as Nazism the novel movement, tackling grandiose, energizing tasks. Although banal careerism was undeniably at work, Eichmann's was a very particular career, made possible only through very particular historically specific circumstances; he was not just following orders but following these particular orders in the context of this extraordinary revolution, entailing unprecedented tasks.

Although he was not a conventional anti-Semite but even something of a Zionist, Eichmann bought into the larger task of racial engineering and sought to rid Germany of Jews. That grandiose project made great demands, but it was essential to see it through even in the face of personal scruples. The sense of elation that even he, the archetypal bureaucrat, conveyed years after the fact reflected that sense of personal worth, even significance, in having played a major role in a project of such magnitude. He had indeed known what he was doing, and that was why he did it. He was not remote from but fully engaged in the new reality that Nazism had created. He contributed to the evil outcome because he had gotten caught up in the great political project, which channeled his banal careerist ambitions in what proved to be a murderous direction.239

At the same time, especially because of the magnitude of the tasks undertaken, the Nazi mode of action did not entail the smooth rational control that the Bauman syndrome suggested. Rather, as we have emphasized, the Nazi dynamic often proved characteristically out of control, and thus response was improvised, helter-skelter. Burleigh and Wippermann noted that "intra-bureaucratic chaos served further to brutalise and radicalise Nazi racial policy."240 It was not the *success* of bureaucracy, as affording predictable, orderly, routinized procedures, but the repeated *inability* to act as planned, the unintended consequences and failure, the incongruence between means and ends, that led to radicalization and brutalization. Still, it mattered that there were moments of bureaucratic calm, when the agents felt not only that they were responding rationally but even that they were collectively in control. Only standing back a step, in retrospect, can we see how even those moments, in interaction with other aspects of the process, fed the wider, out-of-control momentum.

Although they too noted "the self-propelling momentum of bureaucrats," Burleigh and Wippermann cautioned against overdoing the point—and stressed the significance of the underlying motive force, the directions from the top, the functional consensus. This was to remind us how misleading it is to bifurcate the process into visionary gardeners and the segmented bureaucrats who then got caught up in it, shaping it to some extent in their own image as they did so. The several components fed each other as they participated in this developing project that transcended conventional morality. So even to understand how the bureaucratic syndrome came into play, we must grasp the content that emerged in light of the supranational, historically specific break *beyond* generic gardening. We have noted that the energizing sense of involvement did not require, and is not to be conflated with, ideological fanaticism—rabid anti-Semitism, for example. This is a measure of the autonomy and significance of the novel great political layer.

From bureaucratic distancing to face-to-face murder

The central role of the bureaucratic "mass murderers at their desks" has long seemed among the most troubling dimensions of the Holocaust. But the need to encompass quite different dimensions has become clearer over the last fifteen years or so it as we have come to recognize how varied were the modes of killing and death at issue. Raul Hilberg estimated that whereas more than 50 percent of the victims of the Holocaust died in the six camps with systematic gassing facilities, almost a quarter died from such factors as malnutrition, disease, or exhaustion while in transit, in the ghettoes, or in the labor or concentration camps. The rest—more than one-quarter of the victims—were killed individually, mostly by shooting, up close.[241] Here we have anything but the impersonal, bureaucratic efficiency of mass gassing; here we have not distance but skull fragments splattered on the clothing of the killers. Whatever the quantitative measures, such face-to-face killing compels us to encompass mechanisms very different from those associated with the familiar—and too easy—modern bureaucratic syndrome.

The issue was brought forcefully to our attention by Christopher Browning and Daniel Jonah Goldhagen in two of the best-known books on the Holocaust: Browning's focused almost exclusively, Goldhagen's in part, on Hamburg-based Reserve Battalion 101 of the Order Police, sent to assist in the removal of Jews from a remote section of Poland in 1942.[242] We must recognize, first, that a measure of segmentation was at work in this instance as well. Even as they performed their assigned tasks, these policemen had not taken the initiative or made key decisions but were literally following orders—orders that seemed legitimate, emanating from constituted authority. Moreover, some of what they ended up doing, such as rounding up Jews for Ukrainians to kill, or clearing ghettoes for shipment to extermination camps, reflected the more immediate segmentation of the overall process.

But when they first arrived in the obscure village of Józefów on July 13, 1942, and on several occasions thereafter, these ordinary German policemen found themselves charged to shoot large numbers of defenseless Jews one by one. Moreover, when given their collective charge upon their arrival, they were given a chance to "step out," and there proved to be wider scope for each of them, as individuals, to pull back from direct involvement along the way.[243] Yet, to a surprising extent, the men of Battalion 101 proved to be willing, sometimes enthusiastic, face-to-face killers.

Are we to understand this response as ahistorically human, abidingly German, or specifically Nazi? In seeking to account for the mechanisms at work, Browning and Goldhagen agreed up to a point but then diverged in a way that brings out the essential issues—and suggests the need, and the scope, for another step in our effort to understand.

The policemen at issue were "ordinary," often middle-aged Germans who were not simply murderous psychopaths, but neither did their response stem from banal careerist aspirations. Nor, in light of the opportunity to "step out," can the obvious sort of banal fear have been the key. Moreover, their actions cannot be traced to the brutalization that accompanies war; this was anything but a combat situation, and these men had not previously seen combat in this war.[244] They had not been specially selected, and since they were old enough to have been socialized prior to the Nazi era, they would not have been especially susceptible to Nazi indoctrination. The modicum of ideological training that they received surely reinforced Nazi racial stereotypes, including the dehumanization of Jews, but it did not prepare them for the specific task of face-to-face killing. Whereas the *Einsatzgruppen*, before being sent to the Soviet Union, received two months of training explicitly preparing them for systematic murder, the men of Battalion 101 were unprepared and surprised when, upon arriving in Józefów, they learned what they were there to do.[245]

Although Goldhagen made a popular splash, he was roundly criticized by professional historians, several of whom showed that his use of evidence was sometimes tendentious, even sloppy.[246] Many invoked Browning's seemingly more nuanced way of accounting for the response at issue as a more convincing, historiographically responsible alternative to Goldhagen's.[247] But although critics exposed serious weaknesses in his overall argument, Goldhagen usefully insisted that in seeking to account for this episode and other, comparably troubling dimensions of the Holocaust, we have been too quick to resort to the various banal and/or universal categories suggesting that virtually any of us could have done it "under comparable circumstances." He turned up much disturbing evidence that seemed to suggest the inadequacy of the tentative framework that Browning provided, flexible and multidimensional though it was. Even if it was not as widespread as Goldhagen claimed, there proved to be sufficient evidence of unbidden cruelty, for example, to suggest a dimension, beyond the decision for genocide, and beyond any bureaucratic mechanisms, that itself requires explanation—and that proves to illuminate the overall dynamic at work. Indeed, Goldhagen was raising, if only implicitly, central questions about the interaction between ahistorical and historically specific components that his critics, even including Browning, had not adequately addressed. In doing so, he stumbled onto the key terrain for deepening the discussion. Yet he did so almost in spite of himself, in terms of an unsustainable wider thesis.

Goldhagen suggested that even the most ordinary agents, including the members of Battalion 101, were in some sense "willing" in ways that we have failed to recognize as we have resorted to such convenient categories as coercion, conformity, careerism, and bureaucratic distancing.[248] Indeed, as Goldhagen had it, these and other Germans killed Jews because they wanted to, because of their beliefs—because they were such virulent anti-Semites that they believed the Jews ought to die and welcomed the chance to kill them. They differed in the amount of pleasure they took but not over the justice of the enterprise.[249]

In this sense, for Goldhagen the members of Battalion 101 were not ordinary *men* but ordinary *Germans*, manifesting a special eliminationist, even exterminationist, anti-Semitism stemming from a demonic conception of Jews that, Goldhagen contended, had long been endemic in all reaches of German society.[250] So single-mindedly did he insist on this historically specific belief system that even as he stressed what may seem at first merely ahistorical, wanton cruelty, he explicitly minimized the role for sadism, as an ahistorical psychological propensity differentiated across populations. Only something more specific—the demonic German conception of the Jews—could account for the gratuitous cruelty in, for example, the work camps, where making the Jews suffer had normative force and, in that sense, was part of the purpose. Goldhagen found quite telling the contrast with the more clinical way in which the "euthanasia" program, for example, was carried out.[251]

In light of the potential for confusion on this sensitive issue, it is important to note that, although it leaves us with another set of questions, Goldhagen was *not* positing some abiding national character as he insisted on a special German anti-Semitism. It was strictly for long-term historical reasons that the Germans had become such virulent anti-Semites by the late modern period. This meant that the Germans could change again on the historical level, in light of histori- cally specific factors, and as Goldhagen saw it, they had done so after 1945. Indeed, he was quite sanguine about the state of the German democracy since the Second World War. Anti-Semitism had radically diminished, as he saw it, and the remnant had lost its hallucinatory elements.[252] He especially credited postwar American re-education efforts to account for this sudden change—an argument that Ruth Bettina Birn found "almost farcical," for virtually no one else had attributed real influence to this program.[253] If anything, insisted Birn, the program had produced an anti-Semitic backlash. But it is hard to deny that there was indeed significant change on this level in postwar Germany, and although Goldhagen may not convincingly account for it, neither do critics like Birn seem prepared fully to address the questions of historical specificity at issue.

Although Goldhagen was ahead of his critics in certain respects, his tenden- tious overall thesis made it impossible for him to put his insights into useful perspective. He recognized that the exterminationist mindset alleged to charac- terize the earlier Germans was so far removed from our conception of normal that we have had trouble imagining the degree of cultural difference at issue. But he insisted that we take these perpetrators seriously, as moral agents, capable of choices—and thus in their real, irreducible difference, stemming from their belief system. This is to eschew reliance on abstract, ahistorical factors that seem to make them like us so that, conversely, we would have acted just as they did "under certain circumstances."[254] Here Goldhagen was precisely on target. We have indeed been quick to avoid taking the difference seriously, as historically specific, as we have resorted instead to a certain subset of alleged German idiosyncrasies and/or universal psychological propensities or banalities—from fear to careerism to obedience to authority. Insofar as we find even that combi- nation inadequate, we throw up our hands and invoke "the universality of evil." Again and again, Goldhagen's evidence suggested that we must come to terms with a neglected set of historically specific beliefs, a frame of mind different from our own, to understand what fueled the process.

It was especially the possible significance of some such set of beliefs that Goldhagen's critics seemed unprepared to recognize. The problem was that his conception of the source and content of those beliefs was utterly unconvincing. He merely posited an idiosyncratic, long-term German propensity toward a murderous, eliminationist anti-Semitism, without even trying to explain it. To be sure, the notion that some special German anti-Semitism, antedating Nazism, was essential to the Holocaust surely suggests itself as an initial hypothesis. Before relying on such an idiosyncratic tradition for explanation, however, we would need comparative questioning about the depth, extent, and nature of German anti-Semitism, *as well as* a sense of other historically specific factors that might have been at work and that might satisfy Goldhagen's plausible demand for an alternative to the too-easy reliance on ahistorical propensities or generically modern mechanisms like the bureaucratic syndrome.

But, remarkably, Goldhagen sidestepped both comparison and consideration of alternative historically specific factors. He insisted explicitly that his argument did not rest on *demonstrating* German uniqueness through comparative analysis. At some points, in fact, he seemed to be falling into the most egregious circular reasoning. There was also anti-Semitism elsewhere, he said, but its extent and substance were not relevant to explaining what happened in Germany, for only in Germany did a rabidly anti-Semitic movement bent on exterminating Jews come to power—indeed, he insisted gratuitously, get *elected* to power. That alone was sufficient both to confirm a variation on the *Sonderweg* thesis and to assure that German anti-Semitism would have qualitatively different consequences.[255] In other words, German anti-Semitism had to have been special—and the key explanatory factor—because only in Germany was there a regime that produced such consequences, because only the Germans initiated genocide. This was essentially to infer German difference from the fact of the Holocaust itself.

Although the Holocaust was surely special, we have no idea, from Goldhagen's account, whether German anti-Semitism was or was not special and thus to what extent it was the key variable. As we have noted, the overwhelming consensus of recent research is that prior to the advent of the Nazi regime, German anti-Semitism was *not* especially pronounced or virulent. But anti-Semitism was certainly present, and the question is the nature of the connection between that antecedent anti-Semitism and the catastrophic outcome. Even as he eschewed comparative analysis, Goldhagen offered characterizations suggesting, if only implicitly, that what must be understood is the nature of the Nazi revolution itself, the difference it made.[256]

Goldhagen insisted explicitly that whatever its level and virulence, the antecedent anti-Semitism could have produced the genocide only when harnessed to a state policy of violent persecution and killing. At first, he seemed to suggest merely a kind of symbiosis between the Nazi leadership and the German people. Hitler, he said, crossed a moral barrier that ordinary Germans on their own could not have crossed, but then the pre-existing anti-Semitism afforded the willing accomplices that the regime needed. From this perspective, Nazism simply opened the way for the Germans—even those not especially pro-Nazi on other grounds—to do what they had wanted to do in any case.[257] Thus there was nothing twisted about the road to Auschwitz. While admitting Hitler's uncertainty on the level of timing and methods, he insisted that the Führer's apocalyptic mind conceived the exterminationist solution as an urgent but future project.[258] And we can see in retrospect that Hitler took the most radical, the most eliminationist step feasible at each key stage of Nazi Jewish policy. Thus, for Goldhagen "there was no *unintended* cumulative radicalization of policy because of bureaucratic politics or for any other reason."[259] Indeed, he was denying that there was anything "out of control" about the momentum.

But Goldhagen's argument betrayed tensions that suggested a more complex relationship. At some points, Hitler had not merely to tap into or unleash but actively to *mobilize* German anti-Semitism, a notion that raised further questions about the difference that the Nazi framework made.[260] Even on Goldhagen's own terms, in fact, the key variable was the nature—the *content*—of the Nazi revolution itself. Nazism, he contended, was the most profound of modern revolutions, even "the most extreme and thoroughgoing in the annals of Western civilization. It was, above all, a cognitive-moral revolution which reversed processes that had been shaping Europe for centuries."[261] As such, it proved to be the antithesis of Christian morality and Enlightenment humanism. From there, Goldhagen embraced the notion, akin to Arendt's, that the camp world, betraying even a cosmology and ontology radically different from our own, was paradigmatic—the purest expression of the Nazi revolution. All this was to suggest that German society had undergone fundamental moral and cognitive changes during the Nazi period itself. So something beyond the prior anti-Semitism was crucial to the novel set of beliefs at work—and to the radical difference.

Whatever the place of the camps, the first imperative would seem to be to understand the "cognitive-moral revolution" and its relationship with the antecedent anti-Semitism. But having already posited abiding anti-Semitism as the key variable, Goldhagen characterized that revolution only superficially and said nothing about the sources of its anti-Enlightenment and anti-Christian content. We learn only that it entailed a "new ethos" that somehow sanctioned cruelty and mass murder. As we have seen, it was indeed a moral-cognitive revolution that opened the way to mass killing, but because Goldhagen did not grasp the terms of that revolution, he could not assess its place in the process. From within the *a priori* framework that he posited, emphasizing intention and continuity, he could not have recognized the very particular kind of dynamic that resulted from the effort to act in light of the moral-cognitive revolution at issue. Nor could he have recognized how that dynamic exacerbated Germany's unexceptional anti-Semitism and led eventually to the Holocaust.

At some point, the extraordinary exhilaration that Friedländer featured became central to that dynamic. Goldhagen certainly had much the same dimension in mind when he noted that "the overwhelming impression of those who ever witnessed a German ghetto clearing was that they were observing not men who were brought to their tasks reluctantly, but men driven by the passion, determination, tirelessness, and enthusiasm of religious zealots on a holy, redemptive mission."[262] This characterization well supports Goldhagen's insistence on difference, but once we grasp the content and implication of Nazi great politics, we better understand that whereas the action at issue was indeed experienced as "a holy, redemptive mission," even the murderous anti-Semitism was less the underlying cause than an effect, an outcome, of the quest for purification to produce the homogeneity that was seemingly necessary for collective action.

Goldhagen cited the testimony of a member of the *Einsatzgruppen*, in a postwar legal brief, that he and his cohorts had genuinely believed that Germany was in an apocalyptic battle with Bolshevism and that Bolshevism was Jewish. His lawyer argued that Nazism had convinced the overwhelming majority of Germans of this identity. Self-serving though it is, such evidence supports the notion that the variable was not some prior eliminationist anti-Semitism but the momentum of Nazism, with the particular content it entailed.[263] In the same vein, Erwin Graffman, the most forthright of the veterans of Battalion 101, noted in his trial testimony that only after the fact had it occurred to him that the killing had not been right.[264] When acting, he had believed something very different, essentially the rightness of the wider Nazi revolution itself, a belief that rested not on prior anti-Semitism but on the self-justifying action of the Nazi project in course.

Although the appropriate alternative is to specify a *different* historically specific Nazi content, supranational in important respects, the manifest inadequacy of Goldhagen's insistence on abiding German anti-Semitism can easily point us back to some combination of ahistorical factors, taken as exhausting the supranational dimension, and the familiar national triggering mechanisms, taken as exhausting the historically specific dimension. This tendency was clear, for example, in Birn's influential critique of Goldhagen. Her quite plausible effort to counter Goldhagen's way of singling out the Germans led her to emphasize universal ahistorical mechanisms, the sense in which any of us could have done the same. Or, more precisely, under comparable circumstances we would find essentially the same array of responses even from a different population because of universal human psychological mechanisms.[265] This was also to suggest, conversely, that those ordinary Germans were *not* so different from us. But this retreat to the universal psychological level misses the scope for exploring alternative, historically specific bases of difference. For whereas on some level the point about comparable response under comparable circumstances is true virtually *a priori*, the question is what "comparable circumstances" entail—what *were* the circumstances in this case, and where did they come from? We are back to the question of the content of the Nazi revolution. To say that we all could have done it if we had been caught up in the Nazi revolution is trivial.

Criticizing Goldhagen's tendency to generalize about "the Germans" as opposed to differentiating the various roles they played, Birn usefully insisted that a different set of questions was at issue for high- and low-level perpetrators. Ahistorical mechanisms that are obviously insufficient to account for the originators may seem sufficient to account for the "ordinary" agents.[266] In fact, however, we cannot assess even the low-level perpetrators without attending to the dynamic and momentum resulting from the content of the Nazi departure, then asking how the universal psychological layer came to interface with *that*.

We can best understand the place of such ahistorical mechanisms by considering Christopher Browning's alternative to Goldhagen's way of accounting for the responses of the ordinary men of Battalion 101. Whereas Goldhagen sought to force an idiosyncratic German dimension, Browning's account seemed more flexible and nuanced precisely because it showed how such universal mechanisms played into the situation. Emphasizing the agents' scope for choice, he showed that responses ran the gamut from enthusiastic participation to dutiful or regretful compliance to degrees of evasion.[267]

Up to a point, Browning, like Birn, simply concluded that as a result of familiar ahistorical psychological mechanisms—allowing for some degree of variation between individuals—any set of human beings could become killers under comparable circumstances.[268] When faced with the unexpected situation at Józefów, most simply did what they were told, without questioning; because it was sanctioned by legitimate authority, they did not think it wrong. Although they were not regular army members, many had internalized the notion that soldiers were to be tough, to follow orders based on government policy, whatever the content. Moreover, they responded to peer pressure and the dynamic of the unforeseen group situation. They did not want to leave the dirty work to others. They did not want to appear "too good" for the job—or too weak, not least because they would thereby risk isolation in an unfamiliar context. So they tried not to think about what they were doing or masked it through heavy drinking.[269] Taken one by one, and thus isolated in this way, such responses seem self-explanatory and require only minimal reference to the specific situation. Perhaps this, that, or the whole syndrome was less universally human than a male thing, but whatever it was, as characterized up to this point it does not seem to have been even specifically Nazi, let alone specifically German.

For Browning, however, such *ordinary* banal, ahistorical responses did not suffice, because the situation itself was so extraordinary. Seeking the deeper dimension that seemed to be required, he invoked the experiments of Stanley Milgram, which we encountered in connection with Bauman above, and Philip Zimbardo. Each suggested that under certain circumstances a substantial majority of human beings will lapse into cruel, even sadistic behavior.[270] Whereas Milgram tested the capacity to resist authority, the Zimbardo experiment suggested that the polarity of a prison situation, giving some individuals near-total power over others, was itself sufficient to elicit cruel, sadistic responses even from individuals who could not be classified *a priori* as sadistic types. So we slide from familiar, almost self-explanatory factors like conformity to those more troubling like cruelty or sadism. These latter may be comparably universal, as latent human possibilities, although with thresholds varying across populations. But they are less familiar because they come to the fore only under relatively extreme circumstances.

Students of Nazi extremism, from Burleigh and Wippermann to Goldhagen, have questioned the relevance of these experiments, as if they somehow absolved the agents of responsibility.[271] The notion that we "all" could have done it, under the right circumstances, seems to leave us with some vacuous notion of "the universality of evil." Goldhagen could dismiss such experiments because he had another explanation that, if convincing, would indeed render those mechanisms irrelevant. From his perspective, even the ordinary agents in question killed because they believed that it was right; they were all "willing executioners" in the first place. But we have seen that Goldhagen's alternative does not convince. Moreover, Browning, recognizing that responses varied even in the experiments, stressed the scope for choice, so he was hardly absolving of responsibility.

Although such experiments do not afford ready-made answers, it would be unwise to dismiss their findings *a priori*, on moralistic grounds. In principle, they could uncover apparently widespread but normally hidden psychological propensities that could help us to account for what we find most troubling in responses on the level of Battalion 101. Browning noted convincingly that by isolating such factors as role adaptation and deference to authority, Milgram and Zimbardo enabled us better to consider how such mechanisms operated in historically specific instances.[272] And he went on to suggest that, despite some obvious differences, the artificial Milgram situation significantly paralleled the situation that the men of Battalion 101 encountered at Józefów. Circumstances had altered the threshold so that the agents no longer felt responsible for their actions.

But to assess the place of such ahistorical psychological mechanisms, we must first probe the nature of the historically specific situation, asking why and how it could alter the threshold, enabling such mechanisms to become operative. The circumstances at issue in the case at hand were very particular indeed, and we wonder what would count as "comparable." However, those circumstances were not merely idiosyncratic or *sui generis* but had resulted from the momentum of the Nazi revolution, by now partly out of control.

Browning offered some useful indications of the novel features and, on that basis, the difference that the specific Nazi dynamic made as he emphasized the novelty of the experience in the east, a strange area with alien *Ostjuden*, in the context of this war of race and ideology, this atmosphere of violence and dehumanization.[273] But these were only shorthand hints at the crucial connective tissue that Browning tended to leave scattered, in loose interface with the ahistorical mechanisms at issue. So just as Goldhagen charged, a measure of sanitization seemed to result from Browning's account, subtle and nuanced though it was. If we consider the nature of the circumstances more systematically, we see how the troubling aggregate response of these ordinary Germans emerged from within the wider, continuing totalitarian dynamic of Nazism.

Responding to Goldhagen in the second edition of *Ordinary Men*, Browning made more pointedly a theme that had been merely one among others in the first edition. He now agreed that anti-Semitism, negative stereotyping, dehumanization, even hatred, were widespread among the killers of 1942, but he still unequivocally denied that this fuel derived from some longstanding murderous anti-Semitism endemic to Germany.[274] Browning's implication was that, on the contrary, the Nazis had somehow *made* anti-Semitism central to ordinary Germans as it had not been before. The "hate" had *come to be*, in the course of the regime; it was an *outcome*, as opposed to a source, of the ongoing Nazi revolution.

But this was to suggest, yet again, that the key variable was the Nazi revolution itself, which had succeeded in creating "a certain frame of mind" and which entailed a momentum that eventually caught up even these ordinary Germans in essential roles. And in those roles, in light of the extraordinary situation that the unforeseen dynamic had brought into being, they did not merely follow orders but often fell into gratuitous cruelty. They would not have been capable of such cruelty under ordinary circumstances. And that cruelty was indeed directed at Jews, as Jews, precisely as Goldhagen insisted. However, it manifested not an abiding German anti-Semitism but the destructive potential of the new mode of collective action in progress.

Although the antecedent thinking about Jews had not been so different in Germany, we have seen that the Nazi regime's demonization of the Jews, its policies of isolation and discrimination, made a difference from within the framework of concerted action, changing the threshold in the responses of ordinary Germans to the Jews. Especially as the Nazi revolution yielded this apocalyptic war of race, ideology, and annihilation—and encountered unforeseen difficulties in the process—the prior mythology surrounding the Jews took on ever greater salience. But the key variable was not that antecedent and relatively constant mythology but the radicalizing dynamic itself.

That dynamic was by now producing bizarre, unforeseen consequences calling forth further response. When first telling his men of their mission upon their arrival, the commander of Battalion 101 stressed the terror bombing of German cities that had begun by early 1942.[275] His implication was that in response to this development, defying Nazi expectations, the Germans would have to turn it up a notch as they continued the Nazi revolution in an atmosphere of expanding violence. Moreover, it was only in light of this helter-skelter dynamic that these ordinary policemen found themselves in this bizarre situation, calling forth their novel, anything but bureaucratic responses, in the first place. No one had remotely envisioned, let alone intended, middle-aged policemen from Hamburg hunting down and shooting Jews in the woods of eastern Poland. And the surreality of the circumstance itself, the resultant of the out-of-control but strongly contingent Nazi revolution so far, is surely one key to the anomalous side of their response. Seeking to make sense of his own response years later, and despairing of being understood, one of these ordinary perpetrators could say only that "it was a different time and place."[276]

Although all were operating within the framework wrought by Nazism, the members of Battalion 101 responded in different ways, reflecting the expected variables of personality and character. In order to do the face-to-face killing required, some needed actively to dehumanize the victims; others wanted to keep what they did as distant and faceless as possible; still others apparently tried not to think about what they were doing—thus, again, the heavy drinking. They sometimes felt more pity for themselves, having to carry out this unpleasant task in this remote location, than for their victims.[277] At this end of the spectrum, we have anything but "extraordinary exhilaration." But there was plenty of elation as well, or at least a sense of extraordinary enterprise.

Especially telling are the photographs that both Browning and Goldhagen included—photographs that appall us today.[278] The ordinary men took them while doing their extraordinary duty not so that they could forget, obviously, but precisely to retain the memory of participating in what had come to seem a grandiose enterprise beyond experience, defying imagination, on the edge—a whole new edge—in this "greatest of times." The point is not that they had read Nietzsche but that they found themselves called upon to act within a dynamic that reflected the Nietzschean determination of its initiators. And they themselves had gotten sufficiently caught up in it to alter their threshold of response. Thus their participation is not merely to be subsumed within the universal, ahistorical mechanisms of "we all could have done it." Those operating from within the framework of the continuing Nazi revolution, with its particular content, were especially likely to have done it.

In light of these considerations, let us recall Omer Bartov's question to Browning that we pondered in Chapter 1: was the point that literally anyone could have done it? Bartov pointed out, plausibly enough, that Hamburg was not the same as London or New York; aspects of the background and environment of the policemen in question may have made them especially receptive to Nazi policies.[279] Ordinary though they were, we might say, even ordinariness is contextually specific, differentiated. Insisting, quite properly, that we need a deeper understanding of what differentiated these ordinary men, Bartov was raising questions more specific than Browning's about the situation triggering the ahistorical psychological responses in question. And thus, as he stressed, we would like to know more about their background and training. To ask, for example, about the role of some prior authoritarianism in training initiates a line of questioning about the place of nationally specific factors that surely should be part of the mix. But Bartov seemed to assume that the answer would inevitably be found in some form of German *Sonderweg*. In fact, however, we could assess the role of any such nationally specific layer only if we also had a better sense of the supranational, historically specific factors than Browning provided. These ordinary men were operating from within a situation created by a supranational, historically specific departure that took particular form in Germany, reflecting antecedent German traditions, but that demands analysis on its own terms. And it was that departure, not some long-term contextual feature, that most accounts for their *difference* from ordinary men elsewhere.

"Human weakness" and other responses at the outer edge

Even in treating the same evidence about Battalion 101, Goldhagen placed far greater emphasis than Browning on gratuitous violence, and he went well beyond the Order Police to pile up much additional evidence, from the differential treatment of Jews in the labor camps to the incredible late death marches. And although his use of such evidence was sometimes dubious, he undeniably forced to the forefront a significant dimension of wanton, grotesque cruelty, torture, and humiliation that seemingly increased as the war dragged on—and that, whatever its quantitative measure, had not been adequately encompassed in the discussion to that point. Defying any notion of sanitizing distance, efficient bureaucratic control, or "just following orders," this dimension is yet another stage that must be accounted for from within the overall Nazi dynamic.

We noted that even as he featured grotesquely cruel excesses, Goldhagen refused to attribute them to some ahistorical psychological mechanism like sadism, for that would be to play down the strength and sufficiency of the eliminationist anti-Semitism. On this level, too, he was right to insist that we miss something—something about historical specificity and thus difference—insofar as we settle for ahistorical psychological mechanisms or some vacuous "universality of evil." But neither can we simply invoke German eliminationist anti-Semitism as an alternative. We must understand this extreme stage, too, in terms of the interplay of a differentiated ahistorical propensity and the historically specific situation created, brought into the world, by great politics. Although ahistorical, sometimes negative human possibilities were at work at every stage, thresholds and proportions shifted as each step created a new situation, thereby gradually changing the very character of the enterprise.

Although gratuitous violence and cruelty surfaced well before the war, the regime sought to keep it in check or at least to rein it in—as during *Kristallnacht*, for example. Hitler and the Nazi leadership were quite in earnest as they stressed courage, hardness, and self-control. Even with the Holocaust fully in progress, Himmler was serious in lamenting the instances of "human weakness," from petty theft to sadism, that had already occurred, and in seeking to head off further such lapses. The Nazi leadership understood, and explicitly portrayed, sadistic self-indulgence as weakness, as a degeneration. Certainly, wanton cruelty and sadism were not integral to the extermination project, which required speed and efficiency. The testimony of Auschwitz survivors suggests that sadism was evident among only about 5 to 10 percent of SS men in the camps.[280]

Yet grotesque, unbidden cruelty there surely was, and it cannot be understood as mere weakness, as the exception that proves the rule. Such excess seems to have come increasingly to the fore as the Nazi assault on the Jews turned to genocide and as the overall situation grew ever more bizarre and apocalyptic late in the war. In that sense, the excess constituted yet another unforeseen stage of the dynamic. The fact that this ahistorical capacity for cruelty was realized as pervasively as it was tells us nothing about the origins of Nazism, but "Nazism" must be understood precisely as a total dynamic encompassing such unforeseen and unintended stages.[281]

Interviewing Franz Stangl in the late 1960s, Gitta Sereny asked why the seemingly gratuitous humiliation and cruelty if, as Stangl insisted, it was not from anti-Semitism *per se* and if the operation was to be carried out quickly and efficiently. Stangl replied that to whip, to force nakedness, was necessary to dehumanize the victims, to render them weak and passive, to break down any solidarity with them, so that those charged with the extermination could more readily carry it out.[282] Although Stangl's testimony is not always to be credited, his point makes sense of the evidence. It was not as if the perpetrators at the camp level had been lusting after opportunities for sadistic indulgence; rather, they needed to add a dimension to the situation that had already emerged if they were to do their part, carrying forward the grandiose project. But such behavior, changing the overall threshold, then invited further sadistic excess, depending on individual thresholds.

Auschwitz commandant Rudolf Höss, writing, in contrast to Stangl, shortly after the war, was less candid. Although he had used every means available, he claimed, he had been unable to prevent mistreatment of the victims: "One person is no match for the viciousness, depravity, and cruelty of a guard."[283] However, there is evidence that Höss allowed beatings as part of the routine maintenance of discipline.[284] This, too, would have changed the threshold and opened the way for some to take another step into sadistic indulgence.

By the end, in 1945, the stage of cruelty had come to include surreal death marches that would surely have defied the imagination of Hieronymous Bosch himself. These marches developed as German cities were being relentlessly reduced to rubble by Allied bombing and as adversaries approached from both east and west. The Soviets coming from the east were especially to be feared because, responding to the war of racial-ideological annihilation that the Nazis had unleashed, they indulged in a good deal of wanton cruelty of their own. These apocalyptic circumstances called forth unsuspected forms of banality, even on the part of Himmler, who sought to exploit his control over large numbers of Jews to salvage a measure of his own power, even to enhance it, in the face of impending defeat.[285]

With the death marches, the victims were herded out of the camps and into the open, into contact with non-Jewish bystanders, primarily in Germany but also in Poland and Czechoslovakia. To be sure, for all the efforts at secrecy, there had been contact all along between the camp world and those living close by. And there has been much discussion of what these bystanders knew, or could conceive, about the developing genocide and, what, if anything, they might have done to help the victims.

In his study of those living near Mauthausen, in Austria, Bartov noted a combination of fear, indifference, profit, prejudice, humiliation, and guilt, all in the context of the scope for limiting one's focus, not seeing the whole picture. But most striking in Bartov's account was a syndrome noted in other venues as well. People assumed that the camp inmates, who by this point hardly looked human, must be guilty of something terrible.[286] Based on their sense, from all prior experience, of what the world could hold, these bystanders literally could not grasp what was happening; they could only make sense of the evidence in terms of familiar categories. In this light, how do we read the responses of ordinary bystanders when they happened to come into contact with the death marches?

We find not only indifference but instances of further grotesque cruelty—for Goldhagen, yet more evidence of the eliminationist anti-Semitism endemic to Germany.[287] But this phenomenon, too, must be understood as an *outcome* of the overall dynamic in course, as a degeneration possible only once the prior, unforeseen stage had been reached. Moreover, Goldhagen seemed to neglect or explain away the surprisingly numerous cases of ordinary Germans who responded in the opposite way, reaching out to the Jews.[288] And thus he surely skewed the meaning of this apocalyptic final phase. As it became clear that Nazi great politics had merely reduced Germany to rubble, German identification with the Nazi revolution began to dissipate. Thus ordinary Germans became more likely, in defiance of Nazi categories, to experience a common humanity and to respond with acts of simple human kindness.

Great politics and the historicity of evil

We have been concerned throughout with the interplay of historically specific and ahistorical categories. And we noted in Chapter 1 that some have found Nazism, and especially the Holocaust, to be an eruption of ahistorical evil, the core of which no historical explanation can encompass. No one would claim that history can explain the presence of evil. At the same time, few would deny that if, eschewing theodicy, we make moral distinctions between historical phenomena, Nazism proved to be evil on some level and that a historical account can help us to understand how, through Nazism, new evil came into the world. But thus difficult questions open about the interface of the historically specific and whatever we mean by evil in this case. We noted in Chapter 1 the surprise of the distinguished journalist Ron Rosenbaum that professional historians seemed reluctant to impute evil to Hitler and, more generally, to deal in evil when discussing Nazism. Hugh Trevor-Roper's argument that Hitler was convinced of his own rectitude seemed to be the archetypal objection to any emphasis on evil—at least evil intent.

But much of the discussion has dealt in evil at least indirectly. In his pioneering study of Nazi doctors, Robert Jay Lifton emphasized "doubling," the capacity of those involved in the "euthanasia" program and the Holocaust to split between work and peaceful domesticity, as the central mechanism for avoiding facing up to the evil in what they were doing. Indeed, the notion has become a cliché—just another day at the office as a mass murderer while living a normal, even exemplary life, surrounded by a loving family and (almost invariably, it seems) showering kindness on pets. A measure of some such bifurcation was surely at work in many cases. But although Lifton's book usefully expanded our range of categories when it appeared, barely a generation ago, his reliance on doubling mechanisms has come to strike many as incomplete, perhaps disingenuous, diverting us from the key variables.[289]

Rather than resort so quickly to an ahistorical psychological mechanism, we must start by taking the agents more seriously as autonomous moral agents, allowing, again, the scope for individual variation. "Doubling" was not something that happened to them, so that, in their "Mr. Hyde" half, they did not realize what they were doing. Insofar as they "doubled," they often did so because it suited them. First, as we have emphasized, they were often active and willing participants in the wider process, caught up in its momentum. Being part of an enterprise that was both grandiose and illicit in conventional moral terms was genuinely thrilling but also genuinely difficult. Thus many did cling to the Dr. Jekyll self—but as lucid participants. "Doubling" was not a cause but simply describes one of the mechanisms that resulted as these Germans participated in the unprecedented Nazi project.

But we must take another step, for such bifurcation surely declined to zero in some instances. With such grotesque phenomena as the parties at "euthanasia" institutions commemorating the 10,000th killing, the perpetrators were not hiding from but celebrating collectively the work being done. Peremptorily dismissing Lifton, Michael Burleigh insisted that prissy doubling mechanisms are not necessary to understand such central figures in the "euthanasia" program as Friedrich Mennecke and Bodo Gorgass. Far from depending on some bifurcation, such figures often deliberately mixed work and private life, even brought their families into the workplace, partly, said Burleigh, because they were so puffed up with their own importance.[290] But although Burleigh was convincing in eschewing doubling, his alternative relied heavily on moralistic or reductionist put-down. In fact, Mennecke's was not merely the usual, banal careerist self-importance. The fact that he *was* important, in a new, grandiose way defying certain conventional moral categories, was central to the puffing up. Rather than simply explain it away, we should understand the response as yet another indication of the logic of the great political action in progress. It was that logic that made Mennecke's response possible.

But can we thus say that such agency stemmed from an intention to do evil? Also taking on Lifton explicitly was the philosopher Berel Lang, who, like Burleigh, insisted on attributing to such perpetrators a unified self and moral universe. And thus, he argued, we must credit the Nazis for knowledge of evil as evil.[291] Indeed, Lang concluded that "the Nazi genocide involves a knowing commitment to evil in principle beyond the psychological motives of its individual agents." Those agents knew it was wrong and did it "at least in part *because* it was wrong: wrongdoing had assumed for them the status of a principle."[292] At issue was not some sort of collective irrationality or madness; evil, Lang insisted, could be voluntary, intended. As evidence apparently undercutting the notion that the Nazis believed in their own rectitude, Lang adduced their accent on secrecy, their effort to destroy the corpses, the camps, and the records of the process as they retreated from the east. He pointed to their use of euphemisms like *Endlösung* and "pieces" to conceal, even from themselves, what they were in fact doing. To Lang, all this suggested shame—and thus awareness of wrongdoing.

In making this argument, Lang stood opposed not only to Lifton but also to an array from Bauman, who stressed a mechanism that enabled the Nazis to avoid facing the moral implications of what they were doing, to Goldhagen, for whom it was crucial that the Nazis "considered the slaughter to be just."[293] For Lang, in fact, the Nazis wrought an expansion of evil that forces us to confront as never before the historicity of evil itself.[294] Our concept of evil changes over time as, through further historical experience, we learn more about what the world can hold.

Rosenbaum embraced Lang's notion of deliberate evil, emphasizing the conscious relish in the process, as helping to refute the Trevor-Roper rectitude argument that Rosenbaum found so troubling.[295] Rosenbaum found especially telling Lang's insistence that the genocidal project was *not* in fact carried out efficiently, in some clinical way suggesting instrumental, means–ends rationality. The dimension of gratuitous violence itself violated bureaucratic efficiency.[296] Further refuting the "Hitler as Pasteur" argument, Rosenbaum drew out Lang's point to argue that the Nazis did *not* initially think of Jews as germs; they had first consciously and deliberately to reduce them to a subhuman state in order to make the killing palatable. Rosenbaum found a comparable gratuitousness in Hitler's droll reference to the "rumor" of extermination in the east and in the joke of "*Arbeit macht Frei*," the infamous motto on the entry gate to the camp at Auschwitz. For Rosenbaum, following Lang, all this suggested that what characterized Nazism was "evil as an art, the art of evil."[297] One of Rosenbaum's reviewers characterized the argument nicely: "Far from being convinced of their own rectitude, Hitler and his associates knew what they were doing was monstrous, and gloried in the fact—that they were 'artists in evil,' proud of their originality."[298]

It is surely true that Nazism expanded forever what we mean by evil, our sense of the evil that the world can hold. The question is the source of that expansion, how such new evil came into the world. Both Lang and Rosenbaum were quick to retreat to the ahistorical dimension, asserting that the Nazis deliberately did evil as evil, from an implicit sense that there was no other alternative to the rectitude argument, and no way to account, in historically specific terms, for the evidence apparently defying that argument. But to invoke evil so quickly compromises the scope for historical understanding and thus the scope for more complex moral lessons—beyond the need to guard against evil—that are possible through a more consistently historical understanding of this particular evil. And in any case, evil intention is not the only alternative to the rectitude argument, with its disturbing implications of moral relativism.

The issue is difficult partly because it forces us to make distinctions between forms or degrees of evil—and we sometimes see evil as in some sense absolute. If we say, as is tempting, that forced sterilization, or forced emigration stemming from an insistence on ethnic homogeneity, are already evil, how do we differentiate the Holocaust? Rosenbaum and Lang were led to their emphasis on evil intent not because of concern about some particular measure of Nazi policy but from a sense that Nazism itself was somehow evil, expanding what evil can mean. But on what basis? Eugenic and racist measures, for example, were not unique to Germany and would not in themselves have been sufficient to expand our sense of evil in the way that Rosenbaum and Lang had in mind. They were concerned about something more general—an attitude, a frame of mind, a whole mode of action.

What we need, to see beyond both rectitude and intended evil, is a deeper historical account of the connection between belief and action that addresses the interface with moral categories. The point is not simply that they actually believed that what they were doing was right but to grasp what it was they believed, why they believed it, and the implications of believing *that*, especially once they started *acting* on that belief.

Whereas for Lang the Nazis were artists in evil, committed to evil in principle, we note that they did not pick the wrongs they committed at random, perhaps bashing little old ladies over the head while helping them across the street, or enticing children with candy and toys in order to run them down with speeding automobiles. For artists in evil, the possibilities are endless. But obviously Nazi action was more focused, in light of a very particular sense of the challenge.

Certainly, the Nazis knew what they were doing to be *conventionally* evil; thus, in part, the energizing sense of participation in grandiose, unprecedented action. But the point was not merely some titillating pleasure in evil for its own sake; the exhilaration was bound up with transcending conventional morality in ways genuinely conceived as selfless, for a higher purpose. It required toughness and, as with Arthur Koestler's Rubashov in *Darkness at Noon*, the willingness to put aside what seemed mere "bourgeois" scruples. Although not without tensions, the grandiose toughness coexisted with the shame that Lang noted—a syndrome not to be confused with Lifton's doubling. Indeed, shame and toughness fed each other, for the shame was a legacy of the convention to be overcome. Overcoming shame, or doing what had to be done even in the face of shame, indicated hardness and thus afforded further exhilaration.

Because the capacity for hardness was itself energizing, the agents tended to pick the most radical response, the most evil in conventional terms, especially as their grandiose project of ethnic engineering encountered unforeseen obstacles. In this sense, they did indeed increasingly "glory" in doing the monstrous; they were indeed increasingly "proud of their originality." The more different from the mainstream they thereby became, the more sure they were of their superiority.

But the extraordinary mode of action proved not to work. As the project itself proved self-defeating, they were increasingly likely to do what was conventionally seen as evil precisely *because* it was wrong in this sense. But this step was itself a resultant, part of a historically specific dynamic that was not initiated as an effort to do evil as evil in the first place. In that sense, the expansion of evil was the strongly contingent historical outcome of Nazi great politics, of the new mode of action itself. It would in some ways be easier if we could chalk it up to an essentially inexplicable determination on the part of those *Others* to do evil for its own sake in the first place. That such evil could instead have come to be in this twisted, ragged, more deeply historical way through the agency of people who *started out* much like us is surely more troubling—and more admonitory.

Although his critique of the Enlightenment offered some preliminary elements for a more deeply historical treatment, Lang's argument proved limiting precisely because, despite lip service to "history" in an article on the historicity of evil, the sources proved only weakly historical in his account. The historical link to the Enlightenment that he posited proved, like Bauman's, to be too generic. By proceeding in a more deeply historical way, we grasp the steps between the Enlightenment and the Holocaust that made possible a redirection of human moral capacities and then a Nazi revolution that sought to act on the basis of that new possibility. The new collective human agency in a Nietzschean key resulted in a dynamic that proved to make possible actions and outcomes that were not foreseeable, even conceivable, earlier.[299]

Although, as we noted in Chapter 1, Lang offered some helpful observations on the possible role of ideas in subsequent events, he specifically exempted Nietzsche from any connection with Nazism.[300] On the basis of the conventional notion that Nietzsche was concerned with superior individuals, not race and collective struggle, he dismissed, as an "instance of misappropriation," the efforts of Nazi ideologues like Bäumler and Rosenberg to claim Nietzsche. But, as we have seen, although the Nazi appropriation was selective, it was crucial to the Nazi understanding of the scope to go beyond conventional moral categories. Lang's way of exempting Nietzsche made it especially difficult for him to grasp the place of moral categories in the Nazi departure.

It is striking that at least some of the perpetrators gradually came to grasp the implications of what they had done, as if being disenchanted in the literal sense, once the ongoing Nazi action had ended and they were removed from the Nazi framework. Although we may be tempted to dismiss such testimony as self-serving, Rudolf Höss seems genuinely to have come to a new self-understanding when interrogated by a psychologist just after the war. On the eve of his execution in 1947, he claimed to recognize that his actions had been deeply wrong—although he had believed them to be right at the time.[301] Some among the chief Nuremberg defendants, even among those who challenged the court's authority, came to realize the extent of the overall Nazi crime as the trials wore on. They were deeply affected and began to feel guilt.[302] But before the process had run its course, they had been in "a different time and place," engaging the world through a different frame of mind.

This is not to suggest that some mass conversion occurred among the Nazis once their experiment had reached its disastrous end. Ian Kershaw noted that few Nazis showed guilt or contrition after the fact; rather than recognize their own responsibility, they tended to see themselves as having been mesmerized by Hitler.[303] Although the "mesmerization" excuse seems especially reprehensible, certainly many had difficulty sorting out what had gone wrong. They were not prepared to say that the victors, the liberal democracies and/or the Soviet Union, had been right after all. Some sullenly noted that the victors write the history and make the judgments. But the absence of conversion, even in the face of defeat, does not mean that the impulses at work were ahistorical as opposed to historically specific. At issue was what lessons were to be drawn, what had ended and what had not—questions to be addressed in our concluding chapter.

Conclusion: apocalyptic narrowing and myth

The effort at great political action in Nazi Germany produced a strange but characteristic combination by the end. During the course of the war, even some of those most energized by Hitler's seemingly limitless capacity for will came to perceive the flaws in the modes of decision making and organization that had developed during the course of the regime. By 1943, Goebbels had recognized that the regime faced, of all things, a leadership crisis, as Hitler vacillated and neglected domestic issues.[304] But there was little to be done. Possibilities had narrowed with the strongly contingent interaction of forces that had resulted from the new mode of action since 1933. The outcome was a fragmented regime of competing fiefdoms, unable to check Hitler, suffering from both choking bureaucracy and overall administrative chaos.[305]

As Kershaw showed, with the defeat at Stalingrad by early 1943, Hitler was no longer exempt from popular criticism; his responsibility for the debacle was clear. The gulf between the Führer and the people widened thereafter.[306] Yet for Hitler himself it was crucial to steel still further his own will, to maintain an air of invincibility, with no hint of wavering. It remained his faith that resolute will, the strength to hold out, would somehow pay off in the end. The war effort could be renewed through radicalization on the home front, a largely psychological matter based on common austerity and sacrifice.[307] And to what now seems a remarkable extent, Hitler's show of will inspired continued resolve in many of those around him. By this point, however, even the triumph of the will was bound up with narrowing and myth.

Hitler himself increasingly lived in a world of illusion, partly because of what his energized collaborators were telling him about new aircraft, wonder weapons, and the like.[308] The overall Nazi stress on positive thinking, on the susceptibility of the world to willed action, was seriously compromising assessment of the actual prospects.[309] At the same time, the will to continue, to demonstrate the capacity to hold out in the face of incredible odds, was becoming almost an end in itself by the fall of 1944. There still were more specific purposes, but they were changing, narrowing. Continuing the war afforded the occasion to expand the revenge against the Jews, but also to test to the limit the Germans themselves. Defeat would indicate that they had not been worthy of the great task that Hitler had placed before them, not worthy of the Führer's will.[310]

From Hitler's apocalyptic perspective, it was better that Nazi Germany suffer total defeat than capitulate or negotiate from weakness. In light of the world-historical grandeur of the Nazi enterprise, to hold out to the end, then go down in flames, opened the way to validation by history, the only judge.[311] Goebbels noted the positive value of the Allied bombing, which was destroying not the future but only the past, the bourgeois nineteenth century.[312] As the apocalyptic potential of the new historical sense came to the fore, millions died and much of the country was reduced to rubble. Such were the wages of totalitarian great politics in Nazi Germany.

8   The epochal commonality of the three regimes

The framework for rethinking totalitarianism

The three regimes tackled very different projects, and although each failed, they ended in quite different ways. Their lifespans were very different as well. Hitler's "twelve-year Reich" could not possibly have entailed the variety, the ins and outs, of the Soviet experiment, which spanned seventy-four years—longer than the French Third Republic. Although also relatively short-lived, Fascist Italy lasted much longer than Nazi Germany, long enough to face more seriously the challenges of generational change, for example. Yet in following the three cases individually, we noted certain common features that justify, even mandate, treating them together as, at least on one level, participants in a single supranational, historically specific departure—and not merely parallel national departures in chronological proximity.

Grasping the commonality in its historically specific dimension required both backing up and projecting forward to deepen our understanding of how each regime emerged and developed historically. We found it necessary to back up even into the nineteenth century to understand how the originating aspirations emerged from within the new terrain that was settling out through a sort of shifting of tectonic plates by the end of the century. To project forward was to follow the dynamic that resulted from the effort to act on the basis of those aspirations and the new historical-political sense they reflected.

This two-pronged approach revealed certain commonalities in assumptions and priorities, in the respective trajectories, and even in the outcomes in the three cases. In each instance, the enterprise stemmed from a conception of modern challenges and possibilities that differentiated these three from the modern liberal mainstream. That conception cannot be reduced to some combination of ahistorical psychological and idiosyncratic national factors; a sense of certain genuine tensions or creases in the mainstream fueled each departure. In that sense, each was a quest for an alternative modernity. The common elements in the three trajectories followed from the common new mode of action undertaken. In what proved to be a characteristic combination, such action produced certain "successes," defying liberal expectations, but it also encountered unanticipated difficulties that led to a narrowing of participation and purpose, to inflating myth and rhetoric, and to either radicalizing self-destruction or a loss of belief leading to disintegration.

Appropriately recast, "totalitarianism" usefully characterizes the novel aspiration, the new mode of collective action, and the dynamic that ensued, with all its anomalous excesses and disastrous outcomes. To be sure, each dimension defies certain conventional uses of the term, but the earlier totalitarian model, long recognized as unsustainable, is a dead horse that no longer requires flogging.[1] What we come to understand, by backing up and projecting forward, is precisely totalitarianism as a supranational, historically specific departure that led in characteristic directions.

At work was not merely some common desire for total domination or some common technique of rule; nor do we find the key in violence, exclusion, terror, or some "assault on man." As usually invoked, such familiar categories as activism, irrationalism, and "perpetual dynamism" do not convince, but neither does a contrasting emphasis on Enlightenment rationality, totalist ideology, or ideological fanaticism. Still, none of these conventional categories was entirely misplaced; each got at something important about totalitarianism. To understand the place of each, we need the whole trajectory, encompassing both originating aspirations and the ensuing practical dynamic.

The deepest purpose in treating the three cases together is not static comparison, let alone some classificatory schema. Rather, by deepening our understanding of the element of commonality, we illuminate the historically specific modern situation, beyond the idiosyncratic national situations also obviously at issue in each case. To say that each helped to occasion the supranational, historically specific phenomenon is not to suggest that they were "three faces of totalitarianism," as if each merely manifested, in its own particular way, some deeper underlying entity or essence already "there" on some level. "Totalitarianism" was nothing but this three-sided response and the common dynamic that resulted.

But whereas understanding the historical specificity of the aggregate response has been our deepest purpose, attention to the supranational trajectory invites comparison and, by establishing a more appropriate framework, makes more instructive comparisons possible. Indeed, treating the individual cases from within the overarching dynamic brings out differences that remain paramount for certain questions. Doing so can even deepen our understanding of the place of each departure in its respective national history.

Although the originating quest for an alternative modernity must be taken seriously in a non-reductive mode, it betrayed tensions, flaws, and blind spots, evident especially in retrospect, that made certain directions and negative outcomes likely in practice. But whatever our sense that what the totalitarians attempted could not or should not have worked, the situation was sufficiently open that no one could have known at the outset where those experiments would lead. It took the actual experience that resulted from the effort to act on the new basis to reveal the disastrous potential of the originating vision. Put differently, it was only through the history that all the outcomes of totalitarianism, which have so profoundly shaped our self-understanding, came into the world, revealing something previously barely suspected about modern human possibilities. Indeed, it was only the history that *determined* what was to become part of the world, what we would find out about our historically specific situation and *its* possibilities, as a result of the totalitarian moment. Taking the whole trajectory in a more seriously historical way is not to excuse or explain away but precisely to enable us to learn more deeply from this episode in our ongoing political experiment.

By both backing up and projecting forward, we better grasp the need to treat fascism and Soviet Communism in tandem, despite the misuses of the earlier totalitarianism model, and despite certain differences being long taken as decisive even in the face of undoubted elements of convergence on the operational level. In light of the categories then available, those trying to make sense of these departures at the time were likely to start with Marxism, as relatively familiar, and to take fascism as reactive, whatever the value signs placed on each. Even so sophisticated a later observer as Ernst Nolte, seeking to place fascism in the overarching process at work since the Enlightenment, found it reactive, although ultimately against the whole modern emancipatory process, not just its Marxist variant. But any notion that fascism was "revolutionary in its own right" raises questions about Nolte's schema, and our alternative reading of the overarching process at work challenges the assumptions that seemed to warrant positing a fundamental bifurcation between Communism and fascism. The commonalities that emerged especially as the new regimes began seeking to act reflected not just common means but a common aspiration and direction.

Although more directly in Italy than in Germany, generic fascism emerged partly from a sense that the Marxian frame was inadequate to the effort to transcend the liberal mainstream. So fascism had, among other things, to contest Marxism, with its monopolistic claims to the post-liberal terrain. And thus it was bound to be attractive to mere conservatives, a fact that, in turn, enhanced the credibility of the communist claim that fascism was nothing but class reaction. Fascist anti-Communism and Communist anti-fascism fed the more general tendency, among those living through the period, to understand the novel interwar experiments in polarized terms, with the opposition between fascism and Communism fundamental.

Even after the postmodern break, the shadow of that polarized understanding has continued to shape our thinking. However, we have seen that the space for creating an alternative modernity was open to argument, and thus we must be open, as contemporaries often were not, precisely to the scope for such contesting in light of the uncertainties at the time. Following Ruth Ben-Ghiat, we noted that Italian corporativists were genuinely unprepared for the assumption of their French contemporaries, when they met at an international conference in 1935, that Fascism stemmed from right-wing reaction.[2] As the Italians saw it, Fascism had entered a terrain that most of the French seemed yet to have mapped.

We saw that Marxism reached a crossroads around the turn of the century, partly because capitalist society was becoming more open and adaptable. With the responses of Bernstein and Millerand portending all that "social democracy" would become in northern Europe during the century to follow, those like Sorel and Lenin sought desperately to save the possibility of a more systematic and radical alternative. But if there was still the need and scope for revolution to create a post-liberal order, it was not clear how much of the Marxian frame was essential, what had to be jettisoned, and what might be necessary as a supplement. Marxism was a historically specific synthesis that might come apart in light of new challenges and possibilities. Its anti-liberal elements would then be available to be integrated into a new anti-liberal program that might have an altogether different shape. Implicitly at issue, as such reassembling went on, were fundamental questions: what was supposed to have been the purpose of the post-liberal revolution in the first place? Had subsequent experience afforded a deeper understanding of what was desirable—and possible?

The extent to which an anti-liberal revolution required an assault on capitalism was among the issues subject to contest, especially at a point when capitalism had not yet produced all the positive and negative consequences anticipated in orthodox Marxism: it had not yet built up the potential for abundance, arguably a prerequisite for socialism; it had not engendered the experience that would make the working class capable of a genuinely universal role. But such by-products of capitalism were not necessarily prerequisites for a systematic alternative to the liberal mainstream. Conversely, it was not clear what change in economic relations might be required for a post-Marxist anti-liberal revolution. What was most problematic about capitalism: private property? The relentless pursuit of profit? The anarchy of the market? The conditions of production? The fairness of distribution? It was possible to envision a radical change in the liberal relationship between the ethical-political and the economic spheres without altogether eliminating private property. At the same time, it was not clear, in orthodox Marxian terms, what sort of post-bourgeois order would result if private property were in fact abolished in a context in which capitalism had not completed its positive and negative tasks.

The fact that the Soviet regime largely eliminated private property proved to be less significant to its mode of operation and outcomes than the ethical–political change and the effort at collective action on a new basis. Although he certainly mentioned capitalism, Lenin especially emphasized the need to overcome the "bourgeois" principle or mentality. And as a matter of logic, insofar as there was scope to act and even to begin "building socialism" prior to the orthodox crisis of capitalism, the immediate problem was not capitalism but the more general bourgeois orientation, which threatened to undermine the scope for a systematic alternative. So the key was the ethical-political change that the Leninist vanguard was uniquely prepared to spearhead because of its post-liberal consciousness, its spirit, will, discipline, self-sacrifice, and willingness to act. And that syndrome, more than the orthodox ideology, was what continued once the vanguard was in power.

The Marxian accent on "class" was one way of reading beyond the liberal conception of society as a collection of formally equal individuals, which had seemed too mechanical to account either for the social aggregate or for the axes of differentiation within the aggregate. For Marxism, "class" was the key not only to understanding the basis of conflict, past and present, but for conceiving the transition to a post-liberal order. The triumph of the class uniquely situated to play a universal role would usher in a classless society, thereby transcending the form of differentiation that breeds exploitation. But from the start Marxism entailed an element of ambiguity, even potential arbitrariness, in allowing the scope for some, on the basis of consciousness, to break off from the bourgeoisie and join the proletarian side. So even in orthodox terms, consciousness might transcend class—on a basis that was never made clear.

Fascism and Nazism played down the importance of class and stressed unity through race or spirit. It has become a commonplace that any such accent on common race, or even common nationality wound around culture, could only have been an effort to paper over class differences. But this is to afford *a priori* privilege to one of several possible constructs, each of which can be contested. As a constructed category, "class" afforded a characterization of differentiation that seemed relevant with the socio-economic changes that surrounded the French Revolution and the advent of industrial capitalism. But as it was codified in classical Marxism, class was not necessarily the suprahistorically privileged way of characterizing and making sense of exploitative differentiation; nor was it necessarily central as the basis for action to transcend liberalism. The accent, in any case, did not have be exclusive, a matter of either/or; class and a measure of conflicting class interests could be taken as significant but not decisive under particular historical circumstances. The Italian Fascists viewed socio-economic class differences as real and important but thought it possible to harmonize them through post-liberal corporativism. The Nazis sought more systematically to foster classlessness through meritocracy, especially in new institutions like the *Ordensburgen*. The key for each was the scope for mitigating through ethical-political change whatever exploitative effects were inherent in class differentiation.

That the Soviet regime moved more radically beyond traditional class differentiation is undeniable and significant but not evidence that Soviet Communism differed qualitatively from fascism. We noted that the insistence on class and the privilege assigned to proletarian background under Soviet conditions, in the context of elite mobilization, was arbitrary, with no real basis in Marxism, most basically because the Soviet proletariat was not to experience the alienation that, for orthodox Marxism, uniquely leads to a universal consciousness. And the outcome in Soviet practice was not a classless society but a circulation of elites, with differentiation based on function. For the Soviet regime, as for the two fascist regimes, the key was to combine societal unity and differentiation in a post-liberal mode, and the fascists were arguably more lucid in emphasizing functional elite differentiation from within a unified common framework.

Even some of the most indispensable recent accounts tend to reproduce, in ways that prove to be untenable, the longstanding assumption that fascism and Communism were fundamentally different. As we saw in Chapter 5, Steven Kotkin, seeking to account for the consensus and even excitement that accompanied the Stalinist revolution of the 1930s, stressed the participants' sense that, in building socialism, they were transcending capitalism. That sense was powerful, especially in the context of the Depression and the fascist challenge, both widely attributed to capitalism's failings. More particularly, they were building a broad welfare state "in a way," as Kotkin put it, "that contrasted with fascist reaction."[3]

But effective though he was in characterizing the idealism of the period, Kotkin's account of the competition with fascism was one-sided because he saw the Soviet experiment as partaking, despite everything, of Enlightenment reason, justice, and progress, whereas fascism boiled down to reaction against the whole package. Their sense of superiority on some such basis surely energized Soviet citizens during the Stalinist 1930s, but Kotkin, looking at the relationship from his delimited, Soviet-oriented angle, was taking fascism as the Soviets took it, as merely reactive, and thereby missing the deeper basis of the energizing epochal competition. Even as it galvanized enthusiasm, the Soviet assumption of privilege was based on a myth. Not only were the fascists, too, moving toward a species of welfare state, but they claimed to do so on the basis of a more sophisticated understanding of history, society, and the possibilities of modernity. In grasping the array from eugenics to the new social scientific insights of Pareto and Sorel, they were leaving nineteenth-century Marxism behind.

As we noted in Chapter 1, Saul Friedländer argued that the crimes of Stalinism were committed in the name of an ideal that served as an explanation—and as the basis for the Communists' own self-understanding—whereas the Nazi emphasis on secrecy and euphemism suggested something entirely different.[4] But the Communists were no more forthcoming about the terror famine and the *Ezhovshchina* than the Nazis were about the "euthanasia" program and the Holocaust. Insofar as they used conventional Marxian language to justify those episodes to themselves, they too were using euphemism, not facing up to their departure into a new terrain or to the implications of the mode of action that they had adopted.

Although Marxism had emerged from within the Enlightenment deployment to offer its particular version of "the emancipatory process," and although the Communists claimed superiority on that basis, the conditions of possibility had changed by the interwar period, so they were necessarily doing something else, with its own sources and leading eventually to a different self-understanding. That self-understanding emerged in tension with the original Marxist vision but gradually supplanted it—or rendered it sheer myth. It was not clear, especially to them as they clung to the remnants of classical Marxism, when they had shifted onto the new terrain. What they were producing by the 1930s was genuinely anti-bourgeois and post-liberal, but it had no privileged link to some teleological "emancipatory process" with contours discernible *a priori*. The Communists increasingly found themselves on the same terrain as fascism because, in one very general sense, there seemed nowhere else to go as they too sought a systematic alternative to the mainstream in a more deeply historical world. But whether totalitarianism is the only alternative to the liberal mainstream, and vice versa, is central to the lessons to be learned.

Conceiving a new mode of action

In each of our three cases, the originating agency came from a new, self-appointed and self-described elite, defined not by socio-economic place but by consciousness, values, will, and spirit, and claiming a unique capacity to spearhead what it claimed was essential change beyond the liberal mainstream.[5] Their diagnoses and prescriptions, and their sense of their own potential for leadership, reflected the prior intellectual articulation of the new terrain that had emerged by around the turn of the century. Some of the major agents had participated directly in the rethinking, but more generally, the whole elite response drew directly or indirectly, through various layers of influence, from the sense of the challenge and the possibilities that began to crystallize at that point.

The availability of that new framework for understanding meant that those who sensed the scope for a new mode of action in the wake of the war did not have to start from scratch. The earlier innovative responses had yielded categories that helped to shape conceptions of what could and should be done. Although what might result was unpredictable, that prior articulation had introduced a particular, finite framework for understanding even as it had expanded the array of questions and the meaning of such familiar categories as power and freedom.

What those innovators drew from those earlier ideas was not some unified ideology, affording a blueprint. The articulations that followed especially from the waning of developmentalism did not add up to a coherent alternative but were often sketchy, abstract, tension-ridden—perhaps even incompatible among themselves. Indeed, they showed, if only as a by-product, why there could be no coherent blueprint in a world that had come to seem more deeply historical and open-ended. Yet the very fact that humanity seemed more radically on its own suggested possibilities never quite faced before. Even the Soviets, for all their obeisance to a mostly irrelevant Marxism, had no fixed blueprint specifying a course of action for the foreseeable future. Recalling, yet again, Steven Aschheim's respectful play with a characterization by Geoff Eley, what proved to be at issue was precisely a totalitarian "frame of mind"—an appropriate characterization precisely because it is weaker than "ideology."

Most basically, the antecedent layer afforded the originating elites ideas about the modes of collective action necessary to respond to the ongoing challenges of a more deeply historical world. Although distinctive national traditions and concerns, such as Nietzschean hardness, Gentilian idealism, and Russian revolutionary culture, were central to the energizing dimension, the new elites shared a wider determination to act in a new way in light of that overall historical-political sense. And the key to totalitarianism was not this or that particular project but the great political mode of action itself, with the first task precisely to create the collective instrument for ongoing action in that mode.

On the basis of its unique grasp of the challenge and opportunity, each new elite claimed a monopoly of power. Although taking power was experienced as itself legitimizing up to a point, the claim was not simply that "might makes right." Rather, the capacity and willingness to take power indicated the virtues of will, discipline, and organization that were necessary for the ongoing collective action being initiated.

As we discussed in Chapter 4, disaffected elements in Russia, Italy, and Germany had particular reason to embrace the new historical-political ideas and to feel themselves to be moving beyond the mainstream on that basis. From their perspective, the liberals, especially in the smug democracies, were particularly ill-equipped to grasp the need for a radical departure and to discern the direction necessary and possible. As Detlev Peukert stressed, the war's major winners did not feel it necessary to venture ahead precisely because they had been successful from within the modern mainstream. From the perspective of the counter-elites in Russia, Italy, and Germany, that success was superficial, so the aim was not merely to catch up or renew but to break new ground, to assume the forefront, to realize the wider post-liberal aspiration on the basis of their capacity to act politically in unprecedented ways. Drawing on national sensitivities in each of the three cases, the sense of daring what the smug but decadent democracies could not was in itself energizing and fed the confidence to embark on great, unprecedented tasks. But although the self-understanding reflected hubris up to a point, it also entailed shrillness, a sense of risk, and vulnerability. Not only did the present opportunity seem fleeting; to grasp it entailed confronting the relentless endlessness of the challenge in light of the open-endedness of history itself.

So it was not simply that these counter-elites, for one reason or another, were incapable of joining the mainstream. In each case, contextual features had compelled the counter-elite to probe creases in that mainstream, and even in the mainstream quest for a systematic alternative, as those in the mainstream countries were less likely to do. So the energizing aspiration was not only illusion, or myth, or wishful thinking, or atavistic provincialism, any of which would require explanation in other terms, such as national *Sonderweg*, escape from freedom, or banal power hunger. And in each case idiosyncratic national traditions could seem especially relevant to the challenge, and opportunity, at hand. The confident sense of leapfrogging the liberal democrats was then crucial to the elite's effort to galvanize the wider participation essential to the new collective action envisioned.

But even a systematic alternative that addressed genuine creases in an innovative way would not necessarily be desirable in the first place—and might prove disastrous in practice. Moreover, the whole mode of response opened the way to overreaching, to inflating the relevance of national traditions, and to a form of myth making that blinded the agents to real prospects.

Their chronological proximity meant that the three departures developed in interaction, producing a sense of mutual reinforcement that was itself energizing. But, not surprisingly, there was also rivalry, competition, even a sense of epochal struggle for the post-liberal space. Most important was the struggle between Communism and fascism, but more complex modes of interaction developed among all three. Even as the genuine differences among them fed the sense of competition, the competition reinforced the emphasis on the differences at the same time. Moreover, the combination of mutual interaction and competition furthered radicalization in all three cases.

Although the Bolshevik Revolution showed the emerging Fascists in Italy the scope for actual revolution, the advent of the new regime in Russia, with its seemingly wrong-headed yet "imperialistic" claims, made it seem all the more necessary to forge a superior alternative. For both Italian Fascism and German Nazism, the sense of having addressed contemporary political possibilities on a level upon which Marxism, for all its pedigree, was betraying uncertainties—uncertainties that the Marxists themselves papered over—furthered the confidence to challenge the Communist claim to the post-liberal space. But whereas Marxism, from the fascist perspective, afforded no warrant for privilege, the Communist mode of action afforded an energizing example of what could be done, establishing a baseline and certain significant precedents.

Indeed, they all drew precedents from each other as the new action proceeded. Both Mussolini and Hitler took great interest in the Soviet experiment and expressed admiration for their Soviet counterparts, first Lenin, then Stalin. During the 1930s, Mussolini obtained from Stalin, then copied, the stage plan for the Soviet celebrations of May Day and commemorations of the October Revolution.[6] At a Politburo meeting in 1934, Stalin lauded the blood purge that Hitler had initiated on July 30. Hitler, said Stalin, was moving from the revolutionary to the state-building stage; it was time for the Soviet Communists to do the same, adopting, like the Nazis, whatever methods were necessary.[7] At the same time, we noted the importance of Mussolini's example for Hitler and the Nazis, but the Nazis' sense that their movement was different—more dynamic—also energized them, as we will discuss below. Conversely, we saw the significance of the Italian sense of superiority, based on humanistic spirit or culture as opposed to naturalistic race.

The sense of epochal struggle and competition reinforced the tendency to think in quasi-military terms, which the new mode of action seemed to require in any case. The agents had to be courageous, tough, ruthless, willing to use violence, able to steel themselves against squeamishness, even to transcend conventional, merely historically specific moral categories if the essential collective action was to be undertaken. And the epochal circumstances, the birth of each movement or regime from war, civil war, and/or near civil war, also fed the premium on toughness and discipline, the expectation of violence, and the tendency to think in military terms.

The willingness to use violence functioned in a near-Sorelian sense as self-justifying—not, however, as some irrational cult but as an indication of post-liberal commitment. As such, violence reinforced the commitment and forged solidarity. Toughness and the use of violence confirmed their own counter-elite status and the extraordinariness of the departure that they were spearheading—and thus yielded a certain exhilaration. Sorel, Pareto, and, less explicitly, Nietzsche had suggested that the requisite action would have this dimension, thereby helping to establish what proved to be a partly self-fulfilling framework of expectation.

In Russia, the foreign intervention and civil war of 1918–20, coinciding with the fading of hopes for immediate wider revolution, fundamentally shaped Communist perceptions and culture. Feeling itself to be besieged from the outside, fearing war down the road, the regime played up military metaphors, especially with the beginning of the renewed revolutionary push in 1927, partly to exhort ordinary people to sacrifice. At the same time, the brutalities of the civil war changed expectations about the nature of the ongoing struggle and fed a tendency among the Communists to portray the enemy as subhuman.[8]

Although it was spearheaded by the elite, the new ethic of toughness proved to catch up wider circles, precisely as anticipated, in all three cases. Thus, for example, the military trappings in the Soviet Union reinforced the sense of grandiose enterprise even for those too young to have fought in the war or the Russian Civil War. Precisely as with fascism, such activism, with its quasi-military uniforms and style, appealed to youth, especially Komsomol activists.[9]

Grasping the combination of hubris and shrillness enables us to make deeper sense of the "perpetual dynamism," seemingly reflecting some premium on "action for its own sake," that has become almost a cliché in discussions of totalitarianism. The notion was generally portrayed, at least implicitly, as a technique of rule, somehow serving the power drive of the leaders, yet it often seemed merely *sui generis*.[10] Even Detlev Peukert, while suggesting a deeper rationale for totalitarianism, spoke uselessly of "movement for its own sake."[11] J.P. Stern at least suggested a plausible mechanism in arguing that Hitler, with conflict and strife at the core of his ideology, had to seek out or create emergency situations in order to keep the spirit of conflict alive.[12] But even this characterization proves to be problematic. To place such dynamism more convincingly requires approaching the issue from the opposite angle.

Although diametrically opposed to "perpetual dynamism," the notion that the totalitarians sought something like "the security offered by a prison," in J.L. Talmon's characterization, has also become a commonplace. And "perpetual dynamism" is certainly closer to the mark. However valid as a characterization of the eighteenth-century aspirations with which Talmon started, the twentieth-century totalitarians anticipated not some form of repose but more like the contrary, because they sought precisely what Talmon advocated as an antidote to such "cowardice and laziness," namely, "to face the fact that life is a perpetual and never resolved crisis."[13] His notion that, in light of this condition, "all that can be done is to proceed by the method of trial and error" would also have won their assent. What underpinned the totalitarian departure was not some ahistorical psychological propensity but precisely what the agents themselves believed had been learned through the trial and error of the Enlightenment deployment. And part of what they particularly had learned was the impossibility of final repose and the need to keep acting, partly on the basis of what could be learned from trial and error in an ever-provisional world.

In this sense, a kind of relentless dynamism did prove central to totalitarianism. But Stern's notion of creating emergency situations to keep the spirit of conflict alive was to get it almost precisely backwards. From the totalitarian perspective, situations demanding concerted collective response did not have to be manufactured artificially; they endlessly arose in this open-ended historical world. Thus it was constantly necessary to recreate the collective will required for history-making action.

Although some characterize the core aspiration of Nazism as a racial utopia wound around a static *Volksgemeinschaft*, the Nazis sought the capacity for ongoing action. Race struggle was endless. Even the struggle for racial health on the domestic level would have to continue indefinitely. There could be no utopia, no super-race bred once and for all; the Nazi revolution could produce only a more concerted mode of action and a healthier instrument for the ongoing struggle. On one level, there was nothing more to be hoped for than, as Hitler put it, "the survival of a people."

Even as they clung to vestiges of the Marxian telos, the Soviets, too, could only act as if the Communist society had to be deferred indefinitely—just as those Italian Fascists who came from the Marxist Left had concluded around the time of the First World War. There was a revolution to be made, but it was not the revolution, conceived in the nineteenth century, that was to lead to communism and the end of historical struggle. So although the great political alternative was unprecedented and grandiose, it had nothing to do with transcending history altogether, or even with creating the illusion of doing so through some combination of infallible leader and bureaucratic regularity.[14]

In Leninist terms, the bourgeois principle promised to keep returning for the foreseeable future, but it could be kept at bay through the constant effort of collective action that itself nurtured and focused the essential post-bourgeois virtues. For all three regimes, with ends not to be pinned down in advance, there was only the direction instead, or, better, the apparent value of acting in a certain novel mode in response to whatever historically specific challenges arose. Although what might be entailed in practice depended on contingencies, what was required was not just activity for its own sake, nor necessarily the production of enemies that had to be fought in a literal sense. The essential challenges would continue to arise, and the response might include, for example, a "battle for births" or a "battle for grain." And the energizing sense of great collective enterprise in competition with others would help to sustain the collective action.

Because it galvanized the essential virtues, the mode of action was almost self-justifying, and in this sense, especially, the precise tasks were secondary. Even as the totalitarians eschewed teleological thinking and the scope for final repose, they sensed that the new mode of action could achieve some, at least, of the underlying desideratum in the longstanding quest for an alternative modernity. They could create a post-liberal culture, more attuned to the human place in history and thus at once more effective for collective action and more fulfilling to individuals than liberal "self-realization." Participation in history-making enterprise could satisfy the individual need for meaning as the pursuit of short-term individual or even longer-term family interests could not.

It was as post-ideological and post-utopian that the totalitarian frame of mind intertwined with both hubris and doubt. Through will and organization the collective could do more, but it also had to do more, and success was not guaranteed but required extraordinary will and effort to marshal societal energies. But having the appropriate new consciousness in initiating the process, the elite could hope to control and shape what would emerge. Although the assemblage of elements necessary for the new action is often taken as antithetical to "reason," this was in one sense to begin making history "rationally," perhaps even "scientifically," although doing so required above all will, spirit, courage, and toughness. The liberals and the blander socialists could fathom neither the grandiose assurance nor the shrill doubt.

In light of the above, we can usefully return to Claude Lefort's way of assembling the components as he probed totalitarianism on essentially the level at issue for us. We noted in Chapter 2 that he pointed usefully beyond Hannah Arendt in tracing totalitarianism to concerns about the interpenetration of particularism and historical indeterminacy with the break into liberal democracy. Arendt had found the "endless" power generation foreseen by Hobbes to be essential to the modern liberal dispensation, with its premium on endless acquisition.[15] Even as it became the essence of politics, power became separated from the political community it should serve and, as "endless," bound up with relentless dynamism and "motion." This was to open the way to, even to invite, the totalitarian departure, which carried certain tendencies of liberal society to an extreme, even a *reductio ad absurdum.*

For Lefort, too, democracy brought a troubling particularism to the fore, but he found a different set of implications for the historical sense. Such particularism, he argued, revealed the troubling indeterminacy of democratic society as "*historical* society *par excellence.*"[16] Totalitarianism was an attempt to overcome the indeterminacy through a particular way of reunifying power and society. Most basically, to understand the people-as-one confronting some enemy Other was to restore the integrity of the body in the wake of the problematic attempt at self-sustaining unity on a democratic basis. The aspiration yielded characteristic forms of rule, especially the ascendancy of the totalitarian "egocrat" and his substitutes in the bureaucracy. Whereas many have found a tension between leader and bureaucracy, Lefort saw them as complementary. Embodying in purely human terms the unity and coherence of the body, their power re-established some connection with a realm lying beyond mere humanity and history.

Taking the hypertrophy of bureaucracy as essential to totalitarianism, Lefort noted that the bureaucratic fantasy is "to restore the logic of a 'society without history'" by denying the unpredictable—or at least by monitoring the effects of collective societal action in advance—and thereby maintaining continuity with its origin.[17] As he put it elsewhere,

> the idea of the creation, or rather the self-creation of society is accompanied by a prodigious refusal of any innovation that might transgress the limits of an already known future, a reality that in principle is already mastered. In this sense, the image of a history which is being made at every moment proves to be absolutely contradicted by the image of a fixed history. The unknown, the unpredictable, the indeterminable are avatars of the enemy.[18]

As Lefort saw it, the contradictions of totalitarianism in practice revealed that modern indeterminacy cannot be transcended. On the diachronic level, totalitarian bureaucratization stood in tension with the terms of the fundamentally historical world. Whereas the totalitarians clung to the image of a fixed history, history was still being made at every moment through the endless self-creation of society. The practice could not be controlled, routinized. On the synchronic level, the incessant production of enemy Others, apparently required for societal unity, stood in tension with the desire for predictability and control. In any case, such societal unity proved impossible to realize as divisions arose. The overall totalitarian relationship between the head and the body, the leader and society, did not prove to be superior to democracy as a substitute for monarchy but ended up manifesting groundlessness and societal self-referentiality in heightened, we might say garish, form.[19] In light of the loss of transcendence, their interdependence was such that, as Lefort put it, head and body impossibly swallow each other, and thus "the death instinct is unleashed into the closed, uniform, imaginary space of totalitarianism."[20] Yet, writing in 1980, with the Soviet regime clearly in mind, Lefort found that totalitarianism could still cohere on the level of fantasy.[21]

Fanciful though it sometimes was, Lefort's imagery conveyed the impossibility of the totalitarians' putative effort to transcend history in a flattened-out world without transcendence. The denial of history led to the hypertrophy of leadership and bureaucracy, to a potentially self-destructive invention of enemies, and ultimately—although fantasy might mask it for a while—to failure. As an account of the totalitarian reaction against democracy in the context of a deepening sense of the historicity of the world, Lefort's reading was especially valuable. And he was surely on the right track in suggesting that the totalitarian alternative proved to be self-defeating precisely because the totalitarian mode of action was incongruent with the terms of the more deeply historical modern world. But he ended up by misconstruing essential aspects of the totalitarian dynamic in what prove to be highly instructive ways.

For Lefort, the purpose of the new totalitarian concentration of power was essentially to restore something lost with the break into democratic particularism and historicity—the integrity of "the state," as some ahistorical entity, and the symbolic function of power itself, guaranteeing the coherence of the body. Following his logic, we might add that, lacking the monarch's link to the divine, the totalitarian regime could not merely embody power; it had constantly to *demonstrate* power through collective action. But, even from this expanded perspective, the function of power was precisely to be demonstrated, not actually to go on remaking the world. For Lefort, then, even the collective action that power made possible was essentially to serve power itself, by endlessly recreating the power that would afford the essential unity and at least the shadow of transcendence. In that sense, the new collective action was not to make history but to deny history.

We have found a very different relationship between the concentration of power and history. The totalitarian aim was not to deny or transcend history but to face up to it, to be equal to it—and thereby to make it in a new, more effective way. This required, first, concentrating, expanding, even *creating* power as never before by mobilizing and focusing societal energies. But it also required actually *acting* in the new mode, doing new things, particular kinds of things—*not* merely activity for its own sake, simply to prove that the power had been created. Nor, again, did it necessarily require the artificial manufacture of enemies to serve collective mobilization and unity. The grandiose, history-making quality of the tasks to be undertaken—from population engineering to concerted industrial development to international competition and war—was itself the key to the essential collective mobilization.

In light of the most troubling outcomes, it is often assumed that, whether we take the source to be fanaticism, power hunger, or evil, the totalitarian aspiration is to be characterized in the negative, as an "assault on man" to snuff out human freedom and creativity and thereby to produce automatons.[22] At the same time, we sometimes focus on exclusion as the essence of totalitarianism and find the treatment of those excluded archetypal, with the domination of the rest a milder manifestation of the same impulse. But studying the three cases in light of the earlier break suggests that moralism and teleological backloading lurk in such assumptions. The point was not to suppress and to dominate but to nurture and focus human energies and capacities, even ethical capacities, to make the new collective action possible. This was no longer to leave the human ethical potential dispersed in private individuals, encouraged to follow their own desires, but to channel it for supra-individual historical aims by enhancing collective power. With society now more clearly understood as projected into the future, virtue entailed a sense of shared responsibility for society, or the collectivity, in its delimited, concrete, historically specific form as the nation. It entailed a willingness to sacrifice one's immediate interests, and it might demand going beyond conventional moral categories. Such individual capacities could be fostered especially as the community expanded its reach, assuming deeper responsibility for history itself.

Even the Nazis posited ethical-political virtues and capacities that had to be tapped, nurtured, and channeled to maximize collective effectiveness in a mass age. Thus, for example, the requisite cooperation in the quest for racial hygiene included even a willingness to sacrifice family, or oneself, in the event of physiological inadequacy. And thus our way of making sense of the troubling responses of those parents in Nazi Germany who acquiesced in the "euthanasia" of their own children.

We have found that even the element of exclusion cannot be understood as some merely negative assault. Exclusion seemed to be necessary to make possible the deeper homogeneity that, in turn, would underpin the degree of consensus required for the new action. At issue was who could be part of a community capable of acting as one, exercising collective human responsibility in the new "total" way. However arbitrary and repugnant we find the *a priori* principles of exclusion at issue, what must be understood first was not the exclusion *per se* but rather the sense of the world that made such deeper homogeneity, on whatever basis, seem so important in the first place. In other words, the negative moment became important only because, through a historically specific conjuncture, it came to seem necessary and possible to act collectively in a way requiring that deeper homogeneity. And although it is sensitive indeed to suggest any sort of link between exclusion and the ethical, such deeper homogeneity came to seem essential partly because it seemed that only from within such a framework could individual energies and even ethical capacities be marshaled and focused.

Even in the German case, it was not that the Nazis began to demand homogeneity because of the measure of prior anti-Semitism but, rather, that the demand for homogeneity, stemming from a new historical-political sense that emerged independently, led the Nazi counter-elite to seek the exclusion of the Jews. What first requires an accounting, then, is not that the Nazis defined this enhanced homogeneity in terms of race and excluded Jews but the turned-up demand for such homogeneity itself. Even with a measure of anti-Semitism already in the mix, the "Othering" at issue stemmed not merely from some ahistorical "hate" or out-group hostility, even as triggered by Germany's postwar crisis, but from the demand for a deeper homogeneity, which seemed to warrant preclusion and even "scapegoating" as never before.

Homogeneity entailed *some* mode of exclusion in each case, although the totalitarians differed over who could be part of the community, and the differences are obviously crucial for certain questions and outcomes. Political opponents and those who resisted the full-scale participation demanded were obviously self-excluding, but in two of the three cases, belonging was not only a matter of free individual choice. Rather, the necessary homogeneity seemed to require *a priori* exclusion on a naturalistic racial or a materialistic class basis. In these two cases, in fact, the group to be excluded—the Jews and the bourgeoisie, respectively—was deemed not only to be inherently incapable of belonging but also to embody an actively deleterious principle undermining the essential consensus.

The excluded were to be eliminated quickly or perhaps exploited economically but not simply controlled and manipulated—in order to satisfy some will to domination or to confirm some prior ideology. Still, they were often treated brutally, even murderously. Thus the forcible removal of kulaks and Jews, as the most prominent examples. And thus, especially, we may focus first on the exclusion—and the arbitrariness of the criteria—in treating the German and Soviet cases. The Nazi variant seems especially repugnant because racist criteria for membership in the totalitarian community seem far more arbitrary than class. But although exclusion in the Soviet case may seem to entail some residual rationality in comparison, the Communists were often rigid and cruel in excluding "former people," those with the wrong social class backgrounds, some of whom embraced the Communist cause and desperately wanted to belong.[23]

In this company, the Italian case seems relatively benign: until the late 1930s, the only basis of differentiation was "spirit," and anyone could belong through free assent, regardless of class or ethnic background. The essential homogeneity could be created through education and mobilization. Thus, as we saw, the Italian Fascists generally found Nazi and Soviet emphases crudely naturalistic and deterministic. Conversely, the lack of *a priori* criteria of exclusion has made Italian Fascism seem less than totalitarian to some.

Accounts of totalitarianism that start with the German and Soviet cases tend to stress the moment of exclusion, based on putative race or class. Encompassing the very different Italian case helps us to put that exclusionary effort in the wider perspective necessary to get at the deeper basis of the totalitarian aspiration. On this basis, we also better understand what led Abbott Gleason to term Giovanni Gentile "the first philosopher of totalitarianism," even the archetypal totalitarian thinker, and, although he was too quick to do so, to impute Orwellian implications to Gentile's vision.[24] Precisely because of their preoccupations with race and class, respectively, the Nazi and Soviet cases revealed less overtly the negative implications of the "positive" side of the totalitarian vision, with its demand for homogeneity.

Insofar as we understand the underlying totalitarian aspiration not as an "assault on man" but in "positive" terms, as seeking to focus the human ethical capacity, we better grasp the problem. Whereas Gentile may seem more attractive in emphasizing inclusion, the inclusion was *mandatory* and it was to entail, for everyone, a life of total public commitment, total responsibility. As we noted in Chapter 6, he allowed no scope for contemplative withdrawal, or self-cultivation, or mere alienation—let alone for some challenge to the overall vision. Had the Nazis understood their totalitarian community in such a way that Jewish Germans could be included, there would have been no Holocaust, and we would find Nazism less troubling in one crucial sense. But the situation would still have been totalitarian, still demanding constant participation and responsibility.

It is even arguable that insofar as it starts by assuming human freedom and the scope for universal inclusion, the totalitarian enterprise carries the potential for more manipulative education, more constant mobilization, more intrusive vigilance than it does if it starts with *a priori* exclusion based on the putative limitations of race or class. From within this "positive" framework, refusal, as a matter of free choice, constituted a moral fault, more grievous than putatively naturalistic or materialistic limitations. Precisely as free, all were potentially subject to surveillance and judgement at all times. The Nazis and the Soviets, in contrast, tended to assume that those who were not Jews or members of the bourgeoisie, respectively, belonged as a matter of course and that the creation of homogeneity could thus focus on the process of exclusion.

From the start, however, both the Nazis and the Communists had stressed consciousness and will in ways that meshed uneasily with naturalism or materialism. And it gradually became clear that what ultimately was at issue even for the Nazis and the Communists was more a matter of freedom than their respective accents on race and class suggested. This was bound to happen insofar as race and class were not *really* the keys to the desired homogeneity. As the two regimes succeeded in marginalizing or eliminating the Jews and the bourgeoisie, respectively, practice made it clearer that, even as the agents themselves took them, race and class were not *only* material or natural but also afforded a reductive way of making sense of alternative choices, principles, modes of consciousness—and ultimately anything that seemed to impede the community's capacity to act. Just as the Soviets continued to blame the bourgeois principle, the Nazis came close to arguing that all dissidents were Jews, that the Jewish principle accounted for any frustration. At the very least, Jewishness was a principle of division in violation of healthy homogeneity. Conversely, despite its initial emphasis on spirit and freedom, Italian Fascism came to embrace a species of anti-Semitism on the same grounds, seeking some identifiable group to blame as they encountered the difficulties of the new collective action in practice.

In its later phases, the Soviet experiment seemed to have achieved not "socialism" but precisely the conditions of free adherence. Thus dissenters were no longer class enemies, "bourgeois" holdovers in the materialistic sense. Rather, having freely denied the homogeneity now realized, they were guilty of an ethical fault and subject to an ethical-political cure—in a mental hospital.

To stress a set of originating impulses seemingly more benign than exclusion, "total domination," and "assault on man" changes nothing about the direction or the outcomes; nor is it to minimize the murderous potential of the demand for homogeneity. But it enables us better to understand, first, the deeply problematic side of originating aspiration, with the measure of idealism it entailed, then how that aspiration produced a dynamic that yielded terrible outcomes. To understand how a direction experienced as positive, even ethical, led to mass murder surely yields a deeper admonition.

The need for a deeper homogeneity obviously had implications for the elite's relationship with those of the others who were deemed worthy of inclusion. And the relationship between elites and masses has long been at issue in discussions of totalitarianism, or any of the three regimes taken individually. Yet the nature of the relationship has been too quickly sidestepped through categories like myth and domination. At the same time, the conventional dualisms pitting "elitism" against populism, democracy, or egalitarianism also keep us from getting at the self-understanding and objective of the new elites in question.

It is worth recalling, first, that the pioneers of totalitarianism must be distinguished from an array of overt elitists who disliked democracy—members of hereditary elites, for example, or the privileged adepts of a Leo Strauss, or liberals hostile to mass politics like José Ortega y Gasset, or T.S. Eliot, who advocated hereditary "classes" in opposition even to "elitism," which he conflated with the modern meritocracy that, he felt, necessarily bred instability and disruption.[25] Even Ernst Jünger, although he envisioned an anonymous worker-soldier society, proved to be too caught up in quasi-Nietzschean heroic individualism to embrace Nazism. In their different ways, these various elitists were hostile to fascism, Communism, and totalitarianism, which they saw as precisely too mass-based and plebeian. Conversely, the new totalitarian elites did not share the concerns of these elitists.

So it is too simple to view totalitarianism as merely elitist, as if the elite was in itself the embodiment of value and, on that basis, to be protected from mass contamination. Elite satisfaction was not an end in itself because these would necessarily be *functional* elites, whose status was justified only by the wider roles that they uniquely could play. And although egalitarianism and conventional democratic modes of involvement had to be questioned, the totalitarian response stemmed not from the mere "fear of the masses" that Zeev Sternhell emphasized, or that Isaiah Berlin assumed to be a major criterion as he found the origins of fascism in the ideas of Joseph de Maistre.[26] Rather, what defined the elites was a sense of the scope for a new relationship with the masses that would include more effective mobilization for the necessary action.

We saw that Mosca and Pareto, especially, had brought home the apparent inevitability of elites, in defiance of democratic claims and egalitarian ideals. In that light, the effort to conceive a new mode of collective action required fresh thinking about societal differentiation. Although role differentiation was inevitable and essential, the new action required not merely top-down domination but a new and energizing reciprocity between the elites and those deemed capable of belonging to the enhanced community, all of whom were to participate. Ernst Nolte's notion that fascism was an effort to preserve a traditional mode of interaction, even the last gasp of a ruling class deriving its self-image from its opposition to the ruled, particularly misreads the fascist departure from liberal democracy.[27]

Most basically, totalitarianism was to be a post-liberal way of involving the masses, for electoral politics and parliamentary democracy had proved not merely inadequate but actively deleterious, dispersing energies through the pursuit of short-term particular interests. A determination to bypass parliamentary government had long been central even in the Russian case, starting with Lenin's reaction against Bernstein and the Bolsheviks' case against the Mensheviks. In consolidating power, in reconsidering priorities in 1921, and in rekindling the revolution after 1927, the Bolsheviks remained resolute against any backsliding into electoral democracy, which could only undermine the scope for the new kind of action that, as we have emphasized, gradually became their fundamental aim.

From within a framework recognizing the limits of both conventional egalitarianism and representative democracy, it was possible to forge the more constant and direct forms of mass involvement necessary. Michael Burleigh found this new politics to have been very modern, even postmodern, for "Europe's demagogues were archly aware of the manipulative techniques they needed to generate mass faith. . . . These men were artist-politicians."[28] This characterization is effective up to a point, but we must beware of any suggestion that such manipulation was merely to serve some restricted elite interest. The leaders did indeed know what they were doing, but they believed that uniquely through these techniques they could forge the collective instrument for higher collective purposes that they fully shared.

The vexed question of the role of myth obviously intrudes itself at this point. As we noted especially in dealing with the Italian case, myth has long been linked to elites and masses as a manipulative concept. From this perspective, elites cynically used myths that they knew to be *merely* myths, and thus bogus, to satisfy the masses, to keep them in their place while also rendering them "available" to serve the elite's purposes. Myth was simply one of the techniques of totalitarian rule in an age of mass politics. This familiar syndrome makes elites merely cynical, myths merely manipulative, and masses merely exploited.

Myth proved crucial in all three regimes, although not in this delimited, manipulative sense. In helping to furnish the new historical-political space, such thinkers as Sorel, Pareto, and Nietzsche had suggested what the emergence of a genuinely revolutionary instrument for change would have to entail, and thus in each case the new elites had certain expectations about the process in which they were caught up. Rational blueprints were neither possible nor necessary, and something like myth was central to the alternative. Grandiose images of common achievement could draw out ethical-political virtues and inspire the will, discipline, enthusiasm, and sacrifice necessary for successful collective action. Conversely, any "rational" insistence on specifying ends and forging the appropriate means on that basis would impede the capacity to act. Myth in this sense was lucidly embraced by the elites themselves, becoming part of their own self-understanding. In each case, the intersection of the war experience with national idiosyncrasies fueled an epic sense of possibility, a framework of "mythical" expectation, that first crystallized within these elites, affording internal cohesion.

As part of the new interaction, that framework was to be inculcated in the masses. It was partly because ends could not be specified that elites and masses could believe, will, and act together. The sense that grandiose tasks could be undertaken by acting together in this new way was itself energizing. And vague though they were, each of the great energizing projects—building "socialism," or the "totalitarian ethical state," or a healthy racial *Volksgemeinschaft*—afforded an effective galvanizing and unifying myth, as long as both the elite and substantial numbers of the included others continued to believe in the project's world-historical importance. Although such myth proved to be genuinely unifying and energizing at first, only practice would tell where such a mode of action might lead.

The attempt at totalitarian collective action

So what would happen as the new elites began to initiate the new collective action? In this section, we will note a common baseline, some common dilemmas, and some instructive differences in the three efforts. Rather than taking any one direction as defining totalitarianism, we must grasp the scope for certain differences in light of the choices that opened with the new mode of action; the differences at issue emerged from within the common totalitarian departure. In each case, we find a measure of success, but then also, as we will discuss in the next section, a characteristic dynamic leading to narrowing and failure. Only if we keep in mind that the originating aim was a new mode of collective *action*, and *why* it seemed necessary and possible to move in that direction, can we grasp what the resulting dynamic revealed.

Most basically, practice reflected the new embrace of flexibility, trial and error, and improvisation. Thus aspects of practice that have seemed to manifest mere opportunism or sheer activist adventurism in fact stemmed from the new historical-political sense itself. Yet the terms of the apparent challenge also suggested certain priorities and principles of action—and the first steps toward totalitarianism in practice.

On the basis of their claim to a deeper reading of the situation, the originating elites could only be hostile to the established elites, seen as bankrupt, exhausted, unable even to grasp, let alone to spearhead, what needed to be done. In Russia, this meant hostility not only to the tsarist regime but also to the fledgling democratic alternative that emerged in 1917. Thus in each case the new elite claimed a monopoly of political power. And that demand produced intensified opposition, which in turn provoked assault on that opposition—and thus reinforced the demand for a monopoly of power and even suggested the need for a species of "total domination." Although, not surprisingly, opponents, critics, and subsequent scholars tended to take such power and domination as ends in themselves, these simply afforded the foundation for the new collective action and the larger, future-oriented projects that, the originators felt, justified their claim to a monopoly of power in the first place.

In each case, those new elites took political power on the national level. Although the relationship between the nation and the state was often disputed, power on the national level was the first step partly because the nation defined the reach of political organization in each country. At least at that point, human beings could seemingly expand power and thus the freedom to act only in and through the nation. This proved to be true, very early on, even for the Russian Communists, despite their internationalist foundations and their genuinely internationalist aims at the outset. And the Nazis, too, although thinking in terms of race, had first to establish a monopoly of power within the existing German national state, even though many of the world's ethnic-linguistic Germans were not part of the nation governed by that state.

However, at issue was not just a monopoly of political power in a delimited sense. Because the new enterprise required the mobilization and focusing of societal energies, there could be no pluralistic live and let live. Thus it was necessary to coordinate all aspects of the national life, above all by marginalizing the Christian churches. Although each of the new elites took the wider frame of secularization for granted, the churches remained sufficiently powerful to constitute competition—and thus an active obstacle to what seemed to be the essential concentration of human capacities. Conversely, in each case the innovators adopted certain quasi-religious trappings, even fostering an overtly post-Christian "sacralization of politics," in Emilio Gentile's terminology. Although that direction in some ways recalls Durkheim's notion that the ultimate object of religious veneration is society itself, the desideratum, in light of the new historical-political sense, was not simply societal cohesion or a renewed sense of belonging but, again, a new mode of collective *action*. Thus at issue in each case was not merely a cult of society or the state but the sacralization of *politics*, as, in principle, that mode of action.

More generally, the necessary direction entailed the inflation of the political sphere to encompass the whole of life, so that there were no private rights; in principle, in fact, there was no private sphere at all. To be sure, the regimes compromised as expedient, and ordinary people found ways to avoid, evade, or resist, thereby even, on occasion, forcing changes in policy, as with the family plot allowed within the framework of the Soviet collective farms, or the Nazis' willingness to cancel a shipment of Jewish husbands to the east when their non-Jewish wives protested. But none of that should detract from the radicalism of the totalitarian departure in making the public or political sphere all-encompassing in principle. By specifying the Communist Party's authority to intervene in anything, the 1936 Soviet constitution made explicit what had heretofore been implicit but ambiguous in Soviet practice. With Soviet life entirely politicized, every activity was a political act.[29]

In each of the three cases, the elite took it for granted that population policy was a priority and indeed a core aspect of totalitarian responsibility. But different accents were possible, and it is not surprising that there was variation among the three and even a measure of vacillation within each regime as population matters were confronted. Questions of both quantity and quality were at issue. On the quantitative side, the most basic decision concerned natalism or neo-Malthusianism, and all three regimes—in contrast, for example, with Communist China later—actively promoted natalism. In the Soviet Union, the sense of labor shortage led the regime to compromise its earlier egalitarianism in the mid-1930s by promoting fertility and motherhood as well as measures limiting divorce, restricting abortion, and encouraging families.[30]

Concerns with quality could point either to eugenics or to an anti-eugenic emphasis on environmentalism. As they came to insist on environment as opposed to genetics, the Soviet regime cancelled the Seventh International Congress for Genetics, which had been scheduled for Moscow in 1937.[31] By this point, it had begun to conflate genetics, eugenics, and fascism, so its stress on environmentalism reflected the wider tendency of all three regimes to emphasize differences as part of their epochal competition.

The practical effort to organize for the new mode of action encountered more general questions about the role of the leader, the interaction between elites and masses, the relationship between party and state, and the place of various ancillary entities, from the SS to the Komsomol to the Italian Fascist corporative bodies. In addition, each faced questions about the criteria of elite status, about the extent and basis of ongoing differentiation, and about elite openness and replenishment. How were elite institutions to be re-energized to avoid the careerist ossification, the fading of the originating vision and purpose, that Michels had pinpointed as a tendency in any large organization? Was the party to be ever more broadly based as education proceeded, or did it need to remain exclusive, even to undergo periodic purging? How deep and how broad across the society was the new education to be? What was the scope for encompassing specialized experts who had not been part of the originating movement but who now, from within the new framework being created, might make special contributions in areas from public law to public health to the economy?

Whereas Communism stood for egalitarianism in principle, fascism trumpeted ongoing differentiation and hierarchy. But for each some measure of differentiation would remain for the foreseeable future, so each faced precisely the same questions. All three regimes tried various institutional and procedural measures, from the periodic purging in the Soviet Union to the development of the SS as an elite within the elite in Nazi Germany, to address this set of issues. The need for experiment inevitably meant some back and forth within the overall cluster as each regime sought the optimal means of action.

Although all three regimes developed special institutions to rear the next generation of leaders, the results differed in depth and effectiveness. Such Italian Fascist institutions as the Fascist Faculty of Political Science at Perugia and the School of Corporative Studies at Pisa were not insignificant, but Camillo Pellizzi's awe in 1941 upon visiting one of the Nazi *Ordensburgen*, the centers for educating future Nazi leaders, suggests that the Italian institutions were considerably less successful.

The plausible variation in institutional relationships led, most basically, to differences in the respective roles of state and party in the three cases. In all three, the elite was based in a party claiming a monopoly of power, whereas the state was the existing apparatus that was to be transformed for the new mode of action. And each faced the challenge of transforming the state in a context in which elements of the pre-revolutionary state apparatus remained in place. Tensions were inevitable, and the degree of variability between the three regimes is not surprising. The Nazis, for example, sought to bypass the pre-revolutionary bureaucracy to some extent through the "parallel" institutions of the Nazi Party. Italian Fascism was more overtly statist. Although the Soviet leadership, as the beneficiary of a deeper political revolution than the other two, found simply taking over the state less problematic in one sense, it particularly seemed to face a tension between technical competence and ideological commitment as it had to rely on pre-Soviet bureaucratic cadres and experts during the 1920s.

The key for all three was to expand collective action; the institutional locus was secondary and certainly not a decisive criterion of totalitarianism. Yet in light of the scope for variation, once the effort to act led to a particular practical dynamic, disputes over institutional arrangements developed in each case, proving to be a source of unforeseen and debilitating confusion, rivalry, and infighting. Even today, the scope for such variation causes confusion about the commonalities among the three regimes and the basis of the overall totalitarian departure. To get a handle on the issues, we can usefully back up to the interwar period itself, before the marginalization of the Italian case and the Cold War corruption of the totalitarianism category. Especially by attending to the German response, Nazi and anti-Nazi alike, to Italian Fascism, we can recover the combination of confusion and competition that was central at the time—and that fed modes of analysis that continue to impede understanding.

As Abbott Gleason showed, comparison with Italian Fascism was generally popular with prominent Nazis before 1933.[32] The Fascist model was clearly visible as the Nazis began to construct their new regime, and it remained a touchstone of discussion into 1934 as the direction and priorities of the Nazi revolution became clearer. In his remarkable *Behemoth*, published during the Second World War, Franz Neumann noted that top Nazi leaders had initially embraced the Italian notion of totalitarianism. Goebbels, for example, stressed in November 1933 that "the goal of the revolution must be a totalitarian state pervading all spheres of public life."[33] Such noted jurists as Carl Schmitt immediately called for a German version of the Italian totalitarian state.

As we noted in Chapter 4, some of these jurists welcomed the Nazi revolution as a restoration of state authority in response to what seemed the chaotic, excessively pluralistic expansion of state functions during the Weimar period. Thus the notion of totalitarianism became associated in Germany with the top-down coordination—*Gleichschaltung*—that marked the first stage of the revolution.[34] But in responding to the unprecedented Weimar expansion, such a move could not be a mere restoration. And in calling for a German version of the Italian totalitarian state, Schmitt envisioned precisely the extension of state sovereignty to absorb more societal content, essential in light of the Weimar experience.

However, the Nazis came to distance themselves from Italian Fascism and explicitly to reject "totalitarianism" during 1934. Schmitt himself began to stress differences even as Nazi ideologues like Alfred Rosenberg found him still too close to the Italians. Anti-Nazis like Neumann and Herbert Marcuse tended to credit the Nazi way of distinguishing Nazism from Italian Fascism up to a point. In their attention to the Italian package, the Germans took for granted the centrality of Giovanni Gentile's categories and, largely on that basis, associated Italian Fascism with Hegelianism. And they understood totalitarianism, and the Italian emphasis on the totalitarian *state*, in that light. But confusion over party–state relations and the criteria of dynamism led these Germans to misconstrue the thrust of Italian Fascist totalitarianism.

In a brief note published in 1936, Schmitt stressed the intensity and significance of the interchange between German and Italian legal scholars in light of the development of the two new regimes to that point.[35] Noting how closely parallel German and Italian intellectual history had often been, he portrayed the Nazi and Fascist regimes as contending with Soviet-style Communism for the space beyond liberal capitalism. While noting that race was ignored in Italy, he found the key difference between Nazism and Fascism in the Fascist concern to establish the superiority of the state over the party, evidence, as he saw it, of the persistence of the traditional theory of the state in Italy. One way of conceiving the question was whether the living Hegel was to be found in Berlin, in Rome, or even in Moscow. In Schmitt's view, the Italians were saying he lived in Rome. Neumann, too, linked the totalitarian impulse in Italian Fascism to Hegel's idea of the state, including "a bureaucracy that guarantees the freedom of its citizens because it acts on the basis of rational and calculable norms."[36] On those grounds, Nazism appeared to be something quite different.

Although Neumann recognized that postwar economic competition in world markets seemed to mandate a stronger state for Italy, he traced Fascist statism especially to the longstanding weakness of the state in Italy.[37] In the same way, Marcuse suggested that the Fascists had embraced the Hegelian conception of the state, whereas the Nazis rejected it, because of the contrasting historical circumstances of the two countries. By the First World War, the German state, unlike the Italian, was already powerful and firmly established—as a *Rechtsstaat*, a comprehensive rational political system with rights and liberties clearly demarcated and recognized.[38] So whereas the statist direction was genuinely innovative, even revolutionary, in Italy, it still portended conservative subservience to the law, in marked difference from Nazi dynamism.

Thus, although the Germans tended to credit the claim of Mussolini's regime to be "totalitarian," they understood totalitarianism as the advent of a total, legalistic state absorbing even the radical, dynamic party. On that basis, the Nazis found the Italian Fascist direction, even as totalitarian, too static, too merely conservative or authoritarian, and especially too Hegelian. Nazism, in contrast, was a dynamic movement based on race.[39] Because they found totalitarianism insufficiently radical, the Nazis rejected the term altogether.[40]

For Rosenberg, launching a concerted attack on the totalitarian state idea early in 1934, the state was inherently mechanical and aloof. The revolutionary philosophy of National Socialism, having emerged through the movement, was now embodied in the party, which was making the state its mere instrument.[41] Hitler had stressed the limits of the state in comparable terms in *Mein Kampf*. The state was not a moral precept or realization of some absolute idea but merely the servant of the racial people; far from unconditional, obedience to the state was warranted only insofar as the state served the preservation of the people.[42] Even in stressing, at the Nazi Party congress of September 1934, that the Nazi revolution was over, that stability was now essential for success, that permanent revolution would only mean greedy politicians struggling for the spoils, Hitler still attacked the notion of the totalitarian state in his concluding speech.[43]

The Nazi assault on Hegelianism intertwined with and reinforced the assault on totalitarianism. The anti-fascist Marcuse, concerned to rescue Hegel from critics abroad who linked him to both Nazism and Fascism more generally, featured the anti-Hegelianism of the Nazis in his *Reason and Revolution* (1941), which Neumann cited with particular approval.[44] Indeed, Marcuse suggested that because the Nazis, in contrast to many Marxists, took the connection between Hegel and Marx seriously, they understood their own relationship to Hegel better than their critics. As explained by such representative Nazi spokesmen as Rosenberg, Ernst Krieck, and Franz Böhm, Nazism rejected the Hegelian concept of the state as the incarnation of reason, of universally valid laws, calculable in operation, seeking to protect the essential interests of every individual without discrimination. In light of this static conception, the state had come to seem, as the Nazis themselves put it, merely a "soul-less instrument of force" to the masses.[45]

This was to pinpoint nicely the basis of the Nazi rejection of Hegel; the question was whether Marcuse, or any of these German thinkers, was accounting first for the commonality, but then also for the real difference, between the German and Italian departures. Whereas Nazi racism and dynamism were indeed fundamentally incompatible with Hegel's idea of the state, German conflations led them to miss what Nazism had in common with Fascism *vis-à-vis* Hegel. Yet the differences in institutional emphasis were genuine and symptomatic.

The state had indeed developed differently in Germany and Italy, and the difference in historical background is certainly relevant, but we must question the German tendency to reduce the Italian response to relative backwardness. In light of the possibilities that had opened up, the Italian approach, even as statist, was not merely an effort to catch up; it was more innovative and modern than the Germans, viewing the alternatives in dualistic terms, could grasp.

The issue is complicated, however, because the Germans tended to take Italian Fascist totalitarianism as homogeneous whereas, as we noted in Chapter 6, there were major differences even between Giovanni Gentile and Alfredo Rocco, Neumann's major exemplars. In fact, there was much discussion, and disagreement, in Italian Fascist legal theory over party and state, codification and open-ended dynamism. Some, like Rocco and Carlo Costamagna, were closer than others to a statist authoritarianism. They were also the closest to Schmitt, who, as we saw, was marginalized within Nazism as too close to the alleged Hegelian statism of Italian Fascism. Rocco and Costamagna were comparably concerned to encompass new, particularist social forces, especially trade unions, that threatened to undermine or actually replace the state. Still, even Rocco was not seeking merely to order society but insisted on a more dynamic prescription, with the state newly conceived as the instrument for history-making tasks in the long-term national interest.

With Gentile's more radical and open-ended conception, the new post-liberal political order could even less be understood as merely ordering contending social forces in static predictability. Although he focused on the state as opposed to the movement–party, Gentile's was not Hegel's state, understood as the embodiment of reason and thus calculable in operation. Precisely because it was too static, the statist liberalism of the Hegelian tradition had to be transcended in a more deeply historical world. The Gentilian totalitarian state was the living and perpetually changing form or embodiment of the unified political people. As we noted in Chapter 4, Schmitt's emphasis on ordering conflicting social forces, as opposed to channeling them for collective ends, remained "pre-totalitarian" in comparison.

None of these Germans was doing justice to the dynamic, post-Hegelian thrust of Italian totalitarian thinking, but at least Marcuse, concerned to rescue Hegel from association with both Nazism and Fascism, did not accept the Nazi conflation of Italian totalitarian statism with Hegelianism. Indeed, he insisted correctly on Gentile's departure from Hegel—which was to imply that the Nazis had misread Gentile and thus the Fascist totalitarian state as well. But Marcuse could account for Gentile's departure only in terms of an irrational activism that entailed a subservience to what is.[46] Although such activism might seem to be comparable to the Nazi accent on dynamism, Marcuse was missing the nature of the crucial parallel element in the Nazi and the Gentilian departures from Hegel.

Although they differed over the place of the state, Gentile and the Nazis rejected Hegelian statism on much the same grounds—as static, precluding the open-ended dynamism that had come to seem necessary. In fact, Hegel was to be found in *none* of the three capitals at the point Schmitt raised his question, in 1936. Precisely as totalitarian, each regime had moved well beyond Hegel in a way that cannot be grasped in terms of the conventional axis, with the party–state relationship as the crucial variable. Totalitarianism was itself "dynamic" precisely in recognizing that the challenge was to shape an ever-provisional historical world, so even insofar as the totalitarian state was the vehicle, it had constantly to be forged anew.

The key basis of differentiation between Fascism and Nazism was less the party–state relationship than the scope for codification, for fixed laws and proce-dures, in an open-ended world. At issue was, first, the extent to which an emphasis on the state—even a new *totalitarian* state—inherently meant a premium on codification and fixed procedures and, second, the extent to which any such premium was incongruent with the new action necessary. Even *within* each regime such questions occasioned tension—and explicit debate. Whereas Pellizzi, stressing provisionality and openness, portrayed laws as hieroglyphs in the sand, Rocco emphasized codification and the predictability of law even as the state's reach expanded indefinitely.

Rocco's legal rationalism, especially, stood diametrically opposed to the Nazi conception of law, based on race, blood, and the will of the Führer.[47] Although Italian totalitarianism was more dynamic than the Germans tended to recognize, the Nazi vision proved, on balance, more dynamic still, precisely in its resistance to codified law in light of the apparent slipperiness of history. It was precisely their sense of the requirements for the new action that led the Nazis to resist any premium on codification of the law, no matter how wide and even total its compass. Action required flexibility, including the scope for improvised response. In that sense, Nazism did move more radically beyond traditional state ideas, but that is no warrant for concluding, in simple dualistic terms, that Nazism was total-itarian while Fascism was merely traditionalist or authoritarian. To codify the law was indeed less "dynamic" in the sense the Nazis had in mind, but to expand to totality the scope for codified law was no less totalitarian. The criterion of totali-tarianism was not the particular mode of dynamism embraced by the Nazis but the more general determination to act collectively in a newly total way.

Yet partly as a result of the early interaction between the Germans and the Italians, we have long been prone to some such dichotomy pitting the state, taken as conservative and authoritarian, against the movement–party, taken as dynamic and revolutionary.[48] We thereby miss the commonality of all three departures and the terms of the ensuing process in each instance.

Narrowing, myth making, and failure

In all three cases, the elite succeeded, up to a point, in expanding the political sphere and in mobilizing people in the unprecedented ways envisioned. Indeed, as numerous recent authorities have shown, the effort produced a degree of idealism and enthusiasm that we missed as we emphasized first "total domination" and then, when that proved untenable, normality and banality instead. Observers as diverse as Zygmunt Bauman, Steven Kotkin, Mabel Berezin, and Daniel Jonah Goldhagen stressed that these regimes convinced large numbers of ordinary people that something extraordinary, warranting their enthusiastic participation, was taking place. On that basis, each of the regimes made at least some progress on unprecedented tasks—from crash industrialization to politicizing the workplace to re-engineering the population—that were congruent with their originating aims. The fact that ordinary people got caught up in the extraordinary enterprise reinforced the elite's sense of being in the forefront, tackling, as the liberals could not, the most salient issues of the age.

Indeed, as practice developed, there proved to be scope for ordinary people to play active roles barely envisioned at first. Although, as Michael Burleigh, Robert Thurston, and Emilio Gentile all observed, any such accent on the willing participation, and thus responsibility, of such people may offend populist sensibilities, we noted that family initiative or active acquiescence helped to nourish the "euthanasia" program and that even without special selection and indoctrination, ordinary Germans proved surprisingly willing to hunt down and murder Jews in Poland. Moreover, the extent of active participation in all three cases suggests that the human capacities and even virtues galvanized by the grandiose collective action afforded the beginnings of a genuinely post-liberal order, an alternative modernity, unpalatable though we may find it.

To be sure, the demand for hyper-enthusiasm could breed increasing cynicism and disaffection, even, for example, the outright ridicule of the Nazi regime by the Swing Kids and the Edelweiss Pirates at the end of the 1930s. But the situation could never have come to that point without the sense of grandiose enterprise, the inflated claims as the new collective action proceeded. What surprises is not the element of cynicism but the ongoing enthusiasm, which proved more than adequate, for a time, to sustain the collective action even in the face of such cynicism.

Up to a point, in other words, it was possible to act in this newly grandiose way without encountering—and revealing—the limits, the self-defeating nature, of the mode of action itself. But with their sense of the scope to make history through will and epic ambition, the agents set in motion more than they could control. In each case, the effort to maintain the new action encountered an array of largely unforeseen tensions, dilemmas, obstacles, and limits. In the Soviet Union, for example, the sense of great enterprise surrounding crash industrialization produced a tendency to overreach that led, in turn, to bureaucratic difficulties and the doctoring of production figures. Such doctoring unrealistically raised expectations even further, feeding the subsequent tendency to believe that failures could only have been due to wrecking. The effort to master the situation, in light of that belief, produced not only inefficiency and waste but also the Great Terror, with all its long-term implications for the Communist experiment. In the other two regimes as well, the need to respond to unintended consequences produced a new layer of unintended consequences. In the last analysis, the effort to act produced precisely the *in*capacity to act as envisioned, although such incapacity did not mean paralysis.

Even as they differed to some extent, the responses to difficulties in the three cases contributed to a characteristic dynamic and led to a characteristic array of outcomes. As we followed the dynamic in each case, we found again and again the interplay of radicalization and narrowing of both purpose and participation. Such radicalization and narrowing sometimes ensued in sequence, but they could also be simultaneous, even entailing radicalization *as* narrowing. Yet the differences in response among the three were sufficiently significant to help to produce the major differences in both outcomes and modes of ending.

"The law of unintended consequences" is a more general principle, not remotely confined to totalitarianism, but in the totalitarian case it produced pressures in certain characteristic directions. Although genuine contingencies were surely at work, we have been struck again and again by the strength of the tendencies, the pressures, and the momentum in certain directions in light of the initial frame of mind and the mode of action adopted. This is what we characterized as the strong contingency of the resulting dynamic. Still, the outcomes came to be only through that process, which only in retrospect betrays its crazy, characteristically totalitarian logic.

Let us remind ourselves, yet again, that it does not diminish the horror or the tragedy of the most troubling of those outcomes, or the moral culpability for them, to recognize that they emerged in this way, through a historically specific process demanding analysis on its own terms. In each case, the aggregate extreme resulted from a larger process and was not intended, or envisioned, when that process was initiated. More delimited intentions emerged from within that process, in light of the resultants at each step, and in light of the distinctive, historically specific nature of the process itself. Without that process, those intentions would not have emerged as they did, and there would have been no such outcome. Nor is it to deny singularity— the singularity that may matter most for certain questions—to isolate the crucial *historical* dimension in what those outcomes had in common, as resultants of processes that themselves had a characteristic supranational, historically specific element in common.

Even the world of the Soviet and Nazi camps, which for Arendt revealed in microcosm what the totalitarians were trying to achieve, was an unintended by-product in a crucial double sense. First, it was simply more difficult than they had expected to industrialize or to re-engineer the population on the scale attempted within the time they thought history had allotted them. Up to a point, the very fact that things went wrong belied the self-proclaimed capacity of the agents to engineer great politics. But in light of the emphasis on flexibility and trial and error, the fact that grandiose action produced unexpected results would not have to have been fatal. It was especially the inability of the agents to make sense of what was going wrong, and to adjust, that led to bizarre extremes not originally envisioned. In that sense, great politics escaped them.

Although their claim to be addressing creases in the mainstream in new ways was not groundless, the agents' diagnoses and prescriptions proved to be limited partly because their faith in will, spirit, and myth undercut any premium on systematic analysis. Although idiosyncratic national traditions were indeed relevant, the agents tended to overplay them, assuming that they afforded greater privilege than they did. Moreover, having grasped an array of plausible reasons for opposition to liberal democracy, and having pondered the alternatives one at a time, the totalitarians tended to assume that a concerted move beyond liberalism could yield all the advantages of each—a new mode of leadership, a newly committed elite, a more energetic and committed form of mass involvement, a more central role for scientific or technocratic expertise. Partly because they assumed that they could have them all simultaneously, the agents tried to do everything at once, and thus some of the tensions and ambiguities that practice brought to the fore.

The new action was to rest on more effective modes of interaction between the elite and the masses and more effective modes of involvement from below. But what these were to mean was not clear at the outset, and practice revealed dilemmas and limits. Partly at issue was whether meaningful new modes of involvement could be routinized—and if so, on what basis. Perhaps the most significant roles for ordinary people were bound to be extraordinary and *ad hoc* in light of the overall mode of action being attempted.

Fascist Italy placed great store in corporativism—with disappointing results. No comparable claims were made for the closest Nazi equivalent, the German Labor Front, founded under Robert Ley's leadership with the dissolution of the socialist trade union movement in May 1933. The Labor Front quickly proved to be a vehicle for mobilization and propaganda, not for working-class agency.[49] Still, as Franz Neumann, writing before the collapse, was better able than many later observers to recognize, the Nazis, too, sought enhanced, post-liberal modes of involvement, and the endeavor produced much debate. But Neumann stressed the inadequacy of the Nazi effort, despite the generic claim to place the people at the center:

> How the people could act politically was not explained; only the leadership of the "movement" was recognized. Innumerable theorists and pamphleteers stepped forward, calling the people the fountainhead of the state, but none was able to indicate how the people could serve as such, especially since the leader was not bound by plebiscites. Bad metaphysics replaced any rational discussion of the problem.[50]

So, despite the aspiration and the rhetoric, the Nazis never found the basis for sustained collective participation in political action. There was scope instead for mere belonging as a member of the racial community and, on that basis, for participation in ritual and in generically politicized ordinary activity, such as weekend hikes or the weekly one-dish meal. Even that minimal dimension was increasingly empty as the basis of collective action narrowed to Hitler's will and its focus narrowed to war, increasingly war against the Jews.

Such limits meant that the new participation from below was not made systematic and routine but tended to be precisely extraordinary and *ad hoc*—and thus, as it turned out, unsustainable—in all three cases. The new mode of action encouraged initiatives from below that then had to be reigned in but that often served radicalization at the same time. Although such initiative was sometimes "wild," unanticipated and unsanctioned by the leadership, it responded to the momentum that the new elite had initiated. Thus the emphasis on "working toward the Führer" in Nazi Germany and the comparable efforts to serve ongoing revolution in the other two cases. Such initiative was forthcoming especially as the top leaders seemed prone to compromise with the establishment, to tolerate the actual or potential opposition, or to settle for gains already achieved.

In Fascist Italy, the initiatives of local activists, from the rebellion against the Pacification Pact in 1921 to the second wave of violence in 1924 to the assault on Catholic youth organizations in 1931, were essential to sustain the action in progress. In the Nazi case, initiatives from below intensified anti-Semitic policy in 1935 and 1938. In the Soviet Union, comparable initiatives fed the cultural revolution in reaction to the NEP and then, encouraged by the leadership, even the Great Terror, as ordinary workers attacked bureaucratic ineptitude or abuse. Such workers were still taking the initiative to denounce wreckers as the terror was winding down in early 1939.

Because such initiative tended to get out of control, it forced a pull-back by the leadership and thus the characteristic zigzagging that compromised effectiveness in each case. Once the Soviet effort to root out wreckers had spun out of control, producing a potentially ruinous radicalization, the leadership had to impose a deeper mode of control that restricted interaction and narrowed participation. Insofar as something like a system of control resulted, it stemmed not from some originating desire for control for its own sake but from the need to master the process and sustain the ongoing action. Yet those efforts, too, ultimately proved to be inadequate, even self-defeating, for the measures adopted by the end of the 1930s—from bureaucratization to distancing forms of spectatorship to a cult of the leader—tended ultimately to rigidify the Soviet regime.

The narrowing of participation in all three cases meant that, although mobilization continued, it came to revolve around ritual and spectacle and thus to entail real exclusion. At best, what was supposed to have been a new mode of collective doing became a new mode of experience. Participation was held at one remove; deeper societal involvement in the ongoing action came to be indefinitely deferred. What was at issue in Italy, as it came to seem necessary to emphasize the party as opposed to the state, was not actual collective action involving everyone, through the state, but mobilization itself, not quite for its own sake but for *potential* action. The continuing mobilization was not genuinely deepening the society's capacity to act. To be sure, the Italian case showed that the situation could zigzag to a still more grandiose great task, bound up with war making on the European level, but because the country had not been genuinely prepared, this renewed effort at collective action bred disintegration and collapse.

Although obviously in a very different way, the Nazis, too, ended up fatally overreaching themselves in the Second World War. For Woodruff Smith it was especially the lurking contradictions between *Weltpolitik* and *Lebensraum*, the two enduring strands in German expansionism, that led to disaster when war afforded the Nazis the chance to impose their policies on almost the whole of Europe. For the Nazis had not genuinely synthesized the two strands, only papered over the tensions between them, partly in an effort to forge societal consensus, overcoming the fragmentation that resulted from the conflicts among the interest groups for each. As Smith saw it, even temporal and geographical separation did not enable the Nazis to reconcile the conflicting strands during the war. The contradictions were revealed as resettlement in Eastern Europe bumped up against the *Weltpolitik* autarky economic arrangements, then as Nazi Germany ended up fighting not only Britain, which Hitler had viewed as Germany's natural ally, but also the United States.[51] So much, it would seem, for *Lebensraum* in Eastern Europe.

It is certainly true that the maelstrom of the war sucked Nazi Germany in ever deeper, but this was because first Britain, then the Soviet Union, refused to play their assigned roles—roles the Nazis had assigned on the basis of assumptions bound up with the novel mode of action they had adopted. Hitler was not seeking a showdown with the United States, as Smith first seems to suggest, but supported Japan in an effort to deter U.S. intervention in Europe. Within the new European order, it remained possible to distinguish countries that were targets for German expansion, especially Poland and the Soviet Union, from countries like Hungary and Romania to be subjected to German-led *Mitteleuropa* economic arrangements. It was not so much an abiding tension between *Weltpolitik* and *Lebensraum* as the blinkered, mythical thinking bred by the new mode of action itself that led Hitler and the Nazis to miscalculation and the need to respond to unforeseen outcomes, producing ever more reckless action.

In principle, the need for choice and the scope for variation regarding such matters as institutional emphasis, the role for experts, or the extent of party membership would not have to have been seriously debilitating in any of the three cases. We noted that, in principle, exact institutional arrangements were secondary—and certainly not the criterion of totalitarianism. But in light of the difficulties that the new action encountered, the need for choice and the fits and starts on the level of institutional basis produced confusion and rivalry that especially compromised the capacity to act.

Although the efforts to renew commitment and to rear the next generation of leaders differed in depth and effectiveness, the effort itself produced debilitating fissuring in each case. In the Soviet Union, the controversy between Andrei Zhdanov, who wanted the Communist Party to be a relatively open, broadly based educational instrument, and Nikolai Ezhov, who held to a more restrictive, elitist view, was central to Communist practice in the late 1930s and helped to fuel the dynamic that led to the terror.[52] In Italy, questions about elite openness and replenishment grew ever more debilitating especially as the Fascist revolution seemed to bog down. Thus the renewed controversy over educational reform, and thus Adelchi Serena started by restricting party membership as he sought to revitalize Fascism late in 1940. But we noted that Serena's effort only intensified the party–state antagonism and soon had to be called off.

For all three of the originating elites, one point of the new mode of action was to avoid the ossifying tendencies of bureaucracy, as they had been diagnosed especially by Robert Michels. It was partly thus that the Nazis played down the state in favor of the dynamic movement. And thus the Italians, even as they placed greater emphasis on the state, accented corporativism, direct involvement and decision making from the shop floor; bureaucracy could be bypassed by involving those with hands-on knowledge in decisions affecting the sectors of production in which they were directly involved. The Soviet leaders, finding that bureaucracy was expanding as they expanded functions, tried various expedients, including, as early as the mid-1920s, a systematic effort to oversee their own burgeoning bureaucracy.

The problem was that whatever the institutional focus, the new mode of action was itself bound to entail inflating bureaucracy as the range of collective action dramatically expanded. Yet bureaucracy meshed problematically with ongoing revolution and with many aspects of the new mode of action envisioned. Major aspects of the new cluster—relying on the leader, assigning a watchdog or goading role to the party, fostering more direct involvement from below—were intended to head off bureaucratic ossification. And efforts, whether systematic or episodic, to undercut or somehow revivify the bureaucracy were central to the dynamic in each case. But the anti-bureaucratic effort fed radicalization and narrowing in several characteristic ways.

As practice revealed that bureaucratic and careerist tendencies were inherent even in the new mode of action, it became clear that the revolution had to be ongoing, "permanent," not only because of the continuing need for education and the open-endedness of history. Bureaucracy and careerism seemed especially likely to afflict the state, in light of its holdovers from the pre-totalitarian regimes, so those tendencies could seemingly best be countered through a special ongoing role for the party. But even as embodying the revolutionary "movement," even as ongoing educator, goad, and watchdog, the party, too, had to have a bureaucratic structure if it was to be effective; thus the significance of the work of first Roberto Farinacci, then Augusto Turati, in disciplining and structuring the Italian Fascist Party so that it could act, playing its particular roles in the regime.

The weakness of the initial Italian revolution left the greatest potential ongoing role for the pre-Fascist bureaucracy, but thus the increasing restiveness among major sectors of the new Fascist elite, who devised a series of putative antidotes, none very successful. Insofar as the new totalitarian *state* was supposed to be different, the key was to be the corporative system, and ever-new layers were added in an effort to make it work. But especially as it came to encompass layer upon layer, corporativism, too, came to suffer from the inherent bureaucratic element. Moreover, even as the new corporativist institutions encountered resistance from the traditional state bureaucracy, they got caught up in infighting with the party at the same time. So the corporativist effort yielded both bureaucratic rigidity and splintering as the Fascist regime sought to sustain the new mode of action.

We saw that the early Soviet effort to oversee the burgeoning bureaucracy proved simply to add another layer of bureaucracy. Moreover, in light of the apparent tension between technical competence and ideological commitment at the outset, the communists sought to push their own new people into the bureaucracy as soon as possible. But thus those in the massive bureaucracy required for economic planning and directed industrialization were often poorly prepared. The problem stemmed not simply from Russian backwardness; the tasks themselves were grandiose and unprecedented. And in light of the inflated expectations bound up with the mode of action itself, the bureaucrats came to feel especially pressured and thus to emphasize safety and routine even as, to function—even to survive—they found it necessary to take extraordinary measures, circumventing routine, at the same time. The result was a characteristic but debilitating combination of chaos and rigidity.

In Germany, the Nazis sought to avoid bureaucratization first by relying on the supposedly more dynamic party as opposed to the state, but because the Nazi Party particularly included para-state departments for areas from agriculture to foreign affairs, it was especially subject to bureaucratization and careerism of its own. Thus Hitler fostered the SS even at the expense of the party. Yet the SS developed its own bureaucratic dimension, as many scholars have emphasized. The overlapping jurisdictions and notoriously uncertain lines of authority produced not only the well-known "Darwinian" struggle but also chaos and inefficiency. Under the novel circumstances of great political action, however, these chaotic institutional rivalries, and even the overall bureaucratic syndrome itself, fed the tendency toward unanticipated extremes, as we saw especially in connection with Nazi Jewish policy and the Holocaust.

As we noted, Moshe Lewin concluded that the perennial bureaucratic bargaining and infighting in the Soviet Union "actually blocked the system's capacity to act."[53] Although action surely continued to the bitter end in all three cases, the Germans and Italians, too, found that they could not act as envisioned partly because of the bureaucratic syndrome. The overall irony is obvious, since the most general purpose of the totalitarian departure was radically to enhance the capacity for collective action.

The quest for antidotes to the rigidifying effects of bureaucracy fed the zigzagging dynamic as the leaders gave reign to, then had to reign in, initiatives from below. It was especially to keep the functionaries energized and to counter suspected bureaucratic wrecking that the Soviet leadership encouraged ordinary workers to report abuses or incompetence on the part of their superiors. When the resulting momentum got out of hand, feeding the *Ezhovshchina*, renewed bureaucracy seemed to be necessary to restore a modicum of the orderly procedure essential to effective action over the longer term.

In each regime, the need to counter bureaucratization fed the growing reliance on the leader to sustain the action in course. Although archetypal in the Soviet case, the interplay between leader and bureaucracy, as the role of each inflated, proved to be problematic in all three cases. The relationship was not complementary, as Lefort suggested, but tension-ridden. Lewin's classic analysis of the unforeseen dialectic that developed, and its decisive impact on the overall Soviet experiment, also illuminates that wider totalitarian dynamic.

Reliance on the leader grew from the sense, which had developed with the earlier break, that new modes of leadership might serve the new collective action. And although the modes of leadership that emerged differed significantly in the three cases, the measure of personal dictatorship was obviously crucial in each. Thus, of course, the longstanding temptation to resort to some ahistorical megalomania on the part of the leaders to explain these departures. But none of the regimes emerged simply to satisfy some personal power hunger; nor did any of them end up a mere personal dictatorship. Rather, leadership was a function of the new mode of action being adopted, and the role of the leader changed as part of the ensuing dynamic. Despite the momentum toward the outcomes that resulted, we must attend to the overall dynamic to understand how these particular leadership roles emerged.

Still, differences in the fascist and Communist projects, and in their modes of ending, obviously complicate the effort to conceive the role of the leader in terms of the wider dynamic. The increasing emphasis on foreign and military policy in the two fascist experiments proved especially to enhance the roles of the leaders, who increasingly concentrated power, dealt with others merely as individuals, and undermined whatever scope there had been for a new form of genuinely collective action. It is certainly true that, as Aristotle Kallis has stressed, the fate of fascism ended up totally identified with the decisions and fate of the two leaders—with the result a shambles in each case. This outcome may suggest that, whatever the totalitarian pretenses, what in fact resulted was mere authoritarianism as opposed to totalitarianism.[54] However, Emilio Gentile argued convincingly that the overall dynamic—which, after all, initially entailed far more than expansion and war making—must be understood as a three-way interaction between leader, party, and state. Although he was referring especially to Fascist Italy, he insisted explicitly that the other two cases were comparable. And indeed the leader-linked outcome that Kallis noted must be understood in terms of the wider processes at work. As the two experiments narrowed to ever more reckless war making, the leaders sought to make their prerogatives as all-encompassing as possible in the narrow area that remained. But this suggests not that these experiments reduced to mere authoritarianism or personal power hunger but rather that, precisely as totalitarian, they could narrow in this way—with disastrous results.

As the fate of each experiment became ever more narrowly bound up with the will of the leader, some of those who had believed in the wider experiment expressed doubts and criticisms, even began to turn away. Italo Balbo correctly saw the particular triumph of Mussolini as a contraction from within an ongoing experiment.[55] Even Goebbels, on a personal level the ultimate Hitler loyalist, worried about a leadership crisis in Germany in 1943.

The initiating agent was not the leader but the counter-elite, based on its new historical-political sense. So the precise role of the leader was uncertain, and thus there was scope for tension from the outset. In Germany, the effort to imagine an alternative to both liberalism and socialism had long encompassed the leadership principle as central. Thus the Nazis were the most willing to defer to a leader—first on the basis of this generic Führer principle but then especially on the basis of the special attributes of Hitler himself. But even in the German case the leader was to play a functional role, serving the new collective action. He was not merely the symbol of unity or the embodiment of enduring power.

Hitler had to surmount several crises before the Nazi movement became wound around the perceived leadership qualities of this idiosyncratic individual. He triumphed especially because of his strength of will, which seemed to suggest his privileged sense of the requirements for the new action—including the role that he himself would have to play. As Ian Kershaw showed, Hitler, once in power, understood the need to cultivate and maintain a certain aura, not simply to enhance his own power but to sustain the action in progress.[56] Even his way of encouraging rivalry among the other Nazis served that wider indispensable role and not merely, as is often implied, his own power. But the failure, noted by Neumann, to find more genuine modes of participation obviously inflated the reliance on the leader. And reliance on Hitler's will entailed a narrowing of the mode of action that led, in turn, to capriciousness and eventual failure.

Although it yielded flexibility and even dynamism of a sort, the Nazi emphasis on the will of the Führer at the expense of codified law fed the greater tendency toward overt irrationalism in Nazi Germany than in Fascist Italy—and thus the greater tendency toward governmental chaos that Kershaw emphasized. Indeed, Hitler actively undermined Interior Minister Wilhelm Frick's efforts at reform to produce a rational, authoritarian state structure. Yet the overall administrative chaos ended up intensifying the strangling bureaucratic element.[57] Still, as Renzo De Felice showed, there was a marked tendency toward governmental disorder in Fascist Italy too, despite the greater legal rationalism, especially as Mussolini became more reluctant to delegate.

Mussolini personally founded Fascism and, despite the frustrations he quickly encountered, he had the stature when he did so, in 1919, to make a credible effort to rally a new, possibly revolutionary political force from those who embraced the legacy of the war and disliked both liberalism and Marxism. But significant sectors of those who gravitated to his fledgling movement did so on the basis of a vision that seemed to point beyond Mussolini's own. Thus he was subject to pressure from militants that, we have seen, was possibly decisive in maintaining Fascism's revolutionary potential. Conversely, much of Mussolini's effort into the 1930s went toward disciplining the movement/party.

Especially because the content of the originating aspiration had been more heterogeneous in Italy than in Russia or Germany, Mussolini found it necessary to balance and juggle even as he fostered the illusion of dynamism through ritual and spectacle. Yet sharing at least some of the revolutionary aspirations of his movement, he was not satisfied even with the situation that had been established by the early 1930s. Indeed, he understood that the tendency toward impasse and superficiality threatened not only the longer-term revolutionary potential of

Fascism but also the very viability of his regime. Hence the effort at a certain kind of radicalization through imperialism and war. This combination of forces produced the Italian variation on the wider totalitarian tendency toward zigzagging, narrowing, and failure.

In Russian Bolshevism, Lenin had proved to be an indispensable leader, but he actively sought to minimize the role of individual leadership and especially to head off the cult that developed around him in his late years. And as has so often been emphasized, Stalin's initial role did not rest on personal charisma, as did Mussolini's and Hitler's to a considerable extent, and Stalin's "appeal" was not really at issue in his rise to the leadership. But his personal role became crucial precisely as the Soviet experiment came to center on great politics itself, as opposed to the implementation of Marxism or the creation of socialism. The fact that Stalin lacked the charisma of Mussolini and Hitler proved to be a secondary difference once the new Communist regime had been left isolated and the tasks that followed seemed to demand decisive, even ruthless leadership. Trotsky's prediction that the dynamic would lead by stages to the dictatorship of one person is often cited.[58] However, it was not simply Stalin's megalomania that produced this result but the great political dynamic itself—a dynamic to which Trotsky had contributed significantly in its earlier stages.

Stalin, in contrast to Hitler, emerged as leader only through a bruising contest that introduced unforeseen internal opposition and thus fears on his own part, plausible in some measure, that then contributed to the ensuing dynamic. That opposition was exacerbated by the unforeseen difficulties of the great project of crash industrialization based on forced collectivization. Thus even certain potentialities of personality, not evident during the 1920s, came to the fore as Stalin's capacity to play a certain kind of role came to seem central.

It was neither that the times made the man nor vice versa; indeed, our three, very nearly archetypal cases reveal the more complex dialectic that gets us beyond those familiar, too limited, alternatives. Although each of the leaders understood himself as the servant of an ongoing revolution transcending his individual life, the difficulties encountered seemed to dictate that power be concentrated in him, as leader. This historically specific conjuncture then brought forms of ahistorical megalomania to the fore. But even in the German case, this psychological propensity, differentiated among individuals, became so important only because of the historically specific novel mode of action attempted. The overreliance, by the end of the 1930s, on a fallible but ever more megalomaniacal leader soon led Fascism and Nazism to disaster. Although the path was far more circuitous, a comparable overreliance ended up crippling the Soviet experiment as well, as we will discuss when we compare modes of ending.

In each case, the combination of radicalization and narrowing gradually engendered a lack of realism, even a kind of surrealism, and a new order of myth making. As we have emphasized, myth, as an aspect of the new historical-political sense, was central to the whole mode of action from the start; this initial dimension of myth then made a second, less lucid sort of myth making more likely once the new collective action encountered unforeseen difficulties. Although the second dimension was likely to emerge, the two still must be distinguished because the second was an outcome, a resultant of the effort to act, and thus had a different source, a different place in the trajectory, and a different significance.

In each case, the sense of being uniquely positioned to respond to the wider novel modern challenge, though plausible to a degree, was exaggerated from the start, but in light of the initial ambitions and pretensions, as fed by national cultural sensitivities, frustration led not to a more realistic assessment but to hyperbolic rhetoric and the sort of myth making that obscures real circumstances and prospects. The result was a tendency toward inflating claims and expectations, which then made the action still harder to sustain—even as such hyperbole covered over many of the difficulties, at least for a while.

In Italy, the notion that the Fascist Party embodied an ongoing revolution was increasingly a myth as the revolution bogged down in fact. Although it found a role of sorts, the party did not deliver on what had seemed to be the initial promise of Fascism. Operating as if its activity was itself sufficient to continue the Fascist revolution, it fostered a merely superficial mode of involvement through ritual and spectatorship. Even as Serena sought revitalization early in the war, the party remained concerned especially for its own prerogatives. But those like Bottai and Pellizzi who best understood the mythical nature of the party's pretenses clung to their own mythical images of what Fascism could still accomplish.

The Soviet tendency to doctor production figures and to attribute failures to deliberate wrecking fed the surreality, the second layer of myth, which made it ever harder to assess the regime's real prospects even as its purposes began to narrow. Whereas the shared myth of "creating socialism" had earlier galvanized genuine enthusiasm, the Soviet effort was gradually reduced to material advance, catching up with the West, even as the leaders continued to claim to be creating a new and better way.

In Germany, the Nazis' failure seriously to address their inability to find more genuine modes of participation bred the mythical thinking that Neumann characterized, perhaps too charitably, as "bad metaphysics." But in the Nazi case the second-order myth, characteristically combined with both radicalization and narrowing of purpose, was manifested most tragically in the Nazi effort to prolong the war, bringing still greater ruin upon Germany. Although the epochal competition with Communism fed the willingness to fight to the end, much of the leadership sustained the war at least partly in order to kill Jews. The element of putative "revenge" envisioned was ludicrous, but in an attenuated, shriveled way the image of a Europe free of Jews maintained in the Nazis some sense that they were still struggling to realize their original aspiration. Although that aspiration still energized, it was increasingly mythical as it narrowed, for it was not "the Jews" who were arrayed against Germany.

On the part of Nazi leaders, the genocide was bound up with an increasingly apocalyptic sense that even as it also promised to bury the regime itself, the war was destroying the bourgeois order that the whole counter-tradition had aimed to overcome all along. Yet whereas it too helped—absurdly and tragically—to sustain the action, this too was a myth, for although the world would never be the same, mere physical destruction, reducing cities to rubble, could not destroy bourgeois Europe in a way conforming to the longstanding vision of a systematic alternative. On the contrary, the Nazi war helped to discredit the quest for any such alternative.

Extreme outcomes and varied modes of ending

Each of the three departures produced unanticipated extremes, but although each led to failure, they ended in very different ways. The relationship between the extremes and the endings was complex and reveals no particular pattern. Partly because it had spun out of control, the new action led to comparably murderous outcomes in Germany and the Soviet Union. But whereas the Holocaust was bound up with the apocalyptic end of the Nazi regime, the two phases of terror in the Stalinist 1930s had very different places in the Soviet trajectory. Still, the modes of ending in all three cases reflected the increasing radicalization and narrowing bound up with the changing place of myth.

In Italy, the turn to war, itself the strongly contingent response to frustration, revealed the regime's limits and produced efforts at reversal that proved either mythical—such as the faith in the party—or self-defeating—such as the further party–state antagonism. The turn to anti-Semitism was an effort to radicalize, but to fasten upon a bogus issue in a way that seemed to reaffirm the superiority of Fascism over Nazism simply reinforced the narrowing and myth making in progress. As the war effort revealed the hollowness of the regime, myth and energy began to dissipate, although some hung on, in the shadow of Nazi Germany, precipitating a virtual civil war in northern Italy after the first fall of Mussolini in 1943.

Although even the advent of anti-Semitic legislation could mean, in practice, intensified demands for assimilation as opposed to the exclusion of Jews, and although even long-committed Fascists shielded Jews from the Nazis, late Fascism proved to be complicit in the Holocaust. Thus even the Italian case carried the potential for mass murder, revealed as some sought to maintain great political action even in this shrunken and ludicrous final form. Although not the core of totalitarianism, but only one possibility among others, the momentum toward mass murder, too, was strongly contingent, especially in light of the accent on toughness and the willingness to use violence, and especially as circumstances spun partly out of control. We more readily grasp the danger insofar as we place the murderous tendency in the context of the overall totalitarian dynamic, not as first on the agenda but as a strong possibility, in light of the problems with the mode of action itself.

Whereas Italian Fascism, as the result of its wartime failures, reached an ambiguous ending combining disintegration with near civil war, the Nazi experiment ended unambiguously—and still more dramatically. Narrowing to Hitler's will, and fighting to the end against an enemy conceived in mythical terms, the regime went down almost literally in flames. The Soviet experiment ended in something like the opposite way, but its mode of ending, too, was part of a characteristic cluster that became possible only with the overall totalitarian departure.

Although the Communist regime managed to pull back from the Great Terror, that unanticipated extreme seemed to warrant a narrowing of participation and purpose that proved crucial to the subsequent stages of the Soviet experiment. The system survived even the Stalin cult, but fear of a comparable "cult of personality," with all the threatening excesses that it was now known to invite, fed the ascendancy of the bureaucracy, which reached its apogee under Leonid Brezhnev in the 1970s. And this finally yielded a measure of the stability and predictability that bureaucracy was supposed to bring. But in the context of great politics, bureaucratic stability and predictability meant ossification, a further narrowing of purpose, and a loss of commitment and dynamism—all setting the stage for the dissolution of the whole effort.

As Lefort noted, with obvious reference to the Soviet case, the totalitarian mode of action entailed the scope for cohering as fantasy, as "myth," despite the impossibility of its alleged attempt to transcend history. But even as fantasy, Soviet totalitarianism could not cohere for long precisely because, as the experiment settled into bureaucratic routine, as the reality diverged ever more from the myth, the idealism, enthusiasm, and expectation that had sustained the experiment simply dissipated. Even as he recognized that totalitarian practice could not be routinized, Lefort overemphasized bureaucracy as the positive core of totalitarian action. Thus he missed the tendency of bureaucratization to undermine the whole experiment, in light of all that had been necessary to sustain the overall dynamic.

Having won its war against Nazi Germany, the Soviet Union extended the Communist experiment to other countries as a further step in the strongly contingent process. But although the satellite system expanded Soviet power in one sense, it also introduced new tensions and vulnerabilities into the overall experiment. A measure of genuine indigenous enthusiasm certainly accompanied the effort in the satellite states, but the fact that most of these new regimes were in large measure Soviet impositions, and remained subject to an element of Soviet dominance into the 1980s, compromised possibilities. The satellite regimes could not draw on the energizing sense of national pride, of assuming the forefront in light of special national circumstances, that had helped to sustain the totalitarian experiment in Italy, Germany, and the Soviet Union itself. So whereas Soviet dissidents tended either, like Alexander Solzhenitsyn, to reject Marxism–Communism *in toto* as an ill-advised Western import or, like Roy Medvedev, to seek reform and revitalization, the disaffected in the satellite states, especially in the aftermath of the crushing of the Prague Spring in 1968, were better positioned to pinpoint certain problematic and surprising features of the totalitarian dynamic itself.

On that basis, the opposition spearheaded by intellectuals like Leszek Kolakowski, Adam Michnik, and Václav Havel went beyond dissidence to a genuinely *post-totalitarian* perspective by the 1970s. Recognizing that the Communist regimes were losing their last vestiges of commitment and idealism, these intellectuals began to grasp that the whole totalitarian mode of action had become unsustainable. And it seemed to be possible to specify new insights into the limits and possibilities of modern politics on that basis.[59] As Abbott Gleason put it, Polish and Czech dissidents knew "that Soviet ideology no longer had real power over people's minds or hearts."[60] They had come to recognize, in other words, that even the leaders no longer believed in the Communist experiment; not only had it all come to rest on myth, but it turned out that the myth itself could dissipate.

Even has he noted that ideology had long been a mere fig leaf, Timothy Garton Ash nicely pinpointed the hollowing at work as he characterized the residual significance of ideology in the late phase of communism in the satellite states: "However despised and un-credible these structures of organized lying were, they continued to perform a vital blocking function. They no longer mobilized anyone, but they did prevent the public articulation of shared aspirations and common truths."[61] Moreover, Garton Ash went on, they implicated everyone in a double life of feigned belief, the games of outward conformity. This semantic occupation of the public sphere was all that remained of the earlier energizing commitment and belief.

Beginning with several remarkably prescient essays in the late 1980s, Garton Ash pinpointed the ruling elites' loss of confidence in their own right to rule. In Hungary, he noted, the rulers might simply give up power; there was no reason not to.[62] And with Hungary and Poland in the lead, this almost unimaginable outcome soon occurred throughout much of the Soviet bloc.[63] The unraveling in the satellites then contributed to the collapse of the Communist regime in the Soviet Union itself, as the totalitarian dynamic yielded yet another unforeseen outcome.

What had happened, we noted in Chapter 5, was not precisely a drying up of ideology, long a kind of myth, but the end of a dynamic that, it turned out, could narrow and then fizzle as the whole experiment dried up. With even the second-order myth dissipating, the agents lost faith not in the ideology *per se* but in the great political mode of action itself.[64] At the same time, ordinary Soviet people, much like their counterparts in Italy and Germany, had become disenchanted in something like the literal sense, although the process had taken much longer in the Soviet Union. Rather than creating socialism or even catching up with the West, the Soviet Union had simply spent, in the words of one popular refrain, "seventy years on the road to nowhere."

So the effort to do great politics produced quite different trajectories as each regime responded to unforeseen provisional outcomes. There was self-destructive radicalization, but there was also bureaucratic ossification and trivializing spectacle, each of which yielded a waning of idealism and a loss of energy. Different though they were, the ending of the three experiments, as outcomes of the characteristic totalitarian dynamic, themselves formed a characteristic cluster resulting from the mode of action. From a liberal perspective on politics and history, the overall trajectory could only have been bewildering indeed.

Yet even encompassing terror and the Holocaust, totalitarianism was not some mystery or catastrophe, some eruption of "power and evil" defying historical understanding. It happened in historical time and for historical reasons open to our understanding if we think in a sufficiently historical way. The experience of totalitarianism not only demands such deeper historical analysis but also indicates what such historical thinking must encompass. And once we locate totalitarianism in historical time, we can better formulate the lessons and pinpoint the dangers as we recognize that we may still be in the *same* historical time in ways not fully understood. To what extent and in what way become the next questions.

Ending and continuing after the totalitarian moment

Triumphalism, Othering, and deeper doubts

Although they seem strongly contingent in retrospect, the troubling, generally unanticipated phenomena at issue in this study became part of our world only through the history, the particular contingent concatenation that we have explored. Without it, we might never have learned this as opposed to that— about human possibilities, about what the world can hold. Yet a revelation it surely was. And a deeper understanding of totalitarianism in its historical speci- ficity enables us better to formulate the lurking questions about the possibilities before us, and the dangers we face, as we continue in the aftermath.

Most obviously at issue has been the sense in which, the degree to which, "totalitarianism" is an ongoing *modern* possibility, as opposed to either an ongoing ahistorical possibility or an "epochal" phenomenon characteristic of a particular moment now behind us. Of all that the totalitarian experience showed to be possible, what was consumed with the failure of the three classic regimes, and what, among the specifically modern factors that fed into them, seems to have survived them? Insofar as it requires not merely the disastrous outcomes but some deeper learning on our part to put totalitarianism securely behind us, to what extent, and in what sense, have we accomplished it? Such questions have been central to our self-understanding in the aftermath, but even formulating them coherently has proved difficult. The familiar imperative of "never again" suggests our determination to learn, but whereas we now are surely more atten- tive to the dangers of genocide and atrocity, even the object of that imperative is none too clear.

Still, up to a point we surely have learned—and thereby drawn a line between totalitarianism and ourselves. To be sure, it took a while for what may now seem certain of the key lessons to sink in. "Sound stock" arguments for eugenics were still heard in Britain after the Second World War, and forced sterilization continued in Sweden into the 1960s.[1] But the dangers of eugenic thinking are now much clearer. We no longer even contemplate forced sterilization, or killing off the disabled or other "useless eaters," however rational the arguments for economic efficiency. Rather, we assert that no one is superfluous. And although the issue remains contested, and a source of danger, we are less likely to conceive the measure of community or homogeneity essential for societal effectiveness in ethnic as opposed to cultural terms. Indeed, we are far more likely to recognize the positive advantages of multiculturalism. Even insofar as we recognize a societal interest in practices affecting population, we do not specify biologically delimited roles for women as the totalitarians did.

Thanks to the totalitarian experience itself, we now know better to eschew dictatorship and to embrace multi-party pluralism and civil liberties. We understand that, even accepting collective responsibility for an array of issues, we cannot act together as one in the grandiose, great political way; to attempt so much at once is to invite arbitrariness and to set in motion processes beyond control. Totalitarian great politics proved to be a misreading of how history could be made, or made to happen. So quite apart from any particular issue or decision, we proceed more humbly, patiently, cautiously. More generally, we better grasp both the limits of politics and the autonomy of the non-political. Thus, for example, Albert Camus's noted insistence on the autonomy of art in opposition to the totalizing tendencies of Jean-Paul Sartre.[2]

However, from such undeniable lessons we slide easily into a complacent triumphalism, as if there is nothing to be learned from the totalitarian eruption beyond what good liberal democrats knew all along. Whereas the totalitarians fell for ideology and pseudo-science, we follow the rational, moral, or true path. Whereas they sought the security of a prison, we embrace freedom, with all the burdens and messiness that it entails. From there, we simply marginalize the totalitarians through some combination of reductionist categories, usually encompassing ahistorical psychological and contingent contextual factors. From this perspective, national waywardness or backwardness explains the aggregate divergence from normal liberalism, and what continues—and is to be headed off—is especially a set of ahistorical propensities. But thus the imperative can be facile, vacuous, as if the point is simply to guard against the nasty fascist types among us—or evil itself.

Even as the collapse of Communism seemed to suggest the end of the epoch that made totalitarianism possible, the ensuing uncertainties gave a boost to phenomena loosely lumped together as neo-fascism. Apparently encompassing an array from aspiring politicians like Gianfranco Fini in Italy and Jörg Haider in Austria to "lone wolf" terrorists like Oklahoma City bomber Timothy McVeigh, each of its widely differing manifestations raised somewhat different issues. Clearly central, however, were the self-proclaimed neo-Nazi skinheads prominent in the upsurge of violence against immigrants and resident non-citizens in newly reunified Germany during the 1990s. Similar incidents continued—and not only in Germany—into the twenty-first century. Those responsible seemed comparable to white supremacy groups elsewhere that embraced Nazi trappings while betraying fantasies that most found hare-brained, if not clinically paranoid.

This wave of neo-fascism seemed to suggest not the end of an epoch but the continuing possibility of a totalitarian politics, stemming, it would seem, from ongoing psychological propensities.[3] Indeed, it was this new prominence of neo-fascism that prompted Umberto Eco's effort to specify the terms of what he called "ur-fascism."[4] And our way of conceiving neo-fascism obviously has implications for our understanding of original fascism and whatever conditions of possibility might continue.

The visibility of such neo-fascists reinforced our tendency to view "fascism" as an abiding, ahistorical propensity or character type, bound up with hate and paranoia. Such fascist types are always among us, but they are different from us; indeed, we know we are good partly because we are not like them. Insofar as we "Other" them through Eco's "ur-fascism," for example, we seem to serve our imperative of "never again," and we reinforce triumphalism at the same time. Although the danger continues, we know precisely what it is—and that it lies in *them* and not *us*. The imperative is simply to exclude those recognizably neo-fascist, with their characteristic ahistorical psychological patterns.

Although the ahistorical dimension is not negligible, our tendency to inflate it feeds a kind of ahistorical circle that limits our capacity to grasp the historical specificity of *either* original fascism or neo-fascism. Using the "fascist" label ahistorically, we reduce original fascism to the same level as neo-fascism, which, as a recurrence, seems to afford readily accessible keys to the first fascism and to "fascism" in general. By inflating the ahistorical psychological propensity, we skew proportions at the expense of the supranational, historically specific dimension and thereby miss the actual totalitarian dynamic of original fascism. Our failure to sort out the historically specific conditions of possibility then restricts our capacity to consider what has continued and what has ended and thereby to learn all the lessons we might.

At issue is what, on the supranational, historically specific level, might continue not merely in *them* but also in *us*. At issue is how to proceed in a fully post-totalitarian way, having taken totalitarianism seriously and learned the lessons from its supranational, historically specific dimension.

Although we have gotten much mileage from the mutually reinforcing combination of triumphalism and "Othering," we sense that we have more to learn from the totalitarian episode. Indeed, a sense of nervous incompleteness shadows our triumphalism. We feel, most basically, that the ongoing danger may have less to do with ahistorical psychological propensities than with specifically modern conditions of possibility that we have yet fully to confront. Although a recurrence of the classic forms of totalitarianism is unlikely in the extreme, we worry that there remains scope for something comparable, in a form that we cannot anticipate. Insofar as totalitarianism was distinctively modern and we remain confined to the same modern framework, some of the historically specific conditions of possibility necessarily continue, but we are not sure what they are. Indeed, we sometimes note tendencies toward totalism, domination, or the hypertrophy of power that seem to suggest not merely ongoing conditions of possibility but even the realization of negative modern possibilities that our totalitarian predecessors simply put into practice in more extreme and overt form. From this perspective, the ongoing, historically specific danger is not merely the delimited capacity for genocide, as Omer Bartov sometimes seems to suggest.[5] Nor is it simply—one of Arendt's concerns—the putative superfluousness of some human beings, perhaps an increasing number.[6] Precisely because the danger seems more diffuse, we are unsure about what has ended and what continues.

Conversely, we sense that, although the earlier liberal self-understanding remains indispensable in part, it is not enough merely to emphasize rights, interests, and individual self-realization, or even John Stuart Mill's hesitant way of venturing beyond, on the basis of societal utility. Yet what do we need to add or rethink in light of the totalitarian revelation of specifically modern possibilities? Stephen Holmes noted a certain flabbiness in the contemporary liberal self-understanding, the result, he suggested, of the reluctance of contemporary *anti*-liberals to push their diagnoses, prescriptions, and values in the aftermath of totalitarianism.[7] This was indirectly to suggest that a deeper understanding of the earlier totalitarian anti-liberalism might serve to clarify and deepen contemporary liberalism—and contemporary political possibilities more generally.

As it has happened, the totalitarian experience has yielded, alongside triumphalist confidence, something like the opposite, a certain loss of nerve, which has taken various forms. The sense that what continues from the totalitarian era is a more general modern tendency toward totalism, with the hypertrophy of power/knowledge yielding new but related modes of control, has fed a premium in post-totalitarian thought on "little politics" or even edification, gesture, or disruption as opposed to constructive collective action. At the same time, we find ourselves especially reluctant to face responsibility for collective decision and action on certain kinds of question. Rather than deepen our thinking about such matters, we resort to rights and negative liberties—not, from this angle, in a triumphalist mode, but in a nervous, skeptical mode, as if we dare not venture anything more collectively constructive, as if protection against abuse must be the priority. At issue are barely articulated changes in our assumptions about responsibility, the public sphere, and the scope for ethical-political virtue or citizenship; the overall result has been a new skepticism about the scope for acting collectively.

Even as we recognize that "lessons" include something about limits, humility, and pluralism, we still face questions about the positive terms, the scope and purpose of politics, the mode of collective decision making and action, even the scope for "positive" liberty. The loss of nerve has entailed an element of overreaction, from failure to grasp the basis of the totalitarian departure and thus the terms of the continuing challenge. Not only must we avoid mere triumphalism if we are to put totalitarianism securely behind us, but, turning in the other direction, we must counterbalance the loss of nerve with a positive alternative mode of collective responsibility as we recognize that the ongoing modern situation continues to demand collective decision making and action. On that basis, we can proceed in a spirit that is at once humble *and* constructive.

As Holmes implied, the negative outcomes of the totalitarian experiment itself have limited the discourse as we have proceeded in the aftermath. Put differently, the totalitarians contaminated a large area of the terrain that must be explored if we are to specify the terms of a more securely post-totalitarian culture. But the scope to put continuing/ending in better perspective remains. Only on the basis of a deeper grasp of historical totalitarianism itself can we better understand what the totalitarian experience says, and does not say, about *our* challenges and possibilities.

Some anti-triumphalist ways of framing the issue

At issue is the question of ongoing supranational, historically specific conditions of possibility. To understand how better to frame the question, we can usefully begin by considering some influential ways of addressing ending/continuing on the part of those eschewing mere triumphalism. Such pioneering inquirers as Hannah Arendt, Albert Camus, and Ernst Nolte were much concerned with it, as were the Eastern–Central European thinkers who began to see beyond totalitarianism during the 1970s, as well as a number of recent scholars who had not been caught up in totalitarianism directly. But there was little consensus among them. Some featured what has ended, others ongoing dangers. Moreover, the discussion of political priorities in the wake of totalitarianism betrayed certain limits, even a tendency toward overreaction that fed the wider loss of nerve.

Although he was concerned with an epoch of fascism, not totalitarianism, and although some of his key terms do not convince, Nolte suggested clearly what it would mean to conceive fascism as "epochal," emerging at a particular moment in time but also confined to a finite era as the conditions of possibility dissolved or were surmounted. Even though the Soviet regime survived the Second World War, up to a point totalitarianism was surely epochal in his sense, characteristic of the era of the two world wars, bound up with the special features of the First World War and its subsequent, highly idiosyncratic impact on three very different countries at this particular moment, and encompassing the competitive interaction between the Communist and the fascist experiments.[8]

Nolte usefully sought to specify in very particular terms the sense in which the epoch of fascism ended with the Second World War. Indeed, he found Nazism, as the most radical face of fascism, to have been nothing less than the death throes of the old order, which Nolte characterized as "the sovereign, martial, inwardly antagonistic group." Not simply by destroying fascism, but by opening the way to nuclear weapons, new modes of equality and freedom, and new forms of organization on both the international and domestic levels, the Second World War brought about the definitive end of the epoch. Sovereignty and war could not be extolled as such in the same way thereafter. Differentiation and stratification persisted, but nowhere did the ruling class derive its self-image from its opposition to the ruled.[9] It simply was no longer possible to be martial, sovereign, or inwardly antagonistic in the same way.

Still, although he found the epoch to be over in one sense, Nolte concluded that we will "have finally passed into a postfascist era" when we have fully accepted the liberating potential of modernity, which turned out to require meeting an array of complex conditions that he did not fully specify.[10] At the same time, although his response was not merely triumphalist, his account presupposed a master narrative, positing a modern emancipatory process, that is now called into question. So although Nolte was usefully explicit in one sense, his criteria of ending/continuing proved to be at once vague and limited.

We have long found the mainspring of totalitarianism in some variation on utopianism, fanaticism, escape from freedom, or intolerance of ambiguity and multiplicity. The spin could be somewhat positive: even as fanatics, the totalitarians were at least idealists of a sort; or, more negative: the totalitarians could not handle the openness of the modern world.[11] Although ahistorical psychological propensities were obviously implicated, this tradition generally assumed that central aspects of modernity—freedom, openness, secularization, insecurity—actualized those propensities. This was especially likely under idiosyncratic situations of national difficulty. Even insofar as the underlying fuel was some ahistorical utopian human longing for an end to suffering and injustice, that longing could apparently take political form only with the secularization of the modern Enlightenment break, which made it seem possible actually to change the world. So even the utopian impulse can be taken as historically specific in that sense.

In a similar vein, Isaiah Berlin suggested that we find proto-totalitarian implications in the expectation or demand that, with rationality assumed to be universal, all good things, all desirable ends, fit together in a unified system. This notion obviously fed images of utopian social transformation. For Berlin, the antidote was to grasp the heterogeneity of ends and thus the importance of the freedom to choose. The heterogeneity of ends means that conflict and tragedy are never wholly eliminated.[12] From this perspective, the question of continuing/ending is whether we have learned that lesson, or whether some, at least, have yet to do so—perhaps are incapable of doing so.

Many recent students of totalitarian and ancillary impulses find evidence that the earlier fuel has largely dissipated. For Abbott Gleason, Elie Halévy's "era of tyrannies" seems indeed to have ended, at least if we define tyranny in the historically specific sense that Halévy intended. The utopian aim of social transformation has fallen away, and we settle for more traditional statist ambitions instead.[13] As Gleason put it: "Along with the pervasive loss of faith in the statist Left has come, in recent years, a more subtle loss of faith in revolutions to accomplish major and lasting social change in the world, especially through the application of state power."[14]

In the same way, Zygmunt Bauman, even as he stressed that modern bureaucracy continues, found the essential historically specific fuel for Nazism and, by implication, for the wider totalitarian departure of the era to have spent itself. With "the dissipation of the great gardening vision," we no longer seek to devise a perfect society. And thus "the great world-garden has split into innumerable little plots with their own little orders."[15] This smaller scale affords greater scope for Bauman's version of morality, taking face-to-face human encounter as archetypal. Healthy human moral impulses again limit what we are prepared to do to each other. Although not ruling out a return to totalizing visions, Bernard Yack found reason to believe that a new premium on partial reforms and even partial revolutions was resulting from our changing cultural self-understanding.[16]

Even while warning that it might not be definitive, Emilio Gentile noted that the tendency to sacralize politics is receding in the West, partly, although not exclusively, because it has been discredited by totalitarianism.[17] Leszek Kolakowski carried the point a step further. Having himself turned from Marxism a few years before, he traced German Nazism and Soviet Communism, as the two most malignant tyrannies of the century, to Marx and Nietzsche in an essay of 1976. In their different ways, each thinker had fostered a sense of the limitless scope for human self-creation, even self-perfection, while Christianity had weakened in proportion to the universalization of that Promethean faith. Nietzsche had hated Christianity precisely as a confession of human weakness. Much like the array from Gleason to Bauman to Yack, Kolakowski concluded that the Promethean urge appeared to have "passed its zenith." He too was attributing the totalitarian departure to the hubris of perfectibility—and assuming that we had put it all behind us. He went on to suggest that although the weakening of that urge will not necessarily mean a revival of Christianity in traditional forms, it newly fertilizes the soil from which Christianity has always grown.[18]

For all these thinkers, at least implicitly, this waning or ending of the utopian impulse resulted especially from the disastrous outcomes of totalitarianism itself. Indeed, Gleason drew his conclusion largely from the experience in the Soviet bloc, which, as we noted in Chapters 5 and 8, revealed that the assumptions and aspirations underlying totalitarianism could simply dry up as the results of the new mode of action became clear. That fact suggests the extent to which the totalitarian departure rested not simply on ahistorical psychological propensities but on a historically specific vision and aspiration. But precisely *as* historically specific, the idealism could dissipate, and the fact that it seems to have done so would seem to suggest that we have indeed left the totalitarian possibility behind.

Martin Malia, in contrast, traced modern totalitarianism not to such recent figures as Marx and Nietzsche but to an *abiding* utopian impulse, even as he noted that only historically specific modern conditions afforded the scope to try to realize it. So, more cautionary than Gleason, Malia warned against inferring from the Soviet outcome that such utopian politics is finished. Human suffering continues, new and genuine problems intrude themselves, and the utopian impulse springs eternal—indeed, said Malia, is even desirable, despite its inherent dangers. The exaltation of the oppressed at the root of Marxism will continue. The question was what might lead to a comparably salvationist metaphysics that, in turn, could feed something like a new totalitarian politics. Writing in the early 1990s, and fully recognizing the historical specificity of his own perspective, Malia found in "South–North" conflict, in ecological concerns, and in the impulses fueling the various contemporary liberation movements real problems that could readily nourish such a salvationist and neo-totalitarian orientation. Perhaps, he concluded, the Soviet outcome would inoculate us against such extremes, but should a contingent, unforeseen crisis comparable to 1914–18 again befall us, there was no telling what might happen.[19]

By addressing proportions and probing supranational, historically specific content, we found that the totalitarian departure cannot be understood as some utopian effort to transcend the mechanisms of this flawed, frustrating, merely historical world. Conversely, ahistorical suffering surely continues, but it was weak as a source of the totalitarian impulse. Even on the level of national triggering, in Italy and Germany it was not simply greater suffering that produced the originating aspiration or the content of the proffered alternative. Such suffering was more obviously significant in Russia, but even there, the

Communists ended up embracing a mode of collective action that, for a time, elicited enthusiasm on quite different grounds. And the eventual loss of confidence stemmed not from a generic failure to overcome suffering or injustice, whatever that might mean. Nor did it stem from the more specific failure to devise a viable economic alternative to capitalism. Rather, the loss of confidence stemmed from the evident incapacity to mobilize, to sustain enthusiasm, and to act over the long term envisioned.

Just as the totalitarian departure cannot be traced to utopianism, neither was its source in some intolerance of freedom, ambiguity, or the heterogeneity of ends. The new historical consciousness at the root of that departure did not posit the scope for bringing all good things together but recognized ongoing openness and risk. Karl's Popper's way of framing the issue in terms of "the open society and its enemies" has comparably thrown us off. Totalitarianism was not primarily about *closing* society but about seizing the opportunity for a new mode of action in the face of an inherently open and uncertain history. Insofar as we locate the totalitarian departure in whatever variation on utopianism or intolerance of ambiguity, the question of ending/continuing is too easy. We too readily take whatever fueled totalitarianism to have ended, or we at least find it possible, with Malia, to draw relatively clear, thick lines.

Mark Roseman, Omer Bartov, and, with part of his argument, Zygmunt Bauman usefully pointed beyond this syndrome in pinpointing ongoing conditions of possibility that were more deeply historically specific, bound up with continuing aspects of modernity itself. As we noted in Chapter 1, Roseman suggested that wider interwar innovations that had *seemed* modern and progressive, but that had paralleled Nazism, were quietly buried in the aftermath, rendering Nazism all the more incomprehensible in light of the now-sanitized modern tradition.[20] To recognize that we have sidestepped aspects of modernity that prompted the Nazi response was to open deeper questions about ending/continuing. And Roseman's diagnosis suggested the need for greater reflexivity and self-criticism as we ask those questions.

But Roseman quickly resorted to the now-familiar notion of modernity as "domination." As one of its defining features, modernity has seemed to invite the will and scope for control with a good conscience, thanks to the self-confidence that expertise affords. What continues, it would seem, are modes of domination perhaps more differentiated and insidious than we had earlier recognized, in light of our sanitized, triumphalist view of modernity. But our inquiry suggests that the totalitarian response to modernity was not merely to embrace the increased scope for domination. So even as he outlined with particular insight the limits of the earlier way of relating Nazism to modernity, Roseman settled for an alternative that invited a delimited range of new questions.

For Bartov, still more explicitly, the core phenomenon was supranational and historically specific, and the epoch from within which it became possible is by no means over. He noted that what particularly befuddles us about Nazism, with its "incredible mixture of detachment and brutality, distance and cruelty, pleasure and indifference," was precisely the explosive, historically specific interface between modern expertise and "ancient prejudices, hatreds, and violent instincts."[21] In light of our emphasis on layers and their interface in the present study, we note that the abiding ahistorical propensity might have remained latent, even largely harmless, but, as a result of the modern admixture—interfacing with idiosyncratic national factors—that propensity became mobilized, brought to bear in a particular way. And what continues for Bartov is not just those ahistorical impulses but certain aspects, suddenly central with the First World War, of that historically specific modernity. With the Holocaust one outcome, those conditions continued in the several post-1945 instances of genocide, in which physicians and lawyers remained central. Such focus on domination and expertise as the core of the ongoing totalizing potential of modernity has fed the premium on disruption and "little politics" among those seeking firmly anti-totalitarian alternatives.

At least some of the continuing atrocities that bedevil us surely stem partly from the modern processes that Bartov had in mind. Moreover, the indispensability of doctors, lawyers, and other experts to the Holocaust and other totalitarian outcomes has become a commonplace. But the mere availability of experts is obviously a very weak condition of possibility, as are instrumental rationality, bureaucratic momentum, and even the practices readily labeled "domination." We need more differentiation, more steps, a thicker process of connections from the Enlightenment break to the Holocaust and beyond to grasp how each played its role in totalitarianism. Indeed, such factors throw us off if, taking them as the keys, we fail adequately to probe what else was—and might still be—at work. The point is not simply that we still have experts and bureaucrats and even social engineers, or that we would be better off without them, but that insofar as we understand their place in the quest that produced classic totalitarianism, we can more deeply question their place in our wider ongoing collective action. Conversely, although we problematize a wider array of present categories in locating the historically specific side of what continues in expertise, or bureaucratic momentum, or specifically modern "domination," we must problematize a still wider range if we are to grasp the ongoing risks and possibilities.

Even as he focused especially on the modern bureaucratic syndrome, Zygmunt Bauman related a particularly wide range of historically specific factors to the question of lessons and ending/continuing. Thus his wider framework remains especially valuable. Although he found the gardening impulse to be dissipating, he worried that historically specific dangers continued precisely because we had yet to learn the lessons of the Holocaust, a paradigm-shattering event demanding a radical rethinking of the sources of morality. So we must grasp how specifically modern factors affected the human moral sense in ways that not only helped to make the Holocaust possible but that remain dangerous on some level. Bauman found the problem to be bound up with the ongoing modern confidence in social science and instrumental reason, which not only had fed the Holocaust itself but, in continuing, have compromised our ability to learn from the experience. And, by implication, to put totalitarianism behind us required a different cultural self-understanding, replacing the modern overemphasis on social science and instrumental rationality.

The value of the most immediate lesson that Bauman drew from the Holocaust—the danger of the ongoing modern tendency, not confined to formal bureaucracies, toward distancing and segmentation—is surely beyond dispute. In assaulting the Durkheimian conception of morality, moreover, he complemented the prescriptions he had developed earlier, before turning to the Holocaust, for the cultural alternative, based on a kind of humanistic hermeneutics, that he found necessary.[22] But because, as we noted in Chapters 2 and 7, he did not account adequately for the implication of the ethical in totalitarianism and the Holocaust, and because he believed the immediate imperative to be to restore the face-to-face conception of morality he derived from Levinas, even Bauman's treatment of ending/continuing could carry us only so far. We miss too much about ending and continuing if we confine our consideration of modernity, totalitarianism, and the Holocaust to his axes of concern.

So whereas those like Roseman, Bartov, and Bauman, in stressing the historically specific, point us usefully beyond those emphasizing utopianism or other ahistorical propensities, the sense of the historically specific proves to be delimited in each case. Thus further categories are needed. At the same time, such accents as theirs, suggesting that Nazism was "modern" after all, seemed excessive to scholars from Jeffrey Herf to Michael Burleigh who insisted that, in the last analysis, the problem with Nazism was not a surfeit but a deficit of Enlightenment rationality.[23] From this perspective, Nazism, wound around irrational racism, was an atavism, not an alternative modernity based on alternative, arguably more rigorous forms of *both* rationality and domination.

But the question of whether Nazism was modern and rational or atavistic and irrational traps us in an either/or dualism and thus throws us off. The uses and limits of Enlightenment rationality, even what counted as rational and modern, were themselves at issue as totalitarianism emerged. Neither the Nazis nor the other totalitarians sorted it all out clearly, but neither have we. Although Bartov, in noting the combination of modern expertise and ahistorical hatreds and instincts, usefully indicated the uncertainty of the mix, his categories, like those of Roseman, were not broad enough to encompass the counter-insights of those like Herf and Burleigh. Yet the categories of these latter scholars were comparably restricted because, even as they too eschewed mere triumphalism, they missed the historically specific and potentially "modern" place of impulses that they were quick to take as merely reactionary or atavistic.

With their accent on the singularity of Nazism, Burleigh and Wippermann showed convincingly that the Nazi race-hygienic impulse could not be attributed to some generic modern tendency. They were on the right track in suggesting that it stemmed instead from a self-appointed elite, consumed with hatred and intoxicated with violence and the prospect of going beyond conventional morality in pursuing what it took to be therapeutic.[24] But they failed to consider the historical specificity of this syndrome, which, although surely singular, emerged from within a wider cluster of great political responses. We have seen that it was less an atavism than a way of dealing with the new demands and expectations concerning collective action. Thus the ongoing danger is not merely atavistic hatred but the wider, historically specific propensity that we have found to have been at work in Nazism.

Hannah Arendt remains archetypal among those who have taken totalitarianism as at once novel, manifesting a specifically modern crisis, and an ongoing danger.[25] More systematically than those considered above, she sought both to pinpoint the specifically modern, and continuing, conditions of possibility and to show how learning from the totalitarian departure could help us to minimize the scope for something comparable. Her reading proved more differentiated than some that came later because it located the origins of totalitarianism not simply in Enlightenment modernity but in a break from within the ongoing modern deployment, in light of experience to that point. Indeed, for that reason her reading still indicates the direction for the questioning that is necessary. Moreover, because of her more differentiated sense of the problem, she gave more explicit attention to the positive side of the solution, seeking to specify not just what was to be headed off but the changes in our positive self-understanding necessary to proceed in a fully post-totalitarian way.

Although Arendt asserted an ongoing threat without much explanation in her book on totalitarianism, the basis of the claim and the nature of the danger emerged more clearly in her subsequent works. In *Eichmann in Jerusalem* she linked the danger to the superfluousness of perhaps an increasing number of human beings, thanks especially to the convergence of the population explosion and the advent of automation. Under the circumstances, even labor power becomes superfluous, and we might "be tempted to exterminate all those whose intelligence quotient is below a certain level."[26] The unprecedented can become precedent, and now that simply killing the superfluous had been done, its recurrence seemed potentially more tempting—and thus more likely. Because she found prevailing juridical concepts and legal systems inadequate to deal with such administrative massacre by the state, Arendt sometimes seemed to suggest that establishing a wider framework of international penal law was the key to heading off any such recurrence. But certain historically specific frameworks or mentalities are surely more likely than others to open the way to this sort of mass killing, so there is something deeper to be headed off. And Arendt's wider enterprise made clear her sense that the problem was not simply the scope for mass murder resulting from human superfluousness. Thus new institutions or legal systems, even the most visionary, could not afford a sufficient antidote.

As Margaret Canovan has shown, concern with the ongoing possibility of something like totalitarianism proved central to Arendt's whole intellectual enterprise.[27] And even as she emphasized the historical specificity of the problem, Arendt found that that solution required rethinking the nature and purpose of the political sphere itself, for the totalitarian departure seemed to have revealed the inadequacy of our whole tradition of political thought.

Canovan nicely summarized Arendt's sense of the underlying phenomenon to be understood: "The special danger of modernity, as [Arendt] saw it, was that those who felt the impulse to act tended to look for some kind of irresistible trend to side with, some natural or historical force with which they could throw in their lot. She would later diagnose this as the fundamental sin of totalitarianism, but it was a danger that she saw on all sides."[28] Totalitarianism was thus but one manifestation of the ongoing modern tendency to surrender to inhuman or natural forces while pursuing grandiose aims, even omnipotence, necessarily at the price of human plurality and spontaneity.[29] What Arendt found at work, more specifically, was what Canovan called, in a passage worth quoting again:

> a uniquely modern combination of determinism and hubris. Totalitarians simultaneously committed two errors that might on the face of it seem to be incompatible: on the one hand they were determinists, surrendering human freedom to the march of forces they believed to be irresistible; on the other hand they were, in their restless activism, convinced that "everything is possible." The point (as Arendt sees it) is that modern men are tempted to purchase unlimited power at the cost of siding with inhuman forces and giving necessity a helping hand.[30]

As examples of the inhuman forces to which we seem willing to surrender, Arendt had in mind the seemingly irresistible momentum of technology, as with nuclear energy in her own time, and even economic growth. We accept these as forces beyond our decision, to which we must conform our priorities and actions, yet we feel a sense of power, even omnipotence, in doing so.[31] As an antidote to this two-sided modern tendency, Arendt offered, in Canovan's words, "a humanist message of political commitment: commitment to take responsibility for what was happening in the world instead of surrendering in the face of supposedly inevitable trends, and commitment to face up to reality instead of escaping into private or collective fantasies."[32]

For Arendt, then, totalitarianism was one mode of response to the kinds of challenge that continue in a world that seems "in motion," fundamentally historical, as never before. The first key was thus to consider the changing sense of how we collectively are caught up in history, with the implications for political action that followed. More generally at issue was the nature and the range of collective decision, the possibilities and dangers that opened up, in such a world. For as we have stressed, this world has seemed to present us newly—and endlessly—with novel challenges requiring collective decision. As with economic growth and technological progress, we may conceive such phenomena as overarching historical tendencies or forces in motion and conclude that power, and even virtue and rationality, lie in surrender to them, in lining up with them.

Arendt cut to the right level in suggesting that the ongoing danger, *and* the scope for learning deeper lessons, are bound up with the place of human agency in a world that has come to seem more deeply historical in this sense. The key was to specify an alternative that addressed what the totalitarians had sensed about the challenges and possibilities. That alternative had to address the modern tension that Canovan had in mind in juxtaposing determinism and hubris, surrender to necessity and restless activism.

Arendt found it not merely facile but deeply counterproductive to celebrate conventional liberalism in light of the totalitarian experience. We have learned nothing insofar as we simply invoke individual interests, private satisfactions, and negative freedoms or move on to the pluralism of "interest group liberalism." Even securing individual rights is not sufficient. Not only had conventional liberalism been unable to prevent the totalitarian departure, but its weaknesses had actively fed that departure in ways that, she felt, had yet to be adequately understood.

Before considering the uses and limits of Arendt's prescriptions, let us note that her ideas remained central to efforts to rethink politics in light of totalitarianism even as Communism began to decay in the Soviet bloc, and even as the ensuing collapse of Communism bred further triumphalism in the Western mainstream. Although it did not rest, as did Arendt's, on historical analysis of the whole totalitarian epoch, the post-totalitarian thinking that we saw emerging in parts of the Soviet bloc by the 1970s had its own angle on the ending/continuing question—and, if anything, tended to frame it in still more troubling terms. Certainly, thinkers like Adam Michnik, Václav Havel, and Milan Kundera offered no fuel for liberal triumphalism even as they pinpointed the rot in Communist totalitarianism. Decaying totalitarianism revealed ongoing modern totalist tendencies also to be found in the West, but because the East-Central Europeans had experienced those tendencies in garish form, close up, they were especially equipped to prescribe solutions for the whole modern world.[33] For Kundera, the experience of decaying Communism was only the latest phase of the extremely concentrated history that has enabled Central Europe to see beyond the modern mainstream; in Central Europe, most basically, "a lucid form of skepticism has arisen in the midst of our era of illusions."[34] Such arguments betrayed an element of special pleading and even myth making, as had those of the pioneers of totalitarianism in Russia, Italy, and Germany. But there was also a measure of plausibility in the East-Central European claim to be positioned, thanks to idiosyncratic experience, to see wider modern dangers, risks, and possibilities that the triumphant liberal mainstream missed.

The danger was not simply the possibility of recurrence; rather, it was immediate, reflected in present, continuing practices. Kundera began his novel *The Book of Laughter and Forgetting* with the totalitarian control of memory, of the past itself, through enforced forgetting as, with important individuals airbrushed out, even photographs become lies. But he suggested elsewhere that even this notorious, seemingly quintessential totalitarian practice might simply reveal in ludicrous form a wider modern tendency, for, as Kundera put it, "perhaps our entire technical age does this, with its cult of the future, its cult of youth and childhood, its indifference to the past and mistrust of thought."[35]

Havel traced modern totalism to the arrogant anthropocentrism that has resulted from our unprecedented departure from God, our loss of metaphysical certainties. Such anthropocentrism has yielded an impersonal, irresponsible juggernaut of power that produces the sometimes obvious, sometimes hidden mechanisms of totality. This mechanism was producing comparable alienation under state socialism and capitalism; indeed, Havel found people to be manipulated in infinitely more subtle ways in the West. Still, the lurid forms of decaying totalitarianism were especially revelatory—and offered a warning to the Western mainstream. Modern totalizing power tends to reduce individuals to helpless, undifferentiated cogs by means of advertising, manipulation through television, and a consumerist value system that literally "demoralizes," undercutting any sense of societal responsibility.[36] From within this framework, even stable categories and written histories tend simply to serve the power of the victors.[37]

The challenge was clear: man "must extricate himself from this terrible involvement in both the obvious and hidden mechanisms of totality."[38] But in light of all that the decaying communism of East-Central Europe had revealed, it was essential to think beyond mainstream Western mechanisms. There was no evidence that Western democracy could offer a satisfactory alternative for East-Central Europe; even parliamentary democracy could be no more than a transitional step.[39]

Kundera's conclusions were still more skeptical about the scope for any constructive form of politics in the modern world. Indeed, totalitarian practices brought home the weightlessness of history that, Kundera suggested, we moderns have uniquely come to feel.[40] In *The Unbearable Lightness of Being*, first published in 1984, late Communism reveals in sharp relief the texture of the historical world and the stuff of which we construct its public memory. It is a world of capriciousness, contingency, and unintended consequences, in which street names change, the police make unforeseen uses of our photos and the truths we tell them, and the public dimension forever escapes our control.[41] Under the circumstances, public and private are mutually implicated, and communication itself becomes problematic as words fail to convey what was intended. For Kundera's Sabina, "having a public in mind means living in lies." There can be truth only in private, even in secret.[42]

No wonder that history—whatever sense we have of being caught up in history—is anything but the source of the weight we might seek. On the contrary, as Kundera saw it "history is as light as individual human life, unbearably light, light as a feather, as dust swirling in the air, as whatever will no longer exist tomorrow."[43] Rather than suggesting that what we do might have enduring weight, positively affecting what the world becomes, Kundera proposed that "our only immortality is in the police files."[44] Insofar as history is the mode of remembrance as opposed to forgetting, it conflates with public lies, with "official memory," as "written by the victors." Instead of weight we have what Kundera calls "kitsch" in the original sense, excluding shit, contradiction, everything unacceptable.[45] By no means confined to late Communism, kitsch is what becomes of everything we do, including all politics, in the modern world.

In *The Unbearable Lightness of Being*, Kundera was especially concerned with the "Grand March"—shorthand for one especially prominent form of political kitsch. Although it sometimes seems to encompass any accent on history, faith in the Grand March characterizes especially the leftist orientation to which Kundera himself had earlier subscribed but that proves to rest on the facile assumption that all good things fit together, that there could be liberty and justice for all.[46] Having once produced Communism, the modern Grand March had come, by the early 1980s, to yield an equally simplistic anti-Communism. Thanks to kitsch, the Left was able sheepishly to reclassify the Soviet Union as an obstacle to the Grand March and move on.[47]

Overreaction and beyond

Kundera contributed to the wider cultural reaction against historical-mindedness that resulted especially from the totalitarian experience and the apparently ongoing danger of totalism in the aftermath. Indeed, many found a species of totalism to have been a corollary of the new orientation toward history that had helped to define modernity. Pondering the dilemmas of Holocaust memory and commemoration, James E. Young followed Reinhart Koselleck in noting that "even the notion of history as a 'singular collective'—that is, an overarching and singularly meaningful history—is a relatively modern concept."[48] Whereas previously there had been only particular histories of this or that, history as a singular collective became conceivable only in the eighteenth century. As part of the break into modernity, this notion was itself merely historical, historically specific, even contingent—and bound up with hopes for a better world, even redemptive, salvationist aims. To unify history, making it total, was apparently to posit an *a priori* meaning, some telos of freedom, justice, and redemption.

The eruption of totalitarianism, and especially the Holocaust, has seemed to belie, even to shatter, any notion of a unified, meaningful history and thus the scope for orienting ourselves, understanding what we do, in historical terms. Discussing Daniel Libeskind's Berlin Jewish Museum of the late 1990s, Alois Martin Müller noted with approval that Libeskind had "felt obliged not to build a revelatory monument to the 'good' in history, but to keep open a shaft for a historical crime perpetrated in the name of history." And Young, concurring, noted that "by resisting continuous, homogeneous history-housing, Libeskind never allows memory of this time to congeal into singular, salvational meaning."[49] In much thinking along these lines, the implication has been that we have become appropriately postmodern, rejecting or transcending the modern historical sense, especially because of totalitarianism and the Holocaust.

Writing as Soviet-style communism was beginning to collapse, Jeffrey Goldfarb embraced the East-Central European claim of wider relevance in light of ongoing modern dangers and pointed toward a species of postmodernism as the antidote. The West betrayed forms of totalizing thinking and "legitimation through disbelief" that, while by no means identical, were comparable to totalitarian forms in ways that had been missed.[50] Goldfarb claimed to discern the contours of a new third way, beyond the experiences of both East and West, in a synthesis of the new East-Central European thinking and Arendt's earlier ideas about the meaning of politics in light of totalitarianism.[51] He featured Arendt's way of positing freedom, in response to totalitarianism, not as negative and private but as constituted by politics and bound up with action in public, in inter-action with others. But equally valuable was her post-totalitarian sense of limits, which Goldfarb found congruent with, for example, Kundera's accent on self-limitation and ambivalence in stressing the need for both political action and reflection on the limitations of political action.[52]

From this overall perspective, totalitarianism was an extreme form of an ongoing modernism, and to become postmodern is to see beyond triumphalism to grasp that totalitarianism and the modern liberal mainstream shared a capacity and will to domination. It is essential to modernity that concentrated power is bound up with totalism, domination, and a certain embrace of history; it cannot be used in some constructive but non-totalist way. There can be no collective responsibility or responsible collective action that avoids the snares of totalism and domination. Short of quasi-religious disengagement, the appropriate response—the antidote—is a kind of ritualistic disruption of any crystallization of power. Virtue is not bound-up with historical-mindedness but lies in resisting or dissolving an inherently totalizing historical-mindedness. This mode of response feeds a premium on personal edification and gesture as opposed to any premium on collective history making.

In this light, postmodernism has embraced a very different Nietzsche than Leszek Kolakowski had in mind in linking Nietzsche to Nazism. As a prominent prophet of postmodernism, Georges Bataille, noted in 1938, most of Nietzsche pointed beyond the delimited sphere of political action altogether. Indeed, Nietzsche valued, in Bataille's terms, everything beyond the flag and the senseless butchery before which it advances, everything that can be an object of laughter, ecstasy, or sacrifice.[53]

This influential cluster of post-totalitarian ideas operated on the appropriate level and was usefully anti-triumphalist, but it proved to be delimited as a way of addressing historical-political possibilities in light of totalitarianism. Reflecting an inadequate grasp of original totalitarianism, this thinking betrayed uncertainties, tensions, and unwarranted conflations concerning history, necessity, human agency, and collective action in ongoing modernity. Its diagnoses and prescriptions at once reflected and nourished the wider loss of nerve that helps to keep us from a more fully post-totalitarian political culture.

Pinpointing such limits, in light of a deeper understanding of historical totalitarianism, shows what must be clarified and specified. The challenge is to address what continues and ends, or could end, more convincingly on the same level as original totalitarianism, even as we recognize that literal revival is not the issue. How might we adjust to a purely human world while eschewing not only totalitarianism itself but the wider ongoing totalist arrogance that troubled Havel and so many others? How might we encompass the sense of futility, the absurdity of unintended consequences, that led Kundera to posit the weightlessness of history even as we also find a place for power and collective responsibility—but without presupposing some "grand march" or lapsing into liberal triumphalism? Only insofar as we have addressed those questions do we begin to discern how we might proceed in a more fully post-totalitarian spirit, at once humble and constructive.

Much like Havel, Arendt took it for granted that a loss of transcendence is a defining condition of modernity. The retreat from foundational philosophy was the other side of the same coin. Finding ourselves without transcendent guide-posts, we come to recognize that it is up to us to construct whatever moral and political order there is. In doing so, we judge and act without rules from outside and with no guarantee that we get things right.[54] The question, in our terms, is how we go about it in a fully post-totalitarian way. We can hope to do so only insofar as we recognize that the totalitarians were not merely irrationalists, nihilists, or adventurers but, with varying degrees of lucidity, had come to precisely the premise that Arendt would later articulate—that it is up to us. They felt themselves to be facing up to that, and the specifically modern challenges that follow, as the mainstream was not.

For Arendt, the task was bound up with human freedom, which entails a capacity to initiate the new and unpredictable. This capacity is the other side of the world's capacity for novelty, its endless provisionality and incompleteness. There follows a shared, collective human responsibility for what the world becomes. Freedom, then, was not simply a private realm to be protected; rather, freedom was constituted by politics and bound up with action in the public sphere, which afforded the space for free interaction with others.[55]

Arendt tended toward a kind of neo-republicanism as an alternative to *both* liberalism and totalitarianism. As Canovan put it, Arendt "was trying to graft the existentialist sense of the open future that always lies before each individual on to classical republican images of citizens standing shoulder to shoulder in defence of their common freedom."[56] But what was the point of such freedom and free interaction in this more deeply historical world? How do they relate to our exercise of collective responsibility in action, and how are we to understand the relationship between what we do and the endless coming to be of our partic-ular world in history?

Although Arendt was on the right track in fastening upon an oddly bifurcated and tension-ridden historical sense in original totalitarianism, the dichotomies in Canovan's characterization quoted above—determinism and hubris, surrender to necessity and restless activism—do not get at the combination of opportunity and shrillness we found at work. Nor do they adequately characterize what has continued or suggest the terms of the ongoing challenge. We saw that even as she linked the emergence of totalitarianism to a new historical sense, Arendt was quick to trace the totalitarian impulse back to Marxism and social Darwinism, as prior totalist "ideologies of motion," then to stress the putative totalitarian deter-mination to force history, confirming the ideological supersense, by creating readily mobilized automatons. Having encountered the limits of those notions in the preceding chapters, we stressed instead the post-ideological dimensions of the totalitarian departure. But thus we face more difficult questions about ending/continuing. Deeper ending would entail a rejection not merely of ideo-logical thinking, whatever its practical corollaries, but of modes of collective action based on a more subtle, post-ideological understanding of human respon-sibility and its exercise, although still in light of how we are caught up in history. In this sense, again, only insofar as we address the issue and find an alternative on the same level do we move fully beyond totalitarianism.

Just as what we discover through our experience of totalitarianism is not simply the inevitability of choice or the folly of utopianism, neither is it simply to "take responsibility," eschewing some "surrender to necessity." Totalitarianism itself stemmed precisely from a new sense of the need to seize responsibility, to choose, to act collectively, based on the new sense of the human place in history. Indeed, it is not too much of a stretch to say that the totalitarians saw themselves as embracing precisely the imperative that Canovan attributed to Arendt: "commitment to take responsibility for what was happening in the world . . . commitment to face up to reality instead of escaping into private or collective fantasies." Doing so seemed to require not surrendering to necessity, or settling for the *laissez-faire* interplay of immediate individual interests; rather, it required a radically new mode of collective action, a concerted effort to shape history. World making had come to seem more deeply dependent on, and open to, such concerted human effort than ever before. Thus, for example, the Nazis would address population issues through radical new forms of action rather than simply talk, as the parliamentary politicians had done. And such action required the courage to transcend certain conventional ethical principles, as well as such notions as "the rights of man."

From this perspective, the ideological fantasy lay on the other side—in the Christian and/or humanitarian belief that all human life was equally worthy when, by some seemingly obvious measures, it was not. *That* was not facing up to reality. *That* was not accepting human responsibility in what now loomed as a purely secular and historical world. In retrospect, to be sure, aspects of totalitarianism appear precisely as "escaping into . . . collective fantasies"—into all that we associated with myth making in the preceding chapters. But, as we saw, the escapist side of myth was largely the outcome of a dynamic stemming from the effort at a new, putatively responsible form of action. The wider totalitarian departure was not simply a quest for some such escape.

A deeper understanding of that departure forces us back from the too comforting dichotomy between humanistic commitment and responsibility, on the one hand, and some surrender to determinism and/or irrational activism, on the other. At issue was—and is—precisely how to conceive, and collectively exercise, that human responsibility, how we go about deciding and acting. For human responsibility *is* in some sense collective, as are decision and action, and individual morality or virtue is implicated on each level. Yet even as Arendt emphasized openness and responsibility, humility and a tragic sense, her way of conceiving the exercise of that collective responsibility proved to be prejudicial and limiting.

As is well known, Arendt's thinking about human action reflected both her debt to and her reaction against Heidegger, who had lumped together humanism, historicism, and technology, thereby conflating human collective action with fabrication, and who, on that basis, had ended up denigrating the political realm.[57] As Richard Bernstein has argued, Arendt paralleled Hans-Georg Gadamer in developing aspects of praxis and phronesis that Heidegger had concealed.[58]

Reacting against Heidegger's conflation, Arendt famously distinguished between labor, work, and action (or praxis) as she outlined the meaning of political activity. Politics, she insisted, presupposed a plurality of individuals, each capable of initiating, of creating, in concert with others, and thus it required an open public space for debate. As the highest form of human action, politics was thus at once individual and collective. But although Heidegger had carried the point too far, Arendt agreed that the modern embrace of technology had affected our understanding of politics and political action itself. Blurring the distinctions, we had become caught up in fabrication, confidence in the scope for shaping through technology. "Surrender to necessity" was the other side of the same coin. By implication, the concomitant weakening of the autonomous political capacity had opened the way for totalitarianism and remained central to the ongoing danger.

But in seeking to specify the appropriate alternative, Arendt tended to portray the self-assertion of plural individuals as an end in itself rather than connecting individual response to collective decision and historical world making. Even as she stressed the scope for novelty, she worried that to understand action as history-making was to invite hubris and anthropocentric fabrication, understood as some inherently violent effort to shape the world. Indeed, Arendt explicitly conflated any accent on world making with violence and totalitarianism. So even as she departed from Heidegger, the pull of his problematic helped to restrict the range of her thinking. She was playing down or turning from modes of collective shaping that need not be conflated with technology or instrumentality.

Arendt's priorities reflected not only her engagement with Heidegger but also her understanding of the bases of totalitarianism, as was clear especially in her critical treatment of Marx. Indeed, she explicitly suggested that "Marxism could be developed into a totalitarian ideology because of its perversion or misunderstanding of political action as the making of history."[59] In the same vein, she was quick to conflate rationality with deterministic historical blueprints that demand or justify violence.

All in all, Arendt minimized the scope for collective action that might be understood, and experienced, as history-making in a post-totalitarian way. To be sure, in pondering the scope for resistance to Nazi atrocities, she stressed the great potential value of examples like Anton Schmidt, a German army sergeant who had assisted Jewish partisans in Poland for five months until he was arrested and executed in 1942.[60] Her sense of the difference that it would have made had more individuals acted comparably helped to feed her emphasis on moral purity, which was not merely self-justifying but exemplary, capable of inspiring those who followed. Futile though they might be on the immediate level, such actions can have practical effects in the long run. However, such effects do not presuppose *collective* action; nor do they stem from, or require, the actor's informed understanding of the situation in its historical specificity. It is enough that moral response begets moral response.

Although it was crucial that we create and preserve a free political space, for Arendt that space proved to be less the sphere of ongoing collective response to historically specific problems than the arena for differentiated individuals to act in ways that establish their individuality. Although it requires the interaction and recognition that the public political space makes possible, such individual self-assertion proves to be close to an end in itself. Even in standing shoulder to shoulder to preserve the public space for free discussion, the wider purpose is not world building but individual self-assertion. The political sphere also affords the basis for leaving behind an everlasting name in the face of the oblivion that lurks in light of the tragedy of the human situation. Arendt's premium on passing on the memory of one's deeds stands opposed to any premium on the ongoing collective reconstruction of the world.[61]

Even as she showed the inadequacy of liberalism in a world that had yielded totalitarianism, Arendt's alternative fed the wider cultural premium on gesture and edification that reinforced the overall loss of nerve in light of the totalitarian hypertrophy of politics. Indeed, hers was a public sphere afraid of collective decision, largely because any accent on collective world making seemed to conflate with totalitarianism. The challenge is to outline a post-totalitarian politics that is more responsible and constructive even as we grasp the basis for Arendt's emphases on humility, pluralism, risk, and tragedy. Rather than pulling back, having lost our nerve, we proceed on the same level in a different spirit. Only thus do we become fully post-totalitarian.

Whereas Kolakowski found the soil for religious renewal in the move beyond totalitarianism—precisely as a move beyond the arrogant modern anthropocentrism that troubled Havel—Havel himself implied that there could be no turning back from the secular side of modernity. But the self-sustaining momentum of impersonal power was now in crisis, most obviously in East-Central Europe, where people had begun to see through the mechanisms and thus to grasp their own power to withdraw from complicity.[62]

Although his references to power and victors sometimes suggested the familiar bifurcation of dominators and dominated, Havel came to recognize that everyone is both powerful and powerless, both victim and supporter of the system. Thus, even totalitarianism entails universal complicity and responsibility. In his famous greengrocer example, individuals behaving *as if* they believed in the system actually become the system, as everyone going through the motions pressures everyone else to do the same.[63] But thus Havel's now familiar, seemingly revolutionary premise—the apparently powerless have the power to undermine the system simply by living the truth. The greengrocer ceases to play the game, performing rituals in which he does not believe. The ordinary people of East-Central Europe were thereby showing the modern West that we all have the power to stop being reduced to cogs. As we come to grasp the mechanisms of modern totality, the antidote is resistance, living the truth, which is constantly to disrupt systems of power. Renewal, said Havel, is a task confronting each of us at every moment.[64] Congruent with his intellectual beginnings, he sometimes characterized such resistance in quasi-existentialist terms, as a gesture of authenticity. We must avoid the trap of tactical disputes, he tells us, and simply live the truth; "the purity of this struggle is the best guarantee of optimum results."[65]

Whereas Arendt conflated history making with totalitarianism and Kundera seemed to devalue the historical sphere altogether, Havel insisted explicitly that we all contribute to the making of history.[66] He was not advocating, in other words, that we simply pull back to some "inner freedom," as if truth is possible only in private, or even in silence, as Kundera sometimes suggested. Rather, Havel envisioned a sense of positive responsibility to and for the whole. In light of modern consumerist demoralization, however, it would require a kind of existential revolution, the moral reconstitution of society, to engender that sense of responsibility.[67] But something along those lines might seem to have been precisely what Giovanni Gentile and other totalitarians had had in mind in the first place. And some of Havel's emphases pointed in the opposite direction.

The key, said Havel, was to hollow out and defuse power by simultaneously reconstituting civil society. Restoring the human dimension requires decentralization and self-management in the economy and small-scale, *ad hoc* organizations in lieu of bureaucracy.[68] Although such imperatives all sounded noble, there were tensions among them. So how would it be possible to resist power, reconstitute society, exercise collective responsibility, and avoid lapsing back into totalitarian overreach at the same time?

Although Havel recognized that on some level power and complicity are universal, his emphases suggested that the problem is power itself, with its own impersonal, totalizing momentum. Any outcome of power is a "victory"—and thus illegitimate domination. Insofar as all resultants are comparably dehumanizing, disruption becomes the archetypal expression of the ethical. But any such notion is subject to the objection that has been raised against Michel Foucault's thinking, which betrays, as Richard Rorty put it, a "crippling ambiguity" between power as a neutral, descriptive category and power as pejorative, as illegitimate domination.[69]

There may be good reason for a premium on resistance or disruption under certain circumstances, but insofar as power is not merely an impersonal totalizing force but the neutral glue making possible any world at all, disruption cannot be the privileged priority if we are to have constructive, world-making objectives. So whereas Havel also offered some more constructive imperatives, they mesh uneasily with his tendency to conceive power in the pejorative sense and to privilege mere disruption. Partly as a result, his more constructive imperatives seem at once utopian and vague. Insofar as we need an existential revolution if we are to have a sense of positive moral responsibility for the whole community, even living the truth will not suffice. And what would it mean to *exercise* that responsibility?

If, as both Arendt and Havel sometimes recognized, freedom is bound up with constructive responsibility, it cannot be merely negative, mere "freedom from"—pursued by disrupting, resisting, or extricating from systems of power. From this perspective, freedom is positive, "freedom to," and thus is inherently bound up with the exercise of power. At some point, in other words, we must concentrate power and actually use it. The issue is how, in a humble, pluralistic but still constructive way, we are to act together, even through the much-disprized state with its much-disprized but inevitable bureaucracy. So whereas Arendt and Havel certainly sought to prescribe an appropriately post-totalitarian sense of responsibility and the attendant virtues, their reluctance to think more constructively about history and collective action limited what they could offer.

In light of his still more explicit and radical denigration of history, Kundera played down any premium on political response, but he offered several alternative prescriptions. Responding to the tendency of well-meaning German admirers to view her art as political protest, Sabina insists, in *The Unbearable Lightness of Being*, that her enemy is kitsch, not Communism.[70] Futile though it will no doubt prove, an effort to resist or undercut kitsch is valuable essentially as a gesture of truth telling and self-affirmation. Also redeeming are simple acts of kindness, which Kundera contrasted with grand, often grandstanding political gestures that lead who knows where. It is more important to rescue a half-buried crow than to send petitions to the president.[71]

When decaying totalitarianism brings the texture of the public, historical world garishly to the fore, responsibility itself becomes a dead weight. Thus Tomas, in the same novel, is relieved to abandon all sense of mission or vocation, to experience the blissful lightness of forgetting and indifference.[72] Yet such personal lightness, reflecting the weightlessness of history, is itself sometimes unbearable, so through his characters Kundera moves back and forth between modes of response, exploring the paradoxical interplay of lightness and weight, naiveté and cynicism, autonomy and interdependence, mind and body. Balancing feel-good forgetting is the scope for modes of action that either resist, like Sabina's art, or that are sufficiently immediate and personal to stand alone, like rescuing a half-buried crow. But the scope for responsible collective decision and action seems to have dissolved altogether.

Brilliant though his explorations often were, Kundera's prescriptions too often rested on noble-sounding but dubious conflations, as when his Mirek says in the aftermath of the Prague Spring: "The struggle of man against power is the struggle of memory against forgetting."[73] Indeed, the familiar contemporary ways of conflating history with some grand march, of insisting that power controls memory, that history celebrates the victors, that coherence is domination, and that the ethical lies in disruption constitute a syndrome central to the post-totalitarian loss of nerve. Such notions enable us to feel superior even as they confine our sense of responsibility for the world to channels sufficiently delimited to enable us to sidestep wider questions about ongoing collective action. To be sure, moments of doubt and disruption are essential, and Libeskind's museum, for example, is widely accounted a brilliant way of encompassing the tragic absence (or near-absence) of Jews in contemporary Berlin.[74] But as indicated in the gloss by Young and Müller cited above, the wider conception of history surrounding even this project betrayed the now standard conflation and overreaction.

Bataille's way of opposing "laughter" to "senseless butchery" suggests the dualistic thinking that tends to undermine any sense of ongoing responsibility by privileging a sense of absurdity and the premium on personal gesture that it invites. Indeed, Bataille was one source of the later tendency, carried from France into wider postmodernism, to conflate historical-mindedness itself with the teleological assumptions that yield a coercive totalism. But a more accurate understanding of the totalitarian experience and its implications suggests the scope for a mode of collective action that is not merely senseless butchery, that at once fosters and draws on a sense of responsibility for the whole, for the future, for history making.

Experience, learning, and the post-totalitarian alternative

To specify a fully post-totalitarian alternative requires that we find our way beyond the unstable combination of triumphalism and loss of nerve to a deeper understanding of the continuing modern situation—both its limits and its possibilities. A better grasp of the negative—the risks and dangers, the mode of action to be avoided—helps us better to understand the scope for proceeding in a constructive way. Conversely, a better sense of our constructive possibilities helps us better to box out the negative.

Writing well after totalitarianism, Benjamin Barber usefully noted that "politics is what men do when metaphysics fails." Democracy, he went on, is the form of interaction for people who cannot agree on moral absolutes.[75] At the same time, Barber viewed conventional liberal democracy as a thin theory taking democratic politics as a means to exclusively individualistic and private ends, with little concern for civic virtue, participatory citizenship, or public goods. Barber was more optimistic than Arendt about the scope for reforming the democratic tradition, but he had been much less concerned about the continuance of the historically specific conditions of possibility for totalitarianism. The question, then, is the scope for such a new democracy in a fully post-totalitarian mode. If it is to eschew triumphalism, loss of nerve, *and* the totalitarian temptation, that new democracy must reflect an understanding of the whole totalitarian trajectory, grasping all that led the totalitarians, also acting without such guideposts, to reject conventional democracy as a mode of decision, but also grasping how their way of seeking post-liberal involvement and public goods led to excess.

So the first requirement is simply to learn more deeply from the totalitarian experiment itself. This requires not only that we reverse the ahistorical circle in our approach to the totalitarians but also that, on the basis of a deeper, more reflexive sense of our own historicity, we consider how what we learn can orient us for ongoing collective action.

Even as we find less that is ahistorical, including rights and values, to sustain us, we may grasp, with Arendt, our freedom and creativity, our collective capacity to initiate. As a result of those attributes, history does not merely manifest ahistorical possibilities but yields genuine novelty. But thus we are caught up in a situation that is more deeply historically specific than we had recognized—perhaps wanted to recognize. Still, that situation is open to human understanding—on a basis to be considered more fully below. What we have as we proceed is not only our creativity and moral sense but our capacity to learn from history, from our own collective experience. We learn not merely about the scope for actualizing ahistorical possibilities but about the terms of the historically specific world in which we find ourselves.

In our effort to learn more deeply from totalitarianism, we found it essential to sort out sameness and difference more explicitly. Up to a point, we can account for difference in terms of nationally specific factors and for both sameness and difference in terms of ahistorical factors. But in our tendency to overplay those factors, we miss the significance of continuing supranational, historically specific conditions of possibility. Eschewing the Othering, moralism, and triumphalism that take a certain mode of difference for granted, we have sought to understand the responses of people who, when they started out, were not so different, so *Other*, from us. However, the point is not simply that we all confront the same human condition or that we are all sinners capable of evil—or the aggressiveness that troubled Freud. Nor, conversely, does the sameness lie in some abiding axis of *differentiation*, the recognition that there are always fascist or totalitarian types among us, or that the utopian aspiration recurs, or that some people seek escape from freedom and the security of a prison. Although ahistorical sameness is also part of the equation, the key is that we remain caught up in much the same supranational, historically specific experiment that the totalitarians were, the same historical-political channel that opened up at a particular moment from within the broader, ongoing age of politics. From within that channel, the potential for collective responsibility expanded in ways that had not been imagined before. So to learn from the totalitarian episode, we must recognize that we are dealing with people who, starting out, faced comparable challenges on the basis of—swallow hard though we must—comparable moral capacities. In that sense, the experience of our totalitarian predecessors remains *our* experience.

We saw, in fact, that idiosyncratic contextual factors enabled the totalitarians to bring to the fore tensions and possibilities that were less visible elsewhere. Thus those agents addressed, in innovative if often extreme ways, aspects of the modern situation that the mainstream had not addressed—and that we may still prefer to sidestep. The totalitarians were out in front, most basically, in having faced up to the novelty of the situation resulting from the historical-political break. On that basis, they were contemptuous of the smug democracies, which had not grasped the extent to which, the sense in which, modern human beings were on their own in a more deeply historical and open-ended world. It was no longer possible to rely on scientific reason, or suprahistorical values and rights, or tradition and precedent. Yet the need and the scope for collective action seemed to expand dramatically precisely as the world came to seem more open-ended. So it was essential to forge a new instrument for such action—and the means to do so seemed to be available.

In a world that remains in motion, demanding collective decision and action and offering at least the potential for *expanding* collective responsibility and reach, we face the same kinds of questions and challenges. Insofar as we open to this historically specific sameness, we are much better able to learn from the totalitarian experience. Understanding the sense in which, caught in the same channel, we are necessarily responsible and history-making helps us to overcome the confusions concerning power, totalism, and history that have bred the loss of nerve and the premium on mere gesture and disruption. At the same time, we realize that because we are acting within a history that is more open-ended than we had recognized, things can go badly wrong as a result of what *we ourselves*, as opposed to some Others, might do.

In better grasping the historically specific sameness, we understand that the undoubted difference is not to be characterized in such static dualistic terms as moral/immoral, rational/irrational, normal/abnormal, or modern/atavistic. To understand them in a more deeply historical way is to discern how they *became* different, how the differences emerged historically from within the ongoing channel, as a result of the strongly contingent dynamic that ensued from their effort. We saw even that anti-Semitism became central to the Nazi experiment not from ahistorical hate or out-group hostility but from a sense of opportunity and responsibility that seemed to warrant new modes of scapegoating and preclusion. Up to a point, then, we must understand the difference at issue as a resultant of the totalitarian experiment itself, as opposed to ahistorical and idiosyncratic national factors present from the outset.

That historically specific divergence became deeper than we are initially prepared to grasp. "It was a different time," said one of the now notorious "ordinary men" of Hamburg Reserve Police Battalion 101 when under interrogation in the 1960s. He was seeking not so much to make excuses but simply to account, even to himself, for his participation in events that by then had come to seem incredible. It was a different time precisely because he and his fellows were caught up in a dynamic that had led to this unforeseen situation, which not only invited their active participation but made them capable of thinking and acting in genuinely different ways—ways that they themselves would earlier have not thought possible. As we saw in Chapter 7, grasping the emergence of the difference through a historical process from within a historically specific framework affords an antidote to the tendency, evident even in Christopher Browning's notable work, to rely too heavily on universal psychological mechanisms. An insistence that anyone could have done it under comparable circumstances obscures the central role of becoming different.

Insofar as the difference at issue was more historically specific and less ahistorical than we have recognized, that difference could indeed end—even more dramatically than we would have expected—via historical experience itself. We noted that Daniel Jonah Goldhagen drew the ridicule of critics like Ruth Bettina Birn when he credited the victors' re-education efforts after the Second World War for the sudden dissipation of what he took to be the longstanding German eliminationist anti-Semitism.[76] But a measure of change there surely was, and however we assess the weight of the causal factors, there was unexpected scope for change because on the aggregate societal level the difference from us lay not in some specifically German anti-Semitic propensity but in the Nazi departure itself, which had yielded a particular dynamic and a frame of mind that was merely provisional and even potentially ephemeral, depending on what experience itself revealed. With the collapse of the great political enterprise, much of what had fueled both the upsurge of anti-Semitism and the sense of the scope for radical action in fact dissolved. It is arguable that the Germans, more than most, have continued to value ethnic homogeneity, but because they were no longer seeking to act collectively in the same way, they no longer assigned the same priority to exclusion.

This deeper grasp of the place of sameness and difference enables us better to understand what is to be guarded against and, ideally, put behind us. Insofar as we overplay ahistorical sameness at the expense of historically specific sameness and *becoming* different, we miss the generating force and how it may continue in us, how we may continue it. Although racism and anti-Semitism are surely to be guarded against, preoccupation with doing so may lead us to miss the deeper, more general dangers as we continue within the same channel. And only insofar as we address the more general dangers and challenges can we draw thicker lines around the earlier experience and proceed in a positive spirit.

A deeper understanding of sameness and differences also enables us to reverse the ahistorical circle in our approach to "neo-fascism." By conflating, through ahistorical psychological categories, what we call neo-fascism with the earlier forms, we fail to understand what is novel and distinctive in the more recent phenomena at issue and thus even the danger they may pose, or manifest, in some of their guises. The neo-fascists depart from the present mainstream partly in their way of relating to historical fascism. But they also necessarily relate to the deeper ongoing process in a very different way than did historical fascism itself.

The skinhead types fasten upon the symbols and trappings of original fascism even as they know the outcomes—and know that original fascism has become for the mainstream something like the incarnation of evil. Indeed, they play upon and define themselves partly in terms of our eagerness to "other" them as we do. But to embrace something that had already come into the world, only to be defeated and discredited, is altogether different from creating it for the first time, not knowing the outcome. Although obvious and trivial in one sense, it is crucial that the original fascists did not have the same historical experience as a baseline. Even the Nazis, energized though they were by the sense of going beyond conventional good and evil, did not start by embracing something finished and widely deemed evil in the same sense. To embrace the trappings of what the mainstream takes to be evil manifests a very different historical-political sense. This syndrome is not another actualization of an ahistorical possibility but something new, different, itself historically specific, and not "neo" at all. In embracing a kind of warmed-over evil, it is perhaps merely pathetic, although it may portend something dangerous on its own terms.[77]

Although Renzo De Felice, in his famed interview of the mid-1970s, obviously could not address the questions that more recent neo-fascist phenomena have brought to the fore, he seized upon the very different sense of place in history to stress the radical novelty of neo-fascism. Rather than striving, at least, to develop a new political thought, the neo-fascists offered only "a demoniacal affirmation of their own personalities, of their own egos, against everything else." As opposed to struggle for the future, De Felice found "dramatic powerlessness," with fanaticism an end in itself, surrounded by a sense of doom, catastrophe, tragic pessimism, and impending death. Such neo-fascism often entailed a putative embrace of mystical Christianity that was utterly antithetical to original fascism. De Felice thought it no accident that Julius Evola, one of the central figures in this neo-fascism, had been extremely marginal to original fascism.[78]

Nevertheless, concerns about the new Right of the 1990s persuaded Roger Griffin that it was essential to subsume these newer phenomena within generic fascism if they were to be understood and headed off. Thus he was led to stretch and thin his influential earlier definition of fascism and, on that basis, to insist on the contingency of aspects of interwar fascism long taken as definitional. As Griffin had come to see it, the enduring core of "fascism" is a sense of contemporary decadence and a vision of palingenesis that can take many forms and pose an array of dangers—dangers that, he feared, our preoccupation with historical fascism would lead us to miss. Even the "imminence" and "populism" that he emphasized earlier were no longer essential to the fascist ideal of palingenetic rebirth. The modes of action of "lone wolves" like Oklahoma City bomber Timothy McVeigh were as "fascist" as those of the classic regimes. The difference lies merely in what the circumstances allow.[79]

But the original fascist departure rested crucially on a sense of *imminent* possibility, bound up with a new historical-political sense. It entailed a belief that power could be concentrated for new collective action, and it became what it did because it actually concentrated and used power as it did. Moreover, in its quest for a new mode of interaction between leaders and led, fascism was not merely contingently but *essentially* "populist," although also anti-democratic. Insofar as systematic opposition is *not* populist in this sense, insofar as there can be no *collective* response, something other than fascism is at work.[80]

Even a contemporary ideology of racial supremacy cannot be merely conflated with the Nazi view as an instance of the same ahistorical propensity toward "hate" or out-group hostility. By now, to insist on the importance of racial differentiation, not to mention white or "Aryan" superiority, means something different from comparable accents seventy-five years ago. We have had much more experience, including—although not remotely limited to—Nazism itself, and we have probed the issues further. Race thinking no longer has the same degree of seeming plausibility, as scientific, warranted by those credibly taken as experts, as it did then. Although concerns about assimilation, consensus, and the value of tradition are not to be reduced to psychological maladjustment, it is by now less plausible, in light of experience, to find ethnic homogeneity a prerequisite for an effective polity in a mass age. The proportion of ahistorical hate or paranoia in expressions of racism is surely far greater now than before; present-day racism is more justifiably attributed to an ahistorical psychological propensity.

The mutually reinforcing tendencies to view both classic fascism and neo-fascism in terms of ahistorical categories impede understanding of the contours of the ongoing political experiment. Insofar as we take the lesson to be to guard against warmed-over evil or ahistorical hate, to ward off the fascist types, even to keep the Finis and Haiders out of power, we fail to probe deeply enough the supranational, historically specific conditions of possibility of classic fascism, and we cannot grasp what continues and what has been, or might be, superseded on the historically specific level. Thus we cannot assess the possibility that some new departure, different from but comparable to "totalitarianism," would come from within us and not those different Others. Nor, conversely, do we do justice to what is novel in the various "neo-fascisms", the dangers, the new potential for evil, they may manifest *even* insofar as the conditions for classic fascism or totalitarianism have been surmounted.

Our totalitarian predecessors, caught up in the new channel with its seemingly expanded opportunity and responsibility, began to encounter unprecedented choices and decisions in light of trade-offs that newly confronted them. It was partly because of questions concerning population and welfare, labor relations and the interface between politics and economics, that the totalitarian mode of action came to seem required in the first place. Once the issues came to consciousness, it was obvious that they demanded decisions, that decisions were *necessarily* being made, even as they might seem to be sidestepped on the immediate level from within the liberal framework. For once the possibility of an alternative decision had dawned, even an unspoken decision to leave such matters private clearly entailed societal consequences—and thus trade-offs. Although in retrospect we may believe we see a rational or moral basis for such decision, any such basis was not, could not have been, so obvious to them. They could not have known how to make such decisions; they could only experiment through trial and error, pursuing new directions, probing, pushing the trade-offs at issue.

Comparably on our own, facing the same kinds of questions, there is much we have by now decided about what we do or do not do, partly in light of their experience. In pulling back from eugenics, for example, we have decided certain things that had not comparably been settled when the totalitarians began to address what seemed the outstanding challenges to them. In this sense, we have made ourselves different, up to a point. But we tend to misconstrue the basis of our decisions, assuming that we have decided as we have because we are moral, rational, normal, or modern and they were not, or that they were ideological and we are not. Not only do such assumptions feed the triumphalism and Othering that compromise our capacity to learn, they keep us from recognizing that, caught up within the same channel, we too are at risk as we face our decisions. And we magnify the risks insofar as, assuming *we* have access to an ahistorical rationality or moral framework that *they* eschewed, we fail to recognize what in fact we are doing. Although informed by further science up to a point, our decision, in pulling back from eugenics, is arguably no less "ideological" than its contrary. We have moved on in the only way possible, through collective ethical-political decision informed by our understanding of that earlier phase of the ongoing experiment. In making the decisions we have, we have established another historically specific layer that helps sustain to us as we move on from here. Only insofar as we face up to what we necessarily do can we specify the cultural self-understanding from within which we can do it most effectively, minimizing the dangers of totalitarian—or totalist—excess.

But we also face and will continue to face comparable questions that have *not* been decided. The public–private distinction remains permeable, and it is not clear where lines are to be drawn in light of the increasing recognition of the public costs and consequences of private behavior, the ongoing acceptance of societal responsibility for individual welfare, the scope for various forms of societal engineering, the value of pooling risk through insurance, and the scope for some collective mandate as to what insurance must encompass and who must be covered. In light of shared health costs, we have agreed to laws restricting smoking and requiring seat belts, but we now encounter questions about the right to obesity, about modes of healthcare rationing, and about responsibility for child rearing and the social costs of doing it badly. Biomedical advance portends ever-new possibilities for human shaping. We encounter trade-offs between property rights and environmental values and dilemmas concerning the uses and disadvantages of classification, even medical screening, according to "race" or ethnic background. Although not endless, the list is obviously extensive. Such questions are undecidable on any *a priori* grounds, whether characterized in terms of rationality or morality, precepts or rights. Yet they afford us not only the opportunity but the responsibility for collective decision, even if we sometimes decide not to decide.[81]

Understanding that totalitarianism stemmed not from utopianism or some surrender to necessity but from an effort precisely to decide and act collectively in a new way, we probe the totalitarian experience to learn about the limitations and pitfalls entailed in acting from within the continuing channel, with its ongoing demand for collective decision about a seemingly ever-wider array of issues. But in this sense, the deeper question of ending and difference remains unsettled. It concerns whether we can *make ourselves* more genuinely and permanently different from our totalitarian predecessors so that, having drawn thicker lines, we would not get caught up in something comparable. Conversely, we cannot do so unless we face the element of sameness, the ongoing nature of the challenge, the need to decide and act as opposed to invoking rights, values, or precedents. In this sense, learning, ending, and proceeding constructively are all bound up together.

Aspects of our decision making reflect not a triumphalist sense of difference but the loss of nerve that, as we noted, has opened the way to, and been reinforced by, an array of new anti-political emphases, from laughter and disruption to gesture and edification. Moreover, even as our experience of totalitarianism has helped us to decide certain issues, this loss of nerve has made us reluctant to face certain emerging or ongoing problems, from apportioning healthcare to the scope for alternative political–economic arrangements. Thus, for example, Michael Burleigh found it necessary to insist that, because the issues are in fact so different, we can and should debate questions of euthanasia without refer-ence to Nazi Germany.[82] Precisely as two-sided, then, the challenge entails not only minimizing the risks but also grasping the need and scope for ongoing collective decision and action in a constructive, post-totalitarian but non-triumphalist mode.

This more constructive orientation requires recognition of a measure of historical coherence and continuity, even taking history as a unified totality or "singular collective." However, we have seen that the conflation of historical coherence and continuity with totalism and *a priori* meaning has been central to the post-totalitarian loss of nerve. But we also noted, the overreaction involved in the post-totalitarian assault on "history." The cultural framework for a constructive but non-triumphalist post-totalitarian direction requires precisely the alternative orientation toward history that this overreaction misses.

Whereas the notion of history as a "singular collective" is indeed specifically modern, it need not entail some teleological or redemptive baggage. The totali-tarian experience has helped us to see the need to jettison the baggage, but it does not warrant jettisoning the notion of a unified history altogether. There is a singular collective history, even a totality, through which a particular finite world endlessly results through a continuous process. But that world is ever-provisional and contingent; the unity and totality are weak. The coherence and continuity entail neither some readily pilloried grand march nor some telos or *a priori* meaning. The question is the interface of human being, human moral response, even individual experience, with history understood in this weakly totalist way. The focus for the human ethical capacity in such a world is not limited to little plots or face-to-face morality, or to disruption, self-assertion, or gestures of solidarity.

It is in that sense that even Bauman's way of thinking about modernity, totali-tarianism, and the human ethical capacity proves to be limited, despite its enduring value. He was so concerned with distancing and the need for face-to-face morality that he did not attend to the place of the ethical on the level of our ongoing collective decision making. It is not enough to refer to little plots where the moral call is again loud and clear; we must think in terms of what Havel called responsibility to and for the whole—recognizing that it is a moving, future-oriented whole. The challenge lies in operating on *that* level in a fully post-totalitarian mode.

Recognizing that power will inevitably be exercised, structuring the world in some particular way, we plural individuals grasp our share of the collective responsibility for its exercise. We seek not to leave an immortal name but to shape the future through the effects of what we do. In dealing with medical rationing, for example, we surely assert our individuality in contributing to the discussion, but we understand the deeper point to be the collective decision, not the individual self-assertion. In acting, we experience history-making weight as opposed to the lightness of edifying gesture in an unmasterable world where power is everywhere but nowhere. Such participation in collective action entails risk; we never know what will become of what we do.[83] And "laughter" is surely essential as an antidote to the melancholy sense of futility we sometimes feel. But we need not lose our nerve or undermine the sense of shared responsibility for what the world becomes.

We noted that the totalitarian response entailed a particular, tension-ridden embrace of science, will, spirit, and myth that helped to produce the disastrous outcomes. And aspects of that whole syndrome remain in place. But even as we realize that we cannot appeal to suprahistorical reason or *a priori* values in coming to our collective decisions, we find, on the basis of a deeper grasp of the human place in history, that we have the wherewithal to minimize the possibility of such negative outcomes in the future. This is simply to recognize the capacity for historical understanding that falls to us precisely as the agents of our own history. Although it is *merely* historical understanding, it is adequate to prepare action in the sense of affording a rational frame for ethical response, so that what we do is neither a mere shot in the dark nor a mere gesture of personal authenticity. Whereas for Havel the purity of the struggle itself "is the best guarantee of optimum results," the sense of responsibility and weight prompts historical questioning, opens us to learning and understanding, and thereby enables us to minimize the risks as we proceed in a more rational way. Action is responsible, and it transcends the idiosyncrasy of personal moral response, precisely insofar as it is disciplined by historical understanding.

Even as Arendt stressed the importance of cognitive activity, she was prone to privilege philosophy without pondering its relationship to the mode of thinking that affords orientation for action by illuminating the actual historical world.[84] To be sure, we have come to recognize, partly through the totalitarian experience itself, that we construct our histories at least partly from evidence that may seem fatally compromised. Kundera's Tomas, recognizing that the place might be bugged, fears that the police will twist his words, quoting him out of context. And thus he notes that he has no ambition to be quoted by future historians.[85] History becomes light for Kundera partly because we reconstruct historical accounts on the basis of such dubious evidence as this.

It is surely true that historical orientation becomes much more problematic as the present stakes of historical understanding become clearer and people are airbrushed out. We may generate evidence partly with the aim of influencing future historians. But the mechanisms that concerned Kundera do not undermine the scope for true historical understanding, which rests on openness to genuine learning on the part of the inquirer. And our sense of responsibility for action, our care for what the world becomes, opens us to the historical learning that, in turn, affords the orientation we need to act. Kundera was surely right to warn that *a priori* political purposes threaten to compromise historical learning in the modern world, but any implication that we are left with nothing but cynical withdrawal or edifying gesture is part of the overreaction feeding the loss of nerve. The scope for learning depends on us.

Only once we have faced up to our place in an ongoing, weakly unified history can we learn the lessons of the totalitarian disaster and draw thicker lines as we proceed. Understanding how this aspect of our history came to be, we better grasp our limitations and fallibility. But rather than emphasizing rights, interests, and negative freedom, on the one hand, or disruption, gesture, and edification, on the other, we too focus on collective, history-making action as we grasp the ongoing opportunity, responsibility, and positive freedom that now falls to us in the modern world. Although we recognize the dangerous potential of modern power, we are not paralysed but decide and act collectively in a constructive though post-totalitarian spirit.

The question of a new radicalism

The question of what ends with the disastrous outcomes of the totalitarian experiment has a different, some might say opposite, dimension, which concerns the fate of the longstanding radical tradition with its hopes for a systematic alternative. Because that tradition fed the totalitarian departures, we are bound to ask what, if anything, is left of it, and what scope is there for thinking beyond liberalism altogether in a way informed by a deeper understanding of totalitarianism.[86] With the collapse of Soviet-style communism and the end of the Cold War, Francis Fukuyama's suggestion that we had reached "the end of history" immediately brought the issue to the forefront. This notion was often viewed as triumphalist, but somewhat unfairly, for Fukuyama grasped the narrowing of possibilities, the impoverishment of discourse, that the collapse of Communism portended.[87] Hence, whatever the immediate practical relevance, the significance of the question of what, from the earlier radical tradition, has ended, or should have ended, and what might continue, even in the face of the disastrous outcomes of twentieth-century great politics. Perhaps all that is left is the ahistorical utopian impulse or the rebellion against human misery that Malia had in mind. We tend to assume that if, through some bizarre contingency, those acting on the basis of such impulses managed to take political power, they would be doomed to comparable excess and failure. Perhaps, under post-totalitarian circumstances, a fruitful radicalism can aim only at disrupting systems of power.

Insofar as it was indeed utopianism, or the gardening vision, or totalist ideology that fed the quest for an alternative modernity, the outcomes of totalitarianism surely seem to confirm the judgements of those like Gleason and Bauman that the whole radical tradition has burned itself out. But although a sense of the scope for transcending liberalism was essential, we have seen that totalitarianism did not develop primarily from utopianism and the like. Insofar as our understanding of the historically specific sources of totalitarianism has remained incomplete, we may well have misconstrued what the totalitarian experiment revealed about the scope for a systematic alternative. We may have jumped to unwarranted conclusions about our possibilities as one aspect of the wider overreaction and loss of nerve.

Insofar as we eschew triumphalism, there may be scope even for a new radicalism, not confined to ritualistic disruption, from within a weak-totalist post-totalitarian framework, with all its attention to limits, provisionality, and risk. It would entail not some utopian quest to achieve justice, to weave all good things together, or to end history but would simply go beyond mainstream liberalism to address a larger chunk of the historically specific outcome of the overall political experiment so far. This would open a wider range of discussion about our historically specific possibilities. Recognizing the historical specificity of the present conjuncture, the new radicalism would understand any radical diagnosis and prescription as historically specific and provisional. It would thus remain open to *ongoing* historical learning, never claiming to stop the conversation. It would understand itself as one voice in a plurality, and on that basis seek dialogue, eschewing any *a priori* reductionism.[88] Attentive to risk, it would recognize that even the "existential revolution" that Havel thought necessary to nurture a wider sense of responsibility might entail something like Gentilian excess. Avoiding any such excess would be central to the challenge.

In considering the interface between the wider radical tradition and the failed great political experiment, the present study has emphasized the tension, uncertainty, contingency, and often contestation at every step. As it happened, the quest for a post-liberal alternative, reflecting a sense of the scope for a fuller realization of human possibilities, got mixed up with the hegemony of Marxism as the mainstream alternative. Certain categories, and a certain mode of diagnosis and prescription, became central—and came to seem central for all time. But with the partial disaggregation of Marxism, that quest for fuller realization became fused with "great politics," a particular reading of the possibilities and imperatives that became possible only around the end of the nineteenth century. Then the quest got fused with three particular great political enterprises, bound up with the idiosyncrasies of three particular countries, especially in light of their contingent experiences of the Great War and its aftermath. The outcomes of those three experiments then deeply affected our conception of political possibilities and priorities. Because of the complexities of that contingent sequence, the implications of its outcomes for the radical tradition are not easily pinned down.

The difficulty has been compounded immeasurably by the bitter Communist–fascist rivalry central to the totalitarian epoch. Although each was radically opposed to the liberal mainstream, their origins obviously differed, and with Marxism having become dominant within the radical tradition, it was possible to take generic fascism as merely reactionary, "radical" only in its sense that liberal institutions could no longer protect bourgeois interests, that new and extreme measures were necessary. But even if we allow fascism, too, some place within the radical tradition, it obviously originated from a very different place than Communism, and the differences in origins might still seem paramount, whether understood in filo-communist terms, as progressive emancipation versus reactionary delimitation, or in filo-fascist terms, as healthy realism versus utopian abstraction.

Earlier uses of the totalitarian category bridged the Communist–fascist gap in a way, but much of the point was to discredit the earlier departures in the name of a triumphant liberalism. As part of our effort to rethink the historical place of totalitarianism in the present study, we have revisited the relationship between Communism and fascism implicitly throughout and explicitly at several points.

Insofar as the place of the radical tradition is at issue, our way of treating them in tandem is partly to reverse the signs of the earlier totalitarian conflation. The point is not to discredit the radical tradition but to probe the scope for renewing it. This entails recognizing the depth and significance of the parallel between Communism and fascism, despite the obvious and not insignificant differences in their origins. That parallel did not stem primarily from some ahistorical propensity; nor did it entail merely the use of common instruments for radically disparate ends. Rather, it stemmed from the common venture into great politics. And to realize that *both* Communism and fascism went wrong because of the poverty of great politics is to transcend the rivalry between radicals that so long restricted questioning, with echoes still. Learning to let go, to stop fighting those battles, proves to be a crucial aspect of ending/continuing on a basis more deeply informed by our historical experience.

Only thus can we clear the decks sufficiently to reassess the place of the whole multifaceted radical tradition in feeding the totalitarian departures and their disastrous outcomes. Partly as a result of those outcomes, we have tended to sidestep not just the more widespread aspects of modernity that Roseman noted but also some of the perceived *limits* of mainstream modernity that prompted the historically specific dimensions of the radical tradition, even including the great political mode of action itself. So insofar as we better understand the whole totalitarian trajectory, we can better reassess all that prompted frustration with the modern mainstream in the first place. It was not simply the insecurities of freedom or the need to choose between competing goods or the absence of utopian justice. And the alternative was not simply a matter of living happily ever after. Even as we probe the sources of totalitarian excess, we attend to insights, criticisms, and possibilities that got marginalized as they were sucked contingently into the particular totalitarian dynamic. We thereby might ponder, in a way more deeply informed by historical experience, the interface between politics and economics and between public and private, the reach of collective responsibility and the modes of collective decision making, the relationship between collective action and individual self-realization.

The scope for fruitful reconnection, from within a weak-totalist post-totalitarian framework, with the earlier radicalism has yet to be adequately assessed. But any suggestion that a new or ongoing radicalism could *only* reflect ahistorical propensities or some utopian impulse is surely premature.

Whatever the scope for a renewed radicalism, there is surely scope for a weak totalist alternative to post-totalitarian triumphalism, on the one hand, and to post-totalitarian loss of nerve, on the other. While still positing action as history making on the basis of a shared responsibility for the world, that alternative shows how responsibility is exercised in a post-totalitarian way. This humble but constructive post-totalitarianism entails a premium on historical questioning and understanding as well as a reflexive self-consciousness about the place of that understanding in our shared decision and action. On that basis, we draw thicker lines after the totalitarian moment precisely as we learn more deeply from it. On that basis, we continue, a bit more enlightened, in its wake.

Notes

Chapter 1

1 Dan Balz, "Sweden sterilized thousands of 'useless' citizens for decades," *Washington Post*, August 29, 1997, pp. A1, A32. It is striking that this revelation was front-page news in a major American newspaper as late as 1997.

2 Claude Lanzmann, "The obscenity of understanding: an evening with Claude Lanzmann," *American Imago* 48, no. 4 (winter 1991): 473–95, especially 481, 487–8; Emil L. Fackenheim, *To Mend the World: Foundations of Post-Holocaust Jewish Thought* (Bloomington: Indiana University Press, 1994; first published 1982), especially pp. xii–xvi; Laurie McRobert, "Emil L. Fackenheim and radical evil: Transcendent, unsurpassable, absolute," *Journal of the American Academy of Religion* 57, no. 2 (summer 1989): 325–40, especially pp. 338–40; and Ron Rosenbaum, *Explaining Hitler: The Search for the Origins of His Evil* (New York: Random House, 1998), pp. xv–xviii, 281, 284–99. Dominick LaCapra found Lanzmann so obsessed with victimhood that he refused to allow the distance that might make possible a measure of understanding. See Dominick LaCapra, *History and Memory after Auschwitz* (Ithaca, N.Y.: Cornell University Press, 1998), pp. 128–38. Christopher Browning is prominent among historians who have insisted that to explain is not to forgive, that to eschew the effort of understanding is to leave the Holocaust as a one-dimensional caricature. See Christopher R. Browning, *Ordinary Men: Reserve Police Battalion 101 and the Final Solution in Poland*, with a new afterword (New York: HarperCollins, 1998), p. xx.

3 This is the subtitle of Lawrence L. Langer's notable *Holocaust Testimonies: The Ruins of Memory* (New Haven, Conn.: Yale University Press, 1991).

4 Omer Bartov notes—and deplores—what he deems the postwar West German propensity for collective amnesia, evident in the tendency to dwell on "universal evil" or human helplessness in the face of fate and thereby to eschew an encounter with the specifics of German history. His particular target is the filmmaker Alexander Kluge. See Omer Bartov, *Murder in Our Midst: The Holocaust, Industrial Killing, and Representation* (New York: Oxford University Press, 1996), pp. 87–8, 143–52.

5 A major example is the German liberal Erwin von Beckerath's *Wesen und Wenden des faschistischen Staats* (Berlin: Julius Springer, 1927); see especially pp. 146–55 on the parallels between the two new anti-liberal regimes. See also Emilio Gentile, *La via italiana al totalitarismo: Il partito e lo Stato nel regime fascista* (Rome: La Nuova Italia Scientifica, 1995), pp. 15–57, on the developing sense of competition between the new regimes and the efforts of anti-Fascists from Luigi Sturzo and Guido Dorso to Sigmund Neumann to make sense of what was going on. See especially p. 43 on von Beckerath.

6 I am indebted here and throughout to the insightful survey of the concept of totalitarianism by Abbott Gleason, *Totalitarianism: The Inner History of the Cold War* (New York: Oxford University Press, 1995). See also Peter Lassman, "Responses to fascism in Britain, 1930–45: The emergence of the concept of totalitarianism," in Stephen P.

Turner and Dirk Käsler (eds.), *Sociology Responds to Fascism* (London: Routledge, 1992), pp. 214–40, on the embrace of the new concept in an effort to make sense of the surprising new regimes.

7 For a critique of the usual distinction and a way of transcending it that informs the present work, see Hans-Georg Gadamer, "Hermeneutics as a theoretical and practical task," in *Reason in the Age of Science* (Cambridge, Mass.: MIT Press, 1981), pp. 113–38, especially p. 131. We will consider the place of antecedent ideas in concluding the present chapter.

8 In his notable exchange with Saul Friedländer in 1987, Martin Broszat elucidated the need to avoid the foreshortening or backloading that results when we proceed immediately to the Holocaust, assumed to reveal the deepest meaning of Nazism or fascism. This exchange is included in Peter Baldwin (ed.), *Reworking the Past: Hitler, the Holocaust, and the Historians' Debate* (Boston: Beacon Press, 1990), pp. 77–134; see especially pp. 115–16 for the point here. See also Jörn Rüsen, "The logic of historicization: Metahistorical reflections on the debate between Friedländer and Broszat," *History and Memory* 9, nos. 1–2 (fall 1997): 113–44. Responding to some of Friedländer's concerns, Rüsen insisted convincingly that dialogue and "a normal historical empathy," even with the Nazi period, is necessary—but not to domesticate, not to divest the era of its horrors. On the contrary, "the goal should be genuine insight . . . into the era's special terror precisely by entering into the distinctive configurations of its contemporaries' subjectivity"; see pp. 130 and especially 138–9. At the same time, Rüsen disputed Broszat's notion that moral concerns impeded historical understanding; in fact, he noted correctly, such concerns are essential to meaning and learning. See pp. 122–3 and 141–2 n. 8, such concerns, we might add, need not entail *a priori* moralism.

9 At issue is the renewed understanding of historical learning that we owe especially to the philosophical hermeneutics of Hans-Georg Gadamer, who insisted that any genuinely historical thinking takes account of its own historicity, or historical specificity: Hans-Georg Gadamer, *Truth and Method* (New York: Crossroad, 1985), p. 267.

10 Caplan found it anomalous that in the ongoing debate about the fascist sympathies of Martin Heidegger and Paul de Man, there was, as she put it, "a virtually complete silence on both sides about the actual premises and texts of fascist or Nazi ideology: as if all this were coherent, already known, yet somehow insignificant." She went on to propose that the insights of deconstruction might open the way to the deeper approach she had in mind. We need not privilege deconstruction in its narrow sense, as a method focusing on the operation of binaries, to recognize the value of Caplan's overall diagnosis and prescription. Reflexivity in the case of these political extremes simply entails deeper attention to our uses of the by now standard categories. See Jane Caplan, "Postmodernism, poststructuralism, and deconstruction: notes for historians," *Central European History* 22 (September–December 1989): 274–8. The quotation is from p. 276. Writing near the end of the fascist period, Sigmund Neumann made something like the same point as he noted that democratic practice and experience had outgrown the language through which democracy had understood itself: "Our political vocabulary is antiquated and full of misnomers." Totalitarianism had exploited the gaps, sowing confusion in the democratic camp in the process. To address the totalitarian challenge and to renew itself, democracy had "either to acquire a new vocabulary or to renew the old": Sigmund Neumann, *Permanent Revolution: The Total State in a World at War* (New York: Harper & Brothers, 1942), p. xiv; see also pp. vii, x, 306–10.

11 Michael Halberstam, *Totalitarianism and the Modern Conception of Politics* (New Haven, Conn.: Yale University Press, 1999), argues forcefully that we must get beyond conventional liberal categories if we are to learn more deeply from the totalitarian experience about the ongoing possibilities, limits, and dangers of modern politics; see, for example, pp. 39–41, 117.

12 Carl J. Friedrich and Zbigniew K. Brzezinski, *Totalitarian Dictatorship and Autocracy*, 2nd edn, revised by Carl J. Friedrich (New York: Praeger, 1966; (first pub. 1956)). Manfred Funke, "Erfahrung und Aktualität des Totalitarismus: Zur definitorischen Sicherung eines umstrittenen Begriffs moderner Herrschaftslehre," in Konrad Löw (ed.), *Totalitarismus* (Berlin: Duncker & Humblot, 1988), pp. 45–6, is especially good on the reification tendency in what became the standard use of the totalitarianism category. See also Gleason, *Totalitarianism*, pp. 124–5, and Martin Malia, *The Soviet Tragedy: A History of Socialism in Russia, 1917–1991* (New York: Free Press, 1994), pp. 12–14, on the limits of Friedrich and Brzezinski's influential work. However, it should be noted, that, especially in the 1966 edition, this account had more room for the evolution of totalitarianism than is sometimes remembered today. See, for example, Friedrich and Brzezinski, *Totalitarian Dictatorship*, pp. 107–8, 375–6.

13 Hannah Arendt, *The Origins of Totalitarianism* (Cleveland: World [Meridian Books], 1958), p. 456. For exemplary accounts of Arendt's overall interpretation, see Margaret Canovan, *Hannah Arendt: A Reinterpretation of Her Political Thought* (Cambridge: Cambridge University Press, 1992), pp. 17–62; and Gleason, *Totalitarianism*, pp. 108–13.

14 Arendt, *The Origins of Totalitarianism*, p. 318.

15 *Ibid.*, pp. 437–8, 457.

16 Leszek Kolakowski, *Main Currents of Marxism: Its Origins, Growth and Dissolution*, 2: *The Golden Age*, translated by P.S. Falla (Oxford: Oxford University Press, 1981), p. 512.

17 See especially Arendt, *The Origins of Totalitarianism*, pp. 458, 462–6, 470, for her conception of the role of ideology.

18 *Ibid.*, pp. 256–60. A significant exception to the tendency to marginalize Fascist Italy in discussions of totalitarianism was Dante L. Germino, *The Italian Fascist Party in Power: A Study in Totalitarian Rule* (Minneapolis: University of Minnesota Press, 1959).

19 Renzo De Felice, *Fascism: An Informal Introduction to Its Theory and Practice* (an interview with Michael A. Ledeen) (New Brunswick, N.J.: Transaction Books, 1976), pp. 106–7.

20 Arendt, *The Origins of Totalitarianism*, pp. 259–60.

21 See Stephen F. Cohen, *Rethinking the Soviet Experience: Politics and Society since 1917* (New York: Oxford University Press, 1985), pp. 3–37, for a probing critique of the tendency of American Sovietology to misapply the totalitarianism category during the Cold War. See also Les K. Adler and Thomas G. Paterson, "Red fascism: the merger of Nazi Germany and Soviet Russia in the American image of totalitarianism," *American Historical Review* 75, no. 4 (April 1970): 1046–64.

22 To be sure, the history of the historiography on the topic is hardly neat. Roger Griffin pointed to Walter Laqueur (ed.), *Fascism: A Reader's Guide* (1976); Stein Ugelvik Larsen *et al.* (eds.), *Who Were the Fascists* (1980); and Stanley Payne, *Fascism: A Comparative Approach toward a Definition* (1980) as examples of major works of comparison and synthesis produced during the later 1970s. However, the tendency toward nominalism by that point, after the more ambitious works of the 1950s and early 1960s, is undeniable. Two of the works that Griffin cited hardly count as syntheses, because they were collections of the most disparate contributions. Come to think of it, I contributed a piece to the volume edited by Larsen *et al.* Certainly, there was no pretense of thematic unity to the volume. It was this nominalism that prompted, for example, Tim Mason's query of 1989, which we will get to shortly, about whatever happened to "fascism" as a category of analysis. In the same way, R.J.B. Bosworth was among those who pointed to the revival of the totalitarianism model during the Reagan era see R.J.B. Bosworth, *The Italian Dictatorship: Problems and Perspectives in the Interpretation of Mussolini and Fascism* (London: Edward Arnold, 1998), pp. 224–5. However, the vigilance of Jeanne Kirkpatrick did not keep Stephen F. Cohen, Sheila Fitzpatrick, and J. Arch Getty, for example, from publishing influential works further undermining the model during the Reagan years. We will be discussing these revisionists works explicitly in Chapter 5.

23 Barrington Moore Jr, *Social Origins of Dictatorship and Democracy: Lord and Peasant in the Making of the Modern World* (Boston: Beacon Press, 1967).

24 De Felice, *Fascism*, p. 94.

25 Quoted in Michael Burleigh and Wolfgang Wippermann, *The Racial State: Germany 1933–1945* (Cambridge University Press, 1991), pp. 16, 311 n. 39. Taken out of context, this phrasing is sensational and misleading, although it dramatizes the new direction in scholarship at that point. Mommsen outlined his overall argument with particular clarity and force in "Hitler's position in the Nazi system," in Hans Mommsen, *From Weimar to Auschwitz*, translated by Philip O'Connor (Princeton, N.J.: Princeton University Press, 1991), pp. 163–88. And much of that argument remains unassailable.

26 See, for example, Sheila Fitzpatrick, *Education and Social Mobility in the Soviet Union, 1921–1934* (Cambridge, Cambridge University Press, 1979), pp. 242–6; and Sheila Fitzpatrick, "New perspectives on Stalinism," *The Russian Review* 45, no. 4 (October 1986): 357–73, along with her "Afterword: Revisionism revisited" (pp. 409–13), which concludes the important discussion of Stalinism in this issue of the journal. See also Gleason, *Totalitarianism*, pp. 140–2, for a nice summary of Fitzpatrick's place in the debate at this point.

27 See J. Arch Getty, "The politics of repression revisited," in J. Arch Getty and Roberta T. Manning (eds.), *Stalinist Terror: New Perspectives* (Cambridge: Cambridge University Press, 1993), pp. 40–62, for a good introduction to this strand of revisionism in Soviet studies. Also prominent in this revisionist current were Gabor Rittersporn and Robert Thurston, who will be considered along with Getty in Chapter 5. As we will see, there are some important differences between them.

28 See Michael A. Ledeen's introduction to De Felice, *Fascism*, pp. 7–20, on the controversy that this interview occasioned in Italy when it appeared in July 1975. For assessments of De Felice's monumental eight-volume biography of Mussolini, not quite completed upon his death in 1996, see Borden W. Painter Jr, "Renzo De Felice and the historiography of Italian fascism," *American Historical Review* 95, no. 2 (April 1990): 391–405; and Emilio Gentile, "Renzo De Felice: A tribute," *Journal of Contemporary History* 32, no. 2 (April 1997): 139–51. Each of these is generally favorable. For a more critical assessment, see Denis Mack Smith, "Le guerre di Mussolini: Riserve sulla biografia di De Felice," in Pasquale Chessa and Francesco Villari (eds.), *Interpretazioni su Renzo De Felice* (Milan: Baldini & Castoldi, 2002), pp. 29–66.

29 See Richard J. Evans, *In Hitler's Shadow: West German Historians and the Attempt to Escape from the Nazi Past* (New York: Pantheon, 1989), and Charles S. Maier, *The Unmasterable Past: History, Holocaust, and German National Identity* (Cambridge, Mass.: Harvard University Press, 1988), for assessments of the *Historikerstreit* by major English-language experts on modern German history.

30 Burleigh and Wippermann, *The Racial State*, pp. 306–7.

31 Richard Bessel, "Introduction: Italy, Germany and fascism," in Richard Bessel (ed.), *Fascist Italy and Nazi Germany: Comparisons and Contrasts* (Cambridge: Cambridge University Press, 1996), pp. 4–5.

32 Tim Mason, "Whatever happened to 'fascism'?" in Thomas Childers and Jane Caplan (eds.), *Reevaluating the Third Reich* (New York: Holmes & Meier, 1993), pp. 253–62.

33 Bartov, *Murder in Our Midst*, pp. 64–7.

34 Malia, *The Soviet Tragedy*, pp. 499–501. Malia pointed a bit beyond Talmon in insisting that although we can distinguish in principle between exclusivist, nationalistic totalitarianism and inclusive totalitarianism based on Enlightenment traditions and directed to all mankind, fascism and Communism were both outgrowths of mass democracy, for nationalism was itself a product of egalitarian democracy. But this was still within Talmon's range of questions. See J.L. Talmon, *The Origins of Totalitarian Democracy* (New York: W.W. Norton, 1970; first published 1952).

35 Malia found it ironic that the category became current in East-Central Europe precisely as it was being snuffed out in Soviet studies after about 1970 as "a pall of political correctness" gradually settled over the field. See Malia, *The Soviet Tragedy*, p. 12.

36 Michael Burleigh, *The Third Reich: A New History* (New York: Hill and Wang, 2000), pp. 7, 10–11, 14–18.

37 *Ibid.*, pp. 14, 18, 810, 812.

38 *Ibid.*, p. 1.

39 *Ibid.*, pp. 1, 751, 792.

40 Meir Michaelis, "Anmerkungen zum italienischen Totalitarismusbegriff. Zur Kritik der Thesen Hannah Arendts und Renzo De Felices," *Quellen und Forschungen aus italienischen Archiven und Bibliotheken* 62 (1982): 270–302. See especially pp. 276–7, 286, 299–300.

41 Maier, *The Unmasterable Past*, p. 195, n. 56. In one sense, this passage gives new meaning to the phrase "damning with faint praise," for it was merely tucked away in a footnote in a book on the German *Historikerstreit*. The jurist Alfredo Rocco, who came to Fascism from the right-wing Nationalist movement, served as minister of Justice from 1925 to 1932 and in that capacity became a major architect of institutional change in Fascist Italy. He will figure prominently in our discussion of Italian Fascism in Chapter 6.

42 Gleason, *Totalitarianism*, pp. 13–30.

43 *Ibid.*, p. 19. On p. 9, Gleason notes that "the philosopher Giovanni Gentile, operating in the highly abstract vocabulary of conservative Hegelianism, produced a brilliant and premonitory justification of the totalitarian state that seems amazingly like Hannah Arendt's and George Orwell's demonic visions of the later 1940s, only with the value signs inverted." See also pp. 94–5, where the basis for the link to Orwell is clearer.

44 This was to challenge even De Felice's later thinking, which had come to feature a turn to totalitarianism by the mid-1930s. For Gentile, the thrust had been present all along and affords the key to the originating and ongoing aspirations of Italian Fascism. See especially Gentile, *La via italiana al totalitarismo*. Gentile termed Giovanni Gentile the "chief theologian" in the Fascist sacralization of politics. See Emilio Gentile, *The Sacralization of Politics in Fascist Italy* (Cambridge, Mass.: Harvard University Press, 1996), p. 58. Meir Michaelis usefully countered many of the standard reasons for denying the applicability of "totalitarianism" to Italian Fascism in "Anmerkungen zum italienischen Totalitarismusbegriff," especially pp. 286, 300–2.

45 Emilio Gentile, *La via italiana*, pp. 150–1.

46 Prominent examples are Simonetta Falasca-Zamponi, *Fascist Spectacle: The Aesthetics of Power in Mussolini's Italy* (Berkeley: University of California Press, 1997); Barbara Spackman, *Fascist Virilities: Rhetoric, Ideology, and Social Fantasy in Italy* (Minneapolis: University of Minnesota Press, 1996); and Jeffrey T. Schnapp, *Staging Fascism: 18 BL and the Theater of Masses for Masses* (Stanford, Calif.: Stanford University Press, 1996). I have indicated some of the limits of this current in David D. Roberts, "How not to think about fascism and ideology, intellectual antecedents and historical meaning," *Journal of Contemporary History* 35, no. 2 (April 2000): 185–211.

47 Robert W. Thurston, *Life and Terror in Stalin's Russia, 1934–1941* (New Haven, Conn.: Yale University Press, 1996), p. xviii.

48 See, for example, many of the studies collected in Getty and Manning (eds.), *Stalinist Terror*.

49 For astute characterizations of the multiple implications of *Alltagsgeschichte*, see Mary Nolan, "Work, gender, and everyday life: Reflections on continuity, normality, and agency in twentieth-century Germany," in Ian Kershaw and Moshe Lewin (eds.), *Stalinism and Nazism: Dictatorships in Comparison* (Cambridge: Cambridge University Press, 1997), p. 318; and Bartov, *Murder in Our Midst*, p. 66. This is to nuance what seemed the findings of such pioneering efforts at *Alltagsgeschichte* as Detlev J.K. Peukert's *Inside Nazi Germany: Conformity, Opposition, and Racism in Everyday Life* (New

Haven, Conn.: Yale University Press, 1987), which tended to accent the limits of the regime's totalitarian reach. See, for example, Peukert's discussion on pp. 77–9, 188.

50 Also of note in this regard are the "Further reflections on totalitarian and authoritarian regimes" that the political sociologist Juan Linz offered in republishing a work of 1975 on the topic. Although still concerned with taxonomy and the scope for generalization well beyond the Italian, German, and Soviet regimes, Linz accented the need, and the scope, to encompass within the concept much illuminating new research—as well as the surprising collapse of the European Communist experiment. See Juan J. Linz, *Totalitarian and Authoritarian Regimes* (Boulder, Colo.: Lynne Rienner, 2000), pp. 1–48.

51 Talmon, *The Origins of Totalitarian Democracy*, pp. 6–8. Albert Camus's analysis, as he sought to account for rational and irrational forms of state terror, paralleled Talmon's up to a point. See Albert Camus, *The Rebel: An Essay on Man in Revolt* (New York: Random House [Vintage Books], 1956; first published in French in 1951), pp. 177–245. Talmon extended his historical analysis in two subsequent volumes: J.L. Talmon, *Political Messianism: The Romantic Phase* (New York: Praeger, 1960); and J.L. Talmon, *The Myth of the Nation and the Vision of Revolution: The Origins of Ideological Polarization in the Twentieth Century* (London: Secker & Warburg, 1981), published posthumously. For perspectives on Talmon's contribution, see *Totalitarian Democracy and After: International Colloquium in Memory of Jacob L. Talmon, Jerusalem, 21–24 June 1982* (Jerusalem: Magnes Press, The Hebrew University, 1984).

52 Saul Friedländer, *Memory, History, and the Extermination of the Jews of Europe* (Bloomington: Indiana University Press, 1993), pp. 106–7. More generally, from Friedländer's perspective, the difference in the respective languages of the perpetrators suggests an utterly different self-perception.

53 Bartov, *Murder in Our Midst*, pp. 87–8.

54 Malia, *The Soviet Tragedy*, pp. 9–10. Malia notes that after the mid-1960s, Soviet history was systematically rewritten in the West from an "optimistic" social perspective. Even Stephen F. Cohen, himself a leading revisionist, although of a particular stripe, criticized the tendency of those like Sheila Fitzpatrick to accent what was modernizing or progressive "while minimizing or obscuring the colossal human tragedies and material losses" of the 1930s. See Cohen, *Rethinking the Soviet Experience*, pp. 33–4.

55 Although he sought to establish a tradition of significant intellectual antecedents, even Ernst Nolte treated Fascism as fundamentally reactive, not as a revolutionary variant, in his influential *Three Faces of Fascism: Action Française, Italian Fascism, National Socialism*, translated by Leila Vennewitz (New York: Holt, Rinehart and Winston, 1966; first published as *Der Faschismus in seiner Epoch* 1963). A prominent example of the reductive approach is Arno Mayer, *Dynamics of Counterrevolution in Europe, 1870–1956: An Analytic Framework* (New York: Harper & Row, 1971).

56 See Vladimir Brovkin, *Russia after Lenin: Politics, Culture and Society, 1921–1929* (New York and London: Routledge, 1998), for a recent debunking of the Soviet experiment.

57 Stanley G. Payne, *A History of Fascism, 1914–1945* (Madison: University of Wisconsin Press, 1995), p. 494. Payne found the work of Ernst Nolte, George Mosse, Eugen Weber, and Roger Griffin essential in this respect.

58 François Furet, in his *The Passing of an Illusion: The Idea of Communism in the Twentieth Century*, translated by Deborah Furet (Chicago: University of Chicago Press, 1999), offers some of the fresh perspective that we need in light of the end of the Soviet experiment. He notes that fascism was revolutionary and not merely reactive, that it was disputing the anti-bourgeois terrain with the Communists, and that it was long viewed in terms of a double standard, reflecting the dominance of quasi-Marxist modes of understanding. See especially chapter 6 (pp. 156–208), particularly pp. 165–6, 177, 179. However, Furet is too prone to repair to Arendt's categories—the primacy of ideology and terror—to be able to advance the discussion very far. See, for example, pp. 180–2, 185, 191, 205–6.

59 Ernst Nolte addressed the relationship in an innovative way in his classic *Three Faces of Fascism*. And although he surely came too close to apologetics in updating his argu-

ment at the outset of the *Historikerstreit* in the mid-1980s, he continued to bring home the significance of the temporal congruence of these regimes.

60 For one indication, see Arendt, *The Origins of Totalitarianism*, p. 309, on the admiration for the Soviet regime on the part of Hitler and the Nazis. We will return to the issue of mutual influence and competition in Chapters 6, 7, and 8.

61 Stanley G. Payne, "Soviet anti-fascism: theory and practice, 1921–45," *Totalitarian Movements and Political Religions* 4 (no. 2), (autumn 2003): 1–62. See also A. James Gregor, *The Faces of Janus: Marxism and Fascism in the Twentieth Century* (New Haven, Conn.: Yale University Press, 2000).

62 De Felice endorsed Talmon's criteria even as he assigned Fascism, the original movement with totalitarian potential, to the Left. Disputing De Felice, Michaelis insisted that Fascism belongs on the Right, but he well articulated the need to encompass *both* the left–right distinction and totalitarianism in any effort to place Italian Fascism. See Michaelis, "Anmerkungen," pp. 287–9, 300–2.

63 Zygmunt Bauman treats "the Holocaust as a rare, yet significant and reliable, test of the hidden possibilities of modern society." See his *Modernity and the Holocaust* (Ithaca, N.Y.: Cornell University Press, 1991), p. 12.

64 By chance, Ernst Nolte and J. Arch Getty, who have been controversial precisely for claiming, in the face of moralizing pressures, to offer more genuinely historical treatments of the Holocaust and the Soviet terror, respectively, published letters side by side in the same issue of *American Historical Review*, Nolte responding to a review by Richard Wolin, Getty to a letter from Robert Conquest commenting critically on an earlier *AHR* article co-authored by Getty. In their respective letters, Nolte and Getty each usefully addressed what it means to approach these regimes in a seriously historical way, and each plausibly claimed to have done so, in the face of the facile moralism that still lurks in the discussion, seriously impeding historical understanding—and thus even the worthy moral imperative of "never again." See *American Historical Review* 99, no. 3 (1994): 1038–40; and no. 5 (1994): 1821–2.

65 "The universality of evil" is the title of David Bryce-Jones's review of Daniel Jonah Goldhagen's *Hitler's Willing Executioners* in *Wall Street Journal*, March 26, 1996.

66 See, for example, Michael Burleigh, *Death and Deliverance: 'Euthanasia' in Germany, c. 1900–1945* (Cambridge: Cambridge University Press, 1994), p. 178, where the reference to Hitler's "characteristic Chicago gangster mode" seems gratuitous. To be sure, Burleigh and Wippermann plausibly justify characterizing Nazi measures against the asocial as "criminal" because such measures had no legal basis (see *The Racial State*, p. 181), but the will of the Führer had the force of law, and the "criminal" measures at issue were quite consistent with the overall Nazi vision and program—as the thrust of Burleigh and Wippermann's account makes clear. We require still-greater nuance to characterize what we now understand to be the waywardness of these regimes.

67 See Ian Kershaw, *Hitler, 1936–1945: Nemesis* (New York: W.W. Norton, 2000), p. xvii; and Evans, *In Hitler's Shadow*, p. 120, for especially effective statements to this effect.

68 Preoccupation with the Holocaust has been more prevalent in the wider culture than among professional historians dealing with generic fascism. Stanley Payne devotes but two pages to the Holocaust in the 520 text pages of his *A History of Fascism*; see pp. 380–2.

69 Rosenbaum, *Explaining Hitler*, pp. xxii, 208.

70 *Ibid.*, pp. 290–2.

71 Berel Lang, *Act and Idea in the Nazi Genocide* (Chicago: University of Chicago Press, 1990), pp. 26–9, 32–6, 51–6, 99, 148. See Rosenbaum, *Explaining Hitler*, pp. 208–20, for his discussion of (and with) Lang.

72 Umberto Eco, "Ur-fascism," *New York Review of Books*, June 22, 1995, pp. 12–15. A slightly altered version of this piece is included in Umberto Eco, *Five Moral Pieces*, translated by Alastair McEwen (New York: Harcourt, 2001), pp. 65–88; see also pp. x–xi on the circumstances surrounding its genesis.

73 I refer to the famous studies by Erich Fromm, *Escape from Freedom* (1941), and Karl Popper, *The Open Society and Its Enemies* (1945), which account for the negative impulses at issue in very different ways.

74 Talmon, *The Origins of Totalitarian Democracy*, pp. 254–5.

75 Isaiah Berlin, "Joseph de Maistre and the origins of fascism," in his *The Crooked Timber of Humanity: Chapters in the History of Ideas*, edited by Henry Hardy (New York: Random House [Vintage Books], 1992), pp. 91–174. We might compare Stephen Holmes's effort to pinpoint "the permanent structures of anti-liberal thought," although Holmes surely took seriously the arguments of his anti-liberal adversaries. See Stephen Holmes, "The permanent structures of antiliberal thought," in Nancy L. Rosenblum (ed.), *Liberalism and the Moral Life* (Cambridge, Mass.: Harvard University Press, 1989), pp. 227–53.

76 For example, the noted American neo-pragmatist Richard Rorty simply equates "fascism" with sadism or cruelty. See Richard Rorty, *Contingency, Irony, and Solidarity* (Cambridge: Cambridge University Press, 1989), pp. 180n., 183–4. Susan Sontag's "Fascinating fascism," in her *Under the Sign of Saturn* (New York: Farrar Strauss Giroux, 1980), pp. 98–105, is a noted essay on the sexual component in the ongoing fascination with fascism in popular culture. Although concerned primarily with Italy, R.J.B. Bosworth offers some effective observations on the dubious association of Fascism with deviant sexuality, especially in film, as a way of distancing—making the Fascists not like us. See Bosworth, *The Italian Dictatorship*, pp. 165–6, 169.

77 See Chapter 7, pp. 387, 400 for a more detailed discussion and the relevant references.

78 Bauman, *Modernity and the Holocaust*, pp. 152–6.

79 Bartov suggested that forms of education, for example, or even traditions specific to German police training, might need to be considered. See Bartov, *Murder in Our Midst*, pp. 90–3. As we have noted, however, Bartov charged that strategies for avoiding the central questions of agency and responsibility were widespread in contemporary German culture; see especially pp. 139–53. However, István Deák reminds us of the complexity of this issue, noting the prominent roles of Austrians and those who had been raised in the Soviet Union in the Holocaust. See István Deák, "Memories of Hell," *New York Review of Books*, June 26, 1997, pp. 42–3. This was to suggest that we must beware of overemphasizing cultural traditions specific to Germany. The question is what else might have been at work.

80 J. Arch Getty and Roberta T. Manning, "Introduction," pp. 14–15.

81 Thurston, *Life and Terror*, pp. xvii, 228–9.

82 Bartov, *Murder in Our Midst*, p. 67.

83 Luigi Salvatorelli, *Nazionalfascismo* (Turin: Piero Gobetti, 1923).

84 Henry Ashby Turner Jr, "Fascism and modernization," in Henry Ashby Turner Jr, (ed.), *Reappraisals of Fascism* (New York: Franklin Watts [New Viewpoints], 1975), pp. 117–39.

85 De Felice, *Fascism*, pp. 46, 49, 102. See Chapter 4, p. 196, for a further discussion of this issue.

86 See especially A. James Gregor, *The Fascist Persuasion in Radical Politics* (Princeton, N.J.: Princeton University Press, 1974); and A. James Gregor, *Italian Fascism and Developmental Dictatorship* (Princeton, N.J.: Princeton University Press, 1979). Gregor has recently warned that in so far as we seek to head off neo-fascism, we must look not to the advanced but to the developing countries. See A. James Gregor, *Phoenix: Fascism in Our Time* (New Brunswick, N.J.: Transaction Books, 1999).

87 Ruth Ben-Ghiat, *Fascist Modernities: Italy, 1922–1945* (Berkeley: University of California Press, 2001), pp. 2–3, 8, 94–5, 209. This work will be discussed in Chapter 6; see pp. 293–5.

88 For Mabel Berezin, the coherence of Italian Fascism was not on the level of ideology but in its style and emphasis on action. Its ends being malleable, Fascism "repudiated the word and the text" and replaced argumentation, explanation, and rational discourse "with the primacy of feeling and emotion." And because what matters is performance as opposed to text, analysis of ritual action affords the best access to the

Fascist project. See Mabel Berezin, *Making the Fascist Self: The Political Culture of Interwar Italy* (Ithaca, N.Y.: Cornell University Press, 1997), pp. 29–30. I offer a critique of Berezin in Roberts, "How not to think," pp. 204–5.

89 In his influential study of the crisis of Weimar Germany, the late Detlev Peukert noted how hard it was for contemporaries—and remains for us—to distinguish forward-looking from reactionary impulses in responses to the outcome of modernity to that point. See Detlev J.K. Peukert, *The Weimar Republic: The Crisis of Classical Modernity* (New York: Hill and Wang, 1993), pp. 187–8.

90 Malia, *The Soviet Tragedy*, pp. 6–8, 108.

91 Geoff Eley, "The British model and the German road: rethinking the course of German history before 1914," in David Blackbourn and Geoff Eley, *The Peculiarities of German History: Bourgeois Society and Politics in Nineteenth-Century Germany* (Oxford: Oxford University Press, 1984), pp. 37–155. Eley turned to the obvious follow-up question in "What produces fascism: Pre-industrial traditions or a crisis of the capitalist state?" in his *From Unification to Nazism: Reinterpreting the German Past* (Boston: Allen & Unwin, 1986), pp. 254–82.

92 Peukert, *The Weimar Republic*, pp. 34–6, 93–4, 187–8, 271–2. See also Mark Roseman, "National Socialism and modernization," in Bessel (ed.), *Fascist Italy and Nazi Germany*, pp. 197–229, for a probing exploration of the changing approaches to the question of Nazism and "modernity." As we will discuss in Chapter 7, pp. 338–9, Roseman found Peukert's argument incomplete.

93 See Roger Griffin, *The Nature of Fascism* (London: Routledge, 1991), p. 111; Payne, *A History of Fascism*, p. 482; and Robert Proctor, *Racial Hygiene: Medicine under the Nazis* (Cambridge, Mass: Harvard University Press), pp. 223–50, for a few indications.

94 Burleigh and Wippermann, *The Racial State*, pp. 2, 39, 56, 107–8, 167, 304–7.

95 De Felice, *Fascism*, pp. 40–1, 55–6, 94–5.

96 Roseman, "National Socialism and modernization," pp. 204–5, 226–7.

97 Philip Morgan, *Fascism in Europe, 1919–1945* (London: Routledge, 2003), p. 192.

98 In *The Italian Dictatorship*, pp. 228–29, Bosworth notes that "only a purblind and recalcitrant anti-Marxist will want to think about fascism, or the history of the twentieth century, without some reference to class and its discontents." *Some* reference, to be sure, but the question is to what degree we privilege that dimension *a priori*, on the assumption that getting at some putative social "base" is the key to understanding. What else are we prepared to countenance in a non-reductionist way going in?

99 For an influential recent analysis of Fascism that, although brilliant in its way, ends up repairing explicitly to an abiding Fascist psychological type, see Eco, "Ur-Fascism," pp. 65–88.

100 Griffin, *The Nature of Fascism*, pp. 26–8, 32–9, 46–8.

101 Even Karl Dietrich Bracher's way of linking "totalitarianism" to "escape from freedom," as a response from within democracy to a broadly religious crisis, exemplified this "negative" assumption: the question is why *they* could not handle what *we* can. See Karl Dietrich Bracher, "Totalitarianism as concept and reality" (1988), in his *Turning Points in Modern Times: Essays on German and European History* (Cambridge, Mass.: Harvard University Press, 1995), pp. 143–52, especially pp. 144–5, 152.

102 Moshe Lewin, *The Making of the Soviet System: Essays in the Social History of Interwar Russia* (New York: Pantheon, 1985), p. 209.

103 Martin Broszat and Saul Friedländer, "A controversy about the historicization of National Socialism," in Peter Baldwin (ed.), *Reworking the Past: Hitler, the Holocaust, and the Historians' Debate* (Boston: Beacon Press, 1990), pp. 120–1. See also Friedländer, *Memory, History*, pp. 104, 109–11.

104 Burleigh and Wippermann, *The Racial State*, pp. 107–8.

105 For a good statement of the longstanding view that fascism was fundamentally anti-intellectual, that its intellectuals were marginal, that Italian Fascism, for example, "had few true believers who could also write articles and books," see Walter Laqueur, *Fascism: Past, Present, Future* (New York: Oxford University Press, 1996), pp. 96–7. Laqueur went on to note (pp. 219–20) the genuine idealism of classic Fascism; these were not mere gangsters. But this leaves us wondering about the relationships between ideals, ideas, and those who wrote things down. The recent work of Josep R. Llobera, *The Making of Totalitarian Thought* (Oxford: Berg, 2003), which is concerned primarily with the origins of Nazi thinking, does not tackle the wider conceptual issues concerning the importance of antecedent ideas and proves to be too impressionistic to deepen the discussion.

106 Brook Thomas, *The New Historicism and Other Old-Fashioned Topics* (Princeton, N.J.: Princeton University Press, 1991), pp. 233–34, n. 15.

107 Chester McArthur Destler, "Some observations on contemporary historical theory," *American Historical Review* 55 (1950): 504, 517.

108 Steven E. Aschheim, *The Nietzsche Legacy in Germany, 1890–1990* (Berkeley: University of California Press, 1992), p. 318.

109 Eley, *From Unification to Nazism*, pp. 233–7; see pp. 233 and 234 for the passages quoted. Another example, long notorious because of its title, is William Montgomery McGovern, *From Luther to Hitler: The History of Fascist–Nazi Political Philosophy* (Boston: Houghton Mifflin, 1941), a serious work not to be denigrated, even if those of us who find antecedent ideas crucial do not approach the relationship in the same way today.

110 Eley, *From Unification to Nazism*, pp. 235–7; Fritz Stern, *The Politics of Cultural Despair: A Study in the Rise of Germanic Ideology* (Garden City, N.Y.: Doubleday [Anchor], 1965).

111 Lang, *Act and Idea*, pp. 168–70.

112 Although the confusion has remained more or less constant, the sense of anomaly or disconnection has long been noted. George Lichtheim observed in 1965 that with uses of the "ideology" category, "one encounters a terminological vagueness which appears to reflect some deeper uncertainty about the status of ideas in the genesis of historical movements." George Lichtheim, *The Concept of Ideology and Other Essays* (New York: Random House [Vintage Books], 1967), p. 3.

113 However, Sternhell goes on to suggest that "fascism," in its pure ideological form, then got a weird second chance in Vichy France. See Zeev Sternhell, with Mario Sznajder and Maia Asheri, *The Birth of Fascist Ideology: From Cultural Rebellion to Political Revolution*, translated by David Maisel (Princeton, N.J.: Princeton University Press, 1994; original French edn, 1989), p. 256. I have argued elsewhere that Sternhell's reputation as an authority on fascist ideology has impeded our understanding of both fascism and ideology. See Roberts, "How not to think."

114 Schnapp, *Staging Fascism*, pp. 5–7. The quotation is from p. 6.

115 Aschheim, *The Nietzsche Legacy*, pp. 320, 329.

116 Bernard Yack, *The Longing for Total Revolution: Philosophic Sources of Social Discontent from Rousseau to Marx to Nietzsche* (Berkeley: University of California Press, 1992), p. xi.

117 *Ibid.*, pp. xi–xii.

118 *Ibid.*, pp. xxi–xxii.

119 Lang, *Act and Idea*, pp. 167–8. In a similar vein, Lang notes in the same discussion that "as human agents invariably appeal to reasons to explain or even to describe what they do (for this purpose it does not matter that such statements are sometimes mistaken or deceptive), so historical events more generally, if human agency has been involved in them, have an ideational form that serves retrospectively as a representation of the elements comprising the event." See pp. 165–70 and 189–206 for his overall discussion of "the affiliation of ideas."

120 *Ibid.*, p. 194.

Chapter 2

1 J.L. Talmon, *The Origins of Totalitarian Democracy* (New York: W.W. Norton, 1970), pp. 254–5. Talmon remains a baseline even as he has often been used as a foil in recent years. Claude Lefort, for example, denigrates any treatment of totalitarianism "as the product of the phantasies of revolutionary intellectuals, seeking to complete the work of the Jacobins of 1793 in order to reconstruct the world on a *tabula rasa.*" See Claude Lefort, *The Political Forms of Modern Society: Bureaucracy, Democracy, Totalitarianism* (Cambridge, Mass.: MIT Press, 1986), p. 301. Nor did Bernard Yack want any part of the sort of connection between eighteenth-century departures and totalitarianism that Talmon seemed to posit. See Bernard Yack, *The Longing for Total Revolution: Philosophic Sources of Social Discontent from Rousseau to Marx to Nietzsche* (Berkeley: University of California Press, 1992), pp. xviii–xx; see also pp. 13–15. But if Talmon fails to convince today, he at least raised the question of such "deep" or overarching connections. And whereas many simply eschew any analysis on this level, both Lefort and Yack sought to provide an alternative on something like the same level, in light of Talmon's limits. Their efforts will be central to our discussion in this chapter.
2 See Zygmunt Bauman, *Modernity and the Holocaust*, (Ithaca, N.Y.: Cornell University Press, 1992), pp. 218–19, where he argues that the new modern sense of human responsibility made possible not only Auschwitz and the Gulag but also Hiroshima. Any such conflation is especially controversial. The fact that segmentation and distancing were at work in the mass killing in each case surely need not suggest some moral equivalence.
3 See *ibid.*, where Bauman also refers to "devising the perfect world order." See also pp. 70, 91, on the "gardening" impulse.
4 *Ibid.*, p. 91.
5 *Ibid.*, pp. 93 (for quote) and 114.
6 *Ibid.*, pp. 61–2, 65.
7 Meir Michaelis, "Anmerkungen zum italienischen Totalitarismusbegriff. Zur Kritik der Thesen Hannah Arendts und Renzo De Felices," *Quellen und Forschungen aus italienischen Archiven und Bibliotheken* 62 (1982): 298.
8 Zeev Sternhell, *Neither Right Nor Left: Fascist Ideology in France*, translated by David Maisel (Princeton, N.J.: Princeton University Press, 1996; original French ed., 1983); Zeev Sternhell, with Mario Sznajder and Maia Asheri, *The Birth of Fascist Ideology: From Cultural Rebellion to Political Revolution*, translated by David Maisel (Princeton, NJ: Princeton University Press, 1994; original French ed., 1989).
9 Sternhell, *The Birth of Fascist Ideology*, pp. 192–4, 217, 223–5. See also Sternhell, *Neither Right nor Left*.
10 Sternhell, *The Birth of Fascist Ideology*, p. 251.
11 Margaret Canovan, *Hannah Arendt: A Reinterpretation of Her Political Thought* (Cambridge: Cambridge University Press, 1992), p. 42.
12 Yack, *The Longing for Total Revolution*, pp. 14–20, 75, 282, for particularly explicit expressions of this theme, which is the premise of the entire book.
13 Stephen Holmes, *The Anatomy of Antiliberalism* (Cambridge, Mass.: Harvard University Press, 1993).
14 Lefort, *The Political Forms*, p. 303.
15 Michael Halberstam's *Totalitarianism and the Modern Conception of Politics* (New Haven, Conn.: Yale University Press, 1999), part 2 (pp. 57–129) usefully questions the nineteenth-century liberal self-understanding in light of the challenges subsequently posed by totalitarianism. See pp. 49–50 for an effective characterization, following Sigmund Neumann, suggesting that totalitarianism was made possible by, and then exploited, the gaps between the liberal self-representation and reality. See also p. 68 on the limits of reason.
16 Canovan, *Hannah Arendt*, is particularly good in pinpointing the key issues. See especially pp. 22, 32.
17 Giuseppe Mazzini, *The Duties of Man and Other Essays* (London: J.M. Dent & Sons, 1907).

18 Hannah Arendt, *The Origins of Totalitarianism* (Cleveland: World Books (Meridian Books), 1958), pp. 80, 99, 113, 138–9, 146, 148–9, 230, 275. See p. 146 for the reference to Hobbes.

19 Canovan, *Hannah Arendt*, pp. 32–3.

20 Arendt, *The Origins of Totalitarianism*, p. 447.

21 Isaiah Berlin, *Four Essays on Liberty* (London: Oxford University Press, 1969), pp. 131, 136, 148.

22 *Ibid.*, pp. 162–63.

23 *Ibid.*, p. 148n.

24 *Ibid.*, p. 163.

25 As quoted in *ibid.*, p. 151.

26 John Stuart Mill, *On Liberty*, in *Mill*, edited by Alan Ryan (New York: W.W. Norton, 1997), pp. 44, 51.

27 Aileen Kelly, "Leonard Schapiro's Russia," *New York Review of Books*, September 24, 1987, p. 21.

28 Berlin, *Four Essays*, p. 130; José Ortega y Gasset, *Concord and Liberty* (New York: W.W. Norton, 1963; (original Spanish ed. 1940), p. 30.

29 Mill, *On Liberty*, p. 51.

30 Charles Taylor, "What's wrong with negative liberty," in Alan Ryan (ed.), *The Idea of Freedom: Essays in Honour of Isaiah Berlin* (Oxford, Oxford University Press, 1979), pp. 175–93, especially pp. 191–3. The quotations are from p. 193.

31 *Ibid.*, p. 193.

32 Guido De Ruggiero, *The History of European Liberalism*, translated by R.G. Collingwood (Boston: Beacon Press, 1959), pp. 351–9, 381–91, 426–9, 436, 440. Original Italian ed. 1925.

33 José Ortega y Gasset, *The Revolt of the Masses* (New York: W.W. Norton, 1957). Original Spanish ed. 1930.

34 See especially George L. Mosse, *The Nationalization of the Masses: Political Symbolism and Mass Movements in Germany from the Napoleonic Wars to the Third Reich* (Ithaca, N.Y.: Cornell University Press, 1991), p. 4.

35 Without mentioning Durkheim in this connection, Michael Halberstam pinpoints the tension that emerged once the depth of societal conditioning was recognized and earlier notions of individual consent came to seem illusory. Deeper questions about the relationship between societal well-being and individual self-realization were bound to open. See Halberstam, *Totalitarianism and the Modern Conception of Politics*, pp. 114–17, as well as pp. 125–6, for a useful variation on the same tension. Hofmannsthal's sense of the need, and the scope, to aestheticize modern liberal politics is an important theme in Carl E. Schorske's noted *Fin-de-siècle Vienna: Politics and Culture* (New York: Random House [Vintage Books], 1981); see especially pp. 15–22, 134.

36 Sheila Faith Weiss, *Race Hygiene and National Efficiency: The Eugenics of Wilhelm Schallmayer* (Berkeley: University of California Press, 1987), pp. 35–6.

37 François Furet, *The Passing of an Illusion: The Idea of Communism in the Twentieth Century*, translated by Deborah Furet (Chicago: University of Chicago Press, 1999), pp. 4–19, is good on the basis of the hatred that bourgeois society, linked to a premium on interests and money, came to elicit during the nineteenth century.

38 Arendt, *The Origins of Totalitarianism*, p. 464; see also pp. 138, 146, where the link to bourgeois capitalist dynamism is almost explicit.

39 See *ibid.*, pp. 463–4, on Marx and Darwin, accenting the convergence between them.

40 *Ibid.*, p. 458.

41 Yack, *The Longing for Total Revolution*, pp. 22–7.

42 See, for example, *ibid.*, p. 366; there are variations on this phrasing throughout.

43 *Ibid.*, pp. 27, 89, 124, 185–6.

44 *Ibid.*, pp. xviii–xx, 13–14.

45 *Ibid.*, p. xi; this is from the preface to the 1992 paperback edition, which offers a useful retrospective in light of the fall of Communism.

46 *Ibid.*, p. 366.

47 *Ibid.*, pp. 366–9.

48 *Ibid.*, p. 366.

49 *Ibid.*, pp. 286–309, on the essential disjunction in Marxism.

50 *Ibid.*, pp. 295–8, 301–4.

51 *Ibid.*, p. 300.

52 *Ibid.*, pp. 297–8. The quoted passage is from p. 297.

53 *Ibid.*, pp. 368–9.

54 David D. Roberts, *Nothing but History: Reconstruction and Extremity After Metaphysics* (Berkeley: University of California Press, 1995), chapter 4.

55 Arendt, *The Origins of Totalitarianism*, p. 458. See also pp. 407, 417–18 for further explicit discussion of the centrality of "unwavering faith" as opposed to some lust for power or profit. In addition, see Canovan, *Hannah Arendt*, pp. 25–7, 90–1, on this overall set of themes.

56 Arendt, *The Origins of Totalitarianism*, pp. 437–8, 457, 463–6.

57 *Ibid.*, pp. 325–6, 391–2, 398–9, and especially pp. 462–6 for the core point concerning ideology and totalitarian practice, accenting terror and total control.

58 Canovan, *Hannah Arendt*, pp. 12–13.

59 *Ibid.*, p. 26, refers to "an aspiration to omnipotence, the price of which must necessarily be human plurality and spontaneity."

60 Arendt developed her mature theory of labor, work, and action in *The Human Condition* (Chicago: University of Chicago Press, 1958). See Canovan, *Hannah Arendt*, pp. 122–41, for a good summary.

61 Arendt, *The Human Condition*, chapters 3 and 4; Canovan, *Hannah Arendt*, pp. 71–5.

62 Canovan, *Hannah Arendt*, pp. 76–9, 84–5.

63 Hannah Arendt, "The Ex-Communists," *Commonweal* 57, no. 24 (March 20, 1953): 597.

64 Canovan, *Hannah Arendt*, pp. 164–5; see also pp. 71, 76–7, 166 for the same conflation.

65 Canovan, *Hannah Arendt*, p. 78.

66 Lefort, *The Political Forms*, especially pp. 219–22 (1974), 286–9 (1980), 301–6 (1979). Lefort was a one-time Trotskyite who studied with Merleau-Ponty, then worked with Cornelius Castoriadis to analyze the later Soviet system. He also confessed a debt to Freud.

67 *Ibid.*, pp. 219–20, 305. Benjamin R. Barber's account of democratic politics as post-metaphysical makes much the same point from the opposite angle. We will consider this in Chapter 9; see p. 475.

68 Lefort, *The Political Forms of Modern Society*, p. 303.

69 *Ibid.*

70 *Ibid.*, p. 305. This is a slap at Michel Foucault's influential accent on power/knowledge and its variations.

71 Lefort, *The Political Forms*, p. 305.

72 *Ibid.*, pp. 222, 288.

73 This theme is central to the classic study by Robert Wohl, *The Generation of 1914* (Cambridge, Mass.: Harvard University Press, 1979). Ruth Ben-Ghiat usefully traces the Italian Fascist cult of youth to the generational thinking that began around the turn of century in her *Fascist Modernities: Italy, 1922–1945* (Berkeley: University of California Press, 2001), p. 93.

74 Quoted in Martin McCauley, *The Soviet Union Since 1917* (London and New York: Longman, 1981), pp. 72–3.

75 See Melvin Richter, "Durkheim's politics and political theory," in Emile Durkheim *et al.*, *Essays on Sociology and Philosophy*, edited by Kurt H. Wolff (New York: Harper & Row [Harper Torchbooks], 1964), pp. 172, 177, on the critiques of Durkheim's influence by Jean Izoulet and Charles Péguy.

76 Berel Lang, *Act and Idea in the Nazi Genocide* (Chicago: University of Chicago Press, 1990), pp. 183–99, 205–6, for the core of this part of the argument.

77 *Ibid.*, pp. 168–70.

78 Bauman, *Modernity and the Holocaust*, pp. 61–2, 65. See also Zygmunt Bauman, *Modernity and Ambivalence* (Ithaca, N.Y.: Cornell University Press, 1991), p. 1–15, on the modern impulse toward ordering, classification, inclusion, and exclusion.

79 Schorske, *Fin-de-siècle Vienna*, especially chapters 1 and 3. Two of Gabriele D'Annunzio's works from the period that explore these themes are *Il fuoco* (1900) (translated as *The Flame of Life*, 1900) and *La gloria* (1899).

80 Bauman, *Modernity and the Holocaust*, pp. 174–9.

81 *Ibid.*, pp. 178–9, 182–4.

82 *Ibid.*, p. 168; see also pp. 5, 7. Bauman relies especially on the notable work of Nehama Tec in making this point.

83 *Ibid.*, pp. 73, 76–7, 90, 102, 163, 184, 188.

84 Karl Dietrich Bracher, "Totalitarianism as concept and reality" (1988) in his *Turning Points in Modern Times: Essays on German and European History* (Cambridge, Mass.: Harvard University Press, 1995; original German ed. 1992), pp. 143–52. See especially pp. 144–5, 152 on de Tocqueville.

Chapter 3

1 Bernstein's key work is Eduard Bernstein, *Evolutionary Socialism: A Criticism and Affirmation* (New York: Schocken, 1961; 1st German ed., 1899).

2 Bernard Yack, *The Longing for Total Revolution: Philosophic Sources of Social Discontent from Rousseau to Marx to Nietzsche* (Berkeley: University of California Press, 1992), pp. 286–309.

3 Alain Besançon, *The Rise of the Gulag: Intellectual Origins of Leninism*, translated by Sarah Matthews (New York: Continuum, 1981; original French ed., 1977), pp. 176–83, especially pp. 177, 180–1.

4 Emile Durkheim, *The Rules of Sociological Method* (New York: Free Press, 1964; original French edn, 1895). See also Steven Lukes, *Emile Durkheim: His Life and Work: A Historical and Critical Study* (Harmondsworth, UK: Penguin, 1973), pp. 300–1, on the reaction against the notion that society is a collection of self-contained individuals.

5 Emile Durkheim, review of *Formes et essences du socialisme*, by (Francesco) Saverio Merlino, *Revue Philosophique de la France et de l'Etranger* 48 (October 1899): 433–9. The quotation is from p. 437.

6 Emile Durkheim, *Socialism* (New York: Collier, 1962), pp. 246–7; see also pp. 242–3.

7 Durkheim's most important educational writings have been translated into English as Emile Durkheim, *Moral Education: A Study in the Theory and Application of the Sociology of Education*, translated by Everett K. Wilson and Herman Schnurer (New York: Free Press of Glencoe, 1961), based on his first course on education at the Sorbonne, 1902–03, repeated later; and Emile Durkheim, *Education and Sociology*, translated by Sherwood D. Fox (New York: Free Press, 1956), a collection published posthumously.

8 Emile Durkheim, *Suicide: A Study in Sociology*, translated by John A. Spaulding and George Simpson (New York: Free Press, 1966), pp. 373–4, 378–80; Emile Durkheim, "Some notes on occupational groups," preface to the 2nd (1902) ed. of *The Division of Labor in Society* (New York: Free Press of Glencoe, 1964), pp. 1–31. See also Durkheim, *Socialism*, pp. 245–6.

9 Léon Duguit, *Le Droit social, le droit individuel et la transformation de l'État* (Paris: Félix Alcan, 1908), pp. 104, 612–18. See also J.E.S. Hayward, "Solidarist syndicalism: Durkheim and Duguit," 2 parts, *Sociological Review* N.S. 8, no. 1 (July 1960): 17–36 and 8, no. 2 (December 1960): 185–202. Among the other participants in this current were the Austrian Anton Menger and the Italians Enrico Cimbali and Giuseppe Salvioli.

10 Lukes, *Emile Durkheim*, p. 538n., on Duguit's advocacy of integrating the unions into the state.

11 Sergio Panunzio, *Il socialismo giuridico (esposizione—critica)* (Genoa: Libreria Moderna, 1906). See David D. Roberts, *The Syndicalist Tradition and Italian Fascism* (Chapel Hill: University of North Carolina Press, 1979), pp. 318–20, including references, on Panunzio's explicit use of both Duguit and Durkheim, first as he was abandoning Marxism, then during his career as a Fascist publicist.

12 In addition to the references to Durkheim's proto-corporativism in note 7 above, see Lukes, *Emile Durkheim*, pp. 536–8, on Durkheim and "administrative syndicalism."

13 This is Gordon Wright's characterization of Alain in *France in Modern Times: From the Enlightenment to the Present*, 4th ed. (New York: W.W. Norton, 1987), pp. 254–5. Wright both noted the grave demoralizing effects of this sort of individualism and denied that it was a necessary outcome of liberalism. The point for us is that the outcome of liberalism at that point was not at all clear. "Alain" was the pseudonym of Emile Chartier.

14 See, for example, Panunzio's subsequent use of Durkheim in Sergio Panunzio, *La persistenza del diritto* (Pescara: Case Editrice Abruzzese, 1910), p. 163; Sergio Panunzio, *Stato nazionale e sindacati* (Milan: Imperia, 1924), pp. 50–2 (1919) and p. 119 (1923); Sergio Panunzio, *Teoria generale dello Stato fascista*, 2nd ed. (Padua: CEDAM, 1939), p. 23. See also Roberts, *The Syndicalist Tradition*, pp. 62–3, 67, 318.

15 Gaetano Mosca, *The Ruling Class: Elementi di Scienza Politica*, edited by Arthur Livingston, translated by Hannah D. Kahn (New York: McGraw-Hill, 1939), pp. 253–60, esp. pp. 254–5, 259–60.

16 *Ibid.*, p. 481.

17 See especially Gaetano Mosca, "Il pericolo dello Stato moderno," *Corriere della sera*, May 27, 1909. Also influential was Santi Romano, "Lo Stato moderno e la sua crisi," *Rivista di diritto pubblico e della pubblica amministrazione in Italia* 2, no. 1 (1910): 97–114. In addition, see Paolo Ungari, *Alfredo Rocco e l'ideologia giuridica del fascismo* (Brescia: Morcelliana, 1963), pp. 35–9, on the significance of this prewar discussion.

18 Mosca, *The Ruling Class*, pp. 479–82.

19 For a nice short summary, see Maurice Finocchiaro, "Croce and Mosca," in Jack D'Amico, Dain A. Trafton, and Massimo Verdicchio (eds.), *The Legacy of Benedetto Croce* (Toronto: University of Toronto Press, 1999), pp. 121–4.

20 Mosca, *The Ruling Class*, pp. 479–82.

21 *Ibid.*, p. 491.

22 Vilfredo Pareto, *Les Systèmes socialistes*, 2 vols., 2nd ed. (Paris: Marcel Giard, 1926), 1: pp. 62–4, 74–5; and 2: pp. 432–9, 451–4, 460–4. See also Vilfredo Pareto, *The Rise and Fall of the Elites: An Application of Theoretical Sociology*, translated by Hans L. Zetterberg (Totowa, N.J.: The Bedminster Press, 1968), pp. 77, 82–3; Vilfredo Pareto, *The Ruling Class in Italy before 1900* (New York: Howard Fertig, 1974), pp. 82–3; and Vilfredo Pareto, *The Mind and Society: A Treatise on General Sociology*, 4 vols. in 2, translated by Andrew Bongiorno and Arthur Livingstone (New York: Dover, 1963), 3: p. 1293.

23 Pareto, *The Mind and Society*, 4: p. 1532; see also 4: pp. 1533–4.

24 Sorel's "Avenir socialiste des syndicats" is included in Georges Sorel, *Matériaux d'une théorie du prolétariat* (Paris: Marcel Rivière, 1919). See also Roberts, *The Syndicalist Tradition*, pp. 60–1, and, for Sorel on Durkheim, pp. 63 and 333, nn. 44 and 45.

25 Isaiah Berlin, *Against the Current: Essays in the History of Ideas* (New York: Penguin, 1982), pp. 317–18.

26 Such misreading is central to the argument of Zeev Sternhell, with Mario Sznajder and Maia Asheri, *The Birth of Fascist Ideology: From Cultural Rebellion to Political Revolution*, translated by David Maisel (Princeton, N.J.: Princeton University Press, 1994); see, for example, p. 118. For another, less damaging, example of such misuse of Sorel, see George L. Mosse, *The Nationalization of the Masses: Political Symbolism and Mass Movements in Germany from the Napoleonic Wars through the Third Reich* (Ithaca, N.Y.: Cornell University Press, 1991), p. 12. We will be returning to this overall issue in Chapters 6 and 8.

27 Sorel accents individual initiative in discussing "the ethics of producers," for example. See Georges Sorel, *Reflections on Violence*, translated by T.E. Hulme and J. Roth (London: Collier-Macmillan, 1961), chapter 7. Cf. Sternhell, *The Birth of Fascist Ideology*, pp. 127–8, 251. Sternhell is too quick to conflate these themes with what he takes to be subsequent fascism, including "fear of the masses."

28 Isaiah Berlin, *Against the Current*, pp. 309–11.

29 In a noted article on "the death of socialism" in 1911, Sorel's long-time correspondent Benedetto Croce suggested that if socialism were to have come at all, it would have come in the way that Sorel had described. However, Sorel had come to recognize that the unionized workers were not becoming equipped to play a special role after all. Benedetto Croce, "La morte del socialismo," *La voce*, no. 6 (February 9, 1911), 501–2.

30 George Lichtheim, *Marxism: An Historical and Critical Study* (New York: Praeger, 1961), p. 229n.

31 Besançon, *The Rise of the Gulag*, p. 195.

32 *Ibid.*, pp. 195, 281, for the passages quoted. See also pp. 160, 181, 197, and 243, for the same theme.

33 *Ibid.*, pp. 192, 206.

34 Robert C. Tucker, introduction, in Robert C. Tucker (ed.), *The Lenin Anthology* (New York: W.W. Norton, 1975), pp. xxvii, xxxiii, xl.

35 Besançon, *The Rise of the Gulag*, pp. 116, 121, 124–5, 126–35, 152, 168, 193, 226–7. See especially pp. 116, 161, 193 on the enduring importance of Chernyshevski.

36 As Besançon himself accents at several points, e.g., *ibid.*, pp. 150–1, 172–3.

37 Vladimir Ilyich Lenin, "What is to be done?" in Tucker (ed.), *The Lenin Anthology*, pp. 13 and 13n., 20.

38 *Ibid.*, pp. 13–14. Bernstein's key revisionist tract was published in Russian translation in 1901.

39 Lenin, "What is to be done?" pp. 27–9.

40 *Ibid.*, pp. 24–5.

41 Moshe Lewin, *The Making of the Soviet System: Essays in the Social History of Interwar Russia* (New York: Pantheon, 1985), p. 193; Leszek Kolakowski, *Main Currents of Marxism: Its Origins, Growth and Dissolution, 2: The Golden Age*, translated by P.S. Falla (Oxford: Oxford University Press, 1981), pp. 407–9; Alfred G. Meyer, *Leninism* (New York: Praeger, 1962), pp. 117, 119–20, 124–5, 133.

42 Kolakowski, *Main Currents of Marxism*, 2, p. 396; Besançon, *The Rise of the Gulag*, p. 184–5, 187; Tucker, introduction, pp. xxviii–xxix, xlii.

43 Kolakowski, *Main Currents of Marxism*, 2, pp. 384, 389–91, 397–8. Kolakowski also saw as dubious the scope for using the national question.

44 Tucker, introduction, pp. xxxii–xxxiii; Meyer, *Leninism*, pp. 44–7.

45 Besançon, *The Rise of the Gulag*, p. 225.

46 Mayer, *Leninism*, p. 132.

47 *Ibid.*, p. 276–7. See also pp. 279, 288, and especially pp. 290–2. For a similar accent, see Theodore H. Von Laue, *The World Revolution of Westernization: The Twentieth Century in Global Perspective* (New York: Oxford University Press, 1987), p. 87. Cf. Neil Harding's accent on the putative certainty that pertained to Leninism as a distinctive doctrine, forged, as Harding saw it, only during 1914–17. Neil Harding, *Leninism* (Durham, N.C.: Duke University Press, 1996), pp. 113–15.

48 Alex Callinicos, *Theories and Narratives: Reflections on the Philosophy of History* (Durham, N.C.: Duke University Press, 1995), p. 161.

49 Meyer, *Leninism*, p. 78.

50 Lenin, "What is to be done?" pp. 20, 22. Lenin found something comparable in the vanguard role that he believed Russian literature to be assuming at that point.

51 Vladimir Ilyich Lenin, "'Left-wing' communism—an infantile disorder," in Tucker (ed.), *The Lenin Anthology*, p. 554.

52 Vladimir Ilyich Lenin, "On the national pride of the great Russians," in Tucker (ed.), *The Lenin Anthology*, pp. 196–9.
53 Besançon, *The Rise of the Gulag*, pp. 176–83, especially pp. 177, 180–1.
54 Kolakowski, *Main Currents of Marxism*, 2, pp. 395, 417, 479–80, 506–7; Meyer, *Leninism*, pp. 35 and 35n.
55 Lenin, "What is to be done?" pp. 28–9.
56 *Ibid.*, p. 19.
57 See especially the 1919 appendix to the 4th ed. of Sorel's *Réflexions sur la violence*, published in the English edition cited above as "In Defense of Lenin," pp. 277–86. See also Georges Sorel, "Chiaramenti su Lenin," (originally published July 23, 1919), in Georges Sorel, *"Da Proudhon a Lenin" e' "L'Europa sotto la tormenta,"* edited by Gabriele de Rosa (Rome: Edizioni di Storia e Letteratura, 1973), pp. 122–6.
58 Sorel, "Chiaramenti su Lenin," pp. 124–5.
59 Kolakowski stresses the coarseness and aggressiveness of Lenin's style and notes the humorlessness of his mockery. See Kolakowski, *Main Currents of Marxism*, 2, p. 520.
60 *Ibid.*, pp. 432–41. A.A. Bogdanov, for example, sought to adapt the innovative critical positivists Ernst Mach and Richard Avenarius to historical materialism in his three-volume *Empiriomonism* of 1904–06.
61 Kolakowski, *Main Currents of Marxism*, 2, especially pp. 440–1.
62 Steven E. Aschheim, *The Nietzsche Legacy in Germany, 1890–1990* (Berkeley: University of California Press, 1992), pp. 218–19; Edith Clowes, "From beyond the abyss: Nietzschean myth in Zamiatin's 'We' and Pasternak's 'Doctor Zhivago'," in Bernice Glatzer Rosenthal (ed.), *Nietzsche and Soviet Culture: Ally and Adversary* (Cambridge: Cambridge University Press, 1994), p. 314. See also pp. 4–5 in the editor's introduction. In addition, see Bernice Glatzer Rosenthal (ed.), *Nietzsche in Russia* (Princeton, N.J.: Princeton University Press, 1986). We will note Rosenthal's more recent work on Nietzsche and Bolshevism below.
63 Kolakowski, *Main Currents of Marxism*, 2, pp. 451–8, 465. Mikhail Agursky, however, refers plausibly to "Lenin's tacit Nietzscheanism." See Mikhail Agursky, "Nietzschean Roots of Stalinist Culture," in Rosenthal (ed.), *Nietzsche and Soviet Culture*, p. 268.
64 Kolakowski, *Main Currents of Marxism*, 2, pp. 420–3.
65 Gregory Feidin, "Revolution as an esthetic phenomenon: Nietzschean motifs in the reception of Isaac Babel (1923–32)," in Rosenthal (ed.), *Nietzsche and Soviet Culture*, p. 158.
66 Kolakowski, *Main Currents of Marxism*, 2, p. 467. Kolakowski writes of catastrophic decline and disintegration by 1908–11.
67 Max Eastman and others noted Lenin's effect as a speaker. Tucker, introduction, pp. xlviii, lxv–lxviii.
68 *Ibid.*, pp. xlii–xliii, xlix, lxv–lxviii.
69 Gentile was arguably the most distinguished European intellectual to become an out-and-out fascist. For an introduction to recent scholarship, see Gabriele Turi, "Giovanni Gentile: oblivion, remembrance, and criticism," translated by Lydia G. Cochrane, *Journal of Modern History*, 70, no. 4 (December 1998): 913–33. Recent studies of Gentile in English are M.E. Moss, *Mussolini's Fascist Philosopher: Giovanni Gentile Reconsidered* (New York: Peter Lang, 2004), and A. James Gregor, *Giovanni Gentile: Philosopher of Fascism* (New Brunswick, N.J.: Transaction Books, 2001).
70 Giovanni Gentile, *La filosofia di Marx: Studi critici*, 5th ed., revised and expanded, edited by Vito A. Bellezza (Florence, C.G. Sansoni, 1974). This work was originally published in Pisa by Spoerri in 1899. See also Eugenio Garin, "Croce e Gentile interpreti di Marx," in Michele Ciliberto (ed.), *Croce e Gentile fra tradizione nazionale e filosofia europea* (Roma: Riuniti, 1993), pp. 3–13; and Giuseppe Calandra, *Gentile e il fascismo* (Rome and Bari: Laterza, 1987), pp. 33–56, on the centrality of this early encounter and Gentile's ongoing preoccupation with Marx.
71 Gentile, *La filosofia di Marx*, pp. 8–9.

72 Abbott Gleason, *Totalitarianism: The Inner History of the Cold War* (New York: Oxford University Press, 1995), p. 19. As we noted in Chapter 1, Gleason found Gentile's conception of the totalitarian state "extraordinary," "prophetic," and "brilliant and premonitory"—although also proto-Orwellian and profoundly negative. See also pp. 9, 94–5.

73 Here I differ from a major authority, Gennaro Sasso, who denies that Gentile's commitment to Fascism had any connection at all with his antecedent philosophy, despite Gentile's own pretensions to the contrary. For Sasso, what led Gentile to Fascism was a fanciful, tortured reading of Italian history that betrayed an *a priori* determination to construct a distinctively Italian tradition with special contemporary relevance. See Gennaro Sasso, *Le due Italie di Giovanni Gentile* (Bologna: Il Mulino, 1998), especially pp. 280, 286, 568–9. I have challenged Sasso's approach and sought to indicate the scope for an alternative in David D. Roberts, "Maggi's Croce, Sasso's Gentile and the riddles of twentieth-century Italian intellectual history," *Journal of Modern Italian Studies* 7, no. 1 (spring 2002): 116–44.

74 Domenico Settembrini found the ultimate inadequacy of both Croce and Gentile in their pretense to be responding to "the death of God" on a genuinely religious level, with a doctrine of salvation that was purely earthly but still total, without shadows or uncertainties of any kind. See Domenico Settembrini, *Storia dell'idea antiborghese in Italia, 1860–1989* (Rome and Bari: Laterza, 1991), pp. 260–1.

75 Augusto Del Noce, *Giovanni Gentile: Per una interpretazione filosofica della storica contemporanea* (Bologna: Il Mulino, 1990), pp. 123–94 (article originally published 1968); H.S. Harris, *The Social Philosophy of Giovanni Gentile* (Urbana: University of Illinois Press, 1966), pp. 4–7.

76 Gentile establishes the ethical implications of self-knowledge as spirit especially in his *Sommario di pedagogia come scienza filosofica*, first published in 1913 (2 vols., now available in 5th ed., revised, Florence: Sansoni, 1982). See also Calandra, *Gentile e il fascismo*, p. 176, for an effective summary.

77 Gabriele Turi, *Giovanni Gentile: Una biografia* (Florence: Giunti, 1995), p. 105; Daniela Coli, *Croce, Laterza e la cultura europea* (Bologna, 1983), pp. 77–80, 85–6.

78 E.J. Hobsbawm, "The great Gramsci," *New York Review of Books*, April 4, 1974, p. 39.

79 Gentile had already linked philosophy, history, and education in his *L'insegnamento della filosofia nei licei* (1900), the title of which he changed to *Difesa della filosofia* with the 2nd ed., 1921 (now available in 3rd ed., revised, Florence: Sansoni, 1969).

80 Gentile, *La filosofia di Marx*, pp. 94–6, 108–9. See also Garin, "Croce e Gentile inter-preti di Marx," pp. 11–13; and Calandra, *Gentile e il fascismo*, pp. 39, 42.

81 Precisely because Gentile seemed to be more provincial and idiosyncratically Italian than Croce, H.S. Harris noted that "the peculiarly 'national,' and at times almost chauvinistic, character of [Gentile's] culture and . . . genius is one of the factors that has impeded the understanding of his work in foreign countries." See H.S. Harris, introduction to Giovanni Gentile, *Genesis and Structure of Society* (Urbana: University of Illinois Press, 1966), p. 1.

82 Turi, *Giovanni Gentile*, pp. 72–4, 117–18, 128–9, 145, 147, 208.

83 Giovanni Gentile, "Veritas Filia Temporis" (1912), now in his *Il pensiero italiano nel rinascimento* (3rd ed., revised, Florence: Sansoni, 1955), pp. 331–55; see especially pp. 337–9. See also Calandra, *Gentile e il fascismo*, p. 102.

84 Gentile, "Veritas Filia Temporis," pp. 347, 350–3.

85 *Ibid.*, p. 354. On the importance of Vico for Gentile, see also Turi, *Giovanni Gentile*, pp. 72–4, 117–18, 208, and János Kelemen and József Pal (eds.), *Vico e Gentile* (Soveria Mannelli: Rubbettino, 1995). In this latter volume, see especially Eva Ordögh, "Il verum ipsum factum nell'attualismo di Giovanni Gentile," pp. 207–12.

86 Giovanni Gentile, *La riforma della dialettica hegeliana* (3rd ed., Florence: Sansoni, 1975), pp. 1–65 (especially pp. 36–9), 237–40.

87 Giovanni Gentile, *Teoria generale dello spirito come atto puro* (7th ed., revised, Florence: Le Lettere, 1987; first published 1916); translated by Herbert Wildon Carr as *The Theory of Mind as Pure Act* (London: Macmillan, 1922).

88 Benedetto Croce, *Conversazioni critiche*, ser. 2 (Bari: Laterza, 1950), pp. 67–95. See also David D. Roberts, *Benedetto Croce and the Uses of Historicism* (Berkeley: University of California Press, 1987), pp. 105–15, and Calandra, *Gentile e il fascismo*, pp. 91–105, for two of the many treatments of the Croce–Gentile split of 1913 among specialists.

89 See Gentile, *Teoria generale*, pp. 254–65, for Gentile's response to Croce's charge of mysticism.

90 Giovanni Gentile, *Saggi critici*, ser. 2 (Florence: Vallecchi, 1927), p. 29. See also Croce, *Conversazioni critiche*, ser. 2, pp. 68–9.

91 Gentile, *La riforma della dialettica hegeliana*, pp. 247–8, 256–7 (1914).

92 Giovanni Gentile, *Fascismo e cultura* (Milan: Fratelli Treves, 1928), pp. 1–15 (1918).

93 These were tendencies that Francesco De Sanctis had lamented in a famous lecture of 1869, "L'uomo del Guicciardini," now in Francesco De Sanctis, *Scritti critici*, 3 vols. (Bari: Laterza, 1969), 3: 1–25.

94 In addition to Gentile, *Difesa della filosofia*, cited above, see Giovanni Gentile, *The Reform of Education*, translated by Dino Bigongiari (New York: Harcourt, Brace, 1922). This is a translation of a series of lectures that Gentile presented to the schoolteachers of Trieste in 1919, shortly after the city joined Italy as a result of the latter's defeat of Austria in the First World War. See also Turi, *Giovanni Gentile*, pp. 91, 160, 170–2, 181–2, 187, 283–5; and Calandra, *Gentile e il fascismo*, pp. 63–6.

95 The notion was developed especially in *Fondamenti della filosofia del diritto*, 1916, then further in the new chapter 7 added to the 1931 edition. See also Calandra, *Gentile e il fascismo*, pp. 137, 145–6.

96 Especially in treating Gentile's attachment to the poetry of Giacomo Leopardi, Gennaro Sasso nicely characterized Gentile's combination of seeming assurance and underlying doubts. See Sasso, *Le due italie*, pp. 243, 445, 447–51, 455–6. See also Roberts, "Maggi's Croce," pp. 128–9.

97 Gentile, *La filosofia di Marx*, pp. 156–65, especially pp. 161–4.

98 *Ibid.*, pp. 46, 71–8, 118, 156–7. See also Calandra, *Gentile e il fascismo*, pp. 44–6. Gentile was discerning accents now familiar from certain of Marx's works of the early 1840s, works that had not been published when Gentile began trying to make sense of Marx in the mid-1890s.

99 Gentile, *La filosofia di Marx*, pp. 83, 86–92; Turi, *Giovanni Gentile*, p. 63.

100 Calandra, *Gentile e il fascismo*, pp. 49–50, 52. Gentile was surely too quick to equate materialism with an atomistic conception of society—as a mechanical aggregate of individuals—to do justice to the point.

101 Gentile, *La filosofia di Marx*, p. 84.

102 By 1913, a "school" had developed around Gentile at Palermo that included, among others, Giuseppe Lombardo Radice, Adolfo Omodeo, and Guido De Ruggiero, each soon to be a major figure in his own right. By this point, Gentile was also beginning to exert some influence abroad, most notably on the young R.G. Collingwood in England. See Turi, *Giovanni Gentile*, p. 217; and Calandra, *Gentile e il fascismo*, p. 94.

103 Stephen Holmes, *The Anatomy of Antiliberalism* (Cambridge, Mass.: Harvard University Press, 1993), p. 252.

104 Detlev Peukert, "The genesis of the 'Final Solution' from the spirit of science," in Thomas Childers and Jane Caplan (eds.), *Reevaluating the Third Reich* (New York: Holmes & Meier, 1993), pp. 237–8, 240–1, 245–6. Just before his untimely death in 1990, Tim Mason worried that biology was becoming the new paradigm in Nazi studies—one that, from his perspective, was too limited in its neglect of class, capitalism, and the structures of political and economic power. Charles Maier makes clear in his foreword to this volume that Peukert's paper occasioned controversy even at the conference at which it was presented; see pp. xiii–xv. More recently, Michael Burleigh dismissed Peukert's accent on the spirit of science as "pretentious

guff." What science is he talking about, asked Burleigh; what does he know about science? See Michael Burleigh, *Ethics and Extermination: Reflections on Nazi Genocide* (Cambridge: Cambridge University Press, 1997), p. 180. But the point is precisely the admixture of "spirit," not the science itself.

105 Paul Weindling, "The medical profession, social hygiene and the birth rate in Germany," in Richard Wall and Jay Winter (eds.), *The Upheaval of War: Family, Work, and Welfare in Europe, 1914–1918* (Cambridge: Cambridge University Press, 1988), pp. 417–18.

106 Maria Sophia Quine, *Population Politics in Twentieth-Century Europe: Fascist Dictatorships and Liberal Democracies* (London and New York: Routledge, 1996), pp. 101–2, 132.

107 Weindling, "The medical profession," p. 420.

108 Michael Burleigh and Wolfgang Wippermann, *The Racial State: Germany 1933–1945* (Cambridge: Cambridge University Press, 1991), p. 29.

109 Robert Proctor, *Racial Hygiene: Medicine Under the Nazis* (Cambridge, Mass.: Harvard University Press, 1988), pp. 15–17; Sheila Faith Weiss, *Race Hygiene and National Efficiency: The Eugenics of Wilhelm Schallmayer* (Berkeley: University of California Press, 1987), pp. 104–5; Paul Weindling, *Health, Race and German Politics between National Unification and Nazism, 1870–1945* (Cambridge: Cambridge University Press, 1989), pp. 63–89.

110 Weindling, *Health, Race and German Politics*, pp. 112–18; Weiss, *Race Hygiene*, pp. 71, 74, 90. See also Pat Shipman, *The Evolution of Racism: Human Evolution and the Use and Abuse of Science* (Cambridge, Mass.: Harvard University Press, 2002), pp. 131–3, on Ploetz and Schallmayer and the continuity from this period into Nazism.

111 Quine, *Population Politics*, pp. 66–7.

112 *Ibid.*, pp. 27–9.

113 *Ibid.*, pp. 31–3, makes it clear that this was a subject of debate among Italian economists.

114 Weindling, *Health, Race and German Politics*, pp. 393–8.

115 Michael Burleigh, *Death and Deliverance: 'Euthanasia' in Germany, c. 1900–1945* (Cambridge: Cambridge University Press, 1994), pp. 12–15; Weiss, *Race Hygiene*, p. 4.

116 Burleigh and Wippermann, *The Racial State*, p. 31. As early as 1877, Haeckel had called on the Germans to develop a common outlook around evolutionary ideas, thereby overcoming the monstrous beliefs of Christian civilization. See Shipman, *The Evolution of Racism*, pp. 94–5.

117 Weiss, *Race Hygiene*, pp. 110–11.

118 Weindling, "The medical profession," pp. 428–29. Weindling also cites other leaders who explicitly rejected the negative eugenics of Ploetz and Schallmayer.

119 Quine, *Population Politics*, p. 67; Weiss, *Race Hygiene*, pp. 136–40.

120 Stefan Kühl, *The Nazi Connection: Eugenics, American Racism, and German National Socialism* (New York: Oxford University Press, 1994), p. 4.

121 Weiss, *Race Hygiene*, pp. 91–104, esp. p. 100.

122 Proctor, *Racial Hygiene*, pp. 20–30; Weiss, *Race Hygiene*, p. 103.

123 Weiss, *Race Hygiene*, pp. 45–7.

124 Quine, *Population Politics*, p. 104.

125 Weiss, *Race Hygiene*, pp. 36, 50–1.

126 Quine, *Population Politics*, p. 14.

127 Zygmunt Bauman, *Modernity and the Holocaust* (Ithaca, N.Y.: Cornell University Press, 1991), pp. 61–2, 65.

128 Proctor, *Racial Hygiene*, pp. 14–15.

129 Kühl, *The Nazi Connection*, pp. 13, 15–18.

130 See Shipman, *The Evolution of Racism*, pp. 99, 101, 103, on the place of ideology and politics in claims purported to be scientific even before the First World War.

131 Proctor, *Racial Hygiene*, pp. 36–7.

132 Robert Proctor, *The Nazi War on Cancer* (Princeton, N.J.: Princeton University Press, 1999); Alexei Kojevnikov, "Freedom, collectivism, and quasiparticles: social

metaphors in quantum physics," *Historical Studies in the Physical and Biological Sciences* 29:2 (1999): 295–331. See also Alexei Kojevnikov, "Dialogues about knowledge and power in totalitarian political culture," *Historical Studies in the Physical and Biological Sciences* 30:1 (1999): 228–47.

133 Georg Lukács, *The Destruction of Reason* (Atlantic Highlands, N.J.: Humanities Press, 1981), first published in 1962, is a notorious but still-influential example, although it refers not to "totalitarianism" but to fascism, and primarily to Nazism.

134 Bernice Glatzer Rosenthal, *New Myth, New World: From Nietzsche to Stalinism* (University Park: Pennsylvania State University Press, 2002); see especially pp. 1–14, 23–4, 352–5, for the overall argument.

135 See, for example, Benito Mussolini, "La filosofia della forza (Postille alla conferenza dell'on. Treves)" (1908), in *Opera omnia di Benito Mussolini*, edited by Edoardo e Duilio Susmel (Florence: La Fenice, 1951), 1: 174–84; especially pp. 181–3. Mention should also be made of Thomas Harrison (ed.), *Nietzsche in Italy* (Saratoga, Calif.: ANMA Libri, 1988 [Department of French and Italian, Stanford University]), although, as the product of a conference from 1986, it not surprisingly steers clear of the question of Nietzsche's influence on or relationship with Fascism. The exception is Thomas Sheehan's treatment of Julius Evola, who was a highly idiosyncratic late figure in original Fascism, although he became prominent in what passed as "neo-fascism" thereafter.

136 Aschheim, *The Nietzsche Legacy*, pp. 315–16, especially p. 316n., for a criticism of Kaufmann's Nietzsche. See also p. 326n. on the problems with Kaufmann's influential translations of Nietzsche.

137 Philippa Foot, "Nietzsche's immoralism," *New York Review of Books*, June 13, 1991, p. 19.

138 Berel Lang, for example, explicitly exonerates Nietzsche on these grounds in his *Act and Idea in the Nazi Genocide* (Chicago: University of Chicago Press, 1990), pp. 196–8.

139 Jacques Derrida, "Otobiographies: The teaching of Nietzsche and the politics of the proper name," in *The Ear of the Other: Otobiography, Transference, Translation* (Lincoln: University of Nebraska Press, 1988), pp. 30–2. The quotation is from p. 31.

140 Yack, *The Longing for Total Revolution*, pp. 361–2.

141 Georges Bataille, "Nietzsche and the fascists," in *Visions of Excess: Selected Writings, 1927–1939*, edited and translated by Allan Stoekl (Minneapolis: University of Minnesota Press, 1985 [article published January 1937]), pp. 182–6; p. 186 for the passage quoted.

142 Karl Löwith, *From Hegel to Nietzsche* (Doubleday [Anchor], 1967; first published in German 1941), pp. 198–9.

143 Karl Löwith, *My Life in Germany Before and After 1933* (Urbana: University of Illinois Press, 1994), pp. 5–6. Löwith went on to say that Nietzsche's influence in Germany was "boundless," an attraction that the Anglo world, even Italy and France, could not fully comprehend. Nietzsche, like Luther, was "a specifically German phenomenon—radical and fatal" (p. 6).

144 Franz Neumann, *Behemoth: The Structure and Practice of National Socialism, 1933–1944* (New York: Harper & Row [Harper Torchbooks], 1966; from 2nd ed., first published 1944), pp. 127–9.

145 Aschheim, *The Nietzsche Legacy*, pp. 233, 329–30.

146 The key work was Alfred Bäumler, *Nietzsche, der Philosoph und Politiker* (Leipzig: Philipp Reclam, 1931). Note also Alfred Bäumler, *Politik und Erziehung: Reden und Aufsätze* (Berlin: Junker und Dünnhaupt, 1937), as well as the collection of passages from Nietzsche published as *Unschuld des Werdens*, edited by Alfred Bäumler (Leipzig: Kröner, 1931).

147 Bataille, "Nietzsche and the fascists," pp. 190–2.

148 Bäumler, *Nietzsche*, pp. 79–80.

149 Friedrich Nietzsche, *The Will to Power*, translated by Walter Kaufmann and R.J. Hollingdale (New York: Random House [Vintage Books], 1968), no. 687 (p. 366); see also Aschheim, *The Nietzsche Legacy*, pp. 234, 249–50.

150 Bäumler, *Nietzsche*, pp. 180–1.

151 Friedrich Nietzsche, "On the uses and disadvantages of history for life," in his *Untimely Meditations* (Cambridge: Cambridge University Press, 1983), pp. 96–7, 108, 113.

152 *Ibid.*, p. 95.

153 *Ibid.*, pp. 63–7, 100–2, 120–3.

154 Aschheim, *The Nietzsche Legacy*, pp. 227–8, 230.

155 *Ibid.*, p. 14.

156 *Ibid.*, pp. 121–3.

157 *Ibid.*, pp. 120, 122–4, 154.

158 Friedrich Nietzsche, *Ecce Homo*, edited by Walter Kaufmann (with *On the Genealogy of Morals*) (New York: Random House [Vintage Books], 1969), pp. 326–7.

159 Bäumler, *Nietzsche*, pp. 171–3; the quotation is from p. 173.

160 Friedrich Nietzsche, *Beyond Good and Evil: Prelude to a Philosophy of the Future*, edited by Walter Kaufmann (New York: Random House [Vintage Books], 1966), p. 131 (no. 208).

161 Friedrich Nietzsche, *Twilight of the Idols*, in Walter Kaufmann (ed.), *The Portable Nietzsche* (New York: Viking, 1954), p. 543 (no. 39).

162 See Roberts, *Nothing but History*, chapter 4, for a fuller discussion.

163 Nietzsche, *The Will to Power*, p. 548 (no. 1065).

164 Friedrich Nietzsche, *The Gay Science* (New York: Random House [Vintage Books], 1974), pp. 212–13 (no. 233).

165 As quoted by Joan Stambaugh, *Nietzsche's Thought of Eternal Return* (Baltimore: Johns Hopkins University Press, 1972), p. 59. See also Nietzsche, *Beyond Good and Evil*, pp. 117, 136, for examples of Nietzsche's ongoing emphasis on the scope for willed human creation.

166 Friedrich Nietzsche, *Human, All Too Human: A Book for Free Spirits*, translated by R.J. Hollingdale (Cambridge: Cambridge University Press, 1986), p. 97 (no. 210); Nietzsche, *The Will to Power*, pp. 546–50 (nos. 1062–7).

167 Nietzsche, *The Gay Science*, pp. 167–9; Nietzsche, *The Will to Power*, pp. 546–7 (no. 1062).

168 Nietzsche introduced eternal recurrence in 1881, in a famous passage in *The Gay Science*, pp. 273–4 (no. 341). See also Nietzsche, *The Will to Power*, pp. 546–7 (no. 1062), 548–9 (no. 1066); and Roberts, *Nothing but History*, pp. 70–7.

169 Nietzsche, *The Will to Power*, p. 550 (no. 1067).

170 Nietzsche, *Twilight of the Idols*, pp. 499–501. See also Nietzsche, *The Will to Power*, pp. 402–3 (no. 765).

171 Nietzsche, *The Will to Power*, p. 419 (no. 797). See also Nietzsche, *Ecce Homo*, p. 258, on "play," and Friedrich Nietzsche, *Thus Spoke Zarathustra*, in Kaufmann (ed.), *The Portable Nietzsche*, p. 403, on the need to unlearn purposiveness and instrumentality.

172 Friedrich Nietzsche, *The Antichrist*, in Kaufmann (ed.), *The Portable Nietzsche*, pp. 607–9, 614–16.

173 Nietzsche, *The Will to Power*, pp. 35–9 (nos. 55–6).

174 Nietzsche, *Beyond Good and Evil*, pp. 202–4 (nos. 258–9).

175 Nietzsche, *The Antichrist*, p. 646. For a related theme, see *Twilight of the Idols*, p. 555, where Nietzsche argues that greatness pertains to a particular mode of human being, not to effects or public uses.

176 Thus the frivolousness of Hayden White's conflation of Nietzsche, Gentile, and fascism (including Heidegger) around the notion of the historical sublime that he himself was advocating. See Hayden White, "The politics of historical interpretation: Discipline and de-sublimation" (1982), in his *The Content of the Form: Narrative*

Discourse and Historical Representation (Baltimore: Johns Hopkins University Press, 1987), pp. 74–5. I seek to reread the relationships between White, Nietzsche, and Gentile in David D. Roberts, "The stakes of misreading: Hayden White, Carlo Ginzburg, and the Crocean legacy," *Rivista di studi italiani* 20, no. 2 (December 2002): 1–30.

177 As Steven Aschheim has emphasized, Nietzsche underlies Ernst Jünger's vision of a society of hero-workers, the vision that led Jünger to admire both the Soviet and the Italian Fascist experiments as he sought an alternative to the Western mainstream. See Aschheim, *The Nietzsche Legacy*, pp. 199–200.

178 For a rumination on the wider notion that Nietzsche was a "dangerous" thinker, see Sander Gilman, "The Nietzsche murder case; or, what makes dangerous philosophies dangerous," in his *Difference and Pathology: Stereotypes of Sexuality, Race, and Madness* (Ithaca, N.Y.: Cornell University Press, 1985), pp. 59–75.

179 Weiss, *Race Hygiene*, p. 112.

Chapter 4

1 Without the war, said Renzo De Felice, there would have been, could have been, no Fascism: the First World War was "the decisive, explosive fact, the detonator that put the entire process in motion." See Renzo De Felice, *Fascism: An Informal Introduction to Its Theory and Practice* (an interview with Michael A. Ledeen) (New Brunswick, N.J.: Transaction Books, 1976), pp. 106–7. Looking at the Soviet experiment, Martin Malia comparably stresses the decisive importance of the contingent fact of the First World War. See Martin Malia, *The Soviet Tragedy: A History of Socialism in Russia, 1917–1991* (New York: Free Press, 1994), pp. 50, 503–4.

2 As quoted in Jonathan Schell, "The unfinished twentieth century: What we have forgotten about nuclear weapons," *Harper's Magazine*, January 2000, p. 46.

3 Ian Kershaw, *Hitler, 1889–1936: Hubris* (New York: W.W. Norton, 1999), pp. 73, 80.

4 Elie Halévy, *The Era of Tyrannies* (Garden City, N.Y.: Doubleday [Anchor Books], 1965), p. 266 (1936). See also François Furet, *The Passing of an Illusion: The Idea of Communism in the Twentieth Century*, translated by Deborah Furet (Chicago: University of Chicago Press, 1999), pp. 50–3, 207–8, on Halévy and the war.

5 Harold D. Lasswell, *Propaganda Technique in World War I* (Cambridge, Mass., MIT Press, 1971; originally published in 1927 as *Propaganda Technique in the World War*). Finding that "government management of opinion is an inescapable corollary of large-scale modern war," Lasswell recommended that it be carried on openly to avoid breeding suspicion and mistrust. See pp. 10, 14–15.

6 Omer Bartov, *Murder in Our Midst: The Holocaust, Industrial Killing, and Representation* (New York: Oxford University Press, 1996), p. 5; Maria Sophia Quine, *Population Politics in Twentieth-Century Europe: Fascist Dictatorships and Liberal Democracies* (London and New York: Routledge, 1996), p. 68.

7 Quine, *Population Politics*, p. 106; Richard Soloway, "Eugenics and pronatalism in wartime Britain," in Richard Wall and Jay Winter (eds.), *The Upheaval of War: Family, Work, and Welfare in Europe, 1914–1918* (Cambridge: Cambridge University Press, 1988), pp. 369–88.

8 Bartov, *Murder in Our Midst*, pp. 26–32.

9 *Ibid.*, p. 23.

10 Jeffrey Herf, *Reactionary Modernism: Technology, Culture, and Politics in Weimar and the Third Reich* (Cambridge: Cambridge University Press, 1984), pp. 92–4, and overall pp. 70–108, on Jünger.

11 Abbott Gleason, *Totalitarianism: The Inner History of the Cold War* (New York: Oxford University Press, 1995), p. 24.

12 Bartov, *Murder in Our Midst*, pp. 23, 26–7, and (for the passage quoted) p. 42.

13 *Ibid.*, pp. 48–50.
14 Furet, *The Passing of an Illusion*, pp. 167–9, effectively characterizes the paired opposition of Mussolini and Lenin *vis-à-vis* the war.
15 Halévy, *The Era of Tyrannies*, p. 277.
16 Both Neil Harding and Robert Service accentuated the significance of the rethinking that the war occasioned for Lenin, although they drew very different, even incompatible, conclusions about the result. Harding argued that Leninism, as a distinct ideology emerged *only* with the coming of war, and that the rethinking it occasioned was essentially complete by the outbreak of revolution in 1917. Service placed greater emphasis on continuity from the prewar period. Cf. Neil Harding, *Leninism* (Durham, N.C.: Duke University Press, 1996), pp. 113–15; and Robert Service, *Lenin: A Biography* (Cambridge, Mass.: Harvard University Press, 2000), pp. 227–8.
17 Service, *Lenin: A Biography*, pp. 225–6.
18 Vladimir Ilyich Lenin, "Socialism and war," in Robert C. Tucker (ed.), *The Lenin Anthology*, (New York: W.W. Norton, 1975), pp. 183–95. See also Leszek Kolakowski, *Main Currents of Marxism: Its Origins, Growth and Dissolution*, 2: *The Golden Age*, translated by P.S. Falla (Oxford: Oxford University Press, 1981), p. 469.
19 Vladimir Ilyich Lenin, "Imperialism: The highest stage of capitalism," in Tucker (ed.), *The Lenin Anthology*, pp. 204–74. See also Kolakowski, *Main Currents of Marxism*, 2, pp. 471–2, 491–7; and Malia, *The Soviet Tragedy*, pp. 76–7.
20 Service, *Lenin: A Biography*, pp. 244–6.
21 For indications of the significance of Germany's wartime economic experiment for Lenin, see Malia, *The Soviet Tragedy*, p. 81; Alain Besançon, *The Rise of the Gulag: Intellectual Origins of Leninism*, translated by Sarah Matthews (New York: Continuum, 1981), p. 264; and Service, *Lenin: A Biography*, p. 246.
22 Service especially brings out the significance of the 1916 notebooks in his *Lenin: A Biography*, pp. 241–4.
23 Service astutely noted Lenin's refusal to admit that he was essentially reversing the position that had led to his criticism of Bogdanov in 1908. See *ibid.*, p. 244.
24 *Ibid.*, pp. 243–4.
25 Alfred G. Meyer, *Leninism* (New York: Praeger, 1962), p. 144.
26 Kolakowski, *Main Currents of Marxism*, 2, pp. 493–4.
27 Robert C. Tucker, introduction, to Tucker (ed.), *The Lenin Anthology*, p. lii; see also pp. xlix–l.
28 Both statements are quoted in Koppel S. Pinson, *Modern Germany: Its History and Civilization*, 2nd ed. (New York: Macmillan, 1966), p. 337.
29 Kolakowski, *Main Currents of Marxism*, 2, pp. 476–7.
30 Malia, *The Soviet Tragedy*, pp. 95, 105–6.
31 Meyer, *Leninism*, p. 177.
32 Malia, *The Soviet Tragedy*, p. 111.
33 Kolakowski, *Main Currents of Marxism*, 2, pp. 479–80, 503.
34 Moshe Lewin, *The Making of the Soviet System: Essays in the Social History of Interwar Russia* (New York: Pantheon, 1985), pp. 194–5.
35 See Peter Holquist, *Making War, Forging Revolution: Russia's Continuum of Crisis* (Cambridge, Mass.: Harvard University Press, 2002), especially pp. 282–8. On the basis of a study of the Don Territory, Holquist makes clear how decisively the overall experience of war and civil war shaped the subsequent Soviet departure.
36 Richard Stites has shown the depth and range of the early utopianism in his *Revolutionary Dreams: Utopian Vision and Experimental Life in the Russian Revolution* (New York: Oxford University Press, 1991). Sheila Fitzpatrick, *The Russian Revolution*, 2nd ed. (Oxford: Oxford University Press, 1994), p. 84, notes the "comically distorted worldview" of the civil war period.
37 Malia, *The Soviet Tragedy*, pp. 110, 129–32. On p. 112, Malia noted that war communism, far from being a mere aberration, was "the crucial episode that first revealed to

the Bolsheviks who they in fact were." Kolakowski's emphases in *Main Currents of Marxism*, 2: p. 482, are comparable. The radiant vision was clear in Nikolai Bukharin and Evgeny Preobrazhensky's once famous *The ABC of Communism* (1919), published in English translation in 1922.

38 Lewin, *The Making of the Soviet System*, p. 204.

39 Stephen Kotkin, *Magnetic Mountain: Stalinism as a Civilization* (Berkeley: University of California Press, 1995), p. 11.

40 Such major Marxist critics of Bolshevism as Karl Kautsky, Rosa Luxemburg, and Yuli Martov argued along similar lines. Still the best starting point is Kautsky's *The Dictatorship of the Proletariat*, written in 1918. Lenin responded in "The proletarian revolution and the renegade Kautsky," in Tucker (ed.), *The Lenin Anthology*, pp. 461–76, and a significant polemic ensued. See also Kolakowski, *Main Currents of Marxism*, 2, pp. 382, 508–12, 517; and Furet, *The Passing of an Illusion*, pp. 77–89.

41 Leon Trotsky, *Terrorism and Communism: A Reply to Karl Kautsky* (Ann Arbor: University of Michigan Press, 1961), pp. 62–3. The quote is from p. 63.

42 Vladimir Ilyich Lenin, "'Left-wing' communism—an infantile disorder," in Tucker (ed.), *The Lenin Anthology*, p. 609.

43 *Ibid.*, pp. 554–5, 580–1.

44 *Ibid.*, pp. 591, 612.

45 *Ibid.*, p. 564.

46 *Ibid.*, p. 589.

47 *Ibid.*, p. 606.

48 *Ibid.*, pp. 612–14.

49 *Ibid.*, p. 611.

50 *Ibid.*, p. 573.

51 *Ibid.*, pp. 562–3, 577–8, 582.

52 *Ibid.*, pp. 580, 591–4, 596.

53 *Ibid.*, pp. 575, 614.

54 *Ibid.*, pp. 569–70. In the same vein, Lenin noted on p. 590 that even after the nominal overthrow of the bourgeoisie, the proletariat would long remain weaker, partly because of the wider international links that the bourgeoisie had already established, but especially because capitalism and bourgeois modes regenerate spontaneously among small commodity producers.

55 *Ibid.*, p. 574.

56 *Ibid.*, pp. 553, 611.

57 Kolakowski noted that Lenin "was fully aware that the course of events in Russia bore no relation to the traditional Marxist schemata, though he did not consider the theoretical problem in all its bearings. It was a communist revolution in the sense that it transferred state power to the Communist Party, but not in the sense of confirming Marxist predictions as to the fate of capitalist society." Kolakowski, *Main Currents of Marxism*, 2, pp. 479–81. The quotation is from p. 481.

58 Although A. James Gregor surely goes overboard in making Mussolini a consistent ideologue, his *Young Mussolini and the Intellectual Origins of Fascism* (Berkeley: University of California Press, 1979) remains a useful corrective to the notion, still prevalent in some circles, that Mussolini was barely literate. Gregor provides a good sense of Mussolini's range of reading. While not insisting on ideological consistency, Renzo De Felice, in his *Mussolini il rivoluzionario, 1883–1920* (Turin: Giulio Einaudi, 1965), shows that Mussolini was well plugged into the wider intellectual currents of his time. Closer to the usual debunking is the widely read account by Denis Mack Smith, *Mussolini: A Biography* (New York: Random House [Vintage], 1983), which at least recognizes that Mussolini was a talented journalist and propagandist—even a talented actor.

59 A point to be developed in Chapter 6; see p. 298. Mussolini's statement from 1912 about faith moving mountains is discussed in Renzo De Felice, *Mussolini il rivoluzionario, 1883–1920*, p. 128.

60 I have explored this set of issues in greater depth in David D. Roberts, "Croce and beyond: Italian intellectuals and the First World War," *International History Review* 3, no. 2 (April 1981): 201–35.

61 Eugenio Garin, *La cultura italiana tra '800 e '900* (Rome and Bari: Laterza, 1976), pp. 183–4.

62 Perhaps the leading exemplar was the historian and publicist Guglielmo Ferrero, who explicitly blamed Croce for the widespread diffusion of German cultural influence, and who was a major foil for Croce in return. For Ferrero's position, see Guglielmo Ferrero, *La guerra europea: Studi e discorsi* (Milan: Ravà, 1915).

63 Benedetto Croce, *L'Italia dal 1914 al 1918: Pagine sulla guerra*, 4th ed. (Bari: Laterza, 1965), pp. 53–6, 61–4, 158–60.

64 *Ibid.*, pp. 63, 109–12, 131–2.

65 *Ibid.*, pp. 89, 131–2, 141–3.

66 Giovanni Gentile, "Il carattere storico della filosofia italiana" (University of Rome inaugural lecture, January 10, 1918), in Giovanni Gentile, *I problemi della scolastica e il pensiero italiano* (Florence: Sansoni, 1963), pp. 209–18, 235–6.

67 Giovanni Gentile, *Guerra e fede* (Naples: Riccardo Ricciardi, 1919), pp. 158–9 (November 20, 1915).

68 Giovanni Gentile, "Il significato della vittoria" (October 1918), now in his *Dopo la vittoria: Nuovi frammenti politici* (Rome: La Voce, 1920), pp. 3–25, especially pp. 24–25; Gentile, *Guerra e fede*, pp. 158–9, 175, 205–6, 209–12, 217–18, 222–3, 288–90 (in the 3rd ed., Florence, 1989, the key passage is on p. 147).

69 Croce, *L'Italia dal 1914 al 1918*, pp. 95, 107–12, 235–8; Gentile, *Guerra e fede*, pp. 205–6, 209–12, 217–18, 288–90. Gentile established the bases of his political theory, rethinking the relationships between liberty and authority on the one hand, the individual and the state on the other, in his *Filosofia del diritto* of 1916. See also Domenico Settembrini, *Storia dell'idea antiborghese in Italia, 1860–1989: Società del benessere—liberalismo—totalitarismo* (Rome and Bari: Laterza, 1991), p. 266.

70 Giovanni Gentile, *I profeti del Risorgimento italiano* (Florence: Sansoni, 1944), pp. 1–63; Armando Carlini, *Studi gentiliani* (Florence: Sansoni, 1958), pp. 109–12; Raffaele Colapietra, *Benedetto Croce e la politica italiana*, vol. 1 (Bari: Centro del Centro Librario, 1969), p. 302n. In his history of nineteenth-century Italian historiography, written in 1914–15, Croce contemptuously dismissed the notions of Mazzini and Gioberti that Italy had had some special mission to perform. Benedetto Croce, *Storia della storiografia italiana nel secolo decimonono*, vol. 1 (Bari: Laterza, 1964), p. 145.

71 Gentile, *I profeti del Risorgimento*, pp. 1–63, See also Carlini, *Studi gentiliani*, pp. 109–12.

72 Luigi Russo, *Vita e disciplina militare*, 5th ed. (Bari: Laterza, 1946), pp. 7–8, 11–14, 17–18, 21–2, 27–31, 33, 37–8, 69–70, 75–8, 83, 129, 147–8, 158–9. The book went through several editions, with a slight change from the original title. Some later editions included as a preface the laudatory article with which Gentile had greeted the work when it first appeared. For Gentile's review, see *Guerra e fede*, pp. 231–6 (pp. 261–4 in the 1989 edition).

73 Russo, *Vita e disciplina militare*, pp. 14–17, 20.

74 Alfredo Rocco, Manifesto of *Politica*, in Adrian Lyttelton (ed.), *Italian Fascisms from Pareto to Gentile* (New York, Harper & Row [Harper Torchbooks], 1975), p. 262.

75 To recall Hobsbawm's characterization quoted in Chapter 3. Gabriele Turi, *Giovanni Gentile: Una biografia* (Florence: Giunti, 1995), pp. 217, 247, 263–4.

76 Marcello De Cecco, "The economy from liberalism to fascism," in Adrian Lyttelton (ed.), *Liberal and Fascist Italy* (Oxford: Oxford University Press, 2002), pp. 73–5.

77 This is the thrust of the later chapters of David D. Roberts, *The Syndicalist Tradition and Italian Fascism* (Chapel Hill: University of North Carolina Press, 1979); see especially chapters 10 and 11 and the evidence upon which they are based. Zeev Sternhell correctly recognized the centrality of Nationalism and syndicalism to Fascist ideology but missed the ongoing tensions. See Zeev Sternhell, with Mario Sznajder and Maia Asheri, *The Birth of Fascist Ideology: From Cultural Rebellion to Political Revolution*, translated

by David Maisel (Princeton, N.J.: Princeton University Press, 1994; original French ed. 1989); and my critique in David D. Roberts "How not to think about fascism and ideology, intellectual antecedents and historical meaning," *Journal of Contemporary History* 35, no. 2 (April 2000): 185–211.

78 Especially influential was Alfredo Rocco's new journal, *Politica*, launched in 1918. See especially Rocco's introductory "Manifesto" (December 15, 1918) in Lyttelton (ed.), *Italian Fascisms*, pp. 249–68. On pp. 264, 266–7, Rocco noted that an imperial and thus post-national type of civilization was emerging. It would be "democratic" in the sense that the peoples of the world would be the protagonists. But everything would need to be organized and coordinated for imperial struggle.

79 Enrico Corradini, *Il regime della borghesia produttiva* (Rome: L'Italiana, 1918), pp. 45–7, 50; see also pp. 20–1, 30–1, 34, 36–7, 52. See, in addition, Enrico Corradini, *La marcia dei produttori* (Rome: L'Italiana, 1916), pp. 45–54; Enrico Corradini, *Discorsi politici (1902–1923)* (Florence: Vallecchi [1923]), pp. 353–4, 379, 384–90; and Roberts, *The Syndicalist Tradition*, pp. 143–4.

80 Rocco, "Manifesto" of *Politica*, pp. 258–60.

81 Alfredo Rocco, untitled comment in Pier Ludovico Occhini (ed.), *Il Nazionalismo italiano e i problemi del lavoro e della scuola: Atti del secondo convegno Nazionalista a Roma* (Rome: L'Italiana, 1919), pp. 40–3, 98. See also Rocco, "Manifesto of *Politica*" pp. 266–7; and Alfredo Rocco, *Scritti e discorsi politici*, 3 vols. (Milan: A. Giuffrè, 1938), 2, 590–1 (April 24, 1919).

82 Rocco, *Scritti e discorsi*, 2, p. 625 (February 1, 1920); and especially 2, pp. 632, 639–45, "Crisi dello Stato e sindacati" (inaugural lecture, University of Padua, November 15, 1920).

83 Isaiah Berlin, "Joseph de Maistre and the origins of fascism," in his *The Crooked Timber of Humanity: Chapters in the History of Ideas*, edited by Henry Hardy (New York: Random House [Vintage Books], 1992), pp. 91–174.

84 Sternhell notes that the essence of Rocco's thought was "a mystical and organic view of the nation" entailing the "supremacy of the collectivity over the individual"; Sternhell, *The Birth of Fascist Ideology*, p. 230. It is certainly true that Rocco posited the supremacy of the nation over the individual, but this emphasis serves Sternhell as a warrant to subsume Rocco's thinking within the wider French-based package—including myth. Whatever we think of Rocco's priorities, his conception of the relationship between individual and society was no more "mystical," no less rational, than the ideas of 1789. See also p. 251 for Sternhell's overall emphasis on "fear of the masses." For my own assessment of Rocco, see Roberts, *The Syndicalist Tradition*, especially pp. 139–52.

85 Sternhell, *The Birth of Fascist Ideology*, p. 219.

86 Roberts, *The Syndicalist Tradition*, chapter 7 (pp. 153–81).

87 Settembrini, *Storia dell'idea antiborghese*, pp. 277–95.

88 Gaetano Mosca, *The Ruling Class*, edited and revised by Arthur Livingston, translated by Hannah D. Kahn (New York: McGraw-Hill, 1939), pp. 479–82.

89 *Ibid.*, pp. 490–1.

90 Giustino Fortunato, "Dopo la guerra sovvertitrice," in his *Pagine e ricordi parlamentari*, vol. 2, 2nd ed., revised (Rome: Collezione Meridionale Editrice, 1947), pp. 70–1, 82–3. See also Roberts, *The Syndicalist Tradition*, pp. 148–9.

91 Sergio Panunzio "Stato e sindacati," *Rivista internazionale di filosofia del diritto* 3, no. 1 (January—March 1923): 1–20 (originally a lecture at the University of Ferrara, November 1922). Orlando laid out his position most cogently in Vittorio Emanuele Orlando "Lo 'stato sindacale' e le condizioni attuali della scienza di diritto pubblico," *Rivista di diritto pubblico e della pubblica amministrazione in Italia*, ser. 2, 16 (January 1924): 4–18. See also Roberts, *The Syndicalist Tradition*, pp. 242–3.

92 Guido De Ruggiero, "Il trionfo della tecnica" (December 19, 1922), now in his *Scritti politici, 1912–1925*, edited by Renzo De Felice (Bologna: Cappelli, 1963), pp. 595–600. See also Guido De Ruggiero, *The History of European Liberalism*, translated by R.G. Collingwood (Boston: Beacon Press, 1959; first Italian ed., 1925), pp. 382–6, 426–7.

93 Sergio Panunzio, *Stato nazionale e sindacati* (Milan: Imperia, 1924), pp. 143–8, 158; Sergio Panunzio, "Idee sul fascismo," *Critica fascista* 3, no. 6 (March 15, 1925), p. 113. See also Roberts, *The Syndicalist Tradition*, pp. 250–1, 253–6; and Settembrini, *Storia dell'idea antiborghese*, pp. 284–6, on the Panunzio–De Ruggiero exchange.

94 (Luigi Albertini), "I nuovi organi dello Stato: Corporazioni e consigli tecnici," *Corriere della sera*, August 15, 1924, p. 1; (Luigi Albertini), "Stato liberale e Stato organico fascista," *Corriere della sera*, August 16, 1924, p. 1.

95 See Roberts, *The Syndicalist Tradition*, pp. 251–3, for Olivetti's response to the critiques of Albertini and other liberals, and p. 356 n. 31 for the references to Olivetti's articles in *Il popolo d'Italia*, August—October 1924.

96 See Renzo De Felice, *Autobiografia del fascismo: Antologia di testi fascisti, 1919–1945* (Bergamo: Minerva Italica, 1978), p. 162, for an especially effective characterization of the diversity, and often incompatibility, of the cultural tendencies attracted to fascism.

97 Benito Mussolini, "The doctrine of fascism," in Lyttelton (ed.), *Italian Fascisms*, pp. 44–5. See also pp. 48–9.

98 De Felice, *Fascism*, p. 49; see also pp. 46, 102.

99 Emilio Gentile, *La via italiana al totalitarismo: Il partito e lo Stato nel regime fascista* (Rome: La Nuova Italia Scientifica, 1995), pp. 84–5.

100 See Roberts, *The Syndicalist Tradition*, pp. 164–7, on the interface between Pareto and the Italian syndicalists at this point.

101 R.J.B. Bosworth, *The Italian Dictatorship: Problems and Perspectives in the Interpretation of Mussolini and Fascism* (London: Edward Arnold, 1998), pp. 40–1.

102 This is essentially Renzo De Felice's view, endorsed for the most part by Emilio Gentile, even as he departs significantly from De Felice in other respects, as we will discuss below. Coming from very different angles, such scholars as A. James Gregor and MacGregor Knox have emphasized Mussolini's consistency as an ideologue against any emphasis on opportunism, or even his role as a juggler. But the fact that, from there, their pictures differ so dramatically surely gives pause for thought.

103 Dino Grandi, "Il mito sindacalista" (originally published July 1920), in his *Giovani* (Bologna: Nicola Zanichelli, 1941), p. 220.

104 Dino Grandi, "L'uomo più grande," in his *Giovani*. See also Roberts, *The Syndicalist Tradition*, pp. 200–3.

105 Roberts, *The Syndicalist Tradition*, pp. 166–7.

106 Emilio Gentile, "Fascism in power: the totalitarian experiment," in Lyttelton (ed.), *Liberal and Fascist Italy*, p. 145.

107 Gentile, *La via italiana*, pp. 155, 157–9. The 1921 dispute and its outcome are also central to my account of early Fascism in *The Syndicalist Tradition*, pp. 214–23.

108 De Felice, *Fascism*, p. 63. Countering the Marxist and quasi-Marxist reductionist tendencies prominent in the mid-1970s, De Felice insisted that "it is unthinkable that Italy's great economic forces wanted to bring fascism to power. Fascism for them was a 'white guard' that would be sent home once its task had been accomplished. . . . In 1922 the economic world was thinking of solutions with Giolitti, Orlando, or above all Salandra."

109 Roberts, *The Syndicalist Tradition*, p. 237.

110 Renzo De Felice, *Mussolini il fascista: La conquista del potere* (Turin: Giulio Einaudi, 1966): 676.

111 See Ian Kershaw, *Hitler, 1889–1936: Hubris* (New York: W.W. Norton, 1999), pp. 75–6; Detlev J.K. Peukert, *The Weimar Republic: The Crisis of Classical Modernity* (New York: Hill and Wang, 1993), p. 24; and Richard Bessel, "Germany from war to dictatorship," in Mary Fulbrook (ed.), *German History since 1800* (London: Edward Arnold, 1997), p. 237, for various angles on the impact of the sense of harmony of the *Burgfrieden* (wartime peace).

112 Kershaw, *Hitler, 1889–1936*, pp. 98–9.

113 Woodruff D. Smith, *The Ideological Origins of Nazi Imperialism* (New York: Oxford University Press, 1986), pp. 167–8; the quotation is from p. 167.

114 *Ibid.*, p. 187.

115 Quoted in Arno J. Mayer, *Political Origins of the New Diplomacy, 1917–18* (New York: Random House [Vintage Books], 1970), p. 135.

116 Smith, *The Ideological Origins*, p. 196.

117 *Ibid.*, pp. 167–8; the quotation is from p. 167.

118 *Ibid.*, p. 195.

119 *Ibid.*, pp. 206, 212–13. It was argued that degenerative interracial breeding would be limited by a rural setting.

120 *Ibid.*, pp. 218–23; Andrew Gyorgy, *Geopolitics: The New German Science* (Berkeley: University of California Press, 1944).

121 Smith, *The Ideological Origins*, pp. 231, 238, 257.

122 Quine, *Population Politics*, pp. 104–5.

123 Sheila Faith Weiss, *Race Hygiene and National Efficiency: The Eugenics of Wilhelm Schallmayer* (Berkeley: University of California Press, 1987), p. 142.

124 Paul Weindling, "The medical profession, social hygiene and the birth rate in Germany," in Richard Wall and Jay Winter (eds.), *The Upheaval of War: Family, Work, and Welfare in Europe, 1914–1918* (Cambridge: Cambridge University Press, 1988), p. 429.

125 *Ibid.*, pp. 423–4, 426–8. The quotation is from p. 428. See also Weiss, *Race Hygiene*, pp. 140–6.

126 Weindling, "The Medical Profession," p. 430.

127 *Ibid.*, pp. 428, 430, 433; Paul Weindling, *Health, Race and German Politics between National Unification and Nazism, 1870–1945* (Cambridge: Cambridge University Press, 1989), p. 307. See also Quine, *Population Politics*, p. 104.

128 Robert Proctor, *Racial Hygiene: Medicine Under the Nazis* (Cambridge, Mass.: Harvard University Press, 1988), pp. 178–9.

129 Michael Burleigh, *Death and Deliverance: 'Euthanasia' in Germany, c. 1900–1945* (Cambridge: Cambridge University Press, 1994), p. 11.

130 *Ibid.*, pp. 11–12. See also p. 15. Weindling in *Health, Race and German Politics*, p. 395, makes essentially the same point.

131 I refer to the classic works of Clemens von Klemperer (*Germany's New Conservatism: Its History and Dilemma in the Twentieth Century* [Princeton, NJ: Princeton University Press, 1968; first published 1957]) and Fritz Stern (*The Politics of Cultural Despair*, cited in Chapter 1) with the greatest respect.

132 The works of Charles S. Maier remain fundamental; I also have in mind the contributions of Mary Nolan and Atina Grossmann, among many others.

133 Weindling, *Health, Race and German Politics*, pp. 399–405.

134 Bessel, "Germany from war to dictatorship," p. 252. Dieter Langewiesche's argument is comparable despite his greater emphasis on longer-term statist traditions. See Dieter Langewiesche, *Liberalism in Germany*, translated by Christiane Banerji (Princeton, N.J.: Princeton University Press, 2000; original German ed. 1988), pp. 255–6.

135 For this particular point, see Weindling, *Health, Race and German Politics*, p. 348.

136 Peukert, *The Weimar Republic*, pp. 50–1, 130–3, 243–6.

137 Langewiesche, *Liberalism in Germany*, p. 254. See also Atina Grossmann, *Reforming Sex: The German Movement for Birth Control and Abortion Reform, 1920–1950* (New York: Oxford University Press, 1995), pp. 4–5.

138 Peukert, *The Weimar Republic*, pp. 7–8, 18, 93–4; Quine, *Population Politics*, p. 101.

139 Weindling, *Health, Race and German Politics*, especially pp. 343, 356, 480–2.

140 This work was first published in Munich in 1921, then published in an expanded edition in 1923. See Proctor, *Racial Hygiene*, pp. 57–8.

141 *Ibid.*, pp. 25, 48–50. Proctor deemed Lenz the premier racial hygienist during the Weimar and Nazi periods.

142 Weindling, "The medical profession," pp. 431–2; the quotation is on p. 432. Grotjahn was appointed to a university chair in 1920.

143 Steven E. Aschheim, *The Nietzsche Legacy in Germany, 1890–1990* (Berkeley: University of California Press, 1992), pp. 77, 148–53. See also George L. Mosse, *The Crisis of German Ideology: Intellectual Origins of the Third Reich* (New York: Grosset & Dunlap (Universal Library), 1964), pp. 65, 206–8, on Bertram and the transition to Alfred Bäumler, who became the leading Nazi Nietzschean.

144 Aschheim, *The Nietzsche Legacy*, pp. 160–3.

145 Peukert, *The Weimar Republic*, pp. 187–8.

146 Weindling, *Health, Race and German Politics*, p. 348.

147 *Ibid.*, pp. 330, 406, 430–9. The German League for National Regeneration and Heredity, founded in Berlin in March 1925, opposed the sex reform movement and sought, among other things, a prohibition on degenerate procreation. Although its efforts to work with the state found some support, its influence on policy proved limited. The Kaiser Wilhelm Institute for Anthropology, Human Heredity and Eugenics was established in 1927 as a quasi-public entity. In 1936, its director, Eugen Fischer, portrayed it as the key precursor of Nazi policies.

148 Weindling, *Health, Race and German Politics*, pp. 344, 388–93.

149 *Ibid.*, pp. 395–7; Burleigh, *Death and Deliverance*, pp. 15–19; Michael Burleigh, *Ethics and Extermination: Reflections on Nazi Genocide* (Cambridge: Cambridge University Press, 1997), pp. 114–15; Michael Burleigh and Wolfgang Wippermann, *The Racial State: Germany 1933–1945* (Cambridge: Cambridge University Press, 1991), pp. 141–2.

150 Weindling, *Health, Race and German Politics*, p. 389.

151 *Ibid.*, pp. 340, 438.

152 *Ibid.*, chapter 7, "The sick-bed of democracy, 1929–32," pp. 441–87; see especially pp. 444, 449, 454–7.

153 Quine, *Population Politics*, pp. 108–9; Peukert, *The Weimar Republic*, pp. 145–6; Burleigh, *Death and Deliverance*, pp. 23, 33, 36–7; Weiss, *Race Hygiene*, p. 153.

154 Weindling, *Health, Race and German Politics*, pp. 312, 320, 462–70.

155 *Ibid.*, pp. 466–9.

156 *Ibid.*, pp. 431, 452–3.

157 *Ibid.*, pp. 444–5, 447, 476–7.

158 *Ibid.*, pp. 453–4, 462.

159 *Ibid.*, pp. 477, 486.

160 Aschheim, *The Nietzsche Legacy*, p. 163n.

161 Peukert, *The Weimar Republic*, pp. 13, 228–9, 280–1; see also pp. 187–8, as well as Weindling, *Health, Race and German Politics*, p. 441.

162 Peukert, *The Weimar Republic*, pp. 134–6, 271–2.

163 Grossmann, *Reforming Sex*, pp. 153, 161–5. The quotation is from p. 165.

164 Jill Stephenson, "The rise of the Nazis: *Sonderweg* or spanner in the works?" in Fulbrook (ed.), *German History since 1800*, pp. 301–2.

165 Langewiesche, *Liberalism in Germany*, pp. 280–3, 292–3.

166 *Ibid.*, p. 302.

167 George Schwab, "Introduction," in Carl Schmitt, *The Concept of the Political*, translated by George Schwab (Chicago: University of Chicago Press, 1996), pp. 3–16.

168 Joseph W. Bendersky, *Carl Schmitt: Theorist for the Reich* (Princeton, N.J.: Princeton University Press, 1983), pp. 36–9, 54–5, 87.

169 *Ibid.*, p. 165.

170 Franz Neumann, *Behemoth: The Structure and Practice of National Socialism, 1933–1944* (New York: Harper & Row [Harper Torchbooks], 1966; from 2nd ed., first published 1944), pp. 49–51.

171 Carl Schmitt, *State, Movement, People* (Corvallis, Ore.: Plutarch Press, 2001).

172 Bendersky, *Carl Schmitt*, pp. 88–91; Neumann, *Behemoth*, pp. 64–5.

173 Neumann, *Behemoth*, pp. 64–5.

174 Bendersky, *Carl Schmitt*, p. 222.

Chapter 5

1 Martin Malia, *The Soviet Tragedy: A History of Socialism in Russia, 1917–1991* (New York: Free Press, 1994), pp. 153–6.

2 Moshe Lewin, *The Making of the Soviet System: Essays in the Social History of Interwar Russia* (New York: Pantheon, 1985), p. 259.

3 For indications of the significance of this theme, see Malia, *The Soviet Tragedy*, pp. 235–6; Leszek Kolakowski, *Main Currents of Marxism: Its Origins, Growth and Dissolution*, 2: *The Golden Age*, translated by P.S. Falla (Oxford: Oxford University Press, 1981), 2, p. 404; Alain Besançon, *The Rise of the Gulag: Intellectual Origins of Leninism*, translated by Sarah Matthews (New York: Continuum, 1981; original French ed. 1977), pp. 91, 141, 195–6.

4 Stephen Kotkin, *Magnetic Mountain: Stalinism as a Civilization* (Berkeley: University of California Press, 1995), p. 12, nicely links the Communist effort to longstanding Russian desires to play a special role on the basis of putative moral superiority over the West.

5 On the uses and limits of Carr's contribution, see Stephen F. Cohen, *Rethinking the Soviet Experience: Politics and Society since 1917* (New York: Oxford University Press, 1985), pp. 33–4; see also pp. 44–5, on Carr and Isaac Deutscher.

6 Kolakowski, *Main Currents of Marxism*, 2, pp. 501, 516–17.

7 Cohen was especially forceful in emphasizing discontinuity; Stalinism was a radical departure. See Cohen, *Rethinking the Soviet Experience*, p. 62.

8 *Ibid.*, pp. 71–92, especially pp. 85–6, on Bukharin, the NEP, and the enduring significance of Bukharin's legacy. See also Stephen F. Cohen, *Bukharin and the Bolshevik Revolution: A Political Biography, 1888–1938* (New York: Random House [Vintage Books], 1973).

9 Hannah Arendt, *The Origins of Totalitarianism* (Cleveland: World [Meridian Books], 1958), pp. 318–23, especially p. 319.

10 On Tucker's role as a principal critic of the continuity thesis, see Giuseppe Boffa, *The Stalin Phenomenon*, translated by Nicholas Fersen (Ithaca, N.Y.: Cornell University Press, 1992, pp. 41, 44, 54–6.

11 *Ibid.*, pp. 193–4. See also pp. 66, 75.

12 Boffa went on to note that although Stalin did indeed create a new order, it was notable for its costs and waste and had little to do with socialism as envisioned by either Marx or Lenin; *ibid.*, p. 66. See also Giuseppe Boffa (ed.), *Per conoscere Stalin* (Milan: Mondadori, 1970), pp. 18–20 (from Boffa's introduction, pp. 7–37); and Cohen, *Rethinking the Soviet Experience*, p. 47.

13 Kotkin, *Magnetic Mountain*, pp. 4–6.

14 Sheila Fitzpatrick, *The Russian Revolution*, 2nd ed. (Oxford: Oxford University Press, 1994), pp. 144–50, 156; Sheila Fitzpatrick, "Stalin and the making of a new elite" (1979), now in Sheila Fitzpatrick, *The Cultural Front: Power and Culture in Revolutionary Russia* (Ithaca, N.Y.: Cornell University Press, 1992), pp. 149–82. See also Malia, *The Soviet Tragedy*, p. 11; and Abbott Gleason, *Totalitarianism: The Inner History of the Cold War* (New York: Oxford University Press, 1995), pp. 140–2, on the historiographical context, including the role of such other major figures as Merle Fainsod and Jerry Hough.

15 See Boffa, *The Stalin Phenomenon*, pp. 80–1, 86–90, on this developmentalist school, synthesized especially by Jerry Hough.

16 Fitzpatrick, *The Russian Revolution*, pp. 168–70.

17 Lewin, *The Making of the Soviet System*, p. 202 and pp. 258–9 (which includes the passages quoted).

18 *Ibid.*, p. 205.

19 Lewin also emphasized that Lenin's influence within Bolshevism had never been as dogmatic or despotic as had generally been assumed. Moreover, Lenin had long wavered on the extent of capitalist development necessary and on how to sort out the respective

roles of new and old social formations in Russia. He had never come up with a satisfactory understanding of the peasantry. See Lewin, *The Making of the Soviet System*, pp. 291–2.

20 *Ibid.*, pp. 260–1, 299.

21 Moshe Lewin, "Bureaucracy and the Stalinist state," in Ian Kershaw and Moshe Lewin (eds.), *Stalinism and Nazism: Dictatorships in Comparison* (Cambridge: Cambridge University Press, 1997), p. 74; Lewin, *The Making of the Soviet System*, p. 263.

22 Lewin, *The Making of the Soviet System*, p. 208; Lewin, "Bureaucracy and the Stalinist state," p. 54.

23 Lewin, *The Making of the Soviet System*, p. 207.

24 *Ibid.*, pp. 25–32. See also Kotkin's characterization of Lewin in Kotkin, *Magnetic Mountain*, pp. 4–5.

25 Lewin, *The Making of the Soviet System*, p. 274.

26 Boffa (ed.), *Per conoscere Stalin*, pp. 19–20.

27 Kotkin, *Magnetic Mountain*, p. 152.

28 *Ibid.*, pp. 3–6, and pp. 364 and 356 for the passages quoted.

29 For perspectives on the changing understanding of the terror, see *ibid.*, pp. 282–6; and Robert W. Thurston, *Life and Terror in Stalin's Russia, 1934–1941* (New Haven, Conn.: Yale University Press, 1996), pp. xx–xxi.

30 Arendt, *The Origins of Totalitarianism*, p. 318.

31 Stephen F. Cohen, "Stalin's terror as social history," *The Russian Review* 45, no. 4 (October 1986): 357–73. See also Gleason, *Totalitarianism*, pp. 141–2.

32 See Boffa, *The Stalin Phenomenon*, p. 42, and Malia, *The Soviet Tragedy*, p. 261, on this moment in the changing understanding.

33 Roy Medvedev, *Let History Judge: The Origins and Consequences of Stalinism*, translated by Colleen Taylor (New York: Random House [Vintage Books], 1973). Medvedev sought to publish the book in the Soviet Union but was denied, so he authorized publication abroad, by Suhrkamp Verlag, in 1967. Robert Conquest, *The Great Terror: A Reassessment* (New York: Oxford University Press, 1990), updated edition of *The Great Terror: Stalin's Purge of the Thirties*, first published 1968, revised ed. 1973).

34 See, for example, J. Arch Getty and Roberta T. Manning, "Introduction," in J. Arch Getty and Roberta T. Manning (eds.), *Stalinist Terror: New Perspectives* (Cambridge: Cambridge University Press, 1993), pp. 14–15, on the role of Stalin in the context of their case against the orthodox view. For another perspective on the same issues, see Gábor Tamás Rittersporn, *Stalinist Simplifications and Soviet Complications: Social Tensions and Political Conflicts in the USSR, 1933–1953* (Chur, Switzerland: Harwood Academic, 1991), pp. 3–8, 14–18. See also pp. 1–2, 23–4 on the moralizing objections and ready-made answers that impede understanding and even prevent certain questions from coming up at all.

35 See, for example, Geoffrey Hosking's review of Thurston's *Life and Terror* in *Journal of Modern History* 69, no. 4 (December 1997): 897–8. Valuable though it was in many respects, Thurston's account included some overstatement and a few problematic emphases, as we will discuss below.

36 Kotkin, *Magnetic Mountain*, pp. 284–6, 334, tends to caricature Getty and Rittersporn, as if they were portraying the terror as some mysterious, inexplicable descent into chaos. Neither remotely suggested that the process was "mysterious." As for Kotkin, the challenge—if we are not to settle for some Stalinist will to "total domination"—is to find the wider framework from within which we can understood how the terror could have occurred.

37 Malia, *The Soviet Tragedy*, pp. 239–40, 243. For another noted example of the argument that any *Marxism*, never mind the Leninist admixture, and no matter the circumstances in which it was applied, could only have yielded something like the same Stalinist and *totalitarian* outcome, see Leszek Kolakowski, "Marxist roots of Stalinism," in Robert C. Tucker (ed.), *Stalinism: Essays in Historical Interpretation* (New York: W.W. Norton, 1977), pp. 283–98.

38 Gleason, *Totalitarianism*, p. 151.
39 Malia, *The Soviet Tragedy*, p. 16.
40 *Ibid.*, pp. 134–5, 174–5, 503–4.
41 *Ibid.*, pp. 174–5, 495.
42 *Ibid.*, pp. 134–5.
43 *Ibid.*, pp. 50, 503–4.
44 *Ibid.*, pp. 134–5.
45 *Ibid.*, pp. 221–2, 225, 514.
46 *Ibid.*, pp. 12–14.
47 *Ibid.*, pp. 225, 498–9, 503–4.
48 *Ibid.*, pp. 11, 240.
49 *Ibid.*, pp. 261–2.
50 *Ibid.*, pp. 5–12, especially pp. 6–8.
51 *Ibid.*, p. 137.
52 Besançon, *The Rise of the Gulag*, pp. 283–4, 286–7.
53 *Ibid.*, pp. 286–7, 289–90.
54 Cohen, *Rethinking the Soviet Experience*, pp. 66–7.
55 Sheila Fitzpatrick, *Everyday Stalinism: Ordinary Life in Extraordinary Times: Soviet Russia in the 1930s* (New York: Oxford University Press, 1999), pp. 66–8.
56 Kotkin, *Magnetic Mountain*, pp. 86–8.
57 Fitzpatrick, *Everyday Stalinism*, p. 12; Kotkin, *Magnetic Mountain*, p. 81.
58 Kotkin, *Magnetic Mountain*, p. 152.
59 *Ibid.*, p. 153.
60 Besançon, *The Rise of the Gulag*, pp. 225–6.
61 *Ibid.*, p. 290.
62 *Ibid.*, p. 268.
63 Cohen, *Rethinking the Soviet Experience*, p. 52.
64 Alfred G. Meyer, *Leninism* (New York: Praeger, 1962), p. 220, on Lenin's denial that socialism could be achieved in Russia alone.
65 Cf. Besançon, *The Rise of the Gulag*, p. 280.
66 Lev Kopelev, *The Education of a True Believer*, translated by Gary Kern (New York: Harper & Row, 1980), pp. 90–1.
67 *Ibid.*, p. 235; see also pp. 226, 250, for military metaphors and images of ongoing struggle. For further indications of the importance of toughness and military terms, see Vladimir Brovkin, *Russia after Lenin: Politics, Culture and Society, 1921–1929* (New York and London: Routledge, 1998), pp. 12–13.
68 Malia, *The Soviet Tragedy*, pp. 170–1. See also Fitzpatrick, *Everyday Stalinism*, p. 19.
69 Malia, *The Soviet Tragedy*, p. 78, highlighted the appeal of the notion that with the Bolshevik Revolution, Russia, long viewed as the most backward, was now the most advanced.
70 Lenin admitted explicitly that war communism had been a disastrous error. Kolakowski, *Main Currents of Marxism*, 2, pp. 482–4, 495.
71 Ronald Grigor Suny, *The Soviet Experiment: Russia, the USSR, and the Successor States* (New York: Oxford University Press, 1998), pp. 151–4, 156–7. On pp. 152–3, Suny noted that Bukharin was the real author of the economic policies of the 1920s. For an especially clear exposition of Bukharin's position, see N.I. Bukharin, *Selected Writings on the State and the Transition to Socialism*, edited by Richard B. Day (Armonk, N.Y.: M.E. Sharpe, 1982), pp. 245–94, especially pp. 258–63, 266, 273, 284–5, 290–4.
72 Lewin, *The Making of the Soviet System*, p. 204.
73 Brovkin, *Russia after Lenin*, pp. 168–74, 204, 206, 222.
74 *Ibid.*, pp. 168–74, 222 (the quotation is from p. 222).
75 *Ibid.*, pp. 208–10.
76 Fitzpatrick, *The Russian Revolution*, pp. 118–19, 128–9. See also Lewin, *The Making of the Soviet System*, pp. 216–18.

77 Brovkin, *Russia after Lenin*, pp. 190, 192–3, 222.

78 Malia, *The Soviet Tragedy*, pp. 165–7, 188–9, 221, 232–3.

79 Ronald Grigor Suny, "Stalin and his Stalinism: Power and authority in the Soviet Union, 1930–53," in Kershaw and Lewin (eds.), *Stalinism and Nazism*, p. 27. See also Suny, *The Soviet Experiment*, p. 190, for a slightly different way of making the point.

80 Suny, *The Soviet Experiment*, pp. 159, 218–21, especially p. 219; Boffa, *The Stalin Phenomenon*, pp. 83, 218–21.

81 Suny, *The Soviet Experiment*, p. 159. By December 1927, Stalin had a majority in the Politburo.

82 Malia, *The Soviet Tragedy*, pp. 191, 193. Brovkin suggests that the key initiative came later, beginning in fall 1928; see Brovkin, *Russia after Lenin*, p. 205.

83 Malia, *The Soviet Tragedy*, pp. 232–3.

84 *Ibid.*, p. 91; Lewin, *The Making of the Soviet System*, pp. 232–3.

85 Malia, *The Soviet Tragedy*, pp. 184–6, 188–9, 201; Kotkin, *Magnetic Mountain*, pp. 30–1; Suny, *The Soviet Experiment*, p. 234; Jeffrey T. Schnapp, *Building Fascism, Communism, Liberal Democracy: Gaetano Ciocca—Architect, Inventor, Farmer, Writer, Engineer* (Stanford, Calif.: Stanford University Press, 2004), pp. 269–70. See also François Furet, *The Passing of an Illusion: The Idea of Communism in the Twentieth Century*, translated by Deborah Furet (Chicago: University of Chicago Press, 1999), pp. 149–52, 287, on the wide appeal of Soviet planning, especially once the Depression had come to grip the West.

86 Malia, *The Soviet Tragedy*, pp. 185–6.

87 The combination was a radical departure; no Communist faction or leader had advocated anything like it. Stalin was quite aware of having profoundly altered Lenin's NEP policies, yet to counter any alarm, he claimed as late as June 1930—some say even as late as 1931—that this was still the NEP, albeit in a different form. See Boffa, *The Stalin Phenomenon*, p. 38n; and Cohen, *Rethinking the Soviet Experience*, p. 62.

88 Lewin, *The Making of the Soviet System*, p. 227; Suny, *The Soviet Experiment*, p. 190.

89 Fitzpatrick, *Everyday Stalinism*, p. 54.

90 Malia, *The Soviet Tragedy*, pp. 194–6, 201.

91 The speech was followed by a Central Committee resolution to that effect on January 30, 1930. See Kotkin, *Magnetic Mountain*, pp. 80–1; Fitzpatrick, *Everyday Stalinism*, p. 26.

92 Anne Appelbaum, *Gulag: A History* (New York: Doubleday, 2003), pp. 41–57.

93 Malia, *The Soviet Tragedy*, pp. 192–3.

94 Fitzpatrick, *The Russian Revolution*, p. 136. See also Malia, *The Soviet Tragedy*, pp. 190–1; and Fitzpatrick, *Everyday Stalinism*, p. 26.

95 Suny, *The Soviet Experiment*, pp. 224–5.

96 Lynne Viola, "The second coming: Class enemies in the Soviet countryside, 1927–35," in Getty and Manning (eds.), *Stalinist Terror*, pp. 68, 98; Malia, *The Soviet Tragedy*, pp. 197–8. The number of victims of Stalinism has been much in dispute in recent years. Fitzpatrick concluded that there must have been three to four million deaths, devastating enough to affect the birthrate for several years, but some still accept Conquest's figure of six million. Fitzpatrick, *Everyday Stalinism*, p. 41, noted that Conquest's figures were more widely accepted for the terror famine than for the terror of the later 1930s.

97 Malia, *The Soviet Tragedy*, p. 208; Suny, "Stalin and his Stalinism," pp. 44–5; Fitzpatrick, *Everyday Stalinism*, p. 90. The industrialization drive continued, but members of collective farms could own livestock and bring some surplus to market. On all sides, there was more consumption, more dancing—and women were again wearing make-up.

98 Cohen, *Rethinking the Soviet Experience*, pp. 63–4, 67–8, is good on this theme; he follows Moshe Lewin especially. See also Kotkin, *Magnetic Mountain*, p. 41, which also follows Lewin, and p. 279, where Kotkin notes "the perverse assemblage of unintended consequences" that resulted from the Bolshevik economic experiment.

99 Boffa, *The Stalin Phenomenon*, pp. 19–20. This accent on world-historical novelty pervades *The Short Biography of Stalin* (1949).

100 Kopelev, *The Education of a True Believer*, pp. 90–1, 226, 235.

101 Suny, "Stalin and his Stalinism," pp. 36–7; see also p. 39, as well as Suny, *The Soviet Experiment*, pp. 244–5.

102 Malia, *The Soviet Tragedy*, pp. 178 (for quotation), 201.

103 Fitzpatrick, *Everyday Stalinism*, pp. 66–8.

104 Kotkin, *Magnetic Mountain*, pp. 15–16.

105 *Ibid.* pp. 92–3, 149–50, 358.

106 *Ibid.*, p. 203.

107 *Ibid.*, pp. 17, 29–30, 358–9.

108 *Ibid.*, p. 277; in attempting to establish a state-run economy, "the regime took on tasks it did not have the capacity to resolve." Fitzpatrick, *Everyday Stalinism*, p. 54, notes that the malfunctioning of the new distribution system was not surprising, given the scale of what was being attempted. The Communists were not prepared, because that had assumed that their effort would generate abundance.

109 Kolakowski, *Main Currents of Marxism*, 2, pp. 489–90, 513. See also Fitzpatrick, *Everyday Stalinism*, pp. 38–9.

110 Lewin, "Bureaucracy and the Stalinist state," pp. 65–6; Lewin, *The Making of the Soviet System*, p. 301. See also Kotkin, *Magnetic Mountain*, pp. 283–4, on what Kotkin himself found to be the inadequacy of the understanding of party–state interaction even among specialists.

111 Fitzpatrick, *Everyday Stalinism*, pp. 3, 6, 8, 21, 28–9.

112 See Rittersporn, *Stalinist Simplifications*, pp. 18–19, 42–3, on the overall tendency to spin out of control in light of the magnitude of the tasks undertaken. American worker John Scott noted in his memoir the lack of preparation on the part of those left in charge at Magnitogorsk once most of the foreigners had left by 1934; see John Scott, *Behind the Urals: An American Worker in Russia's City of Steel*, enlarged ed. prepared by Stephen Kotkin (Bloomington: Indiana University Press, 1989; original ed., 1942), pp. 174–5. In his "Editor's introduction" to *An American Engineer in Stalin's Russia: The Memoirs of Zara Witkin* (Berkeley: University of California Press, 1991), Michael Gelb provides a brief survey of the first-hand accounts by the many foreigners who came to the Soviet Union during the 1930s, some simply to see for themselves but others, from ordinary workers to engineers and specialists, to partici-pate directly in the Soviet experiment; see pp. 3–6.

113 Lewin, "Bureaucracy and the Stalinist state," p. 70.

114 Arriving in the Soviet Union full of idealistic enthusiasm in 1932, the brilliant young American engineer Zara Witkin (1900–40) left in 1934 disillusioned with the bureaucratic incompetence, the forces for shoddiness, and the disinterest in innova-tion that were coming to seem inherent in the Soviet system. Witkin wrote his memoirs during the late 1930s, after returning to the USA, but he could not find a publisher. See Zara Witkin, *An American Engineer in Stalin's Russia: The Memoirs of Zara Witkin*, edited by Michael Gelb (Berkeley: University of California Press, 1991); and Gelb's introduction, pp. 6–10, for a good summary.

115 Gábor Tamás Rittersporn, "The omnipresent conspiracy: On Soviet imagery of politics and social relations in the 1930s," in Getty and Manning (eds.), *Stalinist Terror*, pp. 102 (for quote), 108–9. See also Rittersporn, *Stalinist Simplifications*, pp. 32–4.

116 Kotkin, *Magnetic Mountain*, pp. 58–9.

117 Fitzpatrick, *Everyday Stalinism*, pp. 70–1; Thurston, *Life and Terror*, p. 170; Kotkin, *Magnetic Mountain*, pp. 45–6.

118 Kotkin, *Magnetic Mountain*, pp. 46, 57, 59, 297.

119 Suny, *The Soviet Experiment*, p. 253; Suny, "Stalin and his Stalinism," pp. 34–5. See also Fitzpatrick, *Everyday Stalinism*, pp. 30–5.

120 Lewin, *The Making of the Soviet System*, p. 265.
121 Lewin, "Bureaucracy and the Stalinist state," pp. 67, 71.
122 Robert C. Tucker, "Introduction: Lenin and revolution," in Robert C. Tucker (ed.), *The Lenin Anthology* (New York: W.W. Norton, 1975), pp. lx–lxi.
123 Malia, *The Soviet Tragedy*, pp. 170, 240–3. See also Kotkin, *Magnetic Mountain*, p. 227, on the embrace of Stalin as the personification of the revolution.
124 Suny, "Stalin and his Stalinism," p. 43. See also Suny, *The Soviet Experiment*, p. 257.
125 Malia, *The Soviet Tragedy*, pp. 219–20.
126 Cohen, *Rethinking the Soviet Experience*, pp. 65–6. See also Boffa, *The Stalin Phenomenon*, p. 105.
127 Lewin, *The Making of the Soviet System*, p. 266.
128 Fitzpatrick, *Everyday Stalinism*, pp. 35–6.
129 Kotkin, *Magnetic Mountain*, pp. 223–5; Thurston, *Life and Terror*, p. 170.
130 Lewin, *The Making of the Soviet System*, pp. 218–21.
131 Malia, *The Soviet Tragedy*, p. 204.
132 Suny, "Stalin and his Stalinism," pp. 44–5.
133 Fitzpatrick, *Everyday Stalinism*, pp. 71–2, 74; James Van Geldern, "The centre and the periphery: Cultural and social geography in the mass culture of the 1930s," in Stephen White (ed.), *New Directions in Soviet History* (Cambridge: Cambridge University Press, 1992), pp. 66–7.
134 Mary Louise Loe, "Gorky and Nietzsche: The quest for a Russian superman," in Bernice Glatzer Rosenthal (ed.), *Nietzsche in Russia* (Princeton, NJ: Princeton University Press, 1986), pp. 251–73. See also Mikhail Agursky, "Nietzschean roots of Stalinist culture," in Bernice Glatzer Rosenthal (ed.), *Nietzsche and Soviet Culture: Ally and Adversary* (Cambridge: Cambridge University Press, 1994), pp. 256–86; and Bernice Glatzer Rosenthal, *New Myth, New World: From Nietzsche to Stalinism* (University Park, Pa.: Pennsylvania State University Press, 2002), pp. 351–422, especially pp. 352–5, 388–93, on the wider fortunes of Gorky and Soviet Nietzscheanism after Nietzsche was officially proscribed in 1933, upon Hitler's appointment as German chancellor.
135 Lewis H. Siegelbaum, *Stakhanovism and the Politics of Productivity in the USSR, 1935–1941* (Cambridge: Cambridge University Press, 1988), pp. 142–3; Thurston, *Life and Terror*, pp. 172–85.
136 Malia, *The Soviet Tragedy*, p. 205.
137 Siegelbaum, *Stakhanovism*, pp. 6–7, 75–6, 127, 296, 298.
138 Kotkin, *Magnetic Mountain*, p. 222; see also pp. 211–13, and Fitzpatrick, *Everyday Stalinism*, p. 106, on the tensions resulting from Stakhanovism.
139 Lewin, "Bureaucracy and the Stalinist state," p. 71.
140 Siegelbaum, *Stakhanovism*, pp. 80, 85–7. See also Rittersporn, *Stalinist Simplifications*, pp. 34–5 on the downside of Stakhanovism.
141 Siegelbaum, *Stakhanovism*, pp. 89–91, 299, 302–3; Roberta T. Manning, "The Soviet economic crisis of 1936–40 and the great purges," in Getty and Manning (eds.), *Stalinist Terror*, pp. 138–9; Robert Thurston, "The Stakhanovite movement: Background to the Great Terror in the factories, 1935–38," in Getty and Manning (eds.), *Stalinist Terror*, pp. 147, 149, 152; Thurston, *Life and Terror*, p. 182.
142 Thurston, "The Stakhanovite movement," pp. 143–5, 154; Thurston, *Life and Terror*, pp. 172–85; Fitzpatrick, *Everyday Stalinism*, p. 200.
143 Rittersporn, "The omnipresent conspiracy," p. 100; Suny, "Stalin and his Stalinism," p. 36; Fitzpatrick, *Everyday Stalinism*, p. 22.
144 Getty and Manning found the outcome in some respects to have been a defeat for Stalin, especially as Beria was forced on Stalin to replace Ezhov as NKVD chief. See their "Introduction" to Getty and Manning (eds.), *Stalinist Terror*, p. 5.
145 Thurston, *Life and Terror*, p. 25.
146 Quoted in Conquest, *The Great Terror*, p. 24.

147 Thurston emphasizes the impact of this event on Stalin; see Thurston, *Life and Terror*, pp. 18–19.
148 Suny, "Stalin and his Stalinism," p. 47; Thurston, *Life and Terror*, pp. 3–4, 6–11, 15.
149 Malia, *The Soviet Tragedy*, pp. 246; Thurston, *Life and Terror*, pp. 19–24. Suny, *The Soviet Experiment*, p. 260, finds it doubtful that Stalin was involved in the killing of Kirov.
150 Manning, "The Soviet economic crisis of 1936–40," pp. 118, 128, 137–8.
151 Getty, *Origins of the Great Purges*, pp. 96–102, 110–11, 118, 199–201; J. Arch Getty, "The politics of repression revisited," in Getty and Manning (eds.), *Stalinist Terror*, p. 50.
152 Fitzpatrick, *Everyday Stalinism*, p. 20.
153 Malia, *The Soviet Tragedy*, pp. 248; Thurston, *Life and Terror*, pp. 32–3, 107–8; Fitzpatrick, *Everyday Stalinism*, p. 192.
154 Thurston, *Life and Terror*, p. 106.
155 Kotkin, *Magnetic Mountain*, pp. 281–2; Fitzpatrick, *Everyday Stalinism*, p. 194; Malia, *The Soviet Tragedy*, p. 256; Thurston, *Life and Terror*, pp. 57–9.
156 Malia, *The Soviet Tragedy*, p. 248.
157 Fitzpatrick, *Everyday Stalinism*, pp. 21, 202–3.
158 Thurston, *Life and Terror*, pp. 38–9, 41–2, 113–14.
159 *Ibid.*, pp. 42, 57–8.
160 For examples of the now consensual notion that they really believed it, see Rittersporn, "The omnipresent conspiracy," pp. 106, 109, 115; and Thurston, *Life and Terror*, pp. 50–8, especially pp. 57–8.
161 Thurston, *Life and Terror*, pp. 81, 117; Thurston, "The Stakhanovite movement," pp. 152 and 152n.
162 Getty, "The politics of repression revisited," p. 59.
163 Thurston, *Life and Terror*, pp. 57–8; see also pp. 43–7.
164 Getty, "The politics of repression revisited," pp. 54, 56, 61–2. See also Getty, *Origins of the Great Purges*, p. 5; and Thurston, *Life and Terror*, pp. 57–8.
165 Thurston, *Life and Terror*, p. 57; see also pp. 43–9, 58, 131–2. In addition, see Getty, "The politics of repression revisited, " pp. 51, 59.
166 Thurston, *Life and Terror*, pp. xvii, 228–9.
167 Roberta T. Manning, "The great purges in a rural district: Belyi Raion revisited," in Getty and Manning (eds.), *Stalinist Terror*, pp. 196–7.
168 Kotkin, *Magnetic Mountain*, p. 343; Thurston, *Life and Terror*, p. 149.
169 Suny, "Stalin and his Stalinism," pp. 26, 50; Thurston, *Life and Terror*, pp. xx, 94, 143–6, 150–1, 154–6; Rittersporn, "The omnipresent conspiracy," pp. 112–13.
170 As Kotkin put it, "that the bosses did in fact have much to answer for was yet another factor contributing to the rationality of the terror." Kotkin, *Magnetic Mountain*, p. 344. See also pp. 341–2.
171 Siegelbaum, *Stakhanovism*, pp. 100, 143–4; Boris A. Starkov, "Narkom Ezhov," in Getty and Manning (eds.), *Stalinist Terror*, p. 33; Thurston, "The Stakhanovite movement," pp. 142–3, 154, 160.
172 To contemplate the limiting *reductio ad absurdum*, one could not cover oneself simply by denouncing everyone (whether above or below) and be done with it. It was bad to blame others, good to judge each on his or her merits. See Thurston, *Life and Terror*, p. 46; Rittersporn, "The omnipresent conspiracy," p. 111.
173 Thurston, *Life and Terror*, p. 151.
174 Getty, "The politics of repression revisited," pp. 59; Malia, *The Soviet Tragedy*, p. 256, Thurston, *Life and Terror*, pp. 62, 81, 112–13.
175 Starkov, "Narkom Ezhov," p. 33.
176 Kotkin, *Magnetic Mountain*, p. 335; Thurston, *Life and Terror*, pp. 90–1.

177 Kotkin, *Magnetic Mountain*, pp. 335–7; Thurston, *Life and Terror*, pp. 83, 87–91. Thurston's argument comes to seem forced when he notes on p. 87 that the NKVD "at least occasionally believed the confessions they obtained."

178 *Ibid.*, pp. 146–7, 159.

179 Starkov, "Narkom Ezhov," p. 36; Manning, "The great purges in a rural district," p. 193.

180 Thurston, *Life and Terror*, pp. 108–13, 120–1, 131; Fitzpatrick, *Everyday Stalinism*, pp. 208, 217.

181 Among the efforts to reassess the numbers are Alec Nove, "Victims of Stalinism: How many?" in Getty and Manning (eds.), *Stalinist Terror*, pp. 261–74; and Stephen G. Wheatcroft, "More light on the scale of repression and excess mortality in the Soviet Union in the 1930s," in Getty and Manning (eds.), *Stalinist Terror*, pp. 275–90. See also Thurston, *Life and Terror*, pp. 68–70; and Malia, *The Soviet Tragedy*, p. 263, for examples of contrasting emphases among leading scholars.

182 Thurston, *Life and Terror*, pp. 106, 128–31, 134–5.

183 Getty, "The politics of repression revisited," p. 62.

184 Suny, "Stalin and his Stalinism," pp. 48–50. See also Suny, *The Soviet Experiment*, p. 267.

185 Fitzpatrick, *The Russian Revolution*, pp. 168–70. The passage quoted is from p. 169.

186 Thurston, *Life and Terror*, pp. 76–7.

187 Rittersporn, "The omnipresent conspiracy," pp. 106, 115; see also pp. 105–9 overall.

188 Manning, "The Soviet economic crisis of 1936–40," p. 141.

189 Suny, *The Soviet Experiment*, p. 266, suggests that the total number of victims during the 1930s was ten to eleven million, including the four–five million victims of the terror famine of 1932–33.

190 Thurston, "The Stakhanovite movement," pp. 154–5. See also Thurston, *Life and Terror*, pp. 138–40, 232.

191 Thurston, *Life and Terror*, pp. 162–3.

192 Fitzpatrick, *Everyday Stalinism*, p. 93.

193 J. Arch Getty and William Chase, "Patterns of repression among the Soviet elite in the late 1930s: a Biographical approach," in Getty and Manning (eds.), *Stalinist Terror*, pp. 242–5; Sheila Fitzpatrick, "The impact of the great purges on Soviet elites: A case study from Moscow and Leningrad telephone directories of the 1930s," in Getty and Manning (eds.), *Stalinist Terror*, p. 256; Fitzpatrick, *Everyday Stalinism*, pp. 7, 192, 212; Thurston, *Life and Terror*, pp. 60–1.

194 Fitzpatrick, *Everyday Stalinism*, pp. 213–16; Kotkin, *Magnetic Mountain*, pp. 348–9.

195 Fitzpatrick, *Everyday Stalinism*, p. 224.

196 Roger R. Reese, "The Red Army and the great purges," in Getty and Manning (eds.), *Stalinist Terror*, pp. 198–214, especially p. 211; Fitzpatrick, *Everyday Stalinism*, p. 212; Thurston, *Life and Terror*, p. 156.

197 Cohen, *Rethinking the Soviet Experience*, pp. 68–9. See also Malia, *The Soviet Tragedy*, pp. 248–9; and Suny, "Stalin and his Stalinism," p. 36. Thurston, unlike most, denied that the terror was connected with generational change within the elite, facilitating the rise of those coming of age under Stalin. See Thurston, *Life and Terror*, pp. 133–4, 146.

198 Thurston, *Life and Terror*, pp. 160–1, 188–98.

199 *Ibid.*, pp. 229–30.

200 Suny, "Stalin and his Stalinism," p. 51.

201 Kopelev, *The Education of a True Believer*, pp. 197–8, noted that the vital forces of the party had been completely routed by 1938–39. By the time he was writing, around 1977, Kopelev found the Communist experiment reduced to mere administration, with no trace of the youthful revolutionary enthusiasm that had inspired his own cohort decades before.

202 Fitzpatrick, *Everyday Stalinism*, p. 217.

203 Cohen, *Rethinking the Soviet Experience*, pp. 143–4.

204 Fitzpatrick, *Everyday Stalinism*, pp. 114, 218–21.

205 Cohen, *Rethinking the Soviet Experience*, pp. 68–9.
206 Fitzpatrick, *Everyday Stalinism*, pp. 21, 28–9.
207 Suny, "Stalin and his Stalinism," p. 36; Suny, *The Soviet Experiment*, p. 252; Fitzpatrick, *Everyday Stalinism*, pp. 178–9.
208 Fitzpatrick, *Everyday Stalinism*, pp. 45, 175–7; Kotkin, *Magnetic Mountain*, pp. 261–3; Van Geldern, "The centre and the periphery," p. 71.
209 Thurston, *Life and Terror*, pp. 192–3. See also Robert W. Thurston, "Reassessing the history of Soviet workers: Opportunities to criticize and participate in decision-making, 1935–41," in White (ed.), *New Directions in Soviet History*, pp. 160–88.
210 Kotkin, *Magnetic Mountain*, pp. 154–5; see also pp. 158–60, 173–6, 223–5, 261–3, 356.
211 Fitzpatrick, *Everyday Stalinism*, pp. 8, 45. See also Thurston, "The Stakhanovite movement," p. 156.
212 Van Geldern, "The centre and the periphery," esp. pp. 71–2; see also pp. 64 and 69 on the vogue of the new Moscow metro and, more generally, the grandiose plan for the rebuilding of Moscow—as an image of the future. Suny explicitly follows and endorses Van Geldern in Suny, "Stalin and his Stalinism," pp. 36, 46. Also valuable is Christel Lane, *The Rites of Rulers: Ritual in Industrial Society—The Soviet Case* (Cambridge: Cambridge University Press, 1981), although it is less historical and is focused especially on the 1960s and 1970s.
213 Lewin, *The Making of the Soviet System*, pp. 305–6; Meyer, *Leninism*, pp. 56, 81n.
214 Fitzpatrick, *Everyday Stalinism*, pp. 105–6, 225–6.
215 Cohen, *Rethinking the Soviet Experience*, p. 145.
216 Lewin, "Bureaucracy and the Stalinist state," pp. 56, 72–3.
217 Cohen, *Rethinking the Soviet Experience*, pp. 147–8.
218 Malia, *The Soviet Tragedy*, pp. 494–5.
219 Suny, "Stalin and his Stalinism," p. 38.
220 Fitzpatrick, *Everyday Stalinism*, p. 107; see also pp. 79, 82, 156–62. Kotkin, *Magnetic Mountain*, pp. 126–7, is also good on differentiation, privilege, and *embourgeoisment*.
221 Fitzpatrick, *Everyday Stalinism*, pp. 95–105, esp. 103–5.
222 Jeffrey C. Goldfarb, *Beyond Glasnost: the Post-totalitarian Mind* (Chicago: University of Chicago Press, 1991), pp. 53–7, 90–1.
223 Fitzpatrick, *Everyday Stalinism*, p. 225.
224 This is Gleason paraphrasing Kolakowski in Gleason, *Totalitarianism*, pp. 175–6.
225 *Ibid.*, pp. 179, 210; see overall pp. 175–80, 182–8.
226 Malia, *The Soviet Tragedy*, pp. 495–6. In the same vein, see George Kennan, "Memorandum for the minister," *New York Review of Books*, April 26, 2001, p. 23 (Kennan's diplomatic dispatch from Riga, Latvia, in August 1932).
227 Gleason, *Totalitarianism*, p. 175.
228 *Ibid.*, p. 210.
229 Malia, *The Soviet Tragedy*, p. 201. See also pp. 218–19.
230 Kotkin, *Magnetic Mountain*, pp. 33 (including the quotation), 48, 50–2, 69–70.
231 Lewin, *The Making of the Soviet System*, pp. 209, 274.
232 Kotkin, *Magnetic Mountain*, p. 298.
233 Rittersporn, "The omnipresent conspiracy," p. 115.

Chapter 6

1 See, for example, Renzo De Felice, *Mussolini il duce*, I: *Gli anni del consenso, 1929–1936* (Turin: Giulio Einaudi, 1974), pp. 534–96, on Mussolini's standing in Europe prior to the invasion of Ethiopia in 1935.
2 Even Roger Griffin, who recognized the seriousness of the original revolutionary aspirations, was quick to adduce structural reasons for Fascism's failure, which thus comes to seem virtually inevitable. See his *The Nature of Fascism* (London:

Routledge, 1993), pp. 78–82, 133. But an element of teleological thinking lurks in Griffin's account, which is thus quick to impute irrelevance and defeat rather than attending to the openness, and thus the degree of contingency, in the Fascist trajectory. We need to follow that trajectory in a more deeply historical way to understand why it took the form it did and yielded the outcomes it did.

3 Abbott Gleason, *Totalitarianism: The Inner History of the Cold War* (New York: Oxford University Press, 1995), pp. 14–20; Emilio Gentile, *La via italiana al totalitarismo: Il partito e lo Stato nel regime fascista* (Rome: La Nuova Italia Scientifica, 1995), pp. 151, 204–5; Meir Michaelis, "Anmerkungen zum italienischen Totalitarismusbegriff. Zur Kritik der Thesen Hannah Arendts und Renzo De Felices," *Quellen und Forschungen aus italienischen Archiven und Bibliotheken* 62 (1982): 292–4.

4 Michaelis, "Anmerkungen," pp. 295–7. Mussolini seems first to have used "totalitarian" in his speech closing the fourth national congress of the Fascist Party in Rome, June 22, 1925. He referred to "our ferocious totalitarian will" in proclaiming that "we want to fascistize the nation." Benito Mussolini, *Opera omnia di Benito Mussolini*, edited by Edoardo e Duilio Susmel, 35 vols. (Florence: La Fenice, 1951–62): 21 (1956), p. 362.

5 "La nostra formula è questa; tutto nello Stato, niente al di fuori dello Stato, nulla contro lo Stato." Mussolini, *Opera omnia* 21 (1956), p. 425 (October 28, 1925).

6 Early in 1925, with Fascism getting a bad press abroad and even still at home, Gentile convened a conference on Fascist culture in Bologna intended to demonstrate that, despite the recent violence, there was no cleft between Fascism and the cultural realm. Gentile was then entrusted by the congress to draft a manifesto justifying Fascism as an innovative departure embodying the best of Italian traditions. Just after the Bologna meeting, the Istituto Nazionale Fascista di Cultura (INFC) was founded with Gentile as president and with its self-proclaimed goal the systematic development of an organic national political consciousness. For Gentile's role, see Gabriele Turi, *Giovanni Gentile: Una biografia* (Florence: Giunti, 1995), pp. 350, 356–7. Gentile's manifesto provoked a famed counter-manifesto from the anti-Fascists Benedetto Croce and Giovanni Amendola. The classic account of this intellectual–political battle is Emilio R. Papa, *Storia di due manifeste: Il fascismo e la cultura italiana* (Milan: Feltrinelli, 1958), which first made clear, after it was all over, the significance of the confrontation. The journalistic organ of the INFC was first *Educazione politica*, which became *Educazione fascista* in January 1927, then *Civiltà fascista* in 1934. Gentile remained in charge, while juggling his many lead roles. With Mussolini's active collaboration, he prepared "The doctrine of Fascism" ("La dottrina del fascismo"), the theoretical section of Mussolini's article on Fascism for the new Treccani *Enciclopedia Italiana* in 1932.

7 Alberto Aquarone, *L'organizzazione dello Stato totalitario* (Turin: Einaudi, 1965), pp. 52–60. See also pp. 366–75 for the corporativist portions of the committee's proposal. On p. 60, Aquarone plays down the impact of the commission's labors on the legislation that followed, noting that in light of the disparate membership, some were concerned simply to strengthen the executive *vis-à-vis* parliament. See David D. Roberts, *The Syndicalist Tradition and Italian Fascism* (Chapel Hill: University of North Carolina Press, 1979), pp. 237–40, on the complex relationship between the commission's labors and the outcome at this point.

8 De Felice, *Mussolini il duce*, I, p. 177.

9 Ruth Ben-Ghiat, *Fascist Modernities: Italy, 1922–1945* (Berkeley: University of California Press, 2001), pp. 175–6. On the origins of this set of impulses, as they developed, most immediately, from Italy's war experience, see Emilio Gentile, *The Sacralization of Politics in Fascist Italy*, translated by Keith Botsford (Cambridge, Mass.: Harvard University Press, 1996), pp. 15–18. Although invaluable in certain respects, Gentile's account affords little sense of the opposition to intervention and the denigration of the war by some in the aftermath. Thus the stakes of the effort to mobilize around the Italian war experience could be clearer.

10 Benito Mussolini, "Il discorso all'Ascensione" (speech to the Chamber of Deputies, May 26, 1927), in Benito Mussolini, *Scritti e discorsi di Benito Mussolini*, vol. 6: *Scritti e discorsi dal 1927-V al 1928-VI—VII E. F.* (Milan: Ulrico Hoepli, 1934), p. 77. This boast concludes Mussolini's lengthy speech.

11 Mabel Berezin, *Making the Fascist Self: The Political Culture of Interwar Italy* (Ithaca, N.Y.: Cornell University Press, 1997), p. 166.

12 Ben-Ghiat, *Fascist Modernities*, p. 19.

13 Luca de Caprariis, "Fascism and Italian foreign policy: 1922–28" (Ph.D. dissertation, University of Wisconsin, Madison, 1998), p. 246.

14 Maria Sophia Quine, *Population Politics in Twentieth-Century Europe: Fascist Dictatorships and Liberal Democracies* (London and New York: Routledge, 1996), pp. 27–8.

15 *Ibid.*, pp. 40–1.

16 This was the *Opera nazionale per la protezione della maternità ed infanzia* (ONMI). See Maria Sophia Quine, *Italy's Social Revolution: Charity and Welfare from Liberalism to Fascism* (Houndmills: Palgrave, 2002), pp. 96–128, on the fortunes of this institution and the Fascist welfare state more generally.

17 Quine, *Population Politics*, pp. 66–7.

18 *Ibid.*, pp. 29–31. Gini was influenced by Charles Darwin and Herbert Spencer in this regard. Together with Giuseppe Sergi, he founded the Italian Eugenic Society in 1912.

19 *Ibid.*, pp. 66–8, 92. Gini was by that point president of the newly formed Italian Society of Genetics and Eugenics.

20 Emilio Gentile, *La via italiana*, pp. 163–4.

21 *Ibid.*, pp. 164–5, 168, 172–5.

22 Gentile, *The Sacralization of Politics*, p. 63; Gentile, *La via italiana*, p. 89–90.

23 Roberts, *The Syndicalist Tradition*, pp. 206–7, 289–91.

24 John F. Pollard, *The Vatican and Italian Fascism, 1929–1932: A Study in Conflict* (Cambridge: Cambridge University Press, 1985), pp. 48–54, 101.

25 Turi, *Giovanni Gentile*, pp. 398–9, 402.

26 Renzo De Felice, *Fascism: An Informal Introduction to Its Theory and Practice* (an interview with Michael A. Ledeen) (New Brunswick, N.J.: Transaction Books, 1976), pp. 60, 70.

27 Quine, *Population Politics*, p. 40.

28 Mabel Berezin, for example, found that the Church was gradually being marginalized in light of the ritual patterns in Verona. See Berezin, *Making the Fascist Self*, p. 176.

29 Gentile, *The Sacralization of Politics*, pp. 69–75, is especially good on this theme.

30 Turi, *Giovanni Gentile*, p. 469.

31 When he came to the years after Ethiopia in his monumental biography of Mussolini, De Felice's choice of subtitle was highly indicative; see Renzo De Felice, *Mussolini il duce*, II: *Lo Stato totalitario, 1936–1940* (Turin: Giulio Einaudi, 1981); see especially pp. 82–93. In his earlier volumes, De Felice had concluded that Mussolini was quite serious about domestic transformation, with corporativism as its core. But by the early 1930s the Duce had come to recognize how potent were the obstacles to any effort to fascistize Italian society directly. Renzo De Felice, *Mussolini il fascista*, II: *L'organizzazione dello Stato fascista, 1925–1929* (Turin: Giulio Einaudi, 1968), pp. 300–1, 359, 363–7; De Felice, *Mussolini il duce*, I, pp. 177–81. See also De Felice, *Fascism*, p. 79; Gentile, *La via italiana*, pp. 114–15; and Michaelis, "Anmerkungen," p. 291.

32 De Felice, *Fascism*, pp. 59–60.

33 *Ibid.*, pp. 49, 54–5, 74–5.

34 *Ibid.*, pp. 102, 106. At this point, De Felice strongly contrasted the Italian Fascist revolutionary aspiration with Nazism, characterized especially by its putatively atavistic racism.

35 De Felice, *Mussolini il duce*, I, pp. 220–8; see especially pp. 227–8. For a typically negative account of the Starace era in English, see Denis Mack Smith, *Mussolini: A Biography* (New York: Random House [Vintage Books], 1983), pp. 175–81.

36 Gentile, *The Sacralization of Politics*, pp. 28, 75–9, 132–3; see also Gentile, *La via italiana*, pp. 144–8, on "the myth of the Duce."

37 Gentile insisted that although comparison reveals differences, they are best understood from *within* a common totalitarian departure. At the same time, the incompleteness of the totalitarianism, so often noted in the Italian case, was true in the other two as well. See Gentile, *La via italiana*, pp. 148–53; especially pp. 149–50. Arguing explicitly against Arendt and De Felice, Michaelis had made much the same overall point in his "Anmerkungen" of 1982, although his understanding of the sources and meaning of the totalitarian thrust was more conventional than Gentile's later.

38 Gentile, *La via italiana*, pp. 148–9.

39 *Ibid.*, pp. 119, 135–6.

40 *Ibid.*, pp. 168–70. See also Emilio Gentile, *Storia del partito fascista, 1919–1922: Movimento e milizia* (Rome and Bari: Laterza, 1989), preface, pp. vii–x, where Gentile nicely locates his own effort in light of what he convincingly deemed the anomalous neglect of the Fascist Party in recent research.

41 Gentile, *La via italiana*, pp. 148–9.

42 *Ibid.*, pp. 117–18.

43 *Ibid.*, pp. 164–5, 168–70, 172–5.

44 Gentile laid out much of this argument in Emilio Gentile, *Il mito dello stato nuovo dall'antigiolittismo al fascismo* (Rome and Bari: Laterza, 1982); see especially pp. 249–52 on Fascism as a political religion. See also Gentile, *The Sacralization of Politics*, pp. 19–31. With these accents, Gentile was moving far from De Felice, who had observed in his famed interview of the mid-1970s (*Fascism*, p. 76) that in Italian Fascism "ritual existed—the salute to the Duce, the call to the fallen heroes—but it does not have a decisive role. Here we have another difference with Germany, where ritual tends to become everything." De Felice was explicitly drawing from George L. Mosse's work on Germany.

45 Gentile, *La via italiana*, pp. 113–19; see especially p. 116.

46 *Ibid.*, pp. 134, 178–91. See also Gentile, *The Sacralization of Politics*, p. 138, on the "grotesque and risible aspects" of the cult of the Duce.

47 Emilio Gentile, *Le religioni della politica: Fra democrazia e totalitarismi* (Rome and Bari: Laterza, 2001), pp. xvii–xviii.

48 For Gentile's overall conception of totalitarianism and political religion, see *ibid.*, pp. 69–102, especially the definition on pp. 70–4. See also Gentile, *The Sacralization of Politics*, p. 160, for some especially cogent remarks on the seriousness of the impulse.

49 Much like Gentile, Mabel Berezin warned that "to ascribe the proliferation of fascist public spectacle to the fanaticism of Starace is to attenuate the extent to which it was part of the fabric of the fascist cultural project. . . . Starace notwithstanding, fascist spectacle sprang from a general agreement among fascist elites, including Mussolini, that the state needed to theatricalize everyday life." See Berezin, *Making the Fascist Self*, p. 65.

50 *Ibid.*, pp. 29–30, 47; Jeffrey T. Schnapp, *Staging Fascism: 18 BL and the Theater of Masses for Masses* (Stanford, Calif.: Stanford University Press, 1996), pp. 5–7.

51 Berezin, *Making the Fascist Self*, p. 46.

52 *Ibid.*, p. 29.

53 *Ibid.*, p. 30.

54 Gentile, *The Sacralization of Politics*, pp. 159–60.

55 Emilio Gentile, *Le origini dell'ideologia fascista (1918–1925)* (Rome and Bari: Laterza, 1975). See Gentile, *The Sacralization of Politics*, pp. 1–18, 153–61, for his way of placing Fascist sacralization on the wider Italian and European levels. Gentile's more recent *Le religioni della politica* extends his discussion of the supranational framework.

56 Stanley G. Payne, *A History of Fascism, 1914–1945* (Madison: University of Wisconsin Press, 1995), p. 494.

57 Zeev Sternhell, with Mario Sznajder and Maia Asheri, *The Birth of Fascist Ideology: From Cultural Rebellion to Political Revolution*, translated by David Maisel (Princeton, NJ: Princeton University Press, 1994; original French ed., 1989), p. 231.

58 Griffin, *The Nature of Fascism*, pp. 38–40, and throughout.

59 See, for example, Gentile, *Il mito dello stato nuovo*, pp. 263–70; Gentile, *La via italiana*, pp. 131–2; and Gentile, *The Sacralization of Politics*, p. 82.

60 Raymond Grew noted the Italian tendency during the pre-Fascist period to view problems that were at least as worrisome elsewhere as distinctively and endemically Italian. See Raymond Grew, "The paradoxes of Italy's nineteenth-century political culture," in Isser Woloch (ed.), *Revolutions and the Meanings of Freedom in the Nineteenth Century* (Stanford, Calif.: Stanford University Press), p. 244.

61 R.J.B. Bosworth, *The Italian Dictatorship: Problems and Perspectives in the Interpretation of Mussolini and Fascism* (London: Edward Arnold, 1998), pp. 5, 179, 204, 225.

62 *Ibid.*, p. 5.

63 *Ibid.*, pp. 21 and 21n., 26–7. Although Bosworth, on p. 24, was surely right to find Mosse the key source of the newly dominant culturalist reading, he went too far in referring to "the curious alliance between the De Feliceans, and especially Emilio Gentile, and American cultural and intellectual historians" (p. 127). Although there are points of contact, partly, indeed, through the influence of Mosse, Gentile is not to be conflated with the American culturalists, most basically because, as noted above, he does not emphasize style *as opposed to* ideological content or substance.

64 *Ibid.*, pp. 133–53 (chapter 6 on "Fascist society") provides a good sense of the issues and the scholarship at issue. See also pp. 28–31, and especially the accent on lingering Catholicism as opposed to new religion on p. 64, a veiled put-down of Mosse and Gentile.

65 *Ibid.*, pp. 99–100.

66 *Ibid.*, pp. 28, 30, 61, 67–8. The tension between Fascism and (Americanist) consumerism is explored in many recent works; see, for example, Ben-Ghiat, *Fascist Modernities*, pp. 71–4.

67 Bosworth, *The Italian Dictatorship*, pp. 225–6.

68 I argue along these lines in David D. Roberts, *Nothing but History: Reconstruction and Extremity After Metaphysics* (Berkeley: University of California Press, 1995). My aim was to head off certain excesses in what is taken to be postmodernism but also to show how the ideas of Derrida, Foucault, Gadamer, and Rorty can contribute to a deeper historical self-understanding in contemporary culture.

69 See for, example, Mussolini's lament to Ottavio Dinale in 1943, as conveyed in Ottavio Dinale, *Quarant'anni di colloqui con lui* (Milan: Ciarrocca, 1953), p. 181. We will consider this example on p. 314.

70 E.J. Hobsbawm, "The great Gramsci," *New York Review of Books*, April 4, 1974, p. 39. See also in Chapter 3, p. 132.

71 For a few examples of such recognition from abroad, see Franz Neumann, *Behemoth: The Structure and Practice of National Socialism, 1933–1944* (New York: Harper & Row [Harper Torchbooks], 1966), pp. 75–7, which cites Rocco, Gentile, and Panunzio along with Mussolini; Herbert Marcuse, *Reason and Revolution: Hegel and the Rise of Social Theory* (Boston: Beacon Press, 1960; first published 1941), p. 403, which finds Panunzio "the official theoretician of the Fascist state"; and Herbert L. Matthews, *The Fruits of Fascism* (New York: Harcourt, Brace, 1943), pp. 151–3, which cites Gentile and Panunzio. Matthews was a *New York Times* correspondent.

72 Giuseppe Calandra, for example, suggested that Fascism embraced Gentile's actu- alism because, in light of the varied, even contradictory quality of Fascist elements, it needed an overarching ideological principle of unification. Gentile's abstract philos- ophy filled the bill. Fascism, for Calandra, was essentially a movement of reaction on the part of erstwhile liberals scared by the new mass politics emerging from the war. See Giuseppe Calandra, *Gentile e il fascismo* (Rome and Bari: Laterza, 1987), especially pp. vii, 4, 12–13, 113, 156.

73 Berezin, *Making the Fascist Self*, p. 246.
74 *Ibid.*, p. 138.
75 Bosworth, *The Italian Dictatorship*, p. 149.
76 Sternhell, *The Birth of Fascist Ideology*. Central to A. James Gregor's effort have been *The Ideology of Fascism: The Rationale of Totalitarianism* (New York: Free Press, 1969); *The Fascist Persuasion in Radical Politics* (Princeton, N.J.: Princeton University Press, 1974); *Italian Fascism and Developmental Dictatorship* (Princeton, N.J.: Princeton University Press, 1979); and *Young Mussolini and the Intellectual Origins of Fascism* (Berkeley: University of California Press, 1979). For a critique of Sternhell that also briefly addresses Gregor, see David D. Roberts, "How not to think about fascism and ideology, intellectual antecedents and historical meaning," *Journal of Contemporary History* 35, no. 2 (April 2000): 185–211.
77 Herbert W. Schneider, *Making the Fascist State* (New York: Howard Fertig, 1968; first published 1928), p. 237.
78 In a study published in 1971, Martin Jänicke did justice to the roles of Gentile, Rocco, and Panunzio as few elsewhere were prepared to do at the time. But although he provided some sense of the changing dynamics of the Fascist regime, he afforded only a limited sense of the differences between the three thinkers and ended up relying too heavily on Panunzio's *Allgemeine Theorie des Fascistischen Staates* (1934), which had made this Fascist thinker particularly well known in Germany. See Martin Jänicke, *Totalitäre Herrschaft: Anatomie eines politischen Begriffes* (Berlin: Dencker & Humblot, 1971), pp. 22–34, 204–6.
79 This is the thrust of Denis Mack Smith's *Mussolini*.
80 Ben-Ghiat, *Fascist Modernities*, p. 9; Bosworth, *The Italian Dictatorship*, p. 175.
81 MacGregor Knox, *Common Destiny: Dictatorship, Foreign Policy, and War in Fascist Italy and Nazi Germany* (Cambridge: Cambridge University Press, 2000), pp. 55–9. See p. 57 for the quoted phrase.
82 This was the title of Knox's first book, *Mussolini Unleashed, 1939–1941: Politics and Strategy in Fascist Italy's Last War* (Cambridge: Cambridge University Press, 1982). Although he has nuanced his argument in recent years, its main lines have remained the same.
83 MacGregor Knox, "Fascism: Ideology, foreign policy, and war," in Adrian Lyttelton (ed.), *Liberal and Fascist Italy* (Oxford: Oxford University Press, 2002), pp. 137–8.
84 *Ibid.*, p. 115.
85 They had only "dei frammenti dove c'è tutto un miscuglio impossibile delle cose più disparate," said Mussolini in a speech to the Fascist militia in Milan on the first anniversary of the March on Rome, now in Mussolini, *Opera omnia di Benito Mussolini*, 20 (1956), pp. 64–5. See also Mussolini, *Opera Omnia di Benito Mussolini*, v. 21 (1956), pp. 422–7 (speech of October 28, 1925, in Milan); and Benito Mussolini, "The doctrine of fascism," in Adrian Lyttelton (ed.), *Italian Fascisms from Pareto to Gentile* (New York, Harper & Row [Harper Torchbooks], 1975), pp. 41, 49, 57.
86 Emilio Gentile, *La via italiana*, p. 143.
87 Bosworth, *The Italian Dictatorship*, p. 22.
88 George L. Mosse, *The Nationalization of the Masses: Political Symbolism and Mass Movements in Germany from the Napoleonic Wars through the Third Reich* (Ithaca, N.Y.: Cornell University Press, 1991); George L. Mosse, *The Fascist Revolution: Toward a General Theory of Fascism* (New York: Howard Fertig, 1999).
89 See, for example, Gentile, *The Sacralization of Politics*, pp. 3, 32–3, on the Fascist abolition of liberty. At the same time, compare his emphasis on "the practice of its politics through myth, ritual, and symbolism" with the Giovanni Gentilian Giorgio Masi's explicit accent on ongoing history making, which Emilio Gentile quotes in stressing the decisive contribution of the Gentilian idealist intellectuals in institutionalizing fascist religion (see pp. 53, 57–8). The Giovanni Gentilean concern with collective history making points well beyond the mode of involvement that an experience of "myth, ritual, and symbolism" would make possible.

90   *Ibid.*, p. 5.
91   Gentile, *La via italiana*, pp. 141–3.
92   *Ibid.*, p. 142.
93   See Simonetta Falasca-Zamponi, *Fascist Spectacle: The Aesthetics of Power in Mussolini's Italy* (Berkeley: University of California Press, 1997), pp. 44, 56, 85, 100, 117, 187–8, for key indications of her overall theme.
94   See especially *ibid.*, pp. 88, 122–4, where Mussolinian Fascism is linked to the Nietzschean "superman," understood as an artist-creator who shapes masses.
95   *Ibid.*, p. 124.
96   *Ibid.*, pp. 186–7, 192. See also pp. 129–35, 144–6 on corporativism.
97   *Ibid.*, pp. 88, 122–4.
98   *Ibid.*, pp. 129–35, 144–6. Even as she quoted both Panunzio and Carlo Costamagna on pp. 134–45, Falasca-Zamponi gave no sense of their crucial differences, which emerged clearly in their important polemic in *Rivista internazionale di filosofia del diritto* during 1926. See Roberts, *The Syndicalist Tradition*, pp. 240–4, on this exchange, and De Felice, *Mussolini il duce*, II, pp. 67–9, for further observations on the significance of the differences between these two Fascists.
99   Falasca-Zamponi *Fascist Spectacle*, p. 124.
100 Ben-Ghiat, *Fascist Modernities*, pp. 4–5, 80, 209.
101 *Ibid.*, pp. 2–3, 8, 94–5, 209.
102 In this connection, let us recall Detlev Peukert's point, noted in Chapters 1 and 4, concerning the difficulty of distinguishing forward-looking from reactionary impulses in responses to "modernity" as of that point. See Detlev J.K. Peukert, *The Weimar Republic: The Crisis of Classical Modernity* (New York: Hill and Wang, 1993), pp. 187–8.
103 Payne, *A History of Fascism*, p. 478. See also Bruno P.F. Wanrooij, "Italian society under fascism," in Lyttelton (ed.), *Liberal and Fascist Italy*, pp. 182–6, for a good brief treatment of the "ruralization" strategy, including its plausible rationale, problematic execution, and essentially failed outcome. Also of interest is Roberto Dainotto, "'Tramonto' and 'Risorgimento': Gentile's dialectics and the prophecy of nationhood," in Albert Russell Ascoli and Krystyna von Henneberg (eds.), *Making and Remaking Italy: The Cultivation of National Identity around the Risorgimento* (Oxford: Berg, 2001), pp. 241–55, on Giovanni Gentile's open-ended dialectic of regional and national culture.
104 Jeffrey T. Schnapp, *Building Fascism, Communism, Liberal Democracy: Gaetano Ciocca—Architect, Inventor, Farmer, Writer, Engineer* (Stanford, Calif.: Stanford University Press, 2004), pp. 76–7, 88, 99.
105 See, for example, Ben-Ghiat, *Fascist Modernities*, pp. 100–1.
106 *Ibid.*, p. 5. See also p. 8.
107 Knox, "Fascism: Ideology, foreign policy, and war," pp. 113–14.
108 *Ibid.*, p. 113; Knox, *Common Destiny*, pp. 57–8. Renzo De Felice, in contrast, maintained that Gentile's ideas constituted "an important and authentic component" in Mussolini's political culture. See De Felice, *Mussolini il duce*, I, p. 35.
109 Knox, *Common Destiny*, p. 58.
110 De Felice, *Mussolini il duce*, I, p. 177.
111 See, for example, Alfredo Rocco, Manifesto of *Politica*, in Lyttelton (ed.), *Italian Fascisms from Pareto to Gentile*, pp. 251–2, 260.
112 See, for example, the speech by the one-time syndicalist Panunzio to the Chamber of Deputies in 1929 on the overtly totalitarian quality of the new Fascist education, published as Sergio Panunzio, *Lo Stato educativo* (Rome: Camera dei Deputati, 1929); see especially p. 11, but also pp. 4–8, 23. For a survey of Fascist education, see Michel Ostenc, *L'éducation en Italie pendant le Fascisme* (Paris: Publications de la Sorbonne, 1980).
113 For well-known examples, see Mussolini's speech in Milan to the Fascist militia on the first anniversary of the March on Rome and his "Discorso di Pesaro" (August

18, 1926), now in Mussolini, *Opera omnia*, 20 (1956), pp. 64–5; and 22 (1957), p. 197. See also Berezin, *Making the Fascist Self*, pp. 104–5, 107.

114 Mussolini, *Opera omnia*, 4 (1952), p. 174.

115 Schnapp, *Building Fascism*, pp. 38, 54–5.

116 Sternhell, *The Birth of Fascist Ideology*, p. 231.

117 Gleason, *Totalitarianism*, p. 19.

118 Giuseppe Bottai, *Esperienza corporativa (1929–1934)* (Florence: Vallecchi, 1934), pp. 584–94.

119 Typical was Mussolini's use of "myth" in his well-known speech in Naples of October 24, 1922, just before the March on Rome, excerpted in Roger Griffin (ed.), *Fascism* (Oxford: Oxford University Press, 1995), p. 44. "We have created our myth . . . the greatness of the nation." Such a myth, Mussolini noted explicitly, need not literally anticipate reality but, bound up with hope, faith, and passion, it affords a stimulus to ongoing action. Although his usage clearly reflects his reading of Sorel, Mussolini was invoking "myth" in a "post-Sorelian" way, reflecting his wider sense of the scope for collective action. Such a lucid embrace of myth was not consistent with Sorel's primitivism, a distinction often missed. See, for example, Philip Morgan's treatment of the same passage in his *Fascism in Europe, 1919–1945* (London: Routledge, 2003), p. 127.

120 See, for example, Sternhell, *The Birth of Fascist Ideology*, p. 118. Mosse, too, fell into the widespread tendency to treat myth as a way to direct and control mass movements; see *Nationalization of the Masses*, p. 12.

121 For one prominent example, see Delio Cantimori, *Conversando di storia* (Bari: Laterza, 1967), pp. 138–9. See also Delio Cantimori, *Politica e storia contemporanea: Scritti (1927–1942)*, edited and with an introduction by Luisa Mangoni (Turin: Giulio Einaudi, 1991). In addition, see Sergio Romano, *Giovanni Gentile: La filosofia al potere* (Milan, 1984), pp. 236–48, 272. Cf. the itineraries of Adolfo Omodeo and Guido De Ruggiero, who, after being deeply influenced by Gentile early on, ended up notable liberals.

122 For example, see G.A. Fanelli, *Contra Gentiles: Mistificazioni dell'idealismo attuale nella rivoluzione fascista* (Rome: Biblioteca del Secolo Fascista, 1933). See also Alessandra Tarquini, "Gli antigentiliani nel fascismo degli anni venti," *Storia contemporanea* 27, no. 1 (February 1996): 5–59; Alessandra Tarquini, "The anti-Gentilians during the fascist regime," *Journal of Contemporary History*, 40(4) (October 2005): 637–62; and the aptly titled conclusion—"Una difficile egemonia" (a difficult hegemony)—to Gabriele Turi's well-researched and carefully balanced biography, *Giovanni Gentile*, pp. 446–526.

123 When the Grand Council of Fascism was made a state entity in 1928, Gentile insisted that it was now time to dispense with the party altogether. All were now fascists—and equal as fascists. See Turi, *Giovanni Gentile*, pp. 412, 416–20; and Gentile, *La via italiana*, p. 170.

124 Even as Gentile's de-emphasis on the party alienated some, it helped to cement his leadership role for others. Especially during the pivotal years just after the Matteotti crisis, when the party was identified with Farinacci, Gentile seemed to be articulating the long-term aims of fascism, beyond the petty everyday politicking. See Turi, *Giovanni Gentile*, p. 371.

125 *Ibid.*, pp. 407–8, 413.

126 Gentile's "L'essenza del fascismo" is included in Giovanni Gentile, *Origini e dottrina del fascismo* (Rome: Libreria del Littorio, 1929), which is included in Giovanni Gentile, *Politica e cultura*, vol. 1, edited by Hervé A. Cavallera (Florence: Le Lettere, 1990), vol. XLV in the standard edition of Gentile's works; see pp. 373–410. The translation, which condenses the original, appeared in *Foreign Affairs* 6 (January 1928): 290–304.

127 George Boas, "Gentile and the Hegelian invasion of Italy," *Journal of Philosophy* 23 (April 1, 1926): 184–8, especially p. 188; Marcuse, *Reason and Revolution*, pp. 402–12,

especially pp. 407–8; Georges Bataille, "Nietzsche and the fascists," in *Visions of Excess: Selected Writings, 1927–1939*, edited and translated by Allan Stoekl (Minneapolis: University of Minnesota Press, 1985; first published 1937), pp. 185–6, 195 n. 12. Zeev Sternhell, widely reputed as an expert on fascist ideology, remarked that among European fascist intellectuals only Gentile produced a body of ideological writings comparable in quality to French fascist literature and thought (Zeev Sternhell, *Neither Right nor Left: Fascist Ideology in France*, translated by David Maisel [Princeton, N.J.: Princeton University Press, 1996; original French ed., 1983], p. 6). But when he turned specifically to Italy, Sternhell offered virtually no analysis of Gentile, and indeed he could not have made sense of Gentile from within his framework, which stressed the French sources of Fascist ideology. Sternhell's readers could only surmise that Gentile, as the leading Fascist ideologue, was part of the "antihumanistic rebellion" that Sternhell attributed to Fascism (Sternhell, *The Birth of Fascist Ideology*, pp. 251–2). But Gentile's vision for Fascism, although explicitly totalitarian, stemmed from arguably the most radical form of philosophically grounded humanism we have known.

128 A prime example is the treatment by Calandra in his *Gentile e il fascismo*, discussed above; see p. 529, n. 72.

129 Gentile, *Il mito dello stato nuovo*, pp. 231–61. See also Gabriele Turi, *Il fascismo e il consenso degli intellettuali* (Bologna, Il Mulino 1980), pp. 5–10.

130 Gentile, *The Sacralization of Politics*, p. 58. Even as he stressed Giovanni Gentile's importance as "chief theologian," Emilio Gentile gave little sense of the basis of Gentile's totalitarian ideal. However, he had treated Gentile in greater detail in his *Le origini dell'ideologia fascista* of 1975; see pp. 343–69. See also Ben-Ghiat, *Fascist Modernities*, pp. 8–9, on Gentile's importance in fostering the notion that Fascism was ethical—and, on that basis, superior to the Soviet regime.

131 Gleason, *Totalitarianism*, pp. 9, 19, 94–95. Even Gabriele Turi, the author of an indispensable, fair-minded biography, fell into misleading commonplaces about coercion and autonomy in an article that, nevertheless, provides a useful orientation in English to the Gentile question. See Gabriele Turi, "Giovanni Gentile: Oblivion, remembrance, and criticism," *Journal of Modern History* 70, no. 4 (December 1998): 928, 930. Despite the recent revival of interest, there remains much point to Norberto Bobbio's comment of 1974 that even in Italy, Gentile's philosophy seems not only dead but literally incomprehensible. Yet Bobbio also noted that not so long before, intelligent, idealistic young Italians had found Gentile's thinking inspiring. Bobbio's characterization is cited, and endorsed, in Maurizio Ferraris, "Il Gentile di Garin," *Aut Aut*, n.s., no. 247 (January–February 1992): 26.

132 Domenico Settembrini, *Storia dell'idea antiborghese in Italia, 1860–1989: Società del benessere—liberalismo—totalitarismo* (Rome and Bari: Laterza, 1991), pp. 269–70.

133 As noted in Chapter 3, the key sources are Giovanni Gentile, *Saggi critici*, ser. 2 (Florence: Vallecchi, 1927), p. 29; and Benedetto Croce, *Conversazioni critiche*, ser. 2 (Bari: Laterza, 1950), pp. 68–9.

134 The quintessential statement of Gentile's fascism is his *Origini e dottrina del fascismo*; see especially pp. 35–53 in the 1929 edition. See also Giovanni Gentile, *Fascismo e cultura* (Milan: Fratelli Treves, 1928), pp. 44–66 (1925).

135 As Gleason noted (*Totalitarianism*, p. 17), Gentile first began to use "totalitarianism" in March 1925 to suggest both the religious character of Fascism and the scope for renewal by penetrating every area of human life. But such a direction was implicit in any translation of Gentilian actualism to politics.

136 Gentile, *Origini e dottrina* (1929 ed.), pp. 35–6, 52–3.

137 The point was made with particular clarity by one of Gentile's most enthusiastic admirers abroad, Aline Lion, a French woman who lived in Italy from 1913 to 1927 and who studied philosophy at Oxford. See Aline Lion, *The Pedigree of Fascism: A Popular Essay on the Western Philosophy of Politics* (London: Sheed & Ward, 1927), pp.

189–210, especially p. 190. See also Aline Lion, *The Idealistic Conception of Religion: Vico, Hegel, Gentile* (Oxford: Clarendon Press, 1932). The whole thrust of Gentile's writings about education pointed in this direction.

138   Gentile, *Origini e dottrina*, pp. 47–8; H.S. Harris, *The Social Philosophy of Giovanni Gentile* (Urbana: University of Illinois Press, 1966), pp. 203, 241n.—2n.

139   Turi, *Giovanni Gentile*, pp. 368–70.

140   Gentile, *Origini e dottrina* (1929 ed.), pp. 43–8, especially pp. 46–8. See also Harris, *Social Philosophy*, pp. 169–70.

141   Cf. Harris, *Social Philosophy*, p. 189, n. 72. Harris accented the convergence of Gentile and Rocco in practice, despite certain differences in emphasis.

142   Gentile, *The Sacralization of Politics*, p. 5.

143   Citing the scope, through corporativism, for involving the individual not as an abstract citizen but as a specialized force of production, Gentile insisted on the democratic character of the Fascist state, in explicit opposition to the Nationalist view. See, for example, Giovanni Gentile, "The origins and doctrine of fascism," as excerpted in Lyttelton (ed.), *Italian Fascisms from Pareto to Gentile*, pp. 310–12. Alfredo Rocco gave that contrasting Nationalist view classic expression in "The political doctrine of fascism," in Henry S. Kariel (ed.), *Sources in Twentieth-Century Political Thought* (New York: Free Press, 1964), pp. 91–115. See especially p. 104 for Rocco's way of combining explicit elitism with an emphasis on mass participation in a subordinate mode.

144   Giovanni Gentile, *Sistema di logica come teoria del conoscere*, 2 vols., 3rd ed. (Florence: Sansoni, 1959), 1: 33–4.

145   Bottai, *Esperienza corporativa*, pp. 569–73 (1930).

146   *Ibid.*, pp. 574–7.

147   *Ibid.*, pp. 577, 583–5.

148   Turi, *Giovanni Gentile*, pp. 351–2, 413. Spirito and Volpicelli quickly emerged as major corporativist advocates, especially through the journals *Nuovi studi di diritto, economia e politica*, which they co-edited, 1927–35, and *Archivio di studi corporativi*, directed by Giuseppe Bottai.

149   De Felice, *Mussolini il duce*, I, p. 177.

150   De Felice noted the contrast with Giuseppe Toniolo (1845–1918), an innovative Catholic social thinker whose vision of a more just social order included medieval elements. See De Felice, *Fascism*, p. 49.

151   The examples are legion, yet there seems to be little interest in dredging them up today. Among them are G. Lowell Field, *The Syndical and Corporative Institutions of Italian Fascism* (New York: Columbia University Press, 1938); and Mihail Manoilescu, *Le Siècle du corporatisme* (Paris: Alcan, 1934). We will consider Paul Einzig below. See also Anthony Galatoli Landi, "Il corporativismo e il *new deal*," in *Il pensiero di Giovanni Gentile*, 2 vols. (Florence: Istituto della Enciclopedia Italiana, 1977), 2: pp. 525–33; and De Felice, *Mussolini il duce*, I, pp. 544–5, for the interest abroad, especially with the advent of the Depression.

152   See, for example, Mussolini's reference to Lenin's artistry and his claim to kinship, even paternity, over aspects of Communism, in his first speech to the Chamber of Deputies, June 21, 1921, in Benito Mussolini, *Scritti e discorsi di Benito Mussolini*, vol. 2: La rivoluzione fascista (23 marzo 1919–28 ottobre 1922) (Milan: Ulrico Hoepli, 1934), pp. 179–80. See also Pier Luigi Bassignana, *Fascisti nel paese dei Soviet* (Turin: Bollati Boringhieri, 2000) on the activities of an array of Fascists who traveled to the Soviet Union and interacted with the Soviets on various levels during the years from 1929 to 1935. Although typically provocative and a bit extreme, A. James Gregor usefully addresses the Fascist understanding of the Soviet trajectory in *The Faces of Janus: Marxism and Fascism in the Twentieth Century* (New Haven, Conn.: Yale University Press, 2000); see especially chapter 7 (pp. 128–48). See also Ben-Ghiat, *Fascist Modernities*, pp. 33–

4, 38–9; and Bosworth, *The Italian Dictatorship*, p. 54; on the overall significance of Fascism's "epochal" competition with the other two regimes.

153 Bottai, *Esperienza Corporativa*, p. 546.

154 Renzo Bertoni, *Il trionfo del fascismo nell'U.R.S.S.* (Rome: Angelo Signorelli, 1934), especially pp. 144, 148–58. Jeffrey Schnapp's *Building Fascism*, on the career of the engineer Gaetano Ciocca, makes particularly tangible the Fascist sense of rivalry with the Soviet experiment. See especially pp. 44–6, on Ciocca's *Giudizio sul bolscevismo* (1933), which related his own experience as an engineer in the Soviet Union, and which drew Mussolini's praise in *Il popolo d'Italia*.

155 Ben-Ghiat, *Fascist Modernities*, p. 119. The implication was that the French, caught up in traditional categories, were not prepared to grasp the innovative thrust of Fascism.

156 See, for example, Bottai's interview with *Deutsche Allgemeine Zeitung* (1929), in Bottai, *Esperienza corporativa*, pp. 669–70.

157 Bottai, *Esperienza corporativa*, p. 683 (1929), praising a recent speech by the veteran syndicalist A.O. Olivetti.

158 For examples, see Perry R. Willson, "Women in fascist Italy," in Richard Bessel (ed.), *Fascist Italy and Nazi Germany: Comparisons and Contrasts*: (Cambridge: Cambridge University Press, 1996), p. 92; and Carl Levy, "From fascism to 'post-fascists': Italian roads to modernity," also in Bessel (ed.), *Fascist Italy and Nazi Germany*, p. 177.

159 Sternhell, *The Birth of Fascist Ideology*, p. 253.

160 See *ibid.*, p. 129, for an example of Sternhell's way of linking market economics to his reductive understanding of corporativism.

161 *Ibid.*, pp. 253–4.

162 Bottai, *Esperienza corporativa*, pp. 40–1, 544. See also Morgan, *Fascism in Europe*, pp. 191–2, which effectively locates corporativism as a modern Italian innovation that attracted the interest of those like Georges Valois, Jacques Doriot, Oswald Mosley, and José Antonio Primo de Rivera.

163 Robert Wohl, *The Generation of 1914* (Cambridge, Mass.: Harvard University Press, 1979), pp. 201–2.

164 Roberts, *The Syndicalist Tradition*, p. 263.

165 The polemic unfolded in *Rivista internazionale di filosofia del diritto*. See *ibid.*, pp. 240–4.

166 See Turi, *Giovanni Gentile*, p. 462, for indications of the important links between Bottai, on the one hand, and Gentile and his followers Spirito and Volpicelli, on the other. Bottai inaugurated *Archivio di studi corporativi* with an article by Gentile in 1930.

167 I offer a brief sketch of Bottai's background in Roberts, *The Syndicalist Tradition*, pp. 203–4. For a full-scale biography, see Alexander J. De Grand, *Bottai e la cultura fascista* (Bari: Laterza 1978).

168 Bosworth, *The Italian Dictatorship*, p. 58n., cites De Felice even as he offers his own put-down of Bottai.

169 Bottai, *Esperienza corporativa*, pp. 684, 686–7. The whole section "Questioni ginevrine," pp. 677–711, is on these themes.

170 *Ibid.*, pp. 593, 635–67. In 1930, in a preface to a 674-page volume marking the International Labor Office's tenth anniversary, Dino Grandi, at this point minister of foreign affairs, stressed the value of the volume itself, which, he said, showed that counter to politically inspired charges, Italy was not hostile to the office. Indeed, Italy was in the forefront, especially in the pioneering socio-economic policy that was the core of Fascism, but also in international collaboration. See Dino Grandi, preface to Giuseppe De Michelis, *L'Italia nell'Organizzazione internazionale del lavoro della Società delle Nazioni* (Pubblicazioni dell'Istituto italiano di diritto internazionale in Roma) (Rome: Edizioni "Sapientia," 1930), pp. xv–xvi.

171 Bottai, *Esperienza corporativa*, pp. 39–40, 601–2.

172 *Ibid.*, p. 685. This basic argument was echoed and developed by countless others during the course of the regime. See, for example, Arnaldo Volpicelli, preface to Carl Schmitt, *Principii politici*, edited by Delio Cantimori (Florence: G.C. Sansoni, 1935), p. x; and Arnaldo Volpicelli, "I fondamenti ideali del corporativismo" (1930), appendix to Ugo Spirito, *Il corporativismo* (Florence: Sansoni, 1970).

173 Bottai, *Esperienza corporativa*, pp. 704–5.

174 *Ibid.*, pp. 37–40, 577–8, 601–2.

175 *Ibid.*, pp. 583–4, 586.

176 *Ibid.*, pp. 546–7.

177 *Ibid.*, pp. 536–8, 542–3 (from pp. 529–47, "La corporazione nella polemica scientifica," Bottai's address to the conference, May 7, 1932). For Spirito's controversial position, see p. 319.

178 See, for example, Gentile, *La via italiana*, pp. 131–2, for the implication that myth was a consciously chosen tool. Especially in *Il mito dello stato nuovo*, pp. 263–5, 268–9, Gentile effectively challenged the reductionist treatment of myth, as a mere propaganda instrument serving political or economic interests.

179 Gentile, *La via italiana*, pp. 134, 136, 206. See also Gentile, *Il mito dello Stato nuovo*.

180 Grandi linked myth to a demand for institutional change in a proto-corporativist direction in "Le origini e la missione del fascismo" (1921), in *Il fascismo*, by Adolfo Zerboglio and Dino Grandi (Bologna: Licinio Cappelli, 1922), pp. 53–4, 63, 69–70. See also Roberts, *The Syndicalist Tradition*, pp. 219–20.

181 See Gentile, *The Sacralization of Politics*, pp. 3, 28–9, 82–4, 104; and Gentile, *La via italiana*, pp. 131–2, 270, for examples of Gentile's liberal and undifferentiated use of myth.

182 Camillo Pellizzi, *Problemi e realtà del fascismo* (Florence: Vallecchi, 1924), pp. 157–65, especially pp. 161 and 164.

183 *Ibid.*, pp. 161, 163–5.

184 *Ibid.* On p. 163, Pellizzi notes that the Fascist formula is: "lo Stato non è, si fa."

185 *Ibid.*, p. 161.

186 *Ibid.*, pp. 157–60. In 1941, Pellizzi was still insisting on the endlessness of the task and thus the open-endedness of the Fascist revolution. Neither the state nor the educational process would ever be finished. See Camillo Pellizzi, *Il partito educatore* (Rome: Studi di *Civiltà fascista*, 1941), pp. 7, 43–4.

187 Quoted in Schnapp, *Building Fascism*, p. 205. See also Ciocca's statement from 1934 quoted on p. 185. Schnapp convincingly portrays Ciocca's case as evidence, counter to the ongoing tendency to denigrate the revolutionary thrust of Fascism, that significant intellectuals found Fascism the vehicle for a revolutionary modernism superior to Soviet Communism (pp. 163–4). Yet Schnapp delimits the notion as, implicitly aligning with A. James Gregor's familiar interpretation, he links this revolutionary modernism to modernization in "third world" dictatorships, which, he suggests, recapitulate aspects of the Italian experience (pp. 164–5). In implying that Fascist revolutionary modernism was about mere catch-up, Schnapp was turning from what he himself seemed to argue throughout the book—that modernity was being contested in the West, and that the Fascist claim to offer an alternative modernity, a third way, must be taken seriously. In doing what he did in the Soviet Union, and in imagining what he did for the United States, Ciocca manifested the energizing confidence that Italy, thanks to Fascism, was now showing even these prominent competitors the most effective modern way.

188 This is the whole thrust of Emilio Gentile's work. Bosworth, blaming the De Felice school's preoccupation with high politics, insists that we have not had sufficient research "from below" to assess the extent and depth of support. See Bosworth, *The Italian Dictatorship*, pp. 131–2.

189 Gentile, *The Sacralization of Politics*, pp. 110–21; especially p. 117. See also Claudio Fogu, *The Historic Imaginary: Politics of History in Fascist Italy* (Toronto:

University of Toronto Press, 2003), pp. 132–64 (see also p. 246 n. 48 for a helpful bibliographical listing on the exhibition). On wartime letters from the front, see Berezin, *Making the Fascist Self*, pp. 222–6; and Ben-Ghiat, *Fascist Modernities*, pp. 180–1.

190 Ottavio Dinale, *Quarant'anni di colloqui con lui* (Milan: Ciarrocca, 1953), p. 181.

191 Quine, *Population Politics*, pp. 45, 48–9, 54.

192 *Ibid.*, p. 49.

193 Turi, *Giovanni Gentile*, pp. 390–1.

194 *Ibid.*, p. 472.

195 Bosworth, *The Italian Dictatorship*, p. 147, following Marzio Barbagli, *Educating for Unemployment* (1982).

196 Turi, *Giovanni Gentile*, pp. 331–2.

197 Ben-Ghiat, *Fascist Modernities*, p. 97.

198 *Ibid.*, pp. 92, 96–7, 102.

199 The Fascist accent on youth and the dilemmas that ensued with the aging of the front generation and the advent of a new youthful cohort have been much discussed in recent years. Although the regime countered claims from the second generation by proclaiming youth to be a state of mind not determined by chronological age, it still sought to keep the older generation from settling into fixed castes by promoting young people. See Bruno Wanrooij, "The rise and fall of Italian fascism as a generational revolt," *Journal of Contemporary History* 22, no. 3 (July 1987): 401–18; and Luisa Passerini, "Youth as a metaphor for social change: Fascist Italy and America in the 1950s," in Giovanni Levi and Jean-Claude Schmitt (eds.), *A History of Young People in the West*, vol. 2: *Stormy Evolution to Modern Times* (Cambridge, Mass.: Belknap Press of Harvard University Press, 1997), pp. 283–303.

200 Ben-Ghiat is especially good on this impulse among leading second-generation Fascists like Gastone Silvano Spinetti, who even organized an anti-idealist conference at the University of Rome in June 1933. See Ben-Ghiat, *Fascist Modernities*, pp. 30, 102–3, 108–9. See also Calandra, *Gentile e il fascismo*, pp. 165–7.

201 Gentile helped to create, for example, the *Istituto italo-germanico* in Cologne, which he inaugurated together with Mayor Konrad Adenauer in October 1931, and subsequently the *Istituto italiano di studi germanici* in Rome. However, subject to increasing pressure from Starace and the Fascist Party, he was finally replaced as head of the *Istituto nazionale fascista di cultura* in 1937 as this entity fell under more immediate party control. See Turi, *Giovanni Gentile*, pp. 436–7, 442.

202 Ben-Ghiat, *Fascist Modernities*, pp. 33, 113–15.

203 Paul Einzig, *The Economic Foundations of Fascism* (London: Macmillan, 1933), v–ix, preface (dated April 1933).

204 De Felice, *Mussolini il duce*, I, pp. 91–8, 193–7; De Felice, *Mussolini il duce*, II, pp. 192–3, 200–20. Cf. the noted and nuanced study by Luisa Passerini, *Fascism in Popular Memory: The Cultural Experience of the Turin Working Class*, translated by Robert Lumley and Jude Bloomfield (Cambridge: Cambridge University Press, 1987). While recognizing a measure of acquiescence, Passerini attributed it primarily to "the forces at work in totalitarian regimes which fragment the personality of the individual" (p. 188). In this case, those forces also produced "a real and ruthless impoverishment of working class culture," which was "reduced to stunted forms of expression" (p. 125). See pp. 74–80, 124–6, 187–9, 196–9.

205 Tobias Abse, "Italian workers and Italian fascism," in Bessel (ed.), *Fascist Italy and Nazi Germany*, pp. 40–60. See especially pp. 44–7 for critiques of first De Felice, then Passerini. But compare Bosworth's more appreciative account of Passerini in *The Italian Dictatorship*, pp. 150–1.

206 For a bitter critique by a veteran syndicalist, see A.O. Olivetti, "Le corporazioni come volontà e come rappresentazione," *La stirpe* 9, no. 4 (April 1931): 145–6. See also Roberts, *The Syndicalist Tradition*, pp. 291, 293–4.

207 Roland Sarti's *Fascism and the Industrial Leadership in Italy, 1919–1940: A Study in the Expansion of Private Power under Fascism* (Berkeley: University of California Press, 1971), remains fundamental on the limited reach of corporativism *vis-à-vis* big business during the 1930s. See especially pp. 118–20 for the point here.

208 Ben-Ghiat, *Fascist Modernities*, pp. 100–1.

209 Augusto Turati, "Il partito e i sindacati" (1928), in Sergio Panunzio *et al.*, *Dottrina e politica fascista* (Venice: La Nuova Italia, 1930). See also Roberts, *The Syndicalist Tradition*, pp. 204–8, 291–2; and De Felice, *Mussolini il fascista*, II, pp. 176, 196–7, 281.

210 Giuseppe Bottai, *Vent'anni e un giorno* (Milan: Garzanti, 1949), pp. 25–35, 42–3, 45.

211 Throughout his multi-volume biography of Mussolini, Renzo De Felice stresses Mussolini's desire to keep his options open, to avoid being cornered—and thus his tendency to become a balancer or juggler on this level.

212 Turi, *Giovanni Gentile*, p. 353.

213 See Roberts, *The Syndicalist Tradition*, pp. 281–3, on the place of the Labor Charter in light of the pulling and tugging already much in evidence by that point.

214 For the proceedings, see Ministero delle Corporazioni, *Atti del secondo convegno di studi sindacali e corporativi: Ferrara, 5–8 maggio 1932*, 3 vols. (Rome: Tipografia del Senato, 1932). Spirito, *Il corporativismo*, incorporates Spirito's key writings on corporativism. See also Roberts, *The Syndicalist Tradition*, pp. 294–7, 363 n. 81.

215 Bottai, *Esperienza corporativa*, pp. 538–43.

216 Roberts, *The Syndicalist Tradition*, pp. 207–10, 234–7.

217 Aquarone, *L'organizzazione dello Stato totalitario*, p. 45n.

218 Curzio Suckert, "La conquista dello Stato nella concezione organica di Sergio Panunzio," *Corriere padano*, December 16, 1925, p. 1.

219 Gentile, *La via italiana*, pp. 169–70.

220 *Ibid.*, p. 136.

221 De Felice, *Fascism*, p. 49.

222 Thus, for example, Gentile noted that Fascism's self-portrayal as a religion afforded both an enduring sense of identity and a significant element of continuity in practice, enabling the party to preserve "the whole complex of myths, rituals, and symbols" that had originated in the *squadristi* experience and that "remained basically unaltered until the fall of the régime." Gentile, *The Sacralization of Politics*, p. 29. See also Gentile, *La via italiana*, p. 270.

223 Roberts, *The Syndicalist Tradition*, pp. 122–8. Writing in *Il popolo d'Italia* in 1924, A.O. Olivetti proposed constructive roles for the new League of Nations in dealing with the problem of Italian emigration, exacerbated by the inequitable distribution of colonial territories—as manifested by France's possession of Tunisia. The Italian situation would be a test of fire for the league. If fair, cooperative solutions could not be worked out, Italy could only turn to imperialism. See A.O. Olivetti ("Lo spettatore"), "Il problema della popolazione: le soluzioni," *Il popolo d'Italia* in 1924, September 2, 1924, p. 3.

224 De Caprariis, "Fascism and Italian foreign policy." By avoiding teleological assumptions, de Caprariis significantly deepens our understanding of the impulses at work and the interplay between them. See also Luca de Caprariis, "Fascism for export? The rise and eclipse of the Fasci Italiani all'Estero," *Journal of Contemporary History* 35, no. 2 (April 2000): 151–83, on the limits to the Fascist effort to "expand" by strengthening cultural ties with Italian immigrant communities abroad.

225 For an example, see Pellizzi, *Problemi e realtà del fascismo*, p. 164. See also De Felice, *Fascism*, pp. 65–6.

226 De Felice, *Fascism*, pp. 40–1.

227 De Felice, *Mussolini il fascista*, II, pp. 359, 363–7.

228 De Felice, *Mussolini il duce*, I, pp. 177–81. See also De Felice, *Fascism*, p. 79; and Michaelis, "Anmerkungen," p. 291.

229 Aristotle A. Kallis, *Fascist Ideology: Territory and Expansionism in Italy and Germany, 1922–1945* (London and New York: Routledge, 2000), pp. 69, 110, 118. Although he featured the novelty of Mussolini's ambitions even during the 1920s, Kallis found the bottom line ambiguous and the results unimpressive as of 1935. And even as he stressed the continuity in ambitions, Kallis did not deny that the Ethiopian turn constituted a tipping point. He notes, for example, that *spazio vitale* arguments became more pronounced from 1935 onwards. See Kallis, *Fascist Ideology*, p. 51, 71–2, 137.

230 Although he focused only on the "expansion" strand of fascist ideology, Aristotle Kallis eschewed any implication of teleological inevitability. Although it was an option prescribed by Fascist ideology, expansion, he insisted, was not the inevitable outcome of either ideology or domestic crisis. Indeed, for him, too, what most basically distinguished Fascism was a mode of activism, not territorial ambitions *per se*. See Kallis, *Fascist Ideology*, pp. 57–9, 157–8.

231 De Felice, *Mussolini il duce*, II, pp. 3–155; Ben-Ghiat, *Fascist Modernities*, pp. 123–4, 127, 130; Berezin, *Making the Fascist Self*, pp. 108–9, 225–6. See also Mack Smith, *Mussolini*, pp. 175–81, for a good account of the Starace era in typically negative mode.

232 Berezin, *Making the Fascist Self*, pp. 65, 137.

233 Gentile, *La via italiana*, pp. 90–2, 188–91, 225, 227–8; Gentile, *The Sacralization of Politics*, pp. 50–1, 63–4.

234 Pellizzi referred to "dimostrazioni spettacolari." See Gentile, *La via italiana*, pp. 273–4, for this passage, the source of which is the Pellizzi Archive. By this point, Pellizzi was director of the Fascist Cultural Institute—and still trumpeting Gentilian themes. Bottai similarly suggested approvingly (although well after the fact) that Starace was finally dismissed because he was obsessed with mere style. See Bottai, *Vent'anni e un giorno*, p. 146.

235 Gentile, *The Sacralization of Politics*, p. 29.

236 In *ibid.*, pp. 132–3, Gentile convincingly distinguished the myth that had developed around Mussolini even before the rise of Fascism from the cult of the Duce that developed later. At the same time, he insisted that as one measure of its richness, the political religion of Fascism was not initially identified with Mussolini; the cult of the Duce derived from the religion but then served to reinforce it. Whereas, up to a point, this line of argument usefully highlights the ongoing process and the scope for change, it betrays Gentile's restricted sense of what the process of change could entail. The cult of the Duce was central to a wider trivialization and narrowing, not just another step in the effort to implement the new political religion. On the changing image and role of Mussolini within Fascism, see also Luisa Passerini, *Mussolini immaginario: Storia di una biografia, 1915–1939* (Rome and Bari: Laterza, 1991); and A.M. Imbriani, *Gli italiani e il duce: Il mito e l'immagine di Mussolini negli ultimi anni del fascismo (1938–1943)* (Naples: Liguori, 1992).

237 Roberto Michels, *First Lectures in Political Sociology*, translated by Alfred de Grazia (New York: Harper & Row [Harper Torchbooks], 1965), pp. 119–33, especially pp. 125–6, 131–2. These lectures were presented at the University of Rome in May 1926 and first published in Roberto Michels, *Corso di sociologia politica* (1927). The English version includes additional material. See also Robert Michels, *Italien von Heute: Politische und wirtschaftliche Kulturgeschichte von 1860 bis 1930* (Zürich and Leipzig: Orell Füssli Verlag, 1930), pp. 266–70.

238 De Felice, *Mussolini il duce*, I, pp. 18–25, 172–81, 221, 227–8, 299–300. De Felice noted the downward phase of a parabola, beginning around 1933, as Mussolini became the prisoner of his own myth.

239 De Felice, *Fascism*, p. 71.

240 Ben-Ghiat, *Fascist Modernities*, pp. 157–9.

241 Gentile, *La via italiana*, pp. 238, 269. See also Vito Panunzio, *Il "secondo fascismo," 1936–1943: La reazione della nuova generazione alla crisi del movimento e del regime* (Milan: Mursia, 1988), for a retrospective account by an energetic member of the second generation. The son of Sergio Panunzio, the young Vito Panunzio called for renewed corporativist revolution in a pamphlet entitled *Fedeltà al sindacato e alla corporazione* (Rome: L'economia italiana, 1942). Against the claim of some historians that mass disaffection was the rule among the youth after 1938, Ben-Ghiat noted that only a small minority had begun to turn from the regime by that point. As she saw it, moreover, it was not the war itself but the defeat that turned younger Italians against the regime (Ben-Ghiat, *Fascist Modernities*, pp. 180–1).

242 Ben-Ghiat, *Fascist Modernities*, pp. 180–3.

243 Gentile, *La via italiana*, chapter 7 (pp. 225–98), especially pp. 226–7, 239, 242, 263, 276. See also p. 211.

244 *Ibid.*, pp. 246, 248–50, 281–2, See also pp. 256–62.

245 *Ibid.*, pp. 137–9, 266–7.

246 *Ibid.*, pp. 239–42, 256–62, 276.

247 *Ibid.*, pp. 250–1, 264–6.

248 *Ibid.*, p. 264. Although Gentile found him typically elusive, Bottai was quite coherent on how to continue the revolution; he simply found the renewed accent on the party and its prerogatives misguided in light of what the revolution was supposed to be about.

249 Pellizzi, *Il partito educatore*, pp. 7–8, 32–3, 44–5. At the same time, Pellizzi's pamphlet drew some harsh criticism, as Emilio Gentile made clear. See Gentile, *La via italiana*, pp. 250–1, 264–6.

250 Gentile, *La via italiana*, p. 266.

251 Indeed, Gentile bordered on incoherence when he stressed that the many young radicals looking hopefully to Serena's effort shared with him the myth of "continual revolution" (*rivoluzione continua*) and the objective of completing the totalitarian state (*ibid.*, p. 270).

252 *Ibid.*, p. 226.

253 *Ibid.*, pp. 288–9.

254 In noting that the absurdities and cruelties that have contributed to the popular image of Fascism came to the fore during the later 1930s, Berezin nicely pinpointed aspects of the trivialization in process. But because she had not done justice to the originating aspirations, she could not convincingly account for those features in terms of the overall trajectory of the regime. See Berezin, *Making of the fascist self*, especially pp. 137–8.

255 Claudio G. Segrè, *Italo Balbo: A Fascist Life* (Berkeley: University of California Press, 1987), pp. 334–62.

256 Kallis, *Fascist Ideology*, pp. 134, 139, 148–9, 153–4, 157.

257 *Ibid.*, pp. 175–81.

258 For a good example of an emphasis on the kinship explicitly as totalitarian, see the jurist Guido Lucatello's "Profilo giuridico dello Stato totalitario," in various authors, *Scritti giuridici in onore di Santi Romano*, vol. 1: *Filosofia e teoria generale del diritto; diritto costituzionale* (Padua: CEDAM, 1940), pp. 575, 580–7.

259 Gentile, *La via italiana*, pp. 273–4. For indications of the radicalization that followed from association with Nazism, see De Felice, *Mussolini il duce*, II, pp. 486–9; and Ben-Ghiat, *Fascist Modernities*, pp. 68–9, 131.

260 Volpicelli, preface to Schmitt, *Principii politici*, p. vii.

261 For examples in the context of the Ethiopian turn, with the link to corporativism explicit, see Roberts, *The Syndicalist Tradition*, p. 305. Note 133 provides references to Bottai and Panunzio. See also Ben-Ghiat, *Fascist Modernities*, pp. 123–4, 126–7, 130, including references to Elio Vittorini and Ruggero Zangrandi.

262 Schnapp, *Building Fascism*, pp. 103–4.

263 For some indications of the flexibility of the concept, especially as invoked by Gaetano Ciocca, see *ibid.*, pp. 40–3, 77, 88, 99, 127.

264 See Roberts, *The Syndicalist Tradition*, pp. 303–4, for the arguments of Sergio Panunzio that Fascist Italy was setting the pace, that Nazism was merely reactionary. Panunzio was the author of a sort of textbook on Fascism for German consumption, *Allgemeine Theorie des Faschistischen Staates* (Berlin: W. de Gryter, 1934).

265 Meir Michaelis, "The current debate over fascist racial policy," in Robert S. Wistrich and Sergio DellaPergola (eds.), *Fascist Antisemitism and the Italian Jews* (Jerusalem: Vidal Sassoon International Center for the Study of Antisemitism, 1995), pp. 79–80; Ben-Ghiat, *Fascist Modernities*, p. 152; Kallis, *Fascist Ideology*, pp. 43–5. Note also Meir Michaelis's still indispensable book, *Mussolini and the Jews: German–Italian Relations and the Jewish Question in Italy, 1922–1945* (Oxford: published for the Institute of Jewish Affairs by Clarendon Press, 1978).

266 Ben-Ghiat, *Fascist Modernities*, p. 152.

267 Michaelis, "The current debate over fascist racial policy," pp. 50, 94.

268 Payne, *A History of Fascism*, pp. 239–40.

269 Michaelis, "The current debate over fascist racial policy," pp. 51–3, 62–3, 81–2, 93; Quine, *Population Politics*, p. 93.

270 Carl Ipsen, *Dictating Demography: The Problem of Population in Fascist Italy* (Cambridge: Cambridge University Press, 1996), pp. 185–94; Quine, *Population Politics*, pp. 93–95; Michaelis, "The current debate over fascist racial policy," p. 94–5; Ben-Ghiat, *Fascist Modernities*, pp. 124, 149, 153. On the overall issue, see also Giorgio Israel and Pietro Nastasi, *Scienza e razza nell'Italia fascista* (Bologna: Il Mulino, 1998).

271 Ben-Ghiat, *Fascist Modernities*, pp. 149, 156–7.

272 Michaelis, "The current debate over fascist racial policy," pp. 66–7.

273 Ruth Ben-Ghiat, "The secret histories of Roberto Benigni's *Life Is Beautiful*," *Yale Journal of Criticism* 14, no. 1 (2001): 262. See also Ben-Ghiat, *Fascist Modernities*, p. 149.

274 Gentile, *The Sacralization of Politics*, p. 101.

275 Here again, my emphasis on narrowing and trivialization is to depart somewhat from Emilio Gentile, who portrayed the anti-Semitic turn as a logical outcome of the ongoing anthropological revolution central to the Fascist totalitarian vision. Totalitarian implementation required the elimination of any separateness. At the same time, Gentile suggested that Mussolini adopted the anti-Semitic laws partly to *enable* the Fascists to claim superiority over Nazism. See Emilio Gentile, "Fascism in power: the totalitarian experiment," in Adrian Lyttelton (ed.), *Liberal and Fascist Italy*, pp. 167–9. While it is convincing to feature competition as opposed to mere imitation, this emphasis, too, needs to be understood in terms of the wider, changing dynamic, which altered the stakes, and the terms, of the epochal competition at work.

276 Michaelis, "The current debate over fascist racial policy," pp. 71–3; Ben-Ghiat, *Fascist Modernities*, pp. 157–9.

277 Those who most explicitly addressed the issue, like Giacomo Acerbo and even the subsequently notorious Julius Evola, explicitly criticized the materialism of Nazi doctrine—and provoked Nazi indignation in response. See Michaelis, "The current debate over fascist racial policy," pp. 73–4. See also Ben-Ghiat, *Fascist Modernities*, p. 150 and especially p. 153, on the importance of the distinction, and point of pride, at issue. Even in 1941, Mussolini noted with satisfaction that, thanks to stepped-up intermarriage, "Jewish" characteristics would disappear in Italy within a generation as Jews were absorbed by the "Aryan" bloodline.

278 Galvano Della Volpe, "Antiromanticismo," *Primato*, May 15, 1941, pp. 2–3. Enzo Paci, another subsequently distinguished intellectual who contributed to *Primato*, similarly favored the Axis cause even as he sought to link Fascism to existentialism. The Axis new order promised an antidote to bankrupt bourgeois civilization. See Ben-Ghiat, *Fascist Modernities*, pp. 169, 183–4.

279 The change in the Fascist "historic imaginary," leaving behind the initial Giovanni Gentilian understanding of "making history," that Claudio Fogu has delineated in *The Historic Imaginary* is best understood in light of this direction—and usefully illuminates that direction at the same time. Put schematically, in coming to stress the perpetual infinitive, suggesting projection into the future as opposed to the ongoing activity suggested by the Gentilian active participial, the Fascists seem to have been covering over their incapacity to make history as envisioned through what was purported to be, in Gentilian terms, a totalitarian ethical state. From this perspective, the rituals and commemorations themselves became the actions and the events, and the concluding phase of the historic imaginary covered over both the failure of the original project and the meaning of what Fascism had by then become.

280 Gentile, *La via italiana*, p. 270, 275–6.

281 *Ibid.*, p. 270.

282 Bosworth, *The Italian Dictatorship*, pp. 106–7.

283 Sarti, *Fascism and the Industrial Leadership*, pp. 1–2, 88–94, 136–8; Charles S. Maier, *Recasting Bourgeois Europe: Stabilization in France, Germany, and Italy in the Decade after World War I* (Princeton, N.J.: Princeton University Press, 1975), pp. 350, 576, 592. See also Bosworth, *The Italian Dictatorship*, pp. 117, 223.

Chapter 7

1 George L. Mosse, *Nazi Culture: Intellectual, Cultural and Social Life in the Third Reich* (New York: Grosset & Dunlap [Universal Library], 1968), pp. xxvi–xxvii; George L. Mosse, *Nationalism and Sexuality: Respectability and Abnormal Sexuality in Modern Europe* (New York: Howard Fertig, 1985), pp. 138, 141,150–2, 157–9, 179–80. See also Steven E. Aschheim, *The Nietzsche Legacy in Germany, 1890–1990* (Berkeley: University of California Press, 1992), p. 329 n.

2 Aschheim, *The Nietzschean Legacy*, p. 330.

3 For just a few indications that we dealing with many of Germany's "best and brightest," see Raul Hilberg, *Perpetrators, Victims, Bystanders: The Jewish Catastrophe, 1933–1945* (New York: HarperCollins [Perennial], 1993), pp. 40, 44–5, on the personnel in the Reich security main office; Berel Lang, *Act and Idea in the Nazi Genocide* (Chicago: University of Chicago Press, 1990), p. 50, on the unusual proportion of higher academic degrees among the SS *Einsatzgruppen*; Robert Proctor, *Racial Hygiene: Medicine Under the Nazis* (Cambridge, Mass.: Harvard University Press, 1988), pp. 5–6, 222; Norman G. Finkelstein, "Daniel Jonah Goldhagen's 'crazy' thesis: A critique of *Hitler's Willing Executioners*," in Norman G. Finkelstein and Ruth Bettina Birn (eds.), *A Nation on Trial: The Goldhagen Thesis and Historical Truth* (New York: Henry Holt, 1998), p. 99; and the pioneering work by Max Weinreich, *Hitler's Professors: The Part of Scholarship in Germany's Crimes Against the Jewish People* (New Haven, Conn.: Yale University Press, 1999; first published 1946).

4 Omer Bartov, *Murder in our Midst: The Holocaust, Industrial Killing, and Representation* (New York: Oxford University Press, 1996), p. 63. Mark Roseman, "National Socialism and modernization," in Richard Bessel (ed.), *Fascist Italy and Nazi Germany: Comparisons and Contrasts* (Cambridge: Cambridge University Press, 1996), p. 219, notes that the Bolshevik success "was surely crucial in creating the 'totalitarian temptation'" in Germany.

5 Ian Kershaw, *Hitler, 1889–1936: Hubris* (New York: W.W. Norton, 1999), pp. 180, 182–3, 289, 343. Kershaw even suggests that comparison with Mussolini was the beginning of the Führer cult surrounding Hitler, which had not been central to Nazism before. See also Philip Morgan, *Fascism in Europe, 1919–1945* (London: Routledge, 2003), pp. 161–3; J.P. Stern, *Hitler: The Führer and the People* (Berkeley: University of California Press, 1975), pp. 35–6, 132, 165; and R.J.B. Bosworth, *The Italian Dictatorship: Problems and Perspectives in the Interpretation of Mussolini and Fascism*

(London: Edward Arnold, 1998), pp. 74 and 74n., 436, on Hitler's ongoing sense of indebtedness to Mussolini.

6 Most famously in Ernst Jünger's works. See his "Untergang oder neue Ordnung?" *Deutsches Volkstum* 15 (1929), pp. 418–19; and *Der Arbeiter* (1932), a best-selling book of early 1933. See also Jeffrey Herf, *Reactionary Modernism: Technology, Culture, and Politics in Weimar and the Third Reich* (Cambridge: Cambridge University Press, 1984), p. 91.

7 Michael Burleigh, *Ethics and Extermination: Reflections on Nazi Genocide* (Cambridge: Cambridge University Press, 1997), pp. 116–17.

8 Detlev J.K. Peukert, *The Weimar Republic: The Crisis of Classical Modernity*, translated by Richard Deveson (New York: Hill and Wang, 1993; first German ed. 1987), pp. 134–6, pp. 271–2.

9 Roseman, "National Socialism and modernization," p. 206; Peukert, *The Weimar Republic*, pp. 187–8.

10 Roseman, "National Socialism and modernization," pp. 215–16, 218–21. Bartov also found Peukert to be overemphasizing biological politics. See *Murder in Our Midst*, p. 208, n. 59.

11 Proctor, *Racial Hygiene*, p. 61.

12 Sheila Faith Weiss, *Race Hygiene and National Efficiency: The Eugenics of Wilhelm Schallmayer* (Berkeley: University of California Press, 1987), pp. 148–51, 153. See also Aschheim, *The Nietzsche Legacy*, p. 163n.

13 Proctor, *Racial Hygiene*, pp. 27, 287, 293–4.

14 Herf, *Reactionary Modernism*, p. 161. See also pp. 154, 186, 199–201, 222, and the whole of chapter 7 on engineers.

15 *Ibid.*, p.175. See also pp. 196, 222–3.

16 Proctor, *Racial Hygiene*, p. 220.

17 Carsten Klingemann, "Social-scientific experts—no ideologues: Sociology and social research in the Third Reich," in Stephen P. Turner and Dirk Käsler (eds.), *Sociology Responds to Fascism* (London: Routledge, 1992), pp. 127–54, especially pp. 136–40.

18 Ian Kershaw, *Hitler, 1936–1945: Nemesis* (New York: W.W. Norton, 2000), pp. 253–4, 510–11; Michael Burleigh, *The Third Reich: A New History* (New York: Hill and Wang, 2000), pp. 164–5. See also Stern, *Hitler*, pp. 70, 122.

19 As for Ron Rosenbaum, *Explaining Hitler: The Search for the Origins of His Evil* (New York: Random House, 1998), to be discussed below.

20 Stern, *Hitler*, p. 167.

21 Although widely accounted a leading functionalist, Hans Mommsen's account of Hitler's place was always highly nuanced. See, for example, Hans Mommsen, "Hitler's position in the Nazi system," in Hans Mommsen, *From Weimar to Auschwitz*, translated by Philip O'Connor (Princeton, N.J.: Princeton University Press, 1991), pp. 163–88.

22 Kershaw, *Hitler, 1889–1936*, p. 243, 252–3.

23 Ian Kershaw stressed that Hitler's speeches by 1930 no longer featured the crude anti-Semitism of the early 1920s but concentrated on attacking Weimar democracy as divisive and ineffectual (Kershaw, *Hitler, 1889–1936*, pp. 330–2). Reviewing the life stories of 581 ordinary party members collected in 1934 and published in Theodore Abel's *Why Hitler Came into Power* (1938, 1986), Kershaw noted that anti-Semitism was the dominant concern for only about one-eighth of them. In the same vein, Detlev Peukert insisted that "anti-Semitism was in no sense . . . an essential instrument in integrating and mobilising the population in a National Socialist direction" (Detlev J.K. Peukert, *Inside Nazi Germany: Conformity, Opposition, and Racism in Everyday Life*, New Haven, Conn.: Yale University Press, 1987, p. 58). This point will be developed further below.

24 Hans Mommsen, "The realization of the unthinkable: The 'final solution of the Jewish question' in the Third Reich," in Gerhard Hirschfeld (ed.), *The Politics of Genocide: Jews and Soviet Prisoners of War in Nazi Germany* (London: Allen & Unwin,

1986), p. 98. See also Hannah Arendt, *Eichmann in Jerusalem: A Report on the Banality of Evil*, revised and enlarged ed. (New York: Viking [Compass], 1965), pp. 30–1, p. 40–1, 83–4, on the basis of Eichmann's claim not to have been anti-Semitic—indeed, quite the contrary, to have been a Zionist.

25 Hans Mommsen, "Anti-Jewish politics and the implementation of the Holocaust," in Hedley Bull (ed.), *The Challenge of the Third Reich: The Adam von Trott Memorial Lectures* (Oxford: Clarendon Press, 1986), p. 130.

26 Stern, *Hitler*, pp. 179, 182. Kershaw's far more detailed study confirms Stern's overall point. See Kershaw, *Hitler, 1889–1936*, pp. 89–97, on Hitler's war experience.

27 Stern, *Hitler*, pp. 18–20.

28 See Kershaw, *Hitler, 1889–1936*, p. 41, 240, 616 (notes 103–6) on Hitler's wide though unsystematic reading, first in Vienna but then also later when in prison in Landsberg.

29 *Ibid.*, p. 156.

30 *Ibid.*, p. 33.

31 See *ibid.*, pp. 149, 316, 330–2, for effective characterizations pointing in this direction.

32 See Kershaw, *Hitler, 1936–1945*, p. xlvi, on Hitler's sense that time was against him—and thus his impatience to act. See also pp. 92, 228–9.

33 Christopher R. Browning, *The Path to Genocide: Essays on Launching the Final Solution* (Cambridge: Cambridge University Press, 1992), p. 24.

34 George L. Mosse, *The Nationalization of the Masses: Political Symbolism and Mass Movements in Germany from the Napoleonic Wars through the Third Reich* (Ithaca, N.Y.: Cornell University Press, 1991; first published 1975), pp. 200–2; George L. Mosse, *The Fascist Revolution: Toward a General Theory of Fascism* (New York: Howard Fertig, 1999), pp. 81–2, 87–8.

35 Stern, *Hitler*, pp. 76–7.

36 *Ibid.*, p. 33.

37 Adolf Hitler, *Mein Kampf*, translated by Ralph Manheim (Boston: Houghton Mifflin [Sentry], 1943), p. 288. Chapter 11, "Nation and race," is the core on struggle as "natural."

38 *Ibid.*, p. 299.

39 Adolf Hitler, *Hitler's Table Talk, 1941–1944: His Private Conversations*, 2nd ed., translated by Norman Cameron and R.H. Stevens (London: Weidenfeld & Nicolson, 1973; published in the United States as *Hitler's Secret Conversations*), p. 332.

40 Kershaw, *Hitler, 1889–1936*, pp. 277–8.

41 *Ibid.*, p. 317.

42 Geoff Eley, "Ordinary Germans, Nazism, and Judeocide," in Geoff Eley (ed.), *The "Goldhagen Effect": History, Memory, Nazism—Facing the German Past* (Ann Arbor: University of Michigan Press, 2000), pp. 22–3.

43 On the implications of Nazi polycracy for the diplomatic sphere, see Aristotle A. Kallis, *Fascist Ideology: Territory and Expansionism in Italy and Germany, 1922–1945* (London and New York: Routledge, 2000), pp. 80–2. Kallis showed that whereas such competition strengthened Hitler's role in one sense, it did not yield a mechanism for carrying out foreign policy effectively.

44 The notion of "working toward the Führer" was adduced by Werner Willikens, state secretary in the Prussian Agricultural Ministry, who stressed at a meeting in February 1934 the duty of all "to try to work toward the Führer along the lines he would wish." See Jeremy Noakes and Geoffrey Pridham (eds.), *Nazism: A History in Documents and Eyewitness Accounts*, vol. 1, *The Nazi Party, State and Society, 1919–1939* (New York: Schocken, 1990), pp. 206–7. For examples of Kershaw's use of the category, as linked to radicalizing "Darwinian" struggle, on the one hand, and to governmental disorder, on the other, see *Hitler, 1889–1936*, pp. 93, 132, 311, 314, 437, 529–32. At the same time, Michael Burleigh plausibly cautioned against overemphasizing the significance

of "Darwinian" struggle as a source of radicalization; the same syndrome, he noted, can be found in democratic states, not to mention institutions like corporations and universities. See Burleigh, *The Third Reich*, pp. 156–7. The question is why, in light of the overall framework that Nazi action established, the wider syndrome contributed to the particular mode of radicalization it did in this case.

45 Ian Kershaw, *The "Hitler Myth": Image and Reality in the Third Reich* (Oxford: Oxford University Press, 1989). See also Kershaw, *Hitler, 1889–1936*, pp. 574–5; Kershaw, *Hitler, 1936–1945*, pp. 185, 374–5.

46 Burleigh, *Ethics and Extermination*, pp. 20–1.

47 Robert Gellately, *The Gestapo and German Society: Enforcing Racial Policy, 1933–1945* (Oxford: Clarendon Press, 1991), pp. 253–6.

48 *Ibid.*, pp. 256–61, esp. pp. 257, 259. See also Burleigh, *Ethics and Extermination*, pp. 3, 167.

49 Omer Bartov, *Hitler's Army: Soldiers, Nazis, and War in the Third Reich* (New York: Oxford University Press, 1992), pp. 3–11 and overall. See also MacGregor Knox, "Expansionist zeal, fighting power, and staying power in the Italian and German dictatorships," in Bessel (ed.), *Fascist Italy and Nazi Germany*, p. 131.

50 Roseman, "National Socialism and modernization," p. 216, noted that recent research has found the regime to have been "astonishingly successful at integrating very heterogeneous social groups into the *Volksgemeinschaft*." See also p. 224. In a sense, this is simply to confirm much of the thrust of Mosse's *Nazi Culture*, which was first published in 1966.

51 Stern, *Hitler*, pp. 44–8 (p. 46 for quotation).

52 Aschheim, *The Nietzsche Legacy*, p. 319n.; Steven E. Aschheim, *Culture and Catastrophe: German–Jewish Confrontations with National Socialism and Other Crises* (New York: New York University Press, 1996), p. 62. In his *Table Talk*, Hitler referred to Kant, Schopenhauer, and Nietzsche as the greatest German thinkers, in comparison with whom, he gloated, the British, French, and Americans had nothing to offer. Hitler credited Nietzsche with far surpassing the pessimism even of Schopenhauer. See *Hitler's Table Talk*, p. 720. See also p. 89.

53 Kershaw, *Hitler, 1889–1936*, p. 240.

54 Kershaw, *Hitler, 1936–1945*, p. 597.

55 Aschheim, *The Nietzsche Legacy*, chapter 8, pp. 232–71, "Nietzsche in the Third Reich"; see especially pp. 234–5, 237, 240, 244, 251, 255.

56 *Ibid.*, pp. 240, 255. See also p. 252. As we noted in Chapter 3, the relationship between Nietzsche and Nazism remains controversial from both sides. Cf. Burleigh, *The Third Reich*, p. 98, on what Burleigh found to have been the superficiality of the Nazi appropriation of Nietzsche. See also pp. 194–5 on what Burleigh judged to have been the pseudo-Nietzscheanism of the SS.

57 George Lichtheim, *Europe in the Twentieth Century* (New York: Praeger, 1972), pp. 151–3 (quotations from pp. 151 and 152). In the same vein, Aschheim suggested that it was as a post-Christian, pitiless, Nietzschean order that the SS appealed even to recruits from outside Germany. See Aschheim, *The Nietzschean Legacy*, pp. 247–8.

58 Aschheim, *The Nietzschean Legacy*, pp. 240–1, p. 243.

59 Stern, *Hitler*, p. 76.

60 Hilberg, *Perpetrators, Victims, Bystanders*, p. 55. Hannah Arendt, in contrast, refused to credit the impulse. Except perhaps for a few brutes, she said, the ideal of toughness "was nothing but a myth of self-deception, concealing a ruthless desire for conformity at any price." This was revealed at Nuremberg, where none had the courage to defend Nazi ideology. See Arendt, *Eichmann in Jerusalem*, p. 175. However, Arendt seemed to assume that only some abiding psychological propensity was at issue; she did not ask about historically specific sources of the accent on hardness. Although "a myth of self-deception" was surely bound up with that accent, even the myth is not so easily dismissed as "nothing but." The question is the source of the whole package

and its place in the overall dynamic. That it could all dissipate once the action was no longer in course is not surprising.

61 Quoted in Gisela Bock, "Racism and sexism in Nazi Germany: Motherhood, compulsory sterilization, and the state," in Renate Bridenthal, Atina Grossmann, and Marion Kaplan (eds.), *When Biology Became Destiny: Women in Weimar and Nazi Germany* (New York: Monthly Review Press, 1984), p. 276. Estimates of the number of undesirables in the population, he noted, ranged from 5 to 30 percent.

62 Rudolf Hoess, *Commandant of Auschwitz: The Autobiography of Rudolf Hoess*, translated by Constantine FitzGibbon (London: Phoenix, 2000), pp. 81–2, 86, 144, 153. See also Steven Paskuly's epilogue to a different version, Rudolf Höss, *Death Dealer: The Memoirs of the SS Kommandant at Auschwitz*, edited by Steven Paskuly, translated by Andrew Pollinger (Buffalo, N.Y.: Prometheus, 1992), p. 202.

63 Detlev Peukert, "The genesis of the 'final solution' from the spirit of science," in Thomas Childers and Jane Caplan (eds.), *Reevaluating the Third Reich* (New York: Holmes & Meier, 1993), p. 247, for a typical characterization.

64 Michael Burleigh, *Death and Deliverance: "Euthanasia" in Germany, c. 1900–1945* (Cambridge: Cambridge University Press, 1994), p. 295.

65 See Burleigh, *The Third Reich*, pp. 157, 160–2, 165 (the quotation is from p. 165). More generally, see pp. 148–215 for the overall section on the demise of the rule of law, and especially 158–77 on "Healthy popular instinct" as the new basis for law.

66 See pp. 435–7.

67 See, for example, Burleigh, *The Third Reich*, p. 196, on Nazism as a sustained assault on Christian values. According to J.P. Stern, Hitler was critical of Alfred Rosenberg's *Mythus des 20. Jahrhunderts* (1930) and other explicit forms of neo-paganism because he was "anxious to postpone a confrontation with the Catholic clergy (who had attacked Rosenberg's book), or at least to choose his own grounds of battle." See Stern, *Hitler*, p. 107. Plausibly enough, Church leaders continued to single out Rosenberg as the most pernicious anti-Christian radical. See Kershaw, *Hitler, 1889–1936*, p. 575.

68 Michael Burleigh and Wolfgang Wippermann, *The Racial State: Germany 1933–1945* (Cambridge: Cambridge University Press, 1991), pp. 210–11.

69 Kershaw, *Hitler, 1936–1945*, pp. 39–40.

70 Burleigh, *Ethics and Extermination*, p. 139.

71 Klaus Scholder, *A Requiem for Hitler and Other New Perspectives on the German Church Struggle*, translated by John Bowden (London: SCM Press, 1989), pp. 174–5, 178–9.

72 *Ibid.*, pp. 179–80.

73 Kershaw, *Hitler, 1936–1945*, pp. 424, 428, 449.

74 See Hitler, *Hitler's Table Talk*, especially pp. 143–6 but also pp. 7, 51, 59, 75, 722, for a few indications. See also Scholder, *A Requiem for Hitler*, p. 180.

75 Martin Bormann, "National Socialist and Christian concepts are incompatible," in Mosse, *Nazi Culture*, pp. 244–7. See also Gitta Sereny, *Into that Darkness: An Examination of Conscience* (New York: Random House [Vintage Books], 1983; first published 1974), p. 281.

76 Hitler, *Mein Kampf*, pp. 400–6; see especially p. 402. See also pp. 255–7, as well as Stefan Kühl, *The Nazi Connection: Eugenics, American Racism, and German National Socialism* (New York: Oxford University Press, 1994), p. 71.

77 Himmler speaking on February 18, 1937, quoted in Burleigh and Wippermann, *The Racial State*, pp. 192–3; see also pp. 177–80.

78 As cited in Karl Dietrich Bracher, *The Nazi Dictatorship: The Origins, Structure, and Effects of National Socialism*, translated by Jean Steinberg (New York: Praeger, 1970), p. 340.

79 Lang, *Act and Idea*, pp. 96–7, notes usefully how language itself became subject to political domination.

80 Even Philip Morgan, in his generally excellent *Fascism in Europe*, refers to Hitler's determination to realize "his vision of a Nazi racial imperialist utopia", then, in the

next paragraph, to the Germanic race's "endless struggle for supremacy with other global racial blocs"; see pp. 181–2. As Ian Kershaw put it, "there would be no end of the struggle in the east, that was clear, even after a German victory"; Kershaw, *Hitler, 1936–1945*, p. 403. See also pp. 504–5, where Kershaw notes Hitler's mixed feelings over the fall of Singapore, which suggested the cracking of the British Empire and the retreat of the white race. Even as he could only admire the Japanese, he considered a showdown with the "yellow" race to be likely at some point. It was clearly necessary to think in centuries.

81 See Burleigh, *Death and Deliverance*, pp. 292–5, on the trajectory of the historiography on eugenics, sterilization, and "euthanasia." Major pioneering works were Ernst Klee, *"Euthanasie" im NS-Staat: Die "Vernichtung lebensunwerten Lebens"* (Frankfurt: S. Fischer Verlag, 1983); and Gisela Bock, *Zwangssterilisation im Nationalsozialismus: Studien zur Rassenpolitik und Frauenpolitik*, (Opladen: Westdeutscher Verlag, 1986).

82 Proctor, *Racial Hygiene*, p. 20.

83 Burleigh and Wippermann tend to conflate biological thinking, even as focused on mere heredity, with "racism." See, for example, *The Racial State*, pp. 172, 181. For another example, see Roseman, "National Socialism and modernization," pp. 207–8.

84 Woodruff D. Smith, *The Ideological Origins of Nazi Imperialism* (New York: Oxford University Press, 1986), pp. 247–8.

85 Kühl, *The Nazi Connection*, pp. xiii–xvii, 65–6, 70. Kühl studied with Bock at Bielefeld.

86 *Ibid.*, pp. 20, 23–5, 37, 85–6.

87 Hitler, *Mein Kampf*, pp. 439–40.

88 Kühl, *The Nazi Connection*, pp. 25–6, 61, 98–9; Proctor, *Racial Hygiene*, pp. 97–101; Maria Sophia Quine, *Population Politics* in Twentieth-Century Europe: *Fascist Dictatorships and Liberal Democracies* (London and New York: Routledge, 1996), p. 111. Stoddard was the author of *The Rising Tide of Color Against White-World Supremacy*, among other works. Also prominent was Madison Grant.

89 Kühl, *The Nazi Connection*, pp. 23–5, 39, 42; Quine, *Population Politics*, pp. 116–17.

90 Bock, "Racism and sexism in Nazi Germany," pp. 271–96; see especially p. 284. See also Quine, *Population Politics*, pp. 113–14.

91 Bock, "Racism and sexism in Nazi Germany," pp. 285, 287–9. Bock concluded that in light of the interpenetration of racism and sexism in assessing the "value" of individual women, the experiences of women differed dramatically. Still, all were subjected to Nazi policy, which was coherent, if double-edged.

92 Proctor, *Racial Hygiene*, pp. 240, 248.

93 Kühl, *The Nazi Connection*, p. 31.

94 Proctor, *Racial Hygiene*, pp. 223–50. See also Robert N. Proctor, *The Nazi War on Cancer* (Princeton, N.J.: Princeton University Press, 1999).

95 Paul Weindling, *Health, Race and German Politics between National Unification and Nazism, 1870–1945* (Cambridge: Cambridge University Press, 1989), pp. 476, 478.

96 Philippe Burrin, *Hitler and the Jews: The Genesis of the Holocaust*, translated by Patsy Southgate (London: Edward Arnold, 1994; original French ed. 1989), p. 45.

97 Bock, "Racism and sexism in Nazi Germany," pp. 279–80. An additional 53,000 had been sterilized in the United States by 1964.

98 Kühl, *The Nazi Connection*, pp. 30–1, 39; Burleigh and Wippermann, *The Racial State*, p. 136.

99 Bock, "Racism and sexism in Nazi Germany," p. 277.

100 Burleigh and Wippermann, *The Racial State*, p. 172; Kühl, *The Nazi Connection*, p. 39. See also Robert Gellately and Nathan Stoltzfus (eds.), *Social Outcasts in Nazi Germany* (Princeton, N.J.: Princeton University Press, 2001), which includes a number of essays that discuss the sterilization of an array of "undesirables."

101 Burleigh and Wippermann, *The Racial State*, pp. 167–82, especially pp. 167–8, 175–6.

102 Kühl, *The Nazi Connection*, pp. 38, 44–5, 51.

103 *Ibid.*, pp. 51–3.

104 *Ibid.*, pp. 32, 75, 79–80, 83, 88, 97.

105 See, for example, Quine, *Population Politics*, p. 118.

106 Burleigh, *Death and Deliverance*, p. 162, and pp. 183–219 for the chapter on film. The discussion on p. 195 is especially striking.

107 *Ibid.*, p. 202.

108 Burleigh and Wippermann, *The Racial State*, p. 142; Burleigh, *Ethics and Extermination*, p. 122.

109 Burleigh, *Death and Deliverance*, pp. 93–4; Proctor, *Racial Hygiene*, pp. 185–6.

110 Burleigh, *Death and Deliverance*, pp. 96, 142; Proctor, *Racial Hygiene*, pp. 181–2.

111 Burleigh, *Death and Deliverance*, pp. 3–4.

112 *Ibid.*, pp. 111–12, 122–3; Burleigh, *Ethics and Extermination*, p. 165.

113 Burleigh, *Death and Deliverance*, p. 160.

114 *Ibid.*, pp. 111, 173, 176–80; Burleigh, *Ethics and Extermination*, pp. 126–8, 140–1; Burleigh and Wippermann, *The Racial State*, pp. 152–3. See also Proctor, *Racial Hygiene*, p. 192.

115 Proctor, *Racial Hygiene*, p. 188.

116 Burleigh, *Death and Deliverance*, p. 97.

117 *Ibid.*, pp. 125, 127. Cf. p. 160, where Burleigh refers to the same sorts as "these rather ordinary people"—an indication of the slipperiness of the "ordinary" category. They were indeed at once different and ordinary, and the basis of each is important.

118 Proctor, *Racial Hygiene*, pp. 189, 193.

119 Burleigh, *Death and Deliverance*, p. 93.

120 *Ibid.*, pp. 4–5, 23, 96–7, 102; Burleigh, *Ethics and Extermination*, p. 3. Proctor, following Götz Aly, similarly noted the broad public support for the "euthanasia" program, even among parents. See Proctor, *Racial Hygiene*, p. 194.

121 Burleigh, *Death and Deliverance*, p. 4.

122 Weiss, *Race Hygiene*, p. 157.

123 See, for example, Christopher Browning's critique of Götz Aly and Suzanne Heim in his *The Path to Genocide*, pp. 59–76. However, it should be noted that the value of their innovative heterodox questioning has come to be widely recognized.

124 Rosenbaum, *Explaining Hitler*, p. xxxix.

125 See especially David Bankier, *The Germans and the Final Solution: Public Opinion under Nazism* (Oxford: Basil Blackwell, 1992). Many recent scholars have emphasized the strong consensus in opposition to Daniel Jonah Goldhagen, *Hitler's Willing Executioners: Ordinary Germans and the Holocaust* (New York: Random House [Vintage Books], 1997), despite the book's popular success. For one prominent example, see Christopher R. Browning's afterword to the new edition of his *Ordinary Men: Reserve Police Battalion 101 and the Final Solution in Poland* (New York: HarperCollins, 1998), pp. 191–223, especially pp. 196–200. See also Finkelstein, "Daniel Jonah Goldhagen's 'crazy' thesis," pp. 18–27, 31–2. We will consider Goldhagen's thesis below.

126 William Sheridan Allen, *The Nazi Seizure of Power: The Experience of a Single German Town, 1922–1945*, revised ed. (New York: Franklin Watts, 1984), pp. 84–6. See also Browning, *Ordinary Men*, p. 198.

127 Browning, *Ordinary Men*, p. 198.

128 Rogers Brubaker, *Citizenship and Nationhood in France and Germany* (Cambridge, Mass.: Harvard University Press, 1992), pp. 132–7.

129 Bartov, *Murder in Our Midst*, p. 9.

130 Proctor, *Racial Hygiene*, p. 196.

131 Bock, "Racism and sexism in Nazi Germany," pp. 283–4, is especially good on the mutually reinforcing interplay between "scientific" racism and "gut" racism, including notions of "Aryan" superiority and the like.

132 See Aschheim, *Culture and Catastrophe*, pp. 45–68, on the longstanding ways of conceiving, and characterizing, "Jewishness" in Germany. See also George L.

Mosse, *Germans and Jews: The Right, the Left, and the Search for a "Third Force" in Pre-Nazi Germany* (New York: Grosset & Dunlap [Universal Library], 1971), pp. 34–76.

133 As Ernst Nolte explored in his *Three Faces of Fascism: Action Française, Italian Fascism, and National Socialism*, translated by Leila Vennewitz (New York: Holt, Rinehart and Winston, 1966; first published in German as *Der Faschismus in seiner Epoche* [Fascism in Its Epoch], 1963), especially pp. 419–25. George Steiner developed this dimension further in his fictionalized *The Portage to San Cristobal of A.H.*, with a new afterword by the author (Chicago: University of Chicago Press, 1999; first published 1981). See also George Steiner, *In Bluebeard's Castle: Some Notes towards the Redefinition of Culture* (New Haven, Conn.: Yale University Press, 1971), pp. 45–7.

134 For example, Daniel Jonah Goldhagen, as evidence for his argument for an abiding exterminationist intention, cited Hitler's speech of August 13, 1920, "Why are we anti-Semites?" in which the future Führer called for the removal of Jews from the German *Volk*. But this was to articulate a vision of racial homogeneity that did not in itself require extermination. See Goldhagen, *Hitler's Willing Executioners*, p. 134.

135 István Deák pointed out that the governments of Poland, Hungary, Greece, Bulgaria, and Turkey actively sought to rid their countries of minority groups. All were acting more assertively to manage populations, especially in light of the changes, territorial and otherwise, that had followed from the First World War. See István Deák, "Memories of hell," *New York Review of Books*, June 26, 1997, p. 43.

136 Noakes and Pridham (eds.), *Nazism: A History in Documents and Eyewitness Accounts*, vol. 2, *Foreign Policy, War and Racial Extermination* (New York: Schocken, 1990), p. 1049.

137 Even as he noted that Hitler's use of bacterial images in *Mein Kampf* suggested the genocidal potential of removal, Ian Kershaw emphasized that the road to Auschwitz was twisted. See Kershaw, *Hitler, 1889–1936*, pp. 244, 290. In *Hitler, 1936–1945*, p. 152, Kershaw stressed that because Hitler used the term "annihilation" (*Vernichtung*) so widely, its use in connection with the Jews did not necessarily indicate an intention for genocide. But the term reflected a mentality that made the genocide possible. Kershaw went on to note that the term *Endlösung* (final solution) was used officially, apparently for the first time, only in June 1941, and even then it meant that some territorial solution was to replace emigration as the basis of Nazi Jewish policy. See Kershaw, *Hitler, 1936–1945*, pp. 321–2.

138 Karl A. Schleunes, *The Twisted Road to Auschwitz: Nazi Policy Toward German Jews, 1933–1939*, new ed. (Urbana: University of Illinois Press, 1990; first published 1970). Based on much new research, Hans Mommsen, especially, advanced this argument during the 1980s. See, for example, Mommsen, "The realization of the unthinkable," pp. 97–144.

139 Lang, *Act and Idea*, p. 9; for the overall point, see pp. 9–11, 188. See also Hilberg, *Perpetrators, Victims, Bystanders*, pp. 53–5; and Zygmunt Bauman, *Modernity and the Holocaust* (Ithaca, N.Y.: Cornell University Press, 1991), p. 85, for this overall theme.

140 The attempted boycott of Jewish shops responded, most immediately, to the developing boycott of German goods in foreign countries in light of German violence against Jews. Although the boycott was not very successful, the day was traumatic for Jews. See Kershaw, *Hitler, 1889–1936*, pp. 472–4; Burleigh and Wippermann, *The Racial State*, pp. 77–8.

141 Burrin, *Hitler and the Jews*, pp. 45–6.

142 *Ibid.*, pp. 48–9, 51; Browning, *Ordinary Men*, p. 199.

143 On the situation surrounding the Nuremberg laws of 1935, see Kershaw, *Hitler, 1889–1936*, pp. 561–73, and Burleigh and Wippermann, *The Racial State*, p. 82.

144 Lang, *Act and Idea*, p. 188; Bauman, *Modernity and the Holocaust*, pp. 188–9.

145 Proctor, *Racial Hygiene*, p. 174.

146 Mommsen, "Anti-Jewish politics," pp. 124–8, esp. pp. 125, 127. See also Arendt, *Eichmann in Jerusalem*, pp. 39–40, 268, on the potential value of the Nuremberg laws from the Jewish perspective at the time. National minority status had been granted to Eastern European minorities by the League of Nations in the wake of the peace settlement.

147 Kershaw, *Hitler, 1936–1945*, p. 42, specifies that even the renewal of anti-Semitism in 1937 was to speed emigration.

148 Burleigh and Wippermann, *The Racial State*, pp. 88–9; Mommsen, "Anti-Jewish politics," p. 124; Arendt, *Eichmann in Jerusalem*, pp. 42–4; Kershaw, *Hitler, 1936–1945*, pp. 145, 147.

149 Kershaw, *Hitler, 1936–1945*, pp. 133–4.

150 For indications of the popular revulsion over *Kristallnacht*, see Saul Friedländer, *Nazi Germany and the Jews*, 1: *The Years of Persecution, 1933–1939* (New York: HarperCollins [Perennial], 1998), pp. 288, 291; Martin Broszat "The Third Reich and the German people," in Bull (ed.), *The Challenge of the Third Reich*, p. 91; Kershaw, *Hitler, 1936–1945*, pp. 142–3, 147; Peukert, *Inside Nazi Germany*, p. 58.

151 Friedländer, *Nazi Germany and the Jews*, 1, pp. 280, 283, 287–8, 290; Mommsen, "Anti-Jewish politics," p. 129; Kershaw, *Hitler, 1936–1945*, pp. 134–5. According to Kershaw, Hitler favored Palestine, although he was nervous about a future Jewish state. More than most authorities, Kershaw links Madagascar and other inhospitable territories to notions of the Jews dying out altogether.

152 Friedländer, *Nazi Germany and the Jews*, 1, pp. 280–91.

153 Kershaw, "German popular opinion and the 'Jewish question'," pp. 369–70.

154 Mommsen, "Anti-Jewish politics," p. 129.

155 The census of May 1939 listed 331,000 Jews in Germany (now including Austria); the number of Jews had dropped by 390,000 since 1933. See Proctor, *Racial Hygiene*, p. 205.

156 Kershaw, "German popular opinion and the 'Jewish question'," pp. 370, 384.

157 Browning, *The Path to Genocide*, p. 7. See also Mommsen, "The realization of the unthinkable," pp. 118–19.

158 Browning, *The Path to Genocide*, pp. 8–9. See also Kershaw, *Hitler, 1936–1945*, pp. 237, 240–8.

159 These figures are difficult to pin down. I follow Dan Cohn-Sherbok, *Atlas of Jewish History* (London: Routledge, 1996), p. 181, which also indicates 3,030,000 Jews in the Soviet Union at that point.

160 Browning, *The Path to Genocide*, p. 25; Mommsen, "Anti-Jewish politics," p. 135.

161 Burrin, *Hitler and the Jews*, p. 75.

162 Browning, *The Path to Genocide*, p. 24.

163 For Himmler's memorandum, see Noakes and Pridham (eds.), *Nazism: A History in Documents*, 2, pp. 932–4.

164 *Ibid.*, pp. 932–3.

165 Browning, *The Path to Genocide*, pp. 11, 14, 16–17.

166 *Ibid.*, pp. 18–19, 32, 127; Kershaw, *Hitler, 1936–1945*, pp. 320–3.

167 Burrin, *Hitler and the Jews*, pp. 78–9, 85.

168 *Ibid.* p. 99; Kershaw, *Hitler, 1936–1945*, pp. 401–3, 462–3.

169 See Browning, *The Path to Genocide*, pp. 28–56, for his chapter on "Nazi ghettoization policy in Poland, 1939–41," featuring the Lodz and Warsaw ghettoes; see especially pp. 30–2 but also p. 89 (for quotation) and p. 152. The Warsaw ghetto was not sealed until November 15, 1940.

170 *Ibid.*, pp. 36, 41–6.

171 *Ibid.*, pp. 22, 33, 36, 38–9.

172 *Ibid.*, p. 160–1; Burleigh and Wippermann, *The Racial State*, p. 102; Mommsen, "Anti-Jewish politics," pp. 135–6.

173 Browning, *The Path to Genocide*, pp. 30, 90.

174 Burleigh, *Ethics and Extermination*, pp. 65–7 (the quotation is from p. 66). See also Kershaw, *Hitler, 1936–1945*, pp. 355–6, 359–60. Burleigh's overall discussion in *Ethics and Extermination*, pp. 37–110, is especially illuminating on German policy in occupied Soviet territories in light of the changing fortunes of the war. On p. 69, he notes that estimates range between 140,000 and 580,000 commissars killed.

175 Browning, *The Path to Genocide*, pp. 99–102; Kershaw, *Hitler, 1936–1945*, pp. 381–2, 463, 468.

176 Browning, *The Path to Genocide*, pp. 110–13.

177 Burleigh, *Ethics and Extermination*, p. 46; Mommsen, "Anti-Jewish politics," pp. 133–5; Kershaw, *Hitler, 1936–1945*, pp. 477–8. Browning, *Ordinary Men*, p. 10; Burrin *Hitler and the Jews*, pp. 138–9

178 The authorization came from Hermann Göring, nominally in charge of Jewish policy, and merely extended earlier mandates to Heydrich. See Noakes and Pridham, *Nazism: A History in Documents*, 2, pp. 1103–4, for the text, prepared by Heydrich's office and signed by Göring; see also Kershaw, *Hitler, 1936–1945*, p. 471. The extent of Hitler's involvement at this pivotal point remains unclear and controversial. Mommsen argued that there was never a formal order, written or oral, from Hitler himself for the systematic killing of all Jews within the Nazi orbit. Indeed, the energy on the level of practice was coming especially from Himmler and Heydrich, although they were operating within the framework of Nazi action already in place, and they had to respond to unforeseen situations resulting from that action. See Mommsen, "The realization of the unthinkable," pp. 110–11, 114, 127–8. Elsewhere, Mommsen insisted that the authorization had no connection with any initiative by Hitler, but he still linked it to the expectation of victory in Russia before winter ("Anti-Jewish politics," p. 133). Ian Kershaw specifies that, in light of the mandates in place, Hitler did not need to be consulted (Kershaw, *Hitler, 1936–1945*, p. 471). Still, Michael Marrus's conclusion of 1987 that the consensus favors a definite Hitler order, as opposed to improvisation and "functionalist" initiatives from below, probably still holds. See Michael R. Marrus, *The Holocaust in History* (New York: New American Library [Meridian Books], 1987), pp. 45–6.

179 Browning, *The Path to Genocide*, p. 113.

180 *Ibid.*, p. 27; see also pp. 81, 121.

181 Burrin, *Hitler and the Jews*, pp. 118, 120. Emigration was still being actively encouraged as of August 21, 1941. See also Browning, *The Path to Genocide*, p. 55.

182 Browning, *The Path to Genocide*, pp. 73–4.

183 *Ibid.*, p. 55.

184 *Ibid.*, pp. 110, 117; Burleigh, *Death and Deliverance*, p. 230.

185 Proctor, *Racial Hygiene*, p. 212.

186 Browning, *The Path to Genocide*, p. 55; Burleigh and Wippermann, *The Racial State*, p. 102.

187 Kershaw, *Hitler, 1936–1945*, pp. 484–5, 838. Over 150,000 Jews died at Chelmno.

188 Kershaw, *Hitler, 1936–1945*, p. 486. The Wannsee conference, initially scheduled for December 9, was postponed in light of the Soviet counter-offensive of December 5 and the Japanese attack on Pearl Harbor of December 7.

189 Burleigh and Wippermann, *The Racial State*, p. 103; Mommsen, "Anti-Jewish politics," p. 137. The fate of those who were one-half or one-quarter Jewish in privileged marriages remained uncertain.

190 Browning, *The Path to Genocide*, pp. 113–14, 117. I have reversed the order of the two quoted passages. The first appears on p. 117.

191 Browning, *Ordinary Men*, pp. 203, 206–7.

192 Bankier, *The Germans and the Final Solution*, pp. 124–38. See also Finkelstein, "Daniel Jonah Goldhagen's 'crazy' thesis," pp. 50–4, 56n.

193 Browning, *The Path to Genocide*, p. 27.

194 Marrus, *The Holocaust in History*, pp. 45–6.

195 Browning, *The Path to Genocide*, p. 121.

196 Burrin, *Hitler and the Jews*, pp. 23–4, 120–1, 127, 146–7, 152. The quoted passages are from p. 147. For a comparable argument linking the Holocaust to the sense of impending defeat, see Sebastian Haffner, *The Meaning of Hitler*, translated by Ewald Osers (Cambridge, Mass.: Harvard University Press, n.d.; original German ed. 1978), pp. 125–45. Also to be mentioned is the more idiosyncratic Arno J. Mayer, *Why Did the Heavens Not Darken? The "Final Solution" in History* (New York: Pantheon, 1988), which portrays the Holocaust as a by-product of the Nazi anti-Bolshevik crusade. Christopher Browning offers a convincing critique in *The Path to Genocide*, pp. 77–85.

197 Kershaw conveys a good sense of the vacillation during 1941–42. See especially Kershaw, *Hitler, 1936–1945*, pp. 411, 415, 441–2, 512. Cf. J.P. Stern, who argued that it was clear from the testimony of military leaders that Hitler knew the war was lost either with the disastrous repulsion of the German armies before Moscow in December 1941 or with Rommel's retreat to Tripolitania at the end of 1942. See Stern, *Hitler*, p. 221.

198 Browning, *The Path to Genocide*, pp. 83–4.

199 Stern, *Hitler*, pp. 29, 32–3; the quoted passage is on p. 33.

200 *Ibid.*, p. 221.

201 *Ibid.*, p. 224.

202 Bartov, *Murder in Our Midst*, pp. 9, 50.

203 Burleigh, *Ethics and Extermination*, p. 223.

204 Burleigh and Wippermann, *The Racial State*, p. 100.

205 Browning, *The Path to Genocide*, p. 54.

206 Mommsen, "Anti-Jewish politics," pp. 128–31. See also Detlev Peukert, "The genesis of the 'final solution' from the spirit of science," p. 237, for an effective statement of the cumulative radicalization point.

207 Burleigh, *Ethics and Extermination*, p. 117.

208 Ruth Bettina Birn, "Revising the Holocaust," in Finkelstein and Birn, *A Nation on Trial*, p. 138.

209 Burleigh, *Death and Deliverance*, p. 233; Proctor, *Racial Hygiene*, pp. 205–12.

210 Browning, *The Path to Genocide*, pp. 141–2.

211 See, for example, Sereny, *Into that Darkness*, p. 201, for "cargo."

212 Mommsen, "Anti-Jewish politics," pp. 138–9.

213 Bauman, *Modernity and the Holocaust*, pp. 73, 90.

214 *Ibid.*, pp. 76–7, 102, 163.

215 *Ibid.*, pp. 188.

216 *Ibid.*, pp. 98–102, 156, 160, 192. See also Browning, *The Path to Genocide*, p. 142, for examples that seem to confirm Bauman's analysis.

217 See Bauman, *Modernity and the Holocaust*, pp. 152–7, 164–6, on the Milgram experiment, which is described in Stanley Milgram, *Obedience to Authority: An Experimental View* (New York, Harper & Row, 1974).

218 Bauman, *Modernity and the Holocaust*, p. 156, for the passage quoted, and pp. 152–6, 164, 166.

219 *Ibid.*, pp. 104–6.

220 Burleigh and Wippermann, *The Racial State*, pp. 84, 94–5.

221 Bauman, *Modernity and the Holocaust*, p. 17.

222 *Ibid.*, pp. 75–6, 186–8.

223 Saul Friedländer, *Memory, History, and the Extermination of the Jews of Europe* (Bloomington: Indiana University Press, 1993), p. 104; see also pp. 105–6. At issue are four Himmler speeches from October 1943 to June 1944.

224 Mommsen, "Anti-Jewish politics," p. 120.

225 Noakes and Pridham (eds.), *Nazism: A History in Documents*, 2, p. 1199. Also especially significant was Himmler's speech of May 5, 1944, on the need to make the extermination total, to keep surviving Jews from taking revenge; see *ibid.*, 2, p. 1200.

226 Friedländer, *Memory, History*, pp. 109–11; the quotation is from p. 110.

227 Cf. Arendt, *Eichmann in Jerusalem*, p. 105. Commenting on Himmler's speech of October 4, 1943, Arendt observed that he hardly ever used ideological justification, and if he did, it was quickly forgotten: "What stuck in the minds of these murderers was simply the notion of being involved in something heroic, grandiose, unique . . . which must therefore be difficult to bear." Arendt also stressed the systematic effort to weed out sadists. Although her thrust here seems to be on target, it seems inconsistent with her put-down of the hardness theme, cited in the context of the Nietzsche discussion (see pp. 545–6.n60). In the same vein, Michael Burleigh sought to make sense of the odd juxtaposition in the SS mentality of "puritanism" about the trivial with a capacity for the monstrous: "This absence of a sense of proportion is a fundamental clue to the workings of the fanatical or zealous mind. It was precisely this combination of moralizing about trivia, absolute self-righteousness, and the utopian doctrine of the perfectibility of mankind through a radical 'quick fix,' which made the twin totalitarianisms of this century and the moralizing zealots who sought to realise them so lethal"; see Burleigh, *The Third Reich*, p. 197. This characterization betrays Burleigh's tendency to retreat to conventional categories rather than confront the historical specificity of the syndrome at issue.

228 Finkelstein, "Daniel Jonah Goldhagen's 'crazy' thesis," p. 61.

229 Sereny, *Into that Darkness*, p. 229.

230 Arendt, *Eichmann in Jerusalem*, p. 109, credits Eichmann's outrage over SS cruelties; it was the cruelty that caused him outrage, not the killing itself.

231 Burleigh, *Death and Deliverance*, p. 221.

232 Burleigh and Wippermann, *The Racial State*, p. 98.

233 Arendt, *Eichmann in Jerusalem*, p. 276. See also p. 272.

234 *Ibid.*, pp. 276, 287.

235 *Ibid.*, pp. 287–8; see also pp. 48–9.

236 *Ibid.*, pp. 53–4 (the quotation is from p. 53).

237 *Ibid.*, p. 247.

238 For an indication of the concern with toughness, see *ibid.*, p. 91–2; Eichmann admitted that others had backed out and that he could have done so as well, but to have done so would not have been admirable. On his idealism, see especially pp. 41–2. Eichmann saw himself as an idealist like the Zionists, as opposed to assimilationist or Orthodox Jews. Yet Arendt found anomalous Eichmann's deal with Dr. Rudolf Kastner in Hungary allowing Kastner to save the putatively best Jewish biological material for settlement in Palestine in exchange for his cooperation in shipping the remaining Jews—hundreds of thousands—to Auschwitz. That Eichmann admired Kastner as a fellow idealist is not anomalous insofar as the point was not anti-Semitism but great politics.

239 The ongoing tendency to accept Arendt's restricted range of categories is evident in Michael Halberstam's discussion, which follows Laura Bilsky on Eichmann and Arendt; see Michael Halberstam, *Totalitarianism and the Modern Conception of Politics* (New Haven, Conn.: Yale University Press, 1999), pp. 163–4. Because we are quick to assume that banal "thoughtlessness" is the alternative to the hatred and/or sadism that were obviously lacking in Eichmann's case, we fail to grasp the role of idealism and exhilaration. Arendt's own evidence indicates that what fueled Eichmann was not merely "the job-holder's concern with success."

240 Burleigh and Wippermann, *The Racial State*, pp. 59, 95–6.

241 Raul Hilberg, *The Destruction of the European Jews*, revised and definitive ed., 3 vols. (New York: Holmes & Meier, 1985), 3, p. 1219 (table B-1: "Deaths by cause").

242 Thanks to prosecutorial inquiries during 1962–72, the interrogations of 210 men from reserve battalion 101 remain in German archives. See Browning, *Ordinary Men*, pp. xvi–xvii, 146.

243 Even as they disagreed on much else, Browning and Goldhagen both stressed the element of genuine choice on the part of the agents as to whether or not to participate. See Browning, *Ordinary Men*, pp. 56–8, 171, 221; and Goldhagen, *Hitler's Willing Executioners*, p. 392.

244 Browning, *Ordinary Men*, pp. 159–61.

245 *Ibid.*, pp. 177–84.

246 For a critique of Goldhagen's use of evidence, see Finkelstein, "Daniel Jonah Goldhagen's 'crazy' thesis," pp. 21n., 30, 68n., 69–72; and Birn, "Revising the Holocaust," pp. 106–7, 111–12, 113n., 127–8, 130. By now, the reception of Goldhagen's book in Germany has its own history—and even metahistory, or reflections on the history. See Robert R. Shandley (ed.), *Unwilling Germans? The Goldhagen Debate* (Minneapolis: University of Minnesota Press, 1998); and Eley (ed.), *The "Goldhagen Effect."*

247 Browning's own afterword to the new edition of his *Ordinary Men*, pp. 191–223, provides an indispensable response to Goldhagen; see also pp. 252–3, notes 1 and 2, for references to other critiques and Goldhagen's responses. See Goldhagen, *Hitler's Willing Executioners*, p. 546, n. 1, for Goldhagen's explicit critique of Browning's *Ordinary Men*.

248 Goldhagen, *Hitler's Willing Executioners*, pp. 237, 279, 385.

249 *Ibid.*, pp. 259–61.

250 *Ibid.*, pp. 14, 419, for particularly pointed statements of this obsessive theme.

251 *Ibid.*, pp. 319–20, 393–4, 398.

252 *Ibid.*, pp. 478, 481–2.

253 Birn, "Revising the Holocaust," p. 146.

254 See Goldhagen, *Hitler's Willing Executioners*, pp. 5–22, 379–93, 460, on the limits of conventional categories, including the Stanley Milgram syndrome. See also pp. 15, 21, 392, 417–18, on the need to take the agents seriously in light of the scope for radical difference.

255 *Ibid.*, pp. 419, 480.

256 Finkelstein, "Daniel Jonah Goldhagen's 'crazy' thesis," pp. 8–10, noted that Goldhagen's way of avoiding comparison by referring to Nazism itself—as essential, and unique—is simply to restate the question of why a movement like Nazism came to power in Germany and not elsewhere. But whereas this is congruent with my point that the key is the Nazi revolution, not anti-Semitism, what must be understood is not merely the coming to power but the content of the Nazi alternative. Especially in insisting that Nazism entailed a "moral–cognitive revolution," Goldhagen was well ahead of many of his critics.

257 Goldhagen, *Hitler's Willing Executioners*, pp. 359, 446–8.

258 *Ibid.*, p. 425; see also pp. 141–3, 162.

259 *Ibid.*, p. 422.

260 *Ibid.*, pp. 417–18.

261 *Ibid.*, pp. 455–61, especially pp. 455–6 for the quotation and the core of the argument.

262 *Ibid.*, p. 396.

263 *Ibid.*, p. 393.

264 *Ibid.*, pp. 279–80.

265 Birn, "Revising the Holocaust," pp. 110, 143–6.

266 *Ibid.*, pp. 139–43.

267 Browning, *Ordinary Men*, p. 221.

268 *Ibid.*, p. 189.

269 *Ibid.*, pp. 184–5, 215–16, 219.

270 *Ibid.*, pp. 167–8, 171–6, 218–19. Here I also draw on Bauman's characterization of the Zimbardo experiment at Stanford, the results of which were published in 1973; see Bauman, *Modernity and the Holocaust*, pp. 166–8, 235 n. 13.

271 Burleigh and Wippermann, *The Racial State*, p. 304.

272 Browning, *Ordinary Men*, pp. 218–19.

273 *Ibid.*, p. 202.

274 *Ibid.*, p. 222. See p. 186 for Browning's original discussion of the issue.

275 *Ibid.*, p. 73. See also Goldhagen's treatment of this theme in *Hitler's Willing Executioners*, pp. 199–200, 212–13, 251–2.

276 Browning, *Ordinary Men*, p. 72.

277 *Ibid.*, pp. 215–16.

278 See also James E. Young, *At Memory's Edge: Afterimages of the Holocaust in Contemporary Art and Architecture* (New Haven, Conn.: Yale University Press, 2000), pp. 58–9, on this theme, including a photograph of perpetrators looking at photographs of what they had done.

279 Bartov, *Murder in Our Midst*, pp. 90–3.

280 Finkelstein, "Daniel Jonah Goldhagen's 'crazy' thesis," pp. 59–66, 74. See also Henry V. Dicks, *Licensed Mass Murder: A Socio-Psychological Study of Some S.S. Killers* (New York: Basic Books, 1973).

281 Hilberg, *Perpetrators, Victims, Bystanders*, pp. 53–5, is especially good on the scope for such vulgarization as a by-product even as he notes that there were also instances of pristine sadism.

282 Sereny, *Into that Darkness*, pp. 101, 201, 222–3.

283 Höss, *Death Dealer*, pp. 183–4.

284 Steven Paskuly, introduction to Höss, *Death Dealer*, pp. 21–2. This is a practice that Höss's successor stopped when Höss himself was promoted to Berlin.

285 Kershaw, *Hitler, 1936–1945*, pp. 716, 819.

286 Bartov, *Murder in Our Midst*, pp. 96–7. Auschwitz survivor Primo Levi noted that outside civilians, mistaking effect for cause, judged the camp inmates worthy of their abasement. See Primo Levi, *Survival in Auschwitz: The Nazi Assault on Humanity*, translated by Stuart Woolf (New York: Simon & Schuster [Touchstone], 1996; original Italian ed., 1958), p. 121.

287 See Goldhagen, *Hitler's Willing Executioners*, pp. 325–71, on the death marches. Although Browning credited Goldhagen for bringing wider attention to this late dimension, he charged that Goldhagen overgeneralized first about the marches themselves from a single example, then about German attitudes from the responses of ordinary bystanders to the marchers. See Browning, *Ordinary Men*, p. 205; and Goldhagen, *Hitler's Willing Executioners*, p. 369, for an indication of Goldhagen's tendency toward such overgeneralization.

288 Finkelstein, "Daniel Jonah Goldhagen's 'crazy' thesis," p. 79; Birn, "Revising the Holocaust," pp. 127–30. See also Kershaw, *Hitler, 1936–1945*, p. 767, on the mixed response of bystanders to the marchers.

289 Robert Jay Lifton, *The Nazi Doctors: Medical Killing and the Psychology of Genocide* (New York: Basic Books, 1986); see especially pp. 418–29 on "doubling." We will encounter objections from Michael Burleigh and Berel Lang below.

290 Burleigh, *Death and Deliverance*, p. 224, see also pp. 154 and 324, n. 88. For Burleigh's put-down of Lifton's "psychohistory over coffee and cake with mass murders," see pp. 294–5.

291 Lang, *Act and Idea*, pp. 51–6.

292 *Ibid.*, pp. 26–9, 32–6, 54–6, 99, 148. See Rosenbaum, *Explaining Hitler*, pp. 208–20, for Rosenbaum's discussion of (and with) Lang.

293 Goldhagen, *Hitler's Willing Executioners*, p. 393.

294 Berel Lang, "The history of evil and the future of the Holocaust," in Peter Hayes (ed.), *Lessons and Legacies: The Meaning of the Holocaust in a Changing World* (Evanston, Ill.: Northwestern University Press, 1991), pp. 84–95, 99–100. A slightly revised version of this essay, retitled "The progress of evil: The past and future of the Holocaust," is included in Berel Lang, *The Future of the Holocaust: Between History and*

Memory (Ithaca, N.Y.: Cornell University Press, 1999), pp. 26–39, along with subsequent essays that further explore the implications of the Holocaust for the historicity of evil.

295 Rosenbaum, *Explaining Hitler*, pp. 218–19.

296 Lang, *Act and Idea*, pp. 42–5, 88; Lang, "The history of evil," pp. 101–2.

297 Rosenbaum, *Explaining Hitler*, pp. 211–15.

298 John Gross, "'A nice pleasant youth'," *New York Review of Books*, December 17, 1998, p. 15.

299 As Christopher Browning put it in *The Path to Genocide*, p. 26, "the reality of Auschwitz was literally inconceivable to its contemporaries." Note also the testimony of Pan Zabecki, one of Gitta Sereny's interviewees, on what he knew of extermination camps early in 1942: "it was beyond—not just experience, but imagination." Sereny, *Into that Darkness*, p. 151.

300 Lang, *Act and Idea*, pp. 196–8.

301 In his epilogue to Höss, *Death Dealer*, p. 205, Steven Paskuly notes that when Höss was confronted with the immorality of his acts by the psychologist G.M. Gilbert at Nuremberg, his began finally to grasp what he had done. For Höss's confession and retrospective self-analysis, see especially Höss, *Death Dealer*, pp. 186 and 192 (this latter from his letter of April 11, 1947, to his wife and five children). It goes without saying that Höss's maudlin confession and self-proclaimed conversion were self-serving on several levels. Yet insofar as something more than ahistorical evil and an ahistorical character type could have been at work, the scope for genuinely turning away is also clear. The proportions are surely undecidable. But the danger for us is not that we will somehow let Höss off by taking his confession too seriously; he was, after all, hanged—and believed he deserved to be hanged. The danger is in cynically minimizing the scope for such conversion—and thus for grasping the historical specificity of the mode of action in question. The point is not that even mass murderers are really good after all but that evil is bound up with historical specificity in ways that we tend to sidestep. We ourselves may thus bring evil into the world in unexpected ways. We will return to this point in the concluding chapter.

302 Scholder, *A Requiem for Hitler*, p. 16.

303 Kershaw, *Hitler, 1936–1945*, p. 838.

304 *Ibid.*, pp. 571–3.

305 *Ibid.*, pp. 566–7, 573–4.

306 *Ibid.*, pp. 551, 556, 565. See also Burleigh, *The Third Reich*, pp. 758–68, on the gap that gradually opened between a leadership determined to go up in flames and an increasingly atomized civilian and military mass ever more bent on personal survival, having lost faith in the rulers. Even before Stalingrad, ordinary Germans found disturbing the American entry into the war.

307 See especially Kershaw, *Hitler, 1936–1945*, p. 554. See also Burleigh, *The Third Reich*, pp. 787–8, for the accent on will. Burleigh also notes, on p. 759, how weary ordinary Germans had become of the repetitive calls to heroism and sacrifice: "The exceptional was reduced to the quotidian, and hence lost its emotional purchase."

308 Kershaw, *Hitler, 1936–1945*, pp. 553, 609–11, 622–3.

309 *Ibid.*, pp. 529, 538, 549, 580–1, 648.

310 *Ibid.*, p. 555; Birn, "Revising the Holocaust," p. 130.

311 Kershaw, *Hitler, 1936–1945*, pp. 696–7, 747. On p. 728, Kershaw took care to note that much of the country had backed Hitler's high-stakes gamble that had led to the situation in fall 1944. At issue, then, is not simply an idiosyncratic Hitler but a mode of action revolving around a particular reciprocity. See Burleigh, *The Third Reich*, pp. 784–93, on this final effort to transform defeat into world-historical spectacle: "The principal actors opted for a tawdry apocalyptic drama, enacted with an eye to posterity" (p. 784).

312 H.R. Trevor-Roper, *The Last Days of Hitler*, 3rd ed. (New York: Collier, 1962), pp. 113–14. See also J.P. Stern, *Hitler*, p. 34. Trevor-Roper's famous account, first published in 1947, finds a nihilistic will to destruction at the core of Nazism all along (pp. 110–14), but we have seen that the destructive will at the end is better understood as a strongly contingent outcome of the mode of action adopted.

Chapter 8

1 As we have noted, such major contemporary scholars as R.J.B. Bosworth and Robert Thurston still find it necessary to take potshots at the concept. See Robert W. Thurston, *Life and Terror in Stalin's Russia, 1934–1941* (New Haven, Conn.: Yale University Press, 1996), p. xviii, as discussed in Chapter 1; and R.J.B. Bosworth, *The Italian Dictatorship: Problems and Perspectives in the Interpretation of Mussolini and Fascism* (London: Edward Arnold, 1998), pp. 106–7, as discussed in Chapter 6.

2 Ruth Ben-Ghiat, *Fascist Modernities: Italy, 1922–1945* (Berkeley: University of California Press, 2001), p. 119. See above, p. 307.

3 Stephen Kotkin, *Magnetic Mountain: Stalinism as a Civilization* (Berkeley: University of California Press, 1995), pp. 20–1, 153–4, 227, 236. See p. 21 for the passage quoted.

4 Saul Friedländer, *Memory, History, and the Extermination of the Jews of Europe* (Bloomington: Indiana University Press, 1993), pp. 106–7.

5 Although concerned only with expansionism in Fascist Italy and Nazi Germany, Aristotle Kallis nicely pinpoints the centrality of the determination to act itself to the overall Fascist departure. For the Italians, that determination was itself innovative—and a manifestation of national vitality. For the Nazis, the capacity for action through will was itself an indication of ideological superiority. See Aristotle A. Kallis, *Fascist Ideology: Territory and Expansionism in Italy and Germany, 1922–1945* (London and New York: Routledge, 2000), pp. 57–9.

6 Emilio Gentile, *The Sacralization of Politics in Fascist Italy*, translated by Keith Botsford (Cambridge, Mass.: Harvard University Press, 1996), p. 86. See also Ian Kershaw, *Hitler, 1936–1945: Nemesis* (New York: W.W. Norton, 2000), p. 401, on Hitler's admiration for Stalin.

7 Martin Malia, *The Soviet Tragedy: A History of Socialism in Russia, 1917–1991* (New York: Free Press, 1994), p. 253.

8 For a few indications of the enduring significance of the civil war experience and of military metaphors, see Sheila Fitzpatrick, *Everyday Stalinism: Ordinary Life in Extraordinary Times: Soviet Russia in the 1930s* (New York: Oxford University Press, 1999), pp. 10, 17; and Thurston, *Life and Terror*, pp. 1–2, 50–8, 66–7.

9 Fitzpatrick, *Everyday Stalinism*, pp. 35–6.

10 As so often, Arendt remains archetypal, although she barely explained what it meant to keep people in motion. See Hannah Arendt, *The Origins of Totalitarianism* (Cleveland: World [Meridian Books], 1958), p. 306; see also p. 464.

11 Detlev J.K. Peukert, *The Weimar Republic: The Crisis of Classical Modernity*, translated by Richard Deveson (New York: Hill and Wang, 1993; first German ed. 1987), p. 236.

12 J.P. Stern, *Hitler: The Führer and the People* (Berkeley: University of California Press, 1975), p. 166.

13 J.L. Talmon, *The Origins of Totalitarian Democracy* (New York: W.W. Norton, 1970), pp. 254–5. See also Chapter 1, p. 28.

14 I refer here to Claude Lefort's account in *The Political Forms of Modern Society: Bureaucracy, Democracy, Totalitarianism* (Cambridge, Mass.: MIT Press, 1986), to be discussed below.

15 Arendt, *The Origins of Totalitarianism*, p. 146.

16 Lefort, *The Political Forms of Modern Society*, pp. 219–20, 305. See also Chapter 2, p. 76.

17 *Ibid.*, p. 222.

18 *Ibid.*, p. 288.

19 *Ibid.*, pp. 220, 222, 297–8.

20 *Ibid.*, p. 306.

21 *Ibid.*, p. 291.

22 This is the implication of Zygmunt Bauman, for example, in his recent *In Search of Politics* (Stanford, Calif.: Stanford University Press, 1999), pp. 87–96; see especially p. 88. Bauman follows Hannah Arendt in part.

23 Fitzpatrick, *Everyday Stalinism*, pp. 115, 130–2, 135.

24 Abbott Gleason, *Totalitarianism: The Inner History of the Cold War* (New York: Oxford University Press, 1995), pp. 9, 19, 94–5, as discussed in Chapter 1; see above, p. 15.

25 For two disparate but archetypal examples of such elitist anti-totalitarian thinking, see José Ortega y Gasset, *The Revolt of the Masses* (New York: W.W. Norton, 1957; first published in Spanish, 1930); and T.S. Eliot, "Notes towards the definition of culture" (1949), in his *Christianity and Culture* (New York: Harcourt, Brace & World [Harvest], 1968), pp. 115–20, 180–1.

26 Isaiah Berlin, "Joseph de Maistre and the origins of fascism," in his *The Crooked Timber of Humanity: Chapters in the History of Ideas*, edited by Henry Hardy (New York: Random House [Vintage Books[, 1992), pp. 91–174; Zeev Sternhell, with Mario Sznajder and Maia Asheri, *The Birth of Fascist Ideology: From Cultural Rebellion to Political Revolution*, translated by David Maisel (Princeton, N.J.: Princeton University Press, 1994; original French ed. 1989), p. 251.

27 Ernst Nolte, *Three Faces of Fascism: Action Française, Italian Fascism, and National Socialism*, translated by Leila Vennewitz (New York: Holt, Rinehart & Winston, 1966), p. 423.

28 Michael Burleigh, *The Third Reich: A New History* (New York: Hill and Wang, 2000), p. 9.

29 Kotkin, *Magnetic Mountain*, pp. 293–4. See also Leszek Kolakowski, *Main Currents of Marxism: Its Origins, Growth and Dissolution*, 2: *The Golden Age*, translated by P.S. Falla (Oxford: Oxford University Press, 1981), pp. 508, 514; and Malia, *The Soviet Tragedy*, pp. 239–40, for accents on Soviet hyper-politics that avoid the long-standing tendency toward reification through reference to some totalitarian "system."

30 Kotkin, *Magnetic Mountain*, pp. 178–9; Moshe Lewin, *The Making of the Soviet System: Essays in the Social History of Interwar Russia* (New York: Pantheon, 1985), p. 220.

31 See Mark B. Adams, "Eugenics in Russia, 1900–1940," in Mark B. Adams (ed.), *The Wellborn Science: Eugenics in Germany, France, Brazil, and Russia* (New York: Oxford University Press, 1990), pp. 153–216, especially pp. 176, 181–200, on the changing place of eugenics in Soviet population policy. See also Stefan Kühl, *The Nazi Connection: Eugenics, American Racism, and German National Socialism* (New York: Oxford University Press, 1994), p. 78.

32 Gleason, *Totalitarianism*, p. 27.

33 Franz Neumann, *Behemoth: The Structure and Practice of National Socialism, 1933–1944* (New York: Harper & Row [Harper Torchbooks], 1966; from 2nd ed., first published 1944), p. 48.

34 *Ibid.*, pp. 49–51.

35 Carl Schmitt, "Faschistische und nationalsozialistische Rechtswissenschaft," *Deutsche Juristen-Zeitung* 41 (1936): pp. 619–20.

36 Neumann, *Behemoth*, pp. 75–80 (the quotation is from p. 78).

37 *Ibid.*, pp. 75–8.

38 Herbert Marcuse, *Reason and Revolution: Hegel and the Rise of Social Theory* (Boston: Beacon Press, 1960; first published 1941), pp. 411–12.

39 Neumann, *Behemoth*, pp. 49, 59–61; Gleason, *Totalitarianism*, p. 29.

40 Gleason, *Totalitarianism*, pp. 15–20.

41 Alfred Rosenberg, *Race and Race History and Other Essays*, edited by Robert Pois (New York: Harper & Row [Harper Torchbooks], 1974), pp. 191–2. Rosenberg had earlier

attacked Hegel in his best-known work, *Der Mythus des 20. Jahrhunderts*, first published in 1930. See also Neumann, *Behemoth*, pp. 63–4.

42 Adolf Hitler, *Mein Kampf*, translated by Ralph Manheim (Boston: Houghton Mifflin [Sentry edition], 1943), pp. 386–94.

43 Neumann, *Behemoth*, pp. 64–5.

44 Marcuse, *Reason and Revolution*, pp. 413, 418–19; Neumann, *Behemoth*, p. 462.

45 Marcuse, *Reason and Revolution*, pp. 411, 413, 416–18.

46 Ibid., pp. 407–8.

47 Paolo Ungari, *Alfredo Rocco e l'ideologia giuridica del fascismo* (Brescia: Morcelliana, 1963).

48 Even Abbott Gleason, despite his particular value and insight, tended to reproduce the longstanding confusion by implicitly endorsing the German notion that to take the state as the focus of totalitarianism inherently meant conservative authority as opposed to radical dynamism. See, for example, Gleason, *Totalitarianism*, pp. 35, 164.

49 Ian Kershaw, *Hitler, 1889–1936: Hubris* (New York: W.W. Norton, 1999), p. 476.

50 Neumann, *Behemoth*, p. 66.

51 Woodruff D. Smith, *The Ideological Origins of Nazi Imperialism* (New York: Oxford University Press, 1986), pp. 245–6, 253–6.

52 J. Arch Getty, *Origins of the Great Purges: The Soviet Communist Party Reconsidered, 1933–1938* (Cambridge: Cambridge University Press, 1985), pp. 96–102, 110–11, 118, 199–201; J. Arch Getty, "The politics of repression revisited," in J. Arch Getty and Roberta T. Manning (eds.), *Stalinist Terror: New Perspectives* (Cambridge: Cambridge University Press, 1993), p. 50.

53 Moshe Lewin, "Bureaucracy and the Stalinist state," in Ian Kershaw and Moshe Lewin (eds.), *Stalinism and Nazism: Dictatorships in Comparison* (Cambridge: Cambridge University Press, 1997), p. 70.

54 Kallis, *Fascist Ideology*, pp. 93–8, 101–3, 190–2.

55 Kallis himself is good on this theme for Balbo and others in Italy. See *ibid.*, p. 96.

56 Kershaw, *Hitler, 1889–1936*, p. 437.

57 *Ibid.*, p. 539; Kershaw, *Hitler, 1936–1945*, pp. 314, 566–7, 573–4.

58 See, for example, Robert C. Tucker, "Introduction: Lenin and revolution," in Robert C. Tucker (ed.), *The Lenin Anthology* (New York: W.W. Norton, 1975), p. xxxviii.

59 See, for example, Václav Havel, "The power of the powerless," in Václav Havel *et al.*, *The Power of the Powerless: Citizens against the State in Central–Eastern Europe* (Armonk, N.Y.: M.E. Sharpe, 1985), pp. 23–96. We will consider that effort in more detail in the next chapter.

60 Gleason, *Totalitarianism*, p. 176; see also p. 178.

61 Timothy Garton Ash, *The Magic Lantern: The Revolution of '89 Witnessed in Warsaw, Budapest, Berlin and Prague* (New York: Random House [Vintage Books], 1993), p. 137.

62 Timothy Garton Ash, "Refolution," in Timothy Garton Ash, *The Uses of Adversity: Essays on the Fate of Central Europe* (New York: Random House [Vintage Books], 1990, with a new postscript), p. 320. See also Garton Ash, *The Magic Lantern*, pp. 141–2.

63 Gale Stokes, *The Walls Came Tumbling Down: The Collapse of Communism in Eastern Europe* (New York: Oxford University Press, 1993). There were differences and complexities, and rulers sometimes maintained themselves in other guises, but Communist monopoly power, based on a claim to a privileged historical-political grasp, had dissipated definitively.

64 The inadequacy of more conventional categories, especially the emphasis on ideology *per se*, is especially evident in François Furet's *The Passing of an Illusion: The Idea of Communism in the Twentieth Century*, translated by Deborah Furet (Chicago: University of Chicago Press, 1999). Furet associates ideology with lies, myths, and fear throughout (e.g., pp. 371, 440, 446, 468, 500), but the relationship between them remains uncertain. Thus he leaves us wondering what had dissipated by the end. As Furet saw it, the regime was already post-totalitarian with the death of Stalin because the universal fear that was a condition of universal silence quickly dissipated (pp. 481, 486). Yet he also notes that

even under Khrushchev, faith in ideology had not weakened, that even Khrushchev believed what he said (p. 449). So in what sense was it all a lie? By the end, *belief* had obviously dissipated—belief in a mode of action that had encompassed an element of myth from the start, but that had become more bound up with myth as it proceeded.

Chapter 9

1 See Denise Riley, "Some peculiarities of social policy concerning women in wartime and postwar Britain," in Margaret Randolph Higonnet *et al.* (eds.), *Behind the Lines: Gender and the Two World Wars* (New Haven, Conn.: Yale University Press, 1987), especially pp. 263–4.

2 Albert Camus, *The Rebel: An Essay on Man in Revolt* (New York: Random House [Vintage Books], 1956; first published in French in 1951), pp. 253–77.

3 Mabel Berezin, for example, found Fini, and even some on the American Right, to be evidence "that the fascist impulse is not . . . 'a parenthesis'." She took it for granted that Fini, in claiming to be *post*-Fascist, could only have been indulging in expediency. See Mabel Berezin, *Making the Fascist Self: The Political Culture of Interwar Italy* (Ithaca, N.Y.: Cornell University Press, 1997), pp. 197, 245–6.

4 Umberto Eco, "Ur-fascism," *New York Review of Books*, June 22, 1995, pp. 12–15. See also Chapter 1, note 72, p. 493.

5 See especially Omer Bartov, *Mirrors of Destruction: War, Genocide, and Modern Identity* (Oxford: Oxford University Press, 2000). This is not in any way to question the value of Bartov's ongoing work on modern atrocity and genocide. We simply need to remember that in light of totalitarianism there are broader challenges to be addressed at the same time.

6 Hannah Arendt, *Eichmann in Jerusalem: A Report on the Banality of Evil*, revised and enlarged ed. (New York: Viking [Compass], 1965), pp. 273, 288–9, 294.

7 Stephen Holmes, *The Anatomy of Antiliberalism* (Cambridge, Mass.: Harvard University Press, 1993), p. 154. For another angle, see Michael Halberstam, *Totalitarianism and the Modern Conception of Politics* (New Haven, Conn.: Yale University Press, 1999), pp. 128, 133. Halberstam suggests that rather than face up to the fact that the liberal political community, like the totalitarian, is dependent on a "nonrational historically shared common sense which is not neutral with regard to competing conceptions of the good," liberals tend simply to invoke the threat of totalitarianism. Among Halberstam's sources was Sigmund Neumann, who, as the Fascist period was nearing its end, noted that the struggle for democracy against totalitarianism could not be simply a matter of preserving the democratic status quo. The democratic self-understanding required renewal, even a new vocabulary: "This is of primary importance for the survival of democracy, which, of all forms of society, is most dependent on 'mutual understanding'." And such renewal required serious engagement with the totalitarian challenge on the conceptual level. See Sigmund Neumann, *Permanent Revolution: The Total State in a World at War* (New York: Harper & Brothers, 1942), p. xiv; see also pp. vii, x, 306–10.

8 Ernst Nolte, *Three Faces of Fascism: Action Française, Italian Fascism, and National Socialism*, translated by Leila Vennewitz (New York: Holt, Rinehart and Winston, 1966; first published in German as *Der Faschismus in seiner Epoche* [Fascism in Its Epoch], 1963). In his subsequent work, Nolte featured the Cold War, which extended the era in a certain sense, even as the conditions for *fascism* seemed to have dissipated. See Ernst Nolte, *Marxism, Fascism, Cold War* (Atlantic Highlands, N.J.: Humanities Press, 1982).

9 Nolte, *Three Faces of Fascism*, pp. 421–3.

10 See *ibid.*, p. 454, for the concluding paragraph, which Roger Griffin pillories in his "Fascism's new faces (and new facelessness) in the 'post-fascist epoch,'" *Erwägen Wissen Ethik* (*EWE*), 15, paragraphs 48 and 51 (2004).

11 We recall Karl Popper's bifurcation in *The Open Society and Its Enemies* (1945) and J.L. Talmon on the totalitarian embrace of the security of a prison. Each helped to establish certain assumptions and categories of understanding.

12 Isaiah Berlin, *Four Essays on Liberty* (London: Oxford University Press, 1969) pp. 154, 168–9, 172.

13 Abbott Gleason, *Totalitarianism: The Inner History of the Cold War* (New York: Oxford University Press, 1995), p. 209.

14 *Ibid.*, p. 210.

15 Zygmunt Bauman, *Modernity and the Holocaust* (Ithaca, N.Y.: Cornell University Press, 1992), p. 219. See also p. 86.

16 Bernard Yack, *The Longing for Total Revolution: Philosophic Sources of Social Discontent from Rousseau to Marx to Nietzsche* (Berkeley: University of California Press, 1992), pp. xiv–xv, 368–9. For another example, see Michael Burleigh, *The Third Reich: A New History* (New York: Hill and Wang, 2000), p. 812: We seem to have learned that there are no quick-fix leaps to happiness; eschewing "ideological fantasy," we settle for a lower register, more pragmatic ambitions.

17 Emilio Gentile, *Le religioni della politica: Fra democrazia e totalitarismi* (Rome and Bari: Laterza, 2001), pp. 217–18.

18 Leszek Kolakowski, *Modernity on Endless Trial* (Chicago: University of Chicago Press, 1990), pp. 90–1 (article originally published in 1976).

19 Martin Malia, *The Soviet Tragedy: A History of Socialism in Russia, 1917–1991* (New York: Free Press, 1994), pp. 516–20.

20 Mark Roseman, "National Socialism and modernization," in Richard Bessel (ed.), *Fascist Italy and Nazi Germany: Comparisons and Contrasts* (Cambridge: Cambridge University Press, 1996), pp. 226–7.

21 Omer Bartov, *Murder in Our Midst: The Holocaust, Industrial Killing, and Representation* (New York: Oxford University Press, 1996), p. 67.

22 See especially Zygmunt Bauman, *Hermeneutics and Social Science* (New York: Columbia University Press, 1978). Since publishing *Modernity and the Holocaust*, Bauman has developed his prescriptions in a number of works, including, for example, *The Individualized Society* (Cambridge: Polity Press, 2001) and *In Search of Politics* (Stanford, Calif.: Stanford University Press, 1999).

23 Jeffrey Herf, *Reactionary Modernism: Technology, Culture, and Politics in Weimar and the Third Reich* (Cambridge: Cambridge University Press, 1984), pp. 233–4; Michael Burleigh and Wolfgang Wippermann, *The Racial State: Germany 1933–1945* (Cambridge: Cambridge University Press, 1991), pp. 2, 39, 107–8, 304–7.

24 Burleigh and Wippermann, *The Racial State*, pp. 46, 98, 107–8, 305–7.

25 Hannah Arendt, *The Origins of Totalitarianism* (Cleveland: World [Meridian], 1958), p. 478. See also p. vii, where she noted: "Never has our future been more unpredictable. . . . It is as though mankind had divided itself between those who believe in human omnipotence (who think that everything is possible if one knows how to organize masses for it) and those for whom powerlessness has become the major experience of their lives." The challenge, obviously, is to find our way beyond those two alternatives by empowering ourselves while eschewing new variations on the totalitarian temptation.

26 Arendt, *Eichmann in Jerusalem*, pp. 273, 288–9, 294. See also Arendt, *The Origins of Totalitarianism*, p. 459, on the ongoing danger of superfluousness if we continue to think in utilitarian terms.

27 Margaret Canovan, *Hannah Arendt: A Reinterpretation of Her Political Thought* (Cambridge: Cambridge University Press, 1992), pp. 86–7.

28 *Ibid.*, p. 11.

29 *Ibid.*, p. 26.

30 *Ibid.*, pp. 12–13; quoted in Chapter 2, p. 74.

31 *Ibid.*, pp. 14, 79, 84. See, for example, Arendt, *Eichmann in Jerusalem*, p. 273, on nuclear power.

32 Canovan, *Hannah Arendt*, p. 11.

33 Gleason, *Totalitarianism*, pp. 176–80. See also pp. 182–8 on Havel.

34 Alain Finkielkraut, "Milan Kundera interview," in Peter Petro (ed.), *Critical Essays on Milan Kundera* (New York: G.K. Hall, 1999), p. 44.

35 Interview with Milan Kundera in Philip Roth, *Shop Talk: A Writer and His Colleagues and Their Work* (Boston: Houghton Mifflin, 2001), pp. 97–8 (based on conversations in London and Connecticut in 1980). The totalitarian airbrushing syndrome begins Kundera's *The Book of Laughter and Forgetting*, translated from the French by Aaron Asher (New York: HarperCollins Perennial Classics, 1999), pp. 3–4. As for such airbrushing in the West, surely the sort of selective memory that Mark Roseman noted in connection with Nazism and modernity qualifies. In this context, George Orwell's observations on what is, and is not, different about the totalitarian manipulation of history are also worth recalling; see "The prevention of literature," in his *Shooting an Elephant and Other Essays* (New York: Harcourt, Brace & World, 1950), pp. 104–21, especially pp. 109–12.

36 Václav Havel, *Disturbing the Peace: A Conversation with Karel Hvízdala,* translated from the Czech by Paul Wilson (New York: Random House [Vintage Books], 1991), pp. 10–11, 13–14, 129, 166; Václav Havel, "The power of the powerless," in Václav Havel *et al., The Power of the Powerless: Citizens against the State in Central–Eastern Europe* (Armonk, N.Y.: M.E. Sharpe, 1985), pp. 27, 38–9, 45.

37 Havel, *Disturbing the Peace,* p. 167.

38 *Ibid.*, p. 11.

39 Havel, "The power of the powerless," pp. 38–9, 89–92.

40 Or we *post*moderns, which we become once we lose confidence in any master narrative and instead experience history as "light, . . . unbearably light." The intricacies of nomenclature need not detain us here. At issue is what ends and what continues from within the specifically *modern* framework that made totalitarianism possible. The point of the present chapter is that this is still being sorted out, whatever Kundera's particular answer, based on his way of assessing historical weight and lightness.

41 For a few examples, see Milan Kundera, *The Unbearable Lightness of Being,* translated from the Czech by Michael Henry Heim (New York: HarperCollins [Perennial], 1991), pp. 141–2, 165–6, 179–84, 187–8, 212, 221–32.

42 *Ibid.*, pp. 112–13. As Kundera put it in an interview, "every evil comes from the moment when a false word is accepted. Capitulation begins there." See Finkielkraut, "Milan Kundera interview," p. 37.

43 Kundera, *The Unbearable Lightness of Being,* p. 223.

44 Kundera, *The Book of Laughter and Forgetting,* p. 120.

45 See Kundera, *The Unbearable Lightness of Being,* p. 248, for the definition, including the explicit use of "shit." See also pp. 248–57, 277–8, for the overall place of "kitsch" in Kundera's sense.

46 The notion that any emphasis on history encompasses faith in the Grand March is implicit throughout Kundera's *The Unbearable Lightness of Being;* see especially pp. 25, 268–9. See, more generally, pp. 257–69, for the "Cambodia protest" and Kundera's withering scorn.

47 The contemporary anti-totalitarian kitsch was just as monochromatic as the earlier embrace of Communism had been. Those opposing totalitarianism, as Kundera put it, "can't function with queries and doubts. They too need certainties and simple truths to make the multitudes understand, to provoke collective tears." See *ibid.*, p. 254; see also p. 261.

48 James E. Young, *At Memory's Edge: Afterimages of the Holocaust in Contemporary Art and Architecture* (New Haven, Conn.: Yale University Press, 2000), p. 182. See also Reinhart Koselleck, *Futures Past: On the Semantics of Historical Time,* translated by Keith Tribe (Cambridge, Mass.: MIT Press, 1985), pp. 92–4; and Alois Martin Müller, "Daniel

Libeskind's muses," in Daniel Libeskind, *Radix–Matrix: Architecture and Writings*, translated by Peter Green (Munich and New York: Prestel Verlag, 1997), p. 117.

49 Young, *At Memory's Edge*, p. 182.

50 Jeffrey C. Goldfarb, *Beyond Glasnost: The Post-Totalitarian Mind* (Chicago: University of Chicago Press, 1991), pp. 53–7, 90–1, 162.

51 *Ibid.*, pp. 16–17, 25–6, 129–31.

52 *Ibid.*, pp. 113–15.

53 Georges Bataille, "Nietzsche and the fascists," in *Visions of Excess: Selected Writings, 1927–1939*, edited and translated by Allan Stoekl (Minneapolis: University of Minnesota Press, 1985), pp. 193–4 (article originally published in 1937).

54 Hannah Arendt, *The Human Condition* (Chicago: University of Chicago Press, 1958), pp. 198–9. See also Halberstam, *Totalitarianism and the Modern Conception of Politics*, p. 129; and Canovan, *Hannah Arendt*, pp. 173–4, 184–5.

55 Hannah Arendt, "What is freedom?" in *Between Past and Future: Eight Exercises in Political Thought* (New York: Viking, 1968), p. 151; Hannah Arendt, "Freedom and politics," in Albert Hunold (ed.), *Freedom and Serfdom: An Anthology of Western Thought* (Dordrecht: Reidel, 1961), p. 198. See also Canovan, *Hannah Arendt*, pp. 178, 213; and Goldfarb, *Beyond Glasnost*, pp. 129–31.

56 Canovan, *Hannah Arendt*, p. 212.

57 For the conflation of historicism and the reign of technology, see Martin Heidegger, *Early Greek Thinking: The Dawn of Western Philosophy*, translated by David Farrell Krell and Frank A. Capuzzi (San Francisco: Harper & Row, 1984; from an essay written in 1946), p. 17. We need not revisit here the question of Heidegger's Nazi affiliations, which occasioned such interest in the late 1980s and early 1990s. I offer a few observations in David D. Roberts, *Nothing but History: Reconstruction and Extremity After Metaphysics* (Berkeley: University of California Press, 1995), pp. 111–13, 125–6, 134, 148, 152.

58 Richard J. Bernstein, *The New Constellation: The Ethical-Political Horizons of Modernity/Postmodernity* (Cambridge, Mass.: MIT Press, 1992), pp. 125–8.

59 Hannah Arendt, "The ex-communists," *Commonweal* 57, no. 24 (March 20, 1953): 597; included in Hannah Arendt, *Essays in Understanding, 1930–1954*, edited by Jerome Kohn (New York: Harcourt Brace, 1994), p. 396. See also Canovan, *Hannah Arendt*, pp. 71, 164–5. Especially as mediated by sympathetic commentators like Canovan, Arendt's sense of action and history led toward prejudicial conflations. On p. 165, Canovan notes that for Arendt "the notion of *making* history, taking one's future in one's hands and shaping it, always entails violence. Fabrication is a violent business." Alternatively, on p. 166, Arendt sought "to present a version of humanist republicanism *without* the model of fabrication, without means–ends thinking, without the sanctification of violence." See also Canovan, *Hannah Arendt*, pp. 76–7, for the tendency toward this particularly prejudicial conflation.

60 Arendt, *Eichmann in Jerusalem*, pp. 230–3.

61 Here I follow especially Canovan's characterizations, which usefully distill Arendt's emphases. See especially Canovan, *Hannah Arendt*, pp. 142, 154, 250–2. Note also the connections between individual agency, history, and remembrance in Arendt, *The Human Condition*, pp. 8–9, 181–8. See also Halberstam, *Totalitarianism and the Modern Conception of Politics*, p. 137, on Arendt's notion that, acting as we do in a complex world of historical significances, we do not project toward a pre-given human nature, as does the Aristotelian subject, but toward the historical judgment of others. The point for us is that those are not the only alternatives in a world of historical significances.

62 Havel, *Disturbing the Peace*, p. 166.

63 *Ibid.*, p. 182; Havel, "The power of the powerless," pp. 27–31, 36–7.

64 Havel, *Disturbing the Peace*, pp. 10–12, 166–7, 182–3. Havel's sense of priorities reflected his conception of the intellectual's role, which is constantly to disturb, to

rebel. As "the chief doubter of systems, of power and its incantations" (p. 167), the intellectual is at odds with those hard and fast categories, which tend to be instruments used by the victors.

65 Havel, "The power of the powerless," p. 89.

66 *Ibid.*, p. 180.

67 *Ibid.*, pp. 78–81, 92.

68 *Ibid.*, pp. 93–4; Havel *Disturbing the Peace*, pp. 15–16, 21.

69 Richard Rorty, *Essays on Heidegger and Others: Philosophical Papers*, vol. 2 (Cambridge: Cambridge University Press, 1991), p. 195. In the same vein, let us recall the implicit put-down of Foucault in Claude Lefort's insistence that power "is not, as a certain contemporary discourse naively repeats, a mere organ of domination: it is the agency of legitimacy and identity." Claude Lefort, *The Political Forms of Modern Society: Bureaucracy, Democracy, Totalitarianism* (Cambridge, Mass.: MIT Press, 1986), p. 305, as quoted in Chapter 2, p. 77.

70 Kundera, *The Unbearable Lightness of Being*, p. 254. See also pp. 102–4.

71 *Ibid.*, pp. 219–20.

72 *Ibid.*, pp. 196–7, 313.

73 Kundera, *The Book of Laughter and Forgetting*, p. 4. The earlier criticism of Robert Boyers is surely on the right track, but in light of the cultural currents still at work, we need a wider historical-political framework to make the point. See Robert Boyers, "Between east and west: A letter to Milan Kundera," in Robert Boyers, *Atrocity and Amnesia: The Political Novel Since 1945* (New York: Oxford University Press, 1985), pp. 212–33.

74 James Young's discussion of the museum in *At Memory's Edge* (pp. 152–83) is deeply appreciative. Berlin's Jewish population is increasing, and something like a Jewish street life is re-emerging in the area of the rebuilt synagogue on Oranienburger Strasse.

75 Benjamin R. Barber, *Strong Democracy: Participatory Politics for a New Age* (Berkeley: University of California Press, 1984), pp. 65, 131.

76 Ruth Bettina Birn, "Revising the Holocaust," in Norman G. Finkelstein and Ruth Bettina Birn, *A Nation on Trial: The Goldhagen Thesis and Historical Truth* (New York: Henry Holt, 1998), p. 146.

77 Walter Laqueur offers a number of effective characterizations of such differences in his *Fascism: Past, Present, Future* (New York: Oxford University Press, 1996); see especially pp. 110, 127, 215, 219–20, 234–5.

78 De Felice, *Fascism: An Informal Introduction to its Theory and Practice* (An interview with Michael A. Ledeen) (New Brunswick: N.J.: Transaction Books, 1976), pp. 98–9, 101, 103–5. The quoted phrase is from p. 104.

79 Griffin, "Fascism's new faces." Griffin had earlier suggested that although Fascism remained a low-level presence in modern society, it was largely the product of a certain configuration in European history that had long passed. See Roger Griffin, *The Nature of Fascism* (London: Routledge, 1993), pp. 203–5, 210.

80 This is the thrust of my response, one of twenty-seven such responses, to Griffin's article. See David D. Roberts, "Understanding fascism as historically specific," *Erwägen Wissen Ethik* (*EWE*), 2004, no. 3 (forthcoming).

81 Although not explicitly concerned with endings and lessons, Robert N. Proctor's reflections in *The Nazi War on Cancer* (Princeton, N.J.: Princeton University Press, 1999), pp. 3–12, are usefully pondered in this context.

82 Michael Burleigh, *Ethics and Extermination: Reflections on Nazi Genocide* (Cambridge: Cambridge University Press, 1997), pp. 142–52. At least as hard-hitting is Burleigh's comparable argument concerning the unwillingness—in Germany, but also elsewhere—to listen to Peter Singer and others with proposals seeming to recall Nazi departures. See Michael Burleigh, *Death and Deliverance: 'Euthanasia' in Germany, c. 1900–1945* (Cambridge: Cambridge University Press, 1994), pp. 291–

8. Also worthy of mention in this context is Pat Shipman, *The Evolution of Racism: Human Evolution and the Use and Abuse of Science* (Cambridge, Mass.: Harvard University Press, 2002), the latter portions of which explore the political and ideological factors, with the Nazi experience constantly lurking, that have limited the scientific discussion of human difference since the Second World War. Yet understanding such difference is crucial to contemporary social policy. See pp. 156–271, especially p. 174, 190–1, 211–20, 243, 245, 257. Shipman insists on the need for open questioning, research, and discussion while also calling for a deeper appreciation of difference, on the one hand, and stressing our collective responsibility to provide equality of opportunity for individuals, on the other. See pp. 196, 219–20, 261, 263–71.

83 See Richard Rorty, *Contingency, Irony, and Solidarity* (Cambridge: Cambridge University Press, 1989), especially p. 41, for an influential contemporary exploration of this sense of risk and its implications. In my view, Rorty's concerns led him to a prejudicially extreme position, including a measure of resentment of history itself and concomitant strategies for one-upping it. In my *Nothing but History*, I suggest a way of understanding such impulses and their interplay with the more constructive relationship with history that I have in mind here; see chapter 9 for my reading of Rorty and pp. 242–3 for this particular point.

84 For one bit of evidence, see Hannah Arendt, "On Hannah Arendt," in Melvyn A. Hill (ed.), *Hannah Arendt: The Recovery of the Public World* (New York: St Martin's Press, 1979), pp. 303–6. See also Canovan, *Hannah Arendt*, pp. 268–9.

85 Kundera, *The Unbearable Lightness of Being*, p. 218.

86 Michael Halberstam addresses this question and offers some useful indications— concerning the limits of John Rawls's influential rethinking of liberalism, for example. See Halberstam, *Totalitarianism and the Modern Conception of Politics*, pp. 205–7. See also pp. 198–9, where Halberstam notes the illegitimacy of any claim that liberalism is the uniquely appropriate response to the groundlessness of the political. But whereas he insists that our thinking about modern political possibilities must be informed more deeply by the totalitarian departure, and whereas he offers some promising indications at first, Halberstam ends up by addressing the issues largely in terms of Arendt's understanding of totalitarianism, worked out in its essentials over half a century ago. Although Arendt remains an indispensable starting point, we cannot seriously rethink the implications of totalitarianism for liberalism—and for the scope for alternatives—if we confine ourselves to her categories to this extent.

87 Francis Fukuyama, *The End of History and the Last Man* (New York: Free Press, 1992). Fukuyama first advanced his thesis in his much-discussed article "The end of history?" *The National Interest* 16 (summer 1989): 3–18.

88 In light of his links to the Frankfurt School legacy, even Jürgen Habermas, who has sought assiduously and effectively to head off the overreaction, has tended to assume that an *a priori* principle of some sort must be specified. Bothered especially by "the hermeneutic claim to universality," he sought to hold to the possibility of rational or enlightened critique by preserving criteria of distinction between distorted and undistorted forms of communication. Writing in 1979, Richard Rorty found something all too metaphysical about Habermas's enterprise: "we need to know more about what counts as 'undistorted.' Here Habermas goes transcendental and offers principles." Richard Rorty, *Consequences of Pragmatism (Essays: 1972–1980)* (Minneapolis: University of Minnesota Press, 1982), p. 173. See also Richard Rorty, *Philosophy and the Mirror of Nature* (Princeton, N.J.: Princeton University Press, 1979), pp. 380–3, 385, for this line of criticism against Habermas. As his thinking developed, Habermas backed ever further away from the sort of substantive claim that would require such a transcendental turn, but even in 1988 Rorty noted that "Habermas would like to ground moral obligation, and thus social institutions, on something universally human." Rorty, *Essays on Heidegger and*

Others, p. 197. In the same vein, Rorty implied that there is little to be said in advance about what counts as undistorted or ideological; thus we can only rely on democratic procedures. See *Rorty, Contingency, Irony, and Solidarity*, pp. 82–4. Habermas summed up his case against Gadamerian hermeneutics with particular clarity in Jürgen Habermas, "The hermeneutic claim to universality," in Joseph Bleicher (ed.), *Contemporary Hermeneutics: Method, Philosophy and Critique* (London: Routledge & Kegan Paul, 1980), pp. 181–211. For his critique of the "postmodern" overreaction, see Jürgen Habermas, *The Philosophical Discourse of Modernity: Twelve Lectures* (Cambridge, Mass.: MIT Press, 1987), chapters 7, 9, and 10, on Foucault and Derrida.

Index